The Language of the Law

To Bubba —

May this book bring
you clarity and grace
for years to come.

Love,
Andy & Hannah

The Language
of the Law

by
DAVID MELLINKOFF

Professor of Law,
University of California at Los Angeles
and
member of the California Bar

Resource *Publications*

An imprint of *Wipf and Stock Publishers*
199 West 8th Avenue • Eugene OR 97401

Resource Publications
 An imprint of Wipf and Stock Publishers
199 West 8th Avenue, Suite 3
Eugene, Oregon 97401

The Language of the Law
By Mellinkoff, David
Copyright©1963 by Mellinkoff, David
ISBN: 1-59244-690-6
Publication date 5/13/2004
Previously published by Little, Brown and Company, 1963

Sir, the law is as I say it is, and so it has been laid down ever since the law began; and we have several set forms which are held as law, and so held and used for good reason, though we cannot at present remember that reason.

FORTESCUE, C.J.[1]

[1] Y.B. 36 Hen. VI, ff. 25b-26 (1458); transl., 3 Holdsworth, *A History of English Law* 626 (3d ed. 1923).

Preface

The law is a profession of words. Yet in a vast legal literature the portion devoted to the language of the law is a single grain of sand at the bottom of a great sea. The profession is properly more concerned with rights, obligations, and wrongs, and the incidental procedures. Even a lawyer and linguist of the highest order, Mr. Justice Holmes, reminds us that "We are not studying etymology, but law."[1] But the main objectives suffer when the principal tool of the whole process is neglected. Legal historians have long recognized that ". . . language is no mere instrument which we can control at will; it controls us."[2] Still, at this writing, the subject of "language" is absent from most law indexes and only in capsule form in the rest. It is certainly not too early, nor is it too late, to commence a systematic examination of the language lawyers use.

To be of any use, the language of the law (as any other language) must not only express but convey thought. With communication the object, the principle of simplicity would dictate that the language used by lawyers agree with the common speech, unless there are reasons for a difference. If there are reasons — old, refurbished, substituted, or brand-new — it is essential that lawyers know those reasons. And this not merely to satisfy an intellectual craving. An ancient and still vital maxim tells us that when the reason ceases, the rule also ceases.[3] When and when not to use particular language is the lawyer's daily decision. If some reason requires special language, the choice is made. If there is no reason for departure from the language of common understanding, the special usage is suspect. If, in addition, a special usage works evil, it should be abandoned, and quickly.

---

[1] Holmes, *The Common Law* 215 (1881), and compare 356, 366. And see also Holmes, "The Theory of Legal Interpretation," 12 Harv. L. Rev. 417 (1899).

[2] 1 Pollock and Maitland, *The History of English Law* 87 (2d ed. 1898). And see too Holmes, *The Common Law* 382 (1881), and 2 Bacon, *Works* 192-193 (Montagu ed. 1825).

[3] Broom, *A Selection of Legal Maxims* 113 (5th American ed. 1864).

This book tells what the language of the law is, how it got that way, and how it works out in the practice. The emphasis is more historical than philosophical, more practical than pedantic. The teachings of history and theory are here tempered by practice. Law today is generally inseparable from ringing telephones, split-second schedules, and daily deadlines. Usually it is more important that a competent practitioner do something as well as he can, than that he do nothing perfectly.

This is no crusade for the propagation of a new language — whether Esperanto or Hohfeld. It is an endeavor to make an existing language better perform its function. For the fate of all language is change: positively, by its own growth; negatively, by taking on a new relationship to its environment.

This is a beginning. The goal is nothing more modest than the rationalization of the language of the law.

The footnotes are for reference only. Anything worth saying has been said in the body of the text.

D. M.

Los Angeles
June 1963

Contents

CHAPTER III

MANNERISMS OF THE LANGUAGE OF THE LAW

PART TWO

HISTORY OF THE LANGUAGE OF THE LAW

CHAPTER IV

SCOPE OF THE HISTORY

CHAPTER V

BEFORE THE NORMANS

CHAPTER X

THREE CENTURIES OF MODERN ENGLISH

P A R T T H R E E

USING THE LANGUAGE OF THE LAW

CHAPTER XII

REASONS GIVEN AND REAL

CHAPTER XIII

MORE PRECISE

CHAPTER XIV

SHORTER

CHAPTER XV

MORE INTELLIGIBLE

CHAPTER XVI

MORE DURABLE

PART ONE

What Is the Language of the Law?

CHAPTER I

An Expanded Definition of the Language of the Law

1. *What it includes*

The *language of the law,* as described in this book, is the customary language used by lawyers in those common law jurisdictions where English is the official language. It includes distinctive words, meanings, phrases, and modes of expression. It also includes certain mannerisms of composition not exclusive with the profession but prevalent enough to have formed a fixed association.

2. *Choice of terminology*

In the first decade of the century Sir William Holdsworth wrote of "the language, or rather languages, of the law," stressing a polyglot origin.[1] Others have emphasized the relationship between language *and* the law.[2] The *language of the law* is a convenient label for a speech pattern with a separate identity.[3] *Law language* is sometimes used here as a shortener; *law words* for individual words in the *language of the law.* These expressions are preferred to *legal parlance,*[4] *legal English,*[5] and *legal language,*[6] for the reason that *legal* is so fre-

---

[1] 2 Holdsworth, *A History of English Law* 478 (3d ed. 1923).

[2] Williams, "Language and the Law" (pts. 1-5), 61 L.Q. Rev. 71, 179, 293, 384 (1945), 62 L.Q. Rev. 387 (1946); Philbrick, *Language and the Law* (1949).

[3] Cairns, "Language of Jurisprudence," in Anshen, ed., *Language* 232 (1957); Frank, *Law and the Modern Mind* 22 (6th print. rev. 1949); 2 Holdsworth, *A History of English Law* 477 (3d ed. 1923); Pei, *The Story of English* 200 (1952); 1 Pollock and Maitland, *The History of English Law* 80 (2d ed. 1898); Rodell, *Woe unto You, Lawyers!* 7 (1939); Winfield, *The Chief Sources of English Legal History* 7 (1925); Lavery, "The Language of the Law" (pts. 1-2), 7 A.B.A.J. 277 (1921), 8 A.B.A.J. 269 (1922).

[4] Pei, *The Story of English* 119 (1952).

[5] Flesch, *The Art of Readable Writing* 152 (1949); Gowers, *Plain Words* 6 (1948); Runes, "Our Obsolete Legal English," 99 N.Y.L.J. 1964 (1938).

[6] Flesch, *The Art of Plain Talk* 36 (1946); J. Last, *Everyday Law Made Simple* 164 (1954); Pei, *The Story of English* 200, 201 (1952); 1 Pollock and Maitland, *The History of English Law* 80, 82 (2d ed. 1898); Rodell, *Woe unto You, Lawyers!* 181 (1939).

quently and properly used to mean *lawful* as to cause confusion at the outset. *Legal lingo*,[7] *legal jargon*,[8] and *legalese*[9] are rejected on the additional grounds of being too sweepingly opprobrious and also too narrow. These objections apply equally to *legalistic jargon*[10] and *argot of the law*.[11]

Swift's acid phrase was "a peculiar Cant and Jargon of their own, that no other Mortal can understand."[12] Bentham had a bag of phrases, applied with uncomplimentary impartiality: *law jargon*,[13] *lawyers' cant*,[14] *lawyers' language*,[15] *flash language*.[16] Opposed to these is the *language of jurisprudence*,[17] dignified but confining. The *language of the law* partakes of some of the essence of all of these diverse characterizations.

3. *The official language: English in England*

The speech of lawyers is conditioned not alone by the law, but also by the prevailing language of their environment. It is the coincidence of dominant common law and dominant English that forms the setting for the language of the law.

In England — the most ancient common law jurisdiction — English is the official language. Today that has a tautological ring. It was not always so. The history of the emergence of English is traced in Part Two.

Customary usage alone could suffice to make English official for England. Yet definition has not been left completely to chance utterance. Legislation on the subject spans seven centuries. Most of these laws have been repealed.[18] Two statutes survive. One expressly re-

---

[7] Oppenheimer, "Legal Lingo," 2 American Speech 142 (1926); Thurber, *The Wonderful O* 58 (1957).

[8] *Benthamiana* 119 (1843); Gowers, *Plain Words* 6 (1948).

[9] Cooper, *Effective Legal Writing* 16 (1953); Littler, "Legal Writing in Law Practice," 31 J.S.B. Calif. 28, 31 (1956).

[10] Hunter, *The Language of Audit Reports* 27 (1957).

[11] Mencken, *The American Language* 424 (4th ed. 1936).

[12] Swift, *Gulliver's Travels* 297 (Crown ed. 1947).

[13] 7 Bentham, *Works* 280 (Bowring ed. 1843).

[14] 7 Bentham, *Works* 282 (Bowring ed. 1843).

[15] 7 Bentham, *Works* 280 (Bowring ed. 1843).

[16] 7 Bentham, *Works* 282 (Bowring ed. 1843).

[17] Cairns, "Language of Jurisprudence," in Anshen, ed., *Language* 232 (1957).

[18] Statute of Pleading, 1362, 36 Edw. III, c. 15, repealed by Statute Law Revision Act, 1863, 26 & 27 Vict., c. 125; Act for turning the Books of the Law . . . into English, 22 November 1650, in 2 *Acts and Ordinances of the Interregnum* 455 (1911), repealed by Stat. (1660) 12 Car. II, c. 3; Proceedings in Courts of Justice, 1731, 4 Geo. II, c. 26, repealed by Civil Procedure Acts Repeal Act, 1879, 42 & 43 Vict., c. 59; Courts in Wales and Chester, 1733, 6 Geo. II, c. 14, repealed by Civil Procedure Acts Repeal Act, 1879, 42 & 43 Vict., c. 59.

quires Crown writs and incidental papers to be in English.[19] The other requires non-British sailors on British ships to have a knowledge of English.[20]

4. The official language: English in the United States generally

English is also the official language in the most populous of common law jurisdictions, the United States. Special situations exist in Louisiana and New Mexico (Section 6). In all other states the tradition of English usage has been reinforced by a host of constitutional or statutory provisions. In one or more jurisdictions, English is the language of statutes,[21] public documents,[22] courts,[23] process,[24] teaching,[25] textbooks,[26] legal newspapers,[27] legal notices,[28] recording,[29] public meetings.[30] It is taught in grade schools[31] and Americanization

[19] Crown Writs to be in English, 1868, 31 & 32 Vict., c. 101, s. 90.
[20] Prohibition of Engagement of Seamen . . . , 1906, 6 Edw. VII, c. 48, s. 12.
[21] Cal. Const., art. IV, §24; Hawaii Rev. Laws, tit. 1, c. 1, §§1-16 (1955); Ill. Const., Sched., §18; Mich. Const., art. XVI, §6; N.J. Stat. Ann. §52:36-4 (1955).
[22] Ky. Rev. Stat. §446.060 (1956); Wis. Stat. §35.68 (1959).
[23] Alaska Comp. Laws Ann. §52-1-12 (1949); Ark. Stat. §22-108 (1947); Cal. Const., art. IV, §24; Cal. Civ. Proc. Code §185; Colo. Rev. Stat. Ann. §37-1-22 (1953); Idaho Code Ann. §1-1620 (1948); Ill. Const., Sched., §18; Mich. Const. of 1908, art. XVI, §6; Mo. Ann. Stat. §476.050 (1949); Mont. Rev. Codes Ann. §93-1104 (1947); Nev. Rev. Stat. §1.040 (1957); N.H. Rev. Stat. Ann. §509:1 (1955); Utah Code Ann. §78-7-22 (1953); Vt. Stat., tit. 4, c. 15, §671 (1959); Wis. Stat. §256.18 (1959).
[24] Alaska Comp. Laws Ann. §52-1-12 (1949); Ark. Stat. §22-108; Mo. Ann. Stat. §476.050 (1949); N. H. Rev. Stat. Ann. §509:1 (1955); Vt. Stat., tit. 4, c. 15, §671 (1959); Wis. Stat. §256.18 (1959).
[25] Ala. Code, tit. 52, §299(c) and §230 (1941); Conn. Gen. Stat. Rev. §10-17 (1958); Guam Govt. Code §11,200 (1952); Hawaii Rev. Laws §40-3 (1955); Iowa Code §280.5 (1958); Kan. Gen. Stat. Ann. §72-1102 (1949); Mich. Const. of 1908, art. XI, §9; Minn. Stat. Ann. §120.10, subd. 2, §126.07 (1960); N.Y. Educ. Law §3204, par. 2; N.C. Gen. Stat. §115-198 (Supp. 1955); N.D. Cent. Code §15-47-03 (1960); Okla. Const., art. I, §5; R.I. Gen. Laws Ann. §16-19-2 (1956); S.D. Code §15.9913 (Supp. 1960); Tex. Pen. Code, art. 288 (1952); Wash. Rev. Code §28.05.010 (1951); W. Va. Code, c. 18, art. 2, §1732 (1961).
[26] Minn. Stat. Ann. §120.10, subd. 2, §126.07 (1960); N.Y. Educ. Law §3204, par. 2; Tex. Pen. Code, art. 288 (1952).
[27] Fla. Stat. §49.01 (1959); Ind. Ann. Stat. §2-4707 (1949) and §2-807 (1933); Iowa Code §618.1 (1958); Minn. Stat. Ann. §331.02, subd. 1 (1947); see N.D. Cent. Code §46-06-02 (1960); S.D. Code §65.0508 (Supp. 1960); Va. Code Ann. §8-81 (1950).
[28] Ind. Ann. Stat. §2-4707 (1949) and §2-807 (1933); Iowa Code §618.1 (1958); Minn. Stat. Ann. §331.02, subd. 5 (1947); Neb. Rev. Stat. §25-523 (1943); Wis. Stat. §324.20 (1959); *Bennett v. Baltimore*, 106 Md. 484, 493 (1907).
[29] N.J. Stat. Ann. §47:1-2 (1940); N.Y. Real Prop. Law §333, par. 2; Okla. Stat., tit. 16, §28 (1961).
[30] Neb. Rev. Stat. §28-741 (1943).
[31] Me. Rev. Stat. Ann., c. 41, §92 (1954); Mass. Ann. Laws, c. 71, §1, and see also §18 (1953); Miss. Code Ann. §6216-02(a) and (b) (1953); Ohio Rev. Code

classes.[32]   It qualifies voters,[33] jurors,[34] public officials,[35] and drivers of vehicles.[36] It has been declared "official." [37]

The federal government joins in. "An understanding of the English language" is a condition of naturalization.[38] English is the court and statute language of the District of Columbia.[39]

The list and citations here are not exhaustive. By these and more circuitous paths we are reminded that America is an English-speaking country. In Guam, we put it bluntly:

> English is the official language of Guam, and all persons employed by the government of Guam shall speak only English during working hours. Other languages must not be spoken except for official interpreting.[40]

In Hawaii, with somewhat more finesse:

> Whenever there is found to exist any radical and irreconcilable difference between the English and Hawaiian version of any laws of the Territory, the English version shall be held binding.[41]

If our history, literature, and common speech ever left the matter in doubt, American legislators have assured the primacy of English.

5. The official language: Is it American in Illinois?

A nominal aberration occurs in Illinois. The state constitution makes English the exclusive medium for "all official writings" and proceed-

---

Ann. §3313.60 (Page's, 1960); R.I. Gen. Laws Ann. §16-19-2 (1956); S.C. Code §21-411 (1952); Tenn. Code Ann. §49-1902 (1956).

[32] Ariz. Rev. Stat. Ann. §15-1041 (1955); Mass. Ann. Laws, c. 69, §9 (1953); R.I. Gen. Laws Ann. §§16-29-1, 16-29-2 (1956); Wyo. Stat. Ann. §21-255 (1957).

[33] Ala. Const., amend. XCI (Dec. 19, 1951); Del. Const. of 1897, as amended, art. V, §2; Ga. Code Ann. §2-704 (1948); Me. Const., art. II, §1; Me. Rev. Stat. Ann., c. 3, §20 (1954); Mass. Const., amends., art. XX (1857); N.Y. Const., art. 2, §1; N.C. Gen. Stat. §163-28 (Supp. 1955); Ore. Const., art. II, §2, and art. VIII, §6.

[34] Cal. Civ. Proc. Code §198; Hawaii Rev. Laws §221-1(d) (1955); Ind. Ann. Stat. §9-1504 (13th) (1949); Neb. Rev. Stat. §25-1601 (1943).

[35] Ariz. Const., art. XX, par. 8th; Ariz. Rev. Stat. Ann. §§11-402, 38-201 (1955); Me. Const., art. II, §1; Mass. Const., amends., art. XX (1857).

[36] Cal. Vehicle Code §12804; S.C. Motor Carrier Safety Regs., Part 1 (1.29), 7 S.C. Code, p. 766 (1952).

[37] Guam Govt. Code §3000 (1952); Neb. Laws 1919-1921, c. 61 (April 14, 1921), held unconstitutional in *Nebraska District of Evangelical Lutheran Synod of Missouri v. McKelvie*, 262 U.S. 404 (1922); see also *Meyer v. Nebraska*, 262 U.S. 390 (1922); *Bennett v. Baltimore*, 106 Md. 484, 493 (1907).

[38] 8 U.S.C.A. §1423 (1952).

[39] D.C. Code Ann. §§13-201, 13-202 (1961).

[40] Guam Govt. Code §3000 (1952).

[41] Hawaii Rev. Laws §1-16 (1955).

ings,[42] and a later statute reads: "The official language of the State of Illinois shall be known hereafter as the 'American' language."[43] This is neither the first nor the last attempt to place a domestic label on our version of the English language.[44] The Illinois courts take a matter-of-fact rather than chauvinistic view, and maintain that for this purpose "English" and "American" mean the same thing.[45]

There are of course numerous differences between the British and American brands of English.[46] The bond of the common law results in minimizing these differences in law language usage. For example, the English *barrister* (our courtroom lawyer) is *called to the bar* (admitted to practice). The English *solicitor* (for the most part, an office lawyer) has clients who *convey* or *transfer by deed* but do not merely *deed* as in America.[47] An English court hands a decision *out* rather than *down*.[48] The English *brief* is a written case summary for the guidance of a barrister; the American *brief* for the guidance of the court.[49]

In the language of the law, as in the language generally, discussion of the differences between American and British usage serves to emphasize the essential similarity. Despite the many differences of usage, and recurrent political differences before and since the Revolutionary War, English continues to be recognized as the basic and official language of the United States, including Illinois.

---

42 Ill. Const., Sched., §18.

43 Act of June 19, 1923, Ill. Ann. Stat., c. 127, §177 (Smith-Hurd, 1953).

44 Mencken, *The American Language* 79-84 (4th ed. 1936); Mencken, *The American Language Supplement I* 136-145 (1945); Carrière, "Early Examples of the Expressions 'American Language' and 'Langue Américaine,'" 75 Modern Language Notes 485-488 (1960).

45 *Leideck v. City of Chicago*, 248 Ill. App. 545, 558 (1928); *Carlin v. Millers Motor Corp.*, 265 Ill. App. 353, 357 (1932).

46 See, for example, collections in: Bartlett, *Dictionary of Americanisms* (4th ed. 1896); *Dictionary of American English* (Craigie and Hulbert ed. 1938-1944); Evans and Evans, *A Dictionary of Contemporary American Usage* (1957); Farmer, *Americanisms* (1889); Fowler, *A Dictionary of Modern English Usage* (3d ed. 1937); Horwill, *Dictionary of Modern American Usage* (2d ed. 1944); Mathews, ed., *A Dictionary of Americanisms* (1951); Mencken, *The American Language* (4th ed. 1936), *Supplement I* (1945), *Supplement II* (1948); Nicholson, *A Dictionary of American-English Usage* (1957); Partridge, *A Dictionary of Slang and Unconventional English* (4th ed. 1951); Partridge, *A Dictionary of the Underworld* (1950); Partridge, *Slang: Today and Yesterday* (3d ed. 1950); Pickering, *A Vocabulary* (1816); Schele De Vere, *Americanisms* (1872); Thornton, *An American Glossary* (1912). Compare *Re La Marquise Footwear's Application*, [1946] 2 All E.R. 497, 498, 499 (Ch. D.).

47 *Oxford English Dictionary*, under *deed*.

48 Mencken, *The American Language* 246 (4th ed. 1936).

49 *Black's Law Dictionary* 240 (4th ed. 1951).

6. *The official language: Variations*

Throughout the American domain there are legal acknowledgments of the fact of multilingual origins.[50] For example, though English is the official language of instruction (Section 4), special provision is made for instruction in Hawaiian (in Hawaii),[51] Italian and Portuguese (in Rhode Island),[52] and Spanish (in Texas[53] and Rhode Island).[54] Yet these are passing nods of courtesy compared to the situation elsewhere.

English is required in the United States District Court for Puerto Rico,[55] but "In all departments of the Commonwealth Government and in all the courts of this island, and in all public offices the English language and the Spanish language shall be used indiscriminately . . ." [56] English is permissive for Puerto Rico pleadings, but those in writing may be required to have Spanish copies, and oral pleadings "should be made through an interpreter." [57]

Spanish and French antecedents have left their mark on Louisiana. On the law side, there are elements of common law present and absent, and important elements from the Code Napoleon.[58] The language picture is likewise mixed. Following the Louisiana Purchase, English was made official,[59] and in certain respects this remains so today. English is the official school language,[60] the language for articles of incorporation[61] and legal notices,[62] a qualification for civil jurors[63] and jury commissioners.[64] A sentence must be recorded in English.[65] But a voter need only be literate and be registered in English or his "mother tongue." [66] A corporate name may be in any language as long as writ-

[50] Mencken, *The American Language Supplement I* 136-145 (1945).
[51] Hawaii Rev. Laws §40-3 (1955).
[52] R.I. Gen. Laws Ann. §16-22-8 (1960).
[53] Tex. Pen. Code, art. 288 (1952).
[54] R.I. Gen. Laws Ann. §16-22-8 (1960).
[55] Puerto Rican Federal Relations Act §42, 1 P.R. Laws Ann. 168 (1954).
[56] P.R. Laws Ann. §51 (1954).
[57] P.R. Laws Ann. §194 (1954).
[58] 1 McMahon, *Louisiana Practice* §1 (1939); 14 *Encyclopaedia Britannica* 428 (1948); see Wigmore, *A Panorama of the World's Legal Systems* 1035 (library ed. 1936).
[59] 14 *Encyclopaedia Britannica* 428 (1948).
[60] La. Const., art. 12, §12.
[61] La. Rev. Stat. §§12:3, 12:103 (1950).
[62] La. Rev. Stat. §§1:52, 43:201, 43:202, 43:204, 47:2181 (1950).
[63] La. Rev. Stat. §13:3041(2) (1950).
[64] La. Rev. Stat. §13:3043 (1950).
[65] La. Rev. Stat. §15:523 (1950).
[66] La. Rev. Stat. §18:31(3) (1950).

ten in "English" letters or characters.[67] The surveyor general "shall possess a thorough knowledge of the English, French, and Spanish languages." [68] A catchall Louisiana statute provides:

> Any act or contract made or executed in the French language is as legal and binding upon the parties as if it had been made or executed in the English language.[69]

In New Mexico, a predominantly common law state,[70] English is one of the official languages. It shares honors with Spanish. The original New Mexico constitution, effective January 6, 1912, provided that for the first twenty years all laws were to be published in both English and Spanish. After that it was left up to the legislature.[71] The 1915 codification of New Mexico law was the first and last published in both languages.[72] But Spanish is still a required subject in grammar school unless there is parental objection.[73] Ballots must be printed in English and Spanish.[74] Publications of proceedings of subdivisions of the state (city councils, school boards, etc.) are required to be published only once. Formerly this was to be in English, but since 1919 in English alone where the populace is 75 per cent English-speaking, in Spanish alone where the same percentage is Spanish-speaking, and in both languages where the percentage using either language is "between" 25 and 75 per cent.[75]

7. Language of the law not English

The great mass of the language used by lawyers is ordinary English. Reciprocally, certain items of the language of the law, e.g., *habeas corpus, prima facie* (Section 11), *plaintiff, defendant* (Section 12), are now accepted as English,[76] *culprit* even invented by the law and abandoned by it to nontechnical English.[77] An assortment of general English idiom also tells its tale of a people long accustomed to settling their

---

[67] La. Rev. Stat. §§12:4(F), 12:104(A) (1950).

[68] La. Rev. Stat. §50:273 (1950).

[69] La. Rev. Stat. §1:51 (1950).

[70] N.M. Stat. Ann. §21-3-3 (1953).

[71] N.M. Const., art. XX, §12.

[72] Poldervaart, *Manual for Effective New Mexico Legal Research* 47 (1955); compare Mencken, *The American Language Supplement I* 141 (1945), and 3 *American Notes & Queries* 173 (1944).

[73] N.M. Stat. Ann. §73-17-2 (1953).

[74] N.M. Stat. Ann. §3-3-7(Ninth) (1953).

[75] N.M. Stat. Ann. §10-2-11 (1953).

[76] See also McKnight, *English Words and Their Background* 79 (1923).

[77] Blount, *A Law-Dictionary and Glossary* (1717); 4 Blackstone, *Commentaries* *339-*340 (Jones ed. 1916); *Black's Law Dictionary* (4th ed. 1951).

quarrels by litigation, e.g., *laughed out of court, hold no brief for,* etc.[78]

But it is a commonplace that that which gives the language of the law its distinctive flavor is something other than the King's or the commoner's English. Laymen are certain that law language is not English. Statutes make the distinction official.

On matters of construction, a statute reads:

> Words and phrases shall be construed according to the common and approved use of the language. Technical words and phrases, and those which have acquired a peculiar and appropriate meaning in the law shall be construed according to such peculiar and appropriate meaning.[79]

When such phraseology is used in a state where English is the official language (Section 4), the antithesis is complete.[80]

Frequently it is not left to inference. A typical item for judicial notice is:

> The true significance of all English words and phrases, and of all legal expressions . . .[81]

On legal papers and courtroom talk:

> All writs, process, proceedings and records in any court shall be in the English language, except that the proper and known name of process and technical words may be expressed in the language heretofore and now commonly used; and shall be made out on paper or parchment, in a fair and legible character, in words at length and not abbreviated; but such abbreviations as are now commonly used in the English language may be used; and numbers may be expressed by Arabic figures or Roman numerals, in the customary way.[82]

Though English is the official language (Sections 3, 4), the language of the law is not officially English.

---

[78] See L. P. Smith, *Words and Idioms* 218 (5th ed. 1943); Simon, "English Idioms from the Law" (pts. 1-2), 76 L.Q. Rev. 429-446, especially 429-430, and 283-305 (1960).

[79] Ariz. Rev. Stat. Ann. §1-213 (1955).

[80] Cal. Civ. Code §13; Kan. Gen. Stat. Ann. §77-201, par. 2 (1949); Ky. Rev. Stat. §446.080(4) (1956); Me. Rev. Stat. Ann., c. 10, §22 I (1954); Minn. Stat. Ann. §645.08(1) (1947); Miss. Code Ann. §702 (1942); N.H. Rev. Stat. Ann. §21:2 (1955); N.J. Stat. Ann. §1:1-1 (1957).

[81] Cal. Civ. Proc. Code §1875(1); Guam Code Civ. Proc. §1875(1).

[82] Ark. Stat. §22-108 (1947); similar language in Mo. Ann. Stat. §476.050 (1949); Wis. Stat. §256.18 (1955); see too Vt. Stat., tit. 9, c. 61, §1265 (1947).

CHAPTER II

Characteristics of the Language of the Law

8. *The uncommon touch*

At what point does the language of the law lose contact with the common speech? What are the hallmarks of the language of the law? The elements overlap. They are intertwined. They affect each other. The composite is a specialized tongue that distinguishes lawyer and non-lawyer. The chief characteristics of the language of the law are these:

(1) Frequent use of common words with uncommon meanings (Section 9).

(2) Frequent use of Old English and Middle English words once in common use, but now rare (Section 10).

(3) Frequent use of Latin words and phrases (Section 11).

(4) Use of Old French and Anglo-Norman words which have not been taken into the general vocabulary (Section 12).

(5) Use of terms of art (Section 13).

(6) Use of argot (Section 14).

(7) Frequent use of formal words (Section 15).

(8) Deliberate use of words and expressions with flexible meanings (Section 16).

(9) Attempts at extreme precision of expression (Section 17). Mannerisms associated with professional expression are separately considered in Chapter III.

9. *Frequent use of common words with uncommon meanings*

Nothing serves better to mark the gulf between the language of the law and the common speech than a listing of common words that mean one thing to the eye or ear of the non-lawyer, and may mean something completely different to the lawyer. The meanings given here are not in every case the only law meanings, but each is peculiar to the law. And in each instance, the meaning — taken or adapted from a standard law dictionary[1] — is one readily understood by the lawyer, and incomprehensible to most nonprofessionals. This list is by no means exhaustive. It is illustrative. The words are of day-to-day use in the practice:

action	law suit
alien	transfer
assigns	assignees
avoid	cancel
consideration	benefit to promisor or detriment to promisee
counterpart	duplicate of a document
covenant	sealed contract
demise	to lease
demur	to file a demurrer
executed	signed and delivered
hand	signature
instrument	legal document
letters	document authorizing one to act
master	employer
motion	formal request for action by a court
of course	as a matter of right
party	person contracting or litigating
plead	file pleadings
prayer	form of pleading request addressed to court
presents	this legal document
provided	word of introduction to a proviso
purchase	to acquire realty by means other than descent
said	mentioned before
save	except
serve	deliver legal papers
specialty	sealed contract
tenement	estate in land
virtue	force or authority, as in "by virtue of"
without prejudice	without loss of any rights

10. *Frequent use of Old and Middle English words once in use but now rare*

Old English is the name given to that form of the English language current in England before the Norman Conquest and down to about 1100. (Sections 28-38.) Middle English covers the period 1100 to about 1500. (Sections 52-53.) Modern English is said to date from about 1500.[2] These are useful approximations, and authorities differ on the dates.[3] Clearly, a classification of Modern English that includes

---

[1] *Black's Law Dictionary* (4th ed. 1951).

[2] *Webster's New International Dictionary* lxxxii-lxxxvi (2d ed. 1934); 1 *Oxford English Dictionary* xxx (1933); Setzler, *The Jefferson Anglo-Saxon Grammar and Reader* 3-4 (1938).

[3] See, e.g., Jespersen, *Growth and Structure of the English Language* iv (Anchor, 9th ed. 1955); 1 Johnson, *A Dictionary of the English Language* (4th ed. 1775), under "History of the English Language"; 8 *Encyclopaedia Britannica* 554 (1948).

Elizabethan must be handled with care in the twentieth century. Under any classification, the general English of today leans heavily on Old and Middle English. But the language of the law retains numerous Old and Middle English words and meanings which have long since passed out of general usage. Some of these same archaic words are preserved in other ancient specialties such as sailing and preaching. The old and essential law sense of *master*, i.e., one having control, is still used at sea; so too *afore*. The ministry, like the law, has never ceased to rely on the literary usages of the King James Bible, e.g., *therefore*,[4] *thereof*,[5] *wherefore*,[6] *whosoever*.[7] Most non-lawyers are exposed to these archaisms on infrequent occasions. For the lawyer they are daily bread. Here is a fair sampling:

aforesaid and *forthwith*
here words: hereafter, herein, hereof, heretofore, herewith
let, as in the law tautology, *without let or hindrance*
said and *such* as adjectives
thence and *thenceforth*
there words: thereabout, thereafter, thereat, thereby, therefor, therefore, therein, thereon, thereto, theretofore, thereupon, therewith
where words, especially *whereas* used in recitals, and *whereby*
witness, in the sense of testimony by signature, oath, etc., as in "In witness whereof, I have set my hand, etc."
witnesseth,[8] meaning to furnish formal evidence of something, the Old English present indicative, third person singular verb form.[9]

11. *Frequent use of Latin words and phrases*

One of the significant features of the English language is its mass borrowing from other languages.[10] The bulk of that borrowing is from Latin directly — or indirectly through French.[11] (Section 58.) Latin has traditionally been recommended for students of English, sometimes as a basis for advanced learning,[12] sometimes as a means of knowing

---

[4] Jer. 42:22; II Cor. 9:5.
[5] Gen. 2:19.
[6] Matt. 14:31.
[7] Matt. 7:24.
[8] *Oxford English Dictionary*, under *witness* (v.).
[9] *Webster's New International Dictionary* (2d ed. 1934), under *archaic;* Bodmer, *The Loom of Language* 259 (Hogben ed. 1944); Sweet, *The Student's Dictionary of Anglo-Saxon* xvi (1896).
[10] *Webster's New International Dictionary* lxxxvi (2d ed. 1934).
[11] *Webster's New International Dictionary* lxxxvi (2d ed. 1934); Whitney, *The Life and Growth of Language* 9 (1875); and see also McKnight, *English Words and Their Background* 116-117 (1923), and Jespersen, *Growth and Structure of the English Language*, pars. 118, 32, 39, and c. 6 (Anchor, 9th ed. 1955).
[12] 1 Howe, *Justice Oliver Wendell Holmes* 6 (1957); Jefferson, *The Complete Jefferson* 668 (Padover ed. 1943); Williston, *Life and Law* 28, 35, 37, 40 (1940).

English, and sometimes as a sort of brain-food.[13]   It has been especially urged upon law students.[14]   Indispensable or not, Latin still crowds the standard law dictionaries.[15]

Some of the Latin found there has become an accepted part of the English language, e.g., *affidavit, alias, alibi, bona fide, proviso,*[16] *quorum.*[17]   Courts sometimes explicitly say so, as for instance with *habeas corpus,*[18] *prima facie,*[19] and *versus.*[20]   A large part of law dictionary Latin is not in active use.   But whether it is rejected, or accepted as English, or permitted in practice as an exception to the rule requiring use of English (Section 7), there remains enough of distinctive Latin in the working law vocabulary to make its own mark on the language of the law.

Some examples are:

ab initio	ex parte	lex fori
ad damnum	ex post facto	lex loci actus
amicus curiae	ex rel.	lex loci contractus
certiorari	haec verba	malum in se
colloquium	in esse	malum prohibitum
coram nobis	in forma pauperis	mandamus
corpus delicti	in invitum	mens rea
cum testamento	in pari delicto	mobilia sequentur
annexo (c.t.a.)	in pari materia	personam
de bonis non	in personam	mutatis mutandis
(d.b.n.)	in propria persona	nil
de minimis non curat	(pro. per.)	nolle prosequi
lex (de minimis)	in re	(nol. pros.)
ejusdem generis	in rem	nolo contendere
et al.	inclusio unius est	nulla bona
ex contractu	exclusio alterius	nunc pro tunc
ex delicto	innuendo	pari passu

[13] Doherty and Cooper, *Word Heritage* x (1929); see, letter to the editor, "How About Latin, Mr. McGowan," 47 A.B.A.J. 1146 (1961).

[14] Doherty and Cooper, *Word Heritage* xi (1929); Jackson, *Law-Latin,* preface (1897); Jefferson, *The Complete Jefferson* 1087 (Padover ed. 1943); *Latin for Lawyers,* preface (2d ed. 1937).

[15] Ballentine, *Law Dictionary with Pronunciations* (2d ed. 1948); *Black's Law Dictionary* (4th ed. 1951); *Bouvier's Law Dictionary and Concise Encyclopedia* (3d rev. 8th ed. 1914); Jowitt, gen. ed., *The Dictionary of English Law* (1959); *Mozley and Whiteley's Law Dictionary* (5th ed. 1930); *Wharton's Law Lexicon* (14th ed. 1938).

[16] McKnight, *English Words and Their Background* 116 (1923).

[17] *Oxford English Dictionary.*

[18] See *People v. Johnson,* 147 Cal. App. 2d 417, 419 (1957).

[19] *People v. Carmona,* 80 Cal. App. 159, 166 (1926); *Leideck v. City of Chicago,* 248 Ill. App. 545, 558 (1928).

[20] *Smith v. Butler,* 25 N.H. 521, 523 (1852).

per capita	quasi	respondeat superior
per quod	qui facit per alium facit	retraxit
per stirpes	per se	sui generis
pro forma	quid pro quo	sui juris
pro rata	re	venire
pro tanto	res gestae	vis major
quantum meruit	res ipsa loquitur (r.i.l.)	
quantum valebant	res judicata	

12. Use of French words not in the general vocabulary

A vast section of the language of the law stems from French sources. (Chapter IX.) Writing in 1895, Pollock and Maitland listed as French words basic to the law vocabulary (even apart from the land law):

action	damage	judges	pleadings
agreement	debt	judgment	pledge
appeal	declaration	jurors	police
arrests	defendant	justice	possession
arson	demand	justices	prisons
assault	descent	larceny	property
attorneys	devise	lien	purchase
battery	easement	marriage	reprieve
bill	evidence	misdemeanour	robbery
claim	execution	(misdemeanor)	sentence
condition	felony	money	servant
constables	gaols (jails)	note	slander
contract	grant	obligation	suit
counsel	guarantee	pardon	tort
count	guardian	parties	treason
court	heir	partner	trespass
covenant	indictment	payment	verdict [21]
crime	infant	plaintiff	

They also listed *burglar, clerk, conviction, master,* and *ward.* But later scholarship credits *conviction* directly to Latin,[22] *clerk* to Old English via Latin[23] (Section 33), splits the credits on *ward* between Old English and French,[24] and suggests a three-way division of honors for *master* and *burglar* between Old English, Latin, and French.[25]

The Pollock and Maitland list cannot now be considered the exclusive property of lawyers. With technical nicety or otherwise, a major-

---

[21] 1 Pollock and Maitland, *The History of English Law* 81 (2d ed. 1898); see also Cairns, "Language of Jurisprudence," in Anshen, ed., *Language* 232, 245-246 (1957).

[22] *Oxford English Dictionary.*

[23] *Oxford English Dictionary; Medieval Latin Word-List* (1934), under *cleric/aliter.*

[24] *Oxford English Dictionary.*

[25] *Oxford English Dictionary; Medieval Latin Word-List* (1934), under *burg/aria.*

ity of those words are in daily use in the press, along with such others as *allege, attorney general, decree, mortgage.*

There is still a substantial group of French words — mostly Old French and Anglo-Norman — which has continued as the special province of lawyers. This is *law French,* distinct alike from English words of French origin and from modern French. (Section 62.) Some of these words which continue to give even educated laymen a sense of not-belonging are:

alien, in the sense of to transfer
chose in action
demurrer
estoppel
estoppel in pais
esquire
fee simple and *fee tail,* which like *attorney general* retain the French
   word order
laches
metes and *bounds*
oyez[26]
quash
roll, as in *judgment roll*
save, in the sense of *except* (Section 9)
specialty, in the sense of *sealed contract* (Section 9)
style, as in the tautology, *name and style*
voire dire (Section 60)

Of less frequent use in the practice, but still virile, are *cestui que trust, de son tort, en ventre sa mere,*[27] and *pur autre vie.*

13. *The use of terms of art*

A *term of art* is a technical word with a specific meaning.[28] Every specialty has its terms of art, whether it be burlesque (*bump,*[29] *grind*[30]), horsemanship (*curb bit, snaffle bit*), or the law. The uninitiated may not understand a term of art even while recognizing it as the mark of a specialty. The Catholic layman may not understand Latin or the Jew Hebrew, yet each knows that these are the official languages of his chosen prayers.

[26] 4 Blackstone, *Commentaries* *341 (Jones ed. 1916); Alderman, "The French Language in English and American Law," 12 Ala. Law. 356, 361-362 (1951); "Language of the Law," 220 L.T. 200, 201 (1955).
[27] *Am. Jur. Pleading and Practice Forms* 3:1059 (1957).
[28] *Webster's New International Dictionary* (2d ed. 1934); 41 *Words and Phrases* (perm. ed. 1940, Supp. 1962).
[29] Mencken, *The American Language Supplement II* 693 (1948).
[30] Mencken, *The American Language Supplement II* 694 (1948).

Not everything that has the sound of the law is a term of art. A large group of law words fails to qualify because not specific. For example, *cause of action* is unadulterated law talk, incomprehensible to laymen and often to lawyers. The first words categorizing the expression in *Black's Law Dictionary* are: "A 'cause of action' may mean one thing for one purpose and something different for another." [31] It is not a matter of one or two well-defined meanings as with *libel,* which may be a tort or a first pleading in admiralty. *Cause of action* is in daily use and in daily controversy. [32]

But, despite endless dispute as to the application of terms of art to particular situations, there are numerous words which lawyers use as a medium of specific and shorthand communication. Some law terms of art are:

agency	felony	master and servant
alias summons	fictitious defendant	month-to-month tenancy
alibi	garnishment	negotiable instrument
amicus curiae	habeas corpus	or order
appeal	injunction	novation
bail	judicial notice	plaintiff
certiorari	jurisdiction in rem	prayer
common counts	laches	principal and surety
comparative negligence	landlord and tenant	publication of summons
contributory negligence	last clear chance	remittitur
defendant	lessee	res judicata
demurrer	lesser included offense	rule in Shelley's Case
dictum	lessor	special appearance
dry trust	letters patent	stare decisis
eminent domain	libelant	tort
ex parte	libelee	voir dire
fee simple	life tenant	
fee tail	mandamus	

14. *Use of argot*

Argot is sometimes used interchangeably with cant, jargon, and slang, especially of the underworld sort. [33] (Section 2.) In its better sense argot is a specialized vocabulary that is common to any group. [34]

---

[31] *Black's Law Dictionary* 279 (4th ed. 1951).

[32] 6 *Words and Phrases* 350-388 (perm. ed. 1940), 128-141 (Supp. 1962); see and compare Clark, *Handbook of the Law of Code Pleading* §19 (1928), and Pomeroy, *Code Remedies* §§412, 413 (5th ed. 1929).

[33] *Webster's New International Dictionary* (2d ed. 1934); *Oxford English Dictionary* (1933).

[34] Evans and Evans, *A Dictionary of Contemporary American Usage* 40 (1957); Mencken, *The American Language* 555 (4th ed. 1936). See contrary view in Fowler, *A Dictionary of Modern English Usage* 307 (3d ed. 1937), and Nicholson, *A Dictionary of American-English Usage* 297 (1957).

Apart from its unsavory background, argot still cannot be used to describe the whole of the language of the law. For argot has the connotation of a language of communication within the group, whether or not deliberately designed to exclude the stranger.[35] The language of the law, sometimes even a particular word, has a dual aspect. Lawyers use language that is intended to speak to lawyers and laymen, as in contracts, jury instructions, notices, and even laws. Lawyers also use language that is intended to speak primarily to each other, in pleadings, opinions, articles, books, argument, the whole gamut of legal papers, and in the day-to-day negotiation and discussion that is the lawyer's life. In this latter aspect, a portion of the language of the law is *argot*, a "professional language." [36]

The other characteristics of the language of the law (Sections 9, 10, 11, 12, 13, 15, 16, 17) individually or in combination often result in argot. For example, lawyers talking to other lawyers (on or off the bench) use the Old French *demur* as a term of art with an uncommon meaning.

At other times argot stands as an independent classification of law phraseology insufficiently technical or specific to qualify as a term of art. For example, the argot of the courtroom:

> FIRST LAWYER: What did he say?
> WITNESS: I told him I wouldn't and he insisted.
> SECOND LAWYER: Move to strike for purpose of making an objection.
> JUDGE: Granted. That may all go out as nonresponsive and a conclusion.
> Mr. Reporter, read the witness the question. [The question is read.]
> WITNESS: He said that I'd better or . . .
> SECOND LAWYER: Objection. Extrajudicial statements not subject to cross.
> FIRST LAWYER: Offered only to show state of mind.
> JUDGE: Overruled. Received for that limited purpose.

As a conversational form, law argot is a code divorced from the common speech. For example:

> FIRST LAWYER: Will you stipulate that the complaint may be amended to negative laches?
> SECOND LAWYER: Unnecessary. This is at law, not equity. My objection is not laches, but that the pleading affirmatively shows the bar of the statute.

---

[35] Mencken, *The American Language* 556 (4th ed. 1936).
[36] Cairns, "Language of Jurisprudence," in Anshen, ed., *Language* 232, 240 (1957).

FIRST LAWYER: Your client has been served.

SECOND LAWYER: But only by publication, and that won't support a personal judgment.

Some further examples of law argot are:

alleged	horse case	raise an issue
alter ego	inferior court	reasonable man
argumentative	issue of fact	record
at issue	issue of law	reversed and remanded
bail exonerated	legal conclusion	set down for hearing
Blackacre	matter	stale claim
breaking and entering	mesne process	superior court
came on for hearing	on all fours	time is of the essence[37]
case	order to show cause	toll the statute
cause of action	pierce the corporate	well settled
court below	veil	Whiteacre
damages	prescriptive right	without prejudice
due care	process	
four corners of the	purported	
instrument	pursuant to stipulation	

15. *Frequent use of formal words*

There is a ceremonial quality to the language of the law achieved by the use of "formal words" [38] — words set apart from the language of street or locker room. The style has been described as solemn, mystical, sacerdotal,[39] dignified, and "assiduously stilted." [40] Whatever its proper name, the effect is derived from the use of formal words: unaccustomed words (Sections 9-14), the polite expressions of former days (*approach the bench* instead of *come here*), euphemisms (*the deceased* and *decedent*), undomesticated Latin and French (*arrested in flagrante delicto* instead of *caught in the act*), and a variety of circumlocutions that make the commonplace exalted. These expressions run throughout the language of the law. For example:

In pleadings —

Comes now the plaintiff
Wherefore, defendant prays that plaintiff take nothing
for such other and further relief as to the court may seem meet and just

In judgments —

---

[37] 4 *California Words, Phrases, and Maxims* 344 (1960); 41 *Words and Phrases* 212-213 (perm. ed. 1940, Supp. 1962); see also Cal. Civ. Code §1492.

[38] Fowler, *A Dictionary of Modern English Usage* 189 (3d ed. 1937); Nicholson, *A Dictionary of American-English Usage* 201 (1957).

[39] Runes, "Our Obsolete Legal English," 99 N.Y.L.J. 1964 (1938).

[40] Rodell, "Goodbye to Law Reviews," 23 Va. L. Rev. 38, 43 (1936).

Now Therefore, It Is Ordered, Adjudged, and Decreed

In court —

oyez, oyez, oyez
hear ye, hear ye, hear ye
Your Honor
may it please the court
plaintiff rests

In contracts —

whereas
time is of the essence
from the beginning of the world
be it remembered
know all men by these presents

In affidavits —

ss
being first duly sworn, deposes and says
further deponent saith not
before me, a notary public

In oaths —

I do solemnly swear (or affirm) that I will faithfully execute the Office
  of President of the United States . . .[41]
the truth, the whole truth, and nothing but the truth, so help you God

Other miscellaneous examples of formal words in the law are:

prior (instead of "before")
subsequent (instead of "after")
strangers to the blood [42]
came on for hearing
set down for hearing
toll the statute
without prejudice
pierce the corporate veil
To All To Whom These Presents Come, Greetings

16. *Deliberate use of words and expressions with flexible meanings*

Popular speech is seldom precise. There is a reluctance to take a
position from which there is no retreat. "Down that ways a piece,"
"fair to middlin'," "mebbe," "we'll see" are expressive of the easygoing
vagueness of daily conversation.

---

[41] U.S. Const., art. II, §1; Lavery, "The Language of the Law," 8 A.B.A.J. 269,
272 (1922).
[42] *Estate of Stanford,* 49 Cal. 2d 120, 159 (1957) (dissenting opinion); 60 *C.J.*
134.

The same tendency in the language of the law is noteworthy for these reasons:

The language of the law is sometimes characterized as one of "extraordinary precision," [43] and "unambiguous." [44] It is also singled out for special condemnation as "equivocal" [45] and full of "weasel words." [46] Lawyers customarily choose their words more carefully than non-lawyers. And it is characteristic of a large part of the selection that there is a deliberate choice of the flexible — a "peculiarly plastic terminology." [47]

This is to be distinguished from the inept, the inadvertent, and the unexpected. The last, for example, may result from the vagary of interpretation of language in the courts, where by circumstance the clear suddenly becomes unclear, a *horse* becomes a *vehicle*,[48] and *white* may mean *black*.[49] Interpretation is discussed in Section 129, precision in Section 17 and Chapter XIII, clarity in Section 20 and Chapter XV.

Here is a fair sample of law words and phrases which are often used because they are flexible or despite their flexibility:

about	clear and convincing	few
abuse of discretion	clearly erroneous	fixture
adequate	commerce	gross
adequate cause	comparable	gross profit
adequate compensation	completion	habitual
adequate consideration	convenient	improper
adequate remedy at law	desire	in conjunction with
and/or	doubtless	in regard to
and others	due care	inadequate
apparently	due process	incidental
approximately	excessive	inconvenience
as soon as possible	existing	intention
available	expenses	intoxicated
average	extraordinary compensation	it would seem
care	extraordinary services	large
clean and neat condition	extreme cruelty	lately
	fair division	luxury
		malice

[43] Cairns, "Language of Jurisprudence," in Anshen, ed., *Language* 232, 258 (1957).

[44] Gowers, *Plain Words* 6 (1948).

[45] Runes, "Our Obsolete Legal English," 99 N.Y.L.J. 1964 (1938).

[46] Chase, *The Tyranny of Words* 324 (1938); Frank, *Law and the Modern Mind* 27 (6th rev. print. 1949).

[47] Maine, *Ancient Law* 368 (new ed. 1930).

[48] *Conrad v. Dillinger*, 176 Kan. 296, 298-299 (1954).

[49] See *Beneficial Fire & Casualty Ins. Co. v. Kurt Hitke & Co.*, 46 Cal. 2d 517, 527 (1956); and see *Mitchell v. Henry*, 15 Ch. D. 181, and especially argument at 188 (1880); see also Swift, *Gulliver's Travels* 296 (Crown ed. 1947).

manifest	proper	technical
many	provide for	temperance
mere	public	temporarily
modify	reasonable care	thereabout
more or less	reasonable man	things
near	reasonable speed	transaction
necessaries	reasonable time	trivial
need	regular	try
negligence	regulate	under the influence
neighborhood	remote	of a person
net profit	reputable	under the influence
nominal sum	resident	of liquor
normal	respecting	understand
notice	safe	understanding
objectionable	satisfaction	undue influence
obscene	satisfactory	undue interference
obstruct	satisfy	undue restraint
obvious	serious and willful	unreasonable
on or about	serious illness	unsafe
ordinary	serious misconduct	unsatisfactory
ought	severe	unsound
overhead	shortly after	unusual
palpable	similar	usual
percentage of the	slight	valuable
gross	sound mind	vicinage
possible	structure	voluntary
practicable	substance	want
preceding	substantial	welfare
prevent	sufficient	wish
profits	suitable	worthless
promptly	take care of	

17. *Attempts at extreme precision*

Opposing themselves to "the inherent vagueness of language," [50] lawyers make many attempts at precision of expression. Their language essays precision by choice of particular words and phrases, and by devices of composition such as numbering, lettering, indexing, and even symbolic logic.[51]

In addition to the use of terms of art (Section 13), there is a recurrent choice of absolutes: *all, none, perpetuity, never, unavoidable, last clear chance, unbroken, uniform, irrevocable, impossible, outright, wherever, whoever.*

There are phrases designed to keep the restricted restricted, e.g.,

[50] Williams, "Language and the Law," 61 L.Q. Rev. 179, 192 (1945).
[51] Allen, "Symbolic Logic: A Razor-edged Tool for Drafting and Interpreting Legal Documents," 66 Yale L.J. 833 (1957); compare Summers, "A Note on Symbolic Logic and the Law," 13 J. Legal Ed. 486 (1961).

and no more, and no other purpose, shall not constitute a waiver, shall not be deemed a consent.

Opposed, there are phrases intended to keep the broad broad, e.g., *including but not limited to, or other similar or dissimilar causes, shall not be deemed to limit, without prejudice, nothing contained herein shall.*

There is the use of multiple specification of legal devices, factual situation, qualifications, applications, exceptions, rights, grievances, e.g., this very sentence, or a formbook general release:

> To all to whom these presents shall come or may come — Greeting:
> Know ye that I, ..., of ...., for and in consideration of .... dollars, to me in hand paid by ...., do by these presents for myself, my heirs, executors, and administrators, remise, release and forever discharge ...., of ...., his heirs, executors, and administrators, of and from any and all manner of action or actions, cause and causes of action, suits, debts, dues, sums of money, accounts, reckonings, bonds, bills, specialties, covenants, contracts, controversies, agreements, promises, trespasses, damages, judgments, executions, claims, and demands whatsoever, in law or equity, which against him I have had, now have, or which my heirs, executors, or administrators, hereafter can, shall, or may have, for or by reason of any matter, cause, or thing whatsoever, from the beginning of the world to the day of the date of these presents, excepting a claim as to ....
> In witness whereof, etc.[52]

There are provisions made against partial invalidity. The facts which together add up to notice are detailed, e.g., *on deposit in the United States mail registered and postage prepaid.* Often a special definition section of a contract or statute will in so many words define terms for the particular occasion, e.g., *words in the singular include the plural and vice versa,*[53] *words used in the masculine gender include the feminine and neuter.*[54] Explicit definition is simply a particular application of the law's major approach to precision, i.e., an attempt to put a brand on the mavericks of speech. Successful or not, the attempts at extreme precision serve to distinguish the language of the law from the common tongue (see Chapter XIII).

[52] Nichols, *Cyclopedia of Legal Forms* 8.273 (1936).
[53] N.Y. Retail Instalment Sales Act §401(18) (1957).
[54] Cal. Civ. Proc. Code §17.

CHAPTER III

Mannerisms of the Language
of the Law

18. No monopoly on mannerisms

The nine characteristics of the language of the law (Sections 9-17) are of universal application to the profession. Taken as a group, those characteristics mark off the language of the law from ordinary speech and from other specialized speech. In addition, widely associated with the language of the law are mannerisms, to which lawyers can claim neither priority nor monopoly. The profession's association with these mannerisms is sufficiently ancient and sufficiently close to justify considering them a part of the language of the law. The language of the law has a strong tendency to be:

    (1) Wordy (Section 19)
    (2) Unclear (Section 20)
    (3) Pompous (Section 21)
    (4) Dull (Section 22)

19. Wordy

> In parchments then, large as his fields, hee drawes
> Assurances, bigge, as gloss'd civill lawes,
> So huge, that men (in our times forwardnesse)
> Are Fathers of the Church for writing lesse.[1]

John Donne said it that way in the sixteenth century. With more or less politeness, others have said the same thing: "Words multiplied for the Purpose," [2] "a viscous sea of verbiage," [3] repetitious,[4] verbose, prolix.[5] The Old English word states it best of all: lawyers are wordy. It takes them a long time to get to the point. Regardless of the reason,

---

[1] John Donne: A Selection of His Poetry 104 (Penguin ed. 1952).
[2] Swift, Gulliver's Travels 296 (Crown ed. 1947).
[3] Chase, The Tyranny of Words 327 (1938).
[4] Evans, The Spoor of Spooks 265 (1954).
[5] Lavery, "The Language of the Law," 7 A.B.A.J. 277 (1921).

the language of the law as customarily written uses too many words. Here is what is meant by wordy:

For	Say
annul	annul and set aside[6]
remove	entirely and completely remove[7]
will	last will and testament [8]
void	totally null and void [9]
without hindrance	without let or hindrance[10]
document	written document [11]
instrument	written instrument [12]

For *the parties agree* use a whole batch of words:

Now Therefore, in consideration of the premises, and the representations, warranties, covenants and undertakings of the parties hereinafter set forth, and for other good and valuable considerations, *the parties agree* among themselves as follows:[13]

Other wordy samplings are in Section 20 and Chapter XIV.

20. *Unclear*

The language of the law is often unclear — plain "muddy." [14] This is not to say that the language is devoid of meaning. Simply that if there is any meaning, it is hard to find. It is puzzling not merely to the untutored non-lawyer. Puzzlement extends to bar and bench. Here is the typical long sentence, loaded with more detail than one period can conveniently carry:

When, without any showing to the contrary, it affirmatively appears, from the record in the trial of a criminal case on an indictment for a felony punishable by confinement in the penitentiary for a period of less than life imprisonment, that the trial court did not comply with the habitual criminal statute then in effect which expressly required that before a sentence of life imprisonment may be lawfully imposed it must be admitted, or by the jury found, that the person convicted on the indictment had previously been twice sentenced in the United States to the penitentiary, a judgment imposing a sentence of life imprisonment upon the convict, based upon the statute, is void, to the extent that it

---

[6] *Schaub's Inc. v. Department of Alcoholic Beverage Control,* 153 Cal. App. 2d 858, 860 (1957).
[7] Nichols, *Cyclopedia of Legal Forms* 8.1415 (1936).
[8] Cooper, *Effective Legal Writing* 190, 201 (1953).
[9] Williams, "Language and the Law," 61 L.Q. Rev. 71, 76 (1945).
[10] *Oxford English Dictionary* (1933), under *let,* sb.
[11] Plucknett, *A Concise History of the Common Law* 548 (5th ed. 1956).
[12] Cal. Civ. Proc. Code §448.
[13] Lindey, *Motion Picture Agreements Annotated* 146 (1947).
[14] Lavery, "The Language of the Law," 7 A.B.A.J. 277 (1921).

exceeds the maximum sentence for the particular offense charged in the indictment, for lack of jurisdiction of the trial court to render it, and the effect of that part of the sentence of life imprisonment, in excess of the maximum sentence for such particular offense will be avoided and its enforcement prevented in a habeas corpus proceeding.[15]

One hundred seventy-six words is by no means a record.[16] But a sentence may be unclear without breaking any records for word count. A shorter, more awkward sentence may be just as muddy:

> Although the will itself was silent as to who would take if the son predeceased the mother, she not having at the time of the son's death remarried, and the son leaving issue at his death, which event occurred, this omission by itself, in the will only, cannot aid the son and defeat the testator's clear intention that the son should take only in the event he survived the death or remarriage of his mother, Lula Kiester.[17]

A tortured metaphor will also help distract the reader:

> The plaintiff argues that the Foundation is the *alter ego* of Macfadden and that its corporate form should be pierced. It is entirely settled that a corporate form will be penetrated by equity where it is used as a shield behind which injustice is sought to be perpetrated or where the corporate cloak is used as a subterfuge to justify wrong.[18]

There are times when the law is explained to non-lawyers. How do you tell a jury about contributory negligence? In one way or another the jurors must be told: "If Mrs. Smith's injury was caused partly by Mr. Jones's negligence and partly by her own negligence, she cannot recover." Here is a typical way of saying this in a form jury instruction:

> You are instructed that contributory negligence in its legal significance is such an act or omission on the part of the plaintiff amounting to a want of ordinary care and prudence as occurring or co-operating with some negligent act of the defendant, was the proximate cause of the collision which resulted in the injuries or damages complained of. It may be described as such negligence on the part of the plaintiff, if found to exist, as helped produce the injury or the damages complained of, and if you find from a preponderance of all the evidence in either of these cases that plaintiff in such case was guilty of any negligence that helped proximately to bring about or produce the injuries of which plaintiff complains, then and in such place the plaintiff cannot recover.[19]

---

[15] *State ex rel. Browning v. Tucker,* 142 W. Va. 830, 838 (1957).

[16] For example, Int. Rev. Code of 1954, §1321(a); Cal. Rev. & Tax. Code §3902(a).

[17] *Kiester v. Kiester,* 3 Ohio Op. 2d 481, 491 (C.P. Montgomery County, 1957).

[18] *Macfadden v. Macfadden,* 46 N.J. Super. 242, 247-248 (1957).

[19] Richardson, *Florida Jury Instructions* §1234 (1954), a partial quote from *Shane v. Saunders,* 129 Fla. 355, 360 (1937).

The language of the law is full of "long sentences, awkward constructions, and fuzzy-wuzzy words." [20]   The result is often nothing less than a failure of communication.   (See Chapter XV.)

21. *Pompous*

In or out of the law, pompous[21] language gives an air of importance out of proportion to the substance of what is said.   Cardozo called the style "magisterial." [22]   Incongruity is its essence, self-esteem its badge.

Pomposity takes many shapes.   One of the most common is the platitude in weighty trappings.   As for instance, the remark of a federal judge addressing law students: "I give it to you as my considered opinion, gentlemen, that this is a government of checks and balances." [23] In the language of the law, thought content is frequently cloaked in words evoking overawed respect: *solemn, supreme, superior, wisdom, wisely, fundamental.*   The effect is heightened when contrary opinion is dismissed with a damning *mere, absurd, subvert, unconscionable.* The pompous style appears in argument of counsel: My client's contention is *obviously correct, clearly justified, overwhelmingly corroborated.*   Your claim is *entirely unsupported, unsound on its face, patently fraudulent,* and *trifles with justice.*   Pomposity also crops up in statutes.   For example: "Law is the solemn expression of the will of the supreme power of the State." [24]   Most often it drapes the opinions of appellate courts.   Here are a few excerpts:

> The people in their wisdom have given appellant board the exclusive power to determine under what circumstances it is or is not contrary to public welfare and morals to issue a liquor license.[25]

> This would be to overthrow, in fact, what was established in theory; and would seem, at first view, an absurdity too gross to be insisted on.[26]

> Nevertheless, this court in a very special sense is charged with the duty of construing and upholding the Constitution; and in the discharge of that important duty, it ever must be alert to see that a doubtful precedent be not extended by mere analogy to a different case if the

[20] Rodell, "Goodbye to Law Reviews," 23 Va. L. Rev. 38, 39 (1936); see also Rodell, *Woe unto You, Lawyers!* 185 (1939).

[21] Beardsley, "Beware of, Eschew and Avoid Pompous Prolixity and Platitudinous Epistles!" 16 J.S.B. Calif. 65 (1941).

[22] Cardozo, *Law and Literature* 10 (1931).

[23] Address at Harvard Law School, Cambridge, Mass., 1939.

[24] Cal. Civ. Code §22.

[25] *Altadena Community Church v. State Board of Equalization,* 109 Cal. App. 2d 99, 106 (1952).

[26] *Marbury v. Madison,* 1 Cranch 137, 177 (U.S. 1803).

result will be to weaken or subvert what it conceives to be a principle of the fundamental law of the land.[27]

From one long opinion pumped full of self-righteousness, here is a working glossary of pomposity, waiting only for the pin prick:[28]

anomalous result
apparent
can be no question
cannot be doubted
cannot in reason be conceived
cannot in reason be said
clear
clearly expressed
clearly pointed out
clearly results
conclusive force of the view we have stated
dispose of the argument
disposed of the reasoning advanced
disposes of the contention
excluded in unmistakable language
fallacy already exposed
irrevocably concluded by previous decisions
it follows
it must follow
it therefore follows
it would follow
made more manifest
no longer open to question
true and controlling principles

The dissent by Mr. Justice Holmes began:

> I do not suppose that civilization will come to an end whichever way this case is decided. But as the reasoning which prevails in the mind of the majority does not convince me, and as I think that the decision not only reverses a previous well-considered decision of this court but is likely to cause considerable disaster to innocent persons and to bastardize children hitherto supposed to be the offspring of lawful marriage, I think it proper to express my views.[29]

22. Dull

Through some professional eyes, a railroad timetable may seem spirited. The consensus would judge it dull. Sufficient interest of reader or listener may infuse life into the most lackluster speech. Yet even granting intense professional interest, too much of the law and discussion about the law is expressed in language bereft of vital juices.

---

[27] *Dimick v. Schiedt*, 293 U.S. 474, 485 (1935).
[28] *Haddock v. Haddock*, 201 U.S. 562 (1906).
[29] *Haddock v. Haddock*, 201 U.S. 562, 628 (1906) (dissent).

It is dull. Wordiness contributes to dullness, as witness the opinion and jury instruction in Section 20, or this one sentence from an opinion:

> The reason for denying an appeal in the latter case is not because the order on the motion to vacate is not within the terms of section 963 of the code allowing appeals, for it may be, and indeed, an order refusing to vacate a final judgment is in its very nature a special order made after judgment, but because it would be virtually allowing two appeals from the same ruling, and would, in some cases, have the effect of extending the time for appealing contrary to the intent of the statute.[30]

Pompous language (Section 21) also contributes to dullness. The combination of wordiness, lack of clarity, and pomposity will almost certainly produce dullness, and it is avoidable. In 1897, as still today, the rule in Shelley's Case was not a laughing matter. Yet in the course of an extended discussion of the rule for the benefit of the bar, Lord Macnaghten found it possible to say:

> That was putting the case in a nutshell.
> But it is one thing to put a case like Shelley's in a nutshell and another thing to keep it there.[31]

The fundamental and still litigated distinction between intentional and negligent wrongs has been expressed by Holmes in eleven lively words:

> . . . even a dog distinguishes between being stumbled over and being kicked.[32]

It is sometimes assumed that an important subject deserves ponderous treatment, and this dread of inappropriate levity has saddled the law with a weight of equally inappropriate dullness.

[30] *Corcoran v. City of Los Angeles*, 153 Cal. App. 2d 852, 855 (1957).
[31] *Van Grutten v. Foxwell*, [1897] A.C. 658, 671.
[32] Holmes, *The Common Law* 3 (1881).

PART TWO

History of the Language of the Law

CHAPTER IV

Scope of the History

23. *How wide and how narrow*

Part One of this book (Sections 1-22) defines the language of the law and describes its characteristics and mannerisms. Part Two gives the history of the language of the law.

Any history of language is of necessity incomplete. It is related to everything within the knowledge of man, and will never be complete until the story of man is fully told. This is truer of the language of the law than of any other specialized language.

The language of the press may carry "All the news that's fit to print"; the language of the law expresses the fit and the unfit, the fleeting and what passes for permanent. No aspect of human affairs is completely isolated from contact with the law. And the history of the language of the law must be connected to law and to non-law. Its history cannot be satisfactorily treated as a mere "digression" [1] from the history of the law, although the two are bound tightly together. The growth of English from a picturesque but riotous assembly of words into a more standardized (if still flexible) speech is at least of equal importance. The tradition of illiteracy which gave birth to the common law; the introduction of printing in England; the development of law as a profession in England and America — these are some of the interwoven elements which are a part of the history of the language of the law. This is neither a history of the law nor a history of the English language, but draws upon both in following the language of the law to its present form.

All history is a matter of the focus of attention. The focus here is on the reasons for the peculiarities of the language of the law: a study of the circumstances which have promoted, channeled, and stunted its development.

---

[1] 1 Pollock and Maitland, *The History of English Law* 87 (2d ed. 1898); 2 Holdsworth, *A History of English Law* 478 (3d ed. 1923); see also Gowers, *Plain Words* 6 (1948).

24. *England as the point of departure*

. As a history has no end, it likewise has no fixed point of beginning. Any selection is arbitrary. Where does the language of the law begin?

The word *law* itself is of Scandinavian origin. It came into Old English about 1000 A.D. from prehistoric Old Norse. (Section 35.) This in turn had been derived from the Old Icelandic word meaning "something laid or fixed." [2] The touchstone of the legal profession, the Latin *res* (thing, matter), with its work-horse forms *re* and *rem*, is related to the ancient Indian word *rati*, meaning "there is." [3] *Deodand*, the primitive notion that a chattel which kills must itself be destroyed, enters the language of the law from the Anglo-French *deodande*. And that was an adaptation of the medieval Latin *deodanum*, properly *deo dandum*, to be given to God. [4] (The forfeited chattel was to be devoted to pious uses. [5]) The practice itself (though not the word) is traceable to the Mosaic code:

> If an ox gore a man or a woman, that they die: then the ox shall be surely stoned, and his flesh shall not be eaten; but the owner of the ox shall be quit. [6]

Three thousand years later, an American statute says that ". . . all forfeitures . . . in the nature of a *deodand* . . . are abolished," [7] but the same jurisdiction continues to personify chattels by forfeiting automobiles that carry narcotics. [8] Also in this twentieth century, automobiles have been burdened with a statutory lien in favor of their victims, [9] despite the disavowal of deodand. [10] And admiralty regularly proceeds against wrongdoing ships. [11]

Wherever one turns the law and the language of the law interlock with the laws and languages of other lands and other times. As Bacon said of "the laws of England":

[2] *Oxford English Dictionary;* Jespersen, *Growth and Structure of the English Language*, par. 74 (Anchor, 9th ed. 1955).

[3] Tur-Sinai, "The Origin of Language," in Anshen, ed., *Language* 71 (1957).

[4] *Oxford English Dictionary.*

[5] 2 Pollock and Maitland, *The History of English Law* 473 (2d ed. 1898).

[6] Ex. 21:28; see also 1 Blackstone, *Commentaries* *301 (Jones ed. 1916), and Holmes, *The Common Law* 7 (1881).

[7] Cal. Pen. Code §2604.

[8] Cal. Health & Safety Code §11,610; *People v. One 1941 Ford*, 26 Cal. 2d 503 (1945).

[9] *Parker-Harris Co. v. Tate*, 135 Tenn. 509, 512, 514-515 (1916).

[10] Tenn. Const., art. 1, §12.

[11] Adm. Rules 9 and 10, 28 U.S.C.A. (1950).

It is true, they are as mixt as our language, compounded of British, Roman, Saxon, Danish, Norman customs. And as our language is so much the richer, so the laws are the more complete . . .[12]

All of this, though, is a matter of finding distant origins for distinctive products — the common law of England and the language of the law. Each has countless collateral relatives as well as a polyglot parentage. But each developed its own personality — in England. The language of the law, nourished and pocked by the words of many cultures, still comes to America directly from England. Without ignoring its far-reaching roots, we concentrate then on the language of the law — as it developed in England, emigrated to America, and here prospered.

[12] 5 Bacon, *Works* 339-340, and see also 359 (Montagu ed. 1826); compare Blackstone, *Commentaries,* introduction °64 (Jones ed. 1916).

CHAPTER V

Before the Normans

25. The Celtic invasion

Long before the birth of Christ, Celtic nomads, who had fought their way from one end of Europe to the other, entered the British Isles. Whether these were the *Pretani*[1] (the painted people), or whether the invader so described the island natives,[2] scholars do not agree, but *Britannia* bears an unmistakable Celtic stamp.[3] Human sacrifice and the blood feud were a part of this ancient Celtic culture. So too was a communal organization related to the later manorial system.[4] All Celtic sons inherited the land — a custom so like the English *gavel-kind*[5] that for years respectable authority gave the word a Celtic origin, derived from the Irish *gabhailcine* for family tenure.[6] (That attribution has since been rejected along with the descriptive folk etymology accepted by Coke, *gave all kind*.[7] *Gavelkind* is now thought to originate in a tenure that was non-military: *gafol* (rent) + *ȝecynd* (nature). This makes it Old English, though not without a dissent from O'Reilly's *Irish Dictionary*.[8])

We are also told of Celtic lawyers, for centuries perpetuating a customary law in a "learnedly archaic language":[9] the learning of law an unchanging ritual, with the slightest departure from the magic of word-for-word accuracy a violation of tribal taboo. Like prayer, the

---

[1] Powell, *The Celts* 56 (1958).

[2] Feiling, *A History of England* 7 (1950); 12 *Encyclopaedia Britannica* 598 (1948).

[3] K. Jackson, *Language and History in Early Britain* 4 (1953); *Oxford English Dictionary*, under *Briton*.

[4] Vinogradoff, *The Growth of the Manor* 35-36 (2d ed. 1932).

[5] Vinogradoff, *The Growth of the Manor* 13 (2d ed. 1932); Coke, *Commentary upon Littleton*, f. 175b (10th ed. 1703).

[6] Skeat, *A Concise Etymological Dictionary* 172 (1882).

[7] Coke, *Commentary upon Littleton*, f. 140a (10th ed. 1703).

[8] Skeat, *An Etymological Dictionary* 236 (new ed. 1909); *Oxford English Dictionary*, under *gavel*, sb.[1], and *gavelkind*; 3 Holdsworth, *A History of English Law* 259 (3d ed. 1923); 1 Pollock and Maitland, *The History of English Law* 186 (2d ed. 1898).

[9] Powell, *The Celts* 78 (1958).

tradition is repetitive and oral. As described in the ancient Irish book of the law, *Senchus Mor,* it is:

"... the joint memory of the ancients, the transmission from one ear to another, the chanting of the poets." [10]

In a passage without present-day support, Coke accepted a notion that "the ancient Brittains" wrote their law in Greek.[11] Though of their Irish kinsmen, he says they had "no law, but a lewd custom," [12] i.e., unlettered. If the Greek writings ever existed, none survive. Better than Coke's "historical judgment" ("worthless," said Pollock),[13] is his rationalization for the supposed practice. For in various forms the same justification echoes through the history of the law:

... they used to do it in the Greek tongue, to the end that their discipline might not be made common among the vulgar.[14]

26. *Celtic survives the Roman occupation*

Celtic was the dominant language of Britain until the Roman occupation in the first century A.D. The Latin interlude ended when the last Roman legions withdrew in 407 A.D., and it was Celtic — not Latin — that greeted the first Anglo-Saxon invaders in the middle fifth century.[15] Before the multitudes of Angles, Saxons, and Jutes, and the vigor of Old English, Celtic was driven into a poor second place. Its chief survial today is in the nationalist tongues of Eire, Scotland, and Wales. Except for place names (e.g., London, Kent), Celtic influence on the English language has been small.[16] Three Celtic words have established some connection with the law.

Whisky, short for *whiskybae,* is the English version of Gaelic *uisge-beatha* (water of life). It is not a law word, but the substantial contributions of *whisky* to the law have been recognized by its inclusion in American law dictionaries.[17]

Unlike *whisky, hubbub* does not appear in the law dictionaries,

[10] Quoted in Powell, *The Celts* 159 (1958).
[11] 5 Holdsworth, *A History of English Law* 459 (1924).
[12] Coke, *Commentary upon Littleton,* f. 141a (10th ed. 1703).
[13] Pollock, *A First Book of Jurisprudence* 304 n.1 (4th ed. 1918).
[14] 2 *Coke's Reports,* pts. III-IV, pp. xiv-xviii (new ed., Butterworth, 1826); see also Maine, *Ancient Law* 11 and Note C at 24 (new ed. 1930).
[15] Vinogradoff, *The Growth of the Manor* 40-42, 120 (2d ed. 1932).
[16] K. Jackson, *Language and History in Early Britain* 256-257 (1953); Skeat, *An Etymological Dictionary* 765 (new ed. 1909).
[17] Ballentine, *Law Dictionary with Pronunciations* (2d ed. 1948); *Black's Law Dictionary* (4th ed. 1951); *Bouvier's Law Dictionary and Concise Encyclopedia* (3d rev. 8th ed. 1914); and see 45 *Words and Phrases* (perm. ed. 1940, Supp. 1962), "whisky" and related words.

though it once had a closer tie to the language of the law. An old Irish warcry, *hubbub* was used in the Plantation Agreement of colonial Rhode Island as a synonym for the common law *hue and cry* (Section 100), the call for villagers to join in hot pursuit of a wrongdoer:

> . . . but if any man raise a hubbub, and there is no just cause, then for the party that raised the hubbub to satisfy men for their time lost in it.[18]

Hubbub added to its own confusion, for New Englanders also so described a noisy Indian game. *Hubbub* has left the law, but continues in general usage, along with the rarer Irish synonym *hubbuboo*.

The Irish *tory* (pursuer) has haunted the border between law and politics since its seventeenth-century origin to describe Irish outlaws. Today, without much choler, *tory* describes an unreconstructed conservative on both sides of the Atlantic. Yet a hundred years ago it stirred men's passions. The Revolution made *tory* a fighting word in America.[19] Judicial opinion of its defamatory character has varied.[20] But the most magnificent achievement of *tory* is that it has occasioned one of the finest pieces of nonjudicial (but not dull) rhetoric ever to escape from the bench. *Tory* was only one of the charges in a free-ranging screed posted on a tree in Georgia. Mr. Justice Lumpkin considered the appeal from a conviction of criminal libel. After purpling the discussion of the incidental accusation of cuckoldry, the judge continued:

> But the enormity of this libel stops not here. As if to involve its victim in the lowest depths of infamy and disgrace, he is accused, not only of being a tory in the war of the Revolution, but with having been punished in the most ignominious manner for the robberies which he then committed. When the name of Washington shall grow old and cold to the ear of the partiot; when it shall be synonymous with that of Arnold; when "the poles of the earth shall be swung round ninety degrees, to a coincidence with the equator," then, and not before, will it cease to be a libel to call a man a plundering tory of the Revolution! [21]

27. A pattern of language mixture

Though Celtic influence on the language of the law is slight (Section 26), the period of the mingling of the Celts with their Anglo-Saxon

---

[18] "Plantation Agreement at Providence" (1640), in 6 F. Thorpe, ed., *The Federal and State Constitutions, Colonial Charters, and Other Organic Laws* (1909).

[19] Mencken, *The American Language Supplement I* 299 and especially n.2 (1945).

[20] See *Hogg v. Dorrah*, 2 Porter 212 (Ala. 1835).

[21] *Giles v. State*, 6 Ga. 276, 284 (1849).

conquerors does supply a clue to the origin of one peculiarity of our law language. One of the sources of tautology is the prolonged presence of two languages side by side. England, for example, is peppered with place names which would read *Hill-hill,* or worse, except that the first *hill* is Celtic (*bre* or *cruc* or *penn*) and the other Old English (*hyll*), for instance, names like *Breedon-on-the-hill, Churchill,*[22] *Penhill, Pendle Hill.* It has been suggested that these formations indicate not knowledge but ignorance: a misunderstanding, in which the invader thinks *penn* is a place name, and adds his own *hill* for identification.[23] Yet whether repetition is deliberate translation to accommodate two cultures or arises through error, it is one of the results of a collision of languages. The English language has survived several such collisions, and the language of the law has been one of the wordy victims. This penchant of English for coupling with foreign synonyms may be traced from Celtic through Scandinavian (Sections 35, 36), Latin (Chapter VII), and French (Section 71). It is by no means a complete explanation of law tautology, but the pattern begins early and stays late.

28. Anglo-Saxon beginnings

A separate language called English gets its name from the invading Angles (Section 31) and dates from around 450 A.D. In that mid-century the Angles and other Teutonic raiders (Saxons and Jutes) left their homes in what is now Denmark and northern Germany and began a serious penetration of the British Isles. Their influence makes English still a predominantly Teutonic speech. In turn, this Teutonic speech is a branch of the hypothetical Indo-European language that also spawned Latin, and then French as a dialect of Latin. So that at a very early date what was later to be English and what was later to be French were related. The law words *robber* and *rob,* which English gained from French in the twelfth and thirteenth centuries, French had earlier received from some distant Teutonic source. The language the Anglo-Saxons brought to England had already within it a nucleus of Latin words, such as the ancestors of *mint* (which meant *money*), *dicker* (ten hides), *inch, pound, mile,*[24] and possibly an earlier form of the legal *seal.*[25]

---

[22] Sheard, *The Words We Use* 151 (1954).
[23] K. Jackson, *Language and History in Early Britain* 245 (1953); compare Coke, *Commentary upon Littleton,* f. 5b (10th ed. 1703).
[24] Sheard, *The Words We Use* 124 (1954).
[25] Serjeantson, *A History of Foreign Words in English* 271 (1935).

The raw materials of words — the letters we use — speak of our remotest past. Thus the first letter of the Hebrew alphabet, the *aleph* (predecessor of *alpha*),[26] means *ox*. In the runic alphabet which the Anglo-Saxons brought to England the letter *F*, called a *feh*, or *feoh*,[27] meant *cattle, money,* and *property*. This Old English *fee* (a later spelling) was the wealth of the Anglo-Saxon as was the *aleph* of the ancient Jews. You were paid in cattle, and the property was movable. Since the O.E. *fee* was movable, the *Oxford English Dictionary* (though not Skeat)[28] rejects a Germanic origin for *fee*, when it means a feudal estate or the absolute ownership of land.[29]   But the mobility of cattle (*chatel* in Old French) did not prevent *chattel* from originally referring to all property, movable or fixed. (Section 38.)   In any event, cattle was king to the Anglo-Saxon: a bargain, a barter, selling, market, price, merchandise were all expressed by another word for cattle, O.E. *ceap* (later *cheap*, a good buy).   And the customary laws of the Anglo-Saxons were adapted to a hunting and cattle-grazing society.   The O.E. form of *own* meant *possess*, for it was possession, not ownership, that was obvious and so protected.[30]   The very words *owner* and *ownership* do not appear in our vocabulary till long after the end of the Anglo-Saxon period.[31]

This Anglo-Saxon society was not only a simple but a savage one.   It was a mark of advancing civilization that family vengeance — the blood feud — could be ended by payment of *wergild*, the price of a man's head (in the ancient proverb, "Buy off the spear or bear it").[32] It was a strange thing for a man to be forced into court, the surrender of an old freedom, and jurisdiction was not readily conceded.   Carefully proved summons, repeated demands, acceptance of repeated excuses for non-appearance, were all a part of the gradual enticement of the savage to settle a dispute by something less than bloodshed.

Once in court (called a *thing* in Old English), the judicial process was still rudimentary.   Guilt or innocence could depend on a litigant's success in carrying in hand a redhot iron.[33]   Under the law, a man

[26] 1 *Encyclopaedia Britannica* 677, 681 (1948).
[27] Earle, *The Philology of the English Tongue* 102 (4th ed. 1887).
[28] Skeat, *An Etymological Dictionary* 210 (new ed. 1909).
[29] *Oxford English Dictionary,* under *fee,* sb.².
[30] Holmes, *The Common Law* 166, 167 (1881).
[31] 2 Pollock and Maitland, *The History of English Law* 153 (2d ed. 1898); 2 Holdsworth, *A History of English Law* 78 (3d ed. 1923); *Oxford English Dictionary,* under *owner* and *ownership.*
[32] Quoted in 2 Holdsworth, *A History of English Law* 45 (3d ed. 1923),
[33] 4 Blackstone, *Commentaries* °344 (Jones ed. 1916).

might lose his tongue for perjuring himself [34] or for speaking a bad word.[35] A word was a dangerous thing — more difficult to handle than a stick or stone, and its effects not as predictable. If a word was dangerous, it could also work magic,[36] and word magic is one of the law's inheritances from its primitive past. (See Section 29.)

29. *Laws for illiterates*

Like the Celts they overran, the Angles, Saxons, and Jutes were largely illiterate. More than a thousand years later — in an England where literacy was still not general [37] — Sir William Blackstone wrote:

> It is true, indeed, that, in the profound ignorance of letters which formerly overspread the whole western world, all laws were entirely traditional, for this plain reason, that the nations among which they prevailed had but little idea of writing.[38]

Illiteracy and an oral tradition are sides of the same coin. There was small place in early Anglo-Saxon England for a law of contract;[39] the open sale before a witness, the pledge of faith with oath and surety, the Biblical handshake[40] — these generally sufficed.[41] Action more than words. And the words spoken important more for their immediate effect than for promise. The solemn words of oath-taking created an immediate relationship, and put in pawn a part of a man's personality. Particular words — not words of inherent precise meaning, but magical words that could stir a God or wreck a soul. Such for example was the oath of fealty (in translation):

> By the Lord, before whom this relic is holy, I will be to N. faithful and true, and love all that he loves, and shun all that he shuns, according to God's law, and according to the world's principles, and never, by will nor by force, by word nor by work, do aught of what is loathful to him; on condition that he me keep as I am willing to deserve, and all that fulfill that our agreement was, when I to him submitted and chose his will.[42]

This was formula, part of a ritual. Its repetition in this exact form — and in no other — would produce the desired effect. It was this way too in an Anglo-Saxon court. Both claim and defense were oral. Each

[34] Tyler, *Oaths* 227 (1834).
[35] Plucknett, *A Concise History of the Common Law* 483 (5th ed. 1956).
[36] Frazer, *The Golden Bough* 284 (abridged ed. 1951).
[37] Watt, *The Rise of the Novel* 37-39 (1957).
[38] Blackstone, *Commentaries*, introduction °63 (Jones ed. 1916).
[39] 1 Pollock and Maitland, *The History of English Law* 43, 44 (2d ed. 1898).
[40] Job 17:3; Proverbs 6:1; 2 Kings 10:15; Tyler, *Oaths* 104-107 (1834).
[41] 2 Holdsworth, *A History of English Law* 81-82 (3d ed. 1923).
[42] 1 B. Thorpe, ed., *Ancient Laws and Institutes of England* 179 (1840).

must use traditional, formal words,[43] oath against oath, with the confidence and fear that a false oath would damn.

The plaintiff swore:

> By the Lord, before whom this relic is holy, so I my suit prosecute with full folk-right, without fraud and without deceit, and without any guile, as was stolen from me the cattle N. that I claim, and that I have attached with N.[44]

And the defendant answered (originally Old English *andswarian,* to swear in reply):

> By the Lord, I was not at rede [counsel] nor at deed, neither counsellor nor doer, where were unlawfully led away N.'s cattle. But as I cattle have, so did I lawfully obtain it. . . . And: as I cattle have, so did it come of my own property, and so it by folk-right my own possession is, and my rearing.[45]

This is traditional, oral pleading. The pleader is the litigant, a nonprofessional, and the words are designed to impress him, his neighbors, and the judges. The ultimate appeal is to the supernatural, and the appeal won't work unless it is worded by the rule. Folk wisdom also takes a hand here. For in an illiterate society only word-for-word repetition will insure survival of ideas too important to risk losing.[46] And if the words are cast in a form pleasing to the ear, retention and repetition are made the easier. (See Section 30.)

30. *The law gets rhythm*

Literature is best adapted to oral transmission when clothed in rhythm. And in common with other primitives, the Anglo-Saxons rose to their literary best with poetry. The classic of Old English is the epic poem ·*Beowulf.*[47] It marks an emphasis on alliteration that has remained a characteristic of English poetry and prose.[48] The law of the Anglo-Saxons picked up the alliterative and rhythmical fashions of the day. Even in modern dress, the old oaths have an impressive poetical roll, words at work for their own sound effect.

Hear the "unbought" witness:

---

[43] 1 Holdsworth, *A History of English Law* 301 (3d ed. 1922); 2 Holdsworth, *A History of English Law* 105 (3d ed. 1923).

[44] 1 B. Thorpe, ed., *Ancient Laws and Institutes of England* 179 (1840).

[45] 1 B. Thorpe, ed., *Ancient Laws and Institutes of England* 179-181 (1840).

[46] Compare Maine, *Ancient Law* 11 (new ed. 1930).

[47] Baugh, *A History of the English Language* 80-83 (1935); see also Quiller-Couch, *On the Art of Writing* 70-73 (1916).

[48] Jespersen, *Growth and Structure of the English Language,* pars. 54, 55, 56 (Anchor, 9th ed. 1955).

In the name of Almighty God, as I here for N. in true witness stand, unbidden and unbought, so I with my eyes oversaw, and with my ears overheard, that which I with him say.[49]

And the ancestor of the allegation on information and belief:

By the Lord, I accuse not N. either for hatred or for envy, or for unlawful lust of gain; nor know I anything soother [truer]; but as my informant to me said, and I myself in sooth believe, that he was the thief of my property.[50]

The vein of rhythm runs through the language of the law, sometimes in traditional oral words, sometimes carried over into what is only written. It is a short step from the most ancient Anglo-Saxon oaths to the redundant but poetic *truth, the whole truth, and nothing but the truth,* Old English words joined in an oath still current. The power of alliteration has also helped preserve in the law tautologies such as *to have and to hold, mind and memory, new and novel, aid and abet, part and parcel, safe and sound, rest, residue, and remainder,* while other rhythms help keep alive the duplicating *remise, release, and forever quitclaim; give, devise and bequeath;* and the more meaningful *ready, willing, and able.* Not all of these combinations are Old English (Section 71), but the tradition of rhythm in the common law begins here in the earliest part of the Old English period.

The tradition includes rhythm not merely for its own sake but also rhythm as an aid to memory and instruction. Littleton used Latin doggerel,[51] and Coke — while liberally salting his writing with verse[52] — a trifle self-consciously rationalized its use:

Verses at the first were invented for the help of memory; and it standeth well with the gravity of our Lawyer to cite them.[53]

Coke's advice was persuasive, and the learning of his Reports was later reduced to rhyming couplets, such as these:

ARCHER, If he for life in feoff in fee:
It bars remainders in contingency.[54]

SHELLEY, Where ancestors a freehold take:
The words (*his heirs*) a limitation make.[55]

---

[49] 1 B. Thorpe, ed., *Ancient Laws and Institutes of England* 181 (1840).
[50] 1 B. Thorpe, ed., *Ancient Laws and Institutes of England* 181 (1840).
[51] Coke, *Commentary upon Littleton,* ff. 236b, 264a, 395a (10th ed. 1703).
[52] Coke, *Commentary upon Littleton,* ff. 64b, 85b, 95b, 140b-141a (10th ed. 1703).
[53] Coke, *Commentary upon Littleton,* f. 237a (10th ed. 1703).
[54] *The Reports of Sir Edward Coke, Kt. in Verse,* pt. I, Case VI, f. 66 (1742).
[55] *The Reports of Sir Edward Coke, Kt. in Verse,* pt. I, Case IX, f. 93 (1742).

A repetitive lilt preserves the sense of many a legal maxim. Thus, *Cessante ratione legis cessat ipsa lex* and *Qui facit per alium facit per se.* The sin of perjury is warned against in *Once forsworn, and ever forlorn.*[56]

Seventeenth-century law dictionaries pointed up definition with rhyme, such as this one to illustrate a form of sealing:

> And in witness that it was sooth,
> He bit the Wax with his foretooth.[57]

This on *deodand* (Section 24):

> What moves to Death, or Kills him dead,
> Is Deodand, and forfeited.[58]

And this one describing the humiliation of an errant tenant in *free bench* (Latin *francus bancus*). By manorial custom a widow would forfeit an estate in her husband's lands if she "commit Incontinency." The land was redeemed if "she will come into Court riding backward on a Black Ram with his tail in her hand," and say:

> Here I am,
> Riding upon a Black Ram,
> Like a Whore as I am.
> And for my *Crincum crancum* [intercourse or v.d.] [59]
> Have lost my *Binkum Bankum*[60]
> And for my Tails Game,
> Have done this Worldly shame.
> Therefore I pray you Mr. Steward let me
> have my Land again.[61]

The rhyming twins Doe and Roe have themselves been immortalized in the eighteenth-century *Pleader's Guide, A Didactic Poem in Two Books:*

> Whom Law United, nor the Grave Can Sever,
> All hail John Doe, and Richard Roe for ever.[62]

And the tradition is still alive:

[56] Tyler, *Oaths* 228 (1834).
[57] *Les Termes de la Ley* (1671), under *fait* (*deed*); compare Jacob, *A New Law-Dictionary* (6th ed. 1750), under *wang.*
[58] Blount, *A Law-Dictionary and Glossary* (1717); compare Blount, *Nomo-Lexikon* (1670).
[59] See *Oxford English Dictionary*, under *crinkum* and *crinkum-crankum;* Partridge, *A Dictionary of Slang and Unconventional English* (4th ed. 1951), under *crinkum* and *crinkum-crankum;* Partridge, *A Dictionary of the Underworld* (1950), under *crinkums.*
[60] See *Oxford English Dictionary*, under *bink.*
[61] Blount, *Nomo-Lexikon* (1670), under *freebench.*
[62] [Anstey], *The Pleader's Guide*, bk. I, p. 79 (1796).

Can women bear at 70? Ask any obstetrician
And he will say: "My dear old fellow! Hawdly!"
But we who know the R.A.P. and Chancery tradition
Will simply smile and cite him *Jee and Audley*.[63]

31. *Anglo-Saxon Old English*

Old English is the term now generally used to describe the immediate ancestor of *Middle English*. It distinguishes the language of
Beowulf from the language of Chaucer. The period of Old English
extends from the mid-fifth-century Teutonic raids (Section 28) to the
Norman Conquest in 1066, generally rounded off at 1100.[64] Some
choose 1150 as an approximate end-date for Old English,[65] taking
cognizance of the fact that a portion of the histories collectively known
as the *Anglo-Saxon Chronicle* (dating from King Alfred's day) continue to 1154.[66] *Webster's New International Dictionary* prefers the
designation *Anglo-Saxon* to *Old English*,[67] though the Angles and
Saxons themselves called their language *Englisc* at least as early as the
ninth century.[68]

By the time of the Norman Conquest, Old English includes as an
integral part of the language not merely words of Anglo-Saxon origin,
but also some Celtic, Latin, and Norse. The Celtic is negligible (Sections 26, 27). Before the Normans, the Latin is just a beginning.
(Sections 28, 33, 34.) And the Old Norse borrowings are basic but
modest. (Section 35.)

Even without these foreign additions, the Old English of the Anglo-
Saxons was an effective speech. *Beowulf* (Section 30) dates from the
eighth century or earlier.[69] Its language is rich in synonym, with two
fistfuls of words for the *sea* and a dozen for *ship*.[70] The Old English

[63] Leach, ed., *Langdell Lyrics of 1938*, p. 14 (1938); see also Swain, *Judicial Jingles* (1955).

[64] *Webster's New International Dictionary* lxxxii-lxxxvi (2d ed. 1934); 1 *Oxford English Dictionary* xxx; 8 *Encyclopaedia Britannica* 554 (1948); Bosworth and Toller, *An Anglo-Saxon Dictionary* i (1898); Setzler, *The Jefferson Anglo-Saxon Grammar and Reader* 3-4 (1938).

[65] Jespersen, *Growth and Structure of the English Language* iv (Anchor, 9th ed. 1955); 1 Johnson, *A Dictionary of the English Language* (4th ed. 1775), under "History of the English Language."

[66] 1 *Encyclopaedia Britannica* 947 (1948).

[67] *Webster's New International Dictionary* (2d ed. 1934), under *English*.

[68] *Oxford English Dictionary*, under *English;* 1 Freeman, *The History of the Norman Conquest of England* 533-548 and especially 542-544 (3d ed. 1877).

[69] 3 *Encyclopaedia Britannica* 425 (1948); 2 Holdsworth, *A History of English Law* 33 (3d ed. 1923).

[70] Sheard, *The Words We Use* 134-135 (1954); compare Jespersen, *Growth and Structure of the English Language*, par. 49 (Anchor, 9th ed. 1955); see also Baugh, *A History of the English Language* 81 (1935).

law oaths as we have them recorded today (Sections 29, 30) probably date from the ninth and tenth centuries.[71] The laws of King Aethelbert of Kent were published in Old English as early as C. 596,[72] two hundred years or more before Old French is classified as a language separate from Vulgar Latin.[73]

Old English had a tremendous capacity for creating words by compounding. For example, you could parlay *cyning* (king) to get *under-cyning* (viceroy), *healhcyning* (chief, God), *cyningdom* (king's power = sovereignty), and many more.[74] Or, for example, common words familiar to the law, *hereafter, herein, hereof, herewith.* (Section 37.) In later days, this flexibility of Old English originals produced such words as *notwithstanding* from the O.E. for *withstand* (Section 53), and *upkeep* from the O.E. for *keep* and *up.* In the Christian era, the language accommodated itself readily to a host of new abstractions. (Section 34.) And even before the Latin of the Church, and additions from Old Norse (Section 35), Old English had an important law vocabulary. (See Section 32.)

32. *Law words from Anglo-Saxon Old English*

The Anglo-Saxon period is too early to properly speak of a language of the law, for there was as yet no distinct profession. But there was an expressive vocabulary, adequate to the demands of the law as it was then known. In this context, to urge that "A primitive system of law has no technical terms" [75] is an overrefinement.

For example, here are some words from the obsolete Anglo-Saxon law list suited to the technicality of their day:

agan	to run out (of a lease)
unagan	not lapsed
boc	book, charter, deed
bocland	land governed by the charter
folcland	land not governed by the special terms of a charter, but by folk custom
hand-haebbende	one caught with the stolen goods (of a thief)
wer	a man (sometimes also used to mean *wergild*)

[71] 1 B. Thorpe, ed., *Ancient Laws and Institutes of England* 178 (1840).
[72] 2 Holdsworth, *A History of English Law* 19, 20 (3d ed. 1923); 1 B. Thorpe, ed., *Ancient Laws and Institutes of England* 2-43 (1840); cf. 1 *P.&M.* 19.
[73] 9 *Encyclopedia Britannica* 760 (1948); 1 Freeman, *The History of the Norman Conquest of England*, n. V, pp. 617-620 (3rd ed. 1877).
[74] Bosworth and Toller, *An Anglo-Saxon Dictionary* 186 (1898); Toller, *An Anglo-Saxon Dictionary: Supplement* 141 (1921).
[75] 2 Holdsworth, *A History of English Law* 43 (3d ed. 1923).

wergild	man compensation: the price of a man's life, graduated by social class (See Section 28.)
wergildþeof	a thief whose criminality had been ended by the payment of his *wergild* (the runic thorn þ equals today's *th*)

Glossaries[76] and Old English dictionaries[77] list numbers of additional words which — like these — have been removed from our law vocabulary by changing legal concepts and French influence.

Other Old English law words of the Anglo-Saxon era have had a partial survival. Here are some of them:

bohr	pledge or surety (lives on in our related *borrow*, which stems from the Anglo-Saxon system of requiring security for the return of borrowed property)
bot	compensation for wrongdoing (has lasted in *bootless*)
bootless	an act that could not be expiated by *bot*
to boot	to the good (in bargaining) (has meant this at least since the year 1000; as a noun *boot* (something to the good) is now part of the tax lawyer's vocabulary)[78]
deem	to pronounce judgment (still means *to consider*)
deemer	a judge (our judges still *deem*, and in the Isle of Man a judge is a *deemster*)
doom	a law, judgment, or decision (from this came the Middle English verb sense, to pronounce judgment)
doombook	judgment book (the modern translation is half French, half Old English) (See Sections 70, 71.)
doomer	a judge (no longer technical; still understandable)
laen	a lease (from a verb form of this we have *lend*; the related *loan* is from Old Norse) (See Section 35.)
wed (noun)	security for performance (survives in the Old English *wedding* and *wedlock*; the ring perhaps is the token security)[79]
wed (verb)	to covenant (in the O.E. form *weddian*)
witan	to know, to be wise (retained in its form *to wit*; the related *witness* belongs in the next category of Anglo-Saxon survivals)

Today's law vocabulary has many more words — some not in the exclusive possession of lawyers — that trace a continuous history to

---

[76] Robertson, ed., *Anglo-Saxon Charters* 544-555 (2d ed. 1956); Robertson, ed. and transl., *The Laws of the Kings of England*, 376-426 (1925); Stubbs, ed., *Select Charters* 535-554 (8th ed. 1905); 2 B. Thorpe, ed., *Ancient Laws and Institutes of England*, glossary (1840).

[77] Bosworth and Toller, *An Anglo-Saxon Dictionary* (1898); Toller, *An Anglo-Saxon Dictionary: Supplement* (1921); Sweet, *The Student's Dictionary of Anglo-Saxon* (1896); see also Blount, *Nomo-Lexikon* (1670); Blount, *A Law-Dictionary and Glosary* (1717); Cowell, *The Interpreter* (1637); *The Student's Law-Dictionary* (1740); *Les Termes de la Ley* (1671 and 1708).

[78] 3 Mertens, *The Law of Federal Income Taxation* §20.144 (rev. ed. 1957).

[79] 2 Holdsworth, *A History of English Law* 89 (3d ed. 1923).

Anglo-Saxon Old English. Despite variation in spelling and meaning, they have had legal significance since the days before the Norman Conquest. These are some of them:

answer	(See Section 29.)
bequeath	
break	to enter a house by force
buy	
child	
deed	an act (as distinguished from an instrument)
drunken	
forgive	to remit a debt; to pardon an offense
free	
gallows	
give	
goods	
guilt	
guilty	
have	to have property
hire	
hold	to have property
kin	
land	
landlord	
let	to rent; hindrance
manslaughter	any homicide
moot	a meeting or court
murder	murder, especially secret killing[80]
name	
oath	
own	to possess (See Section 28.)
right	
sell	
sheriff	
steal	
swear	
theft	
thief	
truth	quality of being true to a person
ward	guard (O.E. *weard*) (See Section 60.)
	to guard (O.E. *weardian*)
wife	
will	an expression of the will as distinguished from the document, but it was used in Old English wills[81]
witness	
writ	something written (in the sense of a legal document, the *Oxford English Dictionary* gives 1122 as the earliest recorded date)[82]

[80] 1 Pollock and Maitland, *The History of English Law* 52-53 (2d ed. 1898).
[81] Robertson, ed., *Anglo-Saxon Charters* 10 (2d ed. 1956).
[82] *Oxford English Dictionary*, under *writ*, sb., No. 3.

33. *Heathen into Christian*

In the later days of the Roman occupation of Britain (Section 26), the Church had made its first halting moves into Britain. The effort had produced martyrdom, and some successes, but — except for remnants in Wales — little of Christianity remained after the Romans departed. In the late sixth century, the process began again, first under Irish impetus and finally — and successfully — with Augustine, who came to friendly Kent in 597. There the Queen of Kent, a Continental, had already been converted to Christianity, and her husband Aethelbert is credited with the earliest written code of Anglo-Saxon law. (Section 31.) One hundred years after Augustine's landing, the conversion was complete — not without lapses from grace, but such unification as England then knew was only in the Church. Political unification was long in following — after two invasions and more than three and a half centuries of intermittent warfare. The Church became a part of England in daily life, in state councils and in courts, in law and in literature, in war and in peace. With the Church came renewed ties with the Continent, an interest in learning, a knowledge of writing, and a reintroduction to Latin. (Section 28.) From that day on, churchmen had an important hand in shaping the common law and its language. It is in this period before the Norman Conquest that the English language acquired from Latin the word which for many practicing lawyers today marks the very center of the court system — the *clerk*. Originally it meant a Catholic priest.

34. *Language influences of Christianity*

The Church did not bring *heaven* and *hell* to England. They were already there as Old English words: *heofon* as the sky and residence of the gods; *hell* as a place of life after death. Christianity gave a new meaning to both words. Hell became a place of torment, inhabited by devils, oathbreakers, and other condemned souls. And it was now understood that a good man might live forever in heaven. This shift of emphasis put considerably more wallop into the oath. (Sections 29, 30.) And a deed (*boc*, Section 32) or will (*cwide*) drawn by a literate clergyman often threatened hell-fire and damnation for those who tried to upset the transfers.

A tenth-century deed, for example, recites the witnesses to the delivery of possession, and adds:

And Archbishop Wulfhelm and all the bishops and abbots who were there assembled excommunicated from Christ and from all the fellowship of Christ and from the whole of Christendom anyone who should ever undo this grant or reduce this estate in pasture or in boundary. He shall be cut off and hurled into the abyss of hell for ever without end. And all the people who stood by said "So be it, Amen, Amen." [83]

Words are not spared. Though redundant, "for ever without end" is both lyrical and impressive.

A charter of King Aethelstan (934) gives a similar forecast of the fate of tamperers:

. . . all those, whoever they be — shall be the companion of Judas, the betrayer of Christ, enduring punishment for all time in the torment of hell.[84]

Written conveyances were still rare, and wills were mostly for the wealthy. Not all these documents are florid, but such excesses as there are must be read with the draftsman's knowledge that enforcement at law was conjectural. Some extra words and a good, strong curse might stay a grasping hand. The doubts which arose in the minds of Anglo-Saxon testators appear plaintively in a ninth-century will, which concludes:

And I entreat the community [i.e., the Church] for the love of God, that the man to whom the community grants the usufruct of the estate carry out the same arrangements with regard to a feast at my anniversary, as my heirs shall have appointed it, and so obtain the divine reward for my soul.[85]

More than literary style reflected the influence of the Church. Through the clergy, Latin words in increasing numbers became a part of the English language. Some of them that now have meaning in the law originally were exclusively religious terms:

cell   in a prison, is kin to the medieval *cell* in a monastery
offer   started out as an offering to God
title   was the inscription on the Cross

The English took a little and gave a little in making their adjust-ment to the language of the new religion. They adopted some of the Latinisms and Greek and Hebrew derivatives, e.g., *bishop* indirectly from Greek, and *Christ* from Latin through Greek as the translation of the Hebrew for "messiah" or "annointed." But numbers of necessary

[83] Robertson, ed., *Anglo-Saxon Charters* 44-45 (2d ed. 1956).
[84] Robertson, ed., *Anglo-Saxon Charters* 46-47 (2d ed. 1956).
[85] Robertson, ed., *Anglo-Saxon Charters* 11 (2d ed. 1956).

theological terms they created anew on their own model, or adapted from existing Old English forms.

Instead of	They used Old English
benediction (Latin)	blessing (in the form bletsung)
evangel (Greek)	gospel (in the form godspel), good tidings
omnipotent (derived from Latin)	almighty

In this process, the blending of the terms of law and religion is again observable.

For the Latin	The Old English was
dies extremi judicii	Doomsday, judgment day[86] (See Section 32.)
penance (through French)	daedbote, act compensation
Pharisee (via Greek and Aramaic)	aelareow, law teacher (alternating with Pharisee itself, which was introduced into O.E. in the ninth century)

The Old English god, which antedated Christianity, was transferred to the new religion along with Old English weard (ward), which now became the heavenly warden. (See Section 32.)

Christianity gave an impetus to scholarship which made England the teacher of Europe. And even in later days when — demoralized by wealth, civil strife, and invasion — the Church had lost its strongest leadership, the spark of learning persisted. The Christian layman King Alfred saw to the translation into English of Bede's *Ecclesiastical History of the English Nation.* It was Alfred, too, who reminded his clergy that they must know Latin, and his administrators that they must be able to read English. Even before the Norman invasion a learned clergy had begun to reassert itself, but in the meantime Old English received a further foreign language infusion. (See Section 35.)

35. Vikings and the "law"

In the late eighth century, the still-heathen Scandinavian kinsmen of the Angles and Saxons commenced an expansionist career which culminated with the Danish King Canute on the English throne (1016) and other Norsemen (Normans) ensconced across the Channel in Normandy. In Normandy, the Vikings eventually spoke a dialect of a

---

[86] See Sheard, *The Words We Use* 158-162 (1954); Baugh, *A History of the English Language* 103 (1935).

dialect — Norman-French (Section 60), a vast departure from their native Teutonic tongue. In England, adaptation was easier, for Old Norse and Old English were so much alike that many words were identical.[87] By the time the Frenchified branch of the family arrived in 1066, Scandinavians had lived in England for more than two centuries: first in scattered settlements; then in a large section of eastern England, the Danelaw; and finally for almost three decades as rulers. Old English prevailed as the general language. But it was an Old English permanently left with a new source of dialect variation, and modified and enriched with Old Norse words and usages.

Before the Vikings came to England, Old English for *law* was *ae* (Section 34), related to a Sanskrit word meaning "course." [88]   *Ae* also meant *marriage*, and *ae* + *breaking* (O.E. *bryce*) could mean ordinary law-breaking or marriage-breaking (adultery),[89] a not very satisfactory situation. Though the written use of *ae* continued as late as the thirteenth century, the word of the new rulers of England prevailed — eventually in the form *law* (Old Norse singular *lag* and probable plural *lagu*). (Section 24.) The law of the Danes was likewise called in Old English by its Scandinavian name, an earlier form of *Danelaw*. (*Danelaw* as the designation of an area, and the name for the tax *Danegeld*, came later.)

Without resort to Norse, the closest approach Old English had to a name for *lawyer* was *forspeaker* (O.E. *forspeca* or *forspreca*), i.e., one who speaks for another, an advocate, a defender.[90] Fortunately this word did not fasten itself upon the profession, since *forspeak* later came to mean *bewitch* or *charm*, and a *forspeaker* became a *witch*.[91] The combining form for the Norse *law* in Old English was *lah*, and on this base were formed *lahmann* (law man) and *lahwita* (one who knows the law). In various spellings, *lawman* has been identified as the O.E. word for *lawyer*,[92] but it has more often been applied to one

---

[87] Baugh, *A History of the English Language* 117-119 (1935).
[88] *Oxford English Dictionary*, under *ae*, sb.2.
[89] Bosworth and Toller, *An Anglo-Saxon Dictionary* (1898), under *aew-bryce;* Toller, *An Anglo-Saxon Dictionary: Supplement* (1921), under *ae-bryce.*
[90] Bosworth and Toller, *An Anglo-Saxon Dictionary* (1898), under *fore-spreca* and *for-speca;* and see 1 Pollock and Maitland, *The History of English Law* 215 (2d ed. 1898); Blount, *A Law-Dictionary and Glossary* (1717), under *forspeaker;* and Jacob, *A New Law-Dictionary* (6th ed. 1750), under *forspeaker.*
[91] *Oxford English Dictionary*, under *forspeak.*
[92] Blount, *Nomo-Lexikon* (1670), under *lawyer*, and compare *lageman;* Blount, *A Law-Dictionary and Glossary* (1717), under *lawyer*, and compare *lageman;* Jacob, *A New Law-Dictionary* (6th ed. 1750), under *lawyer.*

whose duty it was to declare the law,[93] such as *judge*[94] or *jury*.[95] One source equates *lahwita* with *lawyer*.[96] These Old English words cannot apply certainly to practitioners of the law, for common law lawyers had not yet arrived at professional status. The combination of Norse *law* with a suffix indicating *employment* or *profession* (*ier*, *yer*)[97] dates from the fourteenth century, at which time the profession was well established. (Section 59.)

Both law and general dictionaries are full of compounds with *law*, some of ancient vintage, some relatively new. Old Norse *by* (or *byr*) occurs in pre-Conquest England to mean village or habitation,[98] and is a common ending for English place names, e.g., Derby, Whitby, Grimsby. As a result, one explanation of *bylaw* (recorded in the thirteenth and fourteenth centuries) is the linking of these two Old Norse words to mean village or local law.[99] *Byelaw* as the present British name for a municipal ordinance seems to mirror this Norse origin. Still, Old Teutonic supplied Old English with another, the more common *by* (beside or near).[100] This has led to conjecture that *bylaws* are really subordinate rather than local laws,[101] a theory not inconsistent with English practice and more in keeping with the American reference of the word to corporate and association rules.[102]

Outlaw and *inlaw* both originate in the pre-Norman period, *outlaw* from Old Norse *utlagi*. Modeled on that, Old English developed a form of the verb *inlaw*, meaning to restore an outlaw to the fold. In Middle English *inlaw* became a noun opposed to an *outlaw*, and under the influence of canon law, the contrast was made between those related *in law* and those related *in blood*. The first of the resulting *inlaw* combinations to be recorded was *brother-in-law* (about 1300), followed by *father-*, with *mother-* and *sister-* both about 1440. (*Blood*, *brother*, *father*, *sister*, and *mother* are all Common Teutonic found in-

[93] Bosworth and Toller, *An Anglo-Saxon Dictionary* (1898), under *lah-mann;* *Oxford English Dictionary*, under *lawman.*

[94] Kelham, *Domesday Book Illustrated* 247 (1788); see *Medieval Latin Word-List* (1934), under *lagemannus*, and *homo legis* (under *leg/alia*).

[95] *Les Termes de la Ley* (1671), under *lageman.*

[96] Bosworth and Toller, *An Anglo-Saxon Dictionary* (1898).

[97] *Oxford English Dictionary*, under -*ier.*

[98] *Oxford English Dictionary;* and see Coke, *Commentary upon Littleton*, f. 5b (10th ed. 1703).

[99] Skeat, *An Etymological Dictionary* (new ed. 1909); Cowell, *The Interpreter* (1637).

[100] *Oxford English Dictionary*, under *by*, prep., adv., No. 1.

[101] *Oxford English Dictionary*.

[102] *Black's Law Dictionary* (4th ed. 1951).

dependently in O.E. and O.N.)   The somewhat irreverent collective *in-laws* is a nineteenth-century creation attributed to Queen Victoria.[103]

36. *More Old Norse law words*

The contributions of Old Norse do not end with *law* and its variations (Section 35).   The most fundamental contrast in the law is between Old English *right* and Old Norse *wrong*.   An ancient homily (before 1100) speaks of "unjust judges" (expressed by one O.E. word *unrihtdeman*) who turn "wrang to rihte and riht to wrange." [104]   *Gift*, *loan* (Section 32), and *sale* are also Old Norse.

The technical meaning of *trust* is the result of a gradual development; the word itself and its basic concept of confidence is Old Norse. Similarly, the present legal meanings of *bond* are developments of the Middle English and Modern English periods, but the basic concept — something that binds — reflects the origin of *bond* as a "phonetic variation" of Old Norse *band*.[105]

Birth is Old Norse and so is *to die*.   *Bear* and *born*, *death* and *dead* came to Old English from the Common Teutonic ancestor of both languages.

A seafaring people, the Vikings contributed *wreck* to the law (through Anglo-Norman).   Originally exclusively a maritime term,[106] *wreck* has worked its way inland, with emphasis less on locale than damage, to cargo, ships, buildings, institutions, people, and especially automobiles.[107]   No one is eager to claim credit for what Blackstone called "the barbarous and uncouth appellations of *jetsam, flotsam,* and *ligan.*" [108]   Still, there is a possibility that Old Norse may have added to the perils of the sea law in the *ligan* (also *lagan*) part of this otherwise French jumble.[109]

The tendency of a many-languaged society to repeat itself may be

[103] Partridge, *A Dictionary of Slang and Unconventional English* (4th ed. 1951); see also *Oxford English Dictionary.*

[104] Quoted in *Oxford English Dictionary,* under *wrong,* sb.²; see also Serjeantson, *A History of Foreign Words in English* 68 (1935); Bosworth and Toller, *An Anglo-Saxon Dictionary* (1898), under *wrang,* n.

[105] *Oxford English Dictionary,* under *bond,* sb.¹, and *band,* sb.¹.

[106] *Oxford English Dictionary.*

[107] 45 *Words and Phrases* 554-555 (perm. ed. 1940); *Webster's New International Dictionary* (2d ed. 1934).

[108] 1 Blackstone, *Commentaries* °293 (Jones ed. 1916).

[109] *Oxford English Dictionary,* under *lagan;* Skeat, *An Etymological Dictionary* (new ed. 1909), under *lagan;* compare Jowitt, gen. ed., *The Dictionary of English Law* (1959), under *lagan* and *ligan.*

illustrated with Norse as with Celtic. (Section 27.) The place name *Torpenhow* has the distinction of a *hill* in each syllable, the first two Celtic, the last Old Norse.[110] *Self*, an Old English synonym for the Norse *same*, gives emphatic sameness in *selfsame*. Some of this doubled talk has a flavor of the law. An Old Norse *crook* is an Old English *hook*, a bent piece of metal. By 1200, Middle English was using *crook* to mean trickery or deceit. *Crooked* to mean wrong or dishonest is recorded a few years later. By the fourteenth century, the synonyms joined in the unsavory lilt *by hook or by crook*. In time, *to hook* meant to steal, and a *hooker* is still a thief [111] or worse.[112] Then there is *sick* and *ill*. In England, *sick* means about-to-vomit or the act. In the United States, Old English *sick* is a synonym of Old Norse *ill*,[113] and — depending on counsel's mood — a divorce plaintiff may find that mental cruelty makes her ill [114] or makes her sick.[115] The evidence is the same.

37. Common Old English in the language of the law

In the same way that *trust* and *bond* have been alchemized from common Old Norse (Section 36), many words of common Old English have been transformed into law words. Most often the process has been gradual. Words once a part of everyman's stock appear in more formal surroundings. Law use then continues for so long that sometimes the suspicion is born that the words were manufactured for the law. Especially is this the case where nonprofessional use becomes rare.

One of the most valuable pieces of technicality in the law is the *hearsay* rule, a product of the sixteenth and seventeenth centuries.[116] The grammatical construction *saying-heard* is nontechnical Old English nine and a half centuries old; *heard saying* is only a century

110 Skeat, *The Science of Etymology* 80 (1912); and see Coke, *Commentary upon Littleton*, f. 5b (10th ed. 1703).

111 *Oxford English Dictionary*.

112 Partridge, *A Dictionary of Slang and Unconventional English* (4th ed. 1951); Partridge, *A Dictionary of the Underworld* (1950).

113 31 *C.J. ill*, p. 242; 58 *C.J. sick*, p. 706; 42 *C.J.S. ill*, p. 381; 80 *C.J.S. sick*, p. 1276; Evans and Evans, *A Dictionary of Contemporary American Usage* (1957), under *ill; sick;* Fowler, *A Dictionary of Modern English Usage* (3d ed. 1937), under *sick, ill; McAllister v. State*, 28 Ala. App. 213, 215 (1938); *Nelson v. Dean*, 27 Cal. 2d 873, 874 (1946); *Fazekas v. Perth Amboy Holy Mary Roman Catholic Sick Benefit Society*, 13 N.J. Misc. 822, 823 (1935); *Romano v. Masachusetts Bonding & Ins. Co.*, 13 Misc. 2d 209, 213 (N.Y. Mun. Ct. 1956).

114 *Am. Jur. Pleading and Practice Forms* 7:765 (1957).

115 *Am. Jur. Pleading and Practice Forms* 7:768 (1957).

116 9 Holdsworth, *A History of English Law* 214-219 (1926).

younger. A form of *hear-saying*, in the sense of report as opposed to personal knowledge, is recorded as early as 1340. In the sixteenth century *hearsay* is rumor: "I knowe nothyng of it but by here say"; "report and common heare-saie." [117] By the late sixteenth century, a defendant without personal knowledge pleads ". . . that he heard say . . ." [118] Today, the common speech origin is reflected in the rustic's "I hear tell . . ." A sophisticated layman may dismiss gossip as *hearsay*, but the usual use is in the law, and is identified with lawyers.

The trappings of the courtroom also borrow from common Old English. The jury or witness is in the *box*, the witness takes the *stand*, and the judge, who is a member of the *bench*, also sits on it. From this perch he grants a lawyer's motion to *strike*. When — after his labors — counsel (like the Lord) *rests*, it is an Old English *rest* he takes, as distinguished from the French residue *rest* (Section 123).

On the pattern of the O.E. *landlord* (Section 32), sixteenth-century lawyers pieced together common Old English words to give *landlady*. About the same time they joined O.E. *fore* and *man* to get a jury *foreman*, and translated French (*fraunc tenement*) to produce the important *freehold* (Section 32).

More apparent to the layman is the lawyer's passionate adherence to Old English adverbs once in common use, but now bypassed: the *here-* words for example (Section 31), led by the fertile *herein*, which has since lent itself to the manufacture of *hereinbefore, hereinabove*, and *hereinafter*. Of the *there-* words, some have not managed to survive even in the law, beauties like *thereagain* and *thereup*. Many others are preserved in the law, close to their original state except that *th* is used for the Old English þ (Section 32). *Thereof, thereunder*, and most of the other common *there-* words (Section 10) are Old English, except for *therefor, therefore, theretofore*, and *thereupon*, which date from the Middle English period. The *where-* combinations are likewise from Middle English. (Section 53.)

The law's customary use of O.E. *within* as an adjective — *the within lease*, etc.[119] — is now a rare bird in the nonlegal speech where it started.[120]

Adoption, adaptation, and invention based on common Old English

---

[117] Quoted in *Oxford English Dictionary*.
[118] *Burgony v. Machell*, 21 Eng. Rep. 107 (Ch. 1594-1595).
[119] 69 *C.J. within* §6D; 45 *Words and Phrases* 389-390 (perm. ed. 1940).
[120] *Oxford English Dictionary; Webster's New International Dictionary* (2d ed. 1934); and compare *Webster's Third New International Dictionary* (1961).

forms continue today. Tax lawyers have given new life to O.E. *boot* [121] (Section 32), as well as to O.E. *spin* and *off*. When they speak of a *spin-off* for the transfer of corporate assets to a new and controlled corporation,[122] they are adapting common O.E. words to specialized law use in the ancient tradition of Anglo-Saxon compounding (Section 31). The law's figure of speech relates to an earlier description of a procedure in hand spinning. *Spin off* (without the hyphen) was used at least as early as the beginning of the seventeenth century to mean to clear off (a distaff) *by spinning.*[123]

Hit-and-run also combines common O.E. words to depict vividly and briefly the conduct of the automobile driver who fails to stop after an accident. The expression is a twentieth-century creation of the American press, borrowed from baseball journalism of the late nineteenth century.[124] In the course of the present century, the law has embraced it.[125]

38. *The place and problem of Old English*

The preceding pages (Sections 10, 25-37) list only some of the Old English words in the language of the law. Even a partial list demonstrates that many of our most fundamental, a few of our most technical, and many of our most trivial words of the law hail from Old English. It is indeed "too much to say" (as was said in 1895 and repeated in various forms ever since) that:

. . . almost all our words that have a definite legal import are in a certain sense French words.[126]

The importance of French to the language of the law should not be underestimated. (Section 12 and Chapter IX.) The overstressing of French influence discounts the contributions of Old English as well

---

[121] Bosworth and Toller, *An Anglo-Saxon Dictionary* (1898), under *bot*.

[122] CCH U.S. Master Tax Guide ¶582 (1956); see Note, 36 American Speech 283-284 (1961).

[123] *Oxford English Dictionary*, under *spin*, v., No. 5.

[124] Mathews, ed., *A Dictionary of Americanisms* (1951).

[125] *Oden v. District of Columbia*, 65 App. D.C. 50 (1935); *State v. Lee*, 53 Ariz. 295 (1939); *People v. Houston*, 24 Cal. App. 2d 167 (1937); *Ule v. State*, 208 Ind. 255 (1935); *State v. Derosia*, 94 N.H. 228 (1946); *State v. Tarbell*, 64 S.D. 330 (1936); *Herchenbach v. Commonwealth*, 185 Va. 217 (1946).

[126] 1 Pollock and Maitland, *The History of English Law* 80 (2d ed. 1898); and see 2 Holdsworth, *A History of English Law* 478 n.4 (3d ed. 1923); Cairns, "Language of Jurisprudence," in Anshen, ed., *Language* 245 (1957); Sheard, *The Words We Use* 225 (1954); Baugh, *A History of the English Language* 209 (1935); Woodbine, "The Language of English Law," 18 Speculum 395 (1943); Pope, *The Anglo-Norman Element in Our Vocabulary* 3 (1944).

as adaptations direct from Old Norse (Section 36) and from Latin (Sections 11, 28, 33, 34, and Chapter VII). The illusion of uniformity thus created results in the overlooking of a significant contributing factor in tautology, general wordiness, and confusion in the language of the law.

A cursory sampling will give a notion of the intimacy of the language blend:

After a French *marriage* or an Old English *wedding,* you have entered into O.E. *wedlock,* which is the same as French *marriage* (as an institution) or the gratuitous complication *matrimony* (Latin via Old French). You may *buy* a home in Old English or *purchase* it in French, take *possession* in French and *own* it in Old English. You have an Old English *child,* who will also be a French *infant* and a Latin *minor.* You write an O.E. *will* or a Latin *testament.* In it you dispose of your French *property* which was once the same as O.E. *goods* or French *chattels,* until both *goods* and *chattels* were limited to movables.[127]   There was also a time when you could *bequeath* (O.E.) everything you could *devise* (French), and you could once seriously *devise* a bed.[128]   In Old English you *forgive* debts, and at one time you could *pardon* them in French. An O.E. *sheriff* or a French *constable* arrests you for French *larceny* which is the same as O.E. *theft* or *stealing.* You get an English *lawyer* or a French *attorney* who goes to a French *court,* approaches the O.E. *bench,* and speaks to the French *judge.* The O.E. *witnesses* take an O.E. *oath* and *swear* in Old English that their French *evidence* is not English *hearsay.* The O.E. *foreman* of a French *jury* brings in a French *verdict* of O.E. *guilty,* and in a former day you might end up on an O.E. *gallows* or a French *gibbet,* unless you got a French *pardon.*

French penetration of English — in the general speech and in law language — was not a simple matter of a more sophisticated language overpowering a weakened or impotent primitive. Old English was a vigorous, flexible tongue, fully capable of adapting itself to new concepts of law as it had adapted itself to new concepts of religion.[129] (Section 34.) The fact that French took a leading position in law language cannot be explained on the ground that there was something inherent in the language which made it better for the expression of

---

[127] *Oxford English Dictionary.*
[128] *Oxford English Dictionary.*
[129] Jespersen, *Growth and Structure of the English Language,* par. 48 (Anchor, 9th ed. 1955).

law than English. French in the law is more a matter of the accidents of history than of the science of linguistics.

The persistence of English — in the face of repeated infusions of French and Latin — has meant that English and American lawyers have had a greater fund of word material to work with. This has given the language of the law color, flexibility, fine variation of meaning, and also wordiness, ambiguity, and general complexity. A detailing of further conflicts and confusions of merging languages must await a fuller discussion of the introduction into England of French and more Latin. (Chapters VI, VII, IX.)

CHAPTER VI

The Norman Conquest

39. English contact with the Continent before the Conquest

Neither the people nor the language of England had been isolated from Continental influences before the Norman invasion. From their Continental homeland, the Angles and Saxons had brought a sprinkling of Latin (Section 28). Conversion of England to Christianity increased the Latin element in Old English (Sections 33, 34), and also increased intercourse with the rest of Europe.

An English cleric, Alcuin, became adviser to the great King of the Franks, Charlemagne, and elements of Frankish law doubtless influenced the developing law in England.[1] As early as the sixth century, a king of Kent had married a Frankish princess, daughter of the King of Paris. Centuries later, another king in England, Aethelred, married Emma, daughter of the Duke of Normandy, and took temporary refuge there in a dark moment of the Viking raids. The sons of the English Aethelred and the Norman Emma grew to manhood in Normandy. One of them — Edward (Edward the Confessor) — ruled as the French-speaking King of the English from 1042 to 1066.[2]

In those twenty-four troubled years, Normans occupied high place in the English court.[3] Edward introduced the Norman custom of sealing documents,[4] and called his seal keeper and document secretary by the Norman-French name for the office, *cancheler*. (This was the first step in England of the march of the *chancellor* to greatness. This official had gradually worked his way up from an old Roman

---

[1] 1 Pollock and Maitland, *The History of English Law* xxx-xxxi (2d ed. 1898); Holmes, *The Common Law* 17-20 (1881).

[2] 2 Freeman, *The History of the Norman Conquest of England* 300 (3d ed. 1877).

[3] Feiling, *A History of England* 85 (1950); 2 Freeman, *The History of the Norman Conquest of England* 299-311 (3d ed. 1877); Vising, *Anglo-Norman Language and Literature* 8 (1923).

[4] Selden, "The Reverse or Back-Face of the English Janus," in *Tracts Written by John Selden* 52 (Westcot transl. 1683); 2 Holdsworth, *A History of English Law* 29 (3d ed. 1923).

court usher who guarded the latticework bars (in Latin, *cancelli*) which separated judges from the public. Many years later (fifteenth century), the verb meaning to *cancel* a legal document, i.e., by drawing lattice-like lines through it, came into the language through French from the same Latin source.) The few French words which became a part of English in this period were but a token of a trend.[5]

For a brief moment in history, French influence in England waned with the death of Edward in January of 1066. Harold was crowned a few days later, but by October was dead at Hastings, and the French star rose.

40. *William the Conqueror*

In one bloody day the fate of the old England was decided, and before 1066 ended, a Norman sat on the throne. After his death he was dubbed "the Great." For centuries he has been called "the Conqueror." (Some have tried to pull the sting from the word by asserting that *conqueror* here was used in the feudal sense to mean *purchaser* (Section 63) as in Scotland,[6] but this notion is not now credited.[7]) Contemporaries knew him most often as "William the Bastard." It seems likely that this Old French badge, which clung so tenaciously to William that some thought it a surname, was first introduced into the English language in references to the Conqueror.[8] A childhood of danger, a manhood of ruthless and intelligent struggle,[9] and a Norman tradition of legalism[10] (". . . of all nations the most quarrelsome . . ." it was later said),[11] fitted William for the taking (which had been done before) and the keeping of England.

William was no stranger to English shores. Fifteen years before he returned in anger, William paid a state visit to his childless cousin King Edward. Some say that Edward promised to recommend Wil-

---

[5] 5 Freeman, *The History of the Norman Conquest of England* 519 (1876).

[6] 2 Blackstone, *Commentaries* *243-*244 (Jones ed. 1916); 1 Stephen, *New Commentaries* 355 (1841); see also 2 Freeman, *The History of the Norman Conquest of England* 626-627 (3d ed. 1877); Spelman, *Glossarium Archaiologicum* (3d ed. 1687), under *conquestus*.

[7] *Oxford English Dictionary*, under *conquest*.

[8] 2 Freeman, *The History of the Norman Conquest of England* 626 (3d ed. 1877); *Oxford English Dictionary;* Skeat, *An Etymological Dictionary* (new ed. 1909).

[9] 2 Freeman, *The History of the Norman Conquest of England* 164-171 (3d ed. 1877).

[10] 16 *Encyclopaedia Britannica* 495 (1948).

[11] 6 *The Harleian Miscellany* 213 (new ed. 1810).

liam as successor to the English throne.[12]   Some say too that as late
as 1064 Harold had given William his oath to support William's succession.[13]   Mystery surrounds these promises as thick as the unquestioned dissension that overspread England in the days before the Conquest.   The awesome comet of 1066 portended great events.

William's invasion had the Pope's blessing.   And the hostile landing
itself was unopposed.   The Battle of Hastings (inconceivable to the
twentieth century that it was the work of a day!) was followed by
five years of scattered fighting.   But this was a resistance supported
by barons who stood to lose by a change of administration.   It was
not the struggle of united Englishmen, many of whom fought with
William.

From the first William pressed home his rightful and righteous succession, operating through English forms whenever expedient.[14]   In
the new church at Westminster built by Edward the Confessor William
was crowned "King of the English." [15]   William promised the French
and English of London the law as it was in King Edward's day (Section 42),[16] ignoring the brief rule of the oathbreaker Harold as later
Englishmen conveniently skip Cromwell.   The local courts were to
be preserved, administering law in accordance with ancient customs.
The King's Court — "court" here in the broad sense, the gathering of
the King and his courtiers — would decide controversies between the
tenants-in-chief, but this was a group of six hundred or so of William's
loyal followers,[17] mostly Norman.   The estates of traitors (i.e., those
who opposed William) were confiscated and redistributed to the de-
serving, including William.[18]   The areas of these estates and the ancient duties connected with them were carefully recorded in Domesday
Book.   A convenient tax, an old one — the *Danegeld* (Section 35) —
was revived.   William concentrated the loose English feudalism in
the King.[19]   Land was held of him, and the personal relationship
cemented by the Salisbury Oath.

[12] 2 Freeman, *The History of the Norman Conquest of England* 299-311 (3d ed.
1877).
[13] 3 Freeman, *The History of the Norman Conquest of England* 216-255 and
677-707 (2d ed. 1875).
[14] 5 Freeman, *The History of the Norman Conquest of England* 395 (1876).
[15] Shelly, *English and French in England: 1066-1100,* p. 42 (1921).
[16] Stubbs, ed., *Select Charters* 82-83 (8th ed. 1905).
[17] Feiling, *A History of England* 100, 103 (1950).
[18] Kelham, *Domesday Book Illustrated,* bk. 3, pp. 23-24 et seq. (1788).
[19] Compare 5 Freeman, *The History of the Norman Conquest of England* 366-
370 (1876).

If William was firm, he was also circumspect, for both fact and pride required it: Normans in England were a minority, outnumbered 10 to 1 by Englishmen.[20] While the conquest of England did not mean that he ceased to rule in Normandy, yet there was this difference. In Normandy William was Duke, with a knee bent to the Crown of France. In England he was King. This is the background for judgment on the tale of William's hostility to the English language. (Section 41.)

41. The tale that William made French the language of the law

An ancient tale, as current as the latest pocket supplement, relates that William the Conqueror made French the language of the English law. The story has been traced to a writer whose anonymity is so notorious that it has been named — the "pseudo-Ingulphus." [21] (The true Ingulf was an English priest who became secretary to William.) [22] In a "history" since proved to be a fourteenth-century forgery,[23] the false Ingulf wrote that the Normans of 1066 detested the English and abhorred their language. So intense was this antipathy (goes the tale) that "the Laws of the Land" and even "the Statutes of the English Kings" were written and pleaded in French.[24] There are variations in the tale,[25] but this is the legal nub promoted in the fifteenth century by Fortescue[26] and perpetuated in the seventeenth by Selden.[27] Selden later fortified the myth with another unsupported fourteenth-century report: this one repeats the older substance and spices it with

[20] See 3 Freeman, *The History of the Norman Conquest of England* 389 (2d ed. 1875); Vising, *Anglo-Norman Language and Literature* 8-9 (1923); Woodbine, "The Language of English Law," 18 Speculum 395, 407, 408 (1943); Feiling, *A History of England* 97 (1950); 1 *Cambridge Anglo-Norman Texts* xii (1924).

[21] [Palgrave], review in 34 Quarterly Rev. 248, 294 (1826).

[22] 4 Freeman, *The History of the Norman Conquest of England* 598-599 (2d ed. 1876); Shelly, *English and French in England: 1066-1100*, p. 37 (1921); Woodbine, "The Language of English Law," 18 Speculum 395, 403 (1943).

[23] [Palgrave], review in 34 Quarterly Rev. 248-298 (1826); Woodbine, "The Language of English Law," 18 Speculum 395, 403 (1943); compare Luders, "On the Use of the French Language in Our Ancient Laws and Acts of State," Tract VI, *Tracts on Various Subjects in the Law and History of England* 341, 365-366 (1810).

[24] Selden, "The Reverse or Back-Face of the English Janus," in *Tracts Written by John Selden* 54 (Westcot transl. 1683).

[25] 5 Freeman, *The History of the Norman Conquest of England* 507 n.2 (1876); Woodbine, "The Language of English Law," 18 Speculum 395, 403 n.1 (1943).

[26] Fortescue, *De Laudibus Legum Angliae*, cc. 47, 48 (2d ed. 1741).

[27] Selden, "The Reverse or Back-Face of the English Janus," in *Tracts Written by John Selden* 54 (Westcot transl. 1683); and compare Coke, "Le Primer Lecture del Mon Segnior Coke, sur Lestatute de Finibus fait Anno 27 E.I.," in Coke, *Commentary upon Littleton* ff. 2-3 (10th ed. 1703).

the fillip that William wanted "to destroy the Saxon tongue and cause England and Normandy to agree on one speech." [28]   The scarcity of factual history, the apparent logic of a Norman conqueror preferring his own language, and the need for an explanation of the fact that French did later become the language of the law (Chapter IX) led to the general acceptance of the pseudo-Ingulphus' story.

John Lilburn's seventeenth-century petition asking Parliament to put the law into "our Mothers Tongue" considered it

> a Badg of our Slavery to a Norman Conqueror, to have our Laws in the French Tongue, . . .[29]

Seventeenth-century law dictionaries dated French pleading from the Conquest,[30] and in the eighteenth century Giles Jacob's bulky *New Law-Dictionary* indorsed the notion that the Conqueror had decreed French for both the writing and pleading of the law.[31]   In the third volume of his *Commentaries,* the eloquent and authoritative Blackstone (out of the recesses of a retentive mind) wrote of the use of French in court records[32] and "indeed all public proceedings" as a "shameful badge . . . of tyranny and foreign servitude" imposed by "William the Norman and his sons." [33]   Blackstone savored the phrasing, polished it, and (without a word of John Lilburn) worked it into his volume four as a "badge of slavery." [34]   Reeves liked it too.   In his *History of the English Law* (without a nod to either Lilburn or Blackstone), Reeves wrote of:

> . . . the language which the Conqueror had imposed upon our courts (the strongest badge of servitude, perhaps, that could be devised) . . .[35]

[28] Quoted in Woodbine, "The Language of English Law," 18 Speculum 395, 403 n.3 (1943); compare Fortescue, *De Laudibus Legum Angliae* 106n (2d ed. 1741), and Luders, "On the Use of the French Language in Our Ancient Laws and Acts of State," Tract VI, *Tracts on Various Subjects in the Law and History of England* 341, 346 (1810).

[29] Quoted in Jones. *The Triumph of the English Language* 317 (1953); and see also Warr, "The Corruption and Deficiency of the Laws of England" (1649), in 6 *The Harleian Miscellany* 212, 219-220, 222 (new ed. 1810).

[30] See Blount, *Nomo-Lexikon* (1670), under *plea;* Cowell, *The Interpreter* (1637), under *plea.*

[31] Jacob, *A New Law-Dictionary* (6th ed. 1750), under *French.*

[32] 3 Blackstone, *Commentaries* °318 (Jones ed. 1916); compare Stephen, *A Treatise on the Principles of Pleading,* App. Note 14, pp. xxi-xxii (1824), and *James Osborn's Case,* 77 Eng. Rep. 1123, 1128 (K.B. 1614).

[33] 3 Blackstone, *Commentaries* °318-°319 (Jones ed. 1916).

[34] 4 Blackstone, *Commentaries* °416 (Jones ed. 1916).

[35] 3 *Reeves' History of the English Law* 186 (Finlason, new American ed. 1880); compare Stephen, *A Treatise on the Principles of Pleading,* App., Note 14, p. xxi (1824); see also 5 Freeman, *The History of the Norman Conquest of England* 529 (1876).

In 1819, Sir Walter Scott's *Ivanhoe* popularized the theme of Norman hostility to the English speech.[36] Seven years later, less dramatically, the false Ingulf was exposed in a piece of scholarly detective work.[37] Historians tried to set the record straight.[38] But old canards never die readily. To this day works of law reference assert that the language of the law became French with William the Conqueror.[39] Other law reference works say that French then became the language of the courts.[40] And writers on language — some more,[41] some less[42] explicit — have helped to keep the myth alive.

42. *Written language after the Conquest*

The written languages of the law after the Norman Conquest were Latin and English, with Latin far in the lead. French was not yet in the running. At the time of the invasion, acts of the French King's chancery were still recorded in Latin,[43] and we have no records of any Norman laws of that period written in French.[44] In short, French — Norman or otherwise — was not the written language of the law in William's homeland, and there is no evidence that an attempt was made to force French into this unaccustomed role in England. The best and

[36] Shelly, *English and French in England: 1066-1100*, p. 7 (1921); see also Kelham, *Domesday Book Illustrated* 294 n.2 (1788).

[37] [Palgrave], review in 34 Quarterly Rev. 248-298 (1826).

[38] 5 Freeman, *The History of the Norman Conquest of England* 506-528 (1876); 3 Palgrave, *The History of Normandy and of England* 627-629 (1864); and see 1 Pollock and Maitland, *The History of English Law* 82 n.1 (2d ed. 1898).

[39] *Black's Law Dictionary* (4th ed. 1951), under *law French;* 36 *C.J. law* §36; 37 *C.J.S. French*, pp. 183-184 n.43(8) (Supp. 1962); 2 Bouvier, *A Law Dictionary* (Rawle, 15th ed. 1892), under *law French*, and compare 2 *Bouvier's Law Dictionary and Concise Encyclopedia* (3d rev. 8th ed. 1914), under *language*, pp. 1859-1860; Mathew, "Law French," 54 *L.Q. Rev.* 358-359 (1938), cited in Williams, *Learning the Law* 60 n.1 (6th ed. 1957); compare Cohen, *A History of the English Bar* 341-355 (1929).

[40] 2 *Bouvier's Law Dictionary and Concise Encyclopedia* (3d rev. 8th ed. 1914), under *language*, pp. 1859-1860, and compare 2 Bouvier, *A Law Dictionary* (Rawle, 15th ed. 1892), under *law French;* Plucknett, *A Concise History of the Common Law* 400 (5th ed. 1956); Ballentine, *Law Dictionary with Pronunciations* (2d ed. 1948), under *law French.*

[41] Webster, *An American Dictionary of the English Language*, preface (1828); Laird, *The Miracle of Language* 48 (Premier ed. 1957); McKnight, *English Words and Their Background* 123 (1923); Serjeantson, *A History of Foreign Words in English* 104 (1935).

[42] Baugh, *A History of the English Language* 182, 179, and compare with 143 (1935); Vising, *Anglo-Norman Language and Literature* 12-13 (1923).

[43] 9 *Encyclopaedia Britannica* 760 (1948); 1 Pollock and Maitland, *The History of English Law* 66 (2d ed. 1898); and see Luders, "On the Use of the French Language in Our Ancient Laws and Acts of State," Tract VI, *Tracts on Various Subjects in the Law and History of England* 341, 349-350, 353 (1810).

[44] Woodbine, "The Language of English Law," 18 Speculum 404-405 (1943).

earliest that French can show for sure is a late twelfth-century French translation of a Latin collection of William's laws (*Articuli Willellmi*).[45] There is another French compilation (*Leis Willelme*) which one respected scholar dates 1090-1135 and another dates 1150-1170.[46] In either case *Leis Willelme* is not an official document,[47] and the dispute as to whether it is an original or a translation remains unresolved.[48] Some careful writers give it the epithet "so-called." [49]

The case for Latin and English is better documented. Four hundred and eighty-seven official writs and charters survive from the days of the Conqueror and his son William II (1066-1100). None is in French. Nineteen are in English alone. Nine in English and Latin versions. All the rest are in Latin.[50] French language influence may be traced, but the track leads through Latin, where the usages of William's new feudalism began to appear. (Section 45.) Many Old English law terms were also rendered in Latin, yet some are preserved in their virginal state in otherwise Latin documents. For example, Domesday Book uses *utlagh* [51] (outlaw) (Section 35), *wapentac* (the Old Norse equivalent of O.E. *hundred*), and *inland* [52] (in the O.E. sense of land not allotted to tenants). Old English was more than convenient. Its use emphasized the continuity of kingship, law, and property rights. (Section 40.) William's charter to the City of London, though addressed to both his French and English subjects, is in Old English (here interlined with Modern):

> *Will'm kyng gret Will'm bisceop*
> William, king, greets William, bishop,
> *and Gosfregð, portirefan and ealle þa*
> and Gosfrith, portreeve, and all the
> *burhwaru binnan Londone Frencisce and*

---

[45] Robertson, ed. and transl., *The Laws of the Kings of England* 225-226 (1925); Vising, *Anglo-Norman Language and Literature* 50, 69 (1923); Woodbine, "The Language of English Law," 18 Speculum 402 n.1 (1943).

[46] Robertson, ed. and transl., *The Laws of the Kings of England* 227 (1925).

[47] Woodbine, "The Language of English Law," 18 Speculum 402 n.1 (1943); 1 Pollock and Maitland, *The History of English Law* 102-103 n.1 (2d ed. 1898).

[48] 1 Pollock and Maitland, *The History of English Law* 102 (2d ed. 1898); see also Luders, "On the Use of the French Language in Our Ancient Laws and Acts of State," Tract VI, *Tracts on Various Subjects in the Law and History of England* 341, 374-377 (1810).

[49] Robertson, *The Laws of the Kings of England* 252 (1925); Woodbine, "The Language of English Law," 18 Speculum 402 n.1 (1943).

[50] Shelly, *English and French in England: 1066-1100*, pp. 81-83 (1921); 1 Pollock and Maitland, *The History of English Law* 82 (2d ed. 1898).

[51] Kelham, *Domesday Book Illustrated* 364 (1788).

[52] Maitland, *Domesday Book and Beyond* 8 (1921 print.).

burghers within London, French and
Englisce freondlice. and ic kyde eow
English, friendly; and I do you to wit
þat ic wylle þat get beon eallra þaera laga weorðe
that I will that ye two be worthy of all the laws
þe gyt waeran on Eadwerdes daege kynges.
that ye were worthy of in King Edward's day.
and ic wylle þaet aelc cyld beo his
And I will that every child be his
faeder yrfnume. aefter his faederdaege.
father's heir, after his father's day.
and ic nelle geþolian þat aenig man
And I will not endure that any man
eow aenig wrang beode. God eow gehealde.
offer any wrong to you. God keep you.[53]

As the Normans became more firmly entrenched, and the document-writing clergy better organized and educated, English lost ground steadily. After the death of the Conqueror, the use of written English in formal law documents almost disappears, and the field is left to Latin.[54] The first use of French in an official document is not until the thirteenth century, in the year of the Magna Carta.[55]

43. *Spoken language after the Conquest*

The language picture for the days following the Norman Conquest is not as clear for the spoken as for the written language of the law. (Section 42.) But here too the tale that William tried "to destroy the Saxon tongue" and substituted French for English is a distortion. (Section 41.)

In keeping with his official fiction that he was the rightful successor to the English crown,[56] (Section 40), the Conqueror himself attempted to learn English,[57] and at the coronation (Christmas, 1066) he was acclaimed King by the Normans in French and by the natives in

---

[53] Stubbs, ed., *Select Charters* 82-83 (8th ed. 1905); compare Robertson, ed. and transl., *The Laws of the Kings of England* 230-231 (1925), and Blount, *Nomo-Lexikon* (1670), under *port-greve*.

[54] Shelly, *English and French in England: 1066-1100*, p. 81 (1921); Woodbine, "The Language of English Law," 18 Speculum 405 (1943); see Van Caenegem, *Royal Writs in England from the Conquest to Glanvill*, 77 Selden Society 142 (1959).

[55] 5 Freeman, *The History of the Norman Conquest of England* 530 (1876); compare Shelly, *English and French in England: 1066-1100*, p. 81 (1921), and 1 Pollock and Maitland, *The History of English Law* 85 n.6 (2d ed. 1898).

[56] Shelly, *English and French in England: 1066-1100*, p. 53 (1921).

[57] Shelly, *English and French in England: 1066-1100*, pp. 75, 81; 5 Freeman, *The History of the Norman Conquest of England* 892 (1876).

English.[58]   Interracial marriage was encouraged,[59] William giving his own niece in marriage to an Englishman.[60]   Careful scholarship makes it appear most probable that from the earliest days of the Conquest, mixed marriages — mostly of Norman men with English women — produced a generation whose "cradle tongue" was English.[61]   It also appears that even in the reign of William (1066-1087) there was some bilingualism.[62]   Especially was this true of things legal.

The commissioners for the Domesday Book survey were both French and English; testimony was in both languages; and "verdicts" for the survey were given by special juries, half French and half English.[63] Since William was not able to master English,[64] it has appeared to be a reasonable assumption that his Court was conducted in French.[65] Yet he had promised the law as it was "in King Edward's day" (Sections 40, 42), and to determine what that law was he ordered the testimony taken of Englishmen learned in the law.[66]   And even if French were the usual language of William's Court, that assumption does not warrant the additional assumption that the language of the King's Court and the language of the law courts was the same.[67] The King's Court (curia regis) was at this time an all-purpose entity, chiefly administrative, and to a small degree judicial.[68]   The Conqueror preserved the local courts,[69] and these courts accounted for the bulk of the litigation in early post-Conquest England.[70]   Nor were these only trivial matters: high officials of the King's Court personally litigated land titles and rights in local courts.[71]   It appears likely that some local litigation was determined by royal judges unfamiliar with English.   It also appears probable that much more would have been

[58] Shelly, English and French in England: 1066-1100, p. 77; Woodbine, "The Language of English Law," 18 Speculum 409 (1943).
[59] Sheard, The Words We Use 203 (1954).
[60] Shelly, English and French in England: 1066-1100, p. 64 (1921).
[61] Shelly, English and French in England: 1066-1100, p. 93; Woodbine, "The Language of English Law," 18 Speculum 409-410 (1943).
[62] Shelly, English and French in England: 1066-1100, pp. 77-80 (1921).
[63] Shelly, English and French in England: 1066-1100, p. 53 (1921).
[64] 3 Palgrave, The History of Normandy and of England 613-614 (1864).
[65] Woodbine, "The Language of English Law," 18 Speculum 425-426 (1943).
[66] Shelly, English and French in England: 1066-1100, pp. 51-53 (1921).
[67] Compare Vising, Anglo-Norman Language and Literature 12 (1923).
[68] 5 Freeman, The History of the Norman Conquest of England 423-425 (1876).
[69] Robertson, ed. and transl., The Laws of the Kings of England 241, 235, 273 (1925).
[70] Woodbine, "The Language of English Law," 18 Speculum 426 (1943); Fortescue, De Laudibus Legum Angliae 107n (2d ed. 1741).
[71] Shelly, English and French in England: 1066-1100, pp. 51-53; Woodbine, "The Language of English Law," 18 Speculum 426 (1943).

determined according to the pre-Conquest formula under which men of the county and its divisions were the judges and jurors.[72] This was a time-honored duty, and often an onerous one. (For 1130, there is a record of a whole county buying its way out of judge and jury duty.)[73] At this local level there is some evidence that litigation in the post-Conquest days was conducted in English,[74] and none that it was conducted in French.[75] Alongside the oral English and French of the secular courts, oral Latin prevailed in the Church courts. And even in these courts, there is some indication (dating from around 1200) that sometimes oral pleadings might also be in French or English for the better understanding of litigants.[76]

A working conclusion in a matter that will probably never be fully determined is that in the post-Conquest period the spoken language of the law became trilingual — English, French, and Latin.

44. Norman influence on literature and learning

There is the greatest diversity of opinion on the position of Old English literature just before the Conquest. We are told that it was in "a state of languishing depression,"[77] that it was "certainly not rich,"[78] and also that it was "flourishing."[79] On the effect of the Conquest on Old English literature, the comment is almost as confusing. The situation has been overdramatized with:

The shock of the Conquest gave a deathblow to Saxon literature.[80]

Just as it has been oversimplified in the vague footnote to history, that there was a "persistence of written English."[81] This opinion is literally true, and the other is true in a sense.

There are some writings in English that continue through even the immediate turmoil of invasion and conquest. A portion of the *Anglo-*

[72] 1 Holdsworth, *A History of English Law* 10-12 (3d ed. 1922); Shelly, *English and French in England: 1066-1100*, pp. 52-53; 5 Freeman, *The History of the Norman Conquest of England* 449-451 (1876).

[73] 5 Freeman, *The History of the Norman Conquest of England* 441 (1876).

[74] Legge, "French and the Law," in Introduction to *Year Books of Edward II*, 54 Selden Society xxxviii (1935); Fortescue, *De Laudibus Legum Angliae* 107n (2d ed. 1741).

[75] Woodbine, "The Language of English Law," 18 Speculum 433-434 (1943).

[76] Woodbine, "The Language of English Law," 18 Speculum 428 (1943).

[77] Marsh, *The Origin and History of the English Language* 106 (3d ed. 1869).

[78] 5 Freeman, *The History of the Norman Conquest of England* 575 (1876).

[79] 1 *Cambridge Anglo-Norman Texts* x (1924).

[80] Earle, *The Philology of the English Tongue*, par. 40 (4th ed. 1887); see also Trench, *English, Past and Present* 67 (10th ed. 1877).

[81] Woodbine, "The Language of English Law," 18 Speculum 410 n.1 (1943).

Saxon Chronicle continues to 1154 (Section 31), and parts of the chronicles are thought to be political songs, such as one of 1086 titled the "High-Handed Conqueror."[82]   But there is a hiatus in substantial English literature from 1066 till the beginning of the thirteenth century.   English is used to copy works in French, and English writers neglect their own language for French and Latin.[83]

English continued as the popular tongue.[84]   It had written and oral legal uses as a matter of policy and necessity (Sections 42, 43), and through daily contact there was a growing bilingualism of French and English.[85]   English was picked up.   By contrast French and Latin were studied and promoted.   Under noble patronage an Anglo-Norman literature developed.[86]   The languages of learning were Latin and French.   The day-to-day pressure of English was strong, but the mark of the educated man was a knowledge of Latin, and also French[87] — even if it meant getting a tutor from Normandy to learn it properly.[88]

It is now clear that the Norman conquerors of England neither outlawed the English language nor decreed French the language of the law.   English did not vanish from the law with the coming of William, and French did not then become its chief voice.   But a tradition of French as a language of learning and gentility was begun.   And it was this tradition which years later left its lasting mark upon the language of the law.   (Chapter IX.)   In the meantime, the important language for the law was Latin.   (Chapter VII.)

[82] Wells, *A Manual of the Writings in Middle English* 209 (1916).

[83] Wells, *A Manual of the Writings in Middle English*, especially 1, 181, 190, 208, 599 (1916).

[84] Baugh, *A History of the English Language* 140 (1935); Woodbine, "The Language of English Law," 18 Speculum 409-410 (1943).

[85] Shelly, *English and French in England: 1066-1100*, pp. 94-95 (1921); Woodbine, "The Language of English Law," 18 Speculum 408-409 (1943).

[86] Baugh, *A History of the English Language* 144-145 (1935); 5 Freeman, *The History of the Norman Conquest of England* 579-580 (1876); Sheard, *The Words We Use* 202-203 (1954); Vising, *Anglo-Norman Language and Literature* 14 (1923); see 1 *Cambridge Anglo-Norman Texts* x (1924).

[87] Legge, "French and the Law," in Introduction to *Year Books of Edward II*, 54 Selden Society xxxviii (1935); 1 *Cambridge Anglo-Norman Texts* x (1924); Woodbine, "The Language of English Law," 18 Speculum 412 (1943); Baugh, *A History of the English Language* 183 (1935); Vising, *Anglo-Norman Language and Literature* 13 (1923).

[88] Woodbine, "The Language of English Law," 18 Speculum 411 (1943).

CHAPTER VII

The Law and Latin

45. *The Norman impetus to Latin*

Latin was the earliest language beneficiary of the Norman Conquest. Just as Latin was still the language of record in contemporary France (Section 42), so it became the dominant written language for English law — statutes, charters, writs.[1] Some Latin had been used in England before the Normans (Section 34). For example, the Latin to describe a holder of allodial land, an *allodiarius,* an absolute owner as distinguished from the Norman tenant by feudal dues, was known in pre-Conquest England as early as the reign of King Canute.[2] With a revitalized and reorganized Church under a capable civil lawyer — Archbishop Lanfranc — Latin became more general.

The Conqueror separated Church courts from the secular courts,[3] but he did not remove churchmen from the secular courts. Their influence on the law became more, not less. For the most part it was churchmen who were the royal judges and the drafters of documents. *Lay,* which today distinguishes nonprofessional from professional (especially lawyers and doctors), was at this time represented by the Latin *laicalis,* and distinguished the secular from the clerical. Churchmen were the literates, and their literacy was Latin. Into a Latin mold, they poured the terminology of Norman feudalism:

baro	a possible ancestor of the Old French and Middle English *barun,* meant a blockhead in Classical Latin, and had been known in England as early as the eighth century to mean slave. About the time of the Conquest, the Latin word is used to mean tenant-in-chief.
comes	in pre-Conquest England had meant an official or an important person. About the time of the Conquest,

---

[1] Woodbine, "The Language of English Law," 18 Speculum 405 (1943).

[2] *Medieval Latin Word-List* (1934); and see Kelham, *Domesday Book Illustrated* 154 and especially n.2; compare Maitland, *Domesday Book and Beyond* 8 (1921 print.), and Woodbine, "The Language of English Law," 18 Speculum 404 (1943).

[3] Robertson, ed. and transl., *The Laws of the Kings of England* 234-235 (1925).

	comes is used to describe the French *count* (Old French *conte*) and the English *earl* (Old English *eorl*).
comitatus	related to *comes*, this Latin described the earl's domain (French *county* or O.E. *earldom*) and also the county court. (See *scira*, this list.)
homagium	the Latin form for French *homage*, which in Old English was *mannraeden*, man control.
hundredum	the new dress for Old English *hundred*, a division of the shire.
manerium	for French *manor* (Old French *manoir*).
scira	used (in addition to *comitatus*) to describe the English *shire* (O.E. *scir*), which was well identified with place names and in legal usage.
vicecomes	the Latin for the French *viscount* (Old French *visconte*) and the English *sheriff* (Old English *scirzerefa*).

Either English[4] or French could have been adapted to the needs of the Norman legal arrangements, but these were both "vulgar" tongues,[5] as contrasted with Latin, the universal language of medieval learning.[6] Even if it were Latin with a French or English accent, it assumed the classic symmetry, and that was enough to recommend it.

46. *The varieties of Latin*

The metamorphosis of *baro* from a blockhead to a tenant-in-chief (Section 45) is a warning that the important language of the law in Norman England was not the Latin of Caesar, Cicero, and Virgil. In Roman days *misericordia* meant mercy, and in twelfth-century law Latin it had come to mean the discretion (mercy) to impose an arbitrary fine. In such a state of the record, some distinctions are in order:

(1) *Classical Latin.* This is the Latin of the schoolbooks. It is Latin of the period roughly from 80 B.C. to 180 A.D., including the "golden age" and the "silver age" of the Latin language.[7]

(2) *Late Latin.* This is the Latin from the end of the classical period to the end of the fifth century, the beginning of the Middle Ages. It is sometimes used to include Medieval Latin.

(3) *Medieval Latin.* This is the Latin of the period 500-1500, also called *Middle Latin,* and sometimes used interchangeably with *Late*

---

[4] Compare Woodbine, "The Language of English Law," 18 Speculum 404 (1943).

[5] Shelly, *English and French in England: 1066-1100,* p. 90 (1921).

[6] Woodbine, "The Language of English Law," 18 Speculum 411 (1943).

[7] *Webster's New International Dictionary* (2d ed. 1934), under *Latin;* compare 13 *Encyclopaedia Britannica* 745 (1948).

Latin and *Low Latin.* Medieval Latin contains many words of non-Latin origin.[8] It is a language developed principally by the clergy to translate medieval life into a language pattern uniform with the past. Medieval Latin as used in England is sometimes called *Anglo-Latin.*

(4) *Low Latin.* This is sometimes equated with Medieval Latin (and with Late Latin). It refers to "the later stages of the Latin language, including especially the barbarous coinages from French, German, and other tongues." [9]

(5) *Vulgar Latin.* "Vulgar" here is in the classical sense (*vulgaris*), "belonging to the common people." [10] Vulgar Latin is now used to include the language of the masses and "the very different colloquial speech of educated Romans," [11] and was parent to Old French. *Glanvil,* the first great book on the law of England (1189), is described by its author as written in "vulgar Latin." [12]

(6) *New Latin or Modern Latin.* This is Latin of the period since the Renaissance.

(7) *Law Latin.* This is given separate consideration in Section 47.

47. *Law Latin: A definition*

Like its companion *law French* (Section 62), *law Latin* is rarely described in neutral terms. It is "barbarous," [13] "corrupt," [14] "mutilated," [15] "dog Latin," and in an Irish version "bog Latin." [16] The calmest definition is Webster's:

> The kind of Low Latin, containing Latinized English and old French words, used in English law.[17]

Since Low Latin is sometimes used for Medieval Latin (Section 46), this definition could limit law Latin to the period 500-1500. Blackstone imposes a further restriction. He treats "our English legal latinity" as a specialized sort of Medieval Latin, introduced by statute

---

[8] *Webster's New International Dictionary* (2d ed. 1934), under *Latin.*
[9] *Webster's New International Dictionary* (2d ed. 1934), under *Latin.*
[10] Johnson, *Latin Words of Common English* 143 (1931).
[11] *Webster's New International Dictionary* (2d ed. 1934), under *Latin.*
[12] Quoted in Radin, *Handbook of Anglo-American Legal History* 279 (1936).
[13] 2 Bouvier, *A Law Dictionary* (Rawle, 15th ed. 1892), under *law Latin; Oxford English Dictionary,* under *law,* sb.[1], No. 23.
[14] *Black's Law Dictionary* (4th ed. 1951), under *law Latin.*
[15] Ballentine, *Law Dictionary with Pronunciations* (2d ed. 1948), under *law Latin.*
[16] Partridge, *Slang: Today and Yesterday* 188 (3d ed. 1950).
[17] *Webster's New International Dictionary* (2d ed. 1934), under *law Latin.*

in 1362.[18] (Section 65.) Though shaky on detail, Coke more correctly has Latin in English law antedate the Conquest.[19]

Coke placed the peculiar uses of Latin in the law midway between the extremes of "good Latin allowed by grammarians" and "words insensible." In that hallowed middle he made room for

> Words significant, and known to the sages of the law, but not allowed by grammarians . . .

as well as "false or incongruous Latin" with the "countenance of Latin" which would "abate an original writ," but not void other writings if the intent could be determined.[20]

Blackstone vigorously defended law Latin though "not the ridiculous barbarisms sometimes introduced by the ignorance of *modern* practicers." [21] "The truth is," he wrote,

> what is generally denominated law Latin is in reality a mere technical language, calculated for eternal duration, and easy to be apprehended both in present and future times; and on those accounts best suited to preserve those memorials which are intended for perpetual rules of action.[22]

Varying views of law Latin have prevented it from becoming a term of art. Whether it is a matter of putting Classical Latin to new uses, such as *in propria persona* (first recorded in England in 1290), or putting a Latin dress on Old English, as by changing O.E. *morðer* (secret killing) into *murdrum* (c. 1076), *law Latin* is intended to differentiate Latin used in the law from other languages used in the law and also from Latin words used outside of the law. It is in this sense that the term is still used by lawyers to describe the plentiful residue of Latin in the language of the law. (Section 11.) And it is so used in this book unless a different sense is expressly identified. With this meaning, law Latin of the twentieth century is not the same as law Latin of the twelfth and thirteenth centuries. The content of law Latin is constantly shifting. There are additions; old words are dropped or changed (Section 45); and some words cross over.

For example, the Classical Latin *posse* (be able) was used in medieval England to mean *power* or *force* (c. 1114), and the *posse comi-*

---

[18] 3 Blackstone, *Commentaries* *319-*324 (Jones ed. 1916); compare Stephen, *A Treatise on the Principles of Pleading*, App., Note 14, p. xxi (1824).
[19] *James Osborn's Case*, 77 Eng. Rep. 1123, 1128 (K.B. 1614).
[20] *James Osborn's Case*, 77 Eng. Rep. 1123, 1129 (K.B. 1614).
[21] 3 Blackstone, *Commentaries* *321 (Jones ed. 1916).
[22] 3 Blackstone, *Commentaries* *320-*321 (Jones ed. 1916).

tatus was the "effective force of a county" (1234).[23] In this form it is still used today, law Latin and English translation side by side:

> Every male person above 18 years of age who neglects or refuses to join the posse comitatus or power of the county . . .[24]

But the shortened form *posse* (both the starting point and an ancient synonym for *posse comitatus*) is now on the lips of every TV sheriff. It is lost to law Latin and has become a part of the accumulated wealth of general English.

48. Live law Latin: "in-" words

Law Latin is not the dead language of "eternal duration" and easy apprehension pictured by Blackstone. (Section 47.) It partakes of all the vices of the living. It lacks the tidiness of Classical Latin. It is Latin-by-association.

Indebitatus assumpsit (being indebted, he undertook) is law Latin. It is understandable today because it sounds like being in debt. But in Classical Latin it would be *not* in debt, for the *in-* prefix here means *not*. (In the civil law, *indebitum* means not owing.) Unfortunately the Latin prefix *in-* is not always a negative. It can also mean *in* and *into*. Law Latin uses it all ways.

The law deals with property that is *incorporeal* (no body). It also has *incorporate* (into a body), to form a corporation. Dr. Johnson took note of an adjective *incorporate* (unbodied) but said that it was "disused to avoid confusion." [25] Yet until recently Webster listed *incorporate* (not corporate) as a "rare" law usage,[26] so rare it did not appear in the current law dictionaries.

An *indenture* (in teeth) originates in the ancient practice of writing duplicate originals on the same parchment and cutting with a jagged line at the middle of the document. If the teeth fit, the documents are genuine. But in Classical Latin *dentatus* alone meant toothed, and as late as the sixteenth century *indentatus* was not in teeth but no teeth, i.e., toothless.

The *in-* confusion continues current in and out of the law.

The *inflammable* sign on gasoline trucks is the into flame *in-* prefix,

---

[23] *Medieval Latin Word-List* (1934).
[24] Cal. Pen. Code §150.
[25] 1 Johnson, *A Dictionary of the English Language* (4th ed. 1775).
[26] *Webster's New International Dictionary* (2d ed. 1934); compare *Webster's Third New International Dictionary* (1961).

but so many have thought it meant not flammable that the trend is now to use plain *flammable*.[27]

An *inchoate* lien has a Latin origin as in grasp, i.e., only begun. Since something *inchoate* is incomplete, which is not complete, it seemed to follow that *inchoate* was also not choate. And so *Webster 2d* listed *choate* as a "rare" word meaning complete, and *Webster 3d* removed the "rare" tag. The law dictionaries have not yet picked this one up, but the Supreme Court has. In 1946, the United States Supreme Court used *choate* to describe a lien so far perfected as to take priority over a later federal tax lien.[28] This has now become a part of the tax vocabulary[29] along with *choateness*,[30] which has not even made *Webster 3d*. Joseph would turn over.

49. Latin additions and duplications

Some Latin words were introductions to England from the Roman law list. For example, the *notary*[31] (a note taker, a shorthand writer), *protonotary* (chief clerk), *citation* and *exception*,[32] *suborn*[33] and *perjury*.

Other Latin words have been adapted to the expanding needs of the law. It was this way with:

Fieri facias (cause to be made), a writ directing the sheriff to seize goods on execution to make (i.e., realize) enough to cover the judgment; the red-faced sound of this writ has inspired legal puns at least since the end of the sixteenth century;[34] *habeas corpus* (have the body), "the most celebrated writ in the English law," [35] loosely translated by Dickens as a "have-his-carcase";[36] *mandamus* (we command); *quo warranto* (by what warrant); *subpoena* (under a penalty); *supersedeas* (you shall desist); *verdict* (truly said), Latin via French.

---

[27] Evans and Evans, *A Dictionary of Contemporary American Usage* (1957), under *flammable*.

[28] *Ill. ex rel Gordon v. Campbell*, 329 U.S. 362, 371 (1946).

[29] *Shott v. Peoples Bank*, 105 Ohio App. 80, 82 (1957); 7 *Words and Phrases* (perm. ed. 1940, Supp. 1962), "choate," "choate lien," and "choate lien test."

[30] *Gower v. State Tax Commission*, 207 Ore. 288, 296, 297, 298 (1956); Barker, "Federal Tax Lien Priorities," 34 Los Angeles B. Bull. 101, 113 (1959); Plumb, "Federal Tax Liens: Proposed Revision of the Law," 45 A.B.A.J. 351 (1959).

[31] Brooke, *A Treatise on the Office and Practice of a Notary* 2-19 (4th ed. 1876).

[32] Millar, "The Lineage of Some Procedural Words," 25 A.B.A.J. 1023 (1939).

[33] Smith and Hall, *English-Latin Dictionary* (1871).

[34] *Oxford English Dictionary;* see also 3 *The Harleian Miscellany* 74 and especially the note (new ed. 1809); Partridge, *Slang: Today and Yesterday* 188 (3d ed. 1950).

[35] 3 Blackstone, *Commentaries* *129 (Jones ed. 1916).

[36] 2 *The Posthumous Papers of the Pickwick Club* c. 44, p. 257 (Gadshill ed. 1899); see also Holdsworth, *Charles Dickens as a Legal Historian* 110 (1928).

In numerous instances Latin found the field already pre-empted by English usage (Section 38), and the battle for survival has not yet ended. Old English *law* has prevailed over Latin *lex* and *ius*. (Section 53.) Latin *legal* has displaced O.E. *lahlic* and still contends with English *lawful,* sometimes held synonymous and sometimes not.[37] An English *giver* is a Latin *donor,* but over the years the technicality of *donor* has sharpened. Still synonymous,[38] *donor* alone carries the more refined notions of one who gives property in trust or subject to a power of appointment.[39] An O.E. synonym of *give* is *bequeath,* which in Middle English produced *bequest.* Through Old French, Latin has contributed *legacy* as an equivalent of *bequest.*[40] Latin *perjure* has driven O.E. *forswear* out of legal use.[41] O.E. *manslaughter* and Latin *homicide* are both literally man killing, but the Latin has become the more general term,[42] and the Old English the more technical.[43]

O.E. *witness* and its Latin equivalent *testis* have been competitors for centuries. The Old English word once served all purposes. It has lost in court to Latin *testify* and *testimony.* But in court it is still the O.E. *witness.* And out of court, the O.E. *witness* witnesses except when the witness is also a *testator.* The Latin witness is still in the running on another front, the *testament.*

Here the competition with O.E. *will* has been resolved by coupling *will* and *testament,*[44] with Old English *last* thrown into the bargain. Each of these words once had some meaning.

The Roman *testamentum* was a very formal form for an expression of the will (*voluntas*) or last will (*ultima voluntas,* or plain *voluntas*).[45] In a figurative sense — which Coke took for etymology[46] — Justinian called it a *testatio mentis* (a testifying of the mind).[47]

---

[37] 24 *Words and Phrases* 524-526 (perm. ed. 1940), 203 (Supp. 1962).

[38] *Black's Law Dictionary* (4th ed. 1951), under *giver.*

[39] 13 *Words and Phrases* (perm. ed. 1940, Supp. 1962), "donor."

[40] 24 *Words and Phrases* 514 (perm. ed. 1940), 202 (Supp. 1962).

[41] Compare 17 *Words and Phrases* (perm. ed. 1958), "forsworn."

[42] 19 *Words and Phrases* (perm. ed. 1940, Supp. 1962), "homicide."

[43] 26 *Words and Phrases* (perm. ed. 1953, Supp. 1962), "manslaughter."

[44] See Section 38.

[45] Lewis and Short, eds., *A Latin Dictionary* (1879), under *testamentum* and *voluntas;* Justinian, *Institutionum* 114 (Moyle, 5th ed. 1912); Justinian, *The Institutes* 8 (Moyle transl. 5th ed. 1913); Swinburn, *A Brief Treatise of Testaments and Last Willes* 189a (1590).

[46] Coke, *Commentary upon Littleton,* ff. 111a, 322b (10th ed. 1703).

[47] Justinian, *Institutionum* 246 (Moyle, 5th ed. 1912); Swinburn, *A Brief Treatise of Testaments and Last Willes* 2b, 3a (1590); compare 2 Blackstone, *Commentaries* *499 (Jones ed. 1916).

In England, *testament* was used loosely to mean a *covenant*[48] or any *legal instrument*,[49] except that in the probate practice of the Church courts it still partook of some of its Roman formality. A literate consistory judge explained that while a *testament* was indeed a *last will*, a *last will* was not necessarily a *testament* unless it named an executor.[50] This distinction was not rigid in language,[51] and it did not last long in the law.[52]

Old English *will* (like the Latin *voluntas*) was also an expression of the will,[53] and as early as the ninth century it was used — though untechnically — in making a final disposition of property: "min willa is þet min . . . lond . . ."[54] Later, the document in which the will is expressed was itself spoken of as the *will* and *last will*.[55]

The likelihood though is that the expression *last will* is more than a translation of the Latin *ultima voluntas*. Long before the Norman Conquest, the Catholic Church in England paid special attention to a parishioner's dying words, his *last words* — in Latin *novissima verba*,[56] in Old English (singular) *nihsta cwide*.[57] *Cwide*, the ancestor of *bequeath*, by itself meant word, saying, or will[58] — a written will. *Cwide* was the will or last will before either *testament* or the word *will* became current in English law.[59] It gives us the basic sense that a will is a voice from the grave; without a *cwide*, you were *cwide-leas* — which meant both speechless and intestate.[60]

With such profusion of words to choose from, it is little wonder that Englishmen followed no consistent course in their naming of wills:

---

[48] *Oxford English Dictionary*, under *testament*, II.

[49] 2 Pollock and Maitland, *The History of English Law* 317 and especially n.2 (2d ed. 1898).

[50] Swinburn, *A Brief Treatise of Testaments and Last Willes* 2a-3a, 7b, 11b (1590).

[51] 2 Pollock and Maitland, *The History of English Law* 331 (2d ed. 1898).

[52] 3 Holdsworth, *A History of English Law* 536-537 (3d ed. 1923).

[53] *Oxford English Dictionary*.

[54] Robertson, ed., *Anglo-Saxon Charters* 10 (2d ed. 1956).

[55] *Oxford English Dictionary*, under will, sb.1, No. 23.

[56] 2 Pollock and Maitland, *The History of English Law* 318 (2d ed. 1898); 2 Holdsworth, *A History of English Law* 95 (3d ed. 1923); Plucknett, *A Concise History of the Common Law* 739 (5th ed. 1956).

[57] *Oxford English Dictionary*, under *next*, for *nihsta*, especially No. 8; Bosworth and Toller, *An Anglo-Saxon Dictionary* (1898), under *cwide*, II, for *nihsta cwide*. Compare 2 Pollock and Maitland, *The History of English Law* 320 (2d ed. 1898).

[58] Bosworth and Toller, *An Anglo-Saxon Dictionary* (1898); Toller, *An Anglo-Saxon Dictionary: Supplement* (1921).

[59] 2 Holdsworth, *A History of English Law* 95 (3d ed. 1923).

[60] Bosworth and Toller, *An Anglo-Saxon Dictionary* (1898); see also *Medieval Latin Word-List* (1934), under *quideles*.

testamentum (in wills written in Latin),[61] *testament,*[62] *will,*[63] *testament and will,*[64] *testament and last will* [65] (in wills written in English). All of this before the Statutes of Wills[66] made land generally willable, and all without distinction between gifts of lands and gifts of chattels. Writing in French — before these Statutes — Coke's revered Littleton discussed devises of land by borough custom "per son testament." [67] The Statute of Wills (1540) itself speaks indiscriminately of *last will and testament, last will or testament, last will in writing,* etc.[68] After the Statutes, Coke — in an ambiguous passage commenting on the fact that by local custom an oral (*nuncupative*) will may pass lands as well as chattels — wrote:

> But in law most commonly, *Ultima voluntas in scriptis* is used where land or tenements are devised and *testamentum* when it concerneth chattels.[69]

All writers did not accept Coke's dictum;[70] some still cling to it as historical fact without even his qualification "most commonly." [71]

With the terminology itself in confusion, and the law of wills still unsettled,[72] sixteenth-century draftsmen might reasonably indulge in an abundance of caution and words. And this ancient association of Old English and Latin in *last will and testament* continues popular as a rolling law phrase, preferred by lawyers over the adequate but curt *will.* (Section 121.)

50. *Latin names for lawyers*

In addition to an early start in the language lawyers use, Latin placed its lasting mark on the profession itself. The equivocal Old

---

[61] Madox, *Formulare Anglicanum* 421, Form No. 766; 423, Form No. 768 (1702).

[62] Madox, *Formulare Anglicanum* 435, Form No. 779 (1702).

[63] Madox, *Formulare Anglicanum* 438, Form No. 781 (1702).

[64] Madox, *Formulare Anglicanum* 440, Form No. 783 (1702); *Oxford English Dictionary,* under *testament,* No. 1.

[65] *Oxford English Dictionary,* under *testament,* No. 1.

[66] Statute of Wills, 1540, 32 Hen. VIII, c. 1; Statute of Explanation of Statute of Wills, 1542-1543, 34 & 35 Hen. VIII, c. 5.

[67] Coke, *Commentary upon Littleton,* f. 111a (10th ed. 1703).

[68] Statute of Wills, 1540, 32 Hen. VIII, c. 1, s. 1, s. 2, s. 7, etc.

[69] Coke, *Commentary upon Littleton,* f. 111a (10th ed. 1703).

[70] Blount, *Nomo-Lexikon* (1670), under *will;* Blount, *A Law Dictionary and Glossary* (3d ed. 1717), under *will; Les Termes de la Ley* (1708), under *testament.*

[71] *Wharton's Law Lexicon* (14th ed. 1938), under *wills;* compare *Ballentine's Pronouncing Law Dictionary: Supplement* (2d ed. 1954), under *testament; Oxford English Dictionary,* under *will,* No. 23.

[72] 2 Pollock and Maitland, *The History of English Law* 314-356 (2d ed. 1898).

English words for a calling ill-defined before the Conquest (Section 35) met strong competition from Latin that already had roots in the Roman and canon law. With the exception of the English *lawyer* and the French *pleader* (also remotely Latin), all of the current principal equivalents are Latin (mediated by French).

Advocate (kin to the Roman *advocatus*) and *proctor* (short for *procurator*) both have a Church background in England. The *advocate* was a pleader in the Church courts. The *proctor* was an agent for the Church before he became an *attorney* (in the British sense) in matters relating to admiralty, civil, and canon law; "a sort of monkish attorney" Dickens called him.[73]

Attorney comes remotely from Classical Latin *torno* (to turn on a lathe) through Old French *atorner* (turn to, arrange, appoint) and *atorné* (one appointed), with the Norman-French spelling influenced by law Latin *attornatus*. In British usage before the word was abandoned (Section 95), an *attorney* represented clients in legal matters but like the *solicitor* (from Classical Latin *sollicitare*, to stir up) left the court work largely to others. (At one time the *attorney* functioned at common law and the *solicitor* in equity.) *Attorney at law* (to distinguish from *attorney in fact*) follows the medieval law Latin precedent of the *serviens ad legem*, the specialist who serves in matters of law — in French, a *serjeant*.[74]

The etymologies of *the bar* and *barrister* are still in question, but an ancestor of the British *barrister* is the thirteenth-century student pleader known as *apprenticius ad barram* (apprentice at the bar). *The bar* refers to the railing in court,[75] and the *bar* in *barrister* is said to refer originally to "the ancient internal arrangements of the Inns of Court." [76]

Today's *counsel* was the Latin *consilium*, and *counselor* is traceable to Latin *consiliator*.

Some other Latin terms for lawyers have only an indirect survival.

In medieval England, a common law pleader was at one time known as a *narrator*, which in Classical Latin had the same meaning as in present-day general English.

---

[73] 1 *The Personal History of David Copperfield*, c. 23, p. 410 (Gadshill ed. 1897).

[74] Compare *Oxford English Dictionary*, under *sergeant*, No. 6, and Sayles, ed., *Select Cases in the Court of King's Bench Under Edward III*, 76 Selden Society lxv (1958).

[75] *Medieval Latin Word-List* (1934), under *apprenticius ad barram* and *barra; Oxford English Dictionary*, under *bar*, sb.[1], III.

[76] *Oxford English Dictionary*, under *barrister*.

The Latin *ignoramus* (we do not know) was the word once used by the English grand jury when it refused to indict, in contrast to the indorsement *billa vera* (true bill).[77] *Ignoramus*, in the sense of an ignorant person, was introduced into English as the name of a seventeenth-century play lampooning Coke. The title role was an ignorant lawyer bursting with broken Latin.[78] A similar meaning of the word was given added seventeenth-century pompousness by dubbing the lawyer "Sir Ignoramus." [79]

The Medieval Latin *ambidexter* (on both sides righthanded) meant ambidextrous in eighth-century England, but by the thirteenth century it had come to refer also to anyone, lawyer or juror, who took money from both sides of a case.[80] With that unsavory meaning it entered the English language.[81]

Latin with a taint still burdens the profession. *Ambulance chaser* (the first half paradoxically from the Latin for *walking;* the second half Old French) is an American invention, first recorded in the Congressional Record of 1897.[82]

51. *The habit of written Latin*

After a brief nod to English during the reign of the Conqueror (Section 42), law Latin took a commanding position that developed into a two-century monopoly — and a longer habit — as the written language of the law. Even during the heyday of law French (Chapter IX) and even when secular professionals became draftsmen, the Latin habit persisted for most documents of importance.[83]

Latin continued as the language of English statutes through the first half of the thirteenth century (with sometimes a French translation). In the second half of the thirteenth century, Latin statutes predominated but there were also statutes in French. In the fourteenth century French became the regular language of the statutes; yet there was some Latin on the statute books until 1461.[84]

[77] 6 *The Harleian Miscellany* 128 (new ed. 1810).
[78] Bowen, *The Lion and the Throne* 357-359 (1957).
[79] *Oxford English Dictionary*, under *ignoramus*, No. 2.
[80] *Medieval Latin Word-List;* Johnson, *Latin Words of Common English* 249 (1931).
[81] *Oxford English Dictionary; Les Termes de la Ley* (1671 and 1708); Partridge, *Slang: Today and Yesterday* 185 (3d ed. 1950).
[82] Mathews, ed., *A Dictionary of Americanisms* (1951); compare *Oxford English Dictionary Supplement*, under *ambulance*, No. 2.
[83] See generally Madox, *Formulare Anglicanum* (1702).
[84] The Record Commissioners, "An Historical Survey of Ancient English Statutes," in 2 *Select Essays in Anglo-American Legal History* 169, 201 (1908).

In the literature of the law there is a similar pattern. Latin is the language of both of the first important books on English law: in 1189 *Glanvil — Tractatus de legibus et consuetudinibus regni Angliae* (Treatise on the Laws and Customs of the Kingdom of England), and about 1250 *Bracton — De Legibus et Consuetudinibus Angliae* (On the Laws and Customs of England). Latin stands alone into the second half of the thirteenth century in short works bringing *Bracton* up to date (Hengham's *Summa Magna* and *Summa Parva*) and others attempting to abridge and explain *Bracton* for practical use (*Fleta,* and Thornton's *Summa*). At this point French legal literature appeared, but Latin was by no means finished. The Renaissance interest in classicism is reflected in the law. Fortescue's *De Laudibus Legum Angliae* (In Praise of the Law of England) of 1460, and his *De Natura Legis Naturae* (On the Nature of the Law of Nature) in 1464 are Latin, and the first portion of St. Germain's *Doctor and Student* (1523) is also in Latin. (Section 75.)

During all this time the registers of writs (*Registrum Brevium*) were in Latin,[85] and the court records were recognized as appropriately in Latin even when the first statutory protest was made against the unintelligibility of French (1362). (Section 65.) When common law (as distinct from Chancery) pleadings became written, they were in Latin. (Sections 68, 80.) And the formbooks followed suit.[86] (Sections 72-74.) With small variation both remained in Latin, until Latin was tentatively outlawed in the seventeenth century and legislated into a subordinate position in the eighteenth. (Sections 73, 76.) This revolt against Latin did not occur until long after England had cut herself off from the Latin-speaking Church of Rome, and despite official and unofficial attack Latin did not leave the law. With a vigorous and still vocal following,[87] Latin remains in the law under exceptions for "technical" words, and sometimes also as English. (Sections 7, 11.)

[85] Winfield, *The Chief Sources of English Legal History* 286-302 (1925).
[86] Winfield, *The Chief Sources of English Legal History* 304 (1925).
[87] For example, Wickersham, letter, in "An And/or Symposium," 18 A.B.A.J. 574, 575 (1932), and Withers, letter, 47 A.B.A.J. 1146 (1961).

C H A P T E R   V I I I

Some Characteristics of the Middle English Period

52. *Middle English: A definition*

Middle English is the form of the English language used in England in the period 1100-1500.[1] These are the dates usually given, though there is no sharp line of beginning or ending.[2] Middle English arbitrarily fills the gap between Old English (Section 31) and Modern English. Some speak of Old English Transition (twelfth century), Early Middle English (thirteenth century), Late Middle English (fourteenth century), and Middle English Transition (fifteenth century).[3]

Middle English is the language of Chaucer, the high point between *Beowulf* and Shakespeare. It marks the end of the Germanic inflections of Old English. It is the link between a language overwhelmingly Anglo-Saxon and one that incorporates not bits but whole chunks of Latin and French.

The period of Middle English starts with the reign of Henry I, English-born son of the Norman conqueror. It is a time of almost constant warfare — at home (the capitulation of King John at Runnymede; the Revolt of the Barons; the War of the Roses), on the Island (in Wales and in Scotland), and on the Continent (the Hundred Years' War). The battling starts with swords, continues with the crossbow, and ends with the fire of smallarms.

The period sees the introduction of cheaper paper as a substitute for parchment, but it is still hand-made rag paper. And in the last quarter century of the Middle English period, Caxton publishes the first book printed in English in England (1477). By the end of the

---

[1] Setzler, *The Jefferson Anglo-Saxon Grammar* 3-4 (1938); *Webster's New International Dictionary* lxxxii-lxxxvi (2d ed. 1934).

[2] Compare 1 *Oxford English Dictionary* xxx; 8 *Encyclopaedia Britannica* 554 (1948); *Middle English Dictionary*, Plan and Bibliography, ix (Kurath ed. 1954); *A Middle English Dictionary*, title page (Stratmann and Bradley ed. 1891).

[3] 1 *Oxford English Dictionary* xxx.

fifteenth century, English statutes are being printed, and the old proc-lamation of statutes by the sheriffs is through.[4]   The Middle English period closes with the Renaissance, the first Tudor king on the English throne, and the discovery of America.

53. *Middle English: A disorderly language*

If law Latin was not exactly in the classic mold (Sections 46, 47), it did follow a pattern that men of learning recognized.   In contrast, English — expressive enough — was plain disorderly.   Neglected after the Conquest as a language of literature and education (Section 44), Middle English developed without standard or rule.[5]

Not until nearly the end of the Middle English period was there any-thing like a dictionary (as distinguished from a glossary), and that one English-Latin.   The first English language dictionary does not appear until the era of Modern English.[6]   So too with the law.   In the Middle English period a glossary may give some notion in French of Old Eng-lish law words,[7] but there are no English language law dictionaries.

Middle English spelling is a matter of every man for himself.   The same writer may vary the spelling of a word in one document.   Travel by foot or horse over dirt roads or no roads was difficult and discour-aging.   Mass communication was unknown.   Dialect was the rule. And not till the last fifty years of the Middle English period did one of these dialects — East Midland (London) — achieve the status of a standard for written English.[8]   Phonetic spelling and varying degrees of literacy made the simplest word an adventure.   Without change of mood or tense, *did* has been recorded in Middle English as *dede, did, didd, didde, dide, dode, dud, dude, dyd, dyde.*

Law words that came to rest in Middle English met a similar fate. *Law* itself (*laʒu* in Old English — Sections 24, 35) could be spelled a couple dozen ways, including *lach, laewe, lagh, laghe, laha, lau, lauh, law,* and even *laugh.*   *Law* had almost as many meanings as spellings, including:

a particular rule ("a law") = French *loi* and Latin *lex*
a body of rules ("the law") = French *droit* and Latin *ius* (or *jus*)

[4] 4 Holdsworth, *A History of English Law* 308 (1924); 1 Holdsworth, *A History of English Law* 8 (3d ed. 1922); 2 Holdsworth, *A History of English Law* 436 (3d ed. 1923).
[5] Marsh, *The Origin and History of the English Language* 380 (3d ed. 1869).
[6] Hulbert, *Dictionaries British and American* 15-16 (1955); Starnes and Noyes, *The English Dictionary from Cawdrey to Johnson* 1 (1946).
[7] For example, 1 *Reliquiae Antiquae* 33 (1841).
[8] Baugh, *A History of the English Language* 236-244 (1935).

the profession of law (also "the law")
jurisprudence, as in "Goo to oxenford or lerne lawe" [9]
the action of law courts
the custom of the country, as in "law of the land"
justice, as in "right and law" [10]

Basic controversies over the meaning that should be poured into or decanted out of *law* are still not resolved.[11]   But this is not the profession's only legacy from Middle English.

It was an age of experimentation with language.   From Old English *withstand* (oppose), there was fashioned after the model of Medieval Latin *non obstante* (and Old French *non obstant*) the mouth-filling *notwithstanding*, with customary multiple meanings: in spite of, nevertheless, still, yet, although.   It was not a law word to start with, but the law later picked it up and kept it.

In similar style, Middle English formed a couple dozen compounds with *where* such as *whereafterward, wherehence, wherethrough,* and *wheretil.*   Of the many *where-* words then in common use, the law gathered in these:

whereabouts	an approximation
whereas	a ubiquitous creation, usually spelled as two words, and meaning where (in six different senses), in view of the fact that, forasmuch as, inasmuch as
whereby	by means of, so that, how?, near what?
wherefor(e)	with either spelling meaning for what, for which, on account of which, therefore
wherein	in what?, in which, in respect of which
whereof	of what?, of which, wherefore, whereby, in regard to
whereunder	under which
whereupon	upon what?, at what?, wherefore?, whereon, upon which, for what reason, etc.

The unsettled state of the alphabet itself was of no assistance to anyone who groped after consistency in Middle English.

The Old English *thorn* (þ) was still used for the sound *th.*   (Sections 32, 37.)   But alongside the thorn, Middle English began to use *th,* so that in the fourteenth century *there* could be spelled in at least fifteen different ways including þar, þare, þaire, thar, thare, tare,

---

[9] Quoted in *Oxford English Dictionary,* under *law,* sb.[1], No. 3b.
[10] *Oxford English Dictionary,* under *law,* sb.[1], No. 15.
[11] For example, see Frank, *Law and the Modern Mind* (6th rev. print. 1949); Fuller, "The Case of the Speluncean Explorers," 62 Harv. L. Rev. 616 (1949); Hexner, *Studies in Legal Terminology* 14-16 (1941); Kantorowicz, *The Definition of Law* (1958); Kelsen, *What Is Justice?* (1957); Pollock, *A First Book of Jurisprudence* 3-29 (4th ed. 1918).

þer, þere, tere, ther, there. The letter *yogh* was a further complication. Written ʒ and described as an "open-tailed *g*," [12] it could represent *y* at the beginning and *gh* at the end of a word. In Middle English, the yogh was sometimes used and sometimes the *y* (ʒ*e* or *ye*); the yogh was sometimes used and sometimes the *gh* (*toʒ* or *togh* or *tough*).

I and *J* then (and for centuries later), were one letter: *judge* could be *iugge, iuge, iewge, guge,* or *iudge;* the long-tailed, consonant *i* was not written as *j* till the seventeenth century.

U and *V* were also one letter: *overlord* was written *ovyr-lord* and also *our lord.*

Perplexing questions of the appropriateness of particular letters to convey particular sounds added to the strain of writing Middle English. Thus Middle English *where* is a hobgoblin masquerading as *hwaer, huer, quare, gwhare, hwore,* and *whore.* For the greater part of the Middle English period the whimsey of personal choice and personal penmanship was the rule of English grammar.

54. Court hand and abbreviations

The vagaries of the "vulgar" tongues, Middle English (Section 53) and French (Chapter IX), encouraged by contrast the use of written Latin. Another stimulus to Latinism was the fact that the chief body of literates in England was still the Latin-trained clergy. (Sections 45, 51.) The customary test for the right to claim *benefit of clergy*[13] (and so escape the harshness of the King's criminal justice) was the ability to read, later formalized as the ability to read the "neck verse" in Latin: "Miserere mei, Deus" (Have mercy upon me, God).[14]

The documents penned by the clergy (and also by their lay successors) were turned out in various forms of stylized Latin script — at times works of art, but so intricate and so full of abbreviation as to be incomprehensible to any but the initiated. One of these scripts is known as *court hand* and became a much-used medium for Latin legal documents.[15]

Some abbreviations used in court hand and other law scripts are of ancient origin and survive. One of the most famous in the law is *ss,* which stares in silence from the top of every lawyer-drawn affidavit. It has served many purposes and been given many translations (see

---

[12] 1 *Oxford English Dictionary* xxxii.
[13] *Oxford English Dictionary,* under *benefit,* sb., No. 3c.
[14] Psalms 51:1.
[15] 3 Blackstone, *Commentaries* *323 (Jones ed. 1916); compare 10 *Words and Phrases* (perm. ed. 1940), "court hand."

Section 120),[16] but is most widely acknowledged as the abbreviation of the Latin *scilicet* (one may know), in English *towit.* (Section 32.) In this sense it was used in William the Conqueror's *Domesday Book.*[17]

The now standard *ss* is a formalized version of a running style symbol, which in court hand resembled several letter combinations but was not the same as any of them. It was kin to court hand capital *ef*, double long-tailed *ess*, and *st*.[18] If *st* were intended, the *t* would represent one of the court hand conventions for a final *et*.[19] And this would then follow one of the court hand patterns of abbreviation, use of first and last letters,[20] though the script abbreviations were matters of shorthand convenience rather than literal correspondence. A similar scheme was adopted in court hand for another *towit* abbreviation: *viz.* for the Latin *videlicet* (one can see). The *z* in *viz.* is an emaciated version of an ornate court hand Middle English *z*,[21] which — like *t* — was sometimes used as an arbitrary abbreviation of a final *et*.[22] The intricacies of script had to be reduced to standard types by the early printers. Thus the script thorn (þ) which had become confused with script *y* ended up in print as *y* for the *th* sound, giving *ye* for *the*, as in "ye coffee shoppe." [23] It is possible that the printers resolved doubts about *ss* in the same way.

Abbreviations for the Latin *et cetera* (and the rest) also antedated the printing presses — in the form *etc.*[24] and also in a stylized symbol [25] which in print became *&c.* When the day of written pleadings arrived (Section 68), *&c.* was overworked as a substitute for omitted formalities.[26] The ampersand (*&*), a script contraction of the Latin *et* (and), appears in *Domesday Book.*[27]

Other old documents show as standard abbreviations *b.f.* (bona fide), *A.D.* (Anno Domini), *M.* (*mille*, thousand), *ux* (*uxor*, wife),

---

[16] Martin, comp., *The Record Interpreter* 141 (2d ed. 1910); *Black's Law Dictionary* (4th ed. 1951); Bowen, *The Lion and the Throne* 277-278 (1957).

[17] Kelham, *Domesday Book Illustrated* 317 (1788); see 39A *Words and Phrases* (perm. ed. 1953), "SS."; 38 *Words and Phrases* (perm. ed. 1940), "scilicet."

[18] Wright, *Court-Hand Restored*, plates 14, 1, 2, 3, 4 (3d ed. 1786).

[19] Martin, comp., *The Record Interpreter* 154, 163 (2d ed. 1910).

[20] Compare Williams, *Learning the Law* 203-218 (6th ed. 1957).

[21] Wright, *Court-Hand Restored*, plate 7 (3d ed. 1786).

[22] Martin, comp., *The Record Interpreter* viii, 163 (2d ed. 1910).

[23] *Oxford English Dictionary*, under Y.

[24] Martin, comp., *The Record Interpreter* 47 (2d ed. 1910).

[25] Wright, *Court-Hand Restored*, plate 20 (3d ed. 1786).

[26] 3 Holdsworth, *A History of English Law* 630 (3d ed. 1923); see Coke, *Commentary upon Littleton*, ff. 17a, 17b (10th ed. 1703).

[27] Kelham, *Domesday Book Illustrated* 201 (1788).

c. (*cum,* with), *t.* (*testamentum,* will).[28]   These Latin abbreviations had the sanction of long use, which did not apply to written French. A text warned that French, unlike Latin, was not suited to abbreviation.[29]   Yet when law French came into daily court use (Chapter IX), the scribe's familiarity with oft-repeated words, tedium, and need for speed inevitably brought contraction and other abbreviation.[30]   The hurried Year Book law French was shortened to the point where translation rests partly in enlightened conjecture.[31]   As with Latin, French abbreviations were further condensed by the printers.   French abbreviations for *honorable* (written *hon^{ble}*) and *number* (*no^{bre}*) have survived in English as *hon.* and *no.*[32]

Court hand and abbreviation became a part of the legal mysteries. They also became ammunition for the advocates of later legislation to reform the language of the law.   (Sections 73, 76.)   The unfortunate clerk of Chatham in Shakespeare's *Henry the Sixth* is suspect as a man who "can make obligations, and write court-hand."   And when he confesses that he writes his name rather than make a "mark to thyself, like an honest plain-dealing man," he is immediately sentenced to hang "with his pen and ink-horn about his neck."[33]

55. *Land law important*

The Middle English period covers four centuries, and neither the economy nor the law of England remained static.   Yet, as a generalization for the entire period, the important factor in both economy and law was the land.   The law of contract was developing but slowly. Two hundred and fifty years after the Middle English period had ended, "contracts" was still a subordinate and unorganized division of the law.[34]   Commercial transactions were still largely in the hands of Italians and other foreign merchants, who were building up a law of their own outside the courts of common law.

Until expulsion from England in 1290, the Jews (a private and lucra-

---

[28] Martin, comp., *The Record Interpreter* 16, 3, 80, 159, 18, 147 (2d ed. 1910).

[29] Maitland, "Of the Anglo-French Language in the Early Year Books," in Introduction to *Year Books of Edward II,* 17 Selden Society xxxiii, xl (1903).

[30] North, *A Discourse on the Study of the Laws* 14-15 (1824).

[31] Maitland, "Of the Anglo-French Language in the Early Year Books," in Introduction to *Year Books of Edward II,* 17 Selden Society xl-xli (1903).

[32] Martin, comp., *The Record Interpreter* 169, 171 (2d ed. 1910); and see Williams, *Learning the Law* 210 n.3 (6th ed. 1957).

[33] 2 *Henry VI,* act IV, scene II; see also "The Laws Discovery" (1653), in 6 *The Harleian Miscellany* 322, 324 (new ed. 1810).

[34] See, for example, 2 Blackstone, *Commentaries* *296-*298, *442-*470 (Jones ed. 1916); 3 Blackstone, *Commentaries* *153-*166 (Jones ed. 1916).

tive tax preserve for the Crown) had a virtual monopoly of undisguised money-lending, for interest was forbidden to Christians by both the Church and the common law.[35] *Usury* carried its meaning from Classical Latin *usura* — not excessive but any charge for the use of money. Even after Tudor statutes permitted some interest,[36] it was urged that this meant only that the King's courts would not punish the taking of a legal rate of interest, but that:

. . . God will have his Decrees to be kept inviolable, who saith, Lend, looking for nothing thereby, &c.[37]

The Church's threat of the forfeiture of a usurer's chattels upon his death did not end Christian usury. The real property mortgage flourished even though it was by historic definition usurious. Old French *mortgage* was translated into Medieval Latin as *mortuum vadium* (later *morgagium*),[38] a dead pledge. *Glanvil's* explanation of the terminology was that the mortgagee in possession had not merely the land but its profits, and the pledged land was thus dead because its profits were not reducing the debt.[39] Littleton said it was *mort gage* because the pledged land was dead to the borrower if the debt was not paid, and dead to the lender if it was.[40] Coke further distinguished a dead pledge from a living one (*vivum vadium*) where the produce of the land reduced the indebtedness.[41]

But quarrels over mortgages were more concerned with ritual than morals. Ritual land transfer — *livery* of *seisin* (law French for *delivery* of *possession*) — was necessary to put the lender in. And once delivered, the land did not automatically come back to the borrower when the debt was paid; no matter what a document might say. A document was not the "best evidence" of a transfer of land;[42] what counted was the primitive fact of physical transfer of possession. Once this had been memorialized in men's minds by the transfer of bits of the earth and its produce from the hand of the old owner to the hand of the new owner, both physically on the premises.[43] When writings

[35] 1 Pollock and Maitland, *The History of English Law* 468-475 (2d ed. 1898).
[36] Stat. (1536) 27 Hen. VIII, c. 9; Stat. (1571) 13 Eliz., c. 8.
[37] *Les Termes de la Ley* (1671), under *usury;* see Luke 6:34 and 6:35.
[38] *Medieval Latin Word-List* (1934), under *morgagio*.
[39] 2 Pollock and Maitland, *The History of English Law* 119 (2d ed. 1898).
[40] Coke, *Commentary upon Littleton*, f. 205a (10th ed. 1703).
[41] Coke, *Commentary upon Littleton*, f. 205a (10th ed. 1703); compare 2 Pollock and Maitland, *The History of English Law* 119 and especially nn.2, 3 (2d ed. 1898).
[42] 9 Holdsworth, *A History of English Law* 164 (1926).
[43] 2 Pollock and Maitland, *The History of English Law* 84-86 (2d ed. 1898).

came to be used for a symbolic delivery of possession, the document was laid upon the ground, and the deed was picked up instead of the bits of earth. A part of this ancient dream sequence is dimly remembered; today the object of the ritual has changed from the land to the deed, yet it is still delivery — not signing — that is the vital fact of conveyancing.

But for a time during the Middle English period, the feudal forms for transfer of possession of real estate — and the incidents that followed from possession — were jealously guarded. The 1290 statute *Quia Emptores terrarum* (because the purchasers of land) granted tenants the right to sell their lands, but the buyers then owed feudal dues to the seller's lord.

The 1285 statute *De Donis conditionalibus* (concerning conditional gifts) confirmed the right of the landowner to keep his lands within the family circle. He could have a *fee tail* (from Old French *taillier* to cut, shape), i.e., an estate tailor-made, shaped, or cut off as desired.[44] (The ribald seventeenth century found this estate easy to remember: "He gets the French crancums [v.d.], and so knows what it is to have a tenure in taile.")[45] A vast and complicated learning developed around parallel and conflicting efforts to *entail* lands and to *bar entails*. At a later date this polite French expression was joined by a more vivid though repetitious one — with marked similarity to the older custom of docking horse tails. In *docking* the *entail* (i.e., cutting cuttings) the first cut (*dock*) is of uncertain origin but is related to the modern Icelandic for a short, stumpy tail. Still later, French *entails* were unsettled by a third language mixture — the Latin *dis*entail.

One guide through the maze of settling and unsettling estates was a collusive lawsuit brought by the buyer against the seller, *levying a fine* (French, from the Latin for raising an end, or compromise ending a suit).[46] For present purposes the most significant feature of the fine was that it was a conveyance under supervision of the court. If the proposed settlement was frowned upon by the bench, it was revised. And before the fine was entered, it was the considered judgment of colluding counsel and the court that the settlement would hold up.[47] Here was some protection against the twin pitfalls of ambiguity and

---

[44] Plucknett, *A Concise History of the Common Law* 556-557 (5th ed. 1956); Coke, *Commentary upon Littleton*, f. 18b (10th ed. 1703).

[45] Quoted in *Oxford English Dictionary*, under *crankum*.

[46] 3 Holdsworth, *A History of English Law* 222-223 (3d ed. 1923); 2 Pollock and Maitland, *The History of English Law* 86, 98 (2d ed. 1898).

[47] 3 Holdsworth, *A History of English Law* 252-253 (3d ed. 1923).

technicality. It was a protection sorely needed, for the law and its language were growing and changing. Before the end of this Middle English period, the land law had achieved an intricate development, with a variety of feudal estates and a host of intertwined writs and stereotyped oral pleas. The procedures of this age became the base for later expansion and refinement of the land law. They also left a permanent mark on the forms and procedures of the other branches of the law.

56. The phrasing of documents

Because writing was an accomplishment of the few (Sections 45, 54), and because of the parallel historical preference for ritual over writing (Section 29), the Middle English legal matters that ended up in documentary form were limited. As one realistic fourteenth-century judge put it: for small matters "a man cannot always have a clerk at hand to write a deed." [48] Writs and deeds, especially Church deeds, form the biggest proportion of the law documents.

To begin with, a *writ* was no more than a *letter;* the same Medieval Latin *breve* stood for both. And like a letter, a writ started with *salutations* — later translated from Latin into Old English *greetings.* A tenth-century English version of a Pope's letter to King Edwin begins:

Bonefatius papa sende Eadwine gretinge.[49]

In parallel form, a king's writ of entry directed to the Sheriff of Derby begins:

Rex, vicecomiti Derbiae salutem.[50]

With other documents cast in the same mold — deeds,[51] charters of liberties,[52] wills[53] — the intelligence was sometimes made more notorious by multiple greetings. A thirteenth-century deed poll greets:

Omnibus Christi fidelibus, ad quos presens scriptum pervenerit . . .[54]
(All Christ's followers to whom the present writing comes . . .)

And if a man wanted more scope than the "faithful of Christ," a document could begin:

[48] Quoted in another connection in Holmes, *The Common Law* 281 (1881).
[49] Quoted in *Oxford English Dictionary,* under *greeting,* vbl. sb.
[50] 3 Holdsworth, *A History of English Law* 659 (3d ed. 1923).
[51] 3 Holdsworth, *A History of English Law* 667 (3d ed. 1923).
[52] Stubbs, ed., *Select Charters* 82-83, 296 (8th ed. 1905).
[53] Madox, *Formulare Anglicanum* 421, Form No. 767; 438, Form No. 781 (1702).
[54] 3 Holdsworth, *A History of English Law* 669 (3d ed. 1923).

Noverint universi[55]
(Know all men)

A late fifteenth-century will in English adopts the formula of universal greetings and present writing (*presens scriptum*):

> Be yt Kinoven to all men the which this present Writing shall see here or rede, that this is the Wille of me Jane Zowche.[56]

In Medieval Latin *presens scriptum* was shortened so that *presens* would do the work of both words. This shortened form combined with the universal greetings to yield the still-used clause: Know all men by these Presents.[57]

Such introductions to the meat of documents were words of form and not of substance. Both earlier and later simpler beginnings were used. In the ninth century an English will (translated here) began:

> I, Badenoth Beotting, declare and order to be put in writing what I desire to become of my heritable land . . .[58]

And in the thirteenth century:

> *Hec est conventio facta inter* . . .[59]
>
> (This is the agreement made between . . .)

which is the model for a numerous tribe.

After such introductions, some deeds got down to brass tacks, but some continued to indulge in the ecclesiastical obeisances and curses of an earlier era (Section 34). Then followed recitals of reasons for the grant, and a listing of persons present at its making.

In its day, none of this was out of place. The ceremonious aspect of land transfer was still important.[60] (Section 55.) Also, deeds were permitted in evidence before general witnesses could testify to the circumstances of a grant. And here was an early method of preparing and preserving self-serving testimony.[61] It was testimony that something had already been done: *have given and granted;* for the deed only supplemented a completed act of transfer. If the deed went on to say, *and by these presents give and grant*, that made assurance doubly sure, in an age when terms of art were still in the making.

---

[55] Coke, *Commentary upon Littleton*, f. 264b (10th ed. 1703).
[56] Madox, *Formulare Anglicanum* 438, Form No. 781 (1702).
[57] For example, 4 Nichols, *Cyclopedia of Legal Forms Annotated*, par. 4.37 (Ark.), par. 4.40 (Colo.), par. 4.48a (Hawaii), par. 4.100 (S.C.) (1955).
[58] Robertson, ed., *Anglo-Saxon Charters* 10-11 (2d ed. 1956).
[59] 3 Holdsworth, *A History of English Law* 668 (3d ed. 1923).
[60] 2 Pollock and Maitland, *The History of English Law* 90 (2d ed. 1898).
[61] 3 Holdsworth, *A History of English Law* 225 (3d ed. 1923).

If you weren't sure how to describe a fee, you said in detailed thirteenth-century Latin:[62]

> To have and to hold as a freeman and without claim and with honor and peaceably in fee and as an inheritance for himself and his heirs or his assigns and their heirs or whoever and whenever, to give, to sell, to will, or to assign as they might desire forever.

In the late fifteenth century, Littleton — with more technicality and fewer words — could advise that *A aver et tener a luy et a ses heires*[63] (To have and to hold to him and to his heirs) would serve the purpose.

The critical words here were *his heirs*, which made it an estate of inheritance. But mixed in with these words of art, Littleton included medieval boilerplate inherited from a dim past: *to have and to hold.* *Have* and *hold* are Old English synonyms (Section 32) which appear in the same sentence as early as *Beowulf* and are joined with an ampersand as early as the tenth century. In the Old English pattern, saying *have* twice was a more emphatic *have*, and making it swing with alliteration was even more in keeping with the Anglo-Saxon oral tradition (Section 30). What *have* and *hold* lose in alliteration, they gain in rhythmic rumble in the Latin *habendum et tenendum*. And even in law French they retain an end rhyme as *aver et tener.*

To Coke, all of Littleton — even his use of *etc.* — was sacred.[64] So to words of art and to boilerplate alike, Coke gave the sweet sound of reason. Though *have & hold* antedated a centralized feudal tenure in England, *hold*, he said, arose from the fact that:

> . . . all the lands and tenements in England in the hands of subjects, are holden mediately or immediately of the King.

Accordingly, *hold* referred not merely to the estate but to the lord of whom held and the tenure by which held.[65]

The lord part was unnecessary after *Quia Emptores* (1290),[66] and the tenure part became obsolete with the abolition of feudal tenures in 1660.[67] But *to have and to hold* was a strong habit before then. It

---

[62] 3 Holdsworth, *A History of English Law* 228 n.10 (3d ed. 1923).

[63] Coke, *Commentary upon Littleton*, ff. 1a, 302a (10th ed. 1703).

[64] Coke, *Commentary upon Littleton*, ff. 17a, 17b (10th ed. 1703); 5 Holdsworth, *A History of English Law* 467 (1924).

[65] Coke, *Commentary upon Littleton*, ff. 1a, 1b (10th ed. 1703).

[66] 2 Blackstone, *Commentaries* °299 (Jones ed. 1916).

[67] Military tenures, 1660, 12 Car. II, c. 24; Plucknett, *A Concise History of the Common Law* 589 (5th ed. 1956).

was used for anything emphatically possessed (*seised*). Feudal tenure really had nothing to do with it.

You could be seised of a wife, so in 1400:

> He gaffe hym his syster Acheflour,
> To have and to holde.[68]

And in the next century the Book of Common Prayer adopted the rich phrase for the marriage ceremony. You could be seised of a liberty, so the rights of Magna Carta were granted *habendas et tenendas* "to them and their heirs of us and our heirs." [69]   In Anglo-Saxon days an owner could *have* an estate, or he could *hold* it.[70]   In later years a fee could be created without the *hold*, as long as the conveyance said "have to him and his heires." [71]

Like *Know all men* and *these presents, have* and *hold* were not terms of art, not precise, but they were associated with words of art: *and his heirs*.   It came to be sensed — if not understood — that the words *to have and to hold* were a part of the conveyancing ritual.   And they were passed on for flavoring in three languages — English, Latin, and French.   It is to French that our inquiry is now directed.   (Chapter IX.)

[68] Quoted in *Oxford English Dictionary*, under *have*, v., No. 1c.
[69] Stubbs, ed., *Select Charters* 297 (8th ed. 1905).
[70] Robertson, ed., *Anglo-Saxon Charters* 154-155 (2d ed. 1956).
[71] St. Germain, *Doctor and Student*, f. 50a (ed. 1598).

CHAPTER IX

The Rise and Fall of Law French

57. *The spread of bilingualism*

The Norman Conquest did not slam the door on English (Chapter VI), but it did open the door to Frenchmen and the French language. For centuries kings of England were more French than English: with vast real estate holdings in France, owing feudal allegiance to a French crown, marrying French women, preferring French courtiers, and speaking French habitually.

Yet for all the influence of things French, the English language continued strong in the race for survival. From the coronation of the Conqueror on, French and English (and Latin for the learned) were heard side by side in England. At first there were few of either people who spoke both French and English. One tale has it that the sound of English was so strange to the Norman guards outside Westminster Abbey at the coronation, that hearing the English acclamation of William they rushed the Abbey fearing the worst.[1] Linguistic detectives have traced the steady progress of Frenchmen learning English and Englishmen learning French.[2] Though all are not in agreement, the findings for French and English generally (as distinct from the language of the law) may be summarized:

(1) By the end of the twelfth century bilingualism was not uncommon.[3] The upper classes generally had English and French, and the learned Latin as well.[4]

(2) By the middle of the thirteenth century English was becoming general in use among all classes of society,[5] not merely among the

---

[1] Shelly, *English and French in England: 1066-1100*, p. 77 (1921).

[2] E.g., 3 Palgrave, *The History of Normandy and of England* 613-637 (1864); Shelly, *English and French in England: 1066-1100* (1921); Woodbine, "The Language of English Law," 18 Speculum 395 (1943).

[3] 5 Freeman, *The History of the Norman Conquest of England* 527-528, 889-893 (1876); Baugh, *A History of the English Language* 138-154 (1935).

[4] Woodbine, "The Language of English Law," 18 Speculum 395, 399 (1943).

[5] Baugh, *A History of the English Language* 165 (1935); Vising, *Anglo-Norman Language and Literature* 22 (1923); Collas, "Problems of Translation," in Introduction to *Year Books of Edward II*, 70 Selden Society xiii n.1 (1951).

"lower classes." [6]   French was still important to the educated man, and had a prominent place in the Court of Henry III.[7]   While English was thus gaining in England, French of Paris — no longer "a vulgar dialect of Latin" [8] — was becoming the dominant tongue of France,[9] and an influence throughout Europe.[10]   The French of England, Anglo-Norman (Section 61), took an independent course, with unique accents, rhythms, spellings, pronunciations, and meanings increasingly influenced by English.[11]

(3) In the fourteenth century English was the "cradle tongue" of Englishmen generally.   It was the language of common use, and French was now an accomplishment.[12]   Students at Oxford had to be reminded to keep up their French.[13]   In the fourteenth century English began to be taught in the schools.[14]   And in this century also, literature in the English language once again achieved greatness with the works of Chaucer.[15]   English had come into its own, and the deterioration of Anglo-Norman had set in.[16]

(4) In the fifteenth century there was a spreading ignorance of French even among the nobility.[17]   Perhaps almost four hundred years of cross-Channel warring since the Conquest had created a sense of English nationalism that reflected itself in the development of a national language.   Whatever the cause, by the end of the Middle English period there existed a full-blown image of Modern English.   In this century the stream of Anglo-Norman literature petered out.[18]   Except for the law, Anglo-Norman was dead.   And only those French words were saved which became converts to English.

---

[6] 2 Holdsworth, *A History of English Law* 479 (3d ed. 1923).

[7] Baugh, *A History of the English Language* 165-166 (1935).

[8] 1 Pollock and Maitland, *The History of English Law* 82 (2d ed. 1898).

[9] 9 *Encyclopaedia Britannica* 760 (1948).

[10] 5 Freeman, *The History of the Norman Conquest of England* 533 (1876).

[11] 1 *Cambridge Anglo-Norman Texts* xvi-xxvi (1924); Vising, *Anglo-Norman Language and Literature* 33 (1923).

[12] Baugh, *A History of the English Language* 176-182 (1935); 5 Freeman, *The History of the Norman Conquest of England* 535-536 (1876).

[13] Baugh, *A History of the English Language* 170 (1935).

[14] 5 Freeman, *The History of the Norman Conquest of England* 536 (1876); Baugh, *A History of the English Language* 183-185 (1935).

[15] See Louis Untermeyer, Introduction to *The Canterbury Tales* v-vii (Modern Library, Skeat ed. 1929); Wells, *A Manual of the Writings in Middle English* 599 (1916).

[16] 1 *Cambridge Anglo-Norman Texts* xvi (1924).

[17] 5 Freeman, *The History of the Norman Conquest of England* 536-537 (1876); Baugh, *A History of the English Language* 185-187 (1935).

[18] Vising, *Anglo-Norman Language and Literature* 39 (1923).

58. French into general English

At the very time the law was becoming recognized as an independent profession in England (Section 59), the use of the English language was becoming general, French distinctive and on the wane (Section 57). It is in such a period that there is the greatest room for the borrowing of words: for English talkers to pepper their language with "high-class" foreign usage.[19] Also, in a period of shifting language use, translation is sometimes a necessity in order to appeal to a wider audience.[20]

Efforts have been made to identify the time when the largest number of French words became a part of general English. Surveys show that for the first hundred years after the Norman Conquest few French words were taken into English, and that the period of most extensive borrowing of French is 1251-1400.[21] It has been estimated that 40 per cent of the French words in the English language were adopted in that short period.[22] Such statistics must be taken with caution. The datings inevitably reflect only the time when particular words appear in written form. It has been noted that there is a possible time lag of fifty years between first use and the surviving recorded uses — at least for nontechnical words.[23] And even such correction is inadequate. The scarcity of substantial English literature for a considerable period after the Conquest (Section 44) results in a scarcity of recorded borrowing of French during that period.[24] A further correction here would serve only to place the absorption of French and the triumph of English at a still earlier period.

In any event it is certain that during the Middle English period there was ample opportunity for Englishmen to borrow French words, and they took their opportunity. It has been estimated that more than 10,000 French words became English words during the Middle English period, and that about 7500 of these are in use today.[25]

[19] See Jespersen, *Growth and Structure of the English Language*, par. 47 (Anchor, 9th ed. 1955).
[20] Jespersen, *Growth and Structure of the English Language*, par. 98 (Anchor, 9th ed. 1955).
[21] Jespersen, *Growth and Structure of the English Language*, par. 95 (Anchor, 9th ed. 1955); Baugh, *A History of the English Language* 219-220 (1935); compare Marckwardt, *American English* 37 (1958).
[22] Baugh, *A History of the English Language* 220 (1935).
[23] Jespersen, *Growth and Structure of the English Language*, par. 95 (Anchor, 9th ed. 1955).
[24] Laird, *The Miracle of Language* 50 (Premier ed. 1957).
[25] Baugh, *A History of the English Language* 220 (1935).

59. Profession of law and law French ascendant

Strange then, that at the very moment when English is making its big upswing, and French is declining as a separate language in England (Sections 57, 58), the profession of law blossoms and law French with it.

There were lawyers before the time of Edward I (1272-1307), most of them of the cloth.[26] As early as the twelfth century, the right to counsel was recognized, except on accusation of felony.[27] In the thirteenth century there are conflicting complaints about lawyers: They are delaying justice, and so are barred from a local court.[28] They are corrupt; and there are special "rolls of the indictments of attorneys."[29] They are wanting in learning and manners, and only those admitted by the mayor may have a regular practice in the municipal courts of London.[30] A court saves a litigant from incurring "disinheritance on account of the stupidity of his attorney, who through his witlessness made a mistake" in the name of his own client.[31]

In the late thirteenth century, in the reign of Edward I, the practice of the law was regularized. A statute of 1275 punished deceitful practice by a serjeant.[32] And in 1292 a king's writ ordered the justices to provide from each county a fixed number of attorneys and apprentices "of the better and more upright men."[33] In the thirteenth century also, more and more judges were chosen from outside the Church, some of them from the ranks of practitioners at the bar.[34] The law was becoming "a close profession."[35]

Possibly near the end of the reign of Henry III, and certainly early in the reign of Edward I, the profession saw the start of the Year

[26] 1 Pollock and Maitland, *The History of English Law* 211 et seq. (2d ed. 1898).

[27] 1 Pollock and Maitland, *The History of English Law* 211 (2d ed. 1898).

[28] 1 Pollock and Maitland, *The History of English Law* 217 (2d ed. 1898); see also Sayles, ed., *Select Cases in the Court of King's Bench Under Edward III*, 76 Selden Society lxiii (1958).

[29] Sayles, ed., *Select Cases in the Court of King's Bench Under Edward III*, 76 Selden Society lxiii (1958).

[30] 1 Pollock and Maitland, *The History of English Law* 216 (2d ed. 1898).

[31] Sayles, ed., *Select Cases in the Court of King's Bench Under Edward III*, 76 Selden Society lxxxix (1958).

[32] Westminster the First, 1275, 3 Edw. I, c. 29; 1 Pollock and Maitland, *The History of English Law* 216 (2d ed. 1898).

[33] Sayles, ed., *Select Cases in the Court of King's Bench Under Edward III*, 76 Selden Society lxiii (1958).

[34] 1 Pollock and Maitland, *The History of English Law* 205 (2d ed. 1898).

[35] 2 Holdsworth, *A History of English Law* 229 (3d ed. 1923); see also Plucknett, *A Concise History of the Common Law* 217-219 (5th ed. 1956).

Books[36] — unique compounds of uncensored court reporting and shrewd legal and personal comment. The Year Books run from about 1260 to 1535,[37] and from first to last they are French. On the portion of the Year Books thought to be from the reign of Henry III, there is disagreement among scholars as to whether the French writing also reflects oral French court usage.[38] But it is generally agreed that from about 1272, the writers of the Year Books were writing not merely the law language they were accustomed to write, but were writing also the law language they heard spoken in court: law French.[39] The end-date of oral law French trails off in a haze of uncertainty. (See Section 67.)

At about the same time law French took undisputed hold of the courts, it began to compete with Latin in the statutes (Section 51), and became the language of a new legal literature. Practical pleading compilations — Brevia Pleidez (also known as Brevia Placitata, Writs Pleaded) and Fet Asaver (Be It Known). Other pleading tracts, such as La Court de Baron and Le Ple de la Coroune. An unreliable legal critique, the Mirror of Justices. And finally, French made its appearance as the language of an important treatise for the practicing lawyer, Britton (about 1290).

The French trend in the law was contrary to the English trend of the times. Yet from mid-thirteenth century on, at least through the Middle English period, French predominates as the language of the law.

There is no pat explanation of the phenomenon. Most theories time the rise of law French with some other contemporary event.

Thus it has been noted that a new wave of French courtiers (and presumably official French) broke over the English court following Henry III's marriage to Eleanor of Provence in 1236.[40] But it has also been pointed out that this influx of Frenchmen caused a reaction against foreign influence, which led to the Barons' War (1258-1265) and stimulated the growth of English nationalism.[41] If Henry III was

---

[36] Plucknett, A Concise History of the Common Law 268-273 (5th ed. 1956).

[37] Plucknett, A Concise History of the Common Law 273 (5th ed. 1956).

[38] See Plucknett, A Concise History of the Common Law 268 (5th ed. 1956); 1 Pollock and Maitland, The History of English Law 84-85 (2d ed. 1898); compare Woodbine, "The Language of English Law," 18 Speculum 395, 432-433, 427-428 (1943).

[39] Woodbine, "The Language of English Law," 18 Speculum 395, 434 (1943).

[40] Woodbine, "The Language of English Law," 18 Speculum 395, 434, 436 (1943).

[41] Baugh, A History of the English Language 159-164 (1935).

Francophile, Edward I was not. In 1295, in a rousing summons to Parliament, he charged that the King of France:

. . . proposes, if his power is equal to his iniquitous plan, which God forbid, to wipe out the English tongue from the face of the earth.[42]

It has also been suggested that:

French, as the language of the laymen in the king's curia, inevitably became the language of law, when the court and the profession became predominantly secular.[43]

Yet churchmen were not an insignificant group among the king's judges when law French became the language of the courts.[44] And there is evidence that English — not French — was the accustomed tongue of the higher clergy,[45] and also of the bench and bar.[46] Earthy quips from the bench bespeak a rearing in English. For example, this from Hengham "stressing a point of ownership":

Wo so boleth myn kyn, ewerc is the calf myn.[47]
(No matter who bulls my cow, the calf is mine.)[48]

It is most likely that a combination of circumstances resulted in lawyers using French though all others were turning to English. Inertia and self-interest must be listed prominently among those circumstances.

For years French had been the language of education (along with Latin for the clergy and the scholarly). (Section 44.) The more English became the common currency of all classes of society, the more French became the mark of the noble and the wealthy. And it was

[42] See Woodbine, "The Language of English Law," 18 Speculum 395, 424 (1943); Stubbs, ed., *Select Charters* 485 (8th ed. 1905); Baugh, *A History of the English Language* 163-164 (1935); 5 Freeman, *The History of the Norman Conquest of England* 506-507 and especially n.1 (1876).

[43] Radin, *Handbook of Anglo-American Legal History* 290 (1936).

[44] 1 Pollock and Maitland, *The History of English Law* 205 (2d ed. 1898); 2 Holdsworth, *A History of English Law* 318 (3d ed. 1923).

[45] Woodbine, "The Language of English Law," 18 Speculum 395, 424 (1943).

[46] Woodbine, "The Language of English Law," 18 Speculum 395, 434 (1943); see Collas, "Problems of Translation," in Introduction to *Year Books of Edward II,* 70 Selden Society xiii n.1 (1951).

[47] Woodbine, "The Language of English Law," 18 Speculum 395, 431 and especially n.5 (1943); compare *Middle English Dictionary* (Kurath ed. 1958), under *bolen,* pt. B5, p. 1029; and see also Maitland, ed., *Year Books of Edward II,* 17 Selden Society xvi (1903).

[48] See and compare *Middle English Dictionary* (Kurath ed. 1958), under *bolen,* pt. B5, p. 1029, and Vinogradoff, "Ralph of Hengham as C.J. of the Common Pleas," in Little and Powicke, eds., *Essays in Medieval History Presented to Thomas Frederick Tout* 191 (1925); and see also *Oxford English Dictionary,* under *bull,* v.1 No. 1, and Partridge, *A Dictionary of Slang and Unconventional English* (4th ed. 1951), under *bull,* v.

precisely these two groups who sent their sons to the law. No others could afford it. No others had the same interest in knowing the intricacies of the land law.[49] Like other medieval arts organized into guilds, the law was a mystery. And there is no reason to believe that the ruling cliques of England were eager to share the legal mysteries with plebeians.

What better way of preserving a professional monopoly than by locking up your trade secrets in the safe of an unknown tongue? Celtic lawyers had done it before in the British Isles (Section 25). And on the other side of the world a Chinese bureaucracy perpetuated itself through the ages with a language that only the highly educated could hope to master. Comparatively few knew French in mid-thirteenth-century England. It was never the language of the people.[50] And as time passed it would become incomprehensible to any but the initiate. Here indeed was a language for the law. Not that it was deliberately planned that way. Most likely inertia took the place of design, which would explain the absence of any record of a law French conspiracy. And the coincidence of self-interest simply reinforced the normal inclination to leave things as French as they were.

60. *The varieties of French: Old French*

The French used in the law has been called by many names. And there is little agreement on the distinctions that have been made. It all starts with *Old French*. One standard definition labels as Old French the Romance language spoken in northern France in the ninth to fourteenth centuries.[51] Another includes fifteenth-century French in the definition.[52] Old French leads into *Middle French* and contrasts with *Modern French*, which dates from the seventeenth century.[53]

English *contract*, for example, is the Old French form (adapted from Latin *contractus*) as opposed to Modern French *contrat*.

In Modern French *voire* means in truth, but without the *e*, as *voir*, the meaning is to see. A conclusion from Modern French could be that *voir dire* means "to see him speak." [54] But the law words *voir dire*

---

[49] Plucknett, *A Concise History of the Common Law* 225 (5th ed. 1956); 2 Holdsworth, *A History of English Law* 494, 416 n.6, 489-490 (3d ed. 1923).
[50] 1 *Cambridge Anglo-Norman Texts* xv (1924).
[51] 9 *Encyclopaedia Britannica* 760 (1948).
[52] *Middle English Dictionary*, Plan and Bibliography, 7 (Kurath ed. 1954).
[53] 9 *Encyclopaedia Britannica* 760 (1948).
[54] Alderman, "The French Language in English and American Law," 12 Ala. Law. 356, 372 (1951).

(also spelled *voire dire*) carry their Old French meaning to speak the truth,[55] the same meaning as Old French *voir dit*, which ended up in English and Modern French as *verdict*. (Section 49.)

Old French was made up of a fistful of dialects, often mutually unintelligible. Among these were *Francien*, the French of Paris[56] (Section 57), and *Normand*, which we know as *Norman-French*.

Norman-French *gaol* is still the law usage in England,[57] though the language people there prefer the Parisian French *jail*, and both words are pronounced alike.[58]

A more fertile variation is *ward* (northeastern Old French) and *guard* (central Old French). Both of these are from the same Old Teutonic source as Old English *weard*, guard. (Section 32.) From the same root came *warden* and *guardian*, once interchangeable:

> And of Wardiens there are two sorts; namely, Gardian in Right, and Gardian in Deed.[59]

Starting life as synonyms, *ward* and *guard* have developed legal shadings of the original sense, as in prison *warden* and *guard*. They have become opposites in *guardian* and *ward*. And sometimes it is not clear whether we are dealing with synonym, antonym, correlative, or something completely unrelated. In the United States a *guardianship* refers to the job of the guardian,[60] just as the medieval *wardship* emphasized the rights of the one doing the protecting.[61] Guardianship also refers to "the relation . . . between the guardian and ward." [62] And in England, *wardship* (said to be the same as *guardianship*)[63] refers some-

---

[55] *The Law-French Dictionary* (2d ed. 1718); 3 Blackstone, *Commentaries* *332 (Jones ed. 1916); *Oxford English Dictionary; Black's Law Dictionary* (4th ed. 1951); 2 Bouvier, *A Law Dictionary* (1839); 2 Jowitt, gen. ed., *The Dictionary of English Law* (1959).

[56] See Chaucer, *The Canterbury Tales*, prologue, 4 (Modern Library, Skeat ed. 1929).

[57] 1 Jowitt, gen. ed., *The Dictionary of English Law* (1959), under *gaol* and related words; compare 2 Jowitt, gen. ed., *The Dictionary of English Law* (1959), under *jail*.

[58] *Oxford English Dictionary*, under *gaol* and *jail;* Fowler, *A Dictionary of Modern English Usage* (3d ed. 1937), under *gaol*.

[59] *Les Termes de la Ley* (new ed. 1671), under *gardian*.

[60] Ballentine, *Law Dictionary with Pronunciations* (2d ed. 1948); *Black's Law Dictionary* (4th ed. 1951); see also *Wharton's Law Lexicon* (14th ed. 1938).

[61] Ballentine, *Law Dictionary with Pronunciations* (2d ed. 1948); *Black's Law Dictionary* (4th ed. 1951).

[62] *Black's Law Dictionary* (4th ed. 1951).

[63] 2 Jowitt, gen. ed., *The Dictionary of English Law* (1959); *Wharton's Law Lexicon* (14th ed. 1938).

times to "the condition or status of a ward," [64] and sometimes to the position of guardian.[65]

Similar variation of *w* and *gu*, according to French dialect usage, led at a much later date to the law's distinctions between *warranty* and *guaranty* (also *guarantee*), originally the same word.

61. *Legal relatives of Old French*

In addition to basic Old French (Section 60), there are four over-lapping and conflicting classifications of the French that has left its mark upon the law. These are:

(1) *Norman-French*. In one breath Blackstone speaks of "Norman or law French." [66] *Webster 2d* tags three distinct aspects of French with one Norman-French label: the language of the Normans, Anglo-French, and law French.[67] Pollock and Maitland give a glancing and negative definition of Norman-French by objecting to its use to de-scribe either the literary language of the thirteenth century or the "mere 'dog-French'" of the sixteenth-century law reports.[68] Unless otherwise explained, *Norman-French* as used in this book is limited to the dialect of Old French spoken by the Normans in Normandy.

(2) *Anglo-French*. This is another badly cut-up expression, used by a variety of authors to serve many ends. It has been used interchange-ably with Norman-French[69] and Anglo-Norman.[70] Those who prefer Anglo-French to Anglo-Norman as the general name for the variety of Old French used in England after the Norman Conquest point to the fact that other than Norman elements are involved. The *Oxford English Dictionary* describes Anglo-French as a French mixture from the start, including "various Norman and other Northern French dialects." Later, says the O.E.D., it was "mixed with and greatly modified by Angevin, Parisian, Poitevin, and other elements," [71] i.e., by central French. Pollock subdivides Anglo-French into "living" (thirteenth century), "decaying" (sixteenth century), and "degenerate Anglo-

---

[64] 2 Jowitt, gen. ed., *The Dictionary of English Law* (1959).
[65] See *Wharton's Law Lexicon* (14th ed. 1938), under *guardianship*.
[66] 3 Blackstone, *Commentaries* °318 (Jones ed. 1916).
[67] *Webster's New International Dictionary* (2d ed. 1934), under *Norman-French*.
[68] 1 Pollock and Maitland, *The History of English Law* 87-88 n.3 (2d ed. 1898); see also Pollock, *A First Book of Jurisprudence* 296 n.2 (4th ed. 1918).
[69] *Webster's New International Dictionary* (2d ed. 1934), under *Anglo-French* and *Norman-French*.
[70] *Webster's New International Dictionary* (2d ed. 1934), under *Anglo-French* and *Anglo-Norman*.
[71] 1 *Oxford English Dictionary* xxx.

French or 'law-French'" (seventeenth century).[72] *Webster 2d* cuts off Anglo-French at the end of the fourteenth century.[73]

While *Anglo-French* has many other substantial adherents,[74] it is not a term of art, and as a matter of choice the term is not further used in this book except in references to those who do use it.

(3) *Anglo-Norman.* This has become as muddy a description as Anglo-French. It has been used convertibly with Anglo-French as a general designation of the French used in England after the Conquest.[75] Some deny that there is any real distinction between the two expressions.[76] Anglo-Norman has also been used as the equivalent of Norman-French.[77] Some prefer to cut off Anglo-Norman with the start of the reign of Henry II (1154);[78] some with England's loss of Normandy in 1204.[79] Pollock asserts that Anglo-French "had ceased to be Norman before the 13th century." [80]

Even so, *Anglo-Norman* has increased in currency. It has been studied as a special dialect, which influenced and was influenced by the development of English.[81] (Section 57.) And since the pioneer legal studies by Maitland, who used Anglo-French,[82] later respected writers who have studied the language in its relationship to the law have used Anglo-Norman.[83] In this book, *Anglo-Norman* describes the distinctive variety of French used in England after the Norman Conquest, when it becomes necessary to distinguish that usage from French generally, Old French, or Norman-French.

---

[72] Pollock, *A First Book of Jurisprudence* 296-303 (4th ed. 1918).

[73] *Webster's New International Dictionary* (2d ed. 1934), under *Anglo-French.*

[74] For example, Skeat, *An Etymological Dictionary* xlii (new ed. 1909); Weekley, *The English Language* (1952); Maitland, "Of the Anglo-French Language in the Early Year Books," in Introduction to *Year Books of Edward II,* 17 Selden Society xxxiii-lxxxi (1903); "Objects and Work of the Selden Society," in *Select Civil Pleas,* 3 Selden Society 1-28, 17 (following p. 128); see also references in Shelly, *English and French in England: 1066-1100,* especially pp. 9-12 (1921).

[75] Baugh, *A History of the English Language* 172, 214, 215, 216 (1935).

[76] Shelly, *English and French in England: 1066-1100,* pp. 9-12 (1921).

[77] Sheard, *The Words We Use* 194 (1954).

[78] *Webster's New International Dictionary* (2d ed. 1934), under *Anglo-French.*

[79] See Shelly, *English and French in England: 1066-1100,* p. 10 (1921).

[80] Pollock, *A First Book of Jurisprudence* 296 n.2 (4th ed. 1918).

[81] 1 *Cambridge Anglo-Norman Texts* vii-xxviii, 1-12 (1924); see also *Anglo-Norman Political Songs* (1953).

[82] Maitland, "Of the Anglo-French Language in the Early Year Books," in Introduction to *Year Books of Edward II,* 17 Selden Society xxxiii-lxxxi (1903).

[83] For example, Legge, "The Salient Features of the Language of the Earlier Year Books," in Introduction to *Year Books of Edward II,* 52 Selden Society xxxxlii (1934); Legge, "French and the Law," in Introduction to *Year Books of Edward II,* 54 Selden Society xxxviii-xliv (1935); Collas, "Problems of Translation," in Introduction to *Year Books of Edward II,* 70 Selden Society xii-lxiv (1953).

(4) This leaves *law French,* which is discussed in Section 62.

62. *Law French: A definition*

Some treat *law French* as a synonym for *Norman-French.*[84] A late eighteenth-century lawyers' *Dictionary of the Norman or Old French Language* calls it *Norman Law French.*[85] The early eighteenth-century *Law-French Dictionary* does not define it. The yet unborn *Glossary of Law-French*[86] was for some time tentatively called *A Dictionary of Anglo-Norman Legal Terms.*[87] The three standard American law dictionaries date law French from the Norman Conquest (Section 41),[88] though one now calls it *French-Norman.*[89] Law French has also been described as a type of Anglo-Norman of the period commencing in the first half of the fourteenth century.[90]

The epithets tied to *law Latin* (Section 47) have been limited and unimaginative compared to the rich invective heaped on law French. It is not only "barbarous," [91] "corrupt," [92] and a "dog French." [93] It is "degenerate," [94] and "kitchen-," "pigeon-," [95] and "bastard French." [96] Even the tolerant Jespersen describes it as a "curious mongrel language." [97]

But law French is not without its defenders. Though it withered

---

[84] *Black's Law Dictionary* (4th ed. 1951), under *law French;* 3 Blackstone, *Commentaries* °318 (Jones ed. 1916).

[85] Kelham, *A Dictionary of the Norman or Old French Language,* preface (1779).

[86] Announcement in 78 Selden Society following p. 347 (1960).

[87] 54 Selden Society 251 (1935).

[88] Ballentine, *Law Dictionary with Pronunciations* (2d ed. 1948); *Black's Law Dictionary* (4th ed. 1951); 2 Bouvier, *A Law Dictionary* (Rawle, 15th ed. 1892); see 2 *Bouvier's Law Dictionary and Concise Encyclopedia* (3d rev. 8th ed. 1914), under *Language.*

[89] 2 *Bouvier's Law Dictionary and Concise Encyclopedia* (3d rev. 8th ed. 1914), under *Language.*

[90] Legge, "French and the Law," in Introduction to *Year Books of Edward II,* 54 Selden Society xxxviii, xxxix (1935); see Legge, "The Salient Features of the Language of the Earlier Year Books," in Introduction to *Year Books of Edward II,* 52 Selden Society xxx (1934).

[91] 3 Blackstone, *Commentaries* °318 (Jones ed. 1916).

[92] *Oxford English Dictionary,* under *law,* sb.[1], No. 23.

[93] 1 Pollock and Maitland, *The History of English Law* 87 n.3 (2d ed. 1898).

[94] Pollock, *A First Book of Jurisprudence* 300 (4th ed. 1918).

[95] Quoted in Maitland, "Of the Anglo-French Language in the Early Year Books," in Introduction to *Year Books of Edward II,* 17 Selden Society xxxiii, lxxix (1903).

[96] W. Barton Leach, Professor of Law, in Harvard Law School lecture, 1939; see also "Language of the Law," 220 L.T. 200, 220 (1955).

[97] Jespersen, *Growth and Structure of the English Language,* par. 84 n.1 (Anchor, 9th ed. 1955).

with age, "at the time of its introduction it was . . . the best form of the language spoken in Normandy." That is the judgment of two law dictionaries.[98] Holdsworth tells us that:

> The common lawyer had in his law French a technical language equal in precision to that of the civilian.

And he musters Roger North, Fortescue, Coke, and Selden to bulwark the defense.[99] He gives the impression that this characterization is fitting even though — perhaps even because — law French "degenerated into a mere slang." [100]

The varying definitions and views of law French in some instances stem from a failure to distinguish between etymology and law, and in others from a failure to have any sharp focus on a particular time in the history of the language. One thing is certain. With or without capitals and with or without a hyphen, law French — like law Latin — is not a term of art. Yet law French serves a useful purpose when it differentiates French used in the law from other languages used in the law and also from French words used outside of the law. It is so used in this book unless a different sense is expressly identified.

As with law Latin, law French has a changing content. The earliest recorded uses in England of the French *appeal, demand, heir,* and *indictment* were legal uses. They were a part of the law French of their day. They are now sufficiently common in everyday English to render a law French tag superfluous. Old French *voir dire* is still good law French; it has no active life outside of the law, and results in confusion if judged by the standards of Modern French (see Sections 60, 12).

63. *French not at first a technical language*

Whatever its merits from the view of the student of grammar,[101] the French used by the lawyers of England was not at first either an exact or a technical language.[102] The showpiece of law French precision:

---

[98] Quoted in *Black's Law Dictionary* (4th ed. 1951), under *law French.*

[99] 2 Holdsworth, *A History of English Law* 480-482 and especially 482 n.1 (3d ed. 1923).

[100] 2 Holdsworth, *A History of English Law* 481 (3d ed. 1923).

[101] Pollock, *A First Book of Jurisprudence* 298 (4th ed. 1918).

[102] Compare 2 Holdsworth, *A History of English Law* 480-482 (3d ed. 1923), and Greenough and Kittredge, *Words and Their Ways in English Speech* 45 (1902).

"an heir in tail rebutted from his formedon by a lineal warranty with descended assets." [103]

describes land law that came into being almost a century after French became the language of the law.[104] In the beginning the common Anglo-Norman speech (and its sloppy spelling)[105] had to do for the law as well.[106]

In Old French as in Modern, *tort* is a wrong or injustice, and it was so used by English lawyers[107] before it came to mean today's specialized type of wrong.

Old French *devise* was a division, and came to be a giving by will, but not limited to real estate. (See Section 123.) In 1347, an English nobleman writing his will in French determined to *devys* his gold ring to a lady companion.[108]

Seisin (from the same source as *seize*) meant possession generally (Section 56) before it became a term of art in the land law.[109]

Curtesy, another spelling of *courtesy*, meant courteous behavior, before it was politely applied to a widower's estate, "by the curtesy of England." [110] Knighthood was still in flower. A *continuance for settlement* was called a *love-day*. The professional French was thus close

---

[103] Quoted in Maitland, "Of the Anglo-French Language in the Early Year Books," in Introduction to *Year Books of Edward II*, 17 Selden Society xxxiii, xxxvi (1903); quoted in 2 Holdsworth, *A History of English Law* 481 (3d ed. 1923); quoted in Cairns, "Language of Jurisprudence," in Anshen, ed., *Language* 232, 246 (1957).

[104] See 3 Holdsworth, *A History of English Law* 117-118 (3d ed. 1923).

[105] Maitland, "Of the Anglo-French Language in the Early Year Books," in Introduction to *Year Books of Edward II*, 17 Selden Society xxxiii, xliii (1903); Maitland and Baildon, eds., *The Court Baron*, 4 Selden Society 10 (1891); Collas, "Problems of Translation," in Introduction to *Year Books of Edward II*, 70 Selden Society xii, xvi-xxi (1953); compare Turner, ed., *Brevia Placitata*, 66 Selden Society xxxvii (1951).

[106] 2 Pollock and Maitland, *The History of English Law* 31 (2d ed. 1898); see Maitland, *Domesday Book and Beyond* 9 (1921 print.); see also Maitland, "Of the Anglo-French Language in the Early Year Books," 17 Selden Society xxxiii, lxix n.1 (1903); and see also Turner, ed., *Brevia Placitata*, 66 Selden Society xxxv-xxxvii (1951).

[107] Collas, "Problems of Translation," in Introduction to *Year Books of Edward II* xii, xx (1953); Maitland and Baildon, eds., *The Court Baron*, 4 Selden Society 48; compare Woodbine, "The Language of English Law," 18 Speculum 395 n.1 (1943).

[108] *Oxford English Dictionary*, under *devise*, v., No. 4.

[109] 2 Pollock and Maitland, *The History of English Law* 31 et seq. (2d ed. 1898); *Oxford English Dictionary*, under *seisin*, sb.

[110] *Oxford English Dictionary*, under *courtesy*, sb., Nos. 1, 4; 2 Pollock and Maitland, *The History of English Law* 414 et seq. (2d ed. 1898); compare 2 Blackstone, *Commentaries* °126-°127 (Jones ed. 1916).

to the contemporary Anglo-Norman of the classes. And its technical terms were shaky.[111]

Atteindre (an ancestor of *bill of attainder*) could equal the Latin *conviction* and also the consequences of conviction, e.g., the loss of civil rights. An *atteinte* (the process for reversing a jury verdict) could be brought, lie, pass, run, taken, had, sought, granted, or given.

Entendre (an ancestor of today's legal *intent*) could mean what we now know as intention, attention, understanding, hearing, obedience, waiting, meaning, acceptation, purport, assumption, information, thought. It could mean what the draftsman intended, or — what is often the reverse — how he was understood.[112]

Technicality is a slow-formed compound of sophistication in both law and language. And continuity of the form of words gives no assurance of continuity of meaning in or out of the law.[113]

For example, *purchase*.[114] The word, in form and meaning born of the *chase* for wild animals, implied a personal effort to get something. The earliest law uses in French of the twelfth or thirteenth centuries adopted this common understanding. In the thirteenth century law French forms of *purchase* were used in the more specialized senses of obtaining (a writ), and acquiring property other than by inheritance.[115] Since then the law has been refining and expounding this last sense.

In the fifteenth century, Littleton defined *purchase* as the possession a man has not by descent but:

. . . *per son fait, ou per agreement,*

which Coke in the seventeenth century translated:

. . . by his deed or agreement.[116]

In his comment, Coke stated expressly — what Littleton had not — that a gift was also a *purchase*. And Blackstone rounded out the rationalization of Littleton by explaining that one who receives a gift

---

[111] Collas, "Problems of Translation," in Introduction to *Year Books of Edward II*, 70 Selden Society xii, xl (1953); compare 2 Holdsworth, *The History of English Law* 480-482 (3d ed. 1923).

[112] Collas, "Problems of Translation," in Introduction to *Year Books of Edward II*, 70 Selden Society xii-lxiv (1953).

[113] Trench, *A Select Glossary* (4th ed. 1873); Collas, "Problems of Translation," in Introduction to *Year Books of Edward II*, 70 Selden Society xii, xx-xxi (1953).

[114] Compare Woodbine, "The Language of English Law," 18 Speculum 395 n.1 (1943).

[115] *Oxford English Dictionary*, under *purchase*, v., No. 5; compare *Harrap's Standard French and English Dictionary* (1955), pt. 1, under *pourchasser*.

[116] Coke, *Commentary upon Littleton*, ff. 18a, 18b (10th ed. 1703).

. . . comes to the estate by his own agreement, that is, he consents to the gift.[117]

With gift included, the special sense of law French *purchase* is divorced alike from ancient etymology (personal effort) and from the layman's understanding of *purchase* (pay something). The sharp edge of technicality still appears in such phrases as *take by purchase* and *words of purchase*. But *purchase* alone is often used by the law interchangeably with Old English *buy* (Section 38); *purchaser* can mean a buyer or one who takes by purchase, and courts still take time out to identify the difference.[118] In addition, the law has adopted the *buy* sense of *purchase* in such special law terms as *purchase money*, *purchase-money mortgage*, *purchase price*, and *bona fide purchaser* — all truer to the etymology of *purchase* than the land law's term of art.

64. *The growth of technicality*

The constant use of French within the closed ranks of the profession gradually developed specialized meanings that distinguished law French from the prevalent Anglo-Norman (Section 63). And the same process of refinement separated French in the law from the French that became a part of the English language.

In its mass absorption of French (Section 58), English — assisted by lawyers speaking native English and acquired French (Section 59) — also soaked up quantities of French words with legal connotations. This crossing-over began long before there was any official prodding of lawyers to speak English in court. (Section 65.) Of the law words in the Pollock-Maitland list (Section 12), more than half had come into written English with a legal meaning by the middle of the fourteenth century. But most of these with meanings that have remained fairly constant are some of the least technical of the law's vocabulary. Such words as:

court	judge	justices	payment
descent	judgment	marriage	possession
grant	justice	money	property

Many of the early French law words became and remained English words of general use, while the lawyers went on to coin more technical applications.

Slander — of a common origin with *scandal* — crossed over into

---

[117] 2 Blackstone, *Commentaries* °241 (Jones ed. 1916).

[118] 35 *Words and Phrases* (perm. ed. 1940, Supp. 1962), "purchaser"; see also 2 Jowitt, gen. ed., *The Dictionary of English Law* 1446 (1959).

English in the thirteenth century, applied indiscriminately to oral and written defamation. The common speech still clings to this early usage,[119] while the law has made a distinction between actions of slander and libel since the seventeenth century.[120]

In the thirteenth century *partner* was a corrupt spelling of *parcener*, and meant a sharer (still its nontechnical sense) or more specifically the sharer of an inheritance — a *co-heir*. This last sense came to be known as *co-parcener*, and *partner* began to take on its present law sense in the sixteenth century.

Obligation has been an agreement since the thirteenth century, but the special sense of the document that embodies the agreement, though recorded in English in the fourteenth century, is still chiefly legal.

There are a few French words with a long history of some legal technicality — such words as *action, indictment, plaintiff, robbery*, all of these except the distantly Teutonic *robbery* (Section 28) indirectly from Latin. But even here, as with *purchase* (Section 63), there has been refinement further separating the usages of lawyers and laymen.

With *action*, there is the looser *taking* legal action (fourteenth century) and the lawyer's tighter *an* action (fifteenth century).

The accusation of the grand jury was anciently and is still *an indictment;* but familiarity with such accusations led to *the* indictment as the document containing the accusation (sixteenth century).

Robbery, originally a more open as distinguished from a more heinous, clandestine *theft,*[121] is still popularly regarded as a synonym for *theft,*[122] as distinguished from the law's forcible theft from the person.

Plaintiff, as one who starts litigation, dates from the thirteenth century, but it has a common origin with *plaintive* and *complaint*. The *plaintive plaintiff complains* is triply querulous, for all stem from the Latin *plangere* (to lament, to bewail, to beat the breast or head in grief). *Plaintiff* and *plaintive* were originally the same word in both French and English,[123] and for centuries were used interchangeably as a run-of-the-mill complainer or the plaintiff in a lawsuit. *Complaint* is still a lamentation in a generalized way, formalized in the law as the plaintiff's first pleading or the statement of a criminal offense.

---

[119] Under *libel* in Fowler, *A Dictionary of Modern English Usage* (3d ed. 1937), and Evans and Evans, *A Dictionary of Contemporary American Usage* (1957).

[120] Plucknett, *A Concise History of the Common Law* 497 (5th ed. 1956).

[121] 2 Pollock and Maitland, *The History of English Law* 493-494 (2d ed. 1898).

[122] *Webster's New International Dictionary* (2d ed. 1934), under *rob, robber, robbery.*

[123] *Oxford English Dictionary*, under *plaintiff.*

In short, there was no spring blossoming of technicality in the language of the law. And had it not been for the fact that the law used a foreign tongue, protest might have been long delayed.

65. The first regulation of the language of the law

The first national outcry against the language of the law was not that it was technical, but that it was French. This was a time of patriotic animosity: an era of some of England's most celebrated victories over the French — Crecy, Poitiers, Calais. It was also the time of the Black Death, a killing plague of massive proportions. (Estimates of plague deaths run from 40 per cent [124] to more than 75 per cent of England's total population.[125]) This catastrophe contributed to the breakdown of the old feudal order, and strengthened the position of the English-speaking masses.

The popular trend toward English (Section 58) was pointed up for the law at the local level when London required English for court proceedings (1356).[126] Six years later came the Statute of Pleading.[127]

Though the statute deplored French, it was written in French. This is an eighteenth-century translation:

Pleas shall be pleaded in the English tongue, and inrolled in Latin.
Item, Because it is often shewed to the King by the prelates, dukes, earls, barons, and all the commonalty, of the great mischiefs which have happened to divers of the realm, because the laws, customs, and statutes of this realm be not commonly holden and kept in the same realm, for that they be pleaded, shewed, and judged in the French tongue, which is much unknown in the said realm, so that the people which do implead, or be impleaded, in the King's court, and in the courts of other, have no knowledge or understanding of that which is said for them or against them by their serjeants and other pleaders; (2) and that reasonably the said laws and customs the rather shall be perceived and known, and better understood in the tongue used in the said realm, and by so much every man of the said realm may the better govern himself without offending of the law, and the better keep, save, and defend his heritage and possessions: (3) and in divers regions and countries, where the King, the nobles, and other of the said realm have been, good governance and full right is done to every person because that their laws and customs be learned and used in the tongue of the country: (4) the King, desiring the good governance and tranquillity of his people, and to put out and eschew the harms and mischiefs which do or may happen in this behalf by the occasions aforesaid, hath ordained and stablished by the assent aforesaid, that all pleas

124 Baugh, *A History of the English Language* 175 (1935).
125 17 *Encyclopaedia Britannica* 991 (1948).
126 Baugh, *A History of the English Language* 182 (1935).
127 Statute of Pleading, 1362, 36 Edw. III, Stat. I, c. 15.

which shall be pleaded in any courts whatsoever, before any of his justices whatsoever, or in his other places, or before any of his other ministers whatsoever, or in the courts and places of any other lords whatsoever within the realm, shall be pleaded, shewed, defended, answered, debated, and judged in the English tongue, and that they be entered and inrolled in Latin; (5) and that the laws and customs of the same realm, terms, and processes, be holden and kept as they be and have been before this time; (6) and that by the ancient terms and forms of the declarations no man be prejudiced, so that the matter of the action be fully shewed in the declaration and in the writ. (7) And it is accorded by assent aforesaid, that this ordinance and statute of pleading begin and hold place at the fifteenth of St. Hilary next coming.[128]

The cure here does not respond to the diagnosis. Recitals declare that French is "much unknown," litigants don't understand what is "said" in court, and that where law is "learned and used" in the vulgar tongue, violations are less likely and the citizen is better able to protect himself. The statute talks up the vast gains to be derived from the use of English in the law generally. Yet it continues the records in Latin.[129] And ends up with a nibbling requirement of English only for court use, which at the moment meant mostly oral use. Even as to that the statute was not inflexible. If it was more convenient to use "ancient terms and forms" in Latin and French, sections (5) and (6) gave the license.[130]

English-language patriots have hailed the Statute of Pleading as the Magna Carta of the Anglo-Saxon tongue: "the victory of English";[131] "In 1362, a great date indeed, English was made the language of the law-courts; . . ."[132] The rejoicing overwhelms the fact. The statute may have sounded good for public consumption, but it underestimated the power of the bar.

66. Aftermath of the Statute of Pleading

In the century of the statute denouncing French (Section 65), French became the regular language of the statutes of England (Section 51). And French it remained until near the close of the fifteenth century, although in the meantime the broadened base and importance

---

[128] 2 Pickering, ed., *The Statutes at Large from the 15th Year of King Edward III to the 13th Year of King Henry IV, Inclusive* 149, 156 (1762).

[129] *James Osborn's Case*, 77 Eng. Rep. 1123, 1128 (K.B. 1614); compare 3 Blackstone, *Commentaries* *319-*320 (Jones ed. 1916); and see Stephen, *A Treatise on the Principles of Pleading* App., Note 14, p. xxi (1824).

[130] 3 *Reeves' History of the English Law* 186 (Finlason, new American ed. 1880).

[131] 5 Freeman, *The History of the Norman Conquest of England* 536 (1876).

[132] 1 Oliphant, *The New English* 75 (1886).

of Parliament were reflected in a growing use of English in petitions and bills.[133]

With strictly legal literature the dominance of French was even more marked. By the time of the Statute of Pleading the profession had become accustomed to reading its law in French (Section 59). The French of *Britton* had supplanted in popularity the more learned Latin of *Bracton,* and *Glanvil* had long since been translated into French.[134] The French trend continued in the law writings of the fourteenth century. There was the very popular pleading manual *Nova Narrationes;*[135] a book discussing the writs, the *Old Natura Brevium;* and the *Old Tenures.* Fifteenth-century legal literature illustrates the growing specialization of the profession. Of works with a wider readership, in the field of political theory, two by Fortescue were in Latin (Section 51), and — an innovation — one was in English, Fortescue's *Governance of England.* But the "bread and butter" lawbooks were in French: Littleton's *Tenures* and *Statham's Abridgement.*[136]

Both before and after the Statute of Pleading, the all-important writs were in Latin, with copies available in French translation, and the names themselves of the less ancient writs in French, e.g., *formedon,*[137] law French from the law Latin phrase *forma doni* (form of gift). There was nothing written in English of immediate practical value to the practicing common lawyer or law student. Oral study of law at the Inns of Court was also in French.[138]

Thus, the suggestion of the statute (and it was little more than a suggestion) that English be used in pleading had to be weighed by the practitioner against the absence of legal learning in English and the ubiquity of French. The suggestion had also to be weighed against the requirement of rigid adherence to the prescribed form of the writs.

In 1330, a litigant objected that a writ (here in translation) read:

"If the jurors by whom a certain Assize of Novel Disseisin was taken,"

when it should have read:

[133] The Record Commissioners, "An Historical Survey of Ancient English Statutes," in 2 *Selected Essays in Anglo-American Legal History* 169, 198-202 (1908).

[134] Plucknett, *Early English Legal Literature* 79-82 (1958).

[135] Plucknett, *Early English Legal Literature* 89 (1958).

[136] Winfield, *The Chief Sources of English Legal History* 206-220 (1925).

[137] Woodbine, "The Language of English Law," 18 Speculum 395, 435 n.1 (1943).

[138] Thorne, ed., *Readings and Moots at the Inns of Court in the Fifteenth Century,* 71 Selden Society (1954).

"If the jurors of Novel Disseisin by whom such Assize was summoned and taken."

The Court was impressed:

Matthew cannot gainsay this. Therefore let Nicola go quit for the present. Let Matthew procure himself another writ if he will.[139]

So too with oral pleading based on the writs. Plaintiff's oral declaration had to correspond to the writ,[140] and the denials exactly to the charge. A denial (here in translation):

". . . against William, who is there, and the defamation and the damage of 40 s., and every penny thereof and all that he surmiseth against him . . ."

was held fatally defective when it should have said:

". . . against William and against his suit and all that he surmiseth . . ." [141]

The first of a series of statutes designed to prevent disaster through small clerical errors[142] did little to narrow the area of contention. Instead of liberalizing the rules of pleading, it led to insistence on even greater technical correctness at the level one step above the most trivial deviation.[143]

With such a state of the law, and with the current legal learning largely in French (and some Latin), it would have been foolhardy to risk lapse from formula by adventures into untried English. No wonder, then, that most of the pleading continued in French despite the "victory of English" in the Statute of Pleading.[144]

67. Transition from oral French to English

While details are lacking, there appears to be a period of gradual transition from a "somewhat restrained" use of oral French in court after the Statute of Pleading to the time about a hundred years later when law French was "oftener writ than spoken." [145] The best informed surmise is that in the interim the basic pleadings remained

---

[139] Le Taverner v. Le Day, Bedford Eyre (1330), translated in Kiralfy, A Source Book of English Law 49 (1957).

[140] Plucknett, Early English Legal Literature 84 (1958).

[141] Maitland and Baildon, ed., The Court Baron, 4 Selden Society 48-49 (1891).

[142] Jeofail, 1340, 14 Edw. III, Stat. 1, c. 6.

[143] Plucknett, A Concise History of the Common Law 397 (5th ed. 1956); compare 3 Reeves' History of the English Law 185 (Finlason, new American ed. 1880).

[144] 1 Pollock and Maitland, The History of English Law 85 (2d ed. 1898); 2 Holdsworth, A History of English Law 478 (3d ed. 1923).

[145] Fortescue, De Laudibus Legum Angliae 107-108 (2d ed. 1741).

French, but the closely associated argument at the bar was increasingly carried on in English.[146] The oral pleadings must be true to ritual or the cause failed,[147] but ultimately the pleading that was significant was the pleading that came to be entered on the record. In between the opening counting and the pleading issue made on the record, the serjeants jabbed and parried.

Unlike an earlier day when the whole of a lawsuit might be a thing of ritual, oath, ordeal (Section 29), there were now preliminary stages. Maybe it would still all end in ritual — the wager of law, in which a host of oath-takers must recite the proper oaths in the same words, without slightest variation:

The oath that S hath sworn is true, so help me God and the saints.

And a slip of the tongue, or of the hand or lips from the Holy Book, might still mean disaster.[148] But before the moment of decision, the serjeants might speak words and withdraw them, speak words and change them.

As early as 1292, a serjeant had commented in argument:

Every word spoken in Court is not to be taken literally; they are only curial words.[149]

And in the early fourteenth century, a judge had said:

"It is not right that every word a man says should bear force." [150]

As long as pleadings remained oral, misunderstandings could be corrected on the spot. As witness this suggestion from the bench:

"BEREFORD, C.J. — Do you want to abide judgment?
"SCROPE — Take our words just as we say, and we shall abide willingly. . . .
"BEREFORD, C.J. — Take good care for you can have one meaning and perhaps we may have another." [151]

There was latitude to shift a tentative legal position. And much that went on in court (as now) was not technical, precise, or final. It is in the context of such courtroom freedom that English lawyers

---

[146] Maitland, "Of the Anglo-French Language in the Early Year Books," in Introduction to *Year Books of Edward II*, 17 Selden Society xxxiii-xxxv (1903).

[147] See Coke, *Commentary upon Littleton*, ff. 304a, 304b (10th ed. 1703).

[148] Maitland and Baildon, eds., *The Court Baron*, 4 Selden Society 17 (1891).

[149] *Lucy v. Richard*, Y.B. 20, 21 Edw. I (1292), in 1 Horwood, ed. and transl., *Year Books of the Reign of King Edward the First, Years XX and XXI* (1866); compare 3 Holdsworth, *A History of English Law* 630 n.5 (3d ed. 1923).

[150] Quoted in 3 Holdsworth, *A History of English Law* 635 n.3 (3d ed. 1923).

[151] Quoted in 3 Holdsworth, *A History of English Law* 636 n.3 (3d ed. 1923).

began to respond to the encouragement of the Statute to conduct proceedings in their native English.

68. *The start of paper pleadings*

The movement of the law toward the use of English (Section 67) was paralleled by the beginning in the fifteenth century of the change-over from oral to "paper" pleadings. The law of the Church, with a more ancient and intimate contact with the rudiments of literacy, had always placed greater reliance on writings than did the courts of common law. And the practice in Chancery and the King's Council, influenced by churchmen, in turn had its influence on the introduction of written pleadings and the spread of English in the law generally.

The expanding role of Chancery was an answer to the increasing technicality of the common law, its writ-bound remedies, the delays of its procedure, and the high cost of its practitioners. The equitable procedures of Chancery did not operate through the traditionally Latin writs of the common law. And the pressure of meticulous conformity to writ which beset the common law lawyers (Section 66) was relieved on the equitable side. "Equity" came to be distinguished by its English records from Chancery's common law jurisdiction, the "Latin side." [152]   The general preference for English in the country at large (Section 57) was mirrored in the reign of Henry V (1413-1422) in the switch of Chancery petitions from French to English. In the common law courts, written pleadings made a small beginning in the fifteenth century but did not become common until the sixteenth. [153]   In the meantime equity pleadings were experiments in written English.

Documents were peppered with the trivia of language, the *where*[154] and *where as*[155] and *wherefore*[156] (Section 53), *forseid* [157] and *above-seid.*[158]

The French of an earlier day gave way to an English stockpile of formalized piety and lament that has distinguished the language of the law ever since. In entreaties:

---

[152] 1 Holdsworth, *The History of English Law* 450, 515 (3d ed. 1922); 2 Holdsworth, *The History of English Law* 480 (3d ed. 1923).

[153] 3 Holdsworth, *The History of English Law* 641 (3d ed. 1923).

[154] Baildon, ed., *Select Cases in Chancery,* 10 Selden Society 155, 134 (1896).

[155] Baildon, ed., *Select Cases in Chancery,* 10 Selden Society 129, 131, 157 (1896).

[156] Baildon, ed., *Select Cases in Chancery,* 10 Selden Society 129 (1896).

[157] Baildon, ed., *Select Cases in Chancery,* 10 Selden Society 129 (1896).

[158] Baildon, ed., *Select Cases in Chancery,* 10 Selden Society 131 (1896).

. . . for godesake and in the waye of charite . . .[159]

To the reverent fader in God, my lorde the Bisshop of Bathe, Chauncellor of Englond . . .[160]

praying for judgment still seems quite appropriate.[161]

Sir John Damsell humbles himself before the King (1489-1495) and:

Piteously sheweth & complayneth unto your moost noble grace . . .

After reciting his grievances, Sir John continues:

So it is gracioux lord that by reasonn of the seid conjuracion your seid Orator was arrested and kept in prison long tyme contrary to alle ryght & conscience & also lost his service & credence unto this tyme & also spent alle suche goodes as he had to his grete shame & bitter undoyng for ever / so that he is of noun power to sue the comene lawe for his remedy In consideracion whereof please it your highesse to mynyster Justice in this behalve. And he shall during his lyfe pray to god for your most noble & royall estate[162]

In these papers it is possible to see the halting ancestor of Modern English and modern law language. A 1419 writ from Henry V to his Chancellor says:

"Ye doo calle before yow bothe parties specified in the same supplicacion, and thair causes herd, that ye doo unto hem both righte and equitie, and in especial that ye see that the porer partye suffre no wrong." [163]

Untroubled by later pedagogical notions of the double negative,[164] John Wayte says emphatically that he is:

. . . nat gilty of no mater conteyned in the said bille.[165]

English mixed freely with French and Latin. Where a law French petition to Henry IV's (1399-1413) Chancellor spoke of *biens et chateaux*,[166] a Chancery pleading from the reign of Henry VI (1422-1461) combines English and Norman-French to say *godes and catallis*[167] (later changed to Parisian French *chatel*). (Sections 28, 38.) The same pleading joins English and French in *landes and tenementez*. And the

---

159 Baildon, ed., *Select Cases in Chancery*, 10 Selden Society 129 (1896).

160 Baildon, ed., *Select Cases in Chancery*, 10 Selden Society 132 (1896).

161 Baildon, ed., *Select Cases in Chancery*, 10 Selden Society 135, 146 (1896).

162 Bayne and Dunham, eds., *Select Cases in the Council of Henry VII*, 75 Selden Society 108 (1958).

163 Baildon, ed., *Select Cases in Chancery*, 10 Selden Society xiii (1896).

164 Evans and Evans, *A Dictionary of Contemporary American Usage* 143 (1957).

165 Baildon, ed., *Select Cases in Chancery*, 10 Selden Society 136 (1896).

166 Baildon, ed., *Select Cases in Chancery*, 10 Selden Society 100 (1896).

167 Baildon, ed., *Select Cases in Chancery*, 10 Selden Society 135 (1896).

same case has a Latin (or French) *bill*,[168] an Old English *answere*, and an Old French *replicacion*.[169]   Law French was on the move, headed for a career in English.

69. *More law French into English*

The trail of law French into law English became well marked in the fifteenth century.   Development of legal concepts and of the profession is reflected in the adoption by the English language of specialized law uses for long-familiar French words.

Since Middle English of the thirteenth and fourteenth centuries, *defend* had meant to ward off attack.   It now came to be used as an English word in its present law sense, to ward off a legal attack or to defend in court.   Before becoming French, *defendere* had these meanings in Classical Latin, and in law Latin it had meant to deny.   The earliest recorded English law use (1428) couples both French words in "'deny nor defend.'"   Similarly with *defendant*.   This was in common use in the fourteenth century to describe ordinary defense, as in "'. . . hit were him self defendaunt.'"   In the fifteenth century, today's *defendant* became a law word in English.[170]

Classical Latin called our *easement* a *servitus*, something enslaved, and the civil law still translates *easement* as *servitude*.   But Old French had a word *aisement* (something eased), which did for convenience or comfort — or toilet.   Bracton's Medieval Latin used a similar word *aisiamentum* for the law's *easement*, preferred over *servitude* to stress the personal enjoyment rather than the burdened property,[171] a distinction some courts preserve today.[172]   When *easement* became English in the fourteenth century, it meant the process of being relieved from pain, then convenience, comfort, enjoyment.   In the fifteenth century *easement* is recorded to mean a privy and also the relief that a privy affords "'to do one's easement.'"[173]   In the same century *easement* is recorded as an English word with its present specialized law sense.

---

[168] *Oxford English Dictionary*, under *bill*, sb.³; *Medieval Latin Word-List* (1934), under *billa* and *bulla;* compare Millar, "The Lineage of Some Procedural Words," 25 A.B.A.J. 1023, 1025 (1939); Bolland, ed., *Select Bills in Eyre*, 30 Selden Society xi-xv (1914); 2 Holdsworth, *A History of English Law* 339 (3d ed. 1923).

[169] *Oxford English Dictionary;* compare Millar, "The Lineage of Some Procedural Words," 25 A.B.A.J. 1023, 1027 (1939).

[170] Quoted in *Oxford English Dictionary*, under *defendant*, No. 1.

[171] 2 Pollock and Maitland, *The History of English Law* 145 (2d ed. 1898).

[172] 38 *Words and Phrases* (perm. ed. 1940), "servitude," pp. 738-739.

[173] Quoted in *Oxford English Dictionary*.

Many other French words separated into English-language law words in the late fourteenth and in the fifteenth centuries, with law meanings sharper than their earlier general ones. For example, *assault, arrest, counsel, party, process, proof, suit, servant.*

Growth of the law and the conversion of the profession to English usage also introduced into the English language law words of greater technicality than earlier law French contributions (Section 64). Examples are:

bail	in the modern non-French sense of the security given for a prisoner's release pending trial.
detinue	
formedon	see Section 66.
messuage	
release	see Section 71.
remainder	see *reversion*, this list.
remise	see Section 71.
replevin	Latin through French.
reversion	although the distinction between this and *remainder* (this list) was not always clear.[174]
warrant	in the senses of to give warranty of title, to guarantee quality of goods. See Section 60.

The English language and the law were both in ferment. If one or the other had remained still, there might have been bequeathed to us a more certain (and less adequate) language and law. Words in dead Latin and dying Anglo-Norman were little subject to popular influence, except as they were lifted out of their parchments and courts and dropped down into turbulent English. Once in English, crosscurrents were at work. The law mixed up its learning with the common usages, as with *defendant* and *easement*. Technical law words, such as *demand*, were appropriated for popular use, and some were watered down in the process.

English lawyers took *eschete* from Old French, where it had meant inheritance, and made of it the lord's succession to his tenant's land when there were no heirs or by way of forfeit.[175] (The officer who took care of the king's escheats was called in Anglo-Norman an *eschetour*.) In this law French, and in law Latin (*escaeta* or *escheata*), *escheat* might have been secure. But in the fourteenth century *escheat* and *escheator* became English words. They also became English words in clipped forms — *chet* and *cheitur*, with the same technical

---

[174] Plucknett, *A Concise History of the Common Law* 560 (5th ed. 1956).

[175] *Oxford English Dictionary*, under *escheat*; see 2 Pollock and Maitland, *The History of English Law* 23 n.2 (2d ed. 1898).

meanings. In the sixteenth century, by way of popular protest against abuses of the escheat, the shorter words degenerated into the present general senses of *cheat* and *cheater*.[176] A seventeenth-century quotation makes the process clear:

> "Cheaters of mens inheritances, unjust judges . . ."[177]

The law, while clinging to the traditional *escheat,* picked up *cheat* also, and proceeded to use it as a synonym for the Latin *defraudo,* the Old French *deceive,* and for *cozen* (probably French).[178] *Cheat* thus eventually became a law word in its own right, and remains so today.[179]

70. *The grand mixture of languages*

The ancient addiction to language mixture (Section 27) and the Old English relish for synonym (Section 31) joined in the Middle English period to produce word-doubling on an unprecedented scale. With deposits of Celtic (Sections 26, 27) and Norse (Sections 35, 36), Latin (Section 34 and Chapter VII), and now French, the storehouse of word material was filled to overflowing. And overflow it did, scattering bilingual synonyms in every direction, and establishing a habit that has carried into the present. What may have once been rationalized as necessary translation soon became a fixed style.[180]

Thirteenth-century writers went out of their way to translate into English the French *cherite* (luve), *desperaunce* (unhope), *ignoraunce* (unwisdom), *bigamie* (tweiwifing).[181] Their successors reveled in bilingual rhythms, sometimes spiced with alliteration: *wracke and ruine* (Old English: Old French), *poynaunt and sharpe* (O.F.: O.E.), *lord and sire* (O.E.: O.F.),[182] *safe and sound* (French: Middle English). As an ominous precedent, the first book to come from Caxton's printing press in England (1477) bore the tautologous title: *The Dictes and sayenges of the philosophers*[183] — where *dict* is either a shortening of

---

[176] Trench, *On the Study of Words* 118 (21st ed. rev. 1890).

[177] Quoted in *Oxford English Dictionary,* under *cheater,* No. 1.

[178] Compare Skeat, *An Etymological Dictionary* (new ed. 1909), under *cozen,* with *Oxford English Dictionary;* see also under *che,* in *The Law-Latin Dictionary* portion of *The Law-French Dictionary* (1718).

[179] 6 *Words and Phrases* (perm. ed. 1940, Supp. 1962), "cheat."

[180] Earle, *The Philology of the English Tongue* 83-84 (4th ed. 1887).

[181] Jespersen, *Growth and Structure of the English Language,* par. 98 (Anchor, 9th ed. 1955).

[182] Jespersen, *Growth and Structure of the English Language,* par. 98 (Anchor, 9th ed. 1955).

[183] 5 *Encyclopaedia Britannica* 80 (1948); compare *Oxford English Dictionary,* under *dict,* sb., and Steinberg, *Five Hundred Years of Printing* 71 (Pelican, 1955).

Latin *dictum* or straight from Old French, and is followed by the English translation. Poets sometimes mixed Latin, French, and English in the same verse.[184]

Further, the habit of multiplying words was not confined to bilingual combinations. Synonym for its own sake became an ornament of the age in which the legal profession matured.[185] An Old English pair *might and main* can be matched by a French pair *part and parcel*. The habit lent itself to poesy, as in Chaucer's *Knightes Tale*, where Old English synonyms add variety and rhythm:

With *muchel* glorie and *greet* solempnitee . . .[186]

The law got on the bandwagon. (Section 71.)

71. The law's habit of doubling words

With French declining as the principal language of the law (Sections 67, 68), English lawyers — like the population at large — found themselves overstocked with words. Which word would it be?

French	or	English
devise		bequeath
gibbet		gallows
infant		child
larceny		theft
marriage		wedding
property		goods
pledge, gage		borrow

(See Section 38.)

Sometimes for clarity, sometimes for emphasis, and sometimes in keeping with the bilingual fashion of the day (Section 70), they joined synonyms. And what they did not join, their successors did. Here is a token sampling of bilingual synonyms coupled in the law:[187]

acknowledge and confess (Old English: Old French)
act and deed (French or Latin: Old English)
breaking and entering (O.E.: F.)

[184] *Anglo-Norman Political Songs* 161, 165 (1953).
[185] Jespersen, *Growth and Structure of the English Language*, par. 98 n.14 (Anchor, 9th ed. 1955); Collas, "Problems of Translation," in Introduction to *Year Books of Edward II*, 70 Selden Society xii, xxxvi (1953).
[186] Chaucer, *The Canterbury Tales* 23 (Modern Library, Skeat ed. 1929).
[187] Compare Johnson, *Latin Words of Common English* 25 (1931); and compare Millar, "The Lineage of Some Procedural Words," 25 A.B.A.J. 1023, 1029 n.54 (1939); and see also Dickerson, *Legislative Drafting* 75-76 (1954); Jespersen, *Growth and Structure of the English Language*, par. 56 (Anchor, 9th ed. 1955); and Earle, *The Philology of the English Tongue* 82-83 (4th ed. 1887).

deem and consider (O.E.: F.)
final and conclusive (F.: L.)
fit and proper (O.E.: F.)
free and clear (O.E.: O.F.)
give, devise, and bequeath (O.E.: O.F.: O.E.)
goods and chattels (O.E.: O.F.)
had and received (O.E.: F.)
in lieu, in place, instead, and in substitution of (F.: F.: O.E.: O.F. or
    late Latin)
keep and maintain (O.E.: F.)
maintenance and upkeep (French: English)
made and provided (O.E.: L.)
mind and memory (O.E.: O.F.)
new and novel (O.E.: O.F.)
pardon and forgive (F.: O.E.)
peace and quiet (F.: L.)
right, title, and interest (O.E.: O.E.: F.)
save and except (F.: L.)
shun and avoid (O.E.: F.)
will and testament (O.E.: L.)

As with the language generally, doubling became a habit, not confined to law words of diverse origin. Here are some Old English paired synonyms:

by and with	have and hold
each and all	heed and care
each and every	hold and keep
from and after	let or hindrance

And here are some coupled French synonyms, in some instances the French but slight modification of an original Latin:

aid and abet	metes and bounds
aid and comfort	null and void
authorize and empower	pains and penalties
cease and desist	rest, residue, and remainder
fraud and deceit	remise, release, and quitclaim
hue and cry[188]	

It remains for later consideration whether the years have made any of these combinations indivisible. (See Sections 122, 123.)

72. *Tenacity of law French*

The crossing-over of law French into English (Section 69) is a good index of the fact that English was becoming the habitual language of the law. Law French was "decaying," perhaps even "degenerate," [189] but not dead.

---

[188] See *Oxford English Dictionary*.
[189] Pollock, *A First Book of Jurisprudence* 299-300 (4th ed. 1918).

Law French was still heard at the Inns of Court, and occasionally in the law courts,[190] especially in exchanges between bench and bar that did not immediately concern "the lay gents (as we call our clients)." [191] When the Year Books ended in the first half of the sixteenth century, the lawyers who wrote the reports carried on in French.[192] Even though the public expression of law might be in English, the professionals found law French accustomed and useful.

Coke, for example, was at home in all three professional languages. His formbook for lawyers — *A Book of Entries* (1614) — was mostly in Latin, the language of the writs. During his lifetime, he published *Reports* (1600-1615), in French — he said — because that was their customary language. Without disapproval or indorsement of the start of the practice, he related that:

. . . it was not thought fit nor convenient, to publish either those or any of the statutes enacted in those days in the vulgar tongue, lest the unlearned by bare reading without right understanding might suck out errors, and trusting to their conceit, might endamage themselves, and sometimes fall into destruction.[193]

But Coke wished a wider audience for his commentary on Littleton, which he regarded as "an introduction to the knowledge of the national law." [194] So he published the first part of his *Institutes* (1628) in parallel columns of French and English, but with a hedging explanation. He observed that Littleton's French was not like the French of former times:

But this kind of French that our author used, is most commonly written and read, and very rarely spoken, and therefore cannot be either pure or well pronounced.[195]

The translation into English was:

. . . to the end that any of the nobility or gentry of this realm, or of any other estate or profession whatsoever that will be pleased to read him and these Institutes, May understand the language wherein they are written.[196]

---

190 Maitland, "Of the Anglo-French Language in the Early Year Books," in Introduction to *Year Books of Edward II*, 17 Selden Society xxxiii-xxxv (1903).

191 North, *A Discourse on the Study of the Laws* 13 (1824).

192 5 Holdsworth, *A History of English Law* 358-359 (1924).

193 3 Co. Rep. xl (Butterworth, 1826).

194 Coke, *Commentary upon Littleton* xxxviii (Butler, 19th ed. 1832).

195 Coke, *Commentary upon Littleton* xxxix (Butler, 19th ed. 1832).

196 Coke, *Commentary upon Littleton* xxxviii (Butler, 19th ed. 1832).

His letting the mysteries escape into a "vulgar tongue" Coke rationalized with a nod at the recitals of the Statute of Pleading of 1362. He
wrote:

> I cannot conjecture that the general communication of these laws
> into the English tongue can work any inconvenience, but introduce
> great profit, seeing that *Ignorantia juris non excusat*, Ignorance of the
> law excuseth not. And herein I am justified by the wisdom of a par-
> liament . . .[197]

At the same time, Coke was not prepared to junk Littleton's French:

> Yet the change thereof (having been so long customed) should be
> without any profit, but not without danger and difficulty; for so many
> ancient terms and words drawn from that legal French are grown to be
> *vocabula artis*, vocables of art, so apt and significant to express the true
> sense of the laws, and are so woven in the laws themselves, as it is in a
> manner impossible to change them, neither ought legal terms to be
> changed.[198]

As in other fields of learning, said Coke,

> . . . you shall meet with a whole army of words, which cannot defend
> themselves *in bello grammaticali*, in the grammatical war, and yet are
> more significant, compendious, and effectual to express the true sense
> of the matter, than if they were expressed in pure Latin.[199]

Though "in a manner impossible to change them," Coke translated
Littleton's French, carrying much of it into English without change —
a mark of the extent to which technical law French was a part of the
English law vocabulary. French *fee simple* was English *fee simple*.[200]
French *fee taile* was English *fee tail*.[201] French *heires* was English
heirs.[202] *Cy pres* was as yet nontechnical law French, and Coke translated Littleton's words *as near*.[203] A now obsolete form of dower, *de
la pluis beale*, Coke left in its original French,[204] explaining in his comment that it meant *of the most fair*.[205] Coke was neither the last nor
the most extreme in saying a word for law French. As late as the
eighteenth century, the English barrister Roger North gave it as his
opinion:

---

[197] Coke, *Commentary upon Littleton* xxxviii-xxxix (Butler, 19th ed. 1832).
[198] Coke, *Commentary upon Littleton* xxxix (Butler, 19th ed. 1832).
[199] Coke, *Commentary upon Littleton* xxxix-xl (Butler, 19th ed. 1832).
[200] Coke, *Commentary upon Littleton*, f. 1a (10th ed. 1703).
[201] Coke, *Commentary upon Littleton*, f. 18b (10th ed. 1703).
[202] Coke, *Commentary upon Littleton*, f. 1a (10th ed. 1703).
[203] Coke, *Commentary upon Littleton*, f. 219a (10th ed. 1703).
[204] Coke, *Commentary upon Littleton*, f. 38a (10th ed. 1703).
[205] Coke, *Commentary upon Littleton*, f. 38b (10th ed. 1703).

Some may think that because the law French is no better than the old Norman corrupted, and now a deformed hotch-potch of the English and Latin mixed together, it is not fit for a polite spark to foul himself with, but this nicety is so desperate a mistake, that lawyer and law French are coincident; one will not stand without the other. . . . For really the law is scarce expressible properly in English, and, when it is done, it must be *Françoise,* or very uncouth. . . . A man may be a wrangler, but never a lawyer, without a knowledge of the authentic books of the law in their genuine language.[206]

The most celebrated instance of decadent law French is as crude as the frontier justice it records. It is the report of the prisoner being sentenced who:

". . . ject un Brickbat a le dit Justice que narrowly mist, & pur ceo immediately fuit Indictment drawn per Noy envers le prisoner, & son dexter manus ampute & fix al Gibbet sur que luy mesme immediatement hange in presence de Court." [207]

Other practitioners of the style speak of a dog *"profitable pur hunting";*[208] *"beat le dogg";* *"fetch un sword";* and *"knave en l'antient Saxon language est un male child."* [209] This species of law French was personal shorthand rather than a general professional jargon. And it was doomed.

73. *Commonwealth language reform*

Despite substantial inroads of English (Sections 67-72), there was much of the language of the law that was still exotic. More that was esoteric. Some that was both. With law Latin (Chapter VII), court hand and abbreviations (Section 54), technical law French (Sections 64, 69), and degenerate law French (Section 72), the profession had painted itself into a language corner. The grievance recited in the Statute of 1362 (Section 65) was discontenting Englishmen almost two centuries later (1549):

"I have heard suitors murmur at the bar because their attornies pleaded their causes in the French tongue which they understood not." [210]

[206] North, A Discourse on the Study of the Laws 11-14 (1824).

[207] Quoted in Pollock, A First Book of Jurisprudence 301 (4th ed. 1918), from Dyer's Reports (1688) 188b; see also Maitland, Selected Historical Essays 141-142 (1957), and Legge, "French and the Law," in Introduction to Year Books of Edward II, 54 Selden Society xxxviii, xliv (1935); and see translation under Davis's case, 73 Eng. Rep. 415, 416 n.10 (1560).

[208] Quoted in Pollock, A First Book of Jurisprudence 299 (4th ed. 1918).

[209] Quoted in "Language of the Law," 220 L.T. 200-201 (1955).

[210] Quoted in Maitland, "Of the Anglo-French Language in the Early Year Books," in Introduction to Year Books of Edward II, 17 Selden Society xxxiii, xxxv (1903).

A century more, and there was similar complaint. But now the loudest outcry was that the sense of the law itself, as well as its pleading, was denied to the ordinary literate citizen. This meant that Latin, untouched by the first legislation, had become a partner in infamy with French. Court records and writs were still in Latin, and so were the written common law pleadings (Section 51).

John Warr came out with a tractful of rising dudgeon labeled *The Corruption and Deficiency of the Laws of England, Soberly Discovered: Or, Liberty Working up to Its Just Height.*[211] He demanded to know:

> Why is the law still kept in an unknown tongue, and the nicety of it rather countenanced than corrected? [212]

He found an answer in the venality of lawyers, daily becoming more powerful:

> The unknownness of the law, being in a strange tongue; whereas, when the law was in a known language, as before the Conquest, a man might be his own advocate. But the hiddenness of the law, together with the fallacies and doubts thereof, render us in a posture unable to extricate ourselves; but we must have recourse to the shrine of the lawyer, whose oracle is in such request, because it pretends to resolve doubts.[213]

What was needed, said John Jones, was a return to English, more useful than

> . . . the modern custom of hotch potch French and Latine imposed by Lawyers for their own gain to instruct few others of their own generation, to cheat the universalitie of the Nation of their rights and understandings, and make themselves, and their Counsels most learned in others affairs.[214]

St. Edward's Ghost or Anti-Normanism decried the Norman corruption of the English language generally.[215] Change was afoot.[216] And in the reforming mood of the Commonwealth period (1649-1660), the language of the law did not escape.

In 1650, Parliament passed *An Act for turning the Books of the Law, and all Proces and Proceedings in Courts of Justice, into English.* The

---

[211] Reprinted in 6 *The Harleian Miscellany* 212-225 (new ed. 1810).

[212] 6 *The Harleian Miscellany* 221 (new ed. 1810).

[213] 6 *The Harleian Miscellany* 222-223 (new ed. 1810).

[214] Jones, *The New Returna Brevium* 7 (1650).

[215] Reprinted in 6 *The Harleian Miscellany* 90-106, especially 98-99 (new ed. 1810).

[216] See Robinson, "Anticipations Under the Commonwealth of Changes in the Law," in 1 *Select Essays in Anglo-American Legal History* 467-491 (1907).

earlier statute had been directed principally at the language of oral pleading. The new law omitted the preambles of the old one, accepted its premises, and ordered a clean sweep — without the former exceptions — of everything but English in all law writings and proceedings. Except for the Old English words *law, book, writ,* and the half French, half English *court hand,* every law word in the statute is borrowed from either French or Latin. It reads:

> The Parliament have thought fit to Declare and Enact, and be it Declared and Enacted by this present Parliament, and by the Authority of the same, That all the Report-Books of the Resolutions of Judges, and other Books of the Law of England, shall be Translated into the English Tongue: And that from and after the First day of January, 1650, all Report-Books of the Resolutions of Judges and all other Books of the Law of England, which shall be Printed, shall be in the English Tongue onely.
>
> And be it further Enacted by the Authority aforesaid, That from and after the first Return of Easter Term, which shall be in the year one thousand six hundred fifty and one, all Writs, Proces and Returns thereof, and all Pleadings, Rules, orders, Indictments, Inquisitions, Certificates; and all Patents, Commissions, Records, Judgements, Statutes, Recognizances, Roles, Entries, and Proceedings of Courts Leet, Courts Baron, and Customary Courts, and all Proceedings whatsoever in any Courts of Justice within this Commonwealth, and which concerns the Law, and Administration of Justice, shall be in the English Tongue onely, and not in Latine or French, or any other Language then English, Any Law, Custom or Usage heretofore to the Contrary notwithstanding. And that the same, and every of them, shall be written in an ordinary, usual and legible Hand and character, and not in any Hand commonly called Court-hand.
>
> And be it lastly enacted and ordained, That all and every person and persons offending against this Law, shall for every such offense lose and forfeit the full sum of Twenty pounds of lawful English Money; the one moyety thereof to the use of the Commonwealth, and the other moyety to such person and persons as will sue for the same in any Court of Record, by Action of Debt, Suit, Bill, Plaint or Information; in which no Wager of Law, Essoyn, or other Delay shall be admitted or allowed.[217]

The next year Parliament set up a committee to supervise the required translation, and provided that faulty translation would not be error. It also made one slight retreat and permitted use of Latin in "the certifying beyond the Seas" of Admiralty cases.[218]

A separate statute spoke of accepting the "usual and accustomed" tallies in payment of taxes, and someone thoughtfully inserted: "with

[217] II Acts and Ordinances of the Interregnum 455 (1650).
[218] II Acts and Ordinances of the Interregnum 510-511 (1651).

the alteration of the words upon the tally from Latine to English." [219]
This time the reformers felt that they were in earnest.

74. *Aftermath of Commonwealth language reform*

There is evidence that the profession was less than enthusiastic over being ordered to talk and write English (Section 73). Sir John Birkenhead parodied the title of the new law as:

An Act for turning all Lawes into *English,* with a short Abridgement for such new Lawyers as cannot write and read.[220]

William Style had taken his notes in law French, and when his reports were published in English, he assured his fellow lawyers that he did not subscribe to this lay nonsense. In a special introductory note to the profession, Style wrote:

I have made these Reports speak English, not that I believe they will be thereby generally more usefull, for I have been always, and yet am of opinion, that that part of the Common Law which is in English hath only occasioned the making of unquiet spirits contentiously knowing, and more apt to offend others, than to defend themselves; but I have done it in obedinece to authority, and to stop the mouths of such of this English age, who though they be as confusedly different in their Minds and Iudgements, as the builders of *Babel* were in their languages, yet do think it vain, if not impious, to speak or understand more than their own mother-tongue.[221]

Equally testy, Edward Bulstrode shared Style's contempt for the nonprofessional. He told the profession that his reports had long since

. . . been perfected in French, in which language, I did desire it might have seen the light, being most proper for it, and most convenient for the Professors of the law, who indeed are the only competent Judges thereof. For the laws of England, do best commend themselves to them that understand them . . .[222]

Other reporters were also annoyed at the break with tradition. Some welcomed the change.[223] The publisher of Brownlow's English-language formbook took a competitive pride in advising readers that the book was

. . . the quintesence extracted from those vast and unwealdy Volumes, which as now for the most part are rendred uselesse, by reason

---

[219] II Acts and Ordinances of the Interregnum 918-919 (1654).
[220] Quoted in Jones, *The Triumph of the English Language* 319 (1953).
[221] Style, *Narrationes Modernae,* introduction (1658).
[222] Bulstrode, *Reports,* pt. 2, "To the Reader" (2d corrected impression, 1688).
[223] Robinson, "Anticipations Under the Commonwealth of Changes in the Law," in 1 *Select Essays in Anglo-American Legal History* 467, 480 (1907).

as well of their obscurity, being writ in an unknown Tongue, as of the proscription of many Titles now exploded . . .[224]

For the time, the reports that were published conformed to the statute.[225] Though in the shadow land between conformity and contempt, a reporter might let it be known that he remained not merely unconvinced but unsubdued.

Thus, in a landmark case of the language battle, Style reported:

> And for these causes the judgement was reversed, *nisi;* and pronounced by Ierman Iustice (at the prayer of the plaintifs counsel) in English, being the first that was pronounced so in this Court, according to the late Act for proceedings in Law to be in English. Quod nota.[226]

Nearby, his memorandum announcing that

> The first rule of this Court made in English was between White and Keblewhite.

was followed by the notation "*Pasch.* 1651." and — like many another — introduced by the heading "*Pasch.* 1651 *Banc. Sup.*"[227] This abbreviates the Latin *pascha* — by way of Greek from Hebrew — for the Jewish Passover and the Christian Easter. Although *Pasch* by itself, without the period, had already been taken into ordinary English to mean the same thing. It also abbreviates the Latin *Bancus Superior,* for English *Upper Bench,* the Commonwealth name for *King's Bench.*

And even the enthusiastic publisher of Brownlow, in his haste to get an English edition on the market, bobbled the indexing of English forms with such entries as *case sur promise, case upon promise, case sur assumpsit.*[228]

Those who loved "the peculiar dialect of our common law"[229] were under wraps during the remaining years of the Commonwealth. With the Restoration came repeal of Commonwealth legislation. The English-language statute was validated for the period from Easter Term, 1651, to August 1, 1660, and then killed in pique.[230] The reports reverted to French,[231] and the pleading forms to Latin. The "Great Brownlow" rides again, shouted a jubilant publisher — *Brown-*

---

224 Brownlow, *Declarations and Pleadings in English*, p. A2 (1652).
225 5 Holdsworth, *A History of English Law* 360-362 (1924).
226 *Willis v. Bond,* 82 Eng. Rep. 694 (Banc. Sup. 1651).
227 *White v. Keblewhite,* 82 Eng. Rep. 695 (Banc. Sup. 1651).
228 Brownlow, *Declarations and Pleadings in English* 203, 204, 205 (1652).
229 Bridgman, *Reports,* "To the Students . . ." (1659).
230 Pleading, 1660, 12 Car. II, c. 3.
231 5 Holdsworth, *A History of English Law* 362-363 (1924); 6 Holdsworth, *A History of English Law* 552-554 (1924).

low Latine Redivivus. "Unskilfully turned into English" under the Commonwealth, his forms were ". . . Return'd to their Original Language, after a long and unhappy Transmigration . . ." [232]

Yet, without compulsion of statute, and within two decades of the repeal, some reports were once again published in English.[233] English had forced its way into the law, whether the older practitioners liked it or not. Reports that persisted in French had repeatedly to use English when verbatim account was called for, as with the words of a will,[234] or of the statutes[235] — in English since 1489.[236] (See Section 66.) Any account of English defamation also required English words. And a report will drop its French dress to reveal a "scurvy Whore, Jade, & Pocky faced Whore." [237] The incongruity only served to make law French appear more ridiculous:

. . . un libel en Spiritual Court pur disant al auter "thou art an old bawd . . ." [238]

. . . que le Defendant parle ceux parols al auter, My Little Boy in my house is Anne Distols Bastard, I wonder you will keep company with her . . .[239]

After 1704, all the reports are in English,[240] sometimes with a sigh:

Had the Author prepared them for the Press himself, they had appeared in another Dress . . .[241]

The English required by the Commonwealth statute could not be stopped by Restoration repeal. One lifetime later, French and Latin were again outlawed. (Section 76.)

75. Diminishing need for French

After the fifteenth century, French no longer enjoyed its former monopoly of the lawbooks (Section 66). Sixteenth-century books in law French were still important. For example, there were Fitzherbert's *La Graunde Abridgement* (digesting cases) and *La Nouvelle Natura*

---

[232] *Brownlow Latine Redivivus,* title page and "To the Reader" (1693).
[233] 5 Holdsworth, *A History of English Law* 363 (1924); 6 Holdsworth, *A History of English Law* 552-554 (1924).
[234] *Pawling v. Pawling,* 124 Eng. Rep. 279 (C.P. 1631).
[235] *Pomfrayes Case,* 124 Eng. Rep. 187 (C.P. 1629).
[236] The Record Commissioners, "An Historical Survey of Ancient English Statutes," in 2 *Select Essays in Anglo-American Legal History* 169, 201 (1908).
[237] *Thomas Wilcocks Case,* 124 Eng. Rep. 126 (C.P. 1628).
[238] "Language of the Law," 220 L.T. 200, 201 (1955).
[239] *Anne Distols Case,* 124 Eng. Rep. 189 (C.P. 1629).
[240] 6 Holdsworth, *A History of English Law* 552-554 (1924).
[241] Comberbach, *Reports,* dedication (1724).

Brevium (up-to-date writs), and Brooke's *Abridgement* (digesting cases). But English law writings generally were on the increase.

A ruminative work which had a lasting effect on the notion of equity in the law, the treatise known as *Doctor and Student*,[242] was in English by 1532. A formbook titled *Symbolaeographie*[243] (1590) combined Chancery pleadings in English and indictments in Latin. But its sixteenth-century Latin, like the French of the later reports (Section 74), had to dip into English to make sense. In the midst of an indictment for shooting game, the Latin text suddenly jumps to:

Anglice charged with powder & hayleshot.[244]

The Rastells, father John and son William, were interested in both law and printing.[245] Before the middle sixteenth century they had published English abridgments of the statutes.[246] And before century end, the son made a French-English translation[247] of his father's pioneering law dictionary *Expositiones Terminorum Legum Anglorum* (1527). In the early seventeenth, William expanded the translation into the well-known *Les Termes de la Ley*, which ran into numerous bilingual editions.[248] By the end of the seventeenth century there were several useful law dictionaries available to lawyers who dealt only in English.[249]

Sir John Doderidge, who had not always been a majority spokesman,[250] left a posthumous English jab to his colleagues on the King's Bench. He wrote about *The English Lawyer* (1631), observing that:

Judges ought to be learned, especially in the Lawes . . .[251]

---

[242] Christopher St. Germain.

[243] William West.

[244] West, *Three Treatises, of the Second Part of Symbolaeographie* §355 (ed. 1594).

[245] 18 *Encyclopaedia Britannica* 989 (1948).

[246] 4 Holdsworth, *A History of English Law* 311 and especially n.4 (1924); compare 1 Maxwell and Maxwell, comp., *A Legal Bibliography of the British Commonwealth* 565 (2d ed. 1955).

[247] *Exposicions of the termes of the lawes of England* (1563); compare 1 Maxwell and Maxwell, comp., *A Legal Bibliography of the British Commonwealth* 10-11 (2d ed. 1955), with 5 Holdsworth, *A History of English Law* 401 (1924).

[248] 1 Maxwell and Maxwell, comp., *A Legal Bibliography of the British Commonwealth* 11 (2d ed. 1955); compare 5 Holdsworth, *A History of English Law* 401 (1924).

[249] Skene, *De Verborum Significatione* (1597); Cowell, *The Interpreter* (1607); Blount, *Nomo-Lexikon* (1670).

[250] See *Pells v. Brown*, 79 Eng. Rep. 504, 506-507 (K.B. 1620).

[251] Doderidge, *The English Lawyer* 67 (1631).

A learned judge, Sir Matthew Hale, wrote his *Pleas of the Crown* in English (1676). And what did not start out in English was often available in translation,[252] most notably *Littleton* as rendered by Coke (1628). (Section 72.)

In 1622 there appeared a treatise, first of its kind — *Lex Mercatoria or the Ancient Law Merchant.*[253] Its author was not a lawyer, and it was written in English. Here was a portent of change in the law and of the declining monopoly of the law by French-trained professionals. Through the following years of civil commotion the stern discipline of the Inns of Court withered away,[254] and with it one of the last bastions of law French. French was being used infrequently in court (Section 72), and around the turn of the century French law reporting had been finally abandoned. (See Section 74.) Documents of consequence were mostly in Latin (Section 51), or in English[255] — a language now graced by Shakespeare. Despite diehards like Roger North (Section 72), and written advice to law students to know both French and Latin,[256] French was no longer the indispensable tool it had once been. The law French tide had ebbed, leaving words and phrases stranded in English.

76. *The Georgian legislation*

With the arrival of the eighteenth century, the important era of law French was past. Much of it had been absorbed into English. A small part of its former volume was recognizably distinct and active. The rest was dying a natural death (Section 75).[257] By itself law French was hardly worth legislating against. And had it not been associated in the public mind with other vices of law language, law French might have escaped the coup de grâce of further prohibition. But French was part of a parcel that included a heavy burden of Latin and unintelligible court hand. The professional language had also lent itself to calculated word multiplication and ingenious spacing that enormously increased the cost of any contact with the law (Sections 92, 93).

---

[252] 6 Holdsworth, *A History of English Law* 572 (1924).

[253] Gerard Malynes.

[254] 6 Holdsworth, *A History of English Law* 486-499 (1924).

[255] 1 Pollock and Maitland, *The History of English Law* 86 (2d ed. 1898).

[256] W. Phillips, *Studii Legalis Ratio, or Directions for the Study of Law* 28-30 (3d ed. 1675).

[257] Lévy-Ullmann, *The English Legal Tradition* 125 (transl., Mitchell, Goadby ed. 1935).

The clamor for legible English was so strong[258] that it could not be stilled by the Chief Justice of England, Lord Raymond, who rose in the House of Lords to denounce the proposed legislation. He warned that if the traditional language of the law were abandoned, there would be no end to innovation. For even English was not understood by all Britons. In Wales, he predicted, there would be proceedings in Welsh.[259] (Two centuries later this prediction came true.)[260] The plea was in vain.

Without the special focus on French that had characterized the earliest Statute of Pleading (Section 65), a new English-for-lawyers law was passed in 1731, to take effect March 25, 1733. It read:

> *Whereas many and great mischiefs do frequently happen to the subjects of this kingdom, from the proceedings in courts of justice being in an unknown language, those who are summoned and impleaded having no knowledge or understanding of what is alleged for or against them in the pleadings of their lawyers and attornies, who use a character not legible to any but persons practising the law:* To remedy these great mischiefs, and to protect the lives and fortunes of the subjects of that part of *Great Britain* called *England,* more effectually than heretofore, from the peril of being ensnared or brought in danger by forms and proceedings in courts of justice, in an unknown language, be it enacted by the King's most excellent majesty, by and with the advice and consent of the lords spiritual and temporal and commons of *Great Britain* in parliament assembled, and by the authority of the same, That from and after the twenty-fifth day of March one thousand seven hundred and thirty-three, all writs, process, and returns thereof, and proceedings thereon, and all pleadings, rules, orders, indictments, informations, inquisitions, presentments, verdicts, prohibitions, certificates, and all patents, charters, pardons, commissions, records, judgments, statutes, recognizances, bonds, rolls, entries, fines and recoveries, and all proceedings relating thereto, and all proceedings of courts leet, courts baron and customary courts, and all copies thereof, and all proceedings whatsoever in any courts of justice within that part of *Great Britain* called *England,* and in the court of exchequer in *Scotland,* and which concern the law and administration of justice, shall be in the *English* tongue and language only, and not in *Latin* or *French,* or any other tongue or language whatsoever, and shall be written in such a common legible hand and character, as the acts of parliament are usually ingrossed in, and the lines and words of the same to be written at least as close as the said acts usually are, and not in any hand commonly called *court hand,* and in words at length and not abbreviated; any law, custom, or usage heretofore to the contrary thereof notwithstanding: and all and every person or persons offending against this act, shall for every such offence forfeit and pay the sum of fifty pounds to any person who shall sue for the

---

[258] See 8 Foss, *The Judges of England* 77–78 (1864).
[259] Foss, *A Biographical Dictionary of the Judges of England* 548, 549 (1870).
[260] Stat. (1942) 5 & 6 Geo. VI, c. 40.

same by action of debt, bill, plaint, or information in any of his Majesty's courts of record in *Westminster* hall, or court of exchequer in *Scotland* respectively, wherein no essoin, protection or wager of law, or more than one imparlance shall be allowed.[261]

Additional paragraphs repeated the gist of the Commonwealth statute on mistranslation and on Latin certificates in Admiralty (Section 73), and extended the statutes of *jeofails* (Anglo-Norman *I mistake*) to cover errors in English.

Taken at face, the new statute repealed too much of the bar's accumulated learning. As Blackstone put it:

> The translation also of technical phrases, and the names of writs and other process, were found to be so very ridiculous (a writ of *nisi prius,* *quare impedit, fieri facias, habeas corpus,* and the rest, not being capable of an English dress with any degree of seriousness) . . .[262]

Lord Raymond lived on till March 18, 1733, long enough to see the hated law emasculated before its effective date a week later. At the end of an act extending the statute to include Wales, a substantial paragraph watered down the original and extension. It reinstated the customary law abbreviations and technical words, ". . . and has thereby almost defeated every beneficial purpose of the former statute." [263] Under the amendment, all of the writings and proceedings mentioned in the original statute

> . . . may from and after the twenty-fifth day of *March* one thousand seven hundred and thirty-three, be written or printed in a common legible hand and character, and with the like way of writing or printing, and with the like manner of expressing numbers by figures, as have been heretofore or are now commonly used in the said courts respectively, and with such abbreviations as are now commonly used in the *English* language, and that no penalty or punishment shall be incurred, by virtue of the said recited act, for any other offence than for writing or printing in any of the proceedings, or other the matters and things above mentioned, in any hand commonly called *Court Hand,* or in any language except the *English* language, nor shall any such penalty or punishment be extended to the expressing the proper or known names of writs or other process or technical words in the same language as hath been commonly used; so as the same be written or printed in a common legible hand and character, and not in any hand commonly called *Court Hand* . . .[264]

Despite the modification, the profession was not reconciled to the change. When the Act of 1731 was passed, Blackstone was eight years

[261] Records in English, 1731, 4 Geo. II, c. 26.
[262] 3 Blackstone, *Commentaries* °323 (Jones ed. 1916).
[263] 3 Blackstone, *Commentaries* °324 (Jones ed. 1916).
[264] Courts in Wales and Chester, 1733, 6 Geo. II, c. 14.

old, and the groaning of the bar could still be heard when he wrote in middle age:

> This was done, in order that the common people might have knowledge and understanding of what was alleged or done for and against them in the process and pleadings, the judgment and entries in a cause. Which purpose I know not how well it has answered, but am apt to suspect that the people are now, after many years' experience, altogether as ignorant in matters of law as before. On the other hand, these inconveniences have already arisen from the alteration; that now many clerks and attorneys are hardly able to read, much less to understand, a record of even so modern a date as the reign of George the First.[265]

James Burrow, who had become Clerk of the Crown in the Court of King's Bench at about the same time that Latin and court hand were outlawed, was of similar mind. He described the statute as one for converting the common law pleadings

> . . . from a fixed dead Language to a fluctuating living one; and for altering the strong solid compact Hand (calculated to last for Ages) wherein they were used to be written, into a Species of Hand-writing so weak, flimsy and diffuse that (in Consequence and Corruption of this Statute, though undoubtedly contrary to it's Intention,) many a modern Record will hardly out-live it's Writer, and few perhaps will survive much above a Century.[266]

Lord Ellenborough's views were characteristically direct. It is reported he thought the statute "tended to make attorneys illiterate." [267] As indeed it did, if Greek and Latin were to be the test of literacy.[268] The long career of Latin as a major language of the written law was drawing to a close. Having had little to gamble, law French lost little by the Georgian legislation. Like the residue of law Latin (Section 51), law French has lived on in "technical" words and sometimes disguised as English.

[265] 3 Blackstone, *Commentaries* °323 (Jones ed. 1916).
[266] 1 *Burrow's Reports*, pt. 4, p. ii (1766).
[267] Foss, *A Biographical Dictionary of the Judges of England* 549 (1870).
[268] See *Oxford English Dictionary*, under *illiterate*, quoting Lord Chesterfield; compare Johnson, *A Dictionary of the English Language* (4th ed. 1775).

CHAPTER X

Three Centuries of Modern English

77. *The period of Modern English*

For the sake of continuity, the treatment in this book of the law's use of Latin (Chapter VII) and French (Chapter IX) has straddled the nebulous boundary between Middle and Modern English. Neither Latin nor French has penetrated English by schedule. The start is not well marked, and the end is not in sight — even though with an affectation of finality we speak of the advent of Modern English in 1500 (Section 10). That Shakespeare is enjoyed today is some justification for the sweep of the classification *Modern*. That he needs occasional translation, and that his idiom and style are dated, are warnings that *Modern English* is only a title of convenience. This approximation has been subdivided into Early Modern or Tudor English (sixteenth century), Middle Modern English (seventeenth century), and after that, Current English.[1]

Chapter X covers only enough of the Modern English period to set the stage for the development of law language in America. It speaks of the time when the law was reacting to what Maitland called "the three R's — Renaissance, Reformation, and Reception."[2] A time of violence in England, and of revolution — a change from burning Protestants to burning Catholics. Henry VIII's world-shaking divorce. The monasteries broken up and their wealth scattered into select hands. One king was beheaded, and England experimented with uncrowned dictatorship before turning again to a controlled monarchy. The time runs from the Age of Discovery to the very brink of the Industrial Revolution. An expanding economy and an expanding law.

It is in this period that there appeared on the legal horizon a cloud no bigger than a man's hand, the phenomenon reported by Francis Bacon:

---

[1] 1 *Oxford English Dictionary* xxx.
[2] Maitland, "English Law and the Renaissance," in 1 *Select Essays in Anglo-American Legal History* 168, 176 (1907).

. . . there is start up a device called perpetuity . . .[3]

That upstart device had developed enough law and technical language before the American Revolution to keep lawyers busy for years.[4] This was a part of the age when the law was spinning its finest webs, its intricacies doubling, and its expenses multiplying. A field day for lawyers — some of them of literary stature. Outstanding among these was Coke, and much later, Blackstone — both expounders of traditional law. There was also Coke's enemy, the scholarly and devious Bacon, who had a passing vision of the law's improvement.

For all its sophistication, the law still foundered in primitivism. The same Chief Justice, Sir John Popham, who gave judgment in *Chudleigh's Case*[5] construing the involvements of the Statute of Uses, sentenced Sir Walter Raleigh:

> . . . to be hanged and cut down alive, and your body shall be opened, your heart and bowels plucked out, and your privy parts cut off and thrown into the fire before your eyes. . . .[6]

It was a sign of a new dawn that Blackstone could agree with Addison:

> . . . that in general there has been such a thing as witchcraft; though one cannot give credit to any particular modern instance of it.[7]

England had grown in Shakespeare's day to an estimated four and one-half million,[8] up three million from the population at 1066.[9] But only a fraction of the people were speaking the dominant London English — an estimated quarter million in 1600.[10] The language of the law, as the English language generally, had taken on a unique flexibility. It moved freely through Latin and French and other tongues, picking, discarding, uniting. It was an active sharer in an age of increasing literacy. More than all else the age was of the written word. *Written* did not yet include *typing* (see Section 108), but *printing* was part of it — its chiefest glory.

---

[3] 13 Bacon, *Works* 234 (Montagu ed. 1831).
[4] See Leach, "Perpetuities in Perspective: Ending the Rule's Reign of Terror," 65 Harv. L. Rev. 721-749 (1952), and Leach and Tudor, *The Rule Against Perpetuities* (1957).
[5] 76 Eng. Rep. 261 and 270 (K.B. 1589-1595).
[6] Quoted in Bowen, *The Lion and the Throne* 217 (1957).
[7] 4 Blackstone, *Commentaries* °61 (Jones ed. 1916).
[8] Marckwardt, *American English* 11 (1958).
[9] Feiling, *A History of England* 97 (1950); see also 8 *Encyclopaedia Britannica* 462 (1948). See Section 40, note 20.
[10] Marckwardt, *American English* 11 (1958).

78. *The age of the written word*

The era of Modern English is the era of the printing press, which stimulated the growth of a gradually increasing literacy. Increasing but still not general. Sir Thomas More, whose brilliant career was highlighted by the woolsack (1529-1532) and ended by the axe, estimated that two thirds of the population was still illiterate.[11]   Even for late eighteenth-century England, a contemporary estimate puts the reading public at 80,000. And though informed speculation multiplies that figure several times,[12] 80,000 would be progress over a former exclusiveness. The expansion of British enterprise from the land to the city and the sea widened the uses of writing. It was no longer only cleric and lawyer who must be literate. When, in 1648, William Petty advertised his recent invention — "an instrument of small bulk and price . . . whereby any man . . . may write two resembling copies of the same thing at once . . ." — he pitched to a wide market:

> The use hereof will be very great to lawyers and scriveners, for making of indentures and all kinds of counter-parts; to merchants, intelligencers, registers, secretaries, clerks, &c. for copying of letters, accompts, invoices, entering of warrants, and other records; to scholars for transcribing of rare manuscripts, and preserving originals from falsification, and other injuries of time.[13]

There was a vast printed outpouring — newspapers, tracts, broadsides, magazines, books. Shakespeare, Milton, Swift, Richardson, Defoe, Fielding, many others. Of these greats, Fielding was a lawyer — connected with the law by training rather than affection.[14]

If Fielding's law did not at once share in the literary greatness of the age, it did share the addiction to written words. Symbolic of this emphasis was the passage in 1677 of the Statute of Frauds,[15] and — even earlier — the Statute of Wills.[16]

Important procedural changes determined the course of the law in its multiplied contacts with the written word. Late in the sixteenth century, compulsory process was at last available to compel the testimony of disinterested witnesses in the courts of common law. As one

---

[11] Feiling, *A History of England* 522 (1950).

[12] Compare Watt, *The Rise of the Novel* 36 (1957), and Baugh, *A History of the English Language* 246 (1935).

[13] 6 *The Harleian Miscellany* 141 (new ed. 1810).

[14] But see and compare Coley, "Henry Fielding's 'Lost' Law Book," 76 Modern Language Notes 408-413 (1961).

[15] 29 Car. II, c. 3.

[16] 1540, 32 Hen. VIII, c. 1.

consequence, the jury became courtroom listeners instead of a forced muster of oath-swearers alert to neighborhood gossip. The serjeants changed from oral pleaders to skilled examiners of witnesses, no longer vouching to the court for the facts as well as the law of their cases. The pleadings were left mostly to others — at first to court clerks, and then to another branch of the profession. (Section 95.)

Written pleadings became the general rule at law as they had earlier in equity (Section 68), though the form of the written pleadings reflected their oral beginnings. As the clerk's record had once reported — in the third person — what the serjeants had said, the written pleadings now recited with the impersonal third person of the record what the parties contended. A seventeenth-century form complaint in false imprisonment begins:

> Iohn Hathwaye late of, &c. was attached to answer to Richard Bick, of a Plea why by force and armes upon the said Richard at Banbury he made an assault, and him beat, wounded, imprisoned, and evill handled, and him there in Prison being against the Law and Custome of the Realm of our Lord the King of England, a long while did keep, and other injuries to him offered, to the great Damage of the said Richard, and against the Peace of the said Lord the King now, &c. And whereof, &c. he complaines, that the forsaid Iohn the twentieth day of S. . . .[17]

Change in written pleading from that day to this has removed the folksy intimacy of "John" and "Richard" but not the stilted detachment of the third person.

The changeover from oral to written pleadings also had more far-reaching effects on the language of the law. An oral pleading could be nourished and trimmed under the guidance of brother serjeants who sat on the bench. (Section 67.) Written pleadings — like the writs — were prepared outside the courtroom, and the fate of the lawsuit might depend on the proper turn of a written word. Here was the sharpest of urges to use the words that had been used before.

The system of written pleading was intended to reduce decision to a single point. And this decision became — word of words — a *precedent*. The word (from the French for *preceding* in time) is not used in its law sense before the late sixteenth century.[18] And its repute was not established without remonstrance. In the first quarter of the seven-

---

[17] Brownlow, *Declarations, Counts, and Pleadings in English: The Second Part* 216 (1654).

[18] Plucknett, *A Concise History of the Common Law* 348 (5th ed. 1956); compare *Oxford English Dictionary*, under *precedent*, sb., No. 2b.

teenth century, a chancery clerk ticked off *precedent* in his work on *The Abuses and Remedies of Chancery:*

> Some judges, when they seem doubtful what to determine in a cause, will be inquisitive after precedents; which I cannot conceive to what purpose it should be, unless that being desirous to pleasure a friend, and the matter being of that nature that they are ashamed to do it, they would faine know, whether any before them have done so ill as they intended to do.[19]

A century later, the same refrain appears in *Gulliver's Travels:*

> It is a Maxim among these Lawyers, that whatever hath been done before, may legally be done again; And therefore they take special Care to record all the Decisions formerly made against common Justice and the general Reason of Mankind. These, under the Name of *Precedents,* they produce as Authorities; and the Judges never fail of directing accordingly.[20]

It was not until the eighteenth century that the editors of English-language law dictionaries included *precedent* and its companion *stare decisis* (to stand by things decided). But neither written abuse nor neglect could diminish the lure of *precedent.* It was a creature of the printed word. To be sure, it was possible to have precedent without printing. The *Registrum Brevium* (Section 51) recorded the models which had made possible the insistence on meticulous adherence to the form of writs. (Section 66.) But for years these forms were not available to the profession at large. Printing combined with the system of written pleading to place form at ready call in both attack and defense. And the more that was recorded, the more picayune the detail that counsel could ferret out for cavil. (Sections 87, 88, 90.) And higher grew the mountain of precedent.

Not only countless books of form,[21] but reports of decisions became available in print,[22] supplementing recourse to the cumbersome records. Counsel "relied upon presidents," [23] and the judicial conscience was haunted by suggestions of what a predecessor might have decided. See Mr. Justice Roll's afterthought to certainty in *Winn v. Stebbins* (1649):

> Therefore there is no help here . . . Yet let us see the president that Woodward hath to shew, and let the Secondary examine it again.[24]

---

[19] 1 Hargrave, ed., A *Collection of Tracts* 446 (1787).
[20] Swift, *Gulliver's Travels* 296 (Crown ed. 1947).
[21] 1 Maxwell and Maxwell, comps., A *Legal Bibliography of the British Commonwealth* 261-280 (2d ed. 1955).
[22] 5 Holdsworth, A *History of English Law* 358-363 (1924).
[23] *Reckwitch v. Moyle,* 82 Eng. Rep. 763, 764 (Banc. Sup. 1652).
[24] 82 Eng. Rep. 565 (K.B. 1649).

A seventeenth-century disagreement on the bench ends with an order that gives the tone of the period:

> The rule was to bring books to the Judges.[25]

For years the reports did not give "opinions" as we know them today. They were still accounts of oral decision, summarized, discussed, and annotated for the value the reporter thought was in them. Yet even in this form, they swelled a body of law already too fat for some tastes. A half century before Plowden's first reports were published, Thomas More had his say — his views disguised in the cloak of *Utopia* (1516 in Latin, 1551 in English):

> . . . for they think it an unreasonable thing to oblige men to obey a body of laws that are both of such bulk, and so dark as not to be read and understood by every one of the subjects.[26]

By the time Sir Matthew Hale became Lord Chief Justice in 1671, almost three dozen reporters had contributed to the growing mass of published law. Hale viewed with alarm:

> Thus, as the rolling of a snow-ball, it increaseth in bulk in every age, till it become utterly unmanageable. . . . every age did retain somewhat of what was past, and added somewhat of it's own, . . . And this produceth mistakes. . . . It must necessarily cause ignorance in the professors and profession itself; because the volumes of the law are not easily mastered.[27]

The philosopher Locke, son of an attorney, added his voice to the seventeenth-century criticism of the unending multiplication of law. (Section 98.) But the tide had not receded in the eighteenth century when Jonathan Swift echoed More and Hale and Locke, from the security of another mythical land, *Brobdingnag:*

> No law of that Country must exceed in Words the Number of Letters in their Alphabet; which consists only of two and twenty. But indeed, few of them extend even to that Length. They are expressed in the most plain and simple Terms, wherein those People are not Mercurial enough to discover above one Interpretation. And, to write a Comment upon any Law, is a capital Crime. As to the Decision of civil Causes, or Proceedings against Criminals, their Precedents are so few, that they have little Reason to boast of any extraordinary Skill in either.[28]

The satire made not a dent. As well stop the printing presses themselves.

[25] 82 Eng. Rep. 565 (K.B. 1649); see also *Emerson v. Ridley,* 82 Eng. Rep. 595 (K.B. 1649); *Ridley v. Emerson,* 82 Eng. Rep. 625 (Banc. Sup. 1649).
[26] *Utopia,* reprinted in *Ideal Empires and Republics* 203 (1901).
[27] 1 Hargrave, ed., *A Collection of Tracts* 270 (1787).
[28] Swift, *Gulliver's Travels* 152 (Crown ed. 1947).

79. *Languages of the new literacy*

The writing that fed the presses reflected the centuries-long domination by Latin (Chapter VII), and also the sporadic efforts to break Latin's hold. (Section 73-76.) The Latin monopoly in religion had been weakened by Wyclif's fourteenth-century translation of scripture. And shortly before Henry VIII's celebrated divorce, William Tyndale was smuggling in from the Continent his Bible printed in the English language. Separation of England from the Church of Rome further stimulated popular interest in written English, yet an opposing force was active: for the Renaissance had strengthened the scholars' respect for Latin and Greek. Reformation struggled with Renaissance for possession of the language of writing. John Milton, for example, wrote well and often in both Latin and English. He gave his seventeenth-century speech "For the Liberty of Unlicenc'd Printing" the Greek-derived Latin title *Areopagitica*, and then went on to shake an English fist at Latin. He denounced the censor's *Imprimatur:*

> . . . so apishly Romanizing, that the word of command still was set down in Latine . . . for that our English, the language of men ever famous, and formost in the achievements of liberty, will not easily finde servile letters anow to spell such a dictatorie presumption English.[29]

Francis Bacon experienced similar conflicting tugs. For general discussion of the law he used

> . . . the peculiar language of our law . . . a language wherein a man shall not be enticed to hunt after words, but matter . . .[30]

By which he meant mostly English though mixed with snatches of Latin and French. For his maxims it was different:

> . . . the rules themselves I have put in Latin . . . which language I chose, as the briefest to contrive the rules compendiously, the aptest for memory, and of the greatest authority and majesty to be avouched and alleged in argument . . .[31]

Like many others of his day, Bacon was not convinced that English would last.[32] He explained to a friend that he was having his English works translated into Latin:

[29] Milton, *Areopagitica* 40 (English reprints, Arber ed. 1868).
[30] 13 Bacon, *Works* 140 (Montagu ed. 1831).
[31] 13 Bacon, *Works* 140 (Montagu ed. 1831).
[32] Baugh, *A History of the English Language* 321 (1935).

For these modern languages will, at one time or other, play the bankrupt with books: and since I have lost much time with this age, I would be glad, as God shall give me leave, to recover it with posterity.[33]

For the moment English showed no signs of bankruptcy. It was taking its language creditors into the business. During the sixteenth and seventeenth centuries, English was expanding rapidly and inventively, drawing anew on Latin as a source of word material. Some of the formations were grotesque "inkhorn" terms — *obtract, obtrectation, turgidous.* Others once thought grotesque have now become standard — *turgid, clemency, dexterity, scientific.*

Many of the law's terms of art came into English from Latin during this period. For example, *affidavit, alimony, corporation, deponent, minor, to subpoena.* Other words came in as surplus, to cover plainer speaking with the scholarly euphemism of the Renaissance. Old French *bastard* had sufficed for William the Conqueror (Section 40), but Queen Elizabeth was *illegitimate.*[34] So too, the sixteenth century added the Latin *prostitute* to a vocabulary that already included an Old English *whore,* a French *harlot,* and a *strumpet* of undetermined origin.[35] For the Old English *drunk,* the language picked up in the sixteenth century Latin *intoxicated* and in the seventeenth Latin *inebriated,* a continuing problem of confusion and distinction for the law.[36] *Sot* and *soused* (both from Old French) became associated with liquor in ordinary English usage in the same two centuries, but fortunately gained no currency in the law.

The trend of the age was to add words to English: Latin words and Greek words, French (Section 69), Italian (Section 89), and Dutch words. From Greek, for example, came *anonymous, autonomy, didactic, stenography.* A lawyer, Thomas Blount — lexicographer alike to the general public[37] and to the profession[38] — is given credit for first recording as an English word *euphemism,* derived from Greek words

[33] 1 Bacon, *Works* xix (Montagu ed. 1825); cf. 12 Bacon, *Works* 428-429 (Spedding ed. 1874).

[34] *Oxford English Dictionary.*

[35] *Oxford English Dictionary;* Skeat, *An Etymological Dictionary* (new ed. 1909).

[36] 13 *Words and Phrases* (perm. ed. 1940, Supp. 1962), "drunk" to "drunkenness"; 21 *Words and Phrases* (perm. ed. 1960), "inebriate" to "inebriety"; 22A *Words and Phrases* (perm. ed. 1958, Supp. 1962), "intoxicated."

[37] Blount, *Glossographia* (1656); see Starnes and Noyes, *The English Dictionary from Cawdrey to Johnson* 37-47, and notes on 244-246 (1946).

[38] Blount, ed., *Les Termes de la Ley* (1667 and 1671), and Blount, *Nomo-Lexikon* (1670).

meaning to speak fair and of good repute.[39]   In the sixteenth century English acquired from the Dutch *quacksalver* — "one who boasts about the virtues of his salves,"[40] and in the seventeenth century shortened it to *quack*. In that form it has since found a place in medical jurisprudence.[41] The law also picked up in the sixteenth century *loiterer*, to which it added *loiteringly*. Both of these are from Dutch *loiter* — "to wag about (like a loose tooth)" — which had become an English word in the fourteenth or fifteenth century.[42]

From all quarters the new words came. And there were inevitably writers who out of pedantry or for sheer pleasure heaped words on words, multiplying English, French, and Latin synonyms. (Sections 70, 71.) Shakespeare, himself a great innovator, ridiculed the custom of pedantic euphemism in his 1600 *As You Like It*, with Touchstone saying:

> Therefore, you clown, abandon — which is in the vulgar, leave — the society — which in the boorish is company — of this female — which in the common is woman; which together is, abandon the society of this female; or clown, thou perishest; or, to thy better understanding, diest; or, to wit, I kill thee, make thee away, translate thy life into death, thy liberty into bondage . . .[43]

There were still others who opposed any innovation. Yet willy-nilly the vocabulary of English was growing. The language was growing faster than it was being organized, and the law had to function with what was at hand. The language of the law still shows the effects of the too quick accommodation.

80. The translation of Latin

Latin used by the law during the sixteenth and seventeenth centuries was not Latin at its best. Around the close of the sixteenth century a chancery clerk lamented the passing of the old days, when writs were carefully checked for propriety and diction, syllable by syllable, and letter by letter. Now petty clerks worked without "controllement" and "stuffed" their writs with such bad Latin:

> . . . and want of coherence and forme, as is fitt to make both the compounders and the writts themselves ridiculous . . .[44]

[39] *Oxford English Dictionary*.
[40] *Oxford English Dictionary*.
[41] *Black's Law Dictionary* (4th ed. 1951); 35 *Words and Phrases* (perm. ed. 1940, Supp. 1962), "quack."
[42] *Oxford English Dictionary*, under *loiter* and *loitering*.
[43] Act V, scene I.
[44] 1 Hargrave, ed., *A Collection of Tracts* 300-303, 301 (1787).

According to another writer, even "good" Latin of statutes centuries old was not without fault.   In lasting idiom he pointed out that:

> . . . sometymes you maie note in the statute the order of the sentence troubled & the carte sette before the horse, which muste be broughte unto his right order agayne by the iudgement of the reason.[45]

Yet with its failings, Latin — as Bacon had said (Section 79) — had "authority and majesty" compared with the disorder of English.   For hundreds of years the only organized grammar was Latin grammar. Not until the sixteenth century was any serious consideration given to a distinctive English grammar.   In 1580, William Bullokar wrote *A short Introduction or guiding to print, write, and reade Inglish speech* . . . in which he plugged for a thirty-seven letter alphabet.   Two years later, in a book on "the right writing of our English tung," the patriotic grammarian and schoolmaster Richard Mulcaster made his stirring declaration of faith:

> I love Rome, but London better, I favor Italie, but England more, I honor Latin, but I worship the English.[46]

More English grammars appeared in the seventeenth century, but even down into the eighteenth there was much aping of classical precedent.[47]   By the time of the American Revolution, a celebrated scholar was saying:

> The English hath little or no affinity in structure either to the Latin or to the Greek.   It much more resembles the modern European languages, especially the French.[48]

Yet the most popular of the pre-Revolutionary grammarians — Robert Lowth, the Bishop of London — acknowledged that though:

> The English language hath been much cultivated during the last 200 years. . . . it hath made no advance in grammatical accuracy.
>
> It is not the language, but the practice that is in fault.   The truth is, grammar is very much neglected among us . . .[49]

Authoritative Latin was the first language of the written pleadings at common law.   (Section 51.)   And when the Commonwealth (Section

[45] *A Discourse upon the Exposicion & Understandinge of Statutes* 134 (Thorne ed. 1942).

[46] Mulcaster, *The First Part of the Elementarie* 254 (1582).

[47] For example Harris, *Hermes* (5th ed. 1794); see Baugh, *A History of the English Language* 339 (1935); see also 8 Bentham, *Works* 357 (Bowring ed. 1843).

[48] 1 Campbell, *The Philosophy of Rhetoric* 428n (2d ed. 1801).

[49] [Lowth], *A Short Introduction to English Grammar* v-x (2d ed. 1763).

73) and Georgian (Section 76) reforms slowly forced English pleadings on an unwilling profession, the results were not encouraging.

The switch was from a highly inflected Latin to an English that had long since lost most of its inflected forms. (Section 52.) Literal translations failed to take into account that, unlike inflected Latin, intelligible English depends primarily on word order. Accordingly, the Latin predilection for holding a verb in reserve at the end of a sentence[50] made grammatical monstrosities of pleadings translated into English. Here is part of "A Declaration upon Trover" from the Commonwealth version of a Latin formbook:

> And so being thereof possessed, the sayd Beasts out of his hands and possession casually lost, which Beasts afterwards; that is to say, the 19th. day of Decemb. then next following at C. aforesaid to the hands and possession of the foresaid Tho: by finding came, notwithstanding the sayd Tho: knowing the Beasts aforesaid to be the proper Beasts of the said Edw: and to the sayd Edw: of right to belong and appertain, craftily and fraudulently intending the sayd Edw: in that behalf craftily and subtlely to deceive and defraud, the said sheep to the said Edward, though often thereunto requested, hath not delivered . . .[51]

What to do about turning the Latin genitive into an uninflected English possessive was also a problem. Thus it was "Brytton his French" [52] and ". . . Scrope his opynion can not be lawe . . ." [53] The neuter possessive was even more puzzling. *His* was used instead of *its* into the seventeenth century, and the uncertainties of punctuation (Sections 82-84) had *it's* often used for *its* down to the nineteenth.[54]

Following Latin form was not only clumsy but wordy. English made up in articles and prepositions what it lacked in inflection. "For instance," wrote Blackstone,

> these three words, *"secundam formam statutii,"* are now converted into seven, "according to the form of the statute." [55]

As a Scotch contemporary of Blackstone put it:

> The luggage of particles, such as pronouns, prepositions, and auxiliary verbs, from which it is impossible for us entirely to disencumber ourselves, clogs the expression, and enervates the sentiment.

He contrasted the "nervous" brevity of the Latin motto describing the

---

[50] 2 Campbell, *The Philosophy of Rhetoric* 295-297 (2d ed. 1801).

[51] Brownlow, *Declarations, Counts, and Pleadings in English: The Second Part* 482 (1654).

[52] Fraunce, *The Lawiers Logike,* introduction (1588).

[53] *A Discourse upon the Exposicion & Understandinge of Statutes* 155-156 (Thorne ed. 1942).

[54] *Oxford English Dictionary,* under *its.*

[55] 3 Blackstone, *Commentaries* °323 n.y (Jones ed. 1916).

ass fed on thistles, *Pungent dum saturent*, with the "spiritless" verbosity of the English: "Let them sting me, provided they fill my belly." [56]

Copying of Latin form also sometimes ignored procedural change, which had eliminated the reason for the form. In ancient times a plaintiff must produce *secta* — a group of followers to swear merely that the cause of action was genuine.[57] It was a guarantee against frivolous oppression reinforced by Magna Carta.[58] By the time written pleadings were introduced (Section 78), the system of trial had changed, and *secta* was no longer necessary, yet the complaint was made to end with the Latin assurance that the plaintiff brought his *secta*:

Et inde produxit sectam.

In Medieval Latin, a *secta* meant the followers, witnesses, or a lawsuit.[59] And when the Latin was translated, this unsevered appendix came into pleading English as:

And thereof produceth Suit.[60]

Sometimes it was rendered:

And thereof brings his Suit.[61]

And sometimes:

And therefore he brings his suit.[62]

No one could any longer be sure whether the plaintiff was telling why he had started a lawsuit or who was coming to help him.[63]

81. *Background for and/or*

The long neglect of English grammar coupled with the dilution of Latin grammar in England (Section 80) created the necessary climate

---

[56] 2 Campbell, *The Philosophy of Rhetoric* 355-356 and especially the note (2d ed. 1801).

[57] 2 Pollock and Maitland, *The History of English Law* 605-607 (2d ed. 1898); 1 Holdsworth, *A History of English Law* 300-301 (3d ed. 1922); 9 Holdsworth, *A History of English Law* 265, 266, 282-283 (1926).

[58] Magna Carta, par. 38, in Stubbs, ed., *Select Charters* 301 (8th ed. 1905).

[59] *Medieval Latin Word-List* (1934); see *Oxford English Dictionary*, under *sect*, sb.[1], etymology and No. 8, and under *suit*, sb., I and II.

[60] Brownlow, *Declarations, Counts, and Pleadings in English: The Second Part* 473 (1654).

[61] Brownlow, *Declarations, Counts, and Pleadings in English: The Second Part* 472 (1654).

[62] 9 Holdsworth, *A History of English Law* 266 (1926).

[63] See Millar, "The Lineage of Some Procedural Words," 25 A.B.A.J. 1023, 1024 (1939).

of confusion to breed what has since become the great *and/or* controversy.

In the wilderness of English grammar some of the small connectives of language could easily become lost. *And* was relatively secure. It was very old Old English, with a continuous life as a conjunction since at least the eighth century. Even so, in the sixteenth century it slipped out of the corral with a disruptive sense expressing *and also, and others*,[64] as in "There are lawyers and lawyers."

The real maverick was *or*.[65] It does not appear as a conjunction in written English until the thirteenth century, and then as a shortening of Old English *other*.[66] As an adjective *other* early meant *one of two*, as opposed to *either*, which originally meant *each of two*.[67] This forthright antithesis was not destined to last. For in the fourteenth century *either* also came to mean *or*, and the circle was complete. *Or* could connect equivalents, in the sense for which Bentham suggested we use "*or say*."[68] *Or* could also connect alternatives, but to emphasize an alternative *or* was best joined with other words, as in *either . . . or* and *or else* (sometimes spelled *orels*). Some of this history may be reflected in the English dialect expressions *and-aw* (also), *andur* (either), and *andyrs* (other).[69]

As usual, Latin was neater. Latin grammar divided *conjunctions* (i.e., words which join sentences or parts of sentences) into:

>   *copulatives*, which also join meaning; and
>   *disjunctives*, which separate meaning.[70]

The dominant copulative was *et* (and), while on the disjunctive side were a number of words that were all Englished as *or*. Chief among these were:

>   *aut*, which introduced an absolute alternative;
>   *vel* (derived from a form of the verb *volo*, to wish), connecting alternatives which rest in choice; and
>   *sive*, which indicated the speaker was uncertain of the alternatives or indifferent to them.

Anglo-Latin took some of the fine edge off of these distinctions. *Vel* was used to mean *nor* (still a disjunctive), but *vel* was also used to

---

[64] *Oxford English Dictionary*, under *and*, No. 3b.
[65] *Oxford English Dictionary*.
[66] *Oxford English Dictionary*.
[67] *Oxford English Dictionary*.
[68] Ogden, *Bentham's Theory of Fictions* cxxxix (2d ed. 1951).
[69] 1 Halliwell, *A Dictionary of Archaic and Provincial Words* 60 (10th ed. 1881).
[70] See, for example, Harris, *Hermes* 242 (5th ed. 1794).

mean *and,* ignoring the traditional distinction between disjoining and copulating.[71] The laxity was compounded in the use of the disjunctive *seu* (a form of *sive*) to mean *and.*[72]

Partly as a result of these medieval aberrations, there is still scholarly concern over the correct translation of the famous phrase of Magna Carta:

> . . . *nisi per legale judicium parium suorum*
> except by lawful judgment of his peers
> *vel per legem terrae.*[73]
> ? by the law of the land.

Does the *vel* mean *or?* Does it mean *and?* Or does it mean something else? A much indorsed opinion says of this *vel:*

> Often it is like the *and* (*or*) of our mercantile documents. The wording of the clause leaves open the question whether a man can ever be imprisoned or disseised by the law of the land without having had the judgment of his peers.[74]

Holdsworth agrees with the view that *vel* has this split personality. However, as a matter of form he has fastened upon the even more weird — though equally logical — *or/and,* an embodiment which has been not quite universally ignored.[75]

Legal writings of the sixteenth and seventeenth centuries made it clear that the ancient Latin division between copulative and disjunctive was not then meaningful and had not been for centuries. The earliest authenticated treatise on statutory interpretation (about 1571) says that *et* will be treated disjunctively (i.e., *and* = *or*) when:

> . . . two suche thinges so contraryant are coupled together that they can not drawe under one yocke.

and gives instances from Magna Carta and other thirteenth-century statutes.[76] Similar vintage instances are given when "wordes severinge

---

[71] *Medieval Latin Word-List* (1934), under *vel.*

[72] *Medieval Latin Word-List* (1934), under *seu.*

[73] Magna Carta, par. 39, in Stubbs, ed., *Select Charters* 301 (8th ed. 1905).

[74] 1 Pollock and Maitland, *The History of English Law* 173 n.3 (2d ed. 1898) accord: 1 Holdsworth, *A History of English Law* 60-63, especially 61 (3d ed 1922), and Radin, *Handbook of Anglo-American Legal History* 165-167, especially 166 (1936).

[75] 1 Holdsworth, *A History of English Law* 59 (3d ed. 1922); and see, for example, *Olsen Water & Towing Co. v. United States,* 21 F.2d 304, 305 (2d Cir. 1927), cited in Nichols, *Cyclopedia of Legal Forms Annotated* §8.1496 (1936), and compare Nichols, *Cyclopedia of Legal Forms Annotated* §8.1496 (1960); *Ralls v. E. R. Taylor Auto Co.,* 202 Ga. 107 (1947), 75 Ga. App. 136 (1947).

[76] *A Discourse upon the Exposicion & Understandinge of Statutes* 138 (Thorne ed. 1942).

shall be taken ioyntelie," [77] i.e., *or = and*.[78]   Plowden rationalized the interpreting away of the disjunctive-copulative distinction, ". . . in order to make the Words stand with Reason and the Intent of the Parties." He also suggested a rule-of-thumb for deciding when to call an *and* an *or:*

> And in many Cases Words spoken in the Copulative shall be taken in the Disjunctive, if such sense be most strong against those that speak them.[79]

This was authoritative sixteenth-century warning that *and* and *or* were not terms of art. *And* could mean *or* when *or* better served the person who had an *and* dropped into his lap.

Though we span the period of the American Revolution, it must be added here that centuries after Plowden's warning, conjunctions were still being used with abandon[80] when Lord Ellenborough took Plowden seriously. His interpretation of a policy of marine insurance was that a:

> . . . voyage insured to Palermo, Messina, *and* Naples, meant a voyage to *all or any* of the places named . . .[81]   [Emphasis supplied.]

A colleague could not resist a jibe at the draftsman: "It is wonderful," said Mr. Justice Lawrence,

> considering how much property is at stake upon instruments of this description, that they should be drawn up with so much laxity as they are, and that those who are interested should not apply to some man whose habits of life and professional skill will enable him to adapt the words of the policy to the intention professed by the parties.[82]

Having already held that words joined with *and* gave the holder of the *and* an option, Ellenborough a decade later went Plowden one better and decided that adding an *or* did not change the effect. In *Moorsom v. Page*[83] he held that an agreement to load:

> . . . a full and complete cargo of copper, tallow, and hides *or* other goods . . .[84]   [Emphasis supplied.]

was satisfied by a full load of tallow and hides.

[77] A *Discourse upon the Exposicion & Understandinge of Statutes* 139 (Thorne ed. 1942).
[78] See also Coke, *Commentary upon Littleton*, f. 99b (10th ed. 1703).
[79] Plowden, *The Commentaries* 289 (English ed. 1779).
[80] See, for example, *Wright dem. Burrill v. Kemp*, 100 Eng. Rep. 682, 683, 684 (K.B. 1789).
[81] *Marsden v. Reid*, 102 Eng. Rep. 716, 718 (K.B. 1803).
[82] *Marsden v. Reid*, 102 Eng. Rep. 716, 719 (K.B. 1803).
[83] 171 Eng. Rep. 34 (K.B. 1814).
[84] *Moorsom v. Page*, 171 Eng. Rep. 34 (K.B. 1814).

The exact point in time has not yet been fixed when an unsung draftsman consolidated the progress into uncertainty by a formal coupling of *and* with *or*. We do know that Ellenborough was remembered, and it seems likely that Lawrence's nagging challenge was not forgotten. At least as early as 1853, another document of the sea speaks of a voyage "to Sydney $\frac{and}{or}$ Moreton Bay." A mutiny later dragged the document into court, but *and/or* was an unnoticed bystander.[85] In the next two decades *and/or* was caught in a crossfire of conflicting dicta that would have ended the life of any ordinary word.

In 1854 litigation began in *Cuthbert v. Cumming*,[86] where the charterparty followed the general pattern of *Moorsom v. Page*, substituting *and/or* for *or*. The agreement called for a:

. . . full and complete cargo of sugar, molasses$\left\{ \begin{array}{c} and \\ or \end{array} \right\}$other lawful produce,[87]

i.e., A, B, and/or C. Only the trial judge stood with the shipowner. Both appellate courts held that the shipper satisfied his obligation by loading the ship as full as possible of sugar and molasses in customary containers, even though this did not fill the ship. There was no question but that the shipper had an option; as prevailing counsel was pleased to note, *Moorsom v. Page* settled that. What sort of an option? That intriguing question started the dicta flowing. Of the two judges who canvassed the possibilities of *and/or*, one said the shipper could load: A and B and C; *or* A and B; *or* C alone.[88] The other that the option was: A and B and C; *or* A and B.[89] A third judge contented himself with the remark that the shipper had the option to treat the contract as calling for A and B alone.[90] This was a fair beginning.

Fuller justice came in 1875 when the House of Lords in *Stanton v. Richardson*[91] spoke many unnecessary but interesting words over the body. Again a charterparty used the formula A, B, and/or C, requiring a:

85 *Sharp v. Gibbs*, 156 Eng. Rep. 1424 (Ex. 1857).

86 *Cuthbert v. Cumming*, 156 Eng. Rep. 668 (Ex. D. 1855), *aff'd*, 156 Eng. Rep. 889 (Ex. Ch. 1855).

87 *Cuthbert v. Cumming*, 3 C.L.R. 401, and compare 156 Eng. Rep. 668 (Ex. D. 1855), and 10 Exch. 809.

88 *Cuthbert v. Cumming*, 156 Eng. Rep. 668, 670 (Ex. D. 1855).

89 *Cuthbert v. Cumming*, 156 Eng. Rep. 889, 891 (Ex. Ch. 1855).

90 *Cuthbert v. Cumming*, 156 Eng. Rep. 889, 891 (Ex. Ch. 1855).

91 45 L.J.Q.B. (H.L. 1875), *aff'g Stanton v. Richardson* and *Richardson v. Stanton*, L.R. 9 C.P. 390 (Ex. Ch. 1874), *aff'g* L.R. 7 C.P. 421 (1872).

. . . full and complete cargo of sugar in bags, hemp in compressed
bales, $\frac{\text{and}}{\text{or}}$ measurement goods, . . .[92]

Each of the judges who ruminated on the nature of the option that
and/or granted came to different conclusions; each conclusion different
from every answer made in *Cuthbert v. Cumming.* Lord O'Hagan
said it meant "one of the three sorts of cargoes," [93] A or B or C. Lord
Hatherly was at first of the same mind — "evidently it must be taken
in the alternative." But in the course of delivering his opinion, he was
seized by revelation which he shared with assurance: ". . . it appears
to me to be as plain as anything can well be, that the shipper had the
choice of . . ." A *or* A and B *or* A and C.[94] The Chancellor, Lord
Cairns, capped the confusion, pausing "to observe that these words
'and' and 'or' are not without significance," and are "to be read either
disjunctively, or conjunctively." [95] He ultimately explained that this
meant A or B or C, *or* any combination — a blanket more than covering all of the possibilities suggested in both cases. Six judges with six
solutions (all dicta) to the problem posed by two words joined together. As Mr. Justice Lawrence had said: "It is wonderful . . ."

The further history of *and/or* is in Section 120. Its peculiar form is
noticed in the discussion of punctuation. (Section 82.)

82. *Punctuation and the oral tradition*

The scheme of punctuation which Modern English inherited was
inadequate for the era of the printing press. (Section 78.) Developed
at a time when illiteracy was general, punctuation had not been designed to help readers in understanding written words but to reproduce
oral communication in permanent form — to make sure it sounded
right. The oldest Hebrew and Greek writings had been completely
without punctuation; even words were run together. And when the
Greeks began punctuating, their system of dots showed the proper
places for breathing and accent. Similarly, Hebrew punctuation
indentified accent and vowels.[96] This was punctuation as individualistic and variable as only speech can be.

The Romans, and the Latin they bequeathed to the Western world,

---

[92] *Stanton v. Richardson,* L.R. 7 C.P. 421, 423 (1872).

[93] *Stanton v. Richardson,* 45 L.J.Q.B. 78, 85 (H.L. 1875).

[94] *Stanton v. Richardson,* 45 L.J.Q.B. 78, 84-85 (H.L. 1875).

[95] *Stanton v. Richardson,* 45 L.J.Q.B. 78, 82-83 (H.L. 1875).

[96] See, for example, 3 *Encyclopaedia Britannica,* plates I, II following p. 528
(1948).

followed in the oral tradition of Greek rhetoric. From Greek came *period, colon,* and *comma* — originally parts of rhetorical composition rather than the names for marks of punctuation. At the end of a complete sentence (Latin *periodus*), the speaker paused to take on air, and that pause was sometimes indicated with a high dot ˙. A speaker might also pause when he had covered a large portion of a sentence — a member; in Latin this was a *colon,* the same word used for the "great gut." [97] If such a pause were indicated at all in writing, it was as a dot on the line, as the period is now written. A shorter division of a *periodus* was a *comma,* and the pause to catch the breath after a *comma* was sometimes shown in writing by a middle dot ˙. There was no uniformity in this dotting of Latin, for oral delivery might vary greatly, and dots were not intended to supplement the meaning of language: highly inflected Latin could be understood without further mechanical aids. As a result, punctuation sometimes appeared in Latin after every word, sometimes not at all.[98] Occasionally Latin was heavily punctuated, and with apparent care. This is especially noticeable where the precise manner of oral delivery itself became a stereotype, as with the Latin Bible.[99]

By the time printers of the fifteenth and sixteenth centuries — Aldus Manutius in Italy, Gutenberg in Germany, Caxton in England — became interested in punctuation, there were immediate practical doubts more basic than when to use it. What should it look like?

A handwritten dot cannot long remain a dot. It becomes stretched and bent, and takes on gewgaws and curlicues. In the Middle Ages the Greek dots began a metamorphosis that eventually resulted in the modern marks of punctuation. Middle and line dots sometimes teamed up (:) for use as a question mark or a modern colon;[100] the middle dot alone sometimes turned into a modern comma; in turn this comma was sometimes inverted and placed above a dot (:) and sometimes the positions were reversed to form a modern semicolon.[101] To ward off

[97] Lewis and Short, eds., *A Latin Dictionary* (1879).
[98] See, for example, 3 *Encyclopaedia Britannica,* plate II following p. 528 (1948), and Hogben, *From Cave Painting to Comic Strip,* plate at p. 93 (1949).
[99] Hogben, *From Cave Painting to Comic Strip,* plates at p. 131 (1949); 18 *Encyclopaedia Britannica,* plate I following p. 504 (1948); 3 *Encyclopaedia Britannica,* plates III, VI following p. 528 (1948); compare Skelton, *Modern English Punctuation* 161 (1949); and see 3 *Encyclopaedia Britannica* 529 (1948).
[100] See, for example, *Anglo-Saxon Chronicle* in 1 *Monumenta Historica Britannica,* plate XXIII (1848).
[101] See, for example, *Anglo-Saxon Chronicle* in 1 *Monumenta Historica Britannica,* plate XXII (1848).

forgers, there were dashes and double dots, and any number of wiggling lines to fill the blank space of a line snug to the right margin.[102]

There was also the *virgule* (/ or |) — from the Latin for a small rod or wand — a thing of undreamed potential. It could mark an accent, an interruption in poetry, or a pause of the same value as the middle dot or comma.[103] It was the merest stroke, as elusive as the *and* it later joined with *or*. (Sections 81, 120.)

And these were not all. Writings from before the Conquest to the days of the printers give a picture of ancient usage in punctuation overlaid with continuous innovation.[104]

The master printer Aldus Manutius is generally credited with popularizing uniformity in punctuation.[105] And while the product of the Aldine press was persuasively regular, it did not by any means establish a fixed standard of form. Before Manutius, the Gutenberg Bible (1454-1456) used the Greek middle dot,[106] the same as used in an eleventh-century edition of Caedmon's poems[107] and in Bracton's thirteenth-century *De Legibus*.[108] (Section 51.) Manutius used modern commas (1499-1501)[109] and so did Cloverdale's Bible (1535),[110] but Tyndale's Bible (1525) used the virgule[111] — all these marks to similar effect. Caxton (c. 1475) was using the line dot (.) indiscriminately where modern punctuation would use comma, semicolon, or period.[112] His one-time apprentice Wynken de Worde used frequent virgules for commas, modern periods, and modern colons.[113] There was an almost endless variation.

Out of this jumble of contrariety one common principle appears: all of this punctuation was addressed indirectly to the ear rather than

---

[102] For example, *Appendix to Reports,* plates XIV, XXX (1819).

[103] See *Oxford English Dictionary;* Lewis and Short, eds., *A Latin Dictionary* (1879), under *virgula;* 3 *Encyclopaedia Britannica,* plate VI (10) following p. 528 (1948).

[104] See generally plates in 1 *Monumenta Historica Britannica* (1848), Johnson and Jenkinson, *English Court Hand AD 1066 to 1500* (1915), and Jenkinson, *The Later Court Hands in England* (1927).

[105] 18 *Encyclopaedia Britannica* 768 (1948); and see Skelton, *Modern English Punctuation* 159-160 (2d ed. 1949), and Vizetelly, *Punctuation and Capitalization* 9 (1921).

[106] Hogben, *From Cave Painting to Comic Strip,* plate at p. 131 (1949); 18 *Encyclopaedia Britannica,* plate I following p. 504 (1948).

[107] Hogben, *From Cave Painting to Comic Strip,* plate at p. 159 (1949).

[108] Wigmore, *A Panorama of the World's Legal Systems,* plate at p. 1065 (library ed. 1936).

[109] Steinberg, *Five Hundred Years of Printing,* plates 8, 9 (Pelican, 1955).

[110] 3 *Encyclopaedia Britannica,* plate VI (11) following p. 528 (1948).

[111] 3 *Encyclopaedia Britannica,* plate VI (10) following p. 528 (1948).

[112] Hogben, *From Cave Painting to Comic Strip,* plate at p. 156 (1949).

[113] Hogben, *From Cave Painting to Comic Strip,* plate at p. 160 (1949).

the eye. And that continued as the prevailing emphasis in the years between Caxton's press and the American Revolution.

An instructive sampling of sixteenth-century punctuation is a sentence-long passage from Mulcaster's English grammar (Section 80) discussing punctuation. (In the original some of the "n's" and "m's" are ommitted, the omission indicated by a line above the preceding letter, as tūg for tung.)

> Those characts which signify but sound not, ar certain notes, which we vse in the writing of our English tung for the qualifying of our words, & sentences in their pronouncing, by that which is sene in the form of our writing, which be in number thirtene, in name & form these: comma, colon: Period. Parenthesis (.) interrogation ? the longtime - the short time ⌣ the sharp accent ' the flat accent ˪ the streight accent ! the seuerer ‖ the vniter - the breaker = I vse the foren & originall names in most of these, bycause both the notes themselues be of a foren brede, and theie be commonlie best known by their own cuntrie names: I might darken more if I should deuise new names, then by enfranchising of the foren, a thing comon to all speches, which vse the translate terms of anie Art.[114]

Mulcaster found these "characts" helpful in "the right and tunable vttering of our words and sentences." Typical is his description of the *comma:*

> . . . a small crooked point, which in writing followeth some small branch of the sentence, & in reading warneth vs to rest there, & to help our breth a little . . .[115]

By the eighteenth century, the authoritative Robert Lowth, Bishop of London (Section 80), was talking more definitely of "pauses, which depend on the different degrees of connextion," but the stress was still on the oral function of punctuation. "Punctuation," he said,

> is the art of marking in writing the several pauses, or rests, between sentences, and the parts of sentences, according to their proper quantity or proportion, as they are expressed in a just and accurate pronunciation.[116]

He endeavored to reduce punctuation to some order on the analogy of musical notes and rests. Like the full rest, the half, quarter, and eighth:

> . . . The Period is a pause in quantity or duration double of the Colon; the Colon is double of the Semicolon; and the Semicolon is double of the Comma.[117]

---

[114] Mulcaster, *The First Part of the Elementarie* 109 (1582).
[115] Mulcaster, *The First Part of the Elementarie* 148 (1582).
[116] [Lowth], *A Short Introduction to English Grammar* 168 (2d ed. 1763).
[117] [Lowth], *A Short Introduction to English Grammar* 171 (2d ed. 1763).

Here is a good Lowth sentence:

> The precise quantity or duration of each Pause or Note cannot be de-
> fined; for that varies with the Time; and both in Discourse and Music
> the same Composition may be rehearsed in a quicker or a slower Time:
> but in Music the proportion between the Notes remains ever the same;
> and in Discourse, if the Doctrine of Punctuation were exact, the propor-
> tion between the Pauses would be ever invariable.[118]

Besides the . : ; and , Bishop Lowth catalogued ? ! and ( ), and in these
he found an additional oral factor. They ". . . denote a different
modulation of the voice in correspondence with the sense.[119]

If the forms of the basic punctuation marks were well acknowledged
in Bishop Lowth's day, any helpful definition of their appropriate use
was still lacking. As the Bishop said:

> . . . Much must be left to the judgment and taste of the writer.[120]

As a practical matter, punctuation for oral effect produced inter-
minable sentences — waiting, sometimes in vain — for the line dot that
would end the *period* of Greek rhetoric. It also produced composition
that was often sparsely punctuated and usually haphazardly punctuated. There were exceptions in English as there had been in
Latin, particularly when — as in verse — a precise mode of oral
delivery was considered essential. Whether attributable to enlightened
printers or direct intervention of the writer, Shakespearean sonnets
and plays, for example, show a pattern of careful punctuation.[121]
Moreover, there is direct evidence that Shakespeare was keenly aware
that meaning was shaped by punctuation. In *Midsummer Night's
Dream*, produced at the end of the sixteenth century, he dramatizes
the chaos resulting from bad punctuation. The prologue to the play
within the play is rendered:

> If we offend, it is with our good will.
> That you should think, we come not to offend,
> But with good will. To show our simple skill,
> That is the true beginning of our end.
> Consider then we come but in despite.
> We do not come as minding to content you,
> Our true intent is. All for your delight
> We are not here. That you should here repent you,
> The actors are at hand, and by their show
> You shall know all that you are like to know.

---

[118] [Lowth], *A Short Introduction to English Grammar* 172 (2d ed. 1763).
[119] [Lowth], *A Short Introduction to English Grammar* 184 (2d ed. 1763).
[120] [Lowth], *A Short Introduction to English Grammar* 169 (2d ed. 1763.
[121] Simpson, *Shakespearian Punctuation* (1911).

Which brings forth the comment:

> This fellow doth not stand upon points.
> He hath rid his prologue like a rough colt; he knows not the stop. A good moral, my lord: it is not enough to speak, but to speak true.

> His speech was like a tangled chain; nothing impaired, but all disordered.[122]

83. *The tale that English statutes were once unpunctuated*

There is extant in the profession a canard of venerable but undetermined vintage that English statutes were traditionally unpunctuated, and that this is a source of the peculiarity of legal punctuation. For example:

> 1766: It is well known, that in records there is no punctuation . . .[123]

> 1790: . . . and we know that no stops are ever inserted in Acts of Parliament or in deeds.[124]

> 1852: But on the Parliamentary rolls it is well known there were no stops . . .[125]

All of this confident knowing is undocumented.

One English judge studied printed editions of a statute, the first reading:

aliens, duties, customs, and impositions

the other:

aliens' duties, customs, and impositions

a difference he characterized (reflecting unsettled views about the apostrophe[126]):

> . . . but a comma is put on the top of the word *aliens* to mark the genitive case. [Emphasis supplied.] [127]

Taking a quick look at the statute in the uninviting squiggle of the

---

[122] *Midsummer Night's Dream*, act V, scene I.
[123] Barrington, *Observations upon the Statutes* 347 n.y (2d ed. 1766), and 438 n.x (5th ed. 1796); 1 *Words and Phrases: Judicially Defined* 28 (Burrows ed. 1946).
[124] Lord Kenyon, in *Doe dem. Willis v. Martin*, 100 Eng. Rep. 882, 897 (K.B. 1790.).
[125] Maule, J., in *Regina v. Oldham*, 169 Eng. Rep. 587, 588 (Cr. Cas. Res. 1852); accord: 3 Bentham, *Works* 208 (Bowring ed. 1843).
[126] *Oxford English Dictionary*, under *apostrophe*.
[127] Romilly, M.R., in *Barrow v. Wadkin*, 53 Eng. Rep. 384, 385 (Rolls Ct. 1857).

hand-lettered roll, Romilly, M.R., at last found the disputed wording
— bare:

> . . . *Aliens Duties Customs and Impositions* . . .

and felt himself free to adopt the second version of the printed statute,
which he did.   At the same time, he joined in the standard generalization of his day, with language more cautious if not more scholarly:

> 1857:   It seems that in the Rolls of Parliament the words are never
> punctuated.[128]

Thus overlooking (in a sparsely punctuated document) two periods,
twelve hyphens, and — of most importance — three apostrophes[129]
which might have influenced his (and later) decision.[130]

Any tale worth telling deserves embellishment.   And this one is no
exception.   Like most antique yarns it has been garnished to harmonize
with the mores of a later day.   The trimmings here take the form of
rationalization.

Unpunctuated, said Bentham (victimized by the conventions he despised), because:

> The first acts of Parliament were passed at a time when punctuation
> was not in use . . .[131]

Unpunctuated, because it was thought wrong that meaning should
"depend upon the easily transposed 'points,' " [132] a generalization which
claims too much both for punctuation and for the conscience of the
ages which fostered the tale.

Unpunctuated, because the statutes originate in "oral readings"
which would not have included punctuation.[133]   But whatever peculiarity English statutes had on the score of punctuation antedated "oral

---

[128] Romilly, M.R., in *Barrow v. Wadkin*, 53 Eng. Rep. 384, 385 (Rolls Ct.
1857); and see Black, *Handbook on the Construction and Interpretation of the
Laws* 185 (1896); McCaffrey, *Statutory Construction* 53 (1953); *Maxwell on the
Interpretation of Statutes* 42 (10th ed. 1953); Sutherland, *Statutes and Statutory
Construction* 307 (1891).

[129] Stat. (1773) 13 Geo. III, c. 21, in Public Record Office ref. c. 65/939.

[130] See, for example, *Aylwin v. Robertson*, 7 Terr. L.R. 164, 165-167 (Can.
1904).

[131] 3 Bentham, *Works* 208 (Bowring ed. 1843); see also Barrington, *Observations upon the Statutes* 438, 439 n.x (5th ed. 1796).

[132] "Punctuation in the Eye of the Law," 51 Albany L.J. 76 (1895).

[133] Lavery, "Punctuation in the Law," 9 A.B.A.J. 225, 226 (1923), and quoted
in Cook, *Legal Drafting* 82, 83 (1951).

readings" and continued after these "readings" became a formality.[134] The peculiar quality was present in the long years of written petitions whose prayers the king might or might not grant in his own carefully written statutes,[135] and that quality was shared by the leases, deeds, contracts, and other documents of the law never intended for public reading.

The one solid fact in the stew is that legal punctuation is peculiar. But it is the peculiarity of anachronism rather than of extreme individualism. English statutes have been punctuated from the earliest days. And any historic variation of their punctuation from today's fashion stems not from a tradition of "oral readings," but more likely from an opposite cause: that the statutes were intended primarily as a permanent written record, and generally — only incidentally for oral delivery, as for example upon their proclamation.[136]

The oral tradition that has influenced the punctuation of the law is the same oral tradition in which all punctuation originated. Punctuation was once merely an aid to oral delivery, and unless written material were specifically designed for oral delivery in a particular way, punctuation was an indifferent matter, and might be haphazard or even completely omitted. It was not punctuation designed to assist the eye in silent reading, nor was it originally punctuation in its present form. In the matter of form also, legal punctuation has followed generally the historic pattern of all punctuation. (Section 82.)

A convenient starting point for a study of legal punctuation is a comparison of two instruments of ancient Greece: one (of later date but earlier mode) an apparently unpunctuated lease of 350 B.C., with even the words run together; the other a punctuated city-law of 400 B.C.[137] The punctuation is the system of Greek dots, of which England has legal record at least as early as January of 1066, in an Old English writ of Edward the Confessor.[138] William the Conqueror's Charter of

---

[134] See Richardson and Sayles, "The Early Statutes," 50 L.Q. Rev. 540, 544-545 (1934), and May, *A Treatise upon the Law, Privileges, Proceedings and Usage of Parliament* 276-277 (1844), and 441-442 (ed. 1893).

[135] Dwarris, *A General Treatise on Statutes* 3 (2d ed. 1848); May, *A Treatise upon the Law, Privileges and Usage of Parliament* 433-434 (ed. 1893); 2 Holdsworth, *A History of English Law* 421 (3d ed. 1923); Richardson and Sayles, "The Early Statutes," 50 L.Q. Rev. 544-545 (1934).

[136] See Richardson and Sayles, "The Early Statutes," 50 L.Q. Rev. 540, 545-546 (1934).

[137] Wigmore, *A Panorama of the World's Legal Systems*, plate VI.19 at p. 349, plate VI.16 at p. 339 (1936).

[138] Van Caenegem, *Royal Writs in England from the Conquest to Glanvill*, 77 Selden Society, plate I (1959).

London in Old English (Section 42) is lightly punctuated with Greek dots.[139] His Latin *Domesday Book* is heavily dotted.[140] From William's day on to the introduction of printing in England, and beyond, it is possible to trace through legal writings — writs, deeds, charters, enrollments — the same developments in punctuation that occurred in nonlegal writings: the same gradual transition from the Greek system of dots to the modern marks of punctuation.[141] Not everything is punctuated. There are unpunctuated records on the rolls.[142] In that "grammarless string of abbreviated words," [143] the Year books, the remarkable thing is that there is any punctuation at all.[144] No systematic inventory has been made. But the accumulation of punctuated documents of the law is living refutation of any supposed ancient rule of no-punctuation.

For the statutes alone, the record is similar. The *Appendix to Reports* of the Great Britain Record Commission contains facsimiles of twenty-one items under the heading "Statutes of the Realm." [145] The work of the Commissioners has been criticized,[146] but any item in their collection still carries a "presumption in favour of its authority." [147] The *Appendix* spans half a millennium of English statutes — from the second quarter of the twelfth century to the last quarter of the seventeenth. It includes in facsimile Magna Carta, the Charter of the Forest, entries on the Charter Rolls, the Patent Roll, the Statute Roll, the Close Roll, samplings of the commencement of the Statute Roll and of the Parliament Roll, and also the inrollments of seven Acts of Parliament in addition to the Petition of Rights, as consented to by

[139] James, ed., *Facsimiles of National Manuscripts*, pt. I, I following p. 1.

[140] James, ed., *Facsimiles of National Manuscripts*, pt. I, III following p. 1; *Appendix to Reports*, app. BB, plate XXX (1819); 4 *Encyclopaedia Britannica*, plate I following p. 614 (1948); Public Record Office, *Domesday Re-Bound*, plates and figures generally (1954).

[141] See plates generally in Van Caenegem, *Royal Writs in England from the Conquest to Glanvill* (1959), Johnson and Jenkinson, *English Court Hand AD 1066 to 1500* (1915), and Jenkinson, *The Later Court Hands in England* (1927).

[142] See, for example, Johnson and Jenkinson, *English Court Hand AD 1066 to 1500*, plates XXIX, XXXV, XLI(b) (1915).

[143] Maitland, "Of the Anglo-French Language in the Early Year Books," in Introduction to *Year Books of Edward II*, 17 Selden Society lxxxviii (1903).

[144] See, for example, Bolland, *A Manual of Year Book Studies*, app. B, plates I-XI (1925).

[145] *Appendix to Reports*, Nos. I-XXI (1819).

[146] For example, Richardson and Sayles, "The Early Statutes," 50 L.Q. Rev. 201-223, 540, 567-570 (1934); and see 11 Holdsworth, *A History of English Law* 311-312 (1938).

[147] 11 Holdsworth, *A History of English Law* 312 (1938); 2 Holdsworth, *A History of English Law* 428 (3d ed. 1923).

Charles I. Without exception, these exhibits — whether they be in Latin, French, or English — have some punctuation.

The punctuation is neither consistent nor uniform. In some the punctuation is so sparse as to be negligible[148] — "open" or "light" are the proper terms. Occasionally the punctuation is "close" or "heavy." [149] In the earlier statutes, the punctuation is mostly the old system of Greek dots, irregularly used. These dots gradually get mixed up with other forms — virgules, modern commas, modern periods, parentheses, dashes, and even a question mark. According to modern notions of punctuation, some of the punctuation of these statutes is bewildering. Looking at John's Magna Carta, for example, the nineteenth century rendered the Greek line dots variously as comma, period, and semicolon. The Greek middle dot is given as comma, period, and semicolon. One modern form colon is translated as a comma, and another is disregarded.[150]

Even where the marks of punctuation are not strange, the length of some sentences is amazing — if you wait for a period to end a sentence. But if the oral purpose of the punctuation is borne in mind, some of the amazement fades. It was not that these scriveners did not know how to punctuate; they were simply operating under the old rules. If there were a compelling oral reason for punctuation, punctuation would be supplied. In the *Appendix* collection there are two enrolled acts proclaiming days of thanksgiving.[151] Following prayer or preaching, these were to be read aloud in church — in the words of the Guy Fawkes day act — "publikely, distinctly, and playnlie." [152] Both are heavily punctuated, though there are far more commas than sentence-ending periods. In another statute, the oath of allegiance is preceded by an open space and after twenty-nine words ends with a period. The oath of supremacy, three times as long, is also preceded by an open space, includes two commas, and also ends with a period.[153]

The act prescribing the Coronation Oath best illustrates the oral considerations that guided the punctuators of the old statutes.[154] The act starts with a long-winded "whereas" that includes a paren-

---

148 *Appendix to Reports,* plates X, XI, XII, XIV (1819).
149 For example, *Appendix to Reports,* plate XVII (1819).
150 *Appendix to Reports,* plates III, XLIX (1819).
151 *Appendix to Reports,* plate XVI (Act, 1605, 3 James I, c. 1), and plate XVIII (Act, 1660, 12 Car. II, c. 14) (1819).
152 *Appendix to Reports,* plate XVIII (Act, 1660, 12 Car. II, c. 14) (1819).
153 *Appendix to Reports,* plate XIX (Act, 1689, 1 W. & M., c. 1) (1819).
154 *Appendix to Reports,* plate XX (Act, 1689, 1 W. & M., c. 6) (1819).

thetical "(*whome God long preserve/*," punctuated just that way, and ends twenty-five lines later with: ". . . and shall be administered in this manner that is to say." From there on, the precise manner of delivery of the ceremonial words being important, the statute is vigorously and carefully punctuated — an effective script for a state occasion:

> The Archbishop or Bishop shall say. Will you solemnely promise and sweare to governe the people of this Kingdome of England & the Dominions thereto belonging according to the Statute in Parlyament agreed on and the Laws and Customs of the same? The King and Queene shall say, I solemnly promise soe to doe. Archbishop or Bishop. Will you to your power cause Law and Justice in mercy to be executed in all your Judgements. King and Queene, I will. Archbishop or Bishop. Will you to the utmost of your power maintaine the Laws of God the true profession of the Gospell and the Protestant Reformed Religion established by Law? And will you reserve unto the Bishops and Clergy of this Realme and to the Churches committed to their charge all such rights and priviledges as by Law doe or shall appertaine unto them or any of them. King and Queene. All this I promise to doe. After this the King and Queene laying his and her Hand upon the Holy Gospells, shall say. King and Queene, The things which I have here before promised I will performe and keep soe helpe me God. Then the King and Queene shall kisse the Booke. And bee it Further Enacted . . .

The oral drama over, at this point the statute lapses into one long sentence.

Thus, for better or for worse, a system of oral punctuation was used in the English statutes as it was used in other writings legal and nonlegal. Rarely completely absent, this oral punctuation was frequently wide "open." Yet with inflected Latin for so long the written language of the law (Section 51), few felt the need for a system of grammatical or "logical" punctuation.

The silence of the record indicates that lawyers (like the grammarians) were indifferent to punctuation generally, "open" or "close," at least until the beginning of the age of printing. And by that time the English bench and bar were in no position to know whether early statutes were punctuated or not. After years of war and civil confusion, the parchments themselves were not available. What passed for a statute in court might or might not be the original and frequently was not even an accurate copy.[155] Judges took judicial notice of public

---

[155] Plucknett, *A Concise History of the Common Law* 327 (5th ed. 1956); Richardson and Sayles, "The Early Statutes," 50 L.Q. Rev. 540, 553 (1934); Plucknett, *Statutes and Their Interpretation in the First Half of the Fourteenth Century* 103-112 (1922).

acts for the good reason that often the written acts could not have been produced if demanded.[156] Any laws earlier than the first year of the reign of Richard I (1189) were considered beyond the time of legal memory and accepted as a part of the unwritten common law.[157]

The commencement of the printing of the statutes in the 1480's[158] made for a readier availability. But the profession recognized that what was being made available were substitutes, and the distinction was not merely captious. Printed collections differed in the words, clauses, and even sentences of statutes. Translations were inaccurate and inconsistent. Some statutes were entirely omitted.[159] With the body of the law in this disordered state, punctuation of the originals could not have been a major concern to the bar.

The printers of statutes could not slough off questions of punctuation. The penman might hedge with an ambiguous squiggle, but the cutting of type involved decision and art, and the setting of type was not a casual act. Individual notions of punctuation varied. The raw materials the printers worked with were neither uniformly organized or punctuated; and some printers themselves copied copies rather than originals.[160] Each printer according to his own lights attempted to bring order to the disorder of the handwritten statutes, numbering sections, making marginal notes, and improving on the punctuation.[161] These were all labors of typographical composition and not legislation,[162] yet the statutes as fancied up by the printers were the only statutes ordinarily available to the profession. It is in this context — and in the context of the tradition that punctuation was for oral effect anyhow, not for grammatical sense — that it became understood that punctuation was no part of the statute, i.e., that what the printer did could not change the law.[163] In the absence of the originals for comparison (an assist to any canard), it could also be readily believed that if the printer

---

[156] 11 Holdsworth, *A History of English Law* 295 (1938).

[157] Dwarris, *A General Treatise on Statutes* 2 (2d ed. 1848).

[158] 11 Holdsworth, *A History of English Law* 291 (1938).

[159] See 4 Holdsworth, *A History of English Law* 308-310 (1924); 11 Holdsworth, *A History of English Law* 304-310 (1938).

[160] See, for example, 11 Holdsworth, *A History of English Law* 292 n.1 (1938).

[161] For example, *Nova Statuta* (Pynson ed. c. 1500); *Magna Carta Cum Aliis Antiquis Statutis* (Berthelet ed. 1540); W. Rastell, *A Colleccion of all the Statutes* (Tottell ed. 1559); Keble, *The Statutes at Large* (Newcomb ed. 1684), etc.

[162] See 11 Holdsworth, *A History of English Law* 304 and especially n.4 (1938).

[163] See Maxwell, *On the Interpretation of Statutes* 35 (1875); see too *Claydon v. Green*, L.R. 3 C.P. 511, 519, 521-522 (1868), and compare *In re Venour's Settled Estates*, L.R. 2 Ch. D. 522, 525 (1876), and *Sutton v. Sutton*, L.R. 22 Ch. D. 511, 513 (1882).

punctuated, then the statutes must be unpunctuated before the printer got to them. And an occasional glimpse of the vast unpunctuated (or merely dotted) areas of some of the handwritten statutes could serve to confirm this notion. For the scriveners of statutes — even in the eighteenth century — felt no more bound by "rules" of punctuation than did the lawyers. Their style was not only wide open but maverick. One favored the parenthesis,[164] another the dash.[165] Some used the possessive apostrophe,[166] others not.[167] Hyphens were common,[168] periods present but not ubiquitous,[169] great letters often substituting in places where we might use a period or comma.[170]

The generalized result of all this is that principle was born of error: the law does not concern itself with punctuation *because* (it was said) from antiquity the statutes and other legal documents were not punctuated. The practical result for later generations of lawyers and legal scriveners was an indifference to punctuation and an addiction to the long sentence. The long sentence was not a matter of carelessness but of principle. That was the way it had always been done and that was the way to do it. Since the original basis — the oral basis — of punctuation was either not known or forgotten, the long sentence continued in the law despite a change outside the law to "grammatical" or "logical" theories of punctuation. Fortunately, this did not happen without a protest. (Section 84.)

84. Counterpoint: Legal punctuation for meaning

Though punctuation originated as an adjunct to oral delivery (Sections 82, 83), some English lawyers appreciated that punctuation could also affect meaning for the reader. A sixteenth-century treatise

[164] Riot Act, 1714, 1 Geo. I, Stat. 2, c. 5, in Public Record Office ref. c. 65/351a; Records in English, 1731, 4 Geo. II, c. 26, in Public Record Office ref. c. 65/451.

[165] Act (1778) 18 Geo. III, c. 60, s. 4, in Public Record Office ref. c. 65/1025.

[166] Act (1773) 13 Geo. III, c. 21, in Public Record Office ref. c. 65/939; Act (1778) 18 Geo. III, c. 60, s. 4, in Public Record Office ref. c. 65/1025.

[167] Riot Act, 1714, 1 Geo. I, Stat. 2, c. 5, in Public Record Office ref. c. 65/351a; Records in English, 1731, 4 Geo. II, c. 26, in Public Record Office ref. c. 65/451.

[168] Riot Act, 1714, 1 Geo. I, Stat. 2, c. 5, in Public Record Office ref. c. 65/351a; Act (1773) 13 Geo. III, c. 21, in Public Record Office ref. c. 65/939; Act (1778) 18 Geo. III, c. 60, s. 4, in Public Record Office ref. c. 65/1025.

[169] Riot Act, 1714, 1 Geo. I, Stat. 2, c. 5, in Public Record Office ref. c. 65/351a; Records in English, 1731, 4 Geo. II, c. 26, in Public Record Office ref. c. 65/451; Act (1773) 13 Geo. III, c. 21, in Public Record Office ref. c 65/939; Act (1778) 18 Geo. III, c. 60, s. 4, in Public Record Office ref. c. 65/1025.

[170] See all references in note 169, and compare Act (1851) 14 Vict., c. 4, in Public Record Office ref. c. 65/4775.

on statutory interpretation discussed the problem — still troublesome today — of how to deal with a modifier that might attach to only one or to more than one word. For example, receiving goods "stolen or taken by robbers." [171] (See Section 125.) Of the problem (not the example), the anonymous author commented:

And herein the poynctinge & parenthesinge is muche materiall.[172]

So too it was a sixteenth-century judge who called attention to the need of punctuation to make sense of a statute, and proceeded to treat it as if properly punctuated — on the principle that

. . . the words ought to receive such construction as shall not clash with common reason . . .[173]

This precedent was duly noted in a seventeenth-century work attributed to the Lord Chancellor Sir Christopher Hatton.[174]

To another lawyer, Sir James Burrow, goes credit for one of the earliest (1768) essays in the English language stressing the desirability of punctuating writings to make them intelligible. And of all strange places the essay was sandwiched into a volume of reports. This, because the reports were intended for gentlemen, and ". . . no Gentleman ought to be altogether inattentive" to punctuation.[175] Further,

. . . because *most* Writers are (in my Opinion) too careless about it, and Men of the Law, in particular, are apt either to neglect it totally, or to execute it miserably ill . . .[176]

Burrow took notice of the low estate of punctuation. "I know," he wrote,

that there are some *Persons* who affect to *despise* it, and treat this whole Subject with the utmost *Contempt,* as a Trifle far below *their* Notice, and a Formality unworthy of *their* Regard: They do not hold it difficult, but despicable; and neglect it, as being *above* it.[177]

The attitude of the profession generally may be gathered from the opinion of a British judge more than a century later. With patent irri-

---

[171] *Shriedley v. Ohio,* 23 Ohio St. 130, 139-140 (1872); see also *Georgiades v. Glickman,* 272 Wis. 257, 262-264 (1955).

[172] *A Discourse upon the Exposicion & Understandinge of Statutes* 137-138 (Thorne ed. 1942).

[173] Mountague, C.J., in *Partridge v. Strange,* 75 Eng. Rep. 123, 141 (C.P. 1553).

[174] [Hatton], *A Treatise Concerning Statutes* 48-50 (1677).

[175] Burrow, "A Few Thoughts upon Pointing . . ." in *Settlement Cases* 629, 632 (1768).

[176] Burrow, "A Few Thoughts upon Pointing . . ." in *Settlement Cases* 629, 631 (1768).

[177] Burrow, "A Few Thoughts upon Pointing . . ." in *Settlement Cases* 629, 636 (1768).

tation, he said that whether or not the Roll was punctuated, the sense of the statute was too strong for him "to pause at these miserable brackets." [178]

Burrow's position was that the law had need of every possible mechanical aid it could find,

> . . . to assist the *Recollection* of the Writer, to catch the *Apprehension* of the Reader, and to direct the *Pronunciation* of the Speaker.[179]

To this end, he recommended not only the regular marks of punctuation but generous use of underscoring, italics, and capitals.

Burrow also characterized the evil that flowed from the law's neglect of punctuation ("pointing"):

> Very long Writings stand most in Need of its Assistance: And yet it so happens in Fact, that the longest of all are generally (if not Universally) altogether un-pointed. The Original Record of a long Act of Parliament, or a verbose Deed of Conveyance or Marriage Settlement, engrossed upon many Skins of Parchment without a single Point from beginning to End, may be nearly as unintelligible to a Common Reader, as if they were composed in an unknown language.[180]

Meaning likewise suffered when a reader was confronted with ". . . a Report of the Length of several Pages, all huddled together in one single Paragraph . . ." [181]

As bad as no punctuation was improper punctuation. Meaning could be completely changed, ". . . the sense . . . ridiculously perverted by false pointing." Burrow instanced some old nonsense doggerel:

> Every Lady in this Land
> Hath *twenty* Nails on *each* Hand;
> *Five* and *twenty* on Hands *and Feet;*
> And this is *true,* without Deceit.

converted to sense without word change:

> Every Lady in this Land
> Hath *twenty* Nails; on each Hand
> Five; and twenty on Hands *and* Feet;
> And this is true, without Deceit.[182]

---

[178] Fry, L.J., in *Duke of Devonshire v. O'Connor*, 24 Q.B.D. 468, 483 (1890); see also Lord Esher, M.R., at 24 Q.B.D. 468, 478.

[179] Burrow, "A Few Thoughts upon Pointing . . ." in *Settlement Cases* 629, 649 (1768).

[180] Burrow, "A Few Thoughts upon Pointing . . ." in *Settlement Cases* 629, 636 (1768).

[181] Burrow, "A Few Thoughts upon Pointing . . ." in *Settlement Cases* 629, 637 (1768).

[182] Burrow, "A Few Thoughts upon Pointing . . ." in *Settlement Cases* 629, 636-637 (1768); compare *The Oxford Dictionary of Nursery Rhymes* 258 (1951).

He condemned the "too frequent Use of Parentheses" for "The Mind of the Hearer or Reader is thereby put too often in Suspense . . ." There was further abuse of the parenthesis:

> To put one Parenthesis *within* another, is a great Fault in Language: But to *begin* a Parenthesis *only;* and then (within that) to *begin another;* and never to *end* either; is a much greater. And yet the Meaning of a great judge (many of whose sensible and solid Opinions I have endeavoured to represent) was *sometimes* obscured by the latter Incorrectness of his Language. Indeed the justness of his sentiments was *always* much superior to the Language in which he conveyed them.[183]

Burrow was too far ahead of his day. Legal punctuation continued in limbo. "This evil," said Bentham,

> has arisen from a superstitious attachment to ancient customs. . . . We have lived for ages without using stops and figures: why adopt them today? This argument is above all reply.[184]

Sympathetic as Bentham was in principle, he was more interested in language,[185] and his own writings were starved of punctuation. Even a friend has said his ". . . method of punctuation leaves much to be desired." [186]

The absence of clear rules for punctuating (Section 82) did nothing to promote its acceptance by the bar.[187] The punctuation of the law fitted in with the prevailing literary patterns. And there were other problems of greater urgency. Yet, if Burrow's lead was not followed in the documents that came to America as exemplars (Section 99), his thesis that punctuation affects meaning in the law has been a sporadically recurring theme. And it is worth skipping over a hundred and fifty years to light on an incident of high legal drama in which two English judges bothered to concern themselves with the original punctuation of a statute five and a half centuries old.

In the midst of World War I, Sir Roger Casement, patriot to the Irish, was convicted of treason — for conspiring with the Germans to further an Irish insurrection. Casement was in Germany when he conspired, and his counsel (A. M. Sullivan, K. C.) urged against both indictment and conviction that the statute condemned only the traitor

---

183 Burrow, "A Few Thoughts upon Pointing . . ." in *Settlement Cases* 629, 646 (1768).
184 3 Bentham, *Works* 208 (Bowring ed. 1843).
185 6 Bentham, *Works* 461 (Bowring ed. 1843).
186 Ogden, *Bentham's Theory of Fictions* cl (2d ed. 1951).
187 See 6 Bentham, *Works* 461 (Bowring ed. 1843); Burrow, "A Few Thoughts upon Pointing . . ." in *Settlement Cases* 629, 632 et seq. (1768)

who did his work within the Empire. The pertinent portion of the
law French statute (here interlined with English) reads:

> *ou soit aherdant as enemys*
> or be adherent to the enemies
> *nr̄e Seign^r le Roi en le Roialme*
> of our Lord the King in the Realm,
> *donant a eux eid ou confort*
> giving them aid or comfort
> *en son Roialme ou par aillours*[188]
> in his Realm, or elsewhere, . . .

The case was argued by counsel for the defense and the Crown as
though the original French were unpunctuated and another translation
punctuated, as here shown.[189]

Serjeant Sullivan, in a learned presentation which the appellate
bench characterized as "in every way worthy of the greatest traditions
of the King's Courts," [190] insisted that the only way to make sense of
both phrases "in the Realm" and "in his Realm" was to limit the act
to stay-at-home traitors.   Coke, he said, had taken the easy way out,
simply eliminating one of the troublesome phrases.[191]   The attorney
general would solve the problem by treating "giving them aid or comfort in his realm" as a parenthesis.   That, replied Serjeant Sullivan
(and T. Artemus Jones with him), could not be done, for the statute
was unpunctuated.

But Sullivan, for all his meticulous research, had taken at par the
common assumption of the profession.   And he was felled by the
conscientious curiosity of two judges.   In wartime, for the sake of
giving full English justice to a convicted traitor, Justices Darling and
Atkin had quietly taken their dignity across Chancery Lane and
through the iron gates that lead to that solid repository of centuries of
British tradition — the Public Record Office.   There, with magnifying
glass, these two judges examined the time-worn documents.   Let them
tell the story themselves, first Darling, J.:

> My brother Atkin and I have been to the Record Office, and we have
> read the original of this Statute in Norman-French and compared it
> with the Parliamentary Roll of the same date, which probably was writ-
> ten rather before it; and we carefully observed the writing and the
> punctuation, if that is worth anything.[192]

[188] Treason Act, 1351, 25 Edw. III, Stat. 5, c. 2.
[189] *Rex v. Casement*, [1917] 1 K.B. 98, 99n, 134 (1916); see also *Rex v. Casement*, [1917] 86 L.J.K.B. (n.s.) 467, 468 n.1 (1916).
[190] *Rex v. Casement*, [1917] 86 L.J.K.B. (n.s.) 482, 489 (C.A. 1916).
[191] Coke, *Commentary upon Littleton*, f. 261b (10th ed. 1703).
[192] *Rex v. Casement*, [1917] 86 L.J.K.B. (n.s.) 482, 484 (C.A. 1916).

If you look at the Statute Roll and Parliamentary Roll, they are both the same in this respect, that you get the words "adherent as enemies nostre seigniour le Roy," and then there is a break. I mention this because there was a great deal of argument at the trial about commas and brackets. If you look at the original Norman-French, you will find there is a break. You do not see brackets or commas, but they put a transverse line right through. There is a break after "le Roi en le roialme," and then comes "donant a eux eid ou confort en son Roialme ou par aillours." But if you look at the Parliamentary Roll there is just the same break after "en le Roialme," and then comes "donant a eux eid et confort en son Roialme," and then another break, the equivalent of the bracket contended for at the trial by the Attorney-General. That break is drawn right through the line, and you get the words "ou par aillours." If you look at the Statute Roll in that place where there is an undoubted break in the Parliamentary Roll, there is a mark which we looked at carefully with a magnifying glass. It is not certain that it is a break just as it appears in the Parliamentary Roll, but we are inclined to think it was a break — not made with a pen, but a break which had come by the folding in the course of all these six centuries. If you put that break after "donant a eux eid ou confort en son Roialme," it is very much the worse for your argument.[193]

For this development, Serjeant Sullivan was unprepared. His thoughts roamed wildly over the long hours of tedious research, but all that came out was: "I understood brackets did not exist." [194]

The robed detectives would not let off. Darling continued:

They are not brackets, but there is a very distinct line drawn right through the line of writing, and that occurs every here and there where we should now perhaps put what I think are called breaks in the print. Where we should put brackets these old scribes put a transverse line.[195]

And then Atkins, J.:

I think they really are to represent commas; they are reproduced in the reprint of the Statute as commas. The Statute Roll is printed in the Revised Statutes exactly correctly. I suppose you would infer, if there was any importance to be attached to the difference, that they corrected the Parliamentary Rolls from that which is the authority — namely the Statute Roll.[196]

Through these speeches, Serjeant Sullivan had quickly recovered his aplomb. He now swung full circle from his earlier insistence on sticking by the statute as written, and replied:

It ought to be so, but no inference can be drawn from punctuation. The whole matter should be determined without any theory as to punc-

---

[193] *Rex v. Casement*, [1917] 86 L.J.K.B. (n.s.) 482, 486 (C.A. 1916).
[194] *Rex v. Casement*, [1917] 86 L.J.K.B. (n.s.) 482, 486 (C.A. 1916).
[195] *Rex v. Casement*, [1917] 86 L.J.K.B. (n.s.) 482, 486 (C.A. 1916).
[196] *Rex v. Casement*, [1917] 86 L.J.K.B. (n.s.) 482, 486 (C.A. 1916).

tuation arising from a fortuitous circumstance which is not the same in the two rolls, and in dealing with a penal statute crimes should not depend on the significance of breaks or commas. If a crime depended on a comma, the matter should be determined in favour of the accused and not of the Crown.[197]

To which a new adversary, Lawrence, J., observed:

> If you can give an intelligible reading to the words, disregarding them, then that might be so.[198]

Sullivan replied in lawyerly fashion: "The meaning is perfectly clear. The authorities . . ." [199]

But the day had been lost to the ubiquitous virgule. It had supplied the missing link to a tidy rationalization of the statute. The final opinion does not discuss punctuation, and there was the compliment from the bench for Serjeant Sullivan's efforts, but Roger Casement was hanged.

85. *Unhurried prose*

It was not only prevailing style in punctuation which gave encouragement to the long sentence in the law. (Sections 82, 83, 84.) Quite apart from prejudices against punctuating, the popular form of sentence could not be readily chopped up or cut off with convenient shortening periods. At the very moment it was crystallizing into precedent (Section 78), the law was exposed to the flamboyant literary fashions of sixteenth- and seventeenth-century England. Giving it its best, Elizabethan prose was unhurried; those who could read were content to wait for a writer to arrive at his point.

One mode that has left a bad name in literary usage was *euphuism,* so called for the style popularized by John Lyly in *Euphues, or the Anatomy of Wit* (1579). Lyly loved the verbose antithesis dusted with alliteration. Here is a sample of his on-the-other-hand style, immune to cure by punctuation:

> Father and friend (your age sheweth the one, your honestie the other) I am neither so suspitious to mistrust your good wil, nor so sottish to mislike your good counsayle, as I am therefore to thanke you for the first, so it standes me Vpon to thinke better on the latter: I meane not to cauil with you, as one louing sophistrie: neither to controwle you, as one hauing superioritie, the one woulde bring my talke into suspition of fraude, the other conuince me of folly.[200]

[197] *Rex v. Casement*, [1917] 86 L.J.K.B. (n.s.) 482, 486 (C.A. 1916).
[198] *Rex v. Casement*, [1917] 86 L.J.K.B. (n.s.) 482, 486 (C.A. 1916).
[199] *Rex v. Casement*, [1917] 86 L.J.K.B. (n.s.) 482, 486 (C.A. 1916).
[200] Lyly, *Euphues* 40 (English Reprints, 1928).

With that sample from Lyly compare a portion of the introduction to Francis Bacon's reading at Gray's Inn *Upon the Statute of Uses* (1600):

> Herein, though I could not be ignorant either of the difficulty of the matter, which he that taketh in hand shall soon find, or much less of my own unableness, which I had continual sense and feeling of; yet, because I had more means of absolution than the younger sort, and more leisure than the greater sort, I did think it not impossible to work some profitable effect; the rather because where an inferior wit is bent and constant upon one subject, he shall many times, with patience and meditation, dissolve and undo many of the knots, which a greater wit, distracted with many matters, would rather cut in two than unknit . . .[201]

In extenuation, Bacon here wrote for oral delivery. He could also vary his style and write with razor sharpness. But the mass of legal documents of the day was not drafted by men of talent and literary sensibility, indeed most of it not even by lawyers. (Section 95.) And with or without talent, the writer then as now was attune to fashion in prose as in dress. Even when the literary community of England came to laugh at euphuism,[202] there was not the present note of urgency about prose. It is too much to say that nonlegal prose corrupted legal form. It is sufficient that for the moment verbosity in the law was not unique.

86. *The law of evidence*

Without any help from the language styles of the day (Sections 69, 79, 80, 81, 82, 85) the law had its own special urges to involved verbosity. For one thing, the general appearance of the testifying witness (Section 78) swelled the vocabulary of the courtroom.

During the sixteenth and seventeenth centuries, the profession began talking about *hearsay*.[203] It was Old English, old and untechnical in the common tongue (Section 37), but it was useful and stuck. Soon after,[204] from Classical Latin came *res gestae* (things done, a deed or

---

[201] 13 Bacon, *Works* 314 (Montagu ed. 1831).

[202] 1 Oliphant, *The New English* 605 (1886).

[203] 5 Holdsworth, *A History of English Law* 333 (1924); 9 Holdsworth, *A History of English Law* 215, 216 (1926); *Oxford English Dictionary*, under *say, hear,* and *hearsay*.

[204] *The King v. John Hampden*, 3 How. St. Tr. 825, 846, 988 (Ex. 1637), cited in 6 Wigmore, *A Treatise on the Anglo-American System of Evidence* 181 (3d ed. 1940), as *Ship Money Case*.

act).[205] It does not appear in the standard law dictionaries of the seventeenth and eighteenth centuries, and it also was not a technical expression. (Still ". . . not only entirely useless, but even positively harmful," say Wigmore.)[206] The testimony of Sir James Fitzjames Stephen, Q.C., is that *res gestae* ". . . seems to have come into use on account of its convenient obscurity." [207] Thayer concurred in this view, and dated it from the "quite unsettled" state of the law of hearsay in the late eighteenth and early nineteenth centuries:

> . . . lawyers and judges seem to have caught at the term "res gesta" . . . . as one that gave them relief at a pinch. They could not in the stress of business, stop to analyze minutely; this valuable phrase did for them what the "limbo" of the theologians did for them, what a "catch all" does for a busy housekeeper or an untidy one, — some things belonged there, other things might for purposes of present convenience be put there. . . . the singular form of phrase soon began to give place to the plural; this made it considerably more convenient; whatever multiplied its ambiguity multiplied its capacity; it was a larger "catch all." [208]

From a non-lawyer who knew lawyers, Samuel Butler, the law picked up *cross-examine* in the seventeenth century, which Bentham in the early nineteenth converted into *cross-examination.*[209] Examination on *voir dire* (Section 60) is missing from the standard law dictionaries of the seventeenth century, but appears in the early eighteenth.[210]

In the seventeenth century *The Book of Oaths* immortalized in English the rhythmical chant *the truth, and the whole truth, and nothing but the truth.*[211] This was not the earliest use,[212] but it came just at the time when the witness was becoming more important and the written law was becoming more English (Sections 73, 74), and so helped to fix the phrase. Though the form is redundant today (Section

---

[205] Smith and Hall, *English-Latin Dictionary* (1871), under *deed;* Lewis and Short, eds., *A Latin Dictionary* (1879), under *gesta;* Thayer, "Bedingfield's Case: Declarations as a Part of the Res Gesta," 15 Am. L. Rev. 1, 5 (1881); Thayer, *Legal Essays* 207, 238 (1927).

[206] 6 Wigmore, *A Treatise on the Anglo-American System of Evidence* 182 (3d ed. 1940).

[207] Stephen, *A Digest of the Law of Evidence* 156 n.V (2d ed. 1876).

[208] Thayer, "Bedingfield's Case: Declarations as a Part of the Res Gesta," 15 Am. L. Rev. 1, 9-10 (1881); Thayer, *Legal Essays* 207, 243-244 (1927).

[209] *Oxford English Dictionary.*

[210] Blount, *A Law-Dictionary and Glossary* (3d ed. 1717); compare with Blount, *Nomo-Lexikon* (1670).

[211] *The Book of Oaths* 204, 205, 207 (1649); see quote in 6 Wigmore, *A Treatise on the Anglo-American System of Evidence* 291 (3d ed. 1940).

[212] See, for example, *The Laws and Liberties of Massachusetts* 58 (Farrand ed. 1929).

30), in an England still troubled with religious confusions, it recalled to mind that Aquinas in *Summa Theologica* had insisted that an oath to tell the truth did not obligate one to tell "the whole truth." [213]

The rules of evidence which followed in the wake of the testifying witness had the indirect effect of encouraging detail in writings. The most important witnesses to any civil controversy — the parties — were still barred from testifying. The notion persisted that a party's oath was proper only if he would swear once and definitively — as in the old wager of law. (Section 29.)   But if a different sort of determination of truth were to be used — e.g., a trial by a jury passing on evidence — then the party's oath had no place. Also, testimony of parties was patently biased, and simpler than weighing it was the logical expedient of refusing to hear it. Incredible though it now sounds, the English common law — on the civil side — remained substantially that way until the reforms of the nineteenth century.

In the meantime, as in an earlier day (Section 56), a document replete with detail of the circumstances of a transaction was received in evidence.   Since a party to a contract might easily become party to a lawsuit, the more verbose the document the better, lest the party be left to the uneven contest between a curt writing and a voluble disinterested witness.   It was also easier now than in an earlier day to come by someone literate to set down a transaction in permanent form. As a result there was an increasing reliance on documentary evidence.

A corollary to the preference for writings was the expansion of the doctrine of *estoppel*. Known earlier in law French, *estoppel* became an English word in the sixteenth century.   Its Old French form meant a bung or cork. And though Coke's etymology lacked the refined assistance of an *Oxford English Dictionary*,[214] he had the essential notion that an *estoppel* ". . . stoppeth or closeth up his mouth to alledge or plead the truth . . ." [215]   From such an *estoppel* developed the *parol* (French, a spoken word) evidence rule. And this in turn gave further encouragement to draftsmen to get it all in: the document would have to speak for itself. It did. Words upon words. Parchment upon parchment.

In equity the situation was worse than at law. The old simplicity and dispatch were ended. (Section 68.)   By the close of the seventeenth century all testimony in equity cases was taken by deposition

213 See Silving, "The Oath," 68 Yale L.J. 1329, 1346, 1527-1577 (1959).
214 Compare *Oxford English Dictionary*, under *estoppel*, with entry under *stop*.
215 Coke, *Commentary upon Littleton*, f. 352a (10th ed. 1703).

on written interrogatories. Witnesses were examined on these interrogatories by commissioners — outside the presence of the lawyers. Completely inflexible, the interrogatories (even as today) had to be detailed and numerous. The answers were reported in the third person — in the language of commissioners unfamiliar with the controversy.

The attention to detail, the affection for detail, stimulated by the blossoming rules of evidence, in its day was no anomaly. Everything pointed in the same direction. (Sections 87 et seq.)

87. *Lose a syllable, lose the cause*

A maxim said to be derived from Bracton has survived to plague the bar. *Qui cadit a syllaba cadit a tota causa* has been translated:

> He who fails in a syllable fails in his whole cause.[216]

It recalls the infancy of the common law, when it was only by deadly exact formula that men more combative than litigious were gradually wheedled into court. (Section 28.) The maxim was never forgotten in the training of the English bar in the moots of the Inns of Court, nor in the long wrangling years of oral pleading. Even before the day of the printing press, and before the common law pleadings were written, the law was becoming more technical and the distinctions ever finer. (Sections 64, 66.) Now the habit of sharp disputing was reinforced by the Renaissance interest in rhetoric and logic, and armed with ready precedent (Section 78), the English bar embarked on a centuries-long career of hairsplitting.

If — as some classicists thought — the disputations of common lawyers were but ". . . a shadow . . . of the auncient rhetorike," [217] they still followed much of the classical pattern. Though deficient in "Elocution and Pronunciation,"

> Nat withstanding some lawyars, if they be well retayned, wyll in a meane cause pronounce right vehemently.[218]

Even sixteenth-century critics of the common law system conceded:

> . . . the practice of Law to bee the Vse of Logike. . . .[219]

---

[216] *Black's Law Dictionary* 1412 (4th ed. 1951); compare Ballentine, *Law Dictionary with Pronunciations* 1069 (2d ed. 1948), and 3 Bracton, *De Legibus* 138 (Woodbine ed. 1940); 9 Holdsworth, *A History of English Law* 282 (1926).

[217] Elyot, *The Boke Named the Governour* 65 (Everyman's ed. 1937).

[218] Elyot, *The Boke Named the Governour* 66 (Everyman's ed. 1937).

[219] Fraunce, *The Lawiers Logike*, preface (1588).

And to the "sharpe wittes of logitians," [220] the English bar added one of the lasting glories of the common lawyer — a penchant for particularity:

> Instead of geuing a true definition or explication of the nature and essence of any thing in our lawe, these singlesowld Lawyers and golden Asses aunswere . . . put down a particular case, as if I shoulde aske what is a man: A, man, say they, is such a thing as Willy the milman: Robin the pannierman, &c. . . .[221]

A refusal to pour individuals into a generalized mold had its virtues, but it also promoted a slicing away at the general to produce the paper-thin distinction. No distinction was too thin to discourage a try. The gossamer logic of counsel was sometimes too fine — even for a seventeenth-century bench. There was, for example, an attempt to reverse a slander judgment on the ground that the complaint was filed on the day of the tort:

> . . . which was said ought not to be, because the action should be brought after the words spoken, which shall not be intended to be if it be the same day, because the law admits of no fractions of time, which will be, if a day be divided into several parts, as it here must be, for there must be one hour supposed when the words were spoken, and another hour when the plaint was entered. But Roll Iustice said, it was well enough . . .[222]

In another case, an interest in English grammar (Section 80) provided the background for a contest in tenuous distinction. It was slander for saying: *You are a bankrupt skrub* (a *skrub* being "a mean, insignificant fellow"; also, a dwarf).[223] After plaintiff had judgment, it was objected:

> . . . that the words are not actionable, because they are adjective words, and so are not positive enough to ground an action.

Actionable, said the court, spinning finer than the bar,

> . . . for the word banckrupt in it self was not an adjective, and the joyning of it with skrub made it not so, but it should be understood as much as to say, You are a skrub, and also a Banckrupt.[224]

It was this sort of tightrope walking that was lampooned in the eighteenth-century satire, *Law Is a Bottomless Pit*, which publicized the case of *Stradling v. Stiles:*[225]

[220] Elyot, *The Boke Named the Governour* 66 (Everyman's ed. 1937).
[221] Fraunce, *The Lawiers Logike* 62 (1588).
[222] *Symons v. Low*, 82 Eng. Rep. 539 (K.B. 1648).
[223] *Oxford English Dictionary*, under *scrub*.
[224] *Willison v. Crow*, 82 Eng. Rep. 541, 542 (K.B. 1648).
[225] [Arbuthnot], *Law Is a Bottomless Pit* 238-242 (ed. 1732).

Le Recitel del Case: Sir John Swale bequeathed to Stradling "all my black and white Horses." The testator had six black horses, six white horses, and six pyed horses.

Le Point The Debate therefore was whether or no the said Matthew Stradling should have the said pyed horses by virtue of the said Bequest?

Pour le Pl.

.   .   .   .

By the word *Black,* all the Horses that are black are devised; by the word *White,* are devised those that are white; and by the same word, with the conjunction Copulative, *And,* between them, the Horses that are black and white, that is to say Pyed, are devised also.

Whatever is black and white is pyed; and whatever is pyed is black and white; ergo Black and White is Pyed, and vice versa Pyed is Black and White.

If therefore Black and White Horses are devised, Pyed Horses shall pass by such Devise; but Black and White Horses are devised; *ergo,* the Pl. shall have the Pyed Horses.

Pour le Defend.

The Plaintiff shall not have the Pyed Horses by Intendment; for if by the Devise of black and white Horses, not only black and white Horses, but Horses of any Colour between these two Extreams may pass, then not only Pyed and Grey Horses, but also Red or Bey Horses would pass likewise, which would be absurd, and against Reason.

As therefore pyed horses do not come within the Intendment of the Bequest, so neither do they within the letter of the Words.

A pyed Horse is not a white Horse, neither is a pyed a black Horse; how then can pyed Horses come under the words of black and white Horses?

Le Court fuit longement en doubt de cest Matter; et apres grand deliberation eu, Judgment for Plaintiff *nisi causa.*

Motion in Arrest of Judgment that the Pyed Horses are Mares; and thereupon an Inspection was prayed.

Et sur ceo le Court advisare vult [took the matter under submission].

It was both a tribute to the satirist's art and an index of the level of the fierce hairsplitting of the day that some later writers took the humor seriously[226] and that some were not altogether sure that *Stradling v. Stiles* was fiction.[227]

88. *Harshness of the law*

There were reasons besides historical habit and a bent toward argument that accustomed English lawyers to quibbling over the law

---

[226] Lieber, *Legal and Political Hermeneutics* 76, 331-332 n.0 (3d ed. 1880).
[227] *Wilkins vs. Taylor,* 1 Wythe 338, 351-352 (Va. 1799).

and its language. Technicality, for example, was a thinking being's answer to the general acceptance of a primitive brutality.

The enlightened Francis Bacon summarizing the criminal law of England in the first quarter of the seventeenth century listed seventy-one forms of capital offense.[228] These included stealing anything over a shillingsworth, conjuring "wicked spirits," and being a bigamist, an "Egyptian" (a gipsy), or a Catholic priest. Besides hanging or worse (Section 77), there was a forfeiture of property and *corruption of blood* (tainting or spoiling of the whole line of inheritance)[229] — so that the innocent suffered for the guilty. In such dread circumstance, the accused was ordinarily denied counsel. He could speak for himself, but neither he nor his witnesses could be sworn. He could also refuse to say anything, which a puzzled law resolved (in Bacon's words) like this:

> In felony, if the party stand mute, and will not put himself upon his trial . . . he shall have judgment not of hanging, but of penance of pressing to death; but then he saves his lands, and forfeits only his goods.[230]

Harsh criminal laws developed a pattern of meticulous faultfinding. Where counsel was permitted, the lawyers seized on any defect to upset the proceedings. An indictment was quashed because it said a session *was* adjourned instead of *is* adjourned.[231] An indictment for saying:

> That whenever a Burgess of Hull comes to put on his Gown, Satan enters into him,

was quashed because it ended (in Latin) *To the bad example of the inhabitants* instead of *In such a case, to the hurt of a great many of the King's subjects.*[232] An indictment for hiring a servant without clearance from his last master was quashed because it didn't tell what trade was involved, and failed to use the magic words *contra pacem* (against the peace).[233] Detail used to soften rigor.[234]

Even the Crown judges occasionally took the initiative for the accused by an insistence on form. In a case of horse-stealing, the court rejected exceptions taken by counsel,

228 5 Bacon, *Works* 86-98 (Montagu ed. 1826).
229 *Oxford English Dictionary*, under *corruption* and *corrupt;* see also 1 Pollock and Maitland, *The History of English Law* 477 and especially n.6 (2d ed. 1898); 3 Holdsworth, *A History of English Law* 69 (3d ed. 1923).
230 5 Bacon, *Works* 97 (Montagu ed. 1826).
231 *Rex v. Youngman,* 90 Eng. Rep. 526 (K.B. 1702).
232 *King v. Baker,* 86 Eng. Rep. 711 (K.B. 1669).
233 Case 39, Anon., 86 Eng. Rep. 746 (K.B. 1670).
234 See also *King v. Bray,* 82 Eng. Rep. 600 (K.B. 1649).

But Roll chief Iustice took another exception, viz., that the endictment was that the defendant did the fact nuper [lately], and that is so general a word that no answer can be given to it. And for that it was quashed.[235]

In a fourteen-year-old indictment for murder, court-assigned counsel objected that the indictment did not show who was dead, "whether he that was struck or another," and also that,

It doth not appear in what part of the body the wound was given, nor with what weapon.

The court continued the case, with a suggestion

. . . to the councel to take more time to consider of other exceptions, for if these be over-ruled your clyent is gone, viz. must be hanged.[236]

It was not only criminal penalties that stimulated the ingenious exception. There was, for example, the form called *outlawry* for starting a civil suit against an absent defendant. With this process, it was possible that a suit might go to execution without notice to the defendant of the proceedings.[237] Here was a sphere for technicality. Watch your Latin! (Section 47.)

A writ to the sheriff stuttered out: *praecipipimus vobis,* instead of the one syllable shorter *praecipimus vobis* [we command you]. This brought from the Chief Justice:

If the word be *praecipipimus,* then there is no command to the sherif, for that word signifies nothing, therefore let the outlawry be reversed . . .[238]

In another outlawry,

Instead of *proxim,* there is used *px.* for an abbreviation of it, without any dash. 2 ly. Instead of *infra scr.* the abbreviation of *infra scriptam* there is used *infra sr.* And for these exceptions it was quashed.[239]

The finer the distinctions drawn, the more detailed were the documents drafted. Each distinction was reflected in more words. And each rash of words brought still further distinctions — now reduced to print for future lawyers to reproduce. Around and around.

89. *The expanding law*

Despite apparent rigidity and archaism in the laws of England (Section 88), English law continued to grow, adapting itself (if slowly)

---

[235] *King v. Wood,* 82 Eng. Rep. 598 (K.B. 1649).
[236] *King v. Andrews,* 82 Eng. Rep. 556 (K.B. 1649).
[237] 9 Holdsworth, *A History of English Law* 254-255 (1926).
[238] *Griffith v. Thomas,* 82 Eng. Rep. 755 (Banc. Sup. 1652).
[239] *Coswell,* 82 Eng. Rep. 629 (Banc. Sup. 1649); see also *Custodes Libert. &c. v. White,* 82 Eng. Rep. 666 (Banc. Sup. 1650).

to the needs of an age of revolution, discovery, and commerce. (Sections 77, 78.)

Thus there were common law borrowings from the customs of the foreign merchants and traders with whom Englishmen did business, the Italians for instance — whose sixteenth-century *polizza* (schedule, bill) was the first insurance *policy* (French) in England.[240]   This history is still memorialized in English insurance policies which give promise of

> . . . as much Force and Effect as the surest Writing or Policy of Assurance heretofore made in *Lombard-street* . . .[241]

The Italian policies of *assicuranza* (traceable to late Latin words meaning "to make secure") gave English a specialized use outside the land law for the Old French *assurance* — the conveyancer's pet.   In the seventeenth century *assurance* and *insurance* — both with the same meaning — came into general English usage.[242]   (The *assurance* form survives chiefly in England for life policies.)[243]

Early policies of insurance reflected their homely origins.   For the *law merchant* (half Old English, half Old French, from medieval Latin *lex mercatoria*, but English since the fifteenth century)[244] was at first a law practiced not by lawyers but by businessmen and seafarers.   (Section 75.)   A 1692 policy on the cargo of the *Maria* superstitiously and candidly verbalizes the sentiment still present in the minds of insurers:

> Memorandum.   The assurers do hereby covenant, promise and oblidge themselves, their heirs, executors and goods in Case of loss happening (which God forbid) to Satisfie and pay . . .[245]

There was similar piety in the *bill* (*schedule* or *little book*, depending on a disputed Latin or French origin)[246] of *lading* (Old English, loading) — an English expression from the sixteenth century.   At least as late as the eighteenth century, a *bill of lading* read:

---

[240] *Oxford English Dictionary;* compare 5 Holdsworth, *A History of English Law* 79 n.2 (1924).

[241] Park, *A System of the Law of Marine Insurance* 524 (app. No. 1) (1787).

[242] *Oxford English Dictionary,* under *assurance, assure, ensurance, ensure, insurance, insure;* compare 5 Holdsworth, *A History of English Law* 79 n.2 (1924).

[243] 1 Jowitt, gen. ed., *The Dictionary of English Law;* Fowler, *A Dictionary of Modern English Usage* (3d ed. 1937).

[244] *Oxford English Dictionary,* under *merchant,* and compare *law-merchant.*

[245] Burrell, *Reports of Cases Determined by the High Court of Admiralty* 268 (Marsden ed. 1885).

[246] Compare *Oxford English Dictionary,* under *bill,* and *Medieval Latin Word-List* (1934), under *billa,* with Millar, "The Lineage of Some Procedural Words," 25 A.B.A.J. 1023, 1025 (1939).

"Shipped by the Grace of God, in good order . . . and by God's Grace bound for Liverpool . . . And so God send the good ship to her desired port in Safety. Amen."[247]

In the sixteenth century, *bills of exchange* (Anglo-Norman) also became current as an expression in English. In the next century, *negotiate* (from the Latin for "not quiet") and *paper* (Anglo-Norman from Latin for Greek *papyrus*) — both in today's commercial sense — were part of the English language. This wonderful *paper*, endowed with the trader's brevity of trust and immediacy, gave a new and precise seventeenth-century meaning to Old French *order*.

More business activity also pushed forward the law of contract. *Consideration* (Latin, via twelfth-century French) had been in general English as early as Chaucer to mean contemplation. In the fifteenth century, *consideration* had been used by Fortescue as the reason or motive for something.[248] With this sense, it was incorporated in sixteenth-century Latin recitals of indebtedness for a declaration in *indebitatus assumpsit*.[249] (Section 48.) A seventeenth-century English form of this was:

> . . . in consideration that the aforesaid W. at the instance and special request of the said P. would resign all his term and interest . . .[250]

Distinctions appeared. *Good* consideration (natural affection) was different from *valuable* consideration (money). *Consideration* itself — in the course of the seventeenth and eighteenth centuries — became far removed from contemplation and was not merely reason or motive, although Blackstone still spoke of it as

> . . . the reason which moves the contracting party to enter into the contract.[251]

Consideration became the magical essence of contract-ness. In the words of a seventeenth-century dictionary maker, it was

> . . . the materiall cause of a contract, without the which, no contract bindeth.[252]

The land law too was on the move, spurred by violent, revolutionary changes in the ownership of property. The land law was on the move — in a solemn progression of rules and technical evasions. This was

---

[247] Scrutton, *Charterparties and Bills of Lading* 512 (16th ed. 1955).

[248] *Oxford English Dictionary*, under *consideration*.

[249] Plucknett, *A Concise History of the Common Law* 649 and especially n.2 5th ed. 1956).

[250] Brownlow, *Declarations, Counts, and Pleadings in English: The Second Part* 51 (1654).

[251] 2 Blackstone, *Commentaries* °433°444 (Jones ed. 1916).

[252] Cowell, *The Interpreter* (1637); see also Blount, *Nomo-Lexikon* (1670).

the day of the ingenious conveyancer: the computers of the infinite, logical word slicers, dealers in metaphysical wraiths — remainders and reversions, shifting and springing uses, trustees for possibilities yet unborn. This is the period of the blue-ribbon cases of the law of future interests: *Shelley's Case*,[253] *Archer's Case*,[254] *Pells v. Brown*,[255] *The Duke of Norfolk's Case*,[256] *Perrin v. Blake*,[257] etc.[258]

The stars in this drama of word mongering were learned conveyancers of the bar — and Sir Orlando Bridgman led all the rest. Were contingent remainders destructible?[259] Then words by Bridgman would make them indestructible — trustees to preserve contingent remainders.[260] Here is one of his paragraphs, preserved by a faithful clerk in a formbook of Bridgman's precedents ". . . Concerning the Most Considerable Estates in England." It is a single sentence, one that contributed to the legal sharpness and to the literary delinquency of the English bar:

And from and after the determination of that Estate, *To the use* and behoof of H.K. of the *Inner-Temple* L. Gent. his Heirs and Assigns, for and during the Natural life of the said W.P. upon Trust only, for preserving the contingent Uses and Estates herein after-limited, and to make Entries for the same, if it shall be needful: But that the said H.K. his Heirs or Assigns shall not convert the Rents, Issues or Profits thereof, or any part thereof, to his or their own use.[261]

The memory of Sir Francis Moore was kept brighter by his contribution of a device to avoid the Statute of Enrollments.[262] The bargain and sale of a *freehold* must be enrolled, a public record. But for those who desired secrecy, Sir Francis showed that a few more words set the Statute to one side. Don't bargain and sell a freehold. Bargain and sell a *term*, and then *release* to the tenant. Same result, but no enrollment.[263]

253 *Wolfe v. Shelley*, 76 Eng. Rep. 199, 76 Eng. Rep. 206 (K.B. 1579-1581).
254 *Baldwin v. Smith*, 76 Eng. Rep. 139, 76 Eng. Rep. 146 (C.P. 1597).
255 79 Eng. Rep. 504 (K.B. 1620).
256 *Howard v. Duke of Norfolk*, 3 Ch. Cas. 1 (1682).
257 96 Eng. Rep. 392 (K.B. 1769), rev'd, 98 Eng. Rep. 355 (Ex. Ch. 1772).
258 Leach, *Cases and Materials on the Law of Future Interests* (1935).
259 *Archer's Case* (*Baldwin v. Smith*), 76 Eng. Rep. 139, 76 Eng. Rep. 146 (C.P. 1597); *Chudleigh's Case* (*Dillon v. Freine*), 76 Eng. Rep. 261, 76 Eng. Rep. 270 (K.B. 1589-1595).
260 7 Holdsworth, *A History of English Law* 111-114 (ed. 1926).
261 Bridgman, *Sir Orlando Bridgman's Conveyances* 199 (1682).
262 Statute of Enrollments, 1536, 27 Hen. VIII, c. 16; 7 Holdsworth, *A History of English Law* 361 (ed. 1926).
263 See *Lutwich v. Mitton*, 79 Eng. Rep. 516 (Ct. of Wards 1621); 2 Blackstone, *Commentaries* °339 (Jones ed. 1916); 7 Holdsworth, *A History of English Law* 360-362 (ed. 1926).

Bridgman and Moore were using words to avoid the results of other words, working with accepted symbols to effect a client's intent. Could the law carry out that intent even when the wrong symbols were used? Heaven forbid, said the conveyancers.

This was the nub of the bar-shaking controversy over *Perrin v. Blake.*[264] It was a conveyancer — proud of his craft, forceful of language, and careful even of punctuation[265] (Section 84), who stated the case for the *term of art.* This is Charles Fearne (1772) speaking for the Rule in Shelley's Case:

> It must be admitted that those who shall argue against the strict observance of the rule I have been speaking of, may sometimes chance to have the intention of the testator on their side; but let them consider whether a rule of law, inviolably observed for more than three hundred years past, can ever be a decent sacrifice to the presumptive construction of an indetermined or illiterate testator's intention. So long as certain technical expressions shall be allowed their fixed legal import and operation, it is in any man's power to secure the limitation of his property from litigation and precarious construction, by applying to those whose business it is to be acquainted with the force and import of such expressions.
>
> .   .   .   .
>
> If no technical expressions are to be exempt from the operation of an occasional construction, where is the testator who can make his own will? The most careful and guarded endeavours which a man shall exert for that end, will only amount to leaving some precarious instructions behind him, the force and effect of which must depend on the discretion or disposition of those in whom the power of construction shall be reposed for the time being; it is their discernment, humanity, or spirit of improving old laws, must in fact *make* the will of every testator in the kingdom.[266]

The conveyancers taught lessons not always well understood, but never completely lost on future generations of lawyers. The helpful lesson they taught was that rules are made to cover generalities and that proper words can prevent you from becoming a generality. They taught a fierce respect for words that were both so well seasoned and so generally understood that no craftsman could misunderstand them — the term of art (Section 13) — but the same ferocity sometimes came to the defense of words that were only well seasoned. (Section

---

[264] Leach, "Note: The Controversy over Perrin v. Blake," *Cases and Materials on the Law of Future Interests* 134-138 (1935).

[265] Fearne, *An Essay on the Learning of Contingent Remainders and Executory Devises,* errata at p. x, and compare p. 26 (1772).

[266] Fearne, *An Essay on the Learning of Contingent Remainders and Executory Devises* 21-22 (1772).

120.) Finally, they also taught that form — form alone — might triumph over substance.[267]

90. Complex rules of pleading

The intricacy of form (Section 89) was nowhere more apparent than in the rules of pleading, which became more complex as the business of lawyers and the courts increased. Legislation had not yet attained its present standing as a cure-all, so the judges of England, with the assistance — or connivance — of the bar, worked out most of their problems for themselves. Here, as elsewhere (Sections 88, 89), technicality was a substitute for legislation.

Special sets of rules were developed around each of the numerous forms of action. Special sets of rules for each tier of pleading — for declaration, plea, replication, rejoinder, surrejoinder, rebutter, and surrebutter. The only thread of guidance through the labyrinth was form. And this the bench insisted upon. It was not a question of saying it clearly, but of saying it according to pattern. Deviation meant failure.[268] Therefore, use a formbook. (Section 78.) But these, except in the most routine cases, gave only the illusion of security. (Section 94.) The greater the complexity of pleadings, the more paper work, the more delay, and the greater opportunity for small error. In Coke's words (which he applied only to the time of Henry VI, 1422-1461),

. . . the Judges gave a quicker ear to exceptions to pleadings . . .[269]

It was an unimaginative barrister who could not find an undotted *i*.

A declaration in replevin for one hundred sheep was good, but a declaration in replevin for one hundred sheep, ewes and wethers, was bad:

. . . you have made that which was certain, to be incertain by the specification you have made, . . .[270]

Plaintiff had judgment on a verdict in debt. Held: material error,

. . . that the sum demanded to be due for rent was in figures, and not in words, as it ought to be. 2 ly. It is said, that the jury *assideint damna* for *assident damna* [assessed damages].[271]

[267] See Leach, "Perpetuities in Perspective: Ending the Rule's Reign of Terror," 65 Harv. L. Rev. 721-749 (1952).
[268] 9 Holdsworth, *A History of English Law* 284-285 (1926).
[269] Coke, *Commentary upon Littleton*, f. 304b (10th ed. 1703).
[270] *More v. Clipsam*, 82 Eng. Rep. 538 (K.B. 1648).
[271] *Hobson v. Heywood*, 82 Eng. Rep. 552 (K.B. 1648).

Plaintiff had a verdict, slandered by the defendant's words:

. . . Thou mutton-monger theef bring home my stolen hay.

Judgment arrested, for the declaration did not say the words were spoken of the plaintiff. This omission had been supplied before trial, in the replication, but,

> Roll Iustice said, one cannot rejoyn upon words, which are not in the declaration nor in the plea; for if the declaration, and the plea be naught, the replication cannot make them good.[272]

A declaration said that a trespass in the reign of Charles II continued into the reign of James II, and concluded with the words:

contra pacem domini Regis nunc [against the peace of our lord the present King.]

The declaration was held bad on general demurrer, for *against the peace* was matter of substance, not form; it should have said:

> *tam contra pacem dicti nuper Regis,*
> against the peace of the said late King,
> *quam Domini Regis nunc.*[273]
> as well as of our lord the present King.

In trespass, ". . . for digging in his ground, and carrying away 200 load of soyl . . ." Judgment arrested, because the declaration did not say explicitly that the soil carried away came from the ground that was dug:

> . . . an intendment cannot make it good. . . . it is too generallie laid.[274]

An improper denial was a fatal admission. For example, you were sued for rent on a lease of four rooms. It was not enough to plead that it was really a lease of five rooms, that the lessor had put you out of the fifth room, and so wasn't entitled to rent. You must add to this plea: *absque hoc* (without this) or *et non* (and not), that plaintiff leased four rooms only. Otherwise you have admitted the lease of four rooms, and judgment is for the plaintiff.[275] This sort of "diseased

---

272 82 Eng. Rep. 537, 538 (K.B. 1648).
273 *Ingleton v. Burges,* 90 Eng. Rep. 408, 409 (K.B. 1688).
274 *Anon.,* 82 Eng. Rep. 516 (K.B. 1648).
275 *Samon v. Smyth,* 84 Eng. Rep. 293 (1680), 84 Eng. Rep. 295 (1680); se also *Salmon v. Smith* in 5 Bacon, *A New Abridgment of the Law* 383-384 (5 ed. 1798); and see Stephen, *A Treatise on the Principles of Pleading* 188-2 App., Note 50, pp. lvii-lviii (1824).

technicality"[276] made pleaders at the English bar apprehensive and wary. The uneasy feeling of being watched has never left the profession, and is reflected in the language of the law in numerous clauses of precaution: *without prejudice, without admitting, without conceding, if any, claimed, supposed, pretended, purported, imagined, alleged.* (Section 17.)

Similarly, there developed an almost endless multiplication of counts and phrasing to avoid the strict rules on variance. Proof of an indebtedness of £12.0.0 for goods sold, in an action brought to recover £14.0.0 for goods sold, resulted in a reversal of judgment for plaintiff. This was a variance.[277] In one writ a juror was called *Cargenter* and in another writ *Carpenter.* This too was a variance, which arrested a judgment after verdict.[278] To avoid such faultfinding, say the same thing several ways; call a person by a name and an alias; make it long; make it detailed. Thus a habit of singsong verbosity. (See Section 91.)

91. *Three hogsheads of cyder*

The combination of insistence on form (Sections 87, 90), a popular habit of longwindedness (Section 85), Latin inversions (Section 80), and a lack of punctuation (Sections 82-84), resulted in pleadings like this one — a plea of justification to a declaration in trespass and assault. It is taken from the 1741 edition of one of the better formbooks.[279] (Impatient readers may skip to the italicized portion, which gives the essence though not the full flavor of "three hogsheads of cyder.")

> And the said Edward by L.S. his attorney comes and defends the force and injury when &c. and as to the force and arms, the said Edward says, that he is not guilty thereof, as the said William Cooke above against him complains: And of this he puts himself on the Country [trial by jury]: And the said William Cooke thereof likewise: And as to the residue of the trespass aforesaid above supposed to be committed, the same Edward says, that the said William Cooke ought not to have this action against him, because he says, that one Laurence Jersey, at Tyley, otherwise Trinley aforesaid, before the said time when the trespass aforesaid is supposed to be committed, to wit, on the same 29th day of October in the year abovesaid, was possessed of three hogsheads of cyder, as of his own proper goods; and he the said Lau-

---

[276] Pollock, *Essays in Jurisprudence and Ethics* 258-259 (1882), and quoted in 9 Holdsworth, *A History of English Law* 313 n.2 (1926).

[277] *Devereux v. Jackson,* Style 477 (Banc. Sup. 1655), reported *sub nom. Devereux v. Johnson,* 82 Eng. Rep. 876 (Banc. Sup. 1655).

[278] *Kitchinman,* 82 Eng. Rep. 789 (Banc. Sup. 1655).

[279] Lilly, *Modern Entries* 456-457 (2d Eng. ed. 1741).

rence being so as aforesaid possessed of the said three hogsheads of cyder, before the said time when, &c. to wit, on the same 29th day of October, at Tyley, otherwise Trinley, aforesaid, the same three hogsheads of cyder delivered to one Richard Baxter, to be safely kept, and from thence to Gloucester in the County of the same city to be carried; by virtue whereof the said Richard Baxter of the said three hogsheads of cyder was possessed: And farther the same Edward says that the said Richard Baxter being so as aforesaid of the said three hogsheads of cyder possessed, the said William Cooke at the said time when, &c. to wit, on the same 29th day of October abovesaid, at Tyley, otherwise Trinley aforesaid, the said three hogsheads of cyder from the possession and custody of the said R. Baxter would and endeavoured to take and carry away, and on one J. Baxter, the wife of the said R. Baxter, then and there the same three hogsheads of cyder for the same R. Baxter keeping, and the possession thereof preserving, then and there made an assault, and her then and there beat, wounded and abused; wherefore the same Edward, then and there being then the servant of the said Richard Baxter, as the servant of the said Richard Baxter, the said Jane, the wife of the said Richard Baxter his said master, and the possession of the said Richard Baxter his master of the said three hogsheads of cyder, lest the said W. Cooke should the said Jane farther hurt and overpower, and the said three hogsheads of cyder from the custody and possession of the said Richard Baxter, the said master of the said Edward, should take and carry away, and for the preservation of the possession of the said Richard Baxter, the said master of him the said Edward, of the said three hogsheads of cyder, against the said William Cooke did defend, as he lawfully might; and thereupon the said William Cooke on him the said Edward did then and there make an assault, and him the said Edward would have beat and abused, wherefore the same Edward did then and there defend himself against the said William Cooke; which is the same residue of the trespass whereof the said William above thereof now complains; *and so the same Edward says that the injury or damage, if any, then and there happened to the same William Cooke, it arose from the proper assault of him the said William Cooke, and· in defence of the said Jane, the wife of the said Richard Baxter, the master of him the said Edward, and of the possession of the said Richard Baxter, the master of him the said Edward, of the said three hogsheads of Cyder, and in defence of him the said Edward:* And this same Edward is ready to verify: Wherefore he prays judgment if the said William Cooke ought to have his action aforesaid against him, &c.

T. Parker.

One sentence.

92. *The piecework system*

Venality also played a role in stretching the language of the law. This was one of the side effects of a system of corrupt officialdom, which, taking its cue from the top, saw to it that — Magna Carta or no — justice was sold, denied, and delayed.

James, the King of England, intervened in pending litigation through his man Lord Buckingham.   The King's favorite repeatedly and brazenly wrote "My honourable Lord," the Chancellor of England, advising on the course of litigation:

> I have heretofore recommended unto your lordship the determination of the causes between . . .
>
> [January 9, 1617]

> I thank your lordship for your favour to Sir George Tipping . . . I desire your lordship's farther favour . . .
>
> [January 23, 1617]

> . . . desiring you to show him what favour you lawfully may . . .
>
> [April 20, 1618]

> Whereas in Mr. Hansbye's cause, which formerly, by my means, both his majesty and myself recommended to your lordship's favour, your lordship thought good, upon a hearing thereof, to decree some part for the young gentleman . . .
>
> [June 12, 1618] [280]

These were not the only pressures on Francis Bacon.   Before being permanently removed from judicial office, he signed a detailed confession in which he acknowledged receiving from litigants everything from money to gold buttons.[281]   In other writings, Bacon conceded,

> . . . I may be frail, and partake of the abuses of the times . . .[282]

adding later:

> . . . they were not the greatest offenders in Israel upon whom the wall fell.[283]

He yet felt himself ". . . the justest chancellor" in forty years,[284] and could even rationalize a state of moral purity:

> With respect to this charge of bribery, I am as innocent as any born upon St. Innocent's day: I never had bribe or reward in my eye or thought when pronouncing sentence or order.[285]

Courts of Bacon's day were not supported by sufficient public funds to permit of even justice.   Judges were expected to contribute to their

[280] 7 Bacon, *Works* 436-439 (Montagu ed. 1827).
[281] 16 Bacon, *Works* ccclix-ccclxix (Montagu ed. 1834).
[282] 16 Bacon, *Works* ccclxxiii (Montagu ed. 1834).
[283] 16 Bacon, *Works* ccclxxiv n.(a) (Montagu ed. 1834).
[284] 16 Bacon, *Works* ccclxxiii (Montagu ed. 1834).
[285] 16 Bacon, *Works* cccxlv-cccxlvi (Montagu ed. 1834).

own support by the sale of subordinate court offices, and they did.[286] Moreover, like any other group of merchants, the judges tried to make their wares more sought after, their salable offices more profitable, by attracting more of the business of litigation to their particular courts. For example, the court of Common Pleas did a thriving business in *debt*, an action that could not be brought in the court of King's Bench. King's Bench grabbed off some of the business by implying an *assumpsit*, and treating the *debt* as an *indebitatus assumpsit*.[287]   (Section 48.)

The purchaser was seised of a public office as of any other property. It was expected that he would make the property pay for itself, and he entered the market place to do it.   Chief Justice Sir Matthew Hale (d. 1676) noted:

> The scambling and scuffling between the prothonotaries, each one striving to get as many as he can to bring grist to his mill . . .[288]

One of the ways a public office was made to pay for itself was in fees for preparing and filing documents.   The more documents the bigger the fees.   For the sake of fees to the Chancery clerks, litigants were required to pay for *office* (i.e., official) *copies* wanted or not, sometimes paid for whether prepared or not — the so-called *dead copies*.[289] Payment for unwanted, useless, or dead copies was a species of blackmail or bribery to get things moved along, *expedition money* in the vernacular of the early eighteenth century.[290]   Payment of ". . . any sommes of money . . . for expedicion . . ." of documents had been prohibited since the sixteenth century,[291] but down into the nineteenth the evil persisted.   As one solicitor then testified:

> [The registrars] do not take money; but the office copy is the registrar's hood.[292]

Since fees for preparing documents were based on the number of sheets, there was also art in lengthening documents to consume more sheets.   This was a brash and mechanical art — wholly distinct from

---

[286] See 1 Holdsworth, *A History of English Law* 684-686, 686-688 (3d ed. 1922).

[287] Plucknett, *A Concise History of the Common Law* 644-646 (5th ed. 1956).

[288] Hale, "Considerations Touching the Amendment or Alteration of Lawes," in 1 Hargrave, ed., *A Collection of Tracts* 285-287 (1787).

[289] 9 Holdsworth, *A History of English Law* 362 (1926).

[290] 11 *The Harleian Miscellany* 54 (new ed. 1810); compare *Oxford English Dictionary*, under *expedition*.

[291] Quoted in *Oxford English Dictionary*, under *expedition*, No. 4.

[292] Quoted in 1 Holdsworth, *A History of English Law* 442 (3d ed. 1922).

the finer art of word selection. (Section 93.) A seventeenth-century tract gives this description:

> . . . the under-clerks, with their large margins, with their great distances between their lines, with protraction of words, and with their many dashes and slashes, put in places of words, lay their greediness open to the whole world; . . . I did see an answer to a bill of forty of their sheets, which copied out, was brought to six sheets; in which copy there was very sufficient margin left, and good distance between the lines. . . . that copy, which should have cost but four shillings, cost four nobles[293] [more than twenty-five shillings].[294]

Overcharging for blank space was such a patent fraud that measures were early taken to control it. Francis Bacon, as Lord Chancellor (1618-1622), invoked one remedy:

> All copies in chancery shall contain fifteen lines in every sheet thereof, written orderly and unwastefully . . .[295]

A hundred years later, the first Georgian legislation on the language of the law (Section 76) was still laboring the same theme, requiring of legal papers that,

> . . . the lines and words of the same to be written at least as close as the said acts usually are, . . .[296]

Another approach to the evil was to fix the number of words in a sheet. The rule for office copies was ninety words per sheet in Chancery, seventy-eight in the Exchequer, and seventy-two in the court of King's Bench.[297] (Court reporters still base their fees on such a scheme, so much per *folio* — Latin for *leaf* — which in the United States is normally one hundred words.)[298] Interpreted as a requirement of a minimum number of words per sheet, these rules appeared to assure the litigant some relief on fees gauged by the sheet. But the number of words also came to be interpreted as a maximum, for purposes of fixing stamp duties (per sheet) on certain types of documents.[299] So it was a modified relief. Further, as Blackstone pointed out, the per sheet word limitation — coupled with the Georgian ban on Latin (Sections 76, 80) — worsened the litigant's plight:

[293] Carey, "The Present State of England," in 3 *The Harleian Miscellany* 552, 560-561 (new ed. 1809).

[294] See *Oxford English Dictionary*, under *noble*.

[295] "Bacon's Ordinances," par. 67, in 5 Bacon, *Works* 287 (Montagu ed. 1826).

[296] Records in English, 1731, 4 Geo. II, c. 26.

[297] *Denn, ex dimiss. Lucas v. Fulford*, 97 Eng. Rep. 775 (K.B. 1761).

[298] *Oxford English Dictionary*, under *folio*; 17 *Words and Phrases* (perm. ed. 1958), "folio."

[299] See *Denn, ex dimiss. Lucas v. Fulford*, 97 Eng. Rep. 775, 777 (K.B. 1761).

And it has much enhanced the expense of all legal proceedings: for since practicers are confined (for the sake of the stamp duties, which are thereby considerably increased) to write only a stated number of words in a sheet, and as the English language, through the multitude of its particles, is much more verbose than the Latin, it follows that the number of sheets must be very much augmented by the change.[300]

Regulation of lines per sheet and words per sheet were puny challenges to ingenuity. In a venal world, there were those more than ready to confirm the seventeenth-century critic in his opinion:

> Thus you see the old saying true: "If you go to law for a nut, the lawyers will crack it, give each of you half the shell, and chop up the kernel themselves." [301]

93. Padding

A more lasting evil encouraged by the piecework system (Section 92), which no regulation of lines and words per sheet could cure, was the padding of documents with unnecessary words. Here the ground becomes more familiar to the twentieth-century practitioner.

A conservative seventeenth-century statement by a Chief Justice summarizes the vice:

> There are certain unreasonable impertinences used . . . which doth not only exceedingly prejudice the people, but . . . serves for no other use but to swell the attorney's bill, and at present helps fill their prothonotaries' pocket, and to reimburse with advantage the purchase of his place . . .[302]

Lawyers and clerks — both paid by the length of their documents[303] —found one convenient means of increasing the size of document and fee in the *recital*. (The word itself was introduced into English from French or Latin by sixteenth-century legal draftsmen, preceded in the fifteenth century by *recite*, also from legal usage.)[304] The possibilities of the recital were unlimited. An original writ would be repeated without need in the declaration and in the writ summoning the jury, tripling the litigant's expense.[305] A Chancery order would recite without need both the bill and answers, sometimes increasing the cost of

---

[300] 3 Blackstone, *Commentaries* °322-°323 (Jones ed. 1916).

[301] Carey, "The Present State of England," in 3 *The Harleian Miscellany* 552, 558 (new ed. 1809).

[302] Hale, "Considerations Touching the Amendment or Alteration of Lawes," in 1 Hargrave, ed., *A Collection of Tracts* 287 (1787).

[303] 9 Holdsworth, *A History of English Law* 364 (1926).

[304] *Oxford English Dictionary*, under *recital*.

[305] Hale "Considerations Touching the Amendment or Alteration of Lawes," in 1 Hargrave, ed., *A Collection of Tracts* 287 (1787).

preparing the order from thirty shillings to £10 or £15. Court clerks reached out to the bar to add to their supply of recital material:

> And, as instructions for them to act by, they require one of the council's briefs, which necessarily contains the whole state of the case, by which they furnish themselves with matter of lengthening the orders (of which their own interests prompts them to make use) by which means the recitals and allegations are spun out to a tedious length, and oftentimes the whole brief inserted . . .[306]

Orders would recite without need the opposing allegations of counsel,

> . . . which still serves to lengthen them; whence it happens, that the orders often carry in them contradictory, and sometimes very idle and impertinent allegations, for which the order itself has been afterward discharged.[307]

Over the years many expedients were tried in an effort to curtail this custom of verbosity. The most dramatic occurred in the case of *Milward v. Welden*,[308] in 1556. Plaintiff's replication had been stretched from an adequate sixteen pages to one hundred and twenty. The hand of the Chancellor struck, hitting not the draftsman[309] but his hapless client. In addition to a £10 fine and imprisonment,

> "It is therefore ordered that the Warden of the Fleet shall take the said Richard Mylward . . . into his custody, and shall bring him unto Westminster Hall on Saturday next . . . and there and then shall cut a hole in the myddest of the same engrossed replication . . . and put the said Richard's head through the same hole, and so let the same replication hang about his shoulders with the written side outward; and then, the same so hanging, shall lead the same Richard, bare headed and bare faced, round about Westminster Hall, whilst the courts are sitting. and shall shew him at the bar of every of the three courts within the Hall." [310]

Francis Bacon, when Chancellor, extended the threat of punishment to include counsel. Rule 55 of his Chancery Ordinances reads:

> If any bill, answers, replication, or rejoinder, shall be found of an immoderate length, both the party and the counsel under whose hand it passeth shall be fined.[311]

"Immoderate length" was as variable as the length of the chancellor's foot. Lord Chancellor Coventry (1625-1640) tried to be more specific. His Rule 24 said:

[306] 11 *The Harleian Miscellany* 54 (new ed. 1810).
[307] 11 *The Harleian Miscellany* 54 (new ed. 1810).
[308] 21 Eng. Rep. 136 (Ch. 1566).
[309] Compare 5 Holdsworth, *A History of English Law* 233 (1924).
[310] Quoted in 5 Holdsworth, *A History of English Law* 233 n.7 (1924).
[311] 7 Bacon, *Works* 285, and see also 255 (Montagu ed. 1827).

"Whereas, the Masters of the Court do sometimes, by way of inducement, fill a leaf or two of the beginning of their reports, and sometimes
more, with a long and particular recital of the several points of the
orders of reference; they shall forbear such iterations, the same appearing sufficiently in the order, and without any other repetition than thus,
'according to any order' or 'by direction of an order of such a date,'
shall fall directly into the matter of their report, setting down the same
clearly, but as briefly as they can for the ease both of the Court and the
parties." [312]

These and other efforts were equally ineffective. Like trying to stop
a leaky faucet by stuffing it with wadding. (It was not until the reforming nineteenth century that Lord Tenterden published *Models of
Conciseness* . . . , e.g., the common counts, and ordered lawyers to
conform in brevity at the risk of themselves paying the costs for excess
length. See Section 111.)[313] In the meantime matters grew steadily
worse, accompanied by mounting complaint against the law, individual
lawyers, and the whole profession. (Sections 94, 95, 96.)

94. *The unreformed law*

The greatest obstacle to improvement of the language of the law
was the mounting size and disorder of the law itself. Business, exploration, commerce, and religious reform were moving faster than
the law (Section 89), adding new burdens, decisions, and statutes.
(Section 78.) The business of the courts had outdistanced their
capacities. Venality (Sections 92, 93), precedent, and habit blocked
any real reform.

Sir Francis Bacon, when attorney general (1613-1617), had drafted
a proposal for *Compiling and Amendment of the Laws of England*.
He found the confusions of the law so disturbing that with this focus
even his arch enemy looked good:

. . . to give every man his due, had it not been for Sir Edward Coke's
Reports . . . the law, by this time, had been almost like a ship without
ballast; . . .[314]

Bacon envisioned a general overhaul. He said, for example, that the
law was cluttered with overruled cases:

. . . they do but fill the volumes, and season the wits of students in a
contrary sense of law.[315]

---

[312] Quoted in 1 Spence, *The Equitable Jurisdiction of the Court of Chancery*
404 (1846).
[313] 3 Chitty, *A Treatise on Pleading* 1409-1416 (9th American from 6th Lon-
den ed. 1844).
[314] 5 Bacon, *Works* 342 (Montagu ed. 1827).
[315] 5 Bacon, *Works* 348 (Montagu ed. 1827).

Possibly it was Bacon's comment that inspired Henry Fielding to create *Tim Vinegar*, the fifth-year law student at Lincoln's Inn, who gave it as his opinion (1739) that:

> . . . nothing is more hurtful to a perfect knowledge of the law than reading it . . .[316]

The cases, continued Bacon, were ". . . reported with too great prolixity . . ." They should be more tightly reported, ". . . tautologies and impertinences to be cut off . . ."[317]

The law, he said, was full of doubts, and he gave a classification of doubt in the law that has lost none of its vigor in more than three hundred years:

> Mark, whether the doubts that arise, are only in cases not of ordinary experience; or which happen every day. If in the first only, impute it to the fraility of man's foresight, that cannot reach by law to all cases; but if in the latter, be assured there is a fault in the law.[318]

One of the evils of this failure in the law was,

> That the ignorant lawyer shroudeth his ignorance of law, in that doubts are so frequent and many.[319]

Bentham later expanded this point to assert with more vitriol that ". . . the power of the lawyer is in the uncertainty of the law."[320]

Again foreshadowing Bentham (Section 109), Bacon proposed to remove some of the uncertainty with a digest of the laws of England on the model of the civilians.[321] Such a model had been suggested before, but dispite its weaknesses the common law had been vigorous enough to beat off its classic rival. In Maitland's paraphrase, ". . . the live dog may be better than the dead lion."[322] The common lawyers were not prepared to abandon their ". . . wilderness of single instances"[323] in favor of authoritarian principle. A man for the common law was still to be "Willy the milman" (Section 87), and not a bloodless generality.

The alternative that the common law adopted was more of precedent than principle. Precedent was piled high on precedent, flattening out

[316] 1 *The Champion* 127 (Dec. 25, 1739).
[317] 5 Bacon, *Works* 349 (Montagu ed. 1827).
[318] 5 Bacon, *Works* 342 (Montagu ed. 1827).
[319] 5 Bacon, *Works* 342 (Montagu ed. 1827).
[320] 10 Bentham, *Works* 429 (Bowring ed. 1843).
[321] 5 Bacon, *Works* 337-361 (Montagu ed. 1827).
[322] Maitland, "English Law and the Renaissance," in 1 *Select Essays in Anglo-American Legal History* 168, 201 (1907); see Eccl. 9:4.
[323] Tennyson, *Aylmer's Field* (1855).

not only earlier precedent but sometimes principle as well. Precedent on precedent, not merely in reports, but in the multiple forms for conveyancing and pleading, forms whose weight effectively squeezed the remaining literary juices out of the language of the law.

The very existence of the *forms* made it possible for more *form* to be insisted upon, and this in turn required more forms. (Sections 78, 87, 88, 90.)

On this process continued, down into the nineteenth century, when a Parliamentary commission reported:

> "The extreme precision required is scarcely practicable, except in pleadings of well-known character and daily occurrence, in which generations of suitors, having paid costs for the settlement of the law, the pleadings have become easy and intelligible." [324]

The law and its forms were apparently inseparable.

95. *The unreformed profession*

While forms with the force of precedent could serve some useful function (Sections 78, 90, 94), neither precedent nor general utility alone would explain their tight hold on the profession.

The bar's conservatism — inertia — was a factor, here stated by a seventeenth-century Lord Chief Justice of England, Sir Matthew Hale, as incisively as it has ever been put since:

> By long use and custom men, especially that are aged and have been long educated in the profession and practice of the law, contract a kind of superstitious veneration of it beyond what is just and reasonable. . . . They tenaciously and rigorously maintain these very *forms* and proceedings and practices which, though possibly at first they were seasonable and useful, yet by the very change of matters they become not only useless and impertinent, but burthensome and inconvenient and prejudicial to the common justice and the common good of mankind: not considering the *forms* and prescripts of lawes were not introduced for their own sake, but for the use of public justice; and therefore, when they become insipid, useless, impertinent, and possibly derogatory to the end, they may and must be removed. [325]

Hale's argument speaks of men "long educated in the profession and practice of the law." And certainly there were these among the draftsmen and users of the writings of the law. Thus, for example, Henry VIII's divorce left numbers of well-educated and trained members of the English bar unable to appear in court because they refused

---

[324] Quoted in 9 Holdsworth, *A History of English Law* 285 n.2 (1926).
[325] Hale, "Considerations Touching the Amendment or Alteration of Lawes," in 1 Hargrave, ed., *A Collection of Tracts* 264 (1787).

to abandon Catholicism to suit the state.[326] They often became specialists in conveyancing, along with some of their educated Protestant
colleagues. Some men of learning became specialists in the drafting
of pleadings, and others had an intensely practical competence in
pleading precedents. An educated barrister might also advise on the
drafting or polishing of a written pleading, and ultimately he would
sign it.

But the mass of the routine documents of the law being turned out
— pleadings, writs, wills, bonds, leases, covenants, simple contracts —
were not drafted by the best-educated or best-trained English lawyers.
More often, the writings of the law were drafted by the court clerks,
the scriveners, the attorneys (as distinct from barristers), and the
solicitors. The bulk of these papers were being drafted and used by
men either poorly trained for the law, or trained for the law not at all
— many who today would be called "laymen," with no more competence in law (let alone literary usage) than today's real estate
salesman, escrow clerk, or notary public. (Indeed, as late as the
middle eighteenth century the attorneys of London were locked in a
twelve-year battle with the Society of Scriveners to establish the legal
right of attorneys to practice conveyancing. The Scriveners' claim
that the drawing of deeds was part of their ancient art and mystery
was finally decided in favor of the attorneys in 1760.)[327] Most of these
draftsmen could use a form better than the seventeenth-century sheriff
who ruined a good default judgment by using form names for the
sureties:

> . . . the ignorance of sheriffs, who being to make a return, looked into
> some book of precedents for a form; and finding the names of John Doe
> and Richard Roe put down for examples, made their return accord-
> ingly, . . .[328]

There were nonetheless only few who had the educated competence —
in law or language — to improve on the forms or to disregard them,
if they had wanted to do either.[329]

By the late seventeenth century the Inns of Court, though still
governing the bar, were no longer providing any sort of a regular
education in English law for student lawyers. The availability of

---

[326] See Maitland, "English Law and the Renaissance," in 1 *Select Essays in
Anglo-American Legal History* 168, 185 (1907).
[327] *The Records of the Society of Gentlemen Practisers* xii-lxxii, 246-286 (1897).
[328] *Searle v. Long*, 86 Eng. Rep. 859, 860 (C.P. 1677).
[329] See also Style, *Practical Register* 671 (4th ed. 1707).

printed lawbooks had robbed the Inns of their greatest asset — the former imperative necessity for oral instruction. Students were no longer as interested in the Inns; even less so their teachers. The traditional progression to the bench from the teaching ranks of the Inns had been upset by civil chaos and by the corruption of the age. (Sections 92, 93.) Official favorites became judges without the Inns as a steppingstone. Successful barristers were too busy to instruct. Education in the law became a narrow thing, acquired by clerkship and individual discipline, usually more concerned with how it was done than why it was done. Thus even the barristers were less educated than formerly, and with the lesser ranks of the profession it was worse.

Even minimum requirements for admission to practice as an attorney — five years of apprenticeship and good character — were skipped over on the basis of connection. The Society of Gentlemen Practisers, formed around 1739, made efforts to improve this branch of the profession. And they did succeed in having some of the worst removed from practice; for example, an attorney ". . . who had continued to practice while detained in the Fleet prison . . . ,"[330] a solicitor convicted of highway robbery,[331] etc. But the standards of the profession were woefully low. In one notorious case, a turnkey in the King's Bench prison became articled clerk to an attorney, and only after the attorney had represented prisoners there for two years (sixty-three cases) were the articles ordered canceled. The reporter notes with a straight face:

> The Court were *All* very clear that these Articles were *merely collusive*, . . . that the Exercise of the Office of a *Turnkey in a Prison* was . . . a very improper Education for the Profession of an Attorney . . .[332]

We are not told that the attorney was ever disciplined.[333]

Court clerks were attorneys, and attorneys were court clerks. They worked together, and together increased fees at the client's expense. (Sections 92, 93.) So too with the solicitors in Chancery. It was a business more than a profession. Speaking of the attorneys, Matthew Hale observed (seventeenth century):

[330] Robson, *The Attorney in Eighteenth-Century England* 22 (1959).

[331] 12 Holdsworth, *A History of English Law* 59 (1938); Robson, *The Attorney in Eighteenth-Century England* 23 (1959); *The Records of the Society of Gentlemen Practisers* viii-ix (1897).

[332] *Frazer's Case*, 1 Burrow, pt. 4, p. 291, 97 Eng. Rep. 320 (K.B. 1757).

[333] 12 Holdsworth, *A History of English Law* 58 (1938); Robson, *The Attorney in Eighteenth-Century England* 18 (1959).

Their multitude is so great, that they are not able to live one by another; and upon this account they stirr up suits, and shark upon the few clients they have, and are apt to use tricks and knavery to gain themselves credit with those that employ them.

Hale proposed as a partial cure:

A strict and impartial examination in this kind would cast off abundance of rubbish.[334]

Despite criticism the profession of attorney continued to grow, and to grow with business faster than either could be regulated. The nation's business that had legal overtones was in the hands of the attorneys — and more and more in the hands of the solicitors as well. Rents to be gathered in, estates to be managed, justice to be administered in the local courts, loans to be arranged and collected — all the annoying details of business life which the wealthy could hire done. The scurrying about in the dark and small places of the law and business was a principal part of the profession of attorney, and the practitioners' reputations were thoroughly tainted by the contact.

Ancient complaint about the attorney's chicane (Sections 50, 59) was reinforced in the sixteenth century with the addition to the English language of the opprobrious *pettifogger*, to mean a rascally attorney. In the language-mixing mood of the age, the first part of *pettifogger* was from the French, and the second half from someplace else — no one is quite sure where. It has been related to another word of the sixteenth century, *pettifactor*, for "a legal agent who undertakes small cases." [335] *Pettifogger* was also shortened as the sixteenth-century *fogger*, applied mostly to lawyers, but also to others "given to underhand practice for gain." The *Oxford English Dictionary* thinks it probable that this stems from the *Fugger* family, fifteenth- and sixteenth-century German merchants and financiers whose name in a variety of German spellings came to mean (in German) monopolist, usurer, man of great wealth, and in some dialects huckster.[336]

There is ample evidence that the attorneys tried to improve their professional as well as social status.[337] But the very name *attorney*, a reproach since the late fourteenth century,[338] had become by the

---

[334] Hale, "Considerations Touching the Amendment or Alteration of Lawes," in 1 Hargrave, ed., A Collection of Tracts 286 (1787).
[335] Oxford English Dictionary, under pettifactor and pettifogger.
[336] Oxford English Dictionary, under fogger¹.
[337] For example, see The Records of the Society of Gentlemen Practisers vi-ix, 77-78, 82-85, 323-324 (1897), and Robson, The Attorney in Eighteenth-Century England 20-34, 134-154 (1959).
[338] Oxford English Dictionary.

eighteenth a very bad word. Johnson's oft-quoted remark (reproduced but not overheard by Boswell)[339] that

> he did not care to speak ill of any man behind his back, but he believed the gentleman was an attorney,[340]

Boswell attributed to a mood ". . . splenetick, sarcastical, or jocular . . ."[341] It was, thought lawyer Boswell, the sort of remark inspired by a "too indiscriminate admission" to the profession, and "totally inapplicable" to "many very respectable" practitioners.[342]

The sustained effort to deodorize the word *attorney* was later abandoned, and in the nineteenth century it was supplanted in England by *solicitor*.[343] There *solicitor* lacks the offensive American connotation, as in "No peddlers or solicitors."[344] In England *attorney*, for a lawyer, survives only as *the attorney* (the attorney general), while in America the chief respectable lawyer-solicitor is the *solicitor general*.

It is in the context of inadequacies within the profession, in the context of a general lack of good legal education among attorneys and among the even less lawyerly draftsmen such as the scriveners, that the reliance upon forms must be evaluated. For the untrained there was a necessary and uncritical dependence upon the formbooks. Popular law writers capitalized on this weakness, at the same time appealing to the philosopher's and common man's longing for a simpler society in which the intricacies of law would disappear. (Section 78.) They offered books filled with stock forms and "simplified" legal principles as a substitute for a legal education.

One of these books was *Every Man His Own Lawyer*, first published in 1736, with the law (it said),

> . . . so plainly treated of that all Manner of Persons may be particularly acquainted with our Laws and Statutes, concerning Civil and Criminal Affairs, and know how to defend themselves and their Estates and Fortunes; In All Cases Whatsoever.[345]

---

[339] 1 Boswell, *Life of Johnson* 412 (Oxford ed. 1922); compare Robson, *The Attorney in Eighteenth-Century England* 138, 151 and especially n.1 (1959).

[340] 1 Boswell, *Life of Johnson* 420 (Oxford ed. 1922).

[341] 2 Boswell, *Life of Johnson* 565 (Oxford ed. 1922).

[342] 2 Boswell, *Life of Johnson* 565-566 (Oxford ed. 1922).

[343] Judicature Act, 1873, s. 87; 1 Jowitt, gen. ed., *The Dictionary of English Law* (1959), under *attorney;* see Robson, *The Attorney in Eighteenth-Century England* 151-152 (1959).

[344] See Evans and Evans, *A Dictionary of Contemporary American Usage* (1957), under *solicitor,* and compare *attorney.*

[345] Jacob, *Every Man His Own Lawyer,* title page (6th ed. 1765).

In polite circles of the eighteenth century this popularization was looked at askance. *The Critical Review or Annals of Literature* gave it only a passing statistical notice, and the doom:

> This is one of the many productions which reflect disgrace on the profession of Law.[346]

By 1788, the "disgrace" had run through ten editions, and has been followed by similarly titled books to the present day.[347]

Kin to *Every Man* were books of forms and law specially adapted to the needs of the laymen and attorneys who served as justices of the peace. Michael Dalton's *The Countrey Justice* (1618) said right on the title page that it was,

> . . . for the better helpe of such Iustices of Peace as haue not beene much conuersant in the studie of the Lawes of this Realme.

The book included the justice's oath of office with its needling reminders that fines collected were ". . . . to be entred without any concealement (or embesilling) . . ."

> . . . And ye shall not be of counsel of any quarrell hanging before you . . .[348]

Dalton continued as a standard work for more than a century, into the twentieth edition of 1746. Burn's *The Justice of the Peace and Parish Officer* (1754) was similar; in 1869 it was out in a thirtieth edition.

Such books preserved in detail a continuity of archaic English, bad grammar, and deficient punctuation, in form available to every scrivener and dabbler in the law, with or without the slightest knowledge of what he was writing. They gave greater currency to the similar language of the more learned formbooks (Section 91) and of the few archaic forms enshrined for the literate by Blackstone. Where English letters blossomed with originality and sparkle in the eighteenth century, the law was encased in a hard shell of fixed pattern, its language determined by forms and the deadweight of precedent. The mass of misplaced precedent, attached to the forms by coincidence rather than art, dropped into the hands of a legal profession unprepared to

---

[346] Note in "Monthly Catalog," 48 *Critical Review* 79 (1779), and quoted in 1 Maxwell and Maxwell, comps., *A Legal Bibliography of the British Commonwealth* 34 (2d ed. 1955).

[347] For example, *The Complete English Lawyer: Or Every Man His Own Lawyer* (3d ed. 1810); *Every Man's Own Lawyer* (68th ed. 1955).

[348] Dalton, *The Countrey Justice* 10 (1618).

cope with the bulk of its expanding business. The time had not yet come for any mass re-examination; there was too much movement in the law itself to look for more than the show of security. That appearance at least the forms gave, and lawyers embraced the illusion.

CHAPTER XI

Law Language in America

96. *Law and language as the colonists had known them*

For a majority of those who came to America, the recollection of English law was not a pleasant one. It was the remembrance of a legal system mired in precedent, antiquity, and corruption. For laymen who had approached the law its most bristling features were expense and delay, costly delay amounting to a denial of justice. This was the doubled evil the seventeenth-century tract writers bore down on:

> . . . that the price of right is too high for a poor man . . .[1]

> . . . the court of iniquity, alias the Chancery (where a man may be suspended and demurred in his just right, from generation to generation, by the power of the purse) . . .

> . . . delays and labyrinths to dwindle out a bumpkin's patrimony to the last thread.[2]

> . . . and said farther, They have spun me, at length, like a twine thread; and named the number of courts he had been twisted in . . .[3]

> . . . and when either party sees he is like to have the worst, by common law, then they have liberty to remove unto the Chancery, where a suit commonly depends as long as a buff coat will endure wearing, especially if the parties have, as it is said, good stomachs and strong purses . . .[4]

Worst of all, there was no prospect of the law's improvement. The eighteenth-century view affirmed the complaint of the seventeenth, epitomized in the title of the satire *Law Is a Bottomless Pit.* (Section 87.) Despite promises of early judgment, lawsuits went on indefinitely:

---

[1] 6 *The Harleian Miscellany* 212, 220 (new ed. 1810).
[2] 6 *The Harleian Miscellany* 289, 290-291 (new ed. 1810).
[3] Carey, "The Present State of England," in 3 *The Harleian Miscellany* 552, 558 (new ed. 1809).
[4] 7 *The Harleian Miscellany* 25, 29 (new ed. 1810).

. . . but, alas! that final Determination and happy Conclusion was like an inchanted Island, the nearer *John* came to it, the further it went from him; New Tryals upon new Points still arose; new Doubts, new Matters to be cleared; in short, Lawyers seldom part with so good a Cause till they have got the Oyster, and their Clients the Shell.[5]

It was not until the year of the Declaration of Independence that the first solid impetus was given to reform with the opening of Jeremy Bentham's attack on Blackstone. (Section 109.) Even then, reform would be long in coming. It was not a befuddled layman, but a law writer respected by lawyers, who said in 1839:

"No man, as things now stand, can enter into a Chancery suit with any reasonable hope of being alive at its termination, if he has a determined adversary." [6]

The lawyer's repute was at low ebb. (Section 95.) He was considered a conniver in the snail's pace of the judicial process:

All labour in their just vocation,
And each, by kind procrastination,
As one good turn deserves another,
Multiplies business for his Brother.[7]

The language of the lawyers was as unpopular as their profession. Thomas More spoke for many when he described his sixteenth-century uncomplicated *Utopia* (Section 78):

They have no lawyers among them, for they consider them as a sort of people whose profession it is to disguise matters . . .

As for the Utopians, he said,

Every one of them is skilled in their law, for as it is a very short study, so the plainest meaning of which words are capable is always the sense of their laws . . . for it is all one, not to make a law at all, or to couch it in such terms that without a quick apprehension and much study, a man cannot find out the true meaning of it . . .[8]

The seventeenth-century outcry against the "unknown tongue" of the law (Section 73) was coupled with attack on the law's preference for form over substance:

Why are so many men destroyed for want of a formality and punctilio in law? And who would not blush, to behold seemingly grave and

---

[5] [Arbuthnot], *Law Is a Bottomless Pit* 11-12 (6th ed. 1712).

[6] George Spence, quoted in Bowen, "Progress in the Administration of Justice During the Victorian Period," in 1 *Select Essays in Anglo-American Legal History* 516, 529 (1907).

[7] [Anstey], *The Pleader's Guide*, bk. 2, p. 26 (1796).

[8] More, *Utopia*, in *Ideal Empires and Republics* 203-204 (1901).

learned sages to prefer a letter, syllable, or word, before the weight and merit of a cause? [9]

A more savage touch was contributed by Swift (1726):

I said there was a Society of Men among us, bred up from their Youth in the Art of proving by Words multiplied for the Purpose, that *White* is *Black* and *Black* is *White*, according as they are paid. To this Society all the rest of the People are Slaves.[10]

The language of the law, as many of the colonists had experienced it, was the language of oppression for debtors and noncomformists. To boot, in the early days of colonization it was a language yet clothed in nondescript French and — even worse — in Latin. (Sections 73-76.) From some Puritan points of view Latin would remain condemned as the language of the Church at Rome. Moreover, young people must be carefully steered through Latin and Greek, for they were the tongues of

. . . heathenish Authors . . . whose writings are full of the fables, vanities, filthiness, lasciviousness, idolatries, and wickedness of the heathen.[11]

True, the language of the law was also a language that had talked back to tyranny, and could draw on heathen Latin to bulwark the argument. "That wonderful Edward Coke was loose," [12] reminding a would-be autocrat of his place:

. . . With which the King was greatly offended, and said, that then he should be under the Law, which was Treason to affirm, as he said; To which I said, that Bracton saith, *Quod Rex non debet esse sub homine, sed sub Deo & Lege*.[13] [That the King ought not to be under any man, but under God and the law.]

Coke's authoritative position as the exponent of the rule of law was known and respected in colonial America from an early date. (Section 99.) And more would think of him when lawyers became useful in the cause of independence. The popular balance sheet still showed lawyers and their language in the red.

The English language itself — which most of the colonists brought

---

[9] 6 *The Harleian Miscellany* 212, 221 (new ed. 1810).
[10] Swift, *Gulliver's Travels* 295-296 (Crown ed. 1947).
[11] Dell, "A Testimony from the Word" 25, 26, in *The Tryall of Spirits* (1653); see quote in Jones, *The Triumph of the English Language* 304 n.22, and see also 293-323 (1953).
[12] Maitland, "English Law and the Renaissance," in 1 *Select Essays in Anglo-American Legal History* 168, 202 (1907).
[13] *Prohibitions del Roy*, 77 Eng. Rep. 1342, 1343 (K.B. 1608); see also Bowen, *The Lion and the Throne* 303-305 (1950).

with them to pre-Revolutionary America — was yet a backwater language. On the eve of the American Revolution English speakers were only in fifth place in the roll call of the languages of the West, outranked by French, German, Spanish, and Russian.[14] It was a language full of dialect, and in the stream of change. The shift to a new continent cut off Americans from much of the change that continued on in England,[15] and gave rise to that distinctive speech which some call "American English"[16] and others "the American language." (Section 5.)

97. Words of the New World

The English the colonists carried to America was a bubbling mixture of the languages of many nations. (Sections 70, 79.) The Americans now added further seasoning, selected from their immediate surroundings as well as from distant lands and from the distant past.

Their Anglo-Saxon ancestors had brought to England language influenced by the Latin of the frontier trading between Romans and the Teutonic tribes. And the settlers on this new frontier reached back to that ancient frontier on the Continent for a word that fitted their circumstance. The Latin *decuria* (a group of ten), used to number skins in trading with the barbarians, traveled from Europe to England (Section 28), and from there to seventeenth-century Massachusetts, where it appears in the numbering of leather as *dekar*.[17] By the turn of the nineteenth century, Americans had stretched the word into the *dickering* that goes with trade. Its earliest definition has not been improved upon:

> *Dickering* signifies all that *honest* conversation, preliminary to the sale of a horse, where the parties very laudably strive in a sort of gladiatorial combat of lying, cheating, and overreaching.[18]

Some words from the New World had already invaded England before the permanent English settlement of America, and these too came back to American shores. Through Spanish, the native words of Haiti for *canoe* and *tobacco* were known in England before they appeared

---

[14] Marckwardt, *American English* 170-171 (1958).

[15] Marckwardt, *American English* 59-80 (1958).

[16] A *Dictionary of American English* (1938-1944); Mathews, ed., *A Dictionary of Americanisms* vii (1951); Marckwardt, *American English* (1958).

[17] *The Laws and Liberties of Massachusetts* 34 (Farrand, 1929).

[18] 2 *The Port Folio* 238n (1802), quoted in 1 Thornton, *An American Glossary* 249 (1912); see also *Oxford English Dictionary*, under *dicker;* Mathews, ed., *A Dictionary of Americanisms* (1951), under *dicker;* Jowitt, gen. ed., *The Dictionary of English Law* (1959), under *dickar*.

again in seventeenth-century America.[19] Tobacco smoking, "gretlie taken-vp and vsed" in late sixteenth-century England,[20] troubled the Puritan law makers of the Massachusetts Bay Colony. It was a fire hazard, and bothered non-smokers.[21] Worse, it led to idleness. "Tobacco takers" bore special watching.[22]

In the new feudalism which was to be erected in the Carolinas to ". . . avoid creating a numerous democracy . . ."[23] there were to be *caziques* (also spelled *cacique*), the Spanish or French version of the native Haitian word for lord or chief. By the nineteenth century *cacique* was applied with lavish impartiality,

> . . . to chiefs of Indian tribes and now to mayors of New Mexican towns, and any somewhat pompous and self-sufficient man . . .[24]

The Fundamental Constitutions of Carolina also borrowed from the German nobility to create an American *landgrave*.[25] It did not last. (Perhaps in a language where *v* is pronounced *v* the word was too solemn even for ridicule.)

The colonization of America did make a permanent addition to the English vocabulary with *kidnapping*. The first *kidnappers* were those who snatched adults and children to labor in the plantations of seventeenth-century America. So unsavory is the word that no nation has claimed it,[26] though some have handed it to the Dutch,[27] and some make it Scandinavian.[28] Although the crime is an ancient one, *kidnapping* was not listed in English law dictionaries until the eighteenth century;[29] the Authorized Version of the Bible speaks of him that *stealeth a man*.[30] And as an annotation of this biblical expression,

[19] *The Laws and Liberties of Massachusetts* 22, 26 (Farrand, 1929).

[20] Quoted in *Oxford English Dictionary,* under *tobacco.*

[21] *The Laws and Liberties of Massachusetts* 50 (Farrand, 1929).

[22] *The Laws and Liberties of Massachusetts* 26 (Farrand, 1929).

[23] "The Fundamental Constitutions of Carolina — 1669," in 5 F. Thorpe, ed., *The Federal and State Constitutions, Colonial Charters, and Other Organic Laws* 2772 (1909).

[24] Schele De Vere, *Americanisms* 71 (1872); see also *Black's Law Dictionary* (4th ed. 1951), under *cacicazgos,* and *Harrap's Standard French and English Dictionary* (French-English) (new ed. 1955), under *cacique.*

[25] 5 F. Thorpe, ed., *The Federal and State Constitutions, Colonial Charters, and Other Organic Laws* 2772 (1909).

[26] See *Oxford English Dictionary,* under *kidnap, kidnapper, kid, nap.*

[27] Johnson, *A Dictionary of the English Language* (4th ed. 1775), under *kidnap;* Jowitt, gen. ed., *The Dictionary of English Law* (1959), under *kidnapping.*

[28] Skeat, *An Etymological Dictionary* (1909), under *kidnap.*

[29] Jacob, *A New Law-Dictionary* (6th ed. 1750); 2 Bouvier, *A Law Dictionary* (1839), under *manstealing.*

[30] Exodus 21:16.

colonial Massachusetts used the Anglo-Saxon words *man-stealing*.[31] That combination does not occur in Old English, but there was a *mannþeof* which divided authorities translate as *man-stealer*[32] and *horse-thief*.[33]

The *master* of the English common law came to seventeenth-century America,[34] but in the same century came forms of the Dutch equivalent *baas*,[35] which as *boss* was to drive a democratic wedge between the language of the people and the language of the law. Like *master*, *servant* too was redolent of slavery.[36] Although it was used in colonial America[37] and has always been a favorite of the law, the popular tongue came to prefer (eighteenth to early nineteenth centuries) *hired man, -girl, -hand, -help,* as more suited to the freedom of America.[38]

In other ways too, the language of America gave notice of democracy. From Latin *select* and Old English *man*, New England created her elected *selectmen* (1635).[39] The horror of democratic meetings — the *tie* (O.E.) vote — had not yet become known by that name. New England took two Latin elements to create the *equivote* (1641), and in 1648 recorded the first usage of the *casting vote*[40] (as distinguished from an earlier *casting voice*)[41] to break the tie.

Above all the language was flexible. It borrowed from the American Indian, *powwow* for example.[42] It was not embarrassed to call a *backyard* a *backside*[43] though *rump* was a contemporaneous meaning.[44] There was place for the most current usage: *income,* for instance,

---

[31] *The Laws and Liberties of Massachusetts* 6 (Farrand, 1929); see also 2 Bouvier, *A Law Dictionary* (1839); see Bosworth and Toller, *An Anglo-Saxon Dictionary* (1898), under *forstelan* and *mannan forstele.*

[32] Bosworth and Toller, *An Anglo-Saxon Dictionary* (1898).

[33] Jacob, *A New Law-Dictionary* (6th ed. 1750), under *mantheof;* Jowitt, gen. ed., *The Dictionary of English Law* (1959), under *mantheoff.*

[34] *The Laws and Liberties of Massachusetts* 5, 46 (Farrand, 1929).

[35] Mathews, ed., *A Dictionary of Americanisms* (1951).

[36] Marckwardt, *American English* 50 (1958).

[37] *The Laws and Liberties of Massachusetts* 5, 46 (Farrand, 1929).

[38] Mathews, ed., *A Dictionary of Americanisms* 809 (1951); *Oxford English Dictionary,* under *hired.*

[39] *The Laws and Liberties of Massachusetts* 51 (Farrand, 1929); Mathews, ed., *A Dictionary of Americanisms* (1951).

[40] *The Laws and Liberties of Massachusetts* 24 (Farrand, 1929).

[41] *Oxford English Dictionary;* Mathews, ed., *A Dictionary of Americanisms* (1951).

[42] *The Laws and Liberties of Massachusetts* 29 (Farrand, 1929); Mathews, ed., *A Dictionary of Americanisms* (1951); *Oxford English Dictionary.*

[43] *The Laws and Liberties of Massachusetts* 5 (Farrand, 1929).

[44] *Oxford English Dictionary.*

which meant *coming in* in Middle English, had recently been applied in England to *periodic receipts*,[45] and was so used in seventeenth-century America, in a property tax statute.[46]

Puritan morals might be expressed in language, but puritanical restraint did not affect the language itself. The then current English fashion for experiment with language (Section 79) — the sheer joy of words and their sounds — took hold in the New World. The lawyer turned preacher, Nathaniel Ward, besides serving as legislative draftsman (Section 98), carved himself a niche in American letters with *The Simple Cobler of Aggawamm*. This work was written in America but published in London, in 1647, the year Ward permanently returned to the more cultivated life of England. Ward coined *nugiperous* from Latin *nugae* (nonsense or foolish), and also *nudiustertian* from Latin *nudius tertius* (day before yesterday). Both promptly became obsolete. He stumped the *Oxford English Dictionary* for an etymology of *drossock* for "an untidy woman," although they found a similar sixteenth-century *drapsock*.[47] Ward also came up with the rarely used *bullymong*, a mixture of feed grain.[48] These, and more, he combined in such vigorous prose as this diatribe against fashions in dress:

> It is known more than enough that I am neither Nigard, nor Cinick, to the due bravery of the true Gentry: if any man mislikes a bullymong drossock more than I, let him take her for his labour . . . but when I heare a nugiperous Gentledame inquire what dresse the Queen is in this week: what the nudiustertian fashion of the Court; with egge to bee in it in all haste, what ever it be; I looke at her as the very gizzard of a trifle, the product of a quarter of a cypher, the epitome of nothing, fitter to be kickt, if shee were of a kickable substance, then either honour'd or humour'd.[49]

His force was not spent. For some of those who rejected his corner of religion, he had these words:

> They are the very Offall of men, Dregges of Mankind, Reproach of Christendom, the Bots that crawle on the Beasts taile . . .[50]

Thus did the man who boasted, "I have read almost all the Common Law of England, and some statutes . . ."[51] set the pace for the pecu-

[45] *Oxford English Dictionary.*
[46] *The Laws and Liberties of Massachusetts* 20 (Farrand, 1929).
[47] *Oxford English Dictionary.*
[48] *Oxford English Dictionary.*
[49] [Ward], *The Simple Cobler of Aggawamm* 25 (3d ed. 1647).
[50] [Ward], *The Simple Cobler of Aggawamm* 72 (3d ed. 1647).
[51] [Ward], *The Simple Cobler of Aggawamm* 63 (3d ed. 1647).

liarly American tall talk[52] (see Section 26), and become a symbol of the permanent American addiction to word invention and refreshment.

98. *Few lawyers came to America*

The conditions of colonial America were not those to encourage any substantial migration of lawyers. The colonists were first of all largely nonconformists, either in religion or mores, and this was not a lawyerly pigeonhole. More important, practice of the law in the backwoods has never held out the promise of the city. From a safe distance, a successful London lawyer might dabble in a colonial speculation, in Virginia for instance, as did Francis Bacon.[53] Physical presence on the frontier was another matter; it would take strong disquieting inducements at home to make practice in the American wilderness appear attractive. So that the trained lawyers who did come to America came mostly for reasons other than the practice of law. Finally, colonial history provides abundant evidence of early hostility to the profession.

A century before the English settlement of North America, the Spanish colonists had posted the "Not Welcome" sign for lawyers. Four years before trouble with a lawyer cost Balboa his head, the Admiral of the Great South Sea wrote his king (January 20, 1513):

> "One thing I supplicate your majesty: that you will give orders, under a great penalty, that no bachelors of law should be allowed to come here; for not only are they bad themselves, but they also make and contrive a thousand iniquities." [54]

The general disrepute of lawyers in England (Sections 95, 96), buttressed by Thomas More's vision of a lawyerless *Utopia*, evoked similar expression from English colonizers. The philosopher John Locke, son of an attorney, had a laboring hand in drafting *The Fundamental Constitutions of Carolina* (1669). Article Seventy harks back to the Roman and to the medieval religious antipathy to pleading-for-hire;[55] it outlaws the profession of barrister:

> It shall be a base and vile thing to plead for money or reward; nor shall any one (except he be a near kinsman, not farther off than cousin-german to the party concerned) be permitted to plead another man's

---

[52] For example, 2 Thornton, *An American Glossary* app. §§I, II-VII, XXIX, XXXVII, XL (1912).

[53] "Second Charter of Virginia — 1609," in 7 F. Thorpe, ed., *The Federal and State Constitutions, Colonial Charters, and Other Organic Laws* 3790 (1909).

[54] Quoted in Shinn, *Mining Camps* 114 (ed. 1948).

[55] See Yunck, "The Venal Tongue: Lawyers and the Medieval Satirists," 46 A.B.A.J. 267-270 (1960).

cause, till, before the judge in open court, he hath taken an oath that he doth not plead for money or reward, nor hath nor will receive, nor directly nor indirectly bargained with the party whose cause he is going to plead, for money or any other reward for pleading his cause.[56]

Taking a further cue from *Utopia*,[57] perhaps from Justinian,[58] Carolina "absolutely prohibited" any form of "comments and expositions on any part" of the law.[59] And in a final utopian thrust at "multiplicity of laws," it ended all statutes automatically one hundred years after enactment.[60]

Massachusetts, in the *Body of Liberties* (1641), also put pleadings on a pro per or legal free-aid basis:

> Every man that findeth himselfe unfit to plead his owne cause in any court shall have Libertie to imploy any man against whom the Court doth not except, to helpe him, Provided he give him noe fee or reward for his paines.[61]

Without an express prohibition, Pennsylvania noted a preference for nonprofessional court work. Before leaving England, the colonizing group agreed:

> That, in all courts all persons of all persuasions may freely appear in their own way, and according to their own manner, and there personally plead their own cause themselves; or, if unable, by their friends . . .[62]

The Massachusetts ban was not included in *The Lawes and Liberties of Massachusetts* (1648), but prejudice against the profession was still strong. In 1663 lawyers were prohibited from serving in the Massachusetts legislature.[63] Rhode Island at first permitted lawyer legislators, but gave it up as a bad practice in 1729.[64]

---

[56] 5 F. Thorpe, ed., *The Federal and State Constitutions, Colonial Charters, and Other Organic Laws* 2781 (1909).

[57] More, *Utopia*, in *Ideal Empires and Republics* 203 (1901).

[58] Moyle, General Introduction to Justinian, *Imperatoris Iustiniani Institutionum* 75-76 (Moyle, 5th ed. 1912).

[59] "The Fundamental Constitutions of Carolina," art. 80, in 5 F. Thorpe, ed., *The Federal and State Constitutions, Colonial Charters, and Other Organic Laws* 2782 (1909).

[60] "The Fundamental Constitutions of Carolina," art. 79, in 5 F. Thorpe, ed., *The Federal and State Constitutions, Colonial Charters, and Other Organic Laws* 2782 (1909).

[61] Par. 26, in Whitmore, *A Bibliographical Sketch of the Laws of the Massachusetts Colony* 38 (1890).

[62] "Laws Agreed upon in England, &c.," art. VI, in 5 F. Thorpe, ed., *The Federal and State Constitutions, Colonial Charters, and Other Organic Laws* 3060 (1909).

[63] Chafee, Introduction to *Records of the Suffolk County Court 1671-1680*, p. xxiv (1933); "Sketch," in Lechford, *Notebook* xv (1885).

[64] Reinsch, "The English Common Law in the Early American Colonies," in 1 *Select Essays in Anglo-American Legal History* 367, 390 (1907).

Colonial hostility to the profession was general, in New England as in Virginia, where paid lawyers were banned for eleven years (1645-1656),[65] in Pennsylvania as in New York.[66] Few lawyers had the hardihood to give up practice in England for the sake of a practice here. Even the Crown was short of lawyers for the colonies.[67] The first Randolph to become attorney general for Virginia (1694) was a planter and merchant, and held office for four years despite complaint that he was ignorant of the law.[68]

There were nonetheless some men trained in the law who came to seventeenth-century America, some of considerable learning. John Winthrop, son of a lawyer, had studied (without graduation) at Cambridge, had been admitted to Gray's Inn and the Inner Temple; he was a justice of the peace for many years, and had a London practice both "extensive and fairly lucrative." [69] But his practice had declined before he came to America, where he became governor of the Massachusetts Bay Colony. His son John, a governor of Connecticut, had been an Inner Temple barrister, but his fortunes also were drooping when he took ship to the New World. Nathaniel Ward (Section 97), a Cambridge graduate, practiced law in England for a number of years before he was smitten with religion, and it was as the Reverend Nathaniel Ward that he came to Massachusetts. He was the draftsman of the code of law known as the *Body of Liberties.* Bellingham, a judge and lawyer in England, had a part in the preparation of the revised code, the *Laws and Liberties.*[70] Several others in the Massachusetts Bay Colony had studied some law in England.[71] So unlike the Pilgrims at Plymouth who landed with nary a lawyer (Section 100), if the Puritans of Massachusetts Bay were "unfurnished of Lawyers," as the preface to the *Laws and Liberties* recites, it was through choice

[65] Warren, *A History of the American Bar* 41-42 (1911).

[66] Reinsch, "The English Common Law in the Early American Colonies," in 1 *Select Essays in Anglo-American Legal History* 367, 394 (1907); see also Chafee, Introduction to *Records of the Suffolk County Court 1671-1680,* p. xxiii (1933); 1 Osgood, *The American Colonies in the Eighteenth Century* 156-157 (1924); 3 Osgood, *The American Colonies in the Eighteenth Century* 72 (1924).

[67] See, for example, 1 Osgood, *The American Colonies in the Eighteenth Century* 156-157 (1924).

[68] *Dictionary of American Biography,* under "William Randolph."

[69] *Dictionary of American Biography,* under "John Winthrop" (1587-1649); compare Warren, *A History of the American Bar* 59 (1911); Woodbine, "The Language of English Law," 18 *Speculum* 395, 400 n.2 (1943); and Woodbine, review of *Records of the Suffolk County Court 1671-1680,* in 43 Yale L.J. 1036, 1037 (1934).

[70] Whitmore, *A Bibliographical Sketch of the Laws of the Massachusetts Colony* 18; Chafee, Introduction to *Records of the Suffolk County Court 1671-1680,* p. xxvii (1933).

[71] "Sketch," in Lechford, *Notebook* xv (1885).

rather than lack of training. This is not an exhaustive listing of lawyers who came to the colonies, but these were better trained than most of the early colonial practitioners[72] (Section 101), and typically, they did not come to practice their profession.

History does record the unhappy saga of an English attorney (not a barrister) who came to colonial New England with some thought of the practice. Thomas Lechford was a member of Clement's Inn, one of the Inns of Chancery. His practice became involved in the squabbles over religious conformity, and especially in the affairs of the Puritan zealot, earless William Prynne. For this, Lechford "suffered imprisonment, and a kind of banishment," [73] and so sailed for Boston in 1638. While still at sea he discussed with fellow passengers his pet heresies, such as that the Antichrist had not yet come. On land he put his thoughts into writing, and assured himself an unwelcome. For as the ex-lawyer, the articulate Reverend Nathaniel Ward, later wrote:

> It is likewise said, That men ought to have Liberty of their Conscience, and that it is persecution to debarre them of it: I can rather stand amazed then reply to this: it is an astonishment to think that the brains of men should be parboyl'd in such wilfull ignorance . . .[74]

A pariah from the start, Lechford scraped up odd jobs of draftsmanship (some pleading, some copying, some work on the *Body of Liberties*) for small fees. Going beyond the limits of his professional training, he even undertook advocacy — this before the 1641 ban. In the case of *Cole and Cole v. Doughty* (1639), Lechford's advocacy included jury tampering, and his doctrinal enemies were ready for him. It was ordered:

> "Mr. Thomas Lechford, for going to the Jewry & pleading with them out of Court, is debarred from pleading any man's cause hereafter, unlesse his owne, and admonished not to presume to meddle beyond what hee shalbee called to by the Courte." [75]

He later resumed work as attorney.[76] But the pickings were lean and the atmosphere uncongenial. Three years after he arrived in

---

[72] Morris, Introduction to *Select Cases of the Mayor's Court of New York City 1674-1784*, pp. 50-52 (1935); Chafee, Introduction to *Records of the Suffolk County Court 1671-1680*, p. xxvi (1933); compare Haskins, *Law and Authority in Early Massachusetts* 185-186 (1960).

[73] *Dictionary of American Biography*, under "Thomas Lechford."

[74] [Ward], *The Simple Cobler of Aggawamm* 12 (3d ed. 1647).

[75] Quoted in "Sketch," in Lechford, *Notebook* xxi (1885).

[76] Lechford, *Notebook* 168, 169, 322, and "Sketch" at xxi; compare Reinsch, "The English Common Law in the Early American Colonies," in 1 *Select Essays in Anglo-American Legal History* 367, 382 (1907); Woodbine, "The Language of English Law," 18 Speculum 395, 400 n.2 (1943); and Chafee, Introduction to *Records of the Suffolk County Court 1671-1680*, p. xxiii (1933).

Boston, Lechford returned for good to the practice in England, leaving behind him in Boston "his wife and household goods worth £6.13.10." [77]

99. The transplanted language of the law

The scarcity of trained practitioners in the earliest days of colonial life (Section 98) did not prevent the language of the law from gaining a foothold in America. The English bar saw to that. Popham, Dodderidge, and Coke — for instance — all had a hand in the first charter of Virginia,[78] a document which affected title to lands in each of the thirteen original states.[79] This charter of 1606 permanently planted on American soil such expressions as *give and grant, goods and chattels, will and pleasure, time or times,* and *lands, tenements, and hereditaments.* The last sentence of the charter (here in English) suffices to give the familiar flavor of the medieval English land law:

> And finally, we do for Us, our Heirs, and Successors, Grant and agree, to and with the said Sir Thomas Gates, Sir George Somers, Richard Hackliut, Edward-Maria Wingfield, and all others of the said first colony, that, We, Our Heirs and Successors, upon Petition in that Behalf to be made, shall, by Letters Patent under the Great Seal of England, Give and Grant, unto such Persons, their Heirs and Assigns, as the Council of that Colony, or the most part of them, shall, for that Purpose, nominate and assign all the lands, Tenements, and Hereditaments, which shall be within the Precincts limited for that Colony, as is aforesaid, to be holden of us, our heirs and Successors, as of our Manor of East-Greenwich, in the County of Kent, in free and common Soccage only, and not in Capite.[80]

There are similar medieval, one-sentence involvements in other colonial charters.[81] Nor did these documents gather dust unforgotten. Friction with the Crown and with a succession of colonizers and royal agents helped to keep familiar the formal language stereotypes of England.

Furthermore, the introduction of the language of the law into Amer-

---

[77] *Dictionary of American Biography,* under "Thomas Lechford."

[78] Maitland, "English Law and the Renaissance," in 1 *Select Essays in Anglo-American Legal History* 168, 203 and especially n.66 (1907).

[79] F. Thorpe, ed., *The Federal and State Constitutions, Colonial Charters, and Other Organic Laws* (1909), vol. 1, p. 519 (Conn.), p. 557 (Del.); vol. 2, p. 765 (Ga.); vol. 3, p. 1669 (Md.), p. 1827 (Mass.); vol. 4, p. 2433 (N.H.); vol. 5, p. 2533 (N.J.), p. 2623 (N.Y.); p. 2743 (N.C.), p. 3035 (Penn.); vol. 6, p. 3205 (R.I.), p. 3241 (S.C.); vol. 7, p. 3783 (Va.).

[80] 7 F. Thorpe, ed., *The Federal and State Constitutions, Colonial Charters, and Other Organic Laws* 3783, 3789 (1909).

[81] See, for example, F. Thorpe, ed., *The Federal and State Constitutions, Colonial Charters, and Other Organic Laws* (1909), vol. 1, pp. 529-536 (Charter of Connecticut — 1662); vol. 3, pp. 1677-1686 (The Charter of Maryland — 1632); vol. 3, pp. 1621-1625 (A Grant of the Province of Maine — 1622); vol. 3, pp. 1625-1640 (Grant of the Province of Maine — 1639).

ica was not always fortuitous. Amidst the confusions of a strange and savage land, some of the colonists longed for the guidance that was firmly encased in the law's language. In 1647, the General Court of the Massachusetts Bay Colony, " '. . . to the end we may have the better light for making & proceeding about laws . . .' " [82] voted to obtain two copies each of:

> Coke's *Reports,* and his works on *Littleton* and *Magna Carta;*
> "the *Books of Entryes*" — possibly Coke's formbook (Section 72);
> "the Newe *Tearmes of the Lawe*" — possibly the 1642 edition of Rastell's popular dictionary (Section 75);
> and "Daltons *Justice of Peace*" — with its forms (Section 95).

It is not reported that the vote produced the books, nor is such record necessary to trace the beginning influence of English law forms on the language of the law in America. Surviving colonial records give ample evidence that someone brought in hand or head a full collection of the language of the law as it had been known in England. In a short legal career in Massachusetts (Section 98), attorney Thomas Lechford could never have independently come to his artificial wording of a contract, let alone in the same year of his arrival in New England. He could have done it with adaptations from standard formbooks, for example, West's popular *Symbolaeography* (Section 75). Compare

Lechford	*West*
The Condicion of this obligation is such that if the abovebounden John Tinker his heirs executors, administrators and assignes . . .	The condition of this Obligation is such, that if the within bounden A.B. his heirs, executors, or administrators, or any of them . . .[83]
fullfill, performe, keepe and observe all . . .	hold, performe, obserue, fulfill and keep all . . .[84]
this obligation shall be voyd & of none effect, or els it shall be and remaine in full force, strength and vertue.[85]	this present obligation to be utterly voide and of none effect or to stand, remaine and bee of full force, strength, power and vertue.[86]

---

[82] Quoted in Farrand, Introduction to *The Laws and Liberties of Massachusetts* vii (Farrand, 1929).
[83] West, *The First Part of Symboleography* §111 (ed. 1598).
[84] West, *The First Part of Symboleography* §171 (ed. 1598).
[85] Lechford, *Notebook* 8 (1885).
[86] West, *The First Part of Symboleography* §111 (ed. 1598).

Lechford's multilingual synonyms *force* (French, from popular Latin), *strength* (Old English), and *virtue* (Anglo-Norman, from Latin) were in the well-established pattern of the law. (Section 71.) So too with *void* (Anglo-Norman) and *none* (Old English) *effect* (Old French, from Latin).

In the same word-multiplying tradition are *made* (Old English), *ordained* and *appointed* (Old French), and *constituted* (Latin), which show up together in a Massachusetts power of attorney, easily adapted from West. Compare

Massachusetts (1669)	*England (1598)*
Know all men that I . . .	Witnesseth, that the said . . .
have made ordained	hath constituted, made
constituted & appoynted	and ordained, and by these
and doe hereby made ordaine	presents doth constitute,
constitute & appoynt . . .[87]	ordaine and make . . .[88]

The opening words of many colonial documents came in a direct line from the medieval salutations (Section 56), through sixteenth-century English forms. Compare

Massachusetts *(Seventeenth Century)*	*England* *(Sixteenth Century)*
Know all Christian People to whome this pursent writing shall come . . .[89]	To al Christian people &c. . . .[90]
Know all men . . .[92]	To all the faithful of Christ to whome this present writing indented shall come . . .[91]
	Be it knowen unto all men by these presents . . .[93]

A seventeenth-century colonial charterparty commences: *In the name of God Amen,*[94] the same words of piety used in an English policy of marine insurance of the same era.[95]

Seventeenth-century records of the New York Mayor's Court tell the same story, the words of the English lawyer transferred to America:

---

[87] *Records of the Suffolk County Court 1671-1680*, pt. I, pp. 14-15 (1933).
[88] West, *The First Part of Symboleography* §543 (ed. 1598).
[89] *Records of the Suffolk County Court 1671-1680*, pt. I, pp. 388-389 (1933).
[90] West, *The First Part of Symboleography* §539 (ed. 1598).
[91] West, *The First Part of Symboleography* §538 (ed. 1598).
[92] *Records of the Suffolk County Court 1671-1680*, pt. I, p. 14 (1933).
[93] West, *The First Part of Symboleography* §540 (ed. 1598).
[94] *Records of the Suffolk County Court 1671-1680*, pt. I, p. 277 (1933).
[95] Burrell, *Reports of Cases Determined by the High Court of Admiralty* 267 (Marsden ed. 1885).

goods and chattels, made and provided;[96] *all and singular, last will and
testament.*[97]

The working vocabulary of a seventeenth-century English lawyer
is reproduced in the *Laws and Liberties of Massachusetts* (1648) to
an extent that eliminates the possibility of coincidence. The stream
of English law words which connected colonial America to England
appears in this sampling:

acknowledged . . . and recorded
acquittance
alienations
bargain
barratrie
bayle or main-prize
bill of review
bona fide
bond for appearance
common barrater
copartners (i.e., parceners)
deed
distresse
dower
duly received
dures
escheats
exemplification
forge
forgerie
forma pauperis
fraudulent conveyances
hear and determin
heirs males of their bodyes
hereof you are not to fail at your
    peril
hue-and-cries
imbeazling
impannelled

incumbrances
intestate
juries
just and reasonable terms
lyable
master
morgage
mutatis mutandis
non-suted
petty jurie
prescription
prisoners at the Bar
proces
reasonable demand
replevie
replevin
se defendendo
seized of, to his own use, either
    in possession, reversion, or re-
    mainder
summons
tales de circumstantibus
transcript
trespass
truth, the whole truth, and nothing
    but the truth
valuable consideration
wittingly and willingly

100. *Colonial variation*

If the language of the law got an early start in colonial America
(Section 99), it still did not have the field to itself. In greater or
lesser degree, the English colonists brought with them the common
law of England,[98] but in the beginning the details were worked out

---

[96] *King v. Leggitt,* misc. records, N.Y. Mayor's Ct., 1695.
[97] *Dempre v. Ellis,* misc. records, N.Y. Mayor's Ct., 1689.
[98] 1 *Select Essays in Anglo-American Legal History* 367-463 (1907).

mostly by laymen and lay lawyers.[99] The profession was unpopular, trained lawyers were few (Section 98), and there was neither facility nor occasion for training more. In the area of what became the thirteen original colonies, the population in 1625 was less than 2000. Of that total, 1800 were in Virginia, and 180 at Plymouth.[100] (As an aid to perspective, it is worth noting that in 1959, there was one practicing lawyer in Alpine County, California — population 600.) By 1641, there were still only 50,000 English settlers along the whole Atlantic seaboard.[101] There were more wolves than people, and more Indians than English. For the moment food and religion were more important than law. Early colonial life was simple and the outlook of colonials local, with not time enough yet to sniff the scents of nationalism. The wonder is that so much of the law's language arrived so early; variation could be expected.

There was a tendency in the earliest days of colonial New England for briefer and less formal statement than was customary in English documents of the same period. The phenomenon appears in state papers, for example the *Mayflower Compact* (1620) and the *Plantation Agreement at Providence* (1640), as contrasted with the colonial charters drawn in England. (Section 99.)

The lawyerless Pilgrims,[102] "ignorant men," Maitland called them,[103] had a sufficient acquaintance with the law to infuse their Compact with a legalistic flavor; they also were sufficiently untutored in the law to write with a shocking brevity and with disdain for precision. This is the whole thing, window dressing included:

> IN The Name of God, Amen. We, whose names are underwritten, the Loyal Subjects of our dread Sovereign Lord King James, by the Grace of God, of Great Britain, France, and Ireland, King, Defender of the Faith, &c. Having undertaken for the Glory of God, and Advancement of the Christian Faith, and the Honour of our King and Country, a Voyage to plant the first Colony in the northern Parts of Virginia; Do by these Presents, solemnly and mutually, in the Presence of God and one another, covenant and combine ourselves together into a civil Body Politick, for our better Ordering and Preservation, and Furtherance of the Ends aforesaid: And by Virtue hereof do enact, constitute, and frame, such just and equal Laws, Ordinances, Acts, Constitutions, and

---

[99] Chafee, Introduction to *Records of the Suffolk County Court 1671-1680*, p. xxvi (1934).

[100] *Encyclopedia of American History* 442 (Morris ed. 1953).

[101] *Encyclopedia of American History* 442 (Morris ed. 1953).

[102] Bowen, *John Adams and the American Revolution* 145 (1950).

[103] Maitland, Introduction to *Political Theories of the Middle Age* xxxi (Beacon ed. 1958).

Officers, from time to time, as shall be thought most meet and convenient for the general Good of the Colony; unto which we promise all due Submission and Obedience. In Witness whereof we have hereunto subscribed our names at Cape-Cod the eleventh of November, in the Reign of our Sovereign Lord King James, of England, France, and Ireland, the eighteenth, and of Scotland, the fifty-fourth, Anno Domini, 1620.[104]

In Rhode Island, under the influence of Roger Williams, the spirit of libertarianism reigned. Williams had been a favorite of Sir Edward Coke, and for Coke's benefit took shorthand notes of proceedings in the Star Chamber. But Williams strayed from an intended career in the law to religion. Just how far he and his company strayed from the teachings of Coke may be judged from the scarcely intelligible literary style of the Plantation Agreement. For example:

> 2. Agreed. We have with one consent agreed that for the disposeing, of those lands that shall be disposed belonging to this towne of Providence to be in the whole Inhabitants by the choise of five men for generall disposeall, to betrusted with disposeall of lands and also of the towne Stocke, and all Generall things and not to receive in any six days at townesmen, but first to give the Inhabitants notice to consider if any have just cause to shew against the receiving of him as you can apprehend, and to receive none but such as subscribe to this our determination. . . .[105]

Compounding their rejection of the language of the law, the settlers at Providence used the informal Celtic *hubbub* for the French and technical *hue and cry*. Both were noisy; a noisy American Indian game was also called *hubbub;* and for the time it sufficed. (Section 26.)

There is a marked simplicity too in both the substance and style of some enactments, this one for example from the Massachusetts Bay Colony even with its considerable body of English-trained legal talent (Sections 98, 99):

> No Summons pleading Judgement, or any kinde of proceeding in Court or course of Justice shall be abated, arested, or reversed, upon any kinde of cercumstantiall errors or mistakes, If ye person & cause be rightly understood & intended by ye Court.[106]

And this statutory form of summons for debt on a bond:

---

[104] 3 F. Thorpe, ed., *The Federal and State Constitutions, Colonial Charters, and Other Organic Laws* 1841 (1909).

[105] 6 F. Thorpe, ed., *The Federal and State Constitutions, Colonial Charters, and Other Organic Laws* 3205, 3206 (1909).

[106] *Body of Liberties,* par. 25 (1641), in Whitmore, *A Bibliographical Sketch of the Laws of the Massachusetts Colony* 38 (1890).

To (IB) Carpenter, of (D). You are required to appear at the next Court, holden at (b) on the   day of the month next ensuing; to answer the complaint of (NC) for with-holding a debt of   due upon a Bond . . . and hereof you are not to fail at your peril. Dated the   day of the month 1641.[107]

A clear vision of the one true path to salvation also had its influence on the language New England Puritans brought to the law. The men of the Massachusetts Bay Colony were not to be ensnared by the ". . . distinction which is put betweene the Lawes of God and the lawes of men . . ." They rejoiced that in New England,

> . . . Churches, and civil State have been planted, and growne up (like two twinnes) together like that of Israel in the wildernes . . .[108]

There was a constant battle with the devil,[109] and in a homsey-folksey nontechnical way the law was not permitted to forget it. A provision for common schooling so ". . . that Learning may not be buried in the graves of our fore-fathers . . ." was prefaced with this sobering reflection:

> It being one chief project of that old deluder, Satan, to keep men from the knowledge of the Scriptures, as in former times keeping them in an unknown tongue . . .[110]

A seventeenth-century court record recited a sentencing,

> . . . for a foule, & divilish attempt to bugger a cow of Mr. Makepeaces . . .[111]

Even the native inhabitants of New England were reminded that the devil had jurisdictional limits:

> And it is farther ordered and decreed by this Court; that no Indian shall at any time *powaw*, or performe outward worship to their false gods; or to the devil in any part of our Jurisdiction . . .[112]

There was no formbook to tell even an English-trained lawyer how to spell out the Puritan decision that there could be no prescriptive right to sin. The earliest American code — drafted by the lawyer-turned-preacher Nathaniel Ward (Section 98) — said it this way:

---

[107] *The Laws and Liberties of Massachusetts* 55 (Farrand, 1929).

[108] *The Laws and Liberties of Massachusetts,* introductory epistle (Farrand, 1929).

[109] See [Lowell], *The Biglow Papers* xix (1848).

[110] *The Laws and Liberties of Massachusetts* 47 (Farrand, 1929).

[111] Quoted in Whitmore, *A Bibliographical Sketch of the Laws of the Massachusetts Colony* xxx, xxxi (1890).

[112] *The Laws and Liberties of Massachusetts* 29 (Farrand, 1929).

No custome or prescription shall ever prevaile amongst us in any morall cause. our meaneing is maintaine anythinge that canbe proved to bee morallie sinfull by ye word of god.[113]

The tendency to brevity and informality, the simplicity and quaintness of some of the early colonial writings were in conflict from the start with the traditional forms of legal expression. (Section 99.) This conflict continues throughout American history, and the conflict itself has been a factor in shaping today's language of the law. (See Section 109.)

101. *Growth of the profession*

The relative legal naïveté of earliest colonial America had not long to last. The scarcity of people and business had been accompanied by a corresponding scarcity of lawyers. (Sections 98, 100.) When there were more people, there was more business, and — well received or not — there were also more lawyers.

The seventeenth century had opened with the first permanent English settlement in America (1607), and before the close of that century the area of the thirteen colonies held a population of 200,000. By 1715, this figure had more than doubled; 1754 — approximately $1\frac{1}{2}$ million; 1774 — approximately $2\frac{1}{2}$ million.[114] Trade with Great Britain climbed from £551,000 in the first decade of the eighteenth century to £2,739,000 in the last decade before the Revolution.[115]

It has been estimated that in Boston alone the population of 1680 stood between 7000 and 10,000.[116] That was population enough for legal problems, and for lawyers. The Massachusetts Bay Colony ban on paid lawyers had been dropped by 1648 (Section 98). Also, within the next dozen years, the practice of Massachusetts plaintiffs' getting legal counsel in advance from the trial judge was outlawed.[117] Before that, the practice had been condoned as the lesser of evils. If one could not get advice from the judge, what then? As Winthrop wrote:

"We must then provide lawyers to direct men in their causes." [118]

[113] *Body of Liberties,* par. 65 (1641), in Whitmore, *A Bibliographical Sketch of the Laws of the Massachusetts Colony* 46 (1890).

[114] *Encyclopedia of American History* 442 (Morris ed. 1953).

[115] *Encyclopedia of American History* 486 (Morris ed. 1953).

[116] Chafee, Introduction to *Records of the Suffolk County Court 1671-1680,* p. xvii (1934).

[117] Chafee, Introduction to *Records of the Suffolk County Court 1671-1680,* p. xxiv (1934); see also Whitmore, *A Bibliographical Sketch of the Laws of the Massachusetts Colony* 28 (1890).

[118] Quoted in Chafee, Introduction to *Records of the Suffolk County Court 1671-1680,* p. xxiv (1934).

This dreaded alternative brought with it a brisk business in the law, too brisk for the morals of Boston. The Lawyers were a disorderly and litigious lot, tolerated nuisances of poor repute and worse training, they — like the judges — snapping up what education they could from experience.[119] In far-off Virginia, there was a similar story of disorder and ignorance.[120] In New York, taken from the Dutch in 1664, there was an early attempt at regulation by admission to practice; but here too there was no pretense of professional competence.[121]

There are seventeenth-century records of legal writings which give evidence of familiarity with the law. New York, for one, has records of litigation of the period, some reproduced,[122] some unpublished and gradually disintegrating under the dust of the ages. Thus, a crumbling parchment scroll a foot wide and a yard long — carefully hand-lettered on both sides — recites the indictment of an unfortunate Mr. Leggitt, who "by the instigation of the Devill" stole "a certaine Barrow Hogg." [123] It is meticulously full of legal favorites — goods and chattels, made and provided, etc. Massachusetts too has ample stocks of executed seventeenth-century documents of the law, replete with professional wording. Most of this, though, is better evidence of resort to English forms (Section 99) than of any general professional skill.[124] The available data — incomplete though it be — of the general ignorance of those formally and informally in the practice, of the lack of professional standards and control, have led most writers to look upon the seventeenth century as a sort of antediluvian period of the American bar.[125] While it oversimplifies a century of history, there is some justification for the lawyer's dictum that the profession did not begin in America until the eighteenth century.[126]

---

[119] Chafee, Introduction to *Records of the Suffolk County Court 1671-1680*, pp. xxvi-xxvii (1934).

[120] Warren, *A History of the American Bar* 41-42 (1911).

[121] Morris, Introduction to *Select Cases of the Mayor's Court of New York City* 52 (1935).

[122] For example, *Select Cases of the Mayor's Court of New York City 1674-1784* (Morris ed. 1935); Goebel and Naughton, *Law Enforcement in Colonial New York* (1944); *Collections of the New York Historical Society for the Year 1912* (1913).

[123] *King v. Leggitt*, misc. records, N.Y. Mayor's Ct., 1695.

[124] Compare Chafee, Introduction to *Records of the Suffolk County Court 1671-1680*, pp. xxvi, xxviii, xxxi (1934).

[125] Warren, *A History of the American Bar* 15-16 (1911); Harno, *Legal Education in the United States* 18 (1953); Reinsch, "The English Common Law in the Early American Colonies," in 1 *Select Essays in Anglo-American Legal History* 367-415 (1907).

[126] Pound, "Legal Education in the United States," in 13 *Encyclopaedia Britannica* 874 (1948).

Indeed for the greater part of the eighteenth century there was little formal training in the law offered in America. There was nonetheless increasing opportunity for lawyers to escape the stigma of general ignorance and gradually to establish themselves as a "learned profession." Starting with Harvard in 1636, William and Mary (1693), and Yale (1701), ten colleges were in operation by the year of the Boston Massacre (1770).[127] Nine years later the first university law lectures began at William and Mary. Typically, the Professor of Law and Police — George Wythe — had gathered enough scraps of the law from a family friend to be admitted to the bar at age twenty, and had then gone on by his own efforts to become a serious student of the law and its history. Although the president of Yale had outlined a plan for a law professorship as early as 1777,[128] Wythe remained professionally unique in America until after the Revolution.

With a recollection of past greatness, some families of wealth sent sons to England for attachment to the Inns of Court, a connection still impressive to colonials though the training there had slipped. (Section 95.) But the standard approach to the bar in America was reading law in a lawyer's office, and so it remained well into the nineteenth century.

Still in short supply, more and more English lawbooks made their way to America — pre-eminently Blackstone. It was said that the *Commentaries* were selling nearly as well in America as in England,[129] almost 2500 by Independence Day.[130] An American edition was published in Philadelphia (1771-1772).[131] And Blackstone's Vinerian lectures at Oxford (the model for Wythe) had been read by some in America — John Adams for instance — as early as 1759.[132] Reading law with lawyer John Putnam, Adams also labored with Coke's *Institutes, Doctor and Student,* Hale's *History of the Common Law,* Lilly's

---

[127] 22 *Encyclopaedia Britannica* 874 (1948); compare *Encyclopedia of American History* 555 (Morris ed. 1953).

[128] Warren, *A History of the American Bar* 563-566 (1911).

[129] Burke, "Conciliation with America," speech, in 11 Modern Eloquence 368, 385-386 (1903).

[130] Maitland, "English Law and the Renaissance," in 1 *Select Essays in Anglo-American Legal History* 168, 204 (1907); see also Maitland, "History of English Law," in *Selected Historical Essays of F. W. Maitland* 97, 116-117 (Cam ed. 1957).

[131] Hammond, "Bibliography of the Commentaries," in 1 Jones, ed., *Commentaries on the Laws of England by Sir William Blackstone* xxxiv (1916).

[132] Warren, *A History of the American Bar* 179 (1911); Bowen, *John Adams and the American Revolution* 615 (1950); Radin, *Handbook of American Legal History* 287 n.22 (1936).

Abridgment, Finch, Fortescue, miscellaneous English reports. His mentor had a fifteen-book law library, five less than is reported for the Harvard of 1756.[133]

Thomas Jefferson apprenticed five years before admission to the bar. Newly admitted, he could recommend to a student friend not only Coke and Blackstone, but Matthew Bacon's *Abridgement* and several works on equity, and was familiar enough with *Bracton* to discourage its study. He recommended also diligent study of the reports, and a careful abstracting of the cases to fix them "indelibly in the mind" and to aid in acquiring

> . . . the most valuable of all talent, that of never using two words where one will do.[134]

Adams and Jefferson were among that group of colonial lawyers — most of them college graduates — who brought both legal and literary talent into the verbal skirmishing that preceded and accompanied events in the field. Earlier the venerable classicist, Philadelphia lawyer Andrew Hamilton (Zenger trial, 1735)[135] and the learned James Otis and Oxenbridge Thatcher (writs of assistance, 1761),[136] had set the mark of the lawyer at his public-spirited best in the courtroom. In each case the client had shopped for counsel, and the remembered names were second choices, after others had declined the representation.[137] In addition, counsel who had first undertaken the Zenger defense had been disbarred for their efforts in a cause where the bench itself was hostile.[138]

John Adams continued the freedom fight with written words, speaking for the revolutionary conscience of New England as *Novanglus* against the counsel of submission and defeat voiced by *Massachusettensis* (1774-1775). This *Massachusettensis* was an anonymity so well

---

[133] Bowen, *John Adams and the American Revolution* 142 (1950).

[134] *The Complete Jefferson* 1045 (Padover ed. 1943); compare 14 *The Writings of Thomas Jefferson* 57 (1905) and 13 *The Writings of Thomas Jefferson* 166-167 (1905).

[135] *A Treasury of the World's Great Speeches* 101-108 (Peterson ed. 1954); Lewis, "The Right to Complain: The Trial of John Peter Zenger," 46 A.B.A.J. 27, 110 (1960).

[136] See "Letters from the Hon. John Adams," in *Novanglus and Massachusettensis* 229, 230; 233, 235-236; 238, 239; 244-247; 263-265; 267; 284; 293; 296; 304; 306 (1819).

[137] See "Letters from the Hon. John Adams," in *Novanglus and Massachusettensis* 246 (1819); and see *Dictionary of American Biography*, under "Andrew Hamilton" (d. 1741).

[138] *Dictionary of American Biography*, under "Andrew Hamilton" (d. 1741); Lewis, "The Right to Complain: The Trial of John Peter Zenger," 46 A.B.A.J. 27, 30 (1960).

preserved that almost a half century later, Adams thought it concealed his old friend, the Tory lawyer Jonathan Sewall.[139] It has been identified as the pseudonym of another polished Boston lawyer, Daniel Leonard.[140] Leonard drove wedges between leader and follower. He mourned for those ". . . made the dupes of artifice, and the mere stilts of ambition . . ." [141] He warned of the ". . . crossings, windings, and tergiversations of a politician; he is a cunning animal . . ." [142]

Popular demogagues always call themselves the people, and when their own measures are censured, cry out, the people, the people are abused and insulted.[143]

Leonard warned too of inevitable defeat in battle,[144] and of the drawing and quartering[145] that awaited those who ". . . follow the standard of rebellion." [146] With measured defiance, *Novanglus* replied:

Massachusettensis, conscious that the people of this continent have the utmost abhorrence of treason and rebellion, labours to avail himself of the magic of these words. But his artifice is vain. The people are not to be intimidated by hard words, from a necessary defence of their liberties: Their attachment to their constitution so dearly purchased by their own and their ancestors blood and treasure . . . are much deeper rooted than their dread of rude sounds and unmannerly language.[147]

Between these extremes was the more moderate opposition to the Crown of the wealthy and principled Philadelphia lawyer John Dickinson — privately tutored, apprenticed to the law, a Middle Temple man. Like Otis[148] and Adams,[149] he cited Coke in support of American liberties,[150] and rallied waverers with such prose as this:

But while Divine Providence, that gave me existence in a land of freedom, permits my head to think, my lips to speak, and my hand to move, I shall so highly and gratefully value the blessing received, as to take care that my silence and inactivity shall not give my implied assent to

---

139 *Novanglus and Massachusettensis* vi (1819).
140 *Dictionary of American Biography*, under "Daniel Leonard."
141 *Novanglus and Massachusettensis* 151, 152 (1819).
142 *Novanglus and Massachusettensis* 168 (1819).
143 *Novanglus and Massachusettensis* 225 (1819).
144 *Novanglus and Massachusettensis* 226 (1819).
145 *Novanglus and Massachusettensis* 188 (1819).
146 *Novanglus and Massachusettensis* 226 (1819).
147 *Novanglus and Massachusettensis* 26 (1819).
148 See "Letters from the Hon. John Adams," in *Novanglus and Massachusettensis* 287, 295, 297, 298 (1819).
149 *Novanglus and Massachusettensis* 105-110, 111-113, and compare 125-127 (1819).
150 Dickinson, *Letters from a Farmer in Pennsylvania*, letter IV at pp. 20-21, and letter X at p. 61n (1768).

any act, degrading my brethern and myself from the birthright, where-with heaven itself *"hath made us free."* (Gal. 5:1.)[151]

Jefferson echoed Dickinson's sentiment in these lawyer's words of the *Declaration of the Causes and Necessity of Taking up Arms:*

We cannot endure the infamy and guilt of resigning succeeding genera-tions to that wretchedness which inevitably awaits them, if we basely entail hereditary bondage upon them.[152]

There were other lawyers of similar education and standing; there were others neither as educated nor as articulate; the general impor-tance of the profession in the American community had nonetheless risen.   One index is the representation of the profession at the Consti-tutional Convention in 1787.   Of fifty-five delegates, thirty-two were connected with the profession — by training, legal practice, or as judges.[153]   Of these half were graduates of American universities — Harvard, Yale, Columbia (King's College), Princeton (College of New Jersey), William and Mary.   Charles Cotesworth Pinckney of South Carolina had a degree from Oxford which included the lectures given by Blackstone, and James Wilson of Pennsylvania had studied at the universities in Scotland.   Others had had private tutors.   Some, such as William Few and Roger Sherman, the intellectual shoemaker from Connecticut, were strictly self-educated.   At least four of the group had attended the Middle Temple in England;[154] a dozen had absorbed their law from other lawyers — Edmund Randolph of Virginia from his father, a king's counsel.   The rest picked up their law by self-study, practicing law, or judging lawsuits.   A contemporary estimate gave the delegates professional ratings varying from "A" to "C," or worse.   The range was from George Wythe,

. . . the famous Professor of Law at the University of William and Mary.   He is confessedly one of the most learned legal Characters of the present age.[155]

to Houstoun of Georgia:

---

[151] Dickinson, *Letters from a Farmer in Pennsylvania,* letter III, p. 15 (1768).
[152] U.S. Congress, *Documents Illustrative of the Formation of the Union* 10, 15 (1927).
[153] Compare Chroust, "The Dilemma of the American Lawyer in the Post-Revo-lutionary Era," 35 Notre Dame Law. 48 (1959).
[154] *Dictionary of American Biography,* under "John Dickinson," "Jared Inger-soll," "Charles Cotesworth Pinckney," "John Rutledge." See also Warren, *A His-tory of the American Bar* 188-189 (1911).
[155] "Notes of Major William Pierce (Ga.) in the Federal Convention of 1787," in U.S. Congress, *Documents Illustrative of the Formation of the Union* 87, 104 (1927).

As to his legal or political knowledge he has very little to boast of. Nature seems to have done more for his corporeal than mental powers.[156]

102. Lay opinion of the profession

The preponderance of lawyers at the Constitutional Convention helps to measure their new importance in national life (Section 101), but it reflects individual popularity and dependence on lawyers rather than general esteem for the profession. The dependence was recognized and resented. (Section 103.) Respect did not generate affection, and even respect was by no means general. Then as always there were mixed feelings about lawyers; dislike might be tempered by causes championed or won; enthusiasm might be soured by adversity, defeat, or incompetence.

In an expanding economy and a day of intense popular interest in the operation of government, the law was of wide concern. The *Salem Mercury* for Saturday, December 30, 1786, devoted its entire front page and more to the verbatim publication of a tariff act. *The Maryland Journal and Baltimore Advertiser* covered its front page of January 9, 1789, with the text of a statute affecting the organization of Christian churches. A lawyer expressing a popular opinion was spoken of in the press as a "gentleman of the law," [157] and the publisher of a formbook gave weight to anonymity by attributing the work to "a gentleman of the bar." [158]

Selective decision of his opinions has made it appear that Tocqueville confirmed a post-Revolutionary dislike of lawyers.[159] In truth, Alexis de Tocqueville — an impressionable young French lawyer visiting America 1831-1832 — gave a glowing description of lawyers as ". . . the American aristocracy . . . ," [160] ". . . the only enlightened class the people do not mistrust . . . ," [161] and spoke of ". . . the high opinion that is entertained of the ability of the legal profession . . ." [162] These were hardly majority opinions.

[156] "Notes of Major William Pierce (Ga.) in the Federal Convention of 1787," in U.S. Congress, *Documents Illustrative of the Formation of the Union* 87, 108 (1927).

[157] *The United States Chronicle*, Providence, R.I. (April 2, 1789).

[158] *The Attorney's Companion*, title page (1818).

[159] Warren, *A History of the American Bar* 512, 222 (1911); Chroust, "The Dilemma of the American Lawyer in the Post-Revolutionary Era," 35 Notre Dame Law. 48-76 (1959).

[160] 1 Tocqueville, *Democracy in America* 288 (Vintage ed. 1958).

[161] 1 Tocqueville, *Democracy in America* 289 (Vintage ed. 1958).

[162] 1 Tocqueville, *Democracy in America* 287 and generally 282-290 (Vintage ed. 1958).

The colonial prejudice against lawyers (Section 98) was never uniform and never dead, either before or after the Revolution.[163] Another Frenchman (who later became a naturalized American) gave a different, if more equivocal, estimate than Tocqueville. Michel-Guillaume Jean de Crèvecoeur had traveled through America for ten years (1759-1769) before his *Letters from an American Farmer* was first published in 1782. The exact date he composed each of the "letters" included in the book is still uncertain.[164] At one point he writes:

> Here are not aristocratical families, . . .
>
> *Lawyer* or *merchant* are the fairest titles our towns afford . . .[165]

The sweetness evaporates later as Crèvecoeur ponders the fact that Nantucket Island had but one lawyer:

> Lawyers are so numerous in all our populous towns, that I am surprised they never thought before of establishing themselves here: they are plants that will grow in any soil that is cultivated by the hands of others; and when once they have taken root, they will extinguish every other vegetable that grows around them. . . . They are here what the clergy were in past centuries with you; the reformation . . . clipped the clerical wings . . . a reformation equally useful, is now wanted, to relieve us from the shameful shackles and the oppressive burdens under which we groan.[166]

When lawyer John Adams attacked lawyer Daniel Leonard in pre-Revolutionary newspaper debate, both — perhaps prudently — wrote under pseudonyms. (Section 101.) But it was more than prudence that caused each of them to disassociate himself from the profession — in the same town which earlier had made a hero of lawyer James Otis.[167] With incomplete candor *Massachusettensis* Leonard said:

> In mentioning high treason in the course of these papers, I may not always have expressed myself with the precision of a lawyer; they have a language peculiar to themselves. I have examined their books, and

---

[163] Compare Warren, *A History of the American Bar* 212 (1911), and Chroust, "The Dilemma of the American Lawyer in the Post-Revolutionary Era," 35 Notre Dame Law. 48-76 (1959).

[164] *Dictionary of American Biography,* under "Michael-Guillaume Jean de Crèvecoeur."

[165] Crèvecoeur, *Letters from an American Farmer* 43 (misnumbered 34) (ed. 1793).

[166] Crèvecoeur, *Letters from an American Farmer* 146-147 (ed. 1793); compare Warren, *A History of the American Bar* 217 (1911), and Marckwardt, *American English* 120 (1958).

[167] "Letters from the Hon. John Adams," in *Novanglus and Massachusettensis* 247 (1819).

beg leave to lay before you some further extracts, which deserve your attention.[168]

And *Novanglus* Adams, writing of "the people":

> They do not want the advice of an honest lawyer, if such an one could be found, nor will they be deceived by a dishonest one.[169]

John Dickinson too, writing in 1768, covered his polished lawyerhood under a rustic cloak, *Letters from a Farmer in Pennsylvania . . .* (Section 101).

The lawyers' caution was justified. In the pre-Revolutionary youth of John Adams as in the post-Revolutionary days of his son John Quincy Adams, and later, the profession suffered open hostility. Entering his apprenticeship in 1756, John Adams was warned that lawyers "are hated, mistrusted," [170] and he himself soon came to denounce the pettifoggers at the bar.[171] In the year that lawyers crowded into Independence Hall to draft a constitution (1787), young John Quincy Adams recorded in his diary,

> ". . . the mere title of lawyer is sufficient to deprive a man of public confidence . . ." [172]

A mature Jefferson[173] deplored a tendency of law students to pretend mastery of the law when all they had was "a smattering of everything" — out of Blackstone. To a friend he wrote (1812):

> The distinction between these, and those who have drawn their stores from the deep and rich mines of Coke and Littleton, seems well understood even by the unlettered common people, who apply the appelation of *Blackstone lawyers* to these ephemeral insects of the law.[174]

In the early eighteenth century, a Pennsylvania bureaucrat wrote in commendation of Andrew Hamilton that he was,

> ". . . an Ingenious man, and for a lawyer, I believe, a very honest one." [175]

[168] *Novanglus and Massachusettensis* 187, 189 (1819).
[169] *Novanglus and Massachusettensis* 26 (1819).
[170] Bowen, *John Adams and the American Revolution* 140 (1950).
[171] Bowen, *John Adams and the American Revolution* 194-195, 617-618 n.4 (1950).
[172] Quoted in Warren, *A History of the American Bar* 220 (1911).
[173] Compare Section 101.
[174] 13 *The Writings of Thomas Jefferson* 166-167 (Lipscomb ed. 1905); see also 14 *The Writings of Thomas Jefferson* 63 (Lipscomb ed. 1905).
[175] Quoted in Lewis, "The Right to Complain: The Trial of John Peter Zenger," 46 A.B.A.J. 27, 30 (1960); compare 2 *The Papers of Benjamin Franklin* 327-328 (Labaree ed. 1960).

It has been said that Hamilton's later successful defense of Peter Zenger (Section 101) started the currency of *Philadelphia lawyer* as a mark of competence, but this claim has not been substantiated.[176] Some find its origin in Benjamin Franklin's skilled diplomacy;[177] others, in the shrewd assistance given British sailors by the lawyers of Philadelphia.[178] The expression has been said to antedate the Revolution,[179] but it is documented only as early as 1788 in ". . . it would puzzle a Philadelphia lawyer." [180] There is nothing in the collection of early usage to indicate that it was other than the compliment of quality,[181] like *Philadelphia . . . Flower* (1723), *-Butter* (1758), *-Iron* (1790), *-Bricks* (1807),[182] and later *Philadelphia doctor* (1855).[183] But it was the *Philadelphia* that bespoke best, rather than that *lawyer* was praiseworthy, and at some undetermined way point *Philadelphia lawyer* came to shake a derogatory finger at the skilled legal trickster. As with other terms of opprobrium (e.g., "the Spanish gout," "the French disease," etc.),[184] authorities split on national lines in finding place of origin. Americans say *Philadelphia lawyer* originated among the English;[185] the English that it originated among the Americans.[186]

Depending on context, the same quality in the lawyer might evoke admiration or hatred. This ambivalence of fears appears in the first *Biglow Papers* (1848), product of a distinguished lay graduate of the Harvard Law School:

> Ef the bird of our country could ketch him, she'd skin him;
> I seem's though I see her, with wrath in each quill,
> Like a chancery lawyer, afilin' her bill,
> An' grindin' her talents ez sharp ez all nater,
> To pounce like a writ on the back o' the traiter.[187]

[176] Compare Lewis, "The Right to Complain: The Trial of John Peter Zenger," 46 A.B.A.J. 27, 30 (1960), and Funk, *Heavens to Betsy!* 202-203 (1955).

[177] Mathews, ed., *A Dictionary of Americanisms* (1951).

[178] *The Slang Dictionary* (Hotten, 1872); Schele De Vere, *Americanisms* 624 (1872).

[179] Farmer, *Americanisms — Old & New* (1889).

[180] Quoted in Mathews, ed., *A Dictionary of Americanisms* (1951).

[181] *Webster's New International Dictionary* (2d ed. 1934); Partridge, *Slang: Today and Yesterday* 454 (3d ed. 1950).

[182] Mathews, ed., *A Dictionary of Americanisms* (1951).

[183] Taylor and Whiting, *A Dictionary of American Proverbs* (1958), under *Philadelphia doctor*.

[184] Jacobs, *Naming-Day in Eden* 63, and see also 60-68 (1958).

[185] Mathews, ed., *A Dictionary of Americanisms* (1951); Schele De Vere, *Americanisms* 624 (1872).

[186] *Oxford English Dictionary*, Supp.; Partridge, *A Dictionary of Slang and Unconventional English* (4th ed. 1951).

[187] [Lowell], *The Biglow Papers* 47 (1848).

American feelings toward the profession were likewise evidenced in the reasons given for the word *lawyer* attached to miscellaneous wild-life. A bird, the American *avocet* (possibly confused with the French lawyer *avocat*),

". . . from its perpetual clamour and flippancy of tongue, is called by the inhabitants of Cape May, the Lawyer." [1813.][188]

Of another bird:

On the New Jersey coast, it is sometimes called *lawyer*, on account of its "long bill." [189]

Similarly, there is a fish called the *lawyer*,

". . . because he ain't of much use, and the slipp'riest fish that swims." [1857.][190]

And another called the *lake-lawyer*, from its

". . . ferocious looks and voracious habits." [191]

The unkindest verbal stab at American lawyers came in 1846 with the loathsome domestic coinage *shyster*. Its origin is not certain, but the *Dictionary of Americanisms* says it is "Probably from some German slang term based on *sheisse* excrement." [192]   There are other conjectures — none complimentary.   One relates *shyster* to *shy* in the British slang sense, disreputable;[193] another says it describes a lawyer who takes a retainer and then does nothing, avoiding his client, i.e., *fight shy*.[194]

After *shyster, ambulance chaser* in 1897 was relatively mild (Section 50); it merely continued a centuries-long tradition of unfavorable public regard.

103. *The yearning for simplicity*

At the root of the continuing hostility to lawyers, in colonial as in earlier and later days (Sections 50, 59, 95, 102), lay an ancient notion

[188] Quoted in Mathews, ed., *A Dictionary of Americanisms* (1951), under *lawyer*.

[189] Bartlett, *Dictionary of Americanisms* (4th ed. 1896); Schele De Vere, *Americanisms* 380 (1872).

[190] Quoted in Bartlett, *Dictionary of Americanisms* (4th ed. 1896); Schele De Vere, *Americanisms* 383 (1872).

[191] Quoted in Schele De Vere, *Americanisms* 383 (1872).

[192] Mathews, ed., *Dictionary of Americanisms* (1951).

[193] *Oxford English Dictionary;* see also Partridge, *A Dictionary of Slang and Unconventional English* (4th ed. 1951).

[194] Schele De Vere, *Americanisms* 329 (1872); see also Bartlett, *Dictionary of Americanisms* (4th ed. 1896).

that not man himself but the lawyer was responsible for complicating life.[195]

The biblical denunciation:

> Woe unto you, lawyers! for ye have taken away the key of knowledge: ye entered not in yourselves, and them that were entering in ye hindered.[196]

echoes through the history of America. It was condensed in the Old West (Section 108) with the complaint:

> "We needed no law until the lawyers came." [197]

And it was given concrete paraphrase in the eighteenth-century press.

"Caution's" letter to the editor (March 2, 1797) shared with the citizens of Boston a lament over the tendency of lawyers to monopolize position in all branches of the government, especially the judiciary. "If they do not *yet* wholly control the *Judges . . .*" access to the law has become ". . . cloy'd with such numberless difficulties, perplexities, and embarrassments . . ." that a citizen has become largely *"dependent"* on the lawyer to get his rights.[198]

The same day the *Chronicle's* legislative correspondent sympathetically reported an attack on the profession in the Massachusetts senate. The people needed no professional intermediaries between them and God nor between them and the law. What was needed was ". . . a plain system of laws calculated to the understanding and information of the Citizens and that the voluminous code of *British authorities,* should be abolished . . ." In such a "state of simplicity" there would be no need for the

> . . . abstruse and perplexing forms of pleadings, which were practiced in our Courts of Law, by a profession, whose principal study was, to render the laws as intricate as possible, and as far out the reach of *common sense* as professional interest could render them . . .[199]

Poor Richard took to verse to flog the profession and its use of language:

---

[195] See, for example, "A Rod for the Lawyers" (1659), in 7 *The Harleian Miscellany* 25-35 (new ed. 1810), and Warr, "The Corruption and Deficiency of the Laws of England, Soberly Discovered" (1649), in 6 *The Harleian Miscellany* 212-225 (new ed. 1810).

[196] Luke 11:52; see also Luke 11:46; Rodell, *Woe unto You, Lawyers!* (1939).

[197] Quoted in Shinn, *Mining Camps* 113 (ed. 1948).

[198] *The Independent Chronicle & The Universal Advertiser,* Boston.

[199] *The Independent Chronicle & The Universal Advertiser,* Boston (March 2, 1797).

I know you Lawyers can, with Ease,
Twist Words and Meanings as you please;
That Language, by your Skill made pliant,
Will bend to favour ev'ry Client;
That 'tis the Fee directs the Sense
To make out either Side's Pretence;
When you peruse the clearest Case,
You see it with a double Face;
For Scepticism's your Profession;
You hold there's Doubt in all Expression.

Hence is the Bar with Fees supply'd.
Hence Eloquence takes either Side.
Your Hand would have but paultry gleaning;
Could every Man express his Meaning.
Who dares presume to pen a Deed,
Unless you previously are feed?
'Tis drawn, and, *to augment the Cost,*
In dull Prolixity engrost:
And now we're well secur'd by Law,
'Till the next Brother find a Flaw.[200]

One way of returning the law to "every Man" was to keep laymen on the bench who didn't understand the law or its language and didn't care to be instructed. It is related that in the early years of his practice, Jeremiah Mason (who in later courtroom battles was to teach Daniel Webster about pleading)[201] had the temerity to demur in the court of a lay judge of New Hampshire. Demurrers, said Judge John Dudley, were

". . . an invention of the Bar to prevent justice, . . . a cursed cheat. . . . Let me advise you, young man, not to come here with your new-fangled law — you must try your cases as others do, by the court and jury." [202]

The lay desire to perpetuate a "common sense" bench has died hard in America. It was a plainclothes justice of the peace in 1930 who, delighting in the unaccustomed notoriety of presiding over the trial of a movie star, visited the deliberating jury and came out shaking his head. To all who would listen he announced:

. . . it looks to me like they are going to bring in a verdict of guilty. . . .[203]

[200] 2 *The Papers of Benjamin Franklin* 254, and see 244 n.3 (Labaree ed. (1960); and compare 2 *The Papers of Benjamin Franklin* 327-328 (Labaree ed. 1960).

[201] *Dictionary of American Biography,* under "Jeremiah Mason."

[202] Quoted in Warren, *A History of the American Bar* 136 (1911).

[203] "A Call for Messrs. Gilbert & Sullivan," editorial, 4 *Rob Wagner's Script,* No. 95, p. 4 (Dec. 6, 1930, Beverly Hills, Calif.).

More basic than having lay judges to hold lawyers in check was the simpler plan of eliminating the profession entirely. That had been tried and abandoned. (Sections 98, 101.) Even so, before the bar became well organized and professionally well educated, the do-it-yourself tradition got off to a good start in American jurisprudence. In England, the profession began before the printing press promoted literacy and diffused book knowledge of the law. (Sections 59, 78.) In America there was not this early spur to exclusiveness; English printing was better than a century-and-a-quarter old when the first colonists arrived. In New England some compulsory education for children commenced in the seventeenth century. In that same century of the beginning of America a Boston-printed book discussed the jury system,[204] and an American printing press produced its first ready-to-wear legal form.[205] In the course of the next century, these forms became part of the regular stock-in-trade of the printing shop. At the offices of his *Pennsylvania Gazette,* Benjamin Franklin offered for sale in October of 1729 Bibles and bills of lading, psalters and bail bonds, psalm books and apprentice indentures, writs, "summons," arbitration bonds.[206] Other printers carried similar stocks: forms of deeds, wills, mortgages, powers of attorney,[207] letters of agency, charter parties, policies of insurance, "summonses," etc.[208]

Similarly with law formbooks. From a seventeenth-century dependence on those made in England (Section 99), the colonists graduated in the eighteenth century to domestic manufacture.[209] The appeal to the nonprofessional may be observed in such formbooks as the *Scriveners Guide* of 1797. This was edited by the New Jersey lawyer William Griffith, as a diluted version of the English *Scrivener's Guide* (started 1695; 5th edition, 1740). The book was a collection of business forms, the London edition "Useful for all Gentlemen, especially those that Practice the Law . . ."[210] and the American edition simplified for others than "professed Scrivenirs and Conveyancers."[211]

204 Warren, *A History of the American Bar* 158 (1911).
205 Chafee, introduction to *Records of the Suffolk County Court 1671-1680,* p. xxvi (1933).
206 *Pennsylvania Gazette,* No. XL, p. 4 (Sept. 25 to Oct. 2, 1729), reproduced in Franklin, *Autobiography,* following introduction (Pine ed. 1916), reprinted in 1 *The Papers of Benjamin Franklin* 164 (Labaree ed. 1959).
207 *The Pennsylvania Packet and Daily Advertiser,* No. 3208, p. 4 (May 13, 1789).
208 *The Salem Gazette,* vol. II, No. 64, p. 3 (Jan. 2, 1783).
209 See Warren, *A History of the American Bar* 157-159 (1911).
210 1 Covert, *The Scrivener's Guide,* title page (5th London ed. 1740).
211 Griffith, *The Scriveners Guide,* advertisement (Newark, 1797),

Sometimes the formbooks cast a sidelong glance at the profession. In his 1801 *Modern Entries* (conveyancing and pleading), Thomas Harris, Jr., "of the General Court Office, Maryland," sought to compile a book adapted to American practice, ". . . a very desireable object with Gentlemen of the Profession, as well as others . . ."[212] In a becoming prefatory apology, he wrote:

> I flatter myself, however, that it will at least be useful to Young Practitioners, and Clerks of Courts.[213]

Sometimes there was a direct pitch to the booboisie. For instance, this 1818 title page notice, trading on titles already established in England:

> *The Pocket Companion; or Everyman his own lawyer;* containing a variety of precedents, laid down in so plain a manner, that the farmer, mechanic, apprentice or school boy, can draw any instrument of writing without the assistance of an attorney. By a gentleman of the bar. Prefaced with twelve pages of scrip, intended as a copy for those persons who wish to improve their hand writing at leisure hours at home without the instructions of a teacher.[214]

The simplicity of these books lay in their apparent ease of use. Thus in *Precedents* (1822), the instructions for "Numbered *forms* for drafting" are in the now familiar pattern of the ready-to-be-assembled home construction kits:

> To draw a deed, or indenture, for the Conveyance of real estate, take No. 1; after which, if it be intended to recite the original titles from the Commonwealth to the grantor, proceed with the recitals, (for the forms of which refer from No. 18 to 29 inclusive,) continue with Nos. 2 and 3, and conclude with No. 4. The acknowledgment and receipt are then to be appended, for which see Nos. 104 and 107.[215]

As long as a contract could be put together this mechanically, the nicety of the language itself was not important. The formbook was designed to facilitate agreement rather than understanding, calculated to impress laymen and lay lawyers how easy it would be to talk like a lawyer without actually being one. Not always, but generally, the language of these forms was traditional — in the worst tradition of draftsmanship. There was, for example, the clumsy sentence structure,

---

[212] 1 Harris, *Modern Entries,* preface (1801).
[213] 1 Harris, *Modern Entries,* preface (1801).
[214] (Philadelphia, 5th ed. 1918); compare *Pocket Conveyancer; Or Attorney's Useful Companion* (London, 2d ed. 1773), and *Every Man His Own Lawyer* (Poughkeepsie, 1834).
[215] *Precedents* iii-iv (Reading, Getz ed. 1822).

harking back to the inverted word order of Latin translation. (Section 80.) In a form for *Indenture of an Apprentice:*

> During all which term, the apprentice *his* said master faithfully shall serve, his secrets keep, his lawful commands every where readily obey.
>
> .   .   .   .
>
> With *his* own goods nor the goods of others without license from *his* said master, *he* shall neither buy nor sell.[216]

There was also the boilerplate from England:

> Know all men by these presents, . . . have granted, bargained, and sold, and by these presents do grant, bargain and sell . . . To have and to hold the said negro *man,* slave . . .[217] [See Section 56.]

The bilingual tautologies:

> agreement *made* and concluded [218]
> *for* and *during* the term . . .[219]
> last *will* and *testament.*[220]

The yearning was there, indeed, but not the simplicity.

104. *The tenacity of form*

Granted the desire to eliminate the lawyer and his language (Sections 98, 103), Americans soon found the change was easier wished than accomplished. It was possible to speak in language that was no stereotype where substance was not already stereotype. (Section 100.) In a document of consuming public import like the United States Constitution — argued and picked over by lawyers, philosophers, writers, politicians — there could be deliberate choice and rejection of particular words. Language thought superfluous is deleted — *ex officio* before *oath;*[221] the equivocal made explicit — *legally* dropped in favor of *under the Laws thereof;*[222] the "vague" consciously retained — *to regulate Commerce;*[223] and the ambiguous purposefully drawn — the

---

[216] *The Pocket Companion: Or Every Man His Own Lawyer* 29-31 (5th ed. 1818); compare *The Pocket Lawyer, or Self-Conveyancer* 16-18 (5th ed. 1833), *The New American Clerk's Magazine* 42-43 (2d ed. 1807), Griffith, *The Scriveners Guide* 37-39 (Newark, 1797), and 1 Covert, *The Scrivener's Guide* 130-132 (5th London ed. 1740).

[217] *The New American Clerk's Magazine* 148 (2d ed. 1807).

[218] *Practical Forms* 2 (Windsor, Vt. 1823).

[219] *Practical Forms* 140 (Windsor, Vt. 1823).

[220] *Practical Forms* 174 (Windsor, Vt. 1823).

[221] Art. I, §3; "Debates in the Federal Convention," in U.S. Congress, *Documents Illustrative of the Formation of the Union* 721 (1927).

[222] Art. IV, §2, cl. 3; "Debates in the Federal Convention," in U.S. Congress, *Documents illustrative of the Formation of the Union* 734 (1927).

[223] Art. I, §8, cl. 3; "Debates in the Federal Convention," in U.S. Congress, *Documents Illustrative of the Formation of the Union* 730 (1927).

form of subscription designed to give the appearance of unanimity lacking among the delegates — "Done in Convention by the unanimous consent of *the States* present." [224] Madison also records the rejection of attempts at extreme precision —

Layman Elbridge Gerry's suggestion to add to:

> . . . nor any State be formed by the Junction of two or more States, or parts of States, . . .[225]

the words:

> *or a State and part of a State.*[226]

Lawyer John Dickinson's suggestion that the difficult choice between *inhabitant* and *resident* be compromised by not choosing; use both — *inhabitant actually resident for* .... *year.*[227]

Occasionally, even an accepted form was reduced to meaningful simplicity, as in the early wording of the Massachusetts summons. (Section 100.) But generally, where old ground had to be covered, the old way was the easy way. If there had been no wealth of precedent, if the Revolution had come earlier, a different formulary would have developed. As it was, by the time the Revolution gave its spur to Anglophobia in the law as elsewhere, by the time Jeremy Bentham had lent his instructive weight to codification (Section 109), a vast mass of English form had become firmly rooted in America. (Section 99.)

Where the lawyers were earliest established in educated ranks, as in the Maryland haven for persecuted Catholics,[228] the forms bore the strongest markings of tradition. A Maryland formbook of 1801 wallows in the excess wordage of the English declarations, whether in debt,[229] assumpsit,[230] or this one in trover[231] (*which readers of this book may either read or measure*):

---

224 "Debates in the Federal Convention," in U.S. Congress, *Documents Illustrative of the Formation of the Union* 740 (1927).

225 Art. IV, §3.

226 "Debates in the Federal Convention," in U.S. Congress, *Documents Illustrative of the Formation of the Union* 734 (1927).

227 "Debates in the Federal Convention," in U.S. Congress, *Documents Illustrative of the Formation of the Union* 492-494 (1927).

228 Compare Warren, *A History of the American Bar* 51 (1911).

229 1 Harris, *Modern Entries* 552 (1801).

230 1 Harris, *Modern Entries* 119 (1801).

231 1 Harris, *Modern Entries* 698 (1801).

Western shore, state of Maryland, ... county, sc.
S.J. late of .... County, ...,
was attached to answer unto J.G. executor of the testament and last will
of R.G. deceased, in a plea of trespass on the case, and so forth. And
whereupon the said J. by H.S. his attorney, complains, that whereas the
said R., in his life-time, to wit, on the .... day of ....,
in the year of our Lord ...., at .... county
aforesaid, had been possessed of certain cattle, to wit, one bull, &c. of
the price of .... current money, as of his own
proper cattle, and being so possessed thereof, afterwards, to wit, the
same day and year, at .... county aforesaid, casually lost the said cattle out of his hands and possession, which said cattle afterwards, in the life-time of the said R. to wit, on the ....
day of ...., in the year last aforesaid, came to the hands and
possession of the said W by his finding the same; nevertheless the said
W. knowing the said cattle to be the proper cattle of the said R. and of
right to belong and appertain to him the said R. in his life-time, and intending craftily and subtilly to deceive and defraud the said R. in his
life-time in this behalf, hath not delivered the said cattle to the said R.
(although the said W. was, by the said R. in his life-time, often there-
unto required,) but the said W afterwards, in the life-time of the said
R, to wit, on the .... day of ...., in the year aforesaid,
at .... County aforesaid, converted and disposed
of those cattle to the proper use and benefit of the said W. to the delay
of the executor of the testament aforesaid, & to the damage of the said
J. in the sum of .... current money, & therefore he
brings his suit, and so forth, and the said J. brings here into court the
letters testamentary of the said R. by which it appears to the court here,
that he the said J. is executor of the said testament and last will, and
hath the execution thereof, and so forth.

Even discounting the words consumed in alleging Maryland executor-
ship, this form has considerable starch. A contemporary Massachusetts formbook, *American Precedents of Declarations* (1802), decried
"The redundancies of the English forms, however proper in their courts,
where remuneration is proportionate to literal labour . . ." [232] and
gives a shrunken version of the Maryland form in a comparable declaration in trover:

In a plea of the case; for that the Plf., on ...., at
..................................., was possessed of a chest, and several goods
and clothes therein contained, in the schedule hereto annexed particularly mentioned, all of the value of .... dols.; and
being so thereof possessed, thereafterwards, on the same day, lost the
same chest and goods, which thereafterwards, on the same day, came
into the hands & possession of the said A [Dft.] by finding: Yet the said
A, well knowing the same to be the proper goods & chattels of the Plf.,
and of right to appertain to him, though requested, hath not delivered

[232] *American Precedents of Declarations* iii (Macanulty ed. 1802).

the same to the Plf., but thereafterwards, on the same day, converted the same to his own use; to the damage, &c.[233]

Declarations in debt,[234] assumpsit,[235] and deceit[236] were similarly abbreviated.

Such brevity was not to be countenanced. A few years later, *American Precedents of Declarations* (1810) appeared — enlarged and re, vised by a New York counsellor at law. He had in mind,

> . . . the double view of promoting an adherence to the logical accuracy of the antient precedents, and of meeting the diversities in the practice of the several states in the Union.

Many of the forms of the first edition, he said,

> . . . were drawn from approved English Books of Entries, and the remainder were precedents peculiar to the New-England States, and remarkable for their departure from those immemorially observed in England in similar cases. The Editor was of opinion that by subjoining to this latter class the parallel English forms with explanatory notes, the work would be more acceptable to the bar at large, and particularly to the New-England bar.[237]

Accordingly, the irreverently simple form of declaration in trover was repeated, and one in the Maryland pattern added.[238] The original short declaration in debt was repeated,[239] and wordier forms added.[240] To the earlier declaration on an account, which began: "In a plea of the case, . . . ,"[241] the reviser added the note:

> "In a plea of trespass on the case" is the technical expression in the most accurate precedents; "case" is peculiar to the Eastern States.[242]

The result was a fatter book, and a precedent for formbooks in the new federalism. The first edition of *American Precedents of Declarations* was touted ". . . as adapted by form, and qualified by authority, to invite the attention & meet the necessities of every State in the Union,"

---

[233] *American Precedents of Declarations* 248 (Macanulty ed. 1802).
[234] *American Precedents of Declarations* 261 (Macanulty ed. 1802).
[235] *American Precedents of Declarations* 97-98 (Macanulty ed. 1802).
[236] *American Precedents of Declarations* 191 (Macanulty ed. 1802).
[237] Anthon, *American Precedents of Declarations,* advertisement at vii, viii (1810).
[238] Anthon, *American Precedents of Declarations* 316-318 (1810).
[239] Anthon, *American Precedents of Declarations,* No. 1, p. 333 (1810).
[240] Anthon, *American Precedents of Declarations,* e.g., No. 12, p. 336 (1810).
[241] *American Precedents of Declarations,* No. 1, pp. 97-98 (Macanulty ed. 1802).
[242] Anthon, *American Precedents of Declarations,* No. 1, p. 134 (1810).

yet it was acknowledged to be ". . . more immediately applicable to the practice of New England." [243] The revision inaugurated the system of stockpiling forms for the widest possible sale. The method was accumulation rather than selection. Simplicity was more aberrant than desirable. As "bad money drives out good," long forms drove out short forms. In the face of more words collected from the past, the shorter form was suspect. Something must be lacking.

The fatal attraction of all-inclusiveness appeared in the wording of the individual forms as in the harvesting of the forms themselves. When in 1832 the American reviser of a book of English equity forms boldly eliminated the portion on tithes as being "of no use in this Country," he commented:

> Other portions of the work might also have been omitted, but as the practice is different in different states, it was considered better to retain a little which might be of no use here, rather than hazard the loss of something useful elsewhere.[244]

This same awful dread of leaving something out blurred the line between forms intended for the profession and those intended for the laity. (Section 103.) The distinction between lawyer and layman was long a wavering one; the name "lawyer" attached at varied times and places to the "friend" at court, to the uneducated "hanger-on," to the skilled and regulated professional. If the forms were to have the widest appeal (i.e., sale), they must answer to the lowest common denominator; and that was the magic of "precedent." Into that all else divided and dissolved. Prior use was the touchstone — good, bad, involved, sometimes nonsense. On prior use the formbooks flourished, and from this point on the growth was as lush as the growth of America. (See Section 112.)

105. The lawyer's role in the development of language

While some lawyers were helping to turn out those potboilers of the law, the formbooks (Section 104), others were making significant contributions to the intellectual development of the profession and to the growth of the English language itself.

The first law school in America — the Litchfield Law School — opened in 1784, followed by the now oldest established — at Harvard

---

[243] *American Precedents of Declarations* iii-iv (Macanulty ed. 1802).
[244] Van Heythuysen, *The Equity Draftsman*, introduction (Hughes ed. 1832).

in 1817 and Yale in 1826.[245]   Nine years after it was started, the Harvard Law School had less than 2000 volumes in its library; by 1908, more than 100,000.[246]   Included in the growing law libraries were the works of American lawyers, foremost among them the *Commentaries* (1826-1830) of Chancellor Kent, and numerous volumes (*On the Constitution, The Conflict of Laws,* etc.) by the indefatigable Joseph Story.   The lives of both Kent and Story spanned the transition of America from a collection of rebellious colonies to a constitutional democracy convinced of its "Manifest Destiny"[247] to rule at least a continent.

The physical expansion of America was accompanied by a burgeoning interest in language and literature that extended into the age of Jacksonian democracy, and many a lawyer was caught up in this intellectual ferment.   For some, language was affliction, but since colonial times there had been other lawyers with a happy addiction to words that transcended professional obligation.   (Sections 97, 101.)   Thomas Jefferson, a student of languages classical and modern — including Old English — took pride in a simplicity of style,[248] with the Declaration of Independence as his most lasting exemplar.   Gouverneur Morris, who polished the phrasing of the Constitution, graduated from King's College (Columbia) at sixteen and was a lawyer at nineteen. The persuasive *Federalist* papers were mainly the work of lawyers — the chief author Alexander Hamilton with a busy Wall Street practice, and lesser contributions by John Jay and James Madison.   Madison is not recorded as a practitioner, still he had studied the law — having planned to enter a profession where he would ". . . depend as little as possible on the labour of slaves . . ."[249]

Washington Irving for a time kept law offices on Wall Street, but like the lawyer-essayist Joseph Dennie (1768-1812) and the lawyer-poet Joel Barlow (1754-1812) he found literature more satisfying than the practice.   Barlow was of the literary circle known as the "Hartford Wits," a group graced also by John Trumbull, who bears that rarest of encyclopedia tags, "poet and jurist."[250]   Trumbull pro-

---

[245] Harno, *Legal Education in the United States* 29, 35, 37-38 (1953).

[246] 1 *Catalogue of the Library of the Law School of Harvard University,* preface (1909).

[247] Mathews, ed., *A Dictionary of Americanisms* (1951); compare *Encyclopedia of American History* 193 (Morris ed. 1953).

[248] 2 Jefferson, *Papers* 230 and compare 314-315 (Boyd ed. 1950); see also *The Complete Jefferson* 884-888, 1086-1088, 1101-1103 (Padover ed. 1943).

[249] Quoted in *Dictionary of American Biography,* under "James Madison."

[250] *Dictionary of American Biography,* under "John Trumbull," (1750-1831).

gressed from precocious youth (passed the Yale entrance examination at seven, enrolled at thirteen) through comic verse (e.g., *The Progresss of Dulness, M'Fingal*) to an active practice and ultimately to a place on the Connecticut Court of Errors. He is also remembered for his help and encouragement to the language studies of another Yale man and lawyer, Noah Webster.[251]

Neither Webster's brief period of practice (1789-1793) nor his service as justice of the peace (1801-1810) has commended him to posterity, but a commingled interest in law and language appears both in his advocacy of the first American copyright legislation[252] and in his several works on language. Before Webster's day — in 1724 — an English grammar written in America had been published in England.[253] Still in his twenties, Webster undertook *A Grammatical Institute of the English Language*, published piecemeal as a *Spelling Book* (1783), *Grammar* (1784), and in 1785 a *Reader*. A half century after publication, the speller neared the fifteen million mark. The *Grammar*, as Webster conceded, ". . . had its run, but has been superseded by . . ."[254] the very popular *English Grammar* (1795) written by Pennsylvania lawyer Lindley Murray. The Webster *Reader* never achieved the vogue of the McGuffey *Eclectic Readers*, which starting in 1836 ran through various editions to a total of one hundred and twenty-two million copies.[255] Lest we forget, see McGuffey on *Gesture*:

> When a gesture is made with one arm only, the *eye* should be cast in the direction of that arm; not *at* it, but *over* it.[256]

Webster's fame is in the dictionary, a field until then monopolized by the product of England, notably the works of the forthright Nathan Bailey (1721)[257] and the more circumspect Samuel Johnson (1755).[258] In 1806, Webster published a preliminary work, *A Compendious Dictionary of the English Language*, followed twenty-two years later by his monumental two-volume *An American Dictionary of the English*

---

251 Letter to Joel Barlow, October 19, 1807, in Webster, *Letters* 292, and see also 547 (Warfel ed. 1953).

252 *Dictionary of American Biography*, under "Noah Webster"; and see U.S. Library of Congress, *Copyright in Congress* 136 (1905).

253 Jones, *A Short English Grammar* (1724).

254 Letter to Joel Barlow, October 19, 1807, in Webster, *Letters* 292 (Warfel ed. 1953).

255 *Dictionary of American Biography*, under "William Holmes McGuffey."

256 *McGuffey's New Sixth Eclectic Reader* 59 (stereotype ed. 1867).

257 *An Universal Etymological English Dictionary*.

258 *A Dictionary of the English Language*.

Language. From the beginning Webster was under attack, for he not only approved numerous American departures from British usage, but likewise presumed to question the authority and competence of Dr. Johnson as lexicographer. When the critical reviews of the *Compendious Dictionary* began to appear, Webster wrote to a friend:

> I think this an important crisis in our literary history. The question at issue is whether an *American citizen shall be permitted to correct and improve English books* or whether we are bound down to receive whatever the English give us.[259]

Webster was annoyed with "Johnson's *want of just discrimination*," his lawyerly sensibilities aroused by the trifling Johnsonian definition of fraud:

> "*Fraud*," says the author, is "Deceit; cheat; trick, artifice; subtility, stratagem." But a man may use *tricks, artifice, subtility, and stratagems* in a thousand ways without *fraud;* and he may be *deceived* without being *defrauded.* Johnson has defined the word in the loose sense which *fraus* had in Latin, without discriminating between that and the strict technical sense which is most frequent in our language . . .[260]

Webster, as lawyer and American, saw too that the Revolution in fact needed recognition in a revolution of words. The 1775 edition of Johnson's *Dictionary of the English Language* gave a definition of *escheat* with little change from Cowell's seventeenth-century *Interpreter.* Webster eliminated king and nobility. Compare:

Johnson (1775)	Webster (1806)
n.s. Any lands, or other profits, that fall to a lord within his manor by forfeiture, or the death of his tenant, dying without heir general or especial. *Escheat* is also used sometimes for the place in which the king, or other lord, has escheats of his tenants. Thirdly, *escheat* is used for a writ . . .	*n.* The falling of lands to the owner, or to the state by forfeiture or failure of heirs, the lands so falling.
v.a. To fall to the lord of the manor by forfeiture, or for want of heirs.[261]	*v.i.* to fall to the owner or state.[262]

259 Letter to Jedidiah Morse, July 30, 1806, in Webster, *Letters* 268-269 (Warfel ed. 1953); compare Reed, "Noah Webster's Debt to Samuel Johnson," 37 American Speech 95-105 (1962).
260 Letter to David Ramsay, October, 1807, in Webster, *Letters* 282-292 and especially 287-288 (Warfel ed. 1953).
261 Johnson, *A Dictionary of the English Language* (4th ed. 1775); compare Cowell, *The Interpreter* (ed. 1637).
262 Webster, *A Compendious Dictionary of the English Language* (1806).

Webster likewise dropped the royal trappings from *a justice*[263] and *a marshal,*[264] and recognized that in America — unlike England — a *marshal* could be a sort of *sheriff.*[265]

America was unlike England geographically as well as politically. The broad open spaces called for special words, some of them affected with a legal interest. On this, Webster wrote heatedly to a critic:

> You observe, Sir, under the words *locate* and *location* . . . that the verb and one of the significations I have given to the latter word in my Dictionary are not in the English Dictionaries. No, Sir; and this was one reason why I compiled mine. How can the English *locate* lands, when they have no lands to locate! [266]

In the same category were the seventeenth-century *landoffice*[267] and the American sense of Old English *lot,* as in the bilingual tautology *lot or piece* (French) *of land* (O.E.)[268] or the even more grandiose *All that certain lot, tract* (Latin), *or parcel* (F.) *of land situate, lying and being in* . . .[269] *Lot* (like *landoffice*) had been used in the American sense since earliest colonial times,[270] and even the purist approved its use[271] — related to but not the same word as the British *allotment.*[272] The English lawyer continues to use French *parcel,* to which he had become accustomed before America was discovered, and prefers his redundancy weighted more with French, as in *All that piece or parcel of land* . . .[273] We have managed to sell the English our inelegant but descriptive *squatter,* a usage first recorded by Madison in 1788.[274]

Webster's greatest heresy was the simple acknowledgment that people in different areas tend to have different language patterns and

---

[263] Webster, *A Compendious Dictionary of the English Language* (1806); compare Johnson, *A Dictionary of the English Language* (4th ed. 1775).

[264] Webster, *A Compendious Dictionary of the English Language* (1806).

[265] Webster, *A Compendious Dictionary of the English Language* (1806); Mathews, ed., *A Dictionary of Americanisms* (1951); *Oxford English Dictionary.*

[266] Letter to John Pickering, December, 1816, in Webster, *Letters* 341-394 and especially 347 (Warfel ed. 1953).

[267] Mathews, ed., *A Dictionary of Americanisms* (1951); *Oxford English Dictionary,* Supp., under *land;* Webster, *A Compendious Dictionary of the English Language* (1806).

[268] 25A *Words and Phrases* (perm. ed. 1961), "lot or piece of land."

[269] Nichols, *Cyclopedia of Legal Forms Annotated* §4.644B (1955).

[270] *A Dictionary of American English* (1942); *Oxford English Dictionary.*

[271] Pickering, *A Vocabulary* (1816).

[272] Compare Horwill, *A Dictionary of Modern American Usage* (2d ed. 1944), and *Oxford English Dictionary.*

[273] Jowitt, gen. ed., *The Dictionary of English Law* (1959), under *parcels.*

[274] Mathews, ed., *A Dictionary of Americanisms* (1951); *Oxford English Dictionary; Black's Law Dictionary* (4th ed. 1951); Jowitt, gen. ed., *The Dictionary of English Law* (1959).

that nonconformity is not a sin. This affront to the respectable language community brought upon him the wrath of the "lawyer, philologist" [275] John Pickering, who himself had been nursed on Noah Webster's *Spelling Book*.[276] Pickering graduated from Harvard in 1796, and after study and travel abroad commenced the practice of law in 1804. For seventeen years he was city solicitor of Boston, with a reputation as both lawyer and scholar. His learning was such that he published a Greek dictionary and also one of the first collections of Americanisms — his *Vocabulary or Collection of Words and Phrases which have been supposed to be peculiar to the United States of America* (1816). In this, Pickering lamented the frequent departures of language in America from "the English standard" and called upon scholars to

> . . . lose no time in endeavoring to restore it to its purity, and to prevent future corruption . . . by *"setting a discountenancing mark"* upon such of them, as are not rendered indispensably necessary by the peculiar circumstances of our country . . .[277]

The Pickering *Vocabulary* was not devoted to the annihilation of Noah Webster, but some of its sharpest "discountenancing marks" were set upon him. Of Webster's recognition of the lawyer's verb *to deed,* Pickering wrote:

> We sometimes hear this verb used *colloquially;* but rarely, except by illiterate people. It is considered as a low word. None of our *writers* would employ it. It need hardly be observed it is not in the English dictionaries.[278]

Webster replied that with *deed* as with *test* and *advocate,* the formation of verb from noun was ". . . one of the most useful inventions in the structure of language . . ." and criticism ". . . betrayed . . . profound ignorance of the principles on which language is formed . . ."[279] The *Oxford English Dictionary* still lists the verb as "U.S.," [280] and here it is used by layman[281] and lawyer.[282]

[275] *Dictionary of American Biography,* under "John Pickering" (1777-1846).
[276] Webster, *Letters* 528, note under October 28, 1785 (Warfel ed. 1953).
[277] Pickering, *A Vocabulary* 17 (1816).
[278] Pickering, *A Vocabulary* (1816).
[279] Letter to John Pickering, December, 1816, in Webster, *Letters* 341-394 and especially 347-349, 355 (Warfel ed. 1953).
[280] *Oxford English Dictionary,* under *deed.*
[281] *Webster's New International Dictionary* (2d ed. 1934).
[282] See Mencken, *The American Language* 117 (4th ed. 1936), and Mencken, *The American Language Supplement I* 91 (1945); see under *deeded* in 18 C.J. 134, 11 *Words and Phrases* (perm. ed. 1940, Supp. 1962), and Ballentine, *Law Dictionary with Pronunciations* (2d ed. 1948).

There were other words — many of them law words — that were becoming part of the American vocabulary whether Pickering and later language purists liked it or not. For instance, there was *suability* (1793), as in *Chisholm v. Georgia*,[283] an American noun from the older English adjective *suable*,[284] both still alive here,[285] though England manages without our noun.[286] The first written use of *suability* is attributed to John Jay.[287] As first Chief Justice, he placed high court approval on noun and adjective:

> *Suability* and *suable* are words not in common use but they concisely and correctly convey the idea annexed to them.[288]

Alexander Hamilton is credited with the first published use of *constitutionality*,[289] rated by Webster as "well-formed and an excellent word."[290] With her unwritten *constitution,* England had long known *constitutional;* still it is in America that the changes have been rung most vigorously, what with *constitutional amendment, -construction, -law, -lawyer, -right,* and the soon obsolete *Constitution-shrieker,* a Reconstruction era analogue to *glory-shouter.* It was in America too that *unconstitutionality* was born (even before the Constitution)[291] modeled on Blackstone's earlier *unconstitutional.*[292] Without help from abroad, someone in a moment of high political fever stumbled between *unconstitutional* and *unconscionable* to produce the rare bird *unconstitutionable.*[293]

In 1769 a Connecticut scribe wrote down the noun *off-set* for the traditional legal *set-off,* and before long *offset* appeared in the reports as both noun and verb.[294] Pickering commented:

> This is much used by the *lawyers* of America instead of the English term *set-off;* and it is also very common, in popular language, in the sense of an *equivalent.* . . . It is not in the dictionaries.[295]

[283] 2 Dall. 419, 470, 479 (U.S. 1793).
[284] *Oxford English Dictionary.*
[285] Ballentine, *Law Dictionary with Pronunciations* (2d ed. 1948).
[286]Jowitt, gen. ed., *The Dictionary of English Law* (1959), under *suable.*
[287] Mathews, ed., *A Dictionary of Americanisms* (1951); *Oxford English Dictionary;* and see Webster, *A Compendious Dictionary of the English Language* (1806); compare Pickering, *A Vocabulary* (1816).
[288] *Chisolm v. Georgia,* 2 Dall. 419, 470 (U.S. 1793).
[289] Mathews, ed., *A Dictionary of Americanisms* (1951); *Oxford English Dictionary,* Supp.; and see Webster, *A Compendious Dictionary of the English Language* (1806); Pickering, *A Vocabulary* (1816).
[290] Letter to John Pickering, December, 1816, in Webster, *Letters* 341-394 and especially 353 (Warfel ed. 1953).
[291] Mathews, ed., *A Dictionary of Americanisms* (1951).
[292] *Oxford English Dictionary.*
[293] Mathews, ed., *A Dictionary of Americanisms* (1951).
[294] *Oxford English Dictionary* and Supplement.
[295] Pickering, *A Vocabulary* (1816).

On this one, Webster preserved his sarcastic aplomb, merely observing:

> I would leave to the critics the important question, on which side of *set, off* shall be placed . . .[296]

In the 1828 edition of his Dictionary, Webster still declined battle, giving the word both ways. American lawyers continue to use it backwards and forwards, *set-off* customarily retaining its British hyphen,[297] *offset* wobbling indecisively,[298] but more often dropping the hyphen.[299]

Webster agreed with Pickering that it was wrong to use *pled* for *pleaded*.[300] Pickering had noted that it was ". . . in constant use, in the *colloquial* language of the *Bar* in New England" contrary to the centuries-long preference in England, though it was sometimes used even there.[301] It had indeed been used in England, in the form *pled* since the sixteenth century (spelled *plead* since the eighteenth),[302] and survives today in American law and lay usage, variously labeled by the pundits "colloquial," [303] "acceptable," [304] "still used." [305] Similarly with the "antiquated participle" [306] *stricken,* a relic of Old English, preserved by churchmen in one sense ("And Abraham was old, and well stricken in age")[307] and American lawyers in another sense: *I move that all of that be stricken.* Another antiquity, long dead in England but still lively in American legal circles after three hundred years of use, is *decedent. Decedent* and *deceased* originate in the same Latin *decedere,* which even in far-off Roman days was a euphemism, serving both for *depart* and *die*.[308]

---

[296] Letter to John Pickering, December, 1816, in Webster, *Letters* 341-394, 359 (Warfel ed. 1953).

[297] Jowitt, gen. ed., *The Dictionary of English Law* (1959).

[298] See 29 *Words and Phrases* (perm. ed. 1940, Supp. 1962), "offset"; Ballentine, *Law Dictionary with Pronunciations* (2d ed. 1948); *Ballentine's Pronouncing Dictionary: Supplement* (2d ed. 1954).

[299] *Webster's New International Dictionary* (2d ed. 1934); *Black's Law Dictionary* (4th ed. 1951).

[300] Letter to John Pickering, December, 1816, in Webster, *Letters* 341-394, 359 (Warfel ed. 1953).

[301] Pickering, *A Vocabulary* (1816).

[302] *Oxford English Dictionary,* under *plead,* v.

[303] Nicholson, *A Dictionary of American English* (1957), under *plead.*

[304] Evans and Evans, *A Dictionary of Contemporary American Usage* (1957), under *plead.*

[305] Horwill, *A Dictionary of Modern American Usage* (2d ed. 1944), under *plead.*

[306] Pickering, *A Vocabulary* 182 (1816); see Webster, *A Compendious Dictionary of the English Language* (1806), under *stricken.*

[307] Gen. 24:1; see *Webster's New International Dictionary* (2d ed. 1934).

[308] See *decedent* in *A Dictionary of American English* (1940), *Oxford English Dictionary, Black's Law Dictionary* (4th ed. 1951), Ballentine, *Law Dictionary*

Pickering was but one of those who disapproved of Webster and his tampering with "standard" English. There were many traditionalists who in the *War of Dictionaries* sided for long years with Webster's chief American rival, Joseph Emerson Worcester, a non-lawyer from Yale.[309]

Worcester's first dictionary appeared in 1828, the year of publication of Webster's major work. In that same year of language excitement, an upstate New York banker, Alexander Bryan Johnson — who had been admitted to the bar but never practiced — published the first American work on semantics, *The Philosophy of Human Knowledge, or A Treatise on Language.* (A century later Johnson's pioneering and literate work was rescued from an ill-deserved oblivion.)[310]

In all this fretting over words there was surely place for an American law dictionary, especially so since lawyer Webster sometimes seemed more interested in the niceties of language than of law. His 1806 Dictionary confined *mortgage* (verb and noun) to real estate in accordance with the standard common law notion;[311] and while the term *chattel mortgage*, an Americanism, dates only from the second half of the nineteenth century,[312] the mortgage of chattels was not unknown to lawyers of Webster's vintage.[313] The error was repeated in the body of the 1828 Dictionary, but at the very end was corrected in a special note.[314] The 1806 Dictionary also described "one who executes a mortgage" as a *mortgager*.[315] This was one of the two normal English spellings, preferred alike by Johnson[316] and some of the law dictionaries.[317] But it was not the oldest law usage, nor was it the spelling given by Coke and Blackstone[318] and by the popular *New Law-*

---

with *Pronunciations* (2d ed. 1948), Webster, *A Compendious Dictionary of the English Language* (1806); and see Letter to Thomas Dawes, August 6, 1809, in Webster, *Letters* 328-332, 329 (Warfel ed. 1953).

[309] *Dictionary of American Biography,* under "Joseph Emerson Worcester."

[310] See introduction in Johnson, *A Treatise on Language* 3 (Rynin ed. 1959).

[311] Webster, *A Compendious Dictionary of the English Language* (1806).

[312] Mathews, ed., *A Dictionary of Americanisms* (1951); *Oxford English Dictionary,* Supp., under *chattel.*

[313] See, for example, *Ryall v. Rolle,* 26 Eng. Rep. 107, 113, 116 (Ch. 1749); 1 Powell, *A Treatise on the Law of Mortgages* 17a, 18 (6th Eng. ed. with American notes, 1828); *The New American Clerk's Magazine* 230-231 (2d ed. 1807).

[314] 2 Webster, *An American Dictionary of the English Language,* "Corrections" (1828).

[315] Webster, *A Compendious Dictionary of the English Language* (1806).

[316] Johnson, *A Dictionary of the English Language* (4th ed. 1775).

[317] Cowell, *The Interpreter* (ed. 1637); Blount, *Nomo-Lexikon* (1670); Blount, *A Law-Dictionary and Glossary* (3d ed. 1717).

[318] *Oxford English Dictionary.*

Dictionary of Giles Jacob (1750).[319] To make certain that no one took his spelling for inadvertence, Webster characteristically added a belligerent note to the 1828 Dictionary:

Mortgagor is an orthography that should have no countenance.

In 1839, John Bouvier — a French-born Philadelphia lawyer — produced the first of its species (named at length in the style of the day) *A Law Dictionary adapted to the Constitution and Laws of the United States of America, and of the Several States of the American Union.* Without acknowledging debt to Webster, Bouvier had set out to do for American law what Webster had done for American letters. In the Preface to his first edition, Bouvier recalled his plight as a new lawyer ". . . in a labyrinth without a guide . . . ," surrounded by English law dictionaries,

. . . written while the feudal law was in its full vigour, and not fitted to the present times, or calculated for present uses, even in England.[320]

He would compose a dictionary suitable to practice in America; there was not however to be any sharp break with the past. Bouvier did not repeat Webster's heresies in either the law of mortgages or the law spelling of *mortgagor,* and "At the suggestion of a judicious friend . . ."[321] (the work was dedicated to Story) included as an appendix Kelham's *Dictionary of the Norman or Old French Language.* In 1843 Kelham was separately published in Philadelphia, and so was not included in Bouvier's third edition of 1848.[322] Bouvier died — a respected lawyer and judge — in 1851. Time has made the link with the past even more secure; in the hands of others, *Bouvier* — still going strong — has become unexpurgated. (Section 107.)

106. *American punctuation*

During the eighteenth and the first half of the nineteeth centuries, thoughtful men were giving consideration to the words, the spelling, the grammar, the style, the content, the semantics, the organization of the English language in America. (Section 105.) All aspects of literary technique found enthusiastic searchers and teachers, all, that is, except the stepchild of the writing process — punctuation. At the very moment when an increasing use of forms was helping to crystallize

---

[319] See also *The Student's Law-Dictionary* (1740).
[320] 1 Bouvier, *A Law Dictionary* v (1839).
[321] 1 Bouvier, *A Law Dictionary* viii (1839).
[322] 1 Bouvier, *A Law Dictionary, advertisement* (3d ed. 1848).

the usages of law language in America (Sections 103, 104), punctuation enjoyed here the same disrepute and neglect as in England. (Sections 82, 83, 84.)

Even the works of the meticulous Benjamin Franklin and the most literate Thomas Jefferson have had their punctuation doctored to restore order by today's standards.[323] Punctuation was generally deemed unimportant, its rules capricious or nonexistent, its application haphazard. A fitting comment on the wild state of punctuation has been attributed to the Newburyport eccentric "Lord" (by his own decree) Timothy Dexter.[324] Uneducated but shrewd, he made enough money to keep the curious guessing to this day.[325] By his own account, his speculations ran from colonial currency through the sale of warming pans in the "west inges," capped by a flier there in what he spelled "pie eatty." [326] On this, he said, he "made one hundred per cent & littel over" peddling boatloads of depreciated *bibbels* ". . . Run Down in this country nine years gone so low as halfe prise and Dull at that — the bibel I means . . ." [327] In 1802 Dexter published a peck of amusing and popular illiteracy under the title *A Pickle for the Knowing Ones; Or Plain Truths in a Homespun Dress*. A note to the second edition reads:

> fouder mister printer the Nowing ones complane of my book the fust edition had no stops I put in A Nuf here and they may peper and solt it as they plese . . .

This was followed by eleven lines of assorted commas, periods, colons, semicolons, exclamation points, and question marks.[328]

Webster's massive two-volume Dictionary (1828) had room for a forty-six-page essay on language and a twenty-nine-page treatise on grammar, but this included only a scant two pages on punctuation. Webster recognized a relationship between sense and punctuation, with a period marking ". . . completion of the sense . . ." and varying degrees of nearness in sense connection marked by comma, semicolon,

---

[323] 1 *The Papers of Benjamin Franklin* xlii (Labaree ed. 1959); 1 Jefferson, *Papers* xxx (Boyd ed. 1950); see also 1 Adams, *Diary and Autobiography* xlix, lvi-lviii (Butterfield ed. 1961).

[324] *Dictionary of American Biography,* under "Timothy Dexter"; Marquand, *Lord Timothy Dexter* 289-292 (1925); and compare Marquand, *Timothy Dexter Revisited* 301 (1960).

[325] Marquand, *Timothy Dexter Revisited* 149-162 (1960).

[326] Dexter, *A Pickle for the Knowing Ones* 22, and see also 20 (Tucker ed. 1881).

[327] Dexter, *A Pickle for the Knowing Ones* 12-13 (Tucker ed. 1881).

[328] Dexter, *A Pickle for the Knowing Ones* 36 (Tucker ed. 1881).

and colon. Yet his primary concern was with the ancient oral role of these marks. He defined punctuation as

> . . . the marking of the several pauses which are to be observed, in reading or speaking a sentence or continued discourse.

And like his English predecessors (Section 82), Webster attempted to fix a yardstick of pauses:

> With regard to the duration of the pauses, it may be observed that the comma, semicolon, colon, and full point, may bear to each other the proportion of one, two, four, and six; and the interrogation point and exclamation point may be considered each as equal in time to the colon or period.

Finally, though, as had Bishop Lowth, Webster threw up his hands in despair, acknowledging that ". . . no precise rule can be given . . . ," pauses inevitably varying according to content and to the taste of each "judicious speaker." [329]

When John Wilson's *Treatise on English Punctuation* (first published in England in 1844) came out in an American edition (1850), he referred to punctuation as a ". . . despised but useful art . . ." [330] It was still a matter of free choice. This was true of the basic marks, and as for the lesser marks opinion varied sharply. For example, wrote Wilson,

> Some grammarians would unfeelingly lop off the dash, as an excrescence on a printed leaf; but others, again, are so partial to its form and use as to call in its aid on every possible occasion.[331]

Wilson also discussed the ". . . vague and inaccurate conceptions . . ." [332] of the *"exclamative* mark" or "note of exclamation," identified by a British cleric as "notes of admiration" or *"shrieks,"* ". . . strongly suggestive of a gentleman jumping off the ground with amazement." [333] Wilson observed:

> Some writers freely make use of this mark where the sentiments do not contain one iota of emotion, and foist it in on every possible occasion, sometimes in a twofold or a triplicate form; thus vainly trying to hide their lack of pathos or of passion by a bristling array of dagger-like points.[334]

[329] 1 Webster, *An American Dictionary of the English Language,* "Philosophical and Practical Grammar, &c" (1828).
[330] Preface to the Second Edition, in Wilson, *A Treatise on English Pronunciation* vi (13th ed. 1856).
[331] Wilson, *A Treatise on English Punctuation* 12-13 (13th ed. 1856).
[332] Wilson, *A Treatise on English Punctuation* 159 (13th ed. 1856).
[333] Alford, *A Plea for the Queen's English* 101 (ed. 1869).
[334] Wilson, *A Treatise on English Punctuation* 159 (13th ed. 1856).

If punctuation of lay works was disorderly, most law punctuation in America was a shambles. It was not merely a matter of eccentricity, though there was that too. Wilson's remarks on the exclamation point could have been directed at the seventeenth-century Ipswich, Massachusetts lease which said:

> . . . & that they will pay every yeare the summ of 110 pounds. save only that ten pounds more is to bee added to the last yeare! . . .[335]

(Though the emphasis here might record a note of "pathos or passion" in the exaction of that extra £10.) A celebrated historian has commented on the quirk of Freegrace Bendall, a Massachusetts court clerk of the 1670's. Bendall, writes Samuel Eliot Morison,

> . . . had a peculiar habit of using an apostrophe after all plurals', thus, as well as for the possessive case.[336]

A more lasting evil was an inherited one — the general acknowledgment of the supposed English rule that punctuation was out of place in legal documents. (Section 83.) The forms which were passed on to America were single-sentence forms, or at best long-sentence forms. (Sections 91, 99, 104.) Worse yet, authoritative English courts and English law writers had made it clear that this was no aberration, but rather both customary and desirable.

Opposing this line of authority were less well-known English dissenters (Section 84) and also a considerable body of native American legal documents — e.g., the Laws and Liberties of Massachusetts, the Declaration of Independence, the Constitution — which departed materially from English stereotypes not only in substance and form (Section 104), but in punctuation also. Yet such was the neglect of punctuation and so habitual the following of English legal habit that it did not occur to American lawyers that this was an appropriate point to make a further stand for independence.

The leaders in American legal thought followed standard English precedent. Thus, in his *General Abridgement and Digest of American Law* (1823-1829) the respected Nathan Dane set down a close paraphrase of the dictum in *Doe dem Willis v. Martin*[337] (Section 83) uttered by Lord Kenyon (a "famously ignorant" man, Thayer called

---

[335] *Records of the Suffolk County Court 1671-1680*, p. 295 (1933).
[336] Morison, Preface, in *Records of the Suffolk County Court 1671-1680*, p. xii (1933).
[337] 100 Eng. Rep. 882, 897 (K.B. 1790).

him).[338] In Dane's phrasing, the dictum was now unquestioned law:

> Stops are never inserted in statutes or deeds, but the courts of law in construing them must read them with such stops as will give effect to the whole.[339]

Bouvier — who had read Dane — followed the same English dictum in his 1839 *Law Dictionary* (Section 105), finding no inconsistency in the comment that ". . . a written or printed instrument" is to be ". . . construed without any regard to the punctuation . . ."[340] and his recognition that punctuation served a double purpose, ". . . to denote the stops that ought to be made in reading, and to point out the sense."[341]

There is a lingering suspicion of deficiency in grammar or meaning in Bouvier's fuller statement:

> All such instruments are to be construed without any regard to the punctuation; and in a case of doubt, they ought to be construed in such a manner that they may have some effect, rather than in one in which they would be nugatory.[342]

Dane on Kenyon was enshrined in a further dictum in *Cushing v. Worrick* (1857),[343] which helped to fasten upon American law a snatch of concise nonsense:

> . . . for the general rule is that punctuation is no part of a statute.

In the meantime, the United States Supreme Court had had occasion to muse over the shortcomings of punctuation, in a case that had little to do with the punctuation of writing, for *Ewing v. Burnett* (1837) [344] hinged on a charge to the jury. The Court came up with this mild observation:

> Punctuation is a most fallible standard by which to interpret a writing; it may be resorted to, when all other means fail; but the court will first take the instrument by its four corners, in order to ascertain its true meaning; if that is apparent, on judicially inspecting the whole, the punctuation will not be suffered to change it.

Taking "the instrument by its four corners" would not dump out the punctuation, for — as that independent thinker of the Boston bar Joel Prentiss Bishop wrote in 1873 — though punctuation does not control,

---

[338] Thayer, "Bedingfield's Case: Declarations as a Part of the Res Gesta," 15 Am. L. Rev. 1, 10 n.1 (1881); Thayer, *Legal Essays* 244 n.2 (1927).
[339] 3 Dane, *A General Abridgement* 558, §12 (1824).
[340] 2 Bouvier, *A Law Dictionary* (1839), under *punctuation*.
[341] 2 Bouvier, *A Law Dictionary* (1839), under *points*.
[342] 2 Bouvier, *A Law Dictionary* (1839), under *punctuation*.
[343] 75 Mass. 382.
[344] 11 Pet. 41, 54 (U.S.).

Still a judge cannot avoid seeing the marks, and they seem to have been permitted to turn the scale in an evenly balanced case.[345]

The calm sense of *Ewing v. Burnett* was overlooked in *Hammock v. Farmers Loan & Trust Co.* (1881).[346] Lured by the succinct phrase and the temptation of courts to be remembered, the Supreme Court followed in the path of England and Bouvier, making absolute the qualified dictum from Massachusetts:

Punctuation is no part of the statute.

The words stuck, and with them as a corollary, the lawyer's disregard for punctuation generally. This was a part of the climate in which the forms bloomed. While American men of letters experimented with nuances in literary fashions, the style of law language in America hardened into the dullness and muddiness, the monotony and verbosity of the long long sentence.

107. A lawyer's protest against legal form

If American lawyers overlooked the opportunity to improve on the punctuation of the law (Section 106), there were nonetheless lawyer protests against a blind following of English form in other respects. This was criticism different from the layman's longing for a Utopian simplicity (Section 103); here were critics privy to the professional password, who far from advocating self-destruction recognized the responsibility of the profession as best fitted to improve its own usage.

At age thirty-three, Thomas Jefferson was chosen chairman of the committee to revise the laws of Virginia after the Declaration of Independence.[347] His committee pledged itself to draft short bills, ". . . not to insert an unnecessary word, nor omit a useful one."[348] With his draft of a bill on criminal law, Jefferson wrote to his old mentor George Wythe:

> In it's style I have aimed at accuracy, brevity and simplicity, preserving however the very words of the established law, wherever their meaning had been sanctioned by the judicial decisions, or rendered technical by usage. The same matter if couched in the modern statutory language, with all it's tautologies, redundancies and circumlocutions would have spread itself over many pages, and been unintelligible to

[345] Bishop, *Commentaries on the Written Laws and Their Interpretation* 63 (ed. 1882).

[346] 105 U.S. 77, 84; compare Lavery, "Punctuation in the Law," 9 A.B.A.J. 225, 226 (1923).

[347] 2 Jefferson, *Papers* 314 (Boyd ed. 1950).

[348] 2 Jefferson, *Papers* 325 (Boyd ed. 1950).

those whom it most concerns. Indeed I wished to exhibit a sample of reformation in the barbarous style into which modern statutes have degenerated from their antient simplicity.[349]

Jefferson insisted on preserving terms of art, for "new expressions" meant "new questions." At the same time, he once explained, he had no stomach for statutes

. . . which from verbosity, their endless tautologies, their involutions of case within case, and parenthesis within parenthesis, and their multiplied efforts at certainty, by *saids* and *aforesaids,* by *ors* and by *ands,* to make them more plain, are really rendered more perplexed and incomprehensible, not only to common readers, but to the lawyers themselves.[350]

With the bar and Jefferson unconverted, at age seventy-four he was still proposing simplified legislation. Forwarding the draft of a bill to establish elementary schools, Thomas Jefferson — former President of the United States — wrote to a Virginia friend:

I should apologize, perhaps, for the style of this bill. I dislike the verbose and intricate style of the English statutes, and in our revised code I endeavored to restore it to the simple one of the ancient statutes, in such original bills as I drew in that work. I suppose the reformation has not been acceptable, as it has been little followed. You, however, can easily correct this bill to the taste of my brother lawyers, by making every other word a "said" or "aforesaid," and saying everything over two or three times, so that nobody but we of the craft can untwist the diction, and find out what it means; and that, too, not so plainly but that we may conscientiously divide one half on each side. Mend it, therefore, in form and substance to the orthodox taste, and make it what it should be; or, if you think it radically wrong, try something else, and let us make a beginning in some way. No matter how wrong, experience will amend it as we go along, and make it effectual in the end.[351]

Another President of the United States, Jefferson's friend John Adams — at eighty-three — also protested the "immense verbiage" of traditional English legalism, the "useless words" of the colonial charters. He wrote to the biographer of James Otis:

Bishop Butler somewhere complains of this enormous abuse of words in public transactions, and John Reed and Theophilus Parsons of Massachusetts have attempted to reform it. So did James Otis: all with little success. I hope, however, that their examples will be followed, and that common sense in common language will, in time, become fashion-

[349] 2 Jefferson, *Papers* 230 (Boyd ed. 1950); see also 1 *The Writings of Thomas Jefferson* App., Note E, pp. 216-218 (Lipscomb ed. 1905).
[350] 1 *The Writings of Thomas Jefferson* 65 (Lipscomb ed. 1905).
[351] Letter to Joseph C. Cabell, September 9, 1817, in 17 *The Writings of Thomas Jefferson* 417-418 (Lipscomb ed. 1905).

able. But the hope must be faint as long as clerks are paid by the line and the number of syllables in a line.[352]

On a less exalted level was the direct attack on specific usages of law language. Lawyer William Griffith — one of the few modest men ever to write a formbook — apologized for the thinness of his volume. With a bow to the ". . . more voluminous and comprehensive collections . . . ," he said that his work (in 1797) was

> . . . intended to assist such persons as from situation or choice, may not be provided with a more perfect guide: I have attempted (what is indeed uncommon for compilers) to strip the forms of all useless matter, repetitions and circumlocutions; and whilst I hope they be found tolerably correct, I am sure they will be acknowledged more concise, by one third, than any hitherto published.[353]

Firmly wedded to many word forms, e.g., *the day of the date*,[354] *Know all men*,[355] Griffith nonetheless made conscientious effort to cut the length of his English models, whether a general release,[356] an apprenticeship contract,[357] or a power of attorney.[358] Though he persisted in both *making* (Old English) and *appointing* (Old French) an attorney-in-fact,[359] he did not *ordain*,[360] (O.F. from Latin), *constitute* (L.),[361] or *depute* (F. from L.)[362] him. His was a plain *attorney*, instead of a wishfully superfluous *true* and *lawful* one.[363] And Griffith had the attorney do things merely *for me* rather than also *in my Stead* (O.E.) *and Place* (F.) as was customary.[364]

Another who sought to throw off some of the old dross was Bouvier. (Section 105.) In his 1839 *Law Dictionary*, Bouvier would eliminate

---

[352] Letter to William Tudor, September 10, 1818, in *Novanglus and Massachusettensis* 304 (1819).

[353] Griffith, *The Scriveners Guide*, advertisement (1797).

[354] Griffith, *The Scriveners Guide* 5, 38 (1797).

[355] Griffith, *The Scriveners Guide* 5, 20 (1797).

[356] Compare Griffith, *The Scriveners Guide* 5 (1797), and 1 Covert, *The Scrivener's Guide* 121 (5th London ed. 1740).

[357] Compare Griffith, *The Scriveners Guide* 37-39 (1797), and 1 Covert, *The Scrivener's Guide* 130-132 (5th London ed. 1740).

[358] Compare Griffith, *The Scriveners Guide* 20 (1797), and 1 Covert, *The Scrivener's Guide* 146-147, 150 (5th London ed. 1740).

[359] Griffith, *The Scriveners Guide* 20 (1797).

[360] *Records of the Suffolk County Court 1671-1680*, p. 14 (1933).

[361] *Records of the Suffolk County Court 1671-1680*, p. 14 (1933); 1 Covert, *The Scrivener's Guide* 146 (5th London ed. 1740).

[362] 1 Covert, *The Scrivener's Guide* 146 (5th London ed. 1740).

[363] 1 Covert, *The Scrivener's Guide* 146, 150 (5th London ed. 1740).

[364] 1 Covert, *The Scrivener's Guide* 146, 150 (5th London ed. 1740); see also *Records of the Suffolk County Court 1671-1680*, p. 14 (1933).

such useless titles as *abactors, abarnare, abatamentum, abatuda, ab-broachment*.[365] In his lifetime, he suffered *abatuda* and *abbroachment* to return, stigmatized "obsolete."[366] After his death the other titles were welcomed back into the dictionary, along with an *abatuda* no longer marked as a pariah, and an *abbroachment* with the more dignified "Old Eng. law" substituted for a blunt "obsolete."[367] Some other words Bouvier felt would never be missed — *ab, abacista, abandum, abbacy, abbat, abbreviate of adjudication*[368] — have found a new home in *Black's Law Dictionary*.[369]

One of the most forthright of the practical critics of law language in America spoke up from Mississippi in 1852. A. Hutchinson made his point right from the start, in the formbook title: *Manual of Juridical, Ministerial, and Civil Forms, Revised, Americanized, and Divested of Useless Verbiage*. He waggled an experienced finger at ". . . the senseless jargon and cumbrous verbiage of the British forms . . .":

> Those forms are retained, partly, in an abject veneration, and, partly, in the fear lest, by curtailing them, something of substance may be omitted — a fear that ought not to influence any one of conscious skill. In effect, the abuse is a heavy fraud on the people that should be speedily removed.[370]

His own forms were more for court clerks than lawyers, and while he retained much of the old boilerplate, Hutchinson also innovated. On conveyancing, he wrote:

> This Evidence of Transfer may begin *"This Deed of Conveyance,"* or, if you be alarmed about the loss of an old term, you can persevere and begin in a flourish of German text, if you choose, with *This Indenture*. The object of the change is to give truly the actual nature of the Instrument, its date and parties, so as to facilitate the recording clerk in his annotations. An *"Indenture"* means anything. In a Form Book these verbal niceties are not unimportant; come to the thing at once. Say "Deed of Conveyance, donation, lien, mortgage, trust, &c." And in searches, you have no occasion to read a dozen pages in order to find out what the thing is.[371]

---

[365] 1 Bouvier, *A Law Dictionary* v, note (1839).
[366] 1 Bouvier, *A Law Dictionary* (3d ed. 1848).
[367] 1 Bouvier, *A Law Dictionary* (Rawle, 15th ed. 1892).
[368] 1 Bouvier, *A Law Dictionary* v, note (1839).
[369] 4th ed. 1951.
[370] Hutchinson, *Manual of Juridical, Ministerial and Civil Forms*, preface (1852).
[371] Hutchinson, *Manual of Juridical, Ministerial and Civil Forms* 204 (1852).

He preferred *oral* or *orally* to *ore tenus*,[372] *extrinsic the record* to *dehors the record*,[373] and *accessary* or *participant* to *particeps criminis*.[374] The call to order, the Old French *oyez* (hear ye!), which even in Blackstone's day was called out in court as *"O yes,"*[375] Hutchinson thought might be better done by ringing a bell or striking a gong.[376]

None of these critics sharply turned the historic flow of law language. The pace of development of the American economy, the Industrial Revolution, war, and the rapid physical expansion of America both encouraged the keeping of the old usages as a symbol of the stability of law in a changing world (Section 95) and discouraged a general attention of the bar to anything as basic as language. It was not without significance, however, that within the profession there was an awareness of place for improvement. This too has become a part of the American lawyer's tradition.

108. Law language in the Old West

In the Old West there was a brief moment in history when the language of the law was a commoner tongue. For almost two decades before the first federal law on hardrock mining,[377] ". . . prospectors 'had the drop on the army.'"[378] There was no law, and the miners made their own.

In a thousand camps,[379] miners tended to their basic need for order. In Leach and Monroe's cabin, in Wand and Barker's saloon,[380] they made their rules, some with and some without legal advice. By 1849 there were lawyers in the West,[381] but as in the early days of the Massachusetts Bay Colony (Section 98) most lawyers did not come to this frontier to practice law; like other forty-niners, they saw more promise in pick, shovel, and placer pan than in lawbooks. Yet writings of the period give unmistakable evidence of the ubiquity of men who had absorbed the law; even in the rudest circumstances, the frontier im-

---

372 Hutchinson, *Manual of Juridical, Ministerial and Civil Forms* 289 (1852).
373 Hutchinson, *Manual of Juridical, Ministerial and Civil Forms* 289 (1852).
374 Hutchinson, *Manual of Juridical, Ministerial and Civil Forms* 290 (1852).
375 4 Blackstone, *Commentaries* °341 n.u (Jones ed. 1916); see also Stokes, "Directions for Holding Court in Colonial Georgia," 1771, edited by Edwin C. Surrency and reprinted in 2 Am. J. Legal Hist. 321, 323 (1958).
376 Hutchinson, *Manual of Juridical, Ministerial and Civil Forms* 289 (1852).
377 14 Stat. 251 (1866).
378 Davis, *Historical Sketch of Mining Law in California* 12 (ed. 1902).
379 Shinn, *Land Laws of Mining Districts* 49 (1884).
380 Davis, *Historical Sketch of Mining Law in California* 29 (ed. 1902).
381 Shinn. *Mining Camps* 113-115, 168 (Knopf ed. 1948).

patience with delay and formality is streaked with the trace of a tradition of law and a recollection of its language.

The blending appears in express and literate form in the Placer Laws of Alder Gulch, Montana (1864):

> And whereas the rights and interests of the miners of the District are of such a nature as not to admit of a resort to the tedious remedy of the ordinary process of law for every violation of those rights.[382]

Take for instance the case of Dr. Ware, who brought his problem to the Miners Meeting of the Weaverville Mining District in California. Here is a part of the minutes of August 9, 1853, recorded in winter reflection four months later:

> Dr Ware explained the object of the meeting in a few pertenant remarks. He said that McDermot told him on yesterday that unless he gave up one half of the water in the creek aforesaid, that he McDermot would take a body of men and take the water by force of arms and hold the same until he and his men were whiped off the ground. His party as above mentioned have taken possession of the water and are holding it by force of arms, in this dilemma Dr Ware calls upon his fellow miners to assist him in defending his rights, agreeable to the old miners laws, they said that this was a serious affair but they were willing to defend the old and established miners laws and the right.

On motion a committee was appointed to get the facts and ". . . examine the law . . ." and report back at one o'clock. At one, ". . . having thoroughly investigated the laws and customs of the miners of Weaver," the committee reported that

> . . . Dr Ware is fully entitled to all the water in West Weaver except four tom-heads, which is allowed for the bed of the stream, also that the burning of his reservoir and the destruction of his dam and other property and the taking of his water from his race by force of arms are malicious acts and should not be submitted to by those who are in favor of law and order.

The report was received, the committee discharged, and it was

> *Resolved,* that we assist Dr Ware in turning the water into his race and that we sustain him in the last extremity in keeping it in the Race.
> On motion meeting then adjourned for the purpose of carring his reselution into effect.[383]

There was also the note of immediacy plainly spoken in some of the claim notices:

[382] Shinn, *Land Laws of Mining Districts* 57 (1884).

[383] U.S. Dept. of Interior, Census Office, *The United States Mining Laws*, in 14 *Tenth Census* 278-279 (1885).

"*Clame Notise:* Jim Brown of Missoury takes this ground jumpers will be Shot according to the Laws of the Timbuctoo District."

"*Notis* — to all and everybody. This is my claim, fifty feet on the gulch, Cordin to Clear Creek District Law, backed up by shotgun amendments." (Signed) "Thomas Hall"

"*Taken.* — This is my Honest Claim of ten feet each way. (Signed) "Andrew Pesante"

"*To Miners.* — Look further. Respect my claim stakes driven by the rules of Douglas Bar." (Name illegible)

"The undersigned claims this lede with all its driffs, spurs, angels, sinosities, etc., etc., from this staik a 100 fete in each direcshun, the same being a silver-bearing load, and warning is hereby given to awl persons to keepe away at their peril. Any person found trespassing on this claim will be persucuted to the full extent of the law. This is no monky tale butt I will assert my rites at the pint of the sicks shuter if legally Necessary so taik head and good warnin. Accordin to law I post This Notiss. — John Searle" [384]

When it was "time for a change," there was no mincing of words. The proposal of new rules for the Sucker Flat Mining District (1855) was accompanied by a finding that the old laws were ". . . incomplete unintelligible and ill adapted to the wants of the mining community at the present time . . . " [385] Generally, the rules were short and direct, these for instance from the Con Cow Mining District (1851):

Article 1st. It shall be the duty of all persons or Companies intending to hold Claims in Quartz in this district, to have the same recorded by the Recorder of this district, within 30 days after discovery. Which claims can be legally held until such times as machinery can be put upon it. Provided the time does not exceed 6 monthes.

Article 2nd. All person or companies claiming and working a ledge of Quartz, shall be entitled to 150 feet of each Ledge so worked and claimed, also 1 extra claim for discovering the same.

Article 3d. When a company have taken up a ledge they shall be entitled to hold so much ground as they may deem necessary for the purpose of erecting machinery and other needful constructions. With the water privileges thereon. Provided the same has not been previously claimed.

Article 4th. The Recorder elected by this district shall receive for his services the sum of Twenty-five cents for each and every claim he records.

Article 5th. All difficulties arising from holding disputed claims or Mining Ground shall be settled by arbitration.

[384] Quoted in Shinn, *Land Laws of Mining District* 12-13 (1884).
[385] U.S. Dept. of Interior, Census Office, *The United States Mining Laws*, in 14 *Tenth Census* 282 (1885).

All persons buying a claim shall have an indusputable right to the same.[386]

The law words *null* and *void* are used in the rules for Little Humbug Creek Mining District [387] and for Angel's Mining District,[388] but Oregon Gulch Mining District found a down-to-earth substitute:

> That any person or company recording a claim or claims shall be required to specify and distinctly defined the boundaries and location and name, the gulch, ravine, hill or flat, and the particular part of which said claim or claims are located. If not so distinctly described and defined as to be easily found such record shall be considered worthless.[389]

A similar realistic quality is found in the language of Article 7th of the rules of Little Humbug Creek Mining District (1856):

> *Res*, that no persons claim shall be jumpable on the little Humbug while he is sick or in any other way disabled from labor or while he is absent from his claim attending upon sick friends.[390]

The joke was so good that it was repeated six months later in the rules of Main Little Humbug Creek Mining District.[391]

For a time there was a relative simplicity of legal expression even in the cities. It was the simplicity compounded of an uncomplicated life, lawyers with legal memories but few books or forms, and the complete absence of typewriters.

At first law business was plain slow. According to a prejudiced contemporary account of the early 1850's, some San Francisco lawyers,

> . . . to save themselves from the severe pangs of actual want, have been compelled to fish around the wharves for crabs and to enlist themselves in the petty traffic of shrimps and tomcods.[392]

At about the same period, Los Angeles lawyers were advertising for patronage in the columns of the *Los Angeles Star* side by side with

---

[386] U.S. Dept. of Interior, Census Office, *The United States Mining Laws*, in 14 *Tenth Census* 273 (1885).

[387] U.S. Dept. of Interior, Census Office, *The United States Mining Laws*, in 14 *Tenth Census* 291, art. 10 (1885).

[388] U.S. Dept. of Interior, Census Office, *The United States Mining Laws*, in 14 *Tenth Census* 285, art. 9 (1885).

[389] U.S. Dept. of Interior, Census Office, *The United States Mining Laws*, in 14 *Tenth Census* 286, §VII(2) (1885).

[390] U.S. Dept. of Interior, Census Office, *The United States Mining Laws*, in 14 *Tenth Census* 291 (1885).

[391] U.S. Dept. of Interior, Census Office, *The United States Mining Laws*, in 14 *Tenth Census* 293, art. 7th (1885).

[392] Helper, *The Land of Gold*, republished as *Dreadful California* 48, and compare 49 (Beebe and Clegg, 1948); see also Shinn, *Mining Camps* 113-115 (Knopf ed. 1948).

druggists, booksellers, and dealers in drygoods.[393]   One lawyer from Ohio had become a butcher in Los Angeles.[394]

In the first case on file in the old District Court of Los Angeles County, shortly before California was admitted to the Union, the hand-written complaint (assault and false imprisonment) and answer are each under five hundred words.   The hands are distinctively irregular, giving the impression of the impatient personal attention of profes-sional lawyer, amateur penman.   The sentences are long in propor-tion to the total wordage.   There is a scattering of law argot — *for that whereas, force and arms,* etc.   There is also matter not found in today's formbooks.   The defendant justified his arrest of the plaintiff,

> . . . for having committed a public offense upon and against defendant by presenting a pistol at defendant loaded with powder and ball, in the presence of defendant, and having thus assaulted defendant with a deadly weapon, with an intent to inflict upon the person of defendant a bodily injury, without any considerable provocation, and with an abandoned and malignant heart.[395]

Such candor did not last long.   Gold meant wealth, statehood, and litigation.   Disputes raged over land titles.   The Los Angeles butcher went back to the law.[396]   San Francisco lawyers became men of prop-erty.[397]   California offered ". . . so many legal complications that for a time it became the paradise of lawyers." [398]

The complexity of a complaint to partition a vast Spanish land grant could help to offset the encouragement which personal penmanship gave to brevity.   One of the early lawyers of Los Angeles wrote such a pleading on one side of a foolscap roll sixty feet long.   In reply to argument on general demurrer, he mounted a chair, and throwing the complaint to unroll like a giant streamer across the courtroom, ad-dressed the court:

> "If that complaint does not state facts sufficient to constitute a cause of action, then I am incapable of drawing one long enough to do so." [399]

---

[393] *Los Angeles Star,* Aug. 14, 1852, reproduced in Robinson, *Lawyers of Los Angeles,* following p. 30 (1959); see also Rice, *The Los Angeles Star: 1851-1864,* p. 49 (1947).

[394] Robinson, *Lawyers of Los Angeles* 30 (1959).

[395] *Robinson v. Lugo,* Case No. 1, District Court, Los Angeles County (Aug. 9, 1850); see also *People v. McDonald,* 2 Idaho 10, 11 (1881).

[396] Robinson, *Lawyers of Los Angeles* 30 (1959).

[397] Helper, *The Land of Gold,* republished as *Dreadful California* 49 (Beebe and Clegg, 1948).

[398] Shinn, *Mining Camps* 115 (Knopf ed. 1948).

[399] 1 McGroarty, *Los Angeles from the Mountains to the Sea* 349 (1921).

The typewriter manufactured by Philo Remington since 1873 soon made its way to the Pacific coast, the first in Los Angeles owned by a lawyer nicknamed "Diddle Daddle" after its distinctive noise.[400] Before his death in 1889, Remington had sold out the typewriter business as a bad deal. But in the next ten years touchtyping made wide progress, and at the start of the twentieth century verbosity was within the reach of everyone, especially lawyers. Gone were the tedium and expense of handwriting, which had inhibited the verbosity of some lawyers in the East [401] as in the West.[402] It remained only for abundant pattern to make law language West parallel law language East. This was soon achieved with an assist from the formbooks (Section 112), and especially from Jeremy Bentham. (Section 109.)

109. Jeremy Bentham

An ambitious father wanted Jeremy Bentham to become a lawyer and maybe even Lord Chancellor of England. Aged twelve and one-half the boy was entered at Oxford and at sixteen was listening to Blackstone lecture on the glories of the English common law. Bentham early formed an antipathy to the law and lawyers.

His protracted "guerilla war" [403] against the profession (1776-1832) was as wide-ranging as it was bitter. The law was ". . . spun out of cobwebs." [404] It was ". . . wrought up to the highest possible pitch of voluminousness, indistinctness, and unintelligibility . . . intellectual poison." [405] The judge-made common law was no more than "dog-law," i.e., you teach your dog what not to do by beating him after he has done it.[406] The lawyers were "harpies of the law" who understood ". . . the art of poisoning language in order to fleece their clients." [407]

"Law being the subject, whatever tends to keep men in ignorance, is of use to lawyers"; this was the use of the "lawyers' language" (Sec-

[400] 1 McGroarty, *Los Angeles from the Mountains to the Sea* 345 (1921).

[401] See, for example, New York Supreme Court, files, in *Armstrong v. Armstrong* (Dec. 20, 1881), *Stillwell v. Stillwell* (June 24, 1881), and *Young v. Boyd* (Dec. 8, 1881).

[402] See, for example, District Court, Los Angeles County, files, in *Robinson v. Lugo*, Case No. 1 (Aug. 9, 1850), and *Vegar v. Morehead*, Case No. 2 (Aug. 30, 1850).

[403] Quoted in Zagday, "Bentham on Civil Procedure," in *Jeremy Bentham and the Law* 69 (1948).

[404] 5 Bentham, *Works* 485 (Bowring ed. 1843).

[405] 6 Bentham, *Works* 332 (Bowring ed. 1843).

[406] 5 Bentham, *Works* 235 (Bowring ed. 1843).

[407] 5 Bentham, *Works* 233-237, 236 (Bowring ed. 1843).

tion 2), this the "Principle of Jargon or Jargonization."[408]   Law language was "excrementitious matter," "literary garbage."[409]

"Lawyers' cant, besides serving them as a cover and as a bond of union, serves them as an instrument, an iron crow or a pick-lock key, for collecting plunder in cases in which otherwise it could not be collected: . . ."[410]

In all of this, wrote Bentham, the judges were senior partners, delighting in the complexity of a system that frequently produces lawyer errors costly only to their clients:

> This is among the circumstances, that, under the technical system, concur in rendering quirks so pleasant and convenient to the thoroughbred judge. He feels a degree of awkwardness where a decision is to be given upon the merits.[411]

Bentham was not critic alone. He proposed to cleanse the law of its fictions, its barbarity, and costly, antiquated technicality.   The leading semanticist of his day,[412] he proposed to make language itself a better instrument, where necessary for this purpose coining words, e.g., *maximize, minimize, international, utilitarian.*   To many existing words, Bentham first gave legal application: *cross-examination, unilateral, substantive* and *adjective* law, *preponderance, preponderantly,* and *preponderately.*

Preponderancy, preponderant, and *preponderate* are not his creatures though he spoke kindly of that horror of juries, "the *preponderant probability.*"[413]

Bentham's own most beloved coinage was *codify,* and its related *codification* and *codifier.*   It was Bentham's thought that the entire law might be broken down into separate codes, each covering ". . . those parts which are intended for the use of particular classes . . ." Each part would be small enough to be remembered,[414] and written with such clarity that the ordinary citizen ". . . may have presented to his mind an exact idea of the will of the legislator . . ."[415] The prospect was enticing, but the water was cold.

Bentham had less difficulty in persuading English-speakers to adopt

[408] 7 Bentham, *Works* 280 (Bowring ed. 1843).
[409] 3 Bentham, *Works* 260 (Bowring ed. 1843).
[410] 7 Bentham, *Works* 282 (Bowring ed. 1843).
[411] 7 Bentham, *Works* 282 (Bowring ed. 1843).
[412] See Ogden, *Bentham's Theory of Fictions* ix-x (2d ed. 1951).
[413] 7 Bentham, *Works* 191 (Bowring ed. 1843).
[414] 3 Bentham, *Works* 208 (Bowring ed. 1843).
[415] 3 Bentham, *Works* 207 (Bowring ed. 1843).

the words than the concepts. England exhausted its interest in Bentham's legal reforms short of codification. In the reforming atmosphere of America after the Revolution — anti-British and pro-French — there was more interest. Even so, it was in a Louisiana still under the spell of the French civil law that Bentham's urging of codification bore first fruit, the Livingstone code of 1805. Elsewhere Bentham was resisted by the bar. In the year before it adopted the Bentham-influenced Field Code of Civil Procedure, California turned down codification, and turned down a proposal that California adopt the law of the civilians as a substitute for the common law. A state senate committee rejected as "the chimeras of ignorance and folly" the popular notion that the law might be condensed,

> . . . within the compass of a common sized spelling-book — so that every man might become his own lawyer and judge — so that the farmer, the artisan, the merchant, with this "vade mecum" in his pocket, at the plough, in the workshop, or in the counting-house, might be enabled at a moment's warning, to open its leaves and point directly to the very page, section, and line, which would elucidate the darkest case, solve the most abstruse legal problem, clearly define his rights, and prescribe the remedy for his wrongs.[416]

Despite denunciation by the bar, these "chimeras" continued to charm the public. They appealed strongly to the old yearning for simplicity (Section 103), which Bentham had reinforced with philosophical and legal argument. Since the days of the Revolution, law reform of sorts had bubbled in the many legislative pots of America. Now led by the American codifier David Dudley Field, New York adopted the first part of a Code of Civil Procedure (1848), and in the half century that followed, codes spread from coast to coast and border to border.[417]

The Bentham-inspired codes reduced the law to outline form, numbered it for reference, eliminated some of the antique verbiage, shortened it. Bentham tied items into bundles with *as follows* and split categories asunder with:

> Exceptions excepted, let the masculine singular comprehend both genders and numbers.[418]

It has become standard practice to have the singular male include

[416] "Report on Civil and Common Law," February 27, 1850, in Appendix, 1 Cal. 588-604, 591 (1850).
[417] Everett, "Bentham in the United States of America," in *Jeremy Bentham and the Law* 185-201 and especially 200-201 (1948).
[418] 3 Bentham, *Works* 265 (Bowring ed. 1843).

the plural female,[419] and while *exceptions excepted* is not now in vogue, the phrase is a part of Bentham's "substantive-preferring principle" [420] which today permeates legal writing. Bentham believed that "A verb slips through your fingers like an eel, . . ." [421] where a noun may be held — modified, explained, acted upon, made precise[422] — in short, multiplied. The principle

chooses	*instead of*
to give motion to	to move [423]
to give extension to	to extend
to give straightness to	to straighten [424]

and, in Bentham's burlesque of his own system, *to make ringtion* instead of *to ring*.[425] In keeping with Bentham's doctrine, a lawyer frequently

chooses	*instead of*
to make application	to apply [426]
make investigations	investigate
make reports	report
give assistance	assist [427]
to cause abridgement	abridge
to cause annulment	annul [428]

A prejudice against verbs was neither the only nor the worst of Bentham's problems. His legacy also includes sparse punctuation (Section 84) and language so involved that it is embarrassing to friends. In the euphemism of a disciple, after the first decade of the nineteenth century Bentham adopted a style ". . . in which clarity was more important than literary convention." [429] Further, it is said, many of his suggestions for the law were set down by Bentham in fragments and put into form by other hands.[430] Whatever the cause,

---

[419] See, for example, Cal. Code Civ. Proc. §17; and see Rodell, *Woe unto You, Lawyers!* 202 (1939).

[420] 3 Bentham, *Works* 267-268 (Bowring ed. 1843); 10 Bentham, *Works* 569-570 (Bowring ed. 1843); 8 Bentham, *Works* 315 (Bowring ed. 1843).

[421] 10 Bentham, *Works* 569 (Bowring ed. 1843).

[422] 3 Bentham, *Works* 267-268 (Bowring ed. 1843).

[423] 10 Bentham, *Works* 569 (Bowring ed. 1843).

[424] 3 Bentham, *Works* 267 (Bowring ed. 1843).

[425] See 10 Bentham, *Works* 570 (Bowring ed. 1843).

[426] 8 Bentham, *Works* 315 (Bowring ed. 1843); 42 *C.J. motions and orders,* p. 517, §175; *contra,* Dickerson, *Legislative Drafting* 68-69, and 69 n.1 (1954).

[427] See Cal. Code Civ. Proc. §1746.

[428] See 17 U.S.C.A. 8.

[429] Ogden, "Note on Bentham's Method of Composition," in *Bentham's Theory of Fictions* cl (2d ed. 1951).

[430] Ogden, "Note on Bentham's Method of Composition," in *Bentham's Theory of Fictions* cli (2d ed. 1951).

the style in which Bentham was transmitted to posterity did not speak well for his proposals, even if the substance passed muster.

Bentham thought that the desirable qualities in an individual's style were simplicity, compressedness, clearness, impressiveness, and harmoniousness. Here is Bentham's way of saying *Don't use a word that has two confusing meanings:*

> When, for the designation of the idea in question, no other appellative is in use but one which is tainted with ambiguity, presenting in conjunction with the idea required, another which is different from it, and which, on pain of being led into error by it, must be distinguished from it, — substitute another word which is free from ambiguity, presenting to view no idea other than that which is wished and endeavoured to be presented by it.[431]

As a remedy for "longwindedness," Bentham preached "The shorter the sentence the better," [432] and he took out after "legal language" in this one sentence:

> The nomenclature devised in a barbarous age, by a mixture of stupidity, ignorance, error, and lawyer-craft, has, by force of irresistible power, under favour of interest-begotten and authority-begotten prejudice, been interwoven in the language, and been rendered the subject-matter of instruction to the highest educated classes, and the object of admiration and veneration to all classes: — nay, even the more flagrant its inaptitude, the more intense the veneration: for the more flagrant the inaptitude, the greater the labour necessary to the attainment of that incorrect and incomplete conception of the ideas attached to it, which the nature of them admits of; and the greater the labour a man has bestowed upon any subject-matter, be what it may, the greater the value which he of course attaches to the fruits of that labour, whatsoever they may happen to be.[433]

By the standard of some of the works he criticized, e.g., a statute with a sentence thirteen pages long,[434] Bentham was almost succinct. His works, though, have outlived the immediate objects of their criticism and have lived to be judged by the standards of another day.

Worst of all, the codification which Bentham intended as pure blessing made the adoption of pre-packaged law an easy thing. Each code adoption added its drop of precedent to the strength of the form that was there — the bad as well as the good.[435] The neatness of the package discouraged changes in its form; and the apparent interchange-

---

[431] 8 Bentham, *Works* 316 (Bowring ed. 1843).
[432] 3 Bentham, *Works* 264 (Bowring ed. 1843).
[433] 3 Bentham, *Works* 272 (Bowring ed. 1843).
[434] 5 Bentham, *Works* 233-237 and especially 236 (Bowring ed. 1843).
[435] Compare Everett, "Bentham in the United States of America," in *Jeremy Bentham and the Law* 201 (1948).

ability of parts from state to state promoted the spread near and far of word formulas for everything. (Section 112.)

110. *The mountainous law*

Enthusiasm in Western America for Bentham-inspired codes (Section 109) coincided with a Western distrust of delegated authority, whether to legislators or attorneys. The appeal was essentially to the do-it-yourselfers, to the

> . . . somewhat popular doctrine, that in matters of law and legislation, the crude notions of any man, who is not a lawyer, are entitled to a higher consideration than the reflections and ripe experience of the most profound jurist.[436]

This was the tradition of the democracy of Andrew Jackson, frontier lawyer and judge.[437]

The simultaneous fear of lawyers and respect for their power (Section 102) were fostered by the growing complexity of American life. Between Washington's first term and the middle of the nineteenth century, war, purchase, and negotiation had stretched the United States into a two-ocean power, her area more than tripled,[438] her population swollen from less than four million to more than twenty-three million (1880, fifty million plus; 1910, one hundred million plus; 1940, one hundred and fifty million plus).[439]

The Industrial Revolution and the following years of commercial boom and bust brought the common and statute law into new and broad areas of human effort, in both the United States and England. The steam engine, developed in England, floated and harnessed to the paddlewheel by the American Fulton, sailed into the law of the Constitution in 1824 with the commerce clause decision in *Gibbons v. Ogden*.[440] This was a symbol of the changing economy of America. Tied to the soil by British colonial policy, the new nation was still overwhelmingly rural in 1799, when agricultural income exceeded manufacturing by more than seven to one.[441] Toward mid-century

---

[436] "Report on Civil and Common Law," February 27, 1850, in Appendix, 1 Cal. 588 (1850).

[437] See Schlesinger, *The Age of Jackson* 329-333 (1945).

[438] U. S. Bureau of the Census, *Historical Statistics of the United States*, Series B 26-30, p. 25 (1949).

[439] U. S. Bureau of the Census, *Historical Statistics of the United States*, Series B 1-12, p. 25 (1949).

[440] 9 Wheat. 1.

[441] U. S. Bureau of the Census, *Historical Statistics of the United States*, Series A 154-164, p. 14 (1949).

the gap gradually narrowed, and in the first few years after the Civil War manufacturing income came up sharply to hit the billion-dollar mark, alongside agriculture's one and one-half billions in 1869. Twenty years later, manufacturing income had doubled, and for the first time in American history was ahead of agriculture.[442]

These statistics dissolved into the reality of individual controversy in the courtroom, where a change was taking place more important to the law than even the harnessing of steam. The reporting of decisions in colonial America had been — as in England — an avocation, born of a lawyer's notes for the refreshment of him and his friends. Of this character were the notes of young Josiah Quincy, Jr. (published ninety years after his death), who has left us a record of court life in Massachusetts between 1761 and 1772: John Adams and James Otis called to the bar, appearing in "Barristers Habits," "gowns, bands, and tie wigs";[443] a writ abated for a Gentleman sued as a "Yeoman," Otis arguing unsuccessfully that

Lovejoy is certainly no Gentleman by Office; for no Commission from any Governour whatever, can make a Man Gentleman by Office.[444]

The Revolution did not end casual reporting, but the lingering antipathy to things British extended to precedent from English courts (Section 103) and encouraged more reporting of American decisions.[445] Further impetus came from Connecticut, which in 1785 required her judges to file opinions on points of law — a move that resulted in the first formal collection of state decisions, *Kirby's Reports* (1789). When James Kent came to the New York bench in 1799, opinions were still given orally; there were no New York reports, "few American precedents" of any sort, and — as he later recalled — "English authorities did not stand very high in those feverish times . . ."[446] On his own initiative Kent brought written opinions to the decision conferences with his fellow judges, a startling but effective and contagious innovation.

The change from oral to written opinions that began in late eighteenth-century America loosed the floodwaters of precedent as nothing since the change from oral to written pleading at common law in

442 U. S. Bureau of the Census, *Historical Statistics of the United States,* Series A 154-164, p. 14 (1949).

443 *Quincy's Massachusetts Reports* 35 (1865).

444 *Bromfield v. Lovejoy,* Quincy's Mass. Rep. 238 (1767).

445 Warren, *A History of the American Bar* 325-332 (1911).

446 Kent, "An American Law Student of a Hundred Years Ago," in 1 *Select Essays in Anglo-American Legal History* 837, 845 (1907).

sixteenth-century England. (Sections 68, 78.) Conceived in part as a device to democratize the law, to remove its mystery and uncertainty by making it available to all who could read, the written opinion soon overwhelmed writer, reporter, and reader. The writing of opinions became for some an unwelcome, perfunctory duty, hurriedly — often poorly — performed. As in England, most of the early American reports were known by the name of the reporter, some of them distinguished lawyers whose names gave their volumes acceptance with the bar, e.g., George Wythe, Henry Wheaton, William Cranch. But the written opinion had simplified the reporter's task, making it possible for good eyes to substitute for the older requisites — good ears and competence in the law. In time, the critical, living "reporter" was buried under a mass of uncritical, mechanical reproductions; it was the "reports" not the "reporter" that were sought after. With the volume of these no practitioner could hope to keep current. The race of the reports was on, continuing from state to territory to state, from supremest court to town court, from bureau to board, on into reports of unreported cases.[447] No longer would lawyer or judge suffer from want of precedent. Chancellor Kent had once written:

> . . . and I might once and a while be embarrassed by a technical rule,
> but I most always found principles suited to my views of the case . . .[448]

There would now be available not only "principles" of all shades, but matching decisions as well.

Such was the array of reported cases that before the middle of the nineteenth century digests of American decisions made their first tentative volume by volume appearance.[449] The earliest digests divided decisions geographically, but after the Civil War arrangement by subject was begun. One publisher announced the intention of giving fuller treatment to ". . . those decisions . . . which contribute to the progress of legal science . . ."; its digest would be selective:

> Cases which involve only the application of established rules to peculiar
> and unusual facts; opinions which are occupied with recapitulating well

---

[447] Cal. Unreported Cases (1913); Tex. Unreported Cases (1886, 1891).

[448] Kent, "An American Law Student of a Hundred Years Ago," in 1 *Select Essays in Anglo-American Legal History* 837, 843-845 (1907).

[449] *Digest of Decisions, Courts of Common Law and Admiralty, 1754-1846,* vol. 1, Metcalf and Perkins, vols. 2, 3, G. T. Curtis (1840-1846); *Digest of Decisions, Courts of Equity, to 1847,* J. P. Putnam (1851), 2 vols.; *Digest of Decisions, Supplement, 1846-1847,* J. P. Putnam (1847-1861), 2 vols.; *Digest of Decisions, Table of Cases,* G. P. Sanger (1849); *Annual Digest, 1847-1869* (1848-1871), 23 vols.

known principles or accumulating quotations from the authorities, adjudications of local application only; — are to have a briefer treatment.[450]

By the end of the nineteenth century, the criterion of selectivity had been dropped in favor of completeness and meticulous indexing. The fifty-volume Century Edition of the *American Digest* boasted half a million reported cases for the less than two and one-half centuries of law in America (1658-1896), reflecting "The importance which our courts attach to judicial precedents . . ."[451] That mountain of precedent had accumulated at a geologically leisurely rate, compared to the nearly quarter million reported and digested decisions in the next ten years alone. There had been, said the editors, ". . . an extraordinary commercial and industrial development . . ."[452] — twenty-five volumes. The Second Decennial Edition of the *American Digest* (1906-1916) was crowded into twenty-four volumes,[453] and from there on the *American Digest* has paced American science and business, leaving its own editors gasping in wonder. The Third, Fourth, Fifth, and Sixth Decennial *Digests* ran to a total of one hundred and fifty-one volumes, picking up along the way the *automobile*,[454] *workmen's compensation*,[455] the *radio*,[456] *aviation, telecommunications*, and *mental health*.[457] They digested the litigated problems of "unexcelled prosperity" and "widespread depression."[458] The top decade for digesters, 1936-1946 — a period of "unparalleled developments"[459] — produced fifty-two volumes of cases, which in the following decade of "extraordinary change"[460] dwindled to a mere thirty-six. The fifth year of the new decade (1956-1960) has already taken the *Digest* into its thirteenth volume.[461]

The appalling deposit of judge's-words-for-lawyers digested in those two hundred and sixty-three volumes does not take into account the steadily mounting heap of legislation, regulation, and miscellaneous text and periodical literature. As Sir Matthew Hale had said in that

450 *U. S. Digest* (N.S.), *Annual Digest for 1870*, pp. iii-iv (1871). See also *U. S. Digest* (1st Ser.) (1874-1879).
451 1 *Century Edition of the American Digest* iii-v (1897).
452 *1906 Decennial Edition of the American Digest* v (1908).
453 1917 edition.
454 *Third Decennial Edition of the American Digest, 1916-1926* (1928), 29 vols.
455 *Fourth Decennial Digest, 1926-1936* (1937), 34 vols.
456 *Fifth Decennial Digest, 1936-1946* (1947), 52 vols.
457 *Sixth Decennial Digest, 1946-1956* (1957), 36 vols.
458 *Fourth Decennial Digest* v (1937).
459 *Fifth Decennial Digest* iii (1947).
460 *Sixth Decennial Digest* iii (1957).
461 *West's General Digest*, vol. 1, 1956 (1957) to vol. 13, part 1 (May, 1960).

less endowed age almost three hundred years ago, like ". . . the rolling of a snow-ball, it increaseth in bulk in every age, till it become utterly unmanageable." (Section 78.)

111. New words, old habits

The mountain of the law (Section 110) has imbedded within its uneven strata countless words new or become current in the nineteenth and twentieth centuries. These are words deposited by the many language streams of the world, for the reluctance of the lawyer to part with old words has never inhibited him from welcoming new ones from all quarters. And as in ancient times, the new has been piled squarely on top of the old — welding by contact the present comfortably with the past.

An old word like Old French *contract* was once a puny thing in the law, not of great weight with Blackstone,[462] as late as 1798 not even entered as a separate title in the seven volumes of Matthew Bacon's popular *Abridgment*.[463] *Williston* has enshrined *contract;* business has swollen it; and like the amoeba, it has divided without loss of strength into such creatures as the *conditional* (O.F.) *sales* (O.E.) *contract,*[464] the *flooring* (O.E.) *contract,*[465] and the vivid Americanism the *yellow* (O.E.) *dog* (O.E.) *contract.*[466] The ancient *jury* (Anglo-Norman) has been embellished in America with *-box* (O.E.), *-fixer* (L.), *-wheel* (O.E.), and an Old French *blue-ribbon-;*[467] laymen have converted it into a verb *to jury* (an art show).[468]

As in days past (Section 64), the repeated handling by the profession of similar facts has given currency to catch phrases of convenience. A Latin saw derived from Cicero,[469] *res ipsa loquitur* was known in England [470] but ignored by the old dictionaries. The massive use of the phrase in America[471] has bred such intimacy that law-

---

[462] 2 Blackstone, *Commentaries* °440, °442-°470 (Jones ed. 1916); 1 Blackstone, *Commentaries* °439-°440 (Jones ed. 1916).
[463] M. Bacon, *A New Abridgment of the Law* (5th ed. 1798).
[464] 8 *Words and Phrases* (perm. ed. 1951, Supp. 1962).
[465] 17 *Words and Phrases* (perm. ed. 1958), "flooring contracts."
[466] *Black's Law Dictionary* (4th ed. 1951); *Ballentine's Pronouncing Law Dictionary: Supplement* (2d ed. 1954); Mathews, ed., *A Dictionary of Americanisms* (1951).
[467] Mathews, ed., *A Dictionary of Americanisms* (1951), under *blue* and *jury*.
[468] *Encyclopaedia Britannica,* Yearbook 1950, p. 739.
[469] Lewis and Short, eds., *A Latin Dictionary* (1879), under *loquor*.
[470] See Jowitt, gen. ed., *The Dictionary of English Law* (1959).
[471] 37 *Words and Phrases* 481-610 (perm. ed. 1950), 42-59 (Supp. 1962); *Black's Law Dictionary* (4th ed. 1951); Ballentine, *Law Dictionary with Pronunciations* (2d ed. 1948).

yers often speak of a *res ipsa case*, even more familiarly a *resipsy*, and in the bewildering individuality of law student abbreviation[472] *RIL* is fairly standard. Still controversial, *last clear chance* is an overworked ally of the American lawyer;[473] the latest English law dictionary does not list it, though the doctrine is thought to have originated in England.[474]

The law's increasing regard for the intangibles of mind and emotion has produced in America the *right* (O.E.) *of privacy* (L.)[475] and has given special and frequent attention to *mental* (F.) *cruelty* (O.F.)[476] and *mental illness* (O.N.).[477] A related intangible — morality — has been bolstered by the Americanisms *blue* (O.F.) *laws*[478] and *red* (O.E.) *light* (O.E.).[479] Intangible property, widely owned and irregularly peddled, is given recognition in the Americanisms *bucket* (O.F.?)[480] *shop* (O.E.)[481] and *blue sky* (O.N.) *laws*.[482]

Names for lawyers[483] (Sections 50, 102) continue to bubble up out of the depths of the language — *mouthpiece* (O.E. + O.F.) from nineteenth-century England,[484] *lip* (O.E.),[485] *legal* (L.) *beagle* (ori-

---

[472] Compare Williams, *Learning the Law* 203-218 (6th ed. 1957).

[473] 24 *Words and Phrases* 263-287 (perm. ed. 1940), 110-130 (Supp. 1962).

[474] *Davies v. Mann*, 152 Eng. Rep. 588 (Ex. 1842).

[475] 37A *Words and Phrases* (perm. ed. 1950, Supp. 1962).

[476] *Black's Law Dictionary* (4th ed. 1951); 27 *Words and Phrases* (perm ed. 1961).

[477] 27 *Words and Phrases* (perm. ed. 1961).

[478] Mathews, ed., *A Dictionary of Americanisms* (1951); *Oxford English Dictionary*, Supp.; 1 Thornton, *An American Glossary* (1912); Schele De Vere, *Americanisms* (1872); *Black's Law Dictionary* (4th ed. 1951); Ballentine, *Law Dictionary with Pronunciations* (2d ed. 1948); *Ballentine's Pronouncing Law Dictionary: Supplement* (2d ed. 1954).

[479] Mathews, ed., *A Dictionary of Americanisms* (1951); Partridge, *A Dictionary of Slang and Unconventional English* (4th ed. 1951); compare *Oxford English Dictionary*, under *red lamp*, with *Oxford English Dictionary*, Supp., under *red lamp* and *red light;* Ballentine, *Law Dictionary with Pronunciations* (2d ed. 1948); 53 *C.J.* 662 (1931); Cal. Pen. Code §§11225-11235 (Red Light Abatement Law).

[480] *Oxford English Dictionary*.

[481] Mathews, ed., *A Dictionary of Americanisms* (1951); *Oxford English Dictionary; Black's Law Dictionary* (4th ed. 1951); Jowitt, gen. ed., *The Dictionary of English Law* (1959); 5 *Words and Phrases* (perm. ed. 1940).

[482] Mathews, ed., *A Dictionary of Americanisms* (1951); *Oxford English Dictionary*, Supp., under *blue sky;* Ballentine, *Law Dictionary with Pronunciations* (2d ed. 1948); 5 *Words and Phrases* (perm. ed. 1940, Supp. 1962).

[483] See *Dictionary of American Slang* 633 (1960).

[484] Partridge, *A Dictionary of Slang and Unconventional English* (4th ed. 1951); Partridge, *A Dictionary of the Underworld* (1950); *Oxford English Dictionary*, under *mouthpiece*, No. 4b; Mencken, *The American Language* 576 (4th ed. 1936); Mencken, *The American Language Supplement II*, p. 683 (1948); *Dictionary of American Slang* (1960).

[485] Mencken, *The American Language* 576 n.3 (4th ed. 1936); Partridge, *A Dictionary of the Underworld* (1950), under *lip*, n., No. 3.

gin obscure),[486] and *legal eagle* (O.F.)[487] from twentieth-century America.

Warfare between the state and the individual over taxation of *income* (Section 97) and estates and property in general has brought its own distinctive and abundant vocabulary, with *boot* (Section 32), *spin offs* (Section 37), *pour overs*,[488] *leasebacks*,[489] *choate* liens (Section 48), and the *tax ferret*.[490] Lawyers have had drummed into them warnings to consider everything *taxwise*,[491] to keep in mind *tax aspects, -consequences, -cost, -liability, -planning, -purposes*,[492] *-reduction*,[493] *-savings, -treatment*.[494] They speak easily of plans to *minimize taxes*[495] and make ready distinctions between *tax* (O.F.) *avoidance* (Anglo-Norman) and *tax evasion* (F.),[496] although the difference is not everywhere agreed upon. For example, the reprehensible Americanism the *tax dodger* (origin unknown)[497] has been defined as "one who *avoids* paying taxes." [498]

Avoidance also keeps its older law meaning in the pleader's art,[499] as Coke used it in the seventeenth century.[500] So too, with the fifteenth-century *variance* (O.F.), which continues in the pleading sense and has taken on a distinctively twentieth-century use in *zoning variance*.[501] *Zoning* (from Latin and Greek, to gird) was itself new both to the law and to the English language of the twentieth century as

---

[486] *Oxford English Dictionary*, under *beagle; Dictionary of American Slang* (1960), under *beagle*, No. 2, and *legal beagle.*
[487] *Dictionary of American Slang* (1960).
[488] 33 *Words and Phrases* (perm. ed. Supp. 1962), "pour-over will."
[489] Rice, *California Family Tax Planning* 253 (Continuing Education ed. 1959).
[490] 41 *Words and Phrases* (perm. ed. 1940, Supp. 1962), "tax ferret," and (perm. ed. Supp. 1962) "tax ferret contract."
[491] See Strunk, *The Elements of Style* 50, 54 (White ed. 1959).
[492] Rice, *California Family Tax Planning* 29 (Continuing Education ed. 1959).
[493] Magill, *Taxable Income* 434 (1936).
[494] Rice, *California Family Tax Planning* 29 (Continuing Education ed. 1959).
[495] Rice, *California Family Tax Planning* 49 (Continuing Education ed. 1959).
[496] 41 *Words and Phrases* (perm. ed. Supp. 1962), "tax evasion"; see also Magill, *Taxable Income* 254 (1936).
[497] *Oxford English Dictionary*, under *dodger.*
[498] Mathews, ed., *A Dictionary of Americanisms* (1951); and see *Ballentine's Pronouncing Law Dictionary: Supplement* (2d ed. 1954), under *tax evasion* and *moral turpitude.*
[499] 4 *Words and Phrases* (perm. ed. 1940, Supp. 1962); *Black's Law Dictionary* (4th ed. 1951).
[500] Coke, *Commentary upon Littleton*, f. 261b (10th ed. 1703), and cited and quoted in *Oxford English Dictionary*, under *avoidance*, No. 2.
[501] 44 *Words and Phrases* (perm. ed. 1962), "variance" (municipal corporations and zoning.)

applied to municipal planning.[502] In addition to revitalizing *variance*, the *zoning laws* have given rise to the *conditional use*,[503] a latter-day relative of the ancient *conditional fee*.[504]

Science of the atomic age has threatened the old land law's monopoly of a technical use for *re-entry*. With a diminished but still active law life,[505] which began in English (from Latin and French) at least five hundred years ago, *re-entry* — in the second half of the twentieth century — has been given the special meaning:

> The return of a missile to the earth's atmosphere.[506]

Missiles have expanded the profession's horizon and have begun to expand its vocabulary. Less than two centuries after Jeremy Bentham coined *international* (Section 109) as a "more significant" epithet for the law then spoken of as the *law of nations*,[507] other lawyers have started talking of *cosmic* (Greek) *law*[508] and *space* (O.F.) *law*[509] to regulate humans in outer space. And for the possible meeting there between humans and other beings, someone has suggested the pseudo-Greek *metalaw* (beyond law? higher law?).[510]

The production of new law words continues, along with the accumulation of words which come to the law for healing rather than conversion. In seventy volumes, each with an annual pocket part, *Words and Phrases* has still found nothing to go before *A*, but where

502 *Oxford English Dictionary*, Supp.; Horwill, *A Dictionary of Modern American Usage* (2d ed. 1944); *Black's Law Dictionary* (4th ed. 1951); Ballentine, *Law Dictionary with Pronunciations* (2d ed. 1948); *Ballentine's Pronouncing Law Dictionary: Supplement* (2d ed. 1954); 45 *Words and Phrases* (perm. ed. 1940, Supp. 1962).

503 8 *Words and Phrases* (perm. ed. 1951), "conditional use permit"; 8 *Words and Phrases* (perm. ed. Supp. 1962), "conditional use"; 1 *California Words, Phrases, and Maxims* (1960), "conditional use."

504 See 3 Holdsworth, *A History of English Law* 11, 112 (3d ed. 1923); Coke, *Commentary upon Littleton* ff. 18b-19a (10th ed. 1703).

505 36A *Words and Phrases* (perm. ed. 1962).

506 *Encyclopaedia Britannica*, Yearbook 1959, p. 753.

507 *Oxford English Dictionary*, under *international*.

508 "Toward a Cosmic Law: Hope and Reality in the United Nations," 5 N.Y.L.F. 333-347 (1959).

509 *Encyclopaedia Britannica*, Yearbook 1959, p. 753; U. S. Congress, *Survey of Space Law* (House Doc. No. 89, 1959); Hogan, "Legal Terminology for the Upper Regions of the Atmosphere and for the Space Beyond the Atmosphere," 51 Am. J. Int. L. 362-375 (1957).

510 Haley, "Space Law and Metalaw — A Synoptic View," 23 Harv. L. Record 3-5 (Nov. 1, 1956); see *Oxford English Dictionary*, under *meta* and *metaphysics*.

it once stopped at *zoster*,[511] the catalog now continues to *zygoma*.[512] Someday it will surely reach and pass *Zyzzogeton*.[513]

Over the years this wealth of collected word objects and the even vaster assortment of legal prose (Section 110) have overawed lawyers with the immensity of their possessions. Those who regarded themselves as dealers in precedent found their shelves well stocked, with little time to take inventory of quality.

This is not to say that the profession has been wholly insensitive to its language deficiencies; for more than four hundred years individual lawyers and judges have been critical of some phases of law language. (Sections 78, 80, 84, 93, 94, 95, 107, 109.) In an England awakened to an interest in the language of the law by Bentham, Lord Chief Justice Tenterden prescribed short forms for routine complaints.[514] (Section 93.) These *Models of Conciseness in Declarations in Assumpsit and Debt* . . . had most of their excess words squeezed out by Joseph Chitty. It was at the jeopardy of his own purse that a lawyer dared become more verbose over "goods sold" than this:

"Whereas the defendant on ...., at London [or in the County of] was indebted to the plaintiff in £ ...., for the price and value of goods then and there bargained [or 'sold'] and sold [or 'delivered'] by the plaintiff to the defendant at his request." [515]

This was a step, though not an overhaul.

In the American codes, a common provision said that "The complaint must contain: . . . A statement of the facts constituting the cause of action, in ordinary and concise language . . ."[516] The new Federal Rules of Civil Procedure called for pleadings "short and plain,"[517] "simple, concise, and direct."[518] These were expressions of hope, as indefinite as Lord Chancellor Bacon's rule frowning on pleadings of "immoderate length." (Section 93.) They amounted to

[511] 45 *Words and Phrases* (perm. ed. 1940).
[512] 45 *Words and Phrases* (perm. ed. Supp. 1962).
[513] *Webster's New International Dictionary* (2d ed. 1934).
[514] 3 Chitty, *A Treatise on Pleading* 1410 (9th American from 6th London ed. 1844).
[515] Quoted in 3 Chitty, *A Treatise on Pleading* 1409-1416 (9th American from 6th London ed. 1844).
[516] Cal. Civ. Proc. Code §426(2).
[517] *Rules of Civil Procedure for the United States District Courts*, as amended, Rule 8(a)(1) and (b).
[518] *Rules of Civil Procedure for the United States District Courts*, as amended, Rule 8(e)(1).

little more than a reiteration of the general requirement that pleadings be in the English language. (Chapter I.)[519]

Words — their inept or skillful selection, their bumbling or artistic arrangement, their multiplication or restrained use — remained a matter of individual choice. In a sense, this was in the best tradition of the profession: the individual lawyer pitting his skill against the field. Law student, lawyer, or judge — if he sought for it — could find instances of imagination, precision, even beauty to guide his approach to the task of composition. Was there time for this? The harassed law student, reading the casebooks with their mostly unkempt language, was made so busy learning what the books said that he had no time to dwell on the improvement of how it was said. The *how* he picked up in the practice, from busy men who had done likewise, and from forms collected from men who had done likewise. This was the refuge. The forms. This was the only continuing concentration on language to be found within the profession. And in the end, all hands reached for the formbooks. (Section 112.)

112. *The spread of formula*

The market for formbooks in America grew steadily with the growth of American law (Sections 110, 111) and faster with the rapid spread of the codes (Section 109), which made it possible for the same book to have a respectable sale in a number of jurisdictions. These uncomplicated commercial facts resulted in a redoubling of the earlier small efforts to stretch a single formbook beyond state lines. (Section 104.)

An 1858 formbook for New York lawyers looked to a broader horizon. It was said to be ". . . adapted to the new practice in the states of Missouri, California, Wisconsin, Kentucky, Indiana, Ohio, and Alabama: the territories of Oregon and Minnesota, and the island of New Foundland . . ."[520] This was *A Collection of Forms of Plead-*

[519] For *ordinary and concise* see *Stevens v. Kobayshi*, 20 Cal. App. 153, 154 (1912); and also *Moropoulos v. Fuller*, 186 Cal. 679, 685, 688 (1921); *Smith v. Matthews*, 81 Cal. 120-121 (1889); *Green v. Palmer*, 15 Cal. 412, 414, 418 (1860); [Field], untitled manual, reprinted in Cal. Civ. Proc. Code following §426, pp. 162-181 and especially 165-167 (Deering, 1959).

For *short and plain* see *Fleming v. Dierke Lumber & Coal Co.*, 39 F. Supp. 237, 240 (W.D. Ark. 1941); and also *D'Allessandro v. Bechtol*, 104 F.2d 845, 846 (5th Cir. 1939).

For *simple, concise, and direct* see and compare dictum in *Anchor Hocking Glass Corp. v. White Cap Co.*, 47 F. Supp. 451, 454 (D. Del. 1942), and *Kappus v. Western Hills Oil Inc.*, 24 F.R.D. 123 (E.D. Wis. 1959).

[520] Abbott and Abbott, *A Collection of Forms of Pleadings*, title page (1858).

ings . . . , distinguished among formbooks by its originality and candor. Prepared by two lawyers, the "Abbott Brothers," it contained many forms especially designed for code pleading. The editors went out of their way to avoid extravagant claim of adjudicated form.[521] They noted, for example, that a complaint adapted from a case had been used by the successful plaintiffs, and — for whatever inference might be drawn — that no objection had been made to its form.[522] Only eight years later, the same authors produced a less distinguished volume of more general forms, ". . . for the use of The Legal Profession, Business Men, and Public Officers in the United States." [523]   Its geography now included forty-three American jurisdictions — states, territories, and the District of Columbia, with some forms for each.

The long-nurtured hope that if lawyers could not be eliminated, then at least every man could be one (Section 103), now reached its rosiest heights. The 1869 edition of *Everybody's Lawyer and Book of Forms* (prepared by one member of the Philadelphia bar and revised by another) boasted that it covered ". . . The Laws of All the States . . ." on a wide variety of subjects from Administrators through Wills, with, in between, Agreements, Bills of Sale, Liens, Mortgages, Notes, Bills of Exchange, Patents, and many more.[524] *Everybody's Lawyer* made the claim — not made by any other — that though it had been used for years ". . . in public, law and newspaper offices, and in private families . . . In no instance has injury or loss resulted to anyone from its use. Its simplicity," continued the lyrical "Prefatory,"

> is such that persons of the most ordinary capacities or meagre attainments can understand it, while its ability as a whole cannot be gainsayed by the most expert in legal lore. . . . Lawyers, Justices of the Peace, . . . Bankrupts, Creditors, . . . Emigrants, . . . Married Men and Women, and Minors will all find it a faithful and ready counseller, . . .[525]

A more dignified book was produced by an anonymous "corps of able attorneys" in San Francisco. *Revised Law and Form Book for Business Men* . . .[526] was a companion volume to a book of practice

---

[521] Abbott and Abbott, *A Collection of Forms of Pleadings* iii-iv and especially iii (1858).

[522] Abbott and Abbott, *A Collection of Forms of Pleadings* 212-213 n.*u* (1858).

[523] Abbott and Abbott, *The Clerks' and Conveyancers' Assistant,* title page (3d ed. 1911).

[524] Crosby, *Everybody's Lawyer and Book of Forms,* title page (Vandersloot ed. 1869).

[525] Crosby, *Everybody's Lawyer and Book of Forms* 3-4 (Vandersloot ed. 1869).

[526] 1st ed. 1888.

forms for lawyers, and was intended to supplement the publisher's
". . . accurate and incomparable Line of Blanks." [527] Included were
business forms pitched to everyone west of the Mississippi — merchant and mechanic, banker and builder, farmer, miner, lawyer.[528] A
snappy preface denounced competitive forms,

> . . . for the most part either overloaded with cumbersome and obso-
> lete phrases, or stripped so bare that no careful lawyer would venture
> to use them.

That left little ground to stand on, but the publisher claimed to have
found it:

> It has been our endeavor to give no form that does not unite the
> simplicity and brevity of modern statute requirements with the safe,
> established wording of the common law. In this way the form, while
> divested of all useless verbiage, still retains a sufficient amount of tech-
> nical formality to recommend it even to the most thorough and careful
> lawyer. In this matter, safety, and not novelty, has been our aim.[529]

To the end of the nineteenth and on into the present century, formbooks of all dimensions — preserving old formula and old punctuation — blossomed and faded, the withered replaced by the ever larger.
They were larger because the country and the law were larger, and
because it became customary to manufacture books designed for practice in at least every state in the Union; larger too because — with
rare exception — the formbooks became vast, unselective depositaries,
with a form or two for everything.

These collected forms were a far cry from the most ancient forms
of the law, where only the very words handed down from antiquity
would be heard by God, and only a traditional formula would induce
a warrior to give up his right to bloody vengeance. (Sections 28, 29.)
They were also different from the later forms which had to repeat the
exact formula of the king's writs to start the wheels in motion. (Section 66.) They were even different from the still later forms which
were supported only by the claim that one particular formula had the
sanction of precedent (Sections 87, 88, 90), or had become a term of
art. (Section 89.) The new formbooks still asserted the magic blessing of precedent, but it was a blessing scattered indiscriminately over
a dozen ways of saying the same thing. These were not forms so

---

[527] *Revised Law and Form Book for Business Men* iii-iv and especially iii (ed. 1892).

[528] *Revised Law and Form Book for Business Men*, title page (ed. 1892).

[529] *Revised Law and Form Book for Business Men* iii-iv and especially iii (ed. 1892).

much as "skeletons," [530] which could be clothed at will and whose whitened bones were disquieting evidence that here someone had died. These were forms related to the bad days of the profession in England, when a formbook was intended as a substitute for learning in the law. (Section 95.)

In the formbooks one could find everything — the good and the bad, with the accolade of precedent claimed for each. The searching lawyer could be certain with these forms that whichever path he chose someone had been there before. In the midst of merging corporations and exploding rockets, the lawyer would have no feeling of aloneness for he was surrounded by old boilerplate.[531]

Here one could find:

> Know all men by these presents[532]
> Be it known[533]
> in the premises[534]
> whereas[535]
> last will and testament[536]
> party of the first part[537]
> party of the second part[538]
> separate and apart[539]
> false and untrue[540]
> mutually agreed [541]
> for and in consideration of [542]
> said defendant
> aforesaid acts[543]
> and/or[544]

and, until recently, even *or/and* [545] (Section 81).

In the formbooks, *precedent* tended to reassume its earliest French shape — merely preceding in time.[546] The books were filled with

---

[530] See *Black's Law Dictionary* (4th ed. 1951), under *form.*
[531] Compare Psalms 23:4.
[532] Nichols, *Cyclopedia of Legal Forms* §§4.31a, 4.40, 4.48a (1955).
[533] Nichols, *Cyclopedia of Legal Forms* §4.60a (1955).
[534] *Am. Jur. Pleading and Practice Forms* 11:145 (1958).
[535] Nichols, *Cyclopedia of Legal Forms* §4.997 (1955); Lindey, *Motion Picture Agreements,* Forms I-Q, I-A, VI-B (1947).
[536] *Am. Jur. Pleading and Practice Forms* 11:145 (1958).
[537] Nichols, *Cyclopedia of Legal Forms* §6.1018D (Supp. 1956).
[538] *Am. Jur. Legal Forms* 9:88 (1954).
[539] *Am. Jur. Pleading and Practice Forms* 10:1038 (1957).
[540] *Am. Jur. Pleading and Practice Forms* 11:831 (1958).
[541] Nichols, *Cyclopedia of Legal Forms* §8.1503a (Supp. 1956).
[542] *Am. Jur. Legal Forms* 13:1229 (1955).
[543] Hillyer, *Annotated Forms,* No. 3027.1 (Supp. 1954).
[544] *Am. Jur. Legal Forms* 2:964 (1953), 12:650 (1955).
[545] Nichols, *Cyclopedia of Legal Forms* §8.1496 (1936), but not in (1960).
[546] *Oxford English Dictionary.*

forms that had been to court, and dotted with cases often undated, giving the appearance of permanence and uniformity.[547] There were forms that had the aura of seasoned strength of the combat veteran, though some of them had never smelled gunpowder; forms were decorated with decisions that had never passed on the language or arrangement of the form.[548]

There were other forms that definitely had seen action, and emerged so badly shot up as to merit retirement or decent burial.

For instance. Here are the vital statistics of a contract which gave the right to *produce, perform,* and *represent* a play: drawn in 1912; dissatisfied the parties in 1914; litigated 1918-1920; producer wins in District Court;[549] affirmed, with one dissent in the Second Circuit;[550] reversed, with two dissents in the United States Supreme Court;[551] decision pleases no one — holds grant does not give producer motion picture rights, but stops author from using them.[552] This is the *Peg o' My Heart* contract, which in all its substantial detail, its stains of battle unwashed and unnoted, is reproduced in a 1955 formbook.[553]

For instance. A deed conveys land for flowage,[554] to be made into a lake, with a covenant against use

. . . in any manner that would render the remaining lands of [grantor] . . . unsuitable or undesirable for highclass residence purposes . . .[555]

The waters of the made lake undermine grantor's adjacent land. Must this hurt be endured, since the land was being used for the granted

[547] For example, Nichols, *Cyclopedia of Legal Forms* (1936-1960); *Am. Jur. Legal Forms* 4:969, 4:970 (1953), 6:374.1, 6:374.2, 6:374.3, 6:376.1 (Supp. 1962), 6:565 (1954); *Modern Legal Forms* §9128 (1957).

[548] For example, *Am. Jur. Legal Forms* 9:88 (1954), "Adapted from *White Walnut Coal Co. v. Crescent Coal Co.*, 254 Ill. 368, 98 N.E. 668, 42 L.R.A. N.S. 669" (1912); Rodman, *Massachusetts Procedural Forms* §1218 (1949), citing *United States Gypsum Co. v. Carney*, 293 Mass. 581, 200 N.E. 283 (1936); *Am. Jur. Legal Forms* 8:310 (1954), "Adapted from exhibits in *Altman v. Altman*, 297 N.Y. 973, 80 N.E.2d 359" (1948); *Am. Jur. Legal Forms* 9:581 (1954), "Adapted from *World Exhibit Corp. v. City Bank Farmers Trust Co.*, 296 N.Y. 586, 68 N.E.2d 876" (1946); *Am. Jur. Legal Forms* 8:315 (1954), "Adapted from *Jackson Heights, Inc. v. 171-24th Street*, 274 App. Div. 1070, 85 N.Y.S.2d 618" (1949).

[549] *Manners v. Morosco*, 254 Fed. 737 (S.D.N.Y. 1918).

[550] *Manners v. Morosco*, 258 Fed. 557 (2d Cir. 1919).

[551] *Manners v. Morosco*, 252 U.S. 317 (1920).

[552] See case note in 20 Colum. L. Rev. 705-706 (1920).

[553] *Am. Jur. Legal Forms* 12:619 (1955), "Adapted from *Manners v. Morosco*, 254 F. 737" (S.D.N.Y. 1918).

[554] 17 *Words and Phrases* (perm. ed. 1958), "flowage," "flowage right"; *Black's Law Dictionary* (4th ed. 1951); *Ballentine's Pronouncing Law Dictionary: Supplement* (2d ed. 1954).

[555] *McHenry v. Ford Motor Co.*, 146 F. Supp. 896, 899 (E.D. Mich. 1956).

purpose? Or was this the very catastrophe the covenant guarded against? "This issue," said the trial court,

> indicates an ambiguity or uncertainty in the restrictive use covenant in question which must be resolved by ascertaining the intent of the parties, if possible.[556]

The district judge found intent so clearly favored the grantee that he gave summary judgment — round one to the defendant (1956).[557] Round two (1958) — the Sixth Circuit affirmed.[558] Round three (1959) — and by now, this is becoming expensive — the Sixth Circuit reversed; there should not have been a summary judgment, for:

> The District Court held that the grant was ambiguous and that, to determine its meaning, the intention of the parties must be considered. . . . As to the intention of the parties, clearly questions of fact are presented.[559]

The language specifically held ambiguous is now a model for the profession to follow.[560]

It goes on. In *Keene v. Aetna Life Insurance Co.* (1914),[561] the court said:

> The phrase *"payment this day made"* is not so clear, certain, and unambiguous as to preclude evidence to show whether it means "payment which has been this day made" or "payment to be this day made."

The criticized language is taken over into a current formbook, with the notation "Adapted" from the *Keene* case.[562] But the opinion in the *Keene* case shares credit for discovering the ambiguity of such language with an English decision more than a hundred years old. Then the words of the writing were *having this day advanced,* and the judges held them ambiguous enough to let in parol evidence:

> The expression *"this day"* may mean something which has been done, or which is to be done this day.[563]

In *Freeport Journal-Standard Publishing Co. v. Frederic W. Ziv Co.* (1952),[564] the crux of the litigation was the failure of the contract to

---

[556] *McHenry v. Ford Motor Co.*, 146 F. Supp. 896, 900 (E.D. Mich. 1956).
[557] *McHenry v. Ford Motor Co.*, 146 F. Supp. 896 (E.D. Mich. 1956).
[558] *McHenry v. Ford Motor Co.*, 261 F.2d 833, 834 (6th Cir. 1958).
[559] *McHenry v. Ford Motor Co.*, 269 F.2d 18, 23 (6th Cir. 1959).
[560] Nichols, *Cyclopedia of Legal Forms* §3.1246 (Supp. 1958), "From *McHenry v. Ford Motor Co.*, 146 F. Supp. 896" (E.D. Mich. 1956).
[561] 213 Fed. 893, 896 (W.D. Wash. 1914).
[562] *Am. Jur. Legal Forms* 3:1004, 3:1005 (1953).
[563] *Goldshede v. Swan*, 154 Eng. Rep. 65, 67 (Ex. 1847).
[564] 345 Ill. App. 337 (1952).

use plaintiff's corporate name, as distinguished from the description *Radio Station WFJS*, which plaintiff owned. The court held the description adequate, dependent on intention, which calls for the trier to consider ". . . all the facts and circumstances surrounding the making of the contract . . ."[565] Such costly examination is again invited by the repetition of the litigated contract in a formbook, with the owner named only as "Radio Station ...."[566]

The *escalator* clause which caused the litigation in *Beech Aircraft Corp. v. Ross* (1946) has become a "form."[567]

Two separate contracts — in form a management contract — have been denounced by the Chief Justice of the Supreme Court of Washington as ". . . a subterfuge designed to circumvent the covenant against assignment . . ." of a theatre lease.[568] The two contracts were inconsistent, giving ". . . overlapping . . . authority . . ." to the parties, and the court said:

> We hold that the instruments in this case constitute an assignment of the lease and are not a contract of employment.[569]

The substance of the two contracts, now pieced together, with the "overlapping . . . authority," has become a form of contract for the "Management and Operation of Theater."[570]

The formbooks are but one source of the perpetuation of confusion. Tied to the single sentence form of construction that lawyers have used and clients have died with for centuries (see Section 84), the profession can improvise on its own. Here, for example, is the excited mess added by indorsement to a common form of insurance policy, in a moment of alarm over atomic testing:

> 1. Nuclear Clause: The word "fire" in this policy or endorsements attached hereto is not intended to and does not embrace nuclear reaction or nuclear radiation or radioactive contamination, all whether controlled or uncontrolled, and loss by nuclear reaction or nuclear radiation or radioactive contamination is not intended to be and is not insured

[565] *Freeport Journal-Standard Publishing Co. v. Frederic W. Ziv Co.*, 345 Ill. App. 337, 347 (1952).

[566] Nichols, *Cyclopedia of Legal Forms* §7.2135 (1959), "From *Freeport Journal-Standard Pub. Co. v. Frederic W. Ziv Co.*, 345 Ill. App. 337, 103 N.E.2d 153" (1952).

[567] 155 F.2d 615 (10th Cir. 1946); *Modern Legal Forms* §8171 (1957), "From *Beech Aircraft Corp. v. Ross*, C.C.A. 10th, 1946, 155 F.2d 615 . . ."

[568] *Bedgisoff v. Morgan*, 24 Wash. 2d 971, 974 (1946) (concurring opinion), and see earlier opinion in 23 Wash. 2d 737 (1945).

[569] *Bedgisoff v. Morgan*, 23 Wash. 2d 737, 743-746 and especially 746 (1945).

[570] *Am. Jur. Legal Forms* 12:597 (1955), "Adapted from *Bedgisoff v. Morgan*, 23 Wash. 2d 737, 162 P.2d 238, 167 P.2d 422, 163 A.L.R. 513."

against by this policy or said endorsements, whether such loss be direct or indirect, proximate or remote, or be in whole or in part caused by, contributed to, or aggravated by "fire" or any other perils insured against by this policy or said endorsements; however, subject to the foregoing and all provisions of this policy, direct loss by "fire" resulting from nuclear reaction or nuclear radiation or radioactive contamination is insured against by this policy.[571]

This is the sort of language that is sold to policyholders, to preserve in strongboxes if not to read. Will the insurance company pay when the house burns to the ground following some nuclear reaction? Neither the policyholder nor his lawyer will know in advance. Yet they need not await an atomic explosion to become convinced that all is not well with the language of the law.

[571] Clause in policy of Fireman's Fund Insurance Company (1962).

Using the Language of the Law

CHAPTER XII

Reasons Given and Real

113. *Comparison with the common speech*

The argument of this book is that the language of the law should not be different without a reason. (Preface.) Part Two tells how the language of the law (described in Part One) got that way. It sorts out the reasons (causes) from the reasons (explanations). Part Three brings the language of the law down into the practice. Are the reasons (causes) still at work? Are the reasons (explanations) valid or hogwash? Are there any reasons which justify a language of the law different from the language of ordinary good English? The answers to these questions are some concrete suggestions to make the language of the law better serve its purpose.

Part Three focuses on the reasons for a language of the law as compared with the common speech. The language of the law is examined to see if it is:

(1) more precise (Chapter XIII),

(2) shorter (Chapter XIV),

(3) more intelligible (Chapter XV),

(4) more durable (Chapter XVI).

114. *Reasons or literary criticism?*

The discussion here of the reasons for a language of the law is not literary criticism in the sense of judgment on the artistry of lawyers' style. This is no attempt to give a recipe for a savory literary stew — one part four-letter words,[1] two parts color, and a dash of jes' folks — which anyone can cook up in his spare time.[2] Not that the literary artist should be a pariah in the law. (Section 134.) Still, artistry in all its forms is mostly personal, sometimes learned, always untaught.

Professional stylists are ordinarily diffident about giving prescrip-

---

[1] Warren, *Spartan Education* 31 (1942).

[2] Flesch, *The Art of Readable Writing,* end papers (1949).

tions for style,[3] cognizant that they speak of the intimate and that other professionals will look aside sensing a social indiscretion. Or, if they cannot decently avoid comment, will nod and pass on quickly; thus did Holmes dismiss

A book by Quiller-Couch, *On the Art of Writing* — suggestions and prejudices — worth the little time it took but not much more.[4]

Assorted critics have been less reluctant about taking lawyers into their confidence. For centuries the profession has been showered with gratuitous literary advice, accepted with enthusiasm by a stray lawyer here and there,[5] but received generally with profound indifference.

The hardest words of lay critics from Swift to date (Sections 2, 19) — *cant, jargon,*[6] *dull prolixity,*[7] *obsolete,*[8] *stilted,*[9] *wormlike*[10] — have been ignored with aplomb. After all, do *they* know the law? Which is the rhetorical and confident self-assurance that *they* don't know what they are talking about,[11] that this is a preserve for the elite, and trespassers had best keep out.

Literary advice from within the profession has not fared much better, but for different reasons.

First. Lawyers began as advisers and arguers rather than scriveners or literary craftsmen. (Sections 78, 92, 95.) And most of the profession has declined to concede that good writing and proper punctuation (Sections 82, 83, 84, 106) are any part of the business. Lawyers have taken pride in the solidity of their verbiage contrasted with the frothiness of writing generally. Francis Bacon, who rejoiced in the language of the law ". . . wherein a man shall not be enticed to hunt after words, but matter . . ." (Section 79), spoke to the whole literary world in protest against the high-flown literary style of his day. It was a style which he himself sometimes fell into (Section 85), a

---

[3] Quiller-Couch, *On the Art of Writing* 232-248 (1916); Strunk, *The Elements of Style* 52 (White ed. 1959); Orwell, "Politics and the English Language," in *Shooting an Elephant and Other Essays* 100-101 (Secker and Warburg ed. 1950).

[4] 1 *Holmes-Laski Letters* 425, 426, 414 (Howe ed. 1953); see also 2 *Holmes-Pollock Letters* 291 (Howe ed. 1946).

[5] For example, Littler, "Reader Rights in Legal Writing," 25 J.S.B. Calif. 51, 59, 60 (1950); Gerhart, "Improving Our Legal Writing," 40 A.B.A.J. 1057, 1058 n.10, 1059 (1954).

[6] Swift, *Gulliver's Travels* 297 (Crown ed. 1947).

[7] 2 *The Papers of Benjamin Franklin* 254, and see 244 n.3 (Labaree ed. 1960).

[8] Runes, "Our Obsolete Legal English," 99 N.Y.L.J. 1964 (April 23, 1938).

[9] Hunter, *The Language of Audit Reports* 27 (1957).

[10] Flesch, *The Art of Readable Writing* 152 (1949).

[11] See Aiken, "Let's Not Oversimplify Legal Language," 32 Rocky Mt. L. Rev. 358, 361-362 (1960).

style that looked to an abundance of well-turned words more than to substance. "It seems to me," he said,

> that Pygmalion's frenzy is a good emblem or portraiture of this vanity: for words are but the images of matter; and except they have life of reason and invention, to fall in love with them is all one as to fall in love with a picture.[12]

Coke gave similar warning:

> Certainly the fair outsides of enamelled words and sentences do sometimes so bedazzle the eye of the reader's mind with their glittering shew, as they cause them not to see or not to pierce into the inside of the matter; and he that busily hunteth after affected words, and followeth the strong scent of great swelling phrases, is many times (in winding of them in, to shew a little verbal pride) at a dead loss of the matter itself, and so *projicit ampullas et sesquipedalia verba*[13] [Disdain bombast and words half a yard long]: to speak effectually, plainly, and shortly, it becometh the gravity of this profession: . . .[14]

These quotations are themselves the best evidence that their authors never intended them as a rationalization for a neglect of style; yet when they have been observed at all in the law, that has been one of their major influences. Writers in the law disdain style as a nonessential nicety, incompatible with proper legal expression.[15] The lawyer at work on a document is cautioned to ". . . avoid all graces . . ."[16] A legislative draftsman considers punctuation "feminine," and "The dash is the most feminine of all . . ."[17] The fact that historically many law professionals were innocent of liberal education and incapable of literary craftsmanship (Sections 95, 100, 103) puts these rationalizations in a truer perspective.

Second. Coke's direct advice to the profession "to speak effectually, plainly, and shortly" gave the color of formidable authority to the unstated proposition that the criteria of good legal composition can be reduced to generalities. Like Chancellor Bacon's Ordinance against pleadings of *"immoderate length"* (Section 93), Coke's *"effectually, plainly,* and *shortly"* has been followed by similar generalities that neither guide nor intimidate. Lawyers have been advised to use *sim-*

---

[12] 2 Bacon, *Works* 37 (Montagu ed. 1825).

[13] Horace, *Ars Poetica* 97, quoted in Lewis and Short, eds., *A Latin Dictionary* (1879), under *ampulla*.

[14] 2 Co. Rep. xli-xlii (new ed. 1826).

[15] See Schuyler, "Conservative Draftsmanship Is Constructive," in "Drafting Legal Documents," 39 Ill. B.J. 49, 57 (Sept. 1950 Supp.).

[16] Gowers, *The Complete Plain Words* 9 (4th impression, with amends. 1957); Piesse and Smith, *The Elements of Drafting* 12, and see 5 (2d ed. 1958).

[17] Lavery, "Punctuation in the Law," 9 A.B.A.J. 225, 228 (1923).

ple words,[18] *short words,*[19] and *short sentences,*[20] to write *plainly, sensibly, simply,*[21] *clearly, succinctly, interestingly, forcibly.*[22] They have been advised to avoid *verbosity* (Section 107), *big words,*[23] and language *needlessly involved* and *prolix.*[24] They have been told to make their language *understandable.*[25] By the time that statutes came along enjoining draftsmen to make their pleadings *short* and *plain, simple, concise,* and *direct* (Section 111), lawyers had built up a natural immunity to this sort of innocuous nudging. They nodded in agreement and went about their business in the same old ways.

Third. Many of the specific suggestions for changing the pattern of legal style have been offered to the profession with inadequate preparation. They are dropped into the hopper without any reason given, or with reasons that strike lawyers as trifling cause for abandoning old language friends. For example:

["And/or"] . . . is a bastard . . .[26]

"Whereas" seems to be a particularly unpopular word with lay clients.[27]

The customary form of the "whereas" clause is clumsy and obsolete.[28]

There's no such word [as "witnesseth"].[29]

Law language having for long years been accepted by the profession as a part of the law's natural environment, that faith is not to be shaken by name-calling or undocumented caviling in the name of lit-

[18] Witherspoon, "Why Write," 64 Commercial L.J. 152, 154 (1959); Hager, "Let's Simplify Legal Language," 32 Rocky Mt. L. Rev. 74, 85 (1959).
[19] Gerhart, "Improving Our Legal Writing: Maxims from the Masters," 20 Lawyers J. (Manila) 159 (1955).
[20] Witherspoon, "Why Write," 64 Commercial L.J. 152, 154 (1959).
[21] Beardsley, "Beware of, Eschew and Avoid Pompous Prolixity and Platitudinous Epistles!" 16 J.S.B. Calif. 65, 69 (1941).
[22] Gerhart, "Improving Our Legal Writing: Maxims from the Masters," 20 Lawyers J. (Manila) 159 (1955).
[23] Beardsley, "Beware of, Eschew and Avoid Pompous Prolixity and Platitudinous Epistles!" 16 J.S.B. Calif. 65, 69 (1941).
[24] Lindey, "On Legal Style," in *Motion Picture Agreements Annotated* xvii, xviii (1947).
[25] Beardsley, "Wherein and Whereby Beardsley Makes Reply to Challenge," 16 J.S.B. Calif. 106, 107 (1941).
[26] J. W. Davis, letter, in "An and/or Symposium," 18 A.B.A.J. 574, 575 (1932); accord, Viscount Simon, L.C., in *Bonitto v. Fuerst Brothers & Co. Ltd.,* [1944] A.C. 75, 82.
[27] Piesse and Smith, *The Elements of Drafting* 48 (2d ed. 1958).
[28] Lindey, "On Legal Style," in *Motion Picture Agreements Annotated* xvii, xxi (1947).
[29] Beardsley, "Beware of, Eschew and Avoid Pompous Prolixity and Platitudinous Epistles!" 16 J.S.B. Calif. 65, 68 (1941).

erary improvement. Lawyers are trained to demand proof. If proof is furnished, perhaps they will change; without it, they will not budge.

It is to the reasons then that we must turn, the reasons for preferring a language of the law to the common speech.

This is not a question of what is or is not a literary "nicety," but a matter of professional self-respect for the lawyer who daily presumes to ask pay to guide the ignorant. Can he himself work in ignorance, repeat what has been repeated, without considering the consequences? For a lawyer to use language without knowing its reason is to run the risk of using language that is without reason. And in the end, he will be found out — by another lawyer, by a judge, by a client, worst of all by himself.

The reasons discussed in Part Three of this book apply in varying degrees to different parts of the language of the law. And whether one or another or none of the reasons is pertinent varies with the circumstances of the moment. These circumstances include (1) the purpose of the particular language, (2) the person addressed, and (3) the medium of communication.

The order of listing the reasons (Section 113) serves editorial convenience, and does not indicate preference. "More precise" is discussed first because it is the loudest and most lingering reason given for the continuing distinctiveness of the language of the law. (See Chapter XIII.)

CHAPTER XIII

More Precise

115. *Precision unlimited*

The standard answer to any criticism of the language of the law is that this language is *precise.* If the criticism is especially violent, the answer is modified only to the extent of saying that the language of the law is *more precise* than the ordinary speech, but customarily even that modest qualification is omitted. Say that it is *cant, jargon, prolix, obsolete, stilted, wormlike, tedious, polysyllabic, repetitious, cacophonic, humorless.* Charge it with *verbosity* and *big words* and with being *needlessly involved.* (Sections 2, 114.) Call it what you will. *Precise* it is said to be, and that virtue is deemed sufficient, that the clincher in any argument.

In varied phrasings — *apt, significant, certain, exact, technical, unambiguous* — lawyers have been telling each other for so many years that the language of the law is *precise* that they have come to believe it, even though long preoccupation with litigation caused by their language should have by this time made them at least skeptical. Revered authority has from time to time indorsed the precision of some parts of the language of the law — Coke (Section 72), Bacon,[1] Blackstone,[2] Maitland,[3] Holdsworth (Section 62). And the radiance of these names has so covered the whole body of law language with an aura of precision that few within the profession have cared to argue the point.

On both sides of the Atlantic respected lawyers spread the gospel of precision.

An American lawyer writes of the "extraordinary precision" of the law's terminology (Section 16), the "great accuracy" of its vocabulary, and of the great works of the law (Glanvil, Bracton, Littleton, Coke, Blackstone),

---

[1] See Section 79; Bacon, *The Elements of the Common Lawes of England* (1630), preface, in 13 Bacon, *Works* 140-141 (Montagu ed. 1831).

[2] 3 Blackstone, *Commentaries* °319-°322 (Jones ed. 1916).

[3] Maitland, "Of the Anglo-French Language in the Early Year Books," in Introduction to *Year Books of Edward II,* 17 Selden Society xxxvi (1903).

. . . which rank in the exactitude of their language with the classic studies in physics and natural science.[4]

He also tells us:

Nevertheless, for all the accuracy of its vocabulary there seems to be a constant failure of communication within the realm of legal discourse.[5]

A literate barrister, with a following in the United States,[6] has a penetrating eye and a scorching pen for the monstrosities of officialese in the British government service. But turning for a moment to his first love, Sir Ernest Gowers finds that the "inevitable peculiarities" of the language of the law ". . . come from a desire to convey a precise meaning . . ."[7] and in one gloriously succinct rationalization he proclaims it a language ". . . obscure in order that it may be unambiguous . . ."[8] An afterthought makes this ". . . almost necessarily obscure . . ."[9] and a later edition acknowledges ". . . room for improvement . . ."[10]

Lawyers not only believe this talk of precision themselves; they insist that laymen believe it, as though a professional livelihood depended upon its acceptance. The vast nonprofessional majority is sufficiently intimidated by the law itself to refrain from criticism.[11] Lay critics merely vocal, the profession customarily ignores as boisterous ignoramuses. (Section 114.) Those who would change law language by legislation, the profession has cried out against as clumsy meddlers who can take a watch apart but not put it together again. Drastic legislation the profession has emasculated by amendment (Sections 65,

---

[4] Cairns, "Language of Jurisprudence," in Anshen, ed., *Language* 232, 258 (1957).
[5] Cairns, "Language of Jurisprudence," in Anshen, ed., *Language* 232, 259 (1957).
[6] Gowers, *Plain Words* (London, 1948); Gowers, *Plain Words: Their ABC* (New York, 1954); Gowers, *The Complete Plain Words* (4th impression with amends., London, 1957); see also Littler, "Reader Rights in Legal Writing," 25 J.S.B. Calif. 51, 59 (1950); Gerhart, "Improving Our Legal Writing," 40 A.B.A.J. 1057-1060 (1954).
[7] Gowers, *Plain Words* 6 (London, 1948).
[8] Gowers, *Plain Words* 91 (London, 1948).
[9] Gowers, *Plain Words: Their ABC* 120 (New York, 1954).
[10] Gowers, *Plain Words: Their ABC* 20 (New York, 1954).
[11] Bryant, *English in the Law Courts* 295 (1930); Bryant, review of *Language and the Law: The Semantics of Forensic English*, in 24 American Speech 291 (1949); see also "Jargon," editorial in The Listener 584 (April 2, 1959); Linton, *Effective Revenue Writing* 165 (U. S. Treasury Dept., Training No. 83-0, 1961); see and compare Mitgang, "It's Legal — But Is It English?" N.Y. Times Sunday Magazine 73, 76 (Nov. 13, 1960); Philbrick, *Language and the Law: The Semantics of Forensic English* vi (1949).

76) to preserve the law's "precision," or opposed by passive resistance until succor was at hand. (Section 74.)

And the most dangerous of all — the avowedly omniscient lay critics — what of them? Alert to sniff out gobbledygook everywhere but at the fountainhead, least ready to admit ignorance, they have been taken into camp whistling. For one, ". . . the law in action [is] a model of articulate precision . . ." [12] Quick to disavow a fancied slight, he assures the profession:

> There is nothing bad about legal style in its proper place; indeed, it is indispensable, as Sir Ernest Gowers showed in *Plain Words.*[13]

Another, speaking of precision in terms of clarity, makes only a half obeisance:

> The wording of legal documents may be tedious, polysyllabic, repetitious, cacophonic, and humorless, but to anyone not panic-stricken at the sound of "whereas," it usually makes the meaning clearer than it otherwise would be.[14]

Occasional rebels within the profession have been unimpressed with the argument from precision and have said so. Bentham, for instance, in language that has contributed nothing to the British reputation for understatement:

> For this redundancy — for the accumulation of excrementitious matter in all its various shapes . . . for all the pestilential effects that cannot but be produced by this so enourmous a load of literary garbage, — the plea commonly pleaded . . . is, that it is necessary to *precision* — or, to use the word which on similar occasions they themselves are in the habit of using, *certainty*.
> But a more absolutely sham plea never was countenanced, or so much as pleaded, in either King's Bench or Common Pleas.[15]

Though Bentham was hardly an authority on style, his campaigning brought some improvement in the form of legislation (Section 109). Yet neither his efforts nor those of other lawyers who have attacked with broad strokes, mostly semantic,[16] have ended the legend of pre-

---

[12] Barzun, *The House of Intellect* 29 (1959).

[13] Barzun, letter, 44 A.B.A.J. 300 (1958).

[14] Evans, *The Spoor of Spooks* 265 (1954); see also Partridge, *Usage and Abuse-age* 38 (new ed. 1957), under "archaisms or antiques."

[15] 3 Bentham, *Works* 260 (Bowring ed. 1843).

[16] For example: Beutel, "Elementary Semantics: Criticisms of Realism and Experimental Jurisprudence," 13 J. Legal Ed. 67 (1960); Chafee, "The Disorderly Conduct of Words," 41 Colum. L. Rev. 381 (1941); Cohen, "Transcendental Nonsense and the Functional Approach," 35 Colum. L. Rev. 809 (1935); Frank, *Law and the Modern Mind* (6th print. rev. 1949); Hohfeld, "Some Fundamental Legal Conceptions as Applied in Judicial Reasoning," 23 Yale L.J. 16 (1913);

cision in the language of the law. The twentieth century — alert to the weaknesses of all language[17] — finds the lawyer's reliance on the precision of law language stronger than ever. Why is this so?

First. Outside the academy, no profession of words has a longer history of practical effort devoted to refining language. (See Part Two.) Lawyers spend more time talking about being precise than others similarly addicted to words — politicians and the clergy, for example. Listening to these discussions about precision, and contrasting their own concern with the indifference of the street, law students and lawyers come to the effortless conclusion that with so much interest in precision, there must be a lot of it around.

Second. There is a small area of relative precision in the language of the law — mostly terms of art. (Section 13.) This gives color to the argument of a widespread diffusion of precision, especially since the limits of the area of precision have never been carefully marked.

Third. The only organized body of literature devoted to legal style — the formbooks — makes the limits of the area of precision even harder to find, by mixing up in the same forms terms of art and traditional words of law language totally devoid of precision. (Section 112.) Despite warnings that forms are guides only,[18] busy lawyers readily confuse precision of the part for total precision, and swallow the forms whole.

Fourth. Much of the detailed criticism of law language within the profession omits any intimation that the language is not precise.[19] A concentration on other defects often leaves the impression that whatever else is wrong with it, the language of the law is at least precise.

Hohfeld, "Fundamental Legal Conceptions as Applied in Judicial Reasoning," 26 Yale L.J. 710 (1917); "The Language of Law, a Symposium," 9 W. Res. L. Rev. 115 (1958); Levin, "Language, Symbol Cycles, and the Constitution," 71 U.S.L. Rev. 258 (1937); Probert, "Law and Persuasion: The Language Behavior of Lawyers," 108 U. Pa. L. Rev. 35 (1959); Rodell, *Woe unto You, Lawyers!* (1939); Weissman, "'Supremecourtese': A Note on Legal Style," 14 Law. Guild Rev. 138 (1954); Weissman, "The 'No-Nonsense, Straight-from-the-Shoulder' School: Another Note on Legal Style," 20 Law. Guild Rev. 24 (1960); Williams, "Language and the Law," 61 L.Q. Rev. 71-86, 179-195, 293-303, 384-406 (1945), 62 L.Q. Rev. 387-406 (1946).

[17] For example, Korzybski, *Science and Sanity* (2d ed. 1941); Ogden and Richards, *The Meaning of Meaning* (6th ed. 1944); Hayakawa, *Language in Action* (1941); Chase, *The Tyranny of Words* (1938); Arnold, *The Folklore of Capitalism* (1937).

[18] For example, 1 *Am. Jur. Legal Forms*, preface (1953); 1 *Am. Jur. Pleading and Practice Forms* v (1956); 1 Nichols, *Cyclopedia of Legal Forms* iii (1936).

[19] See Section 114; and see Rossman, "The Lawyer's English," 48 A.B.A.J. 50 (1962).

Thus, the frequent complaint of wordiness tacitly admits that law language is precise though wordy.[20]   Most lawyers read no further.   Extra words?   A small price to pay for precision.

Fifth.   Philosophical criticism has pointed up a lack of precision in the language of the law as a facet of the basic deficiency of all language.   Locke,[21] Bentham (Section 109), Hohfeld,[22] the school of general semantics,[23] the devotees of symbolic logic,[24] have annoyed some lawyers sufficiently to make them skeptical of hackneyed usage.   More will be touched.   Eons, not lifetimes, are involved in such fundamental reappraisals.   In the finite interim these critiques stimulate an interest in better language and are a help to legal analysis.   But thus far, they do not solve the lawyer's daily problem of word choice.   They may arouse suspicions about traditional law language, but they don't enable the practitioner to reject the traditional with any considerable degree of confidence that judges and other lawyers will know just what it is he is talking about.

Sixth.   Buttressing all the other reasons for belief in the precision of the language of the law is fear.   The fear not merely of changing, but of being weakened by doubt of the correctness of a whole pattern.   For the profession, this is no ordinary conservative fear.   Lurking in the dark background is the always present, rarely voiced lawyer's fear of what will happen if he is not "precise" — in the way that the law has always been "precise."   Consider, you lawyers, ". . . 'plain and simple' language . . ." and ". . . the possible liability of lawyers for negligence who use too much of it." [25]

. . . forms have been carefully put together by experts in the light of a myriad of interpretive court decisions that have attempted to fix

[20] See, for example, Beardsley, "Beware of, Eschew and Avoid Pompous Prolixity and Platitudinous Epistles!" 16 J.S.B. Calif. 65 (1941); Beardsley, "Wherein and Whereby Beardsley Makes Reply to Challenge," 16 J.S.B. Calif. 106 (1941).

[21] 2 Locke, *An Essay Concerning Human Understanding* 3-164 (Fraser ed. 1894); see Levin, "Language, Symbol Cycles, and the Constitution," 71 U.S.L. Rev. 258, 260, 265 (1937).

[22] Hohfeld, "Some Fundamental Legal Conceptions as Applied in Judicial Reasoning," 23 Yale L.J. 16 (1913); Hohfeld, "Fundamental Legal Conceptions as Applied in Judicial Reasoning," 26 Yale L.J. 710 (1917); see Williams, "Language and the Law," 61 L.Q. Rev. 179, 180 (1945).

[23] See, for example, "The Language of Law, a Symposium," 9 W. Res. L. Rev. 115 (1958); compare Tollett, "Verbalism, Law, and Reality," 37 U. Det. L.J. 226 (1959).

[24] See, for example, Allen, "Symbolic Logic: A Razor-edged Tool for Drafting and Interpreting Legal Documents," 66 Yale L.J. 833 (1957).

[25] Morton, "Challenge Made to Beardsley's Plan for Plain and Simple Legal Syntax," 16 J.S.B. Calif. 103 (1941).

the legal import of certain words and combinations of words. Can these safely be omitted or tampered with? [26] . . .

Not to mention the possibility that our lawyer one day may find himself in court trying to explain why he used language too plain and simple to be clear and unambiguous, or so plain and simple as to be devoid of legal meaning, or both.[27]

That is the fear that freezes lawyers and their language. It is precise now. We are safe with it now. Leave us alone. Don't change. Here we stay till death or disbarment.

Let us plant a seed of doubt right now. A new and more terrible fear. The fear that using "precise" law language as it is can — often does — lead the lawyer headlong into disaster.

116. *What is "precise"?*

The word *precise* is itself as loose as water, and this paradox has helped to keep alive the dogged belief of lawyers in the precision of their language. (Section 115.) Though rarely distinguished, two distinct meanings of *precise* are active in the law. *Precise* can be exact meaning or exactly-the-same-way.[28] The first sense is the fixing of sharp definition; the second is repetition; and though one sense does not exclude the other, the two are not the same.

Except when context makes another sense clear, this book uses *precise = exact meaning*.[29] That is what lawyers and others think they are talking about when they say that the language of the law is *precise* or has *precision*. It is exact meaning which distinguishes the *terms of art* (Section 13), which enables lawyers to communicate briefly to each other on some subjects so that they may argue endlessly on others. The words *the rule in Shelley's Case* stir up polite murmurs of recognition from common law lawyers. Agreeing on what those words say, the bar passes on quickly to argue for centuries about their application to specific cases. (Sections 22, 89.)

---

[26] Morton, "Challenge Made to Beardsley's Plan for Plain and Simple Legal Syntax," 16 J.S.B. Calif. 103, 105 (1941).

[27] Morton, "Challenge Made to Beardsley's Plan for Plain and Simple Legal Syntax," 16 J.S.B. Calif. 103, 105 (1941); see also Lindey, "Let's Write Better Contracts," 3 Prac. Law. 32, 38 (1957); Schuyler, "Conservative Draftsmanship Is Constructive," in "Drafting Legal Documents," 39 Ill. B.J. 57 (Sept. 1950 Supp.).

[28] See *Webster's New International Dictionary* (2d ed. 1934); *Oxford English Dictionary*.

[29] See *Black's Law Dictionary* (4th ed. 1951); 33 *Words and Phrases* (perm. ed. 1940).

It is also a characteristic striving after exact meaning (Section 17) that is caught up in the phrase ". . . the precision of a lawyer . . ." [30] Flattering, this phrase, confirming the lawyer's pride in an ability to talk law terms of art over the heads of laymen. But this *precise* is properly applied to only the smallest part of the language of the law.

Of far greater application in the law and its language is the other use of *precise = exactly-the-same-way.* This wider *precise* is the exactness of literal repetition; here anything to do with precision is coincidental. This *precise* is related to magic, and to the religious ritual which was the birth of the language of the law. (See Section 29.)

Exactly-the-same-way may not yield exact meaning or any meaning at all. It may be boundless nonsense in exactly-the-same-way. There may be centuries of *precise* repetition without ever an approach to *precision.* There is, for instance, *ss.* Lawyers have been using *ss* for nine hundred years (Section 54) and still are not sure what it means. (Section 120.)

There are three overlapping categories of exactly-the-same-way "precise" law language that have no necessary relation to precision. Taken together, they include the bulk of the language of the law. Each a euphemism for *repetition,* they are:

(1) The *traditional* way of saying things, such as *ss, last will and testament* (Section 49), *to have and to hold* (Section 56), and the great mass of habitual tautologies. (See Section 71.)

(2) The way of *precedent,* which sometimes leads one way and yields a term of art, but more often furnishes a path to follow in any direction. There are the myriad collected cases which tell us, for example, that *cause of action* means the facts, or — if it better suits our purpose — that *cause of action* means rights;[31] that *cancellation* means *termination,*[32] and does not mean *termination.*[33]

(3) Finally, there is the *required* way, by which is meant the form prescribed by legislation or an order as distinguished from case law. A statute may prescribe the exact form of a verdict — *for the people* or *for the defendant*[34] — or of an oath.[35] The wording of a particular

---

[30] Adams [and Leonard], *Novanglus and Massachusettensis* 187, 189 (1819); see also Kennedy, *Profiles of Courage* xviii (1956).

[31] 6 *Words and Phrases* 350-388 (perm. ed. 1940), 128-141 (Supp. 1962).

[32] 6 *Words and Phrases* 36-37 (perm. ed. 1940), 10-11 (Supp. 1962).

[33] 6 *Words and Phrases* 36-37 (perm. ed. 1940); see also Maxwell, "Oil and Gas Lessee's Rights on Failure to Obtain Production . . ." in *Rocky Mountain Mineral Law Institute: Third Annual* 133, 157 n.66 (1957).

[34] Cal. Pen. Code §1151.

[35] Cal. Pen. Code §911.

sort of contract may require official approval, e.g., a surety bond,[36] an employment agency contract.[37] The size of type used for the printing of a ballot may be specified by statute.[38]

Exactly-the-same-way, in each of its forms — tradition, precedent, requirement — may sometimes be the exact meaning. To be sure, the distinction between these two senses of *precise* is not always an easy or an apparent one. Repetition by way of tradition and precedent at one time made *and his heirs* a term of art, the magic words which created a fee. (Section 56.) They came to be precise words that a lawyer could count on, regardless of what a testator had in mind. (See Section 89.) And the fact that the repeated may also sometimes be exact has befuzzed the distinction between what is exact and what is merely repeated.

The distinction must nonetheless be made if lawyers are to avoid confusing not merely laymen but themselves. Sooner or later the lawyer's genius for making distinctions must be applied to the distinction between what is called *precise* because it does have well-defined limits and what is called *precise* only because it is repeated again and again. For the lawyer's decision to use or not to use words because they are said to be *precise* will vary with the kind of *precise* he is talking about. And the truth of the assertion of *precision* may be tested in different ways. (Section 117.)

117. *"Exact" or "exactly-the-same-way"?*

In the daily routine of legal analysis the lawyer sifts the grist of client woes to separate *contract* from *no-contract, sue* from *settle, not guilty* from *guilty, timely* from *barred, fee* from *no-fee.* In the process the lawyer unconsciously asks himself a hundred questions to focus his accumulated learning on the problem of the moment.

Too often, the choice of "precise" language goes by default — without notice that any problem exists. Yet the same process of silent questioning can guide the lawyer in deciding whether language that others have used and language that he contemplates using is exact or merely exactly-the-same-way it has been used some place before. The questioning will also help to determine whether the particular language is appropriate or inexcusable.

Here are some of the pertinent questions.

[36] Cal. Pen. Code §1295.5.
[37] Cal. Lab. Code §1628.
[38] Mellinkoff, "How to Make Contracts Illegible," 5 Stan. L. Rev. 418, 429 (1953).

(1) *Is it a term of art?* (Sections 13, 128.)

    (a) Did I ever learn "law" about this expression?

    (b) Are its edges sharp or soft?

    (c) Is that the only way it can be used?

    (d) Is it used in this instance as a term of art?

    (e) Are there other words can serve as well?

    (f) Will even slight variation change its legal effect?

(2) *Is this the traditional way of saying it?* (Section 118.)

    (a) Did it ever have a definite meaning? (Sections 119, 120.)

    (b) Does it have a definite meaning now? (Section 121.)

    (c) Does this way make meaning more exact than ordinary English? (Sections 122, 123.)

    (d) Is there any good reason for saying it this way now?

(3) *Does precedent support this usage?* (Section 126.)

    (a) Is it decision or dictum?

    (b) Is the precedent decisive or persuasive in this jurisdiction?

    (c) How fresh is this precedent?

    (d) Would it be followed today?

    (e) Are there other precedents the other way?

    (f) Does it make sense?

(4) *Is there some requirement that it be said this way?* (Section 127.)

    (a) What sort of requirement is it — statute, ordinance, rule of court, administrative order, or something Charley the filing clerk insists upon?

    (b) What are the consequences of departure from rote?

    (c) Has it ever been interpreted?

    (d) Has it been tested — recently?

    (e) Would it be enforced today?

If enough of these questions are asked (and habit can make the asking and answering rapid), the massive word-for-word repetitions of the law "dictated" by tradition, precedent, and other requirements turn out to have very little to do with being precise. The chief pretender to precision in the law goes by the name of "tradition," and it deserves first consideration.

118. *The traditional way*

This section and Sections 119 through 125 discuss the confusion of *tradition* and *precision*. Other aspects of tradition in the language of the law are mentioned in Section 126 and in Chapter XVI.

The pattern of saying things in the same way is ancient in the law, and antedates by far the system of precedent as we know it today. Tradition sometimes finds support in the cases, but it is not dependent upon them. It has a closer relationship to the older formbooks which called themselves "precedents," [39] but tradition also antedated such collections.

In the ancient Anglo-Saxon oaths which are a part of the earliest days of the common law (Sections 29, 30, 67), all of the words were equally important. It was not a question of the meaning of a word but of the effect produced by a formula. All or nothing. If the oath called for the word *shun, shun* it must be; *avoid,* or some other synonym no matter how inseparable in meaning, was completely inadequate. Tradition called for exactly-the-same-way, not exact meaning.

If long-continued use of a whole formula of words produced only a given result, the ritual words could become not only repetitive but precise. For all language is arbitrary (*cat* rather than *glunk*), and if it takes fifty words of indifferent meaning to say *swear,* the fifty together may be as precise as one. It was all the same to Ali Baba that the cave door was operated by the name of an herb. *Open sesame!* worked in an exact way. Thus an inflexible primitive insistence on word-for-word repetition could make the traditional the precise.

Repetition gave precision to the English writs[40] and to the pleading of the English writs. (Section 66.) As long as only the very words of the traditional writ — and no others — meant action of a specified sort, a writ was precise and its pleading precise, though the individual words of the writ might not be. The traditional phrase of the old writs, *ne inde clamorem audiam amplius* ("that I hear no further complaint thereof"),[41] has more the sound of an harassed schoolteacher than of a royal lawyer straining after fineness of meaning.

If society had remained as primitive as it was when the ordeal by hot iron settled controversies (Section 28), and if a profession of learned and thinking men had never arisen to mediate the controver-

---

[39] For example: West, *The First Part of Symboleography, Which May Bee Termed the Art, or Description, of Instruments and Presidents* (ed. 1598); *Sir Orl. Bridgman's Conveyances: Being Select Precedents of Deeds and Instruments Concerning the Most Considerable Estates in England* (1682); Covert, *The Scrivener's Guide: Being Choice and Approved Forms of Precedents* . . . (5th London ed. 1740).

[40] See Van Caenegem, *Royal Writs in England from the Conquest to Glanvill,* 77 Selden Society 166 (1959).

[41] Van Caenegem, *Royal Writs in England from the Conquest to Glanvill,* 77 Selden Society 512, No. 190, and see also 147 and especially n.8 (1959); compare Jacob, *A New Law-Dictionary* (6th ed. 1750), under *recto.*

sies of the untutored, the law might also have remained nothing but ritual, with *tradition* and *precision* as equivalents. It did not happen that way. The profession of law itself doomed this old-style precision. Arguing lawyers early rejected the notion that all words must have the irrevocable effect of ritual. (Section 67.) And over the years — slowly — they haggled out for themselves some words of habitual use whose sharpness of meaning distinguished them from other words of habitual use. (Sections 63, 64.)

But the recollection of the law's past, when a whole formula could make sense though its parts did not, carried beyond the time when the law had begun to make precise sense of individual words. The clerks and scriveners who prepared documents and "precedents" of forms were often not lawyers but laymen. (Section 95.) They repeated the repeated because it had been repeated without appreciation of the weight of words. They impartially preserved the gradually emerging terms of art and the often completely imprecise words, not even law words, which encased the terms of art like a cocoon. (Section 56.) Like the spreading of primitive taboo, anything close to the sacred became sacred.[42]

The printing press gave wider circulation and a greater appearance of authority and permanence to all these preserved words. (Section 78.) And both before the printing press and after, it was imagined that a continuity of Latin form also gave assurance of some sort of ancient authoritativeness. Though Medieval Latin and law Latin were vagabond relatives of respected and dead Classical Latin (Chapter VII), the fact that for years law words were "Latin" added to the feeling that these words must be as exact, as unchanging as a sentence from Caesar. (Sections 79, 80, 88.)

It was similar with law French. A persistent and false belief that the language of the law became French with William the Conqueror (Sections 41-44) gave a wrong sense of the antiquity of law language, and pushed backwards into the mists the dating of the development of technical precision in the law. (Sections 63, 64.) The added error — that all essential law words were French (Section 38) — has promoted the belief that law language (not merely the law itself) was a monolith, steady and unchanging in a sea of swirling English.

Supporters of this thesis could readily prove half their case by

---

[42] See Maine, *Ancient Law* 17 (new ed. 1930); Frazer, *The Golden Bough* 269 (abridged ed. 1951); Freud, *The Basic Writings* 828 (Brill, Modern Library ed. 1938).

"waving the bloody shirt." In the formative years of the law, the English language was indeed an unruly instrument. (Section 53.) Any insistence on constancy (real or pretended) in the language of the law might seem a reassuring gesture in the direction of order.

The pretense of precision appealed too to thinking men of the law, who found in the traditional insistence on rigid adherence to any form an answer to the harshness of the laws of England (Section 88), and a guide through the wilderness of pleading. (Section 90.) And for the ignorant who once practiced in great number, a belief in the precision of forms was nothing less than the self-assurance that they could practice law without an education. (Section 95.)

The few trained lawyers of colonial America were glad enough in the isolation of the wilderness to cling to the support of British form. (Sections 99, 104.) And the laity, while resenting the whole profession, were still fearful enough of the unknown to have the confidence of ignorance in the magic of the law's formulas. (Sections 102-104.) In the wild ferment of American expansion, who would listen to the earnest few who spoke out for change in the language of the law? (Section 107.) Form spread.

The proliferation of form (Section 112) coincided with the proliferation of law (Section 110). Lawyers — skilled and unskilled alike — have found themselves too pinched for time, too surrounded by repeated assurance that their language is precise, too oppressed by the fear of change (Section 115) to examine the ground on which they stand.

119. *Did it ever have a definite meaning?*

Many of the words that lawyers traditionally use never have had any definite meaning. Foremost among these are the deliberately flexible and some of the archaic.

Words like *reasonable, substantial, satisfactory* (Section 16), blatantly flaunt their lack of precision. They merit attention under other reasons for the language of the law (Section 135), and should not even receive passing notice here but for a tendency to consider them precise by association. The flexibles have for so long been a part of a language described as precise it is easy to forget that lack of precision is their only reason for existence.

Take *reasonable,* for instance. English, via Old French, since the fourteenth century,[43] it was not originally nor is it exclusively a law

43 *Oxford English Dictionary.*

word. In an earlier Latin form, Glanvil used it in the context of *reasonable time* (*rationabile terminum*) for payment of a mortgage debt when there had been no express agreement.[44] The 1215 Magna Carta spoke of a *reasonable aid* (*rationabile auxilium*),[45] in an attempt to put some vague limit on the unspecified tax the king or lord might levy to defray the expenses of ransom, knighting his oldest son, and marrying off his oldest daughter — once. Leaving it at *reasonable* proved unsatisfactory even seven hundred years ago. And before long a definite limit was fixed on *reasonable aid*,[46] though the tax continued to be called by that euphemism.[47]

 ̄ In our day, when *reasonable* stands alone, there is general agreement that it cannot be hog-tied and branded.[48] It is the byword of that most unprecise of encounters, the family argument — *Be reasonable, dear!*

But the law doesn't deal with unattached *reasonable*'s. And when *reasonable* in one form or another is hitched onto another word, sound men grow giddy with the excitement. It is assumed that the attachment can work a reformation, and that a word wild and amorphous can suddenly become tame and purposeful.

Take, for example, *reasonable doubt* and *beyond a reasonable doubt*. Because they are so often repeated — as a matter of tradition, and precedent,[49] and statute[50] — it is assumed that they must have some definite meaning, that in this context *reasonable* is precise.

Few have had the courage to say with England's Chief Justice Goddard:

---

[44] 3 Holdsworth, *A History of English Law* 129 n.1 (3d ed. 1923); 2 Pollock and Maitland, *The History of English Law* 120 and especially n.1 (2d ed. 1898).

[45] Stubbs, ed., *Select Charters* 298, par. 12; 299, par. 15; and see also 297, par. 4 (8th ed. 1905).

[46] Stat. (1275) 3 Edw. I, Stat. I, c. 36; Stat. (1350) 25 Edw. III, Stat. 5, c. 2; 3 Holdsworth, *A History of English Law* 66-67 (3d ed. 1923); 1 Pollock and Maitland, *The History of English Law* 349-351 (2d ed. 1898).

[47] Cowell, *The Interpreter* (ed. 1637), under *reasonable ayde*.

[48] 75 *C.J.S. reasonable*, p. 634; see *Black's Law Dictionary* (4th ed. 1951); Ballentine, *Law Dictionary with Pronunciations* (2d ed. 1948).

[49] 5 *Words and Phrases* 409-419 (perm. ed. 1940), 81 (Supp. 1962), "beyond a reasonable doubt"; 1 *California Words, Phrases, and Maxims* (1960), "beyond a reasonable doubt"; 34 *Words and Phrases* (perm. ed 1957, Supp. 1962), "proof beyond a reasonable doubt"; 3 *California Words, Phrases, and Maxims* (1960), "proof beyond a reasonable doubt"; 36 *Words and Phrases* 483-544 (perm. ed. 1962), 5 (Supp. 1962), "reasonable doubt"; 3 *California Words, Phrases, and Maxims* (1960), "reasonable doubt"; 4 *Words and Phrases: Judicially Defined* (Supp. 1960), "reasonable doubt"; 16 *C.J. criminal law* §§2395-2412.

[50] For example, Cal. Pen. Code §1096; Ga. Code §38-110.

I have never yet heard any court give a real definition of what is a "*reasonable doubt*," and it would be much better if that expression was not used.[51]

But many *reasonable men*[52] have warned lawyers at least to leave well enough alone, to stop trying to tell juries what a *reasonable doubt* really is. Sometimes self-restraint is urged on the ground that

There are no words plainer than "reasonable doubt," and none so exact to the idea meant.[53]

Sometimes on the practical ground that explanations do not clarify,[54] and instead give "misleading refinements"[55] which

. . . darken more minds, of the classes from whom our jurors are mainly drawn, than it will enlighten.[56]

Other *reasonable men* load the books with pages of words aimed at making something which is not certain have the show of certainty.[57] An influential definition comes from mid-nineteenth-century Massachusetts, in a case heavy with circumstantial evidence:

It is not mere possible doubt; because every thing relating to human affairs, and depending on moral evidence, is open to some possible or imaginary doubt. It is that state of the case, which, after the entire comparison and consideration of all the evidence, leaves the minds of jurors in that condition that they cannot say that they feel an abiding conviction, to a moral certainty, of the truth of the charge.[58]

[51] *R. v. Summers*, [1952] 1 All E.R. 1059, 1060 (C.C.A.); compare Jowitt, gen. ed., *The Dictionary of English Law* (1959), under *presumption of innocence*.

[52] 36 *Words and Phrases* (perm. ed. 1962), "reasonable man," "reasonable men"; 3 *California Words, Phrases, and Maxims* (1960), "reasonable man."

[53] 1 Bishop, *New Criminal Procedure* §1094.1, p. 682 (4th ed. 1895); see also *Sims v. State*, 203 Ga. 668, 670 (1948); *Brock v. State*, 91 Ga. App. 141, 178 (1954); *People v. Schoos*, 399 Ill. 527, 534 (1948); *State v. Wong Sun*, 114 Mont. 185, 197 (1943).

[54] See *Holland v. United States*, 348 U.S. 121, 140 (1954); *Miles v. United States*, 103 U.S. 304, 309 (1880).

[55] *State v. Smith*, 65 Conn. 283, 285 (1894).

[56] 1 Bishop, *New Criminal Procedure* 683 (4th ed. 1895); see also *People v. Lenon*, 79 Cal. 625, 631 (1889).

[57] For example, *State v. Seeney*, 21 Del. 142 (1904); *Commonwealth v. Kluska*, 333 Pa. 65, 74 (1939); Mathes, "Some Suggested Forms for Use in Criminal Cases," 20 F.R.D. 231, 238, Form No. 4, and compare notes at 238-239 and especially 238; 1 *Wharton's Criminal Evidence* §12, p. 31 (Anderson, 12th ed. 1955).

[58] *Commonwealth v. Webster*, 59 Mass. 295, 320 (1850); Cal. Pen. Code §1096; *California Jury Instructions: Criminal* 39 (rev. ed. 1958); compare *People v. Matthai*, 135 Cal. 442, 445 (1902), and *People v. Soldavini* 45 Cal. App. 2d 460, 463 (1941); see also *Pitts v. State*, 140 Ala. 77 (1903); *State v. McDowell*, 228 Iowa 182, 187 (1940); *State v. Abbott*, 64 W. Va. 411, 413 (1908).

These are the words of metaphysics for philosophers to wrestle with. These are sounds to titillate appellate benches and benumb jurors. After all the effort to make a silk purse, *reasonable doubt* remains a sow's ear.

The law is full of deliberately flexible words which lawyers will continue to live with. These words should not be used at all when precision is aimed at. When using flexible words, lawyers should know in their immediate consciousness — not only vaguely in some deep recess — what it is they are doing. It ought to be done knowingly, and for reasons other than precision, for against the charge of uncertainty the flexibles are defenseless. And most lawyers — when they think about it — know that this is so.

With some of the archaic words of the law (Section 10), it is different. To those accustomed to the cadence of law language, the archaic words mean law and its precision. The fact that they are archaic is a recommendation, as it once was with French and Latin in the law. (Sections 59, 72, 74, 76.) The deader the better; that means they can't move around. "Archaic" is taken as another way of saying that these words haven't changed since Coke, and anything that old must be good. Not so. Many words that old have simply been bad longer. (See Section 120.)

120. *Some continuously vague archaisms*

Here is a sampling of some law words which have been used long and often, with never a healthy smell of precision about them. They are flabby words; and, in addition, many of them are treacherous, for unlike such as *reasonable* (Sections 16, 119) and *substantial* (Section 16) they are not obviously vague. Were it not for the fact that they have been used repeatedly, traditionally by other lawyers, no lawyer alive would independently choose any of these words. Yet, except for one variant (*or/and*), all are in such common professional use as to be considered by the profession indispensable. And, except for one device (*ss*), these are litigious words, eager — though unready — for battle, tricky, ducking, bobbing words. None of them is worth saving, and their deaths should serve as a warning. A warning that unless a lawyer has learned some law which justifies a peculiar usage, peculiar usage is suspect.

Aforesaid

This lay combination from Middle English[59] has been causing trouble for more than three hundred years. Its purpose is to refer to something that has been said,[60] and its chief vice is that you can't be sure what it refers to.[61]

Coke recognized this defect, and warned that *aforesaid* (Latin, *praedictus*) was no good when precision was called for, because it was not clear that *aforesaid* always referred to what went immediately before.[62] Despite Coke, lawyers have permitted *aforesaid* to give the same ambiguous directions ever since. It may refer to what is next-before,[63] to the next-to-the-next-before,[64] or to everything that has gone before.[65]

As a kind of fetish supposed to endow with precision whatever it stuck to, *aforesaid* has been glued to everything — the day and month, the year, the name of a town,[66] "F.P., sheriff as aforesaid," [67] "for the purposes aforesaid," [68] "detained . . . as aforesaid," "paid as aforesaid," [69] "the aforesaid icing dock," [70] "my said will so made as aforesaid." [71] But *aforesaid* gives only the appearance of precision.[72] It is a nervous habit, become so chronic that *aforesaid* is occasionally thrown in with nothing to refer to — as in a will giving land to "my aforesaid nephews and nieces," with not a nephew or niece named in the will.[73] Of old, such lapses were sometimes fatal.[74] And they still may cause

---

[59] *Oxford English Dictionary.*

[60] *Black's Law Dictionary* (4th ed. 1951); 2A *Words and Phrases* (perm. ed. 1955, Supp. 1962); 1 *California Words, Phrases, and Maxims* (1960).

[61] 2 *C.J.S. aforesaid*, p. 1007.

[62] Coke, *Commentary upon Littleton*, f. 20b and compare f. 46b (10th ed. 1703).

[63] *Black's Law Dictionary* (4th ed. 1951); 1 *Words and Phrases: Judicially Defined* (1946); *Allentown v. Pennsylvania Public Utility Commission*, 173 Pa. Super. 219, 222 (1953); *State v. Youngblood*, 199 Tenn. 519, 523 (1955); *contra: State v. Fields*, 70 Kan. 391, 393 (1904).

[64] *Sanborn v. Camberlin*, 101 Mass. 409, 418 (1869).

[65] *In re Pearsons*, 98 Cal. 603, 608 (1893); *Central National Bank v. Pratt*, 115 Mass. 539, 545 (1874); *Doe dem Gibson v. Gell*, 107 Eng. Rep. 535 (K.B. 1824).

[66] *King v. Fearnley*, 99 Eng. Rep. 1115 (K.B. 1786).

[67] Hillyer, *Annotated Forms*, No. 2739 (1938).

[68] Hillyer, *Annotated Forms*, No. 2735 (1938).

[69] Hillyer, *Annotated Forms*, No. 2735 (1938).

[70] Hillyer, *Annotated Forms*, No. 3559.6 (Supp. 1954).

[71] *Estate of Dubois*, 94 Cal. App. 2d 838 (1949).

[72] Compare Piesse and Smith, *The Elements of Drafting* 57-58 (2d ed. 1958).

[73] *Campbell v. Bouskell*, 54 Eng. Rep. 127, 128, 129 (Rolls Ct. 1859); compare *Chapman v. Groton*, 20 Conn. Supp. 333, 336 n.1, 337 n.2 (1956).

[74] *King v. Fearnley*, 99 Eng. Rep. 1115, 1117 (K.B. 1786); 2 Hawkins, *A Treatise of the Pleas of the Crown*, c. 25, §72, pp. 320, 321 (8th ed. 1824).

unnecessary litigation, even though *aforesaid* is ultimately labeled "sheer redundance" and disregarded.[75]

If there is only one possible reference for *aforesaid*, it is usually unnecessary — as when an answer refers to the only action there is, "the action aforesaid." [76] If *aforesaid* can by any chance refer to more than one thing, or to nothing, its long history of uncertain reference marks it as dangerous. In either case, no aid to precision.[77]

If a definite reference is necessary, the antecedent should be repeated when the antecedent is short and the references not numerous. When the antecedent is long (e.g., land boundaries) or references will be numerous, a convenient identification may be made on first mention and used uniformly — e.g., "Blackacre," "John Smith, mortgagor," "Adam Baker, the vendor," [78] "this writing is called 'the Building Contract,'" "called in this answer 'the '59 Chevvy,'" etc. (See also *said* in this list.) [79]

And/or

This unfortunate expression[80] ("happy," [81] "useful," [82] say its friends) has been clouding the law for more than one hundred years[83] and has roots that go centuries deeper into the confusions of English translation of Latin conjunctions.[84] The good-usage people are all critical of it, though in varying degrees,[85] with the weathervane school de-

---

[75] *Estate of Dubois*, 94 Cal. App. 2d 838, 842 (1949); *accord: Finnegan v. United States*, 231 Fed. 561, 565 (6th Cir. 1916); *Campbell v. Bouskell*, 54 Eng. Rep. 127, 128, 129 (Rolls Ct. 1859); and see *Commonwealth v. O'Hearn*, 132 Mass. 553, 555 (1882).

[76] Hillyer, *Annotated Forms*, No. 3317 (1938); compare Piesse and Smith, *The Elements of Drafting* 47-48 (2d ed. 1958).

[77] Dickerson, *Legislative Drafting* 75 (1954); National Conference of Commissioners on Uniform State Laws, *Handbook* 255 (1959); compare Strunk, *The Elements of Style* 33 (White ed. 1959).

[78] Piesse and Smith, *The Elements of Drafting* 58 (2d ed. 1958).

[79] Page 318.

[80] *In re Lewis*, [1942] L.R. Ch. D. 424, 425.

[81] Note, "In Defense of 'and/or,'" 45 Yale L.J. 918-919 (1936).

[82] Note, "Words and Phrases — Meaning of Words 'and/or,'" 20 Marq. L. Rev. 101, 102 (1936).

[83] Section 81; compare Parsons, "And/or," 10 J.S.B. Calif. 77 (1935); "An and/or Symposium," letters, 18 A.B.A.J. 574, 576 (1932); and Welch, "And/or," 44 Mass. L.Q. 98 (1959).

[84] Section 81.

[85] Gowers, *The Complete Plain Words* 26 (4th impression with amends. 1957); Nicholson, *A Dictionary of American-English Usage* (1957); compare Partridge, *The Concise Usage and Abusage* (1955), and Partridge, *Usage and Abusage* (new ed. 1957), with Partridge, *A Dictionary of Clichés* 22, 65, 114, 124, 154, 183, 188, 192, 195, 198, 240, 241 et seq. (4th ed. 1950); Strunk, *The Elements of Style* 34 (White ed. 1959).

claring it validated by mass use.[86] For lawyers, *and/or* is "traditional" in the sense that it has become habitual — appearing in statutes,[87] rules,[88] pleadings,[89] contracts,[90] etc. — in complete disregard of unfavorable precedent [91] and general condemnation.[92] It has belligerent enthusiasts within the profession,[93] although the very first time it was called into question, in 1854, *and/or* was given not one but three meanings (Section 81), and ever since it has been the repeated and direct cause of uncertainty, litigation, and courtroom failure.[94] That *and/or* is loved so intensely and rejected so bitterly argues against its claim to precision, and is some evidence of the appropriateness of its having been called "bastard" by careful lawyers on two continents.[95]

What does *and/or* mean?

(1) One understanding is that it includes every possibility imaginable with *and* alone plus every possibility imaginable with *or* alone.[96]

---

[86] Evans and Evans, *A Dictionary of Contemporary American Usage* (1957).

[87] 47 U.S.C.A. §§152, 311; *State v. Dudley*, 159 La. 871, 877 (1925).

[88] Rules of the Los Angeles Municipal Court, Revised Rule 42 (1959); *Brown v. Guaranty Estates Corp.*, 239 N.C. 595, 599, 604 (1954); see also *Baum v. Baum*, 51 Cal. 2d 610, 612 (1959).

[89] *Vilardo v. County of Sacramento*, 54 Cal. App. 2d 413, 415-418 (1942); *Shadden v. Cowan*, 213 Ga. 29 (1957); and see *In re Bell*, 19 Cal. 2d 488, 530 (1942); *Underhill v. Alameda Elementary School District*, 133 Cal. App. 733, 736 (1933).

[90] *Sproule and/or Fidelity Life Ins. Co. v. Taffe*, 294 Ill. App. 374, 374-376 (1938); *Fadden v. Deputy Federal Commissioner of Taxation*, 68 Commw. L.R. 76 (Austl. 1943); compare *Gurney v. Grimmer*, 44 Lloyd's List L.R. 189, 194-195 (Eng. 1932).

[91] See generally 3 *Words and Phrases* 640-647 (perm. ed. 1953), 33 (Supp. 1962), "and/or."

[92] *In re Bell*, 19 Cal. 2d 488, 499-500 (1942); *City National Bank & Trust Co. v. Davis Hotel Corp.*, 280 Ill. App. 247, 252-253 (1935); *Tarjan v. National Surety Co.*, 268 Ill. App. 232, 238-241 (1932); "And/or," editorial, 18 A.B.A.J. 456 (1932); "And/or -iana," editorial, 18 A.B.A.J. 524 (1932); letters in "An and/or Symposium," 18 A.B.A.J. 574, 575-577 (1932); Notes, "And/or," 118 A.L.R. 1367 (1939), 154 A.L.R. 866 (1945); National Conference of Commissioners on Uniform State Laws, *Handbook* 255 (1959).

[93] Letters in "An and/or Symposium," 18 A.B.A.J. 574, 574-575 (1932); letters in "For and/or on Behalf of; Or Against and/or," 10 J.S.B. Calif. 89-91, 95, and letters contra on 91-93, 95 (1935); Mumper, "The Unfair Tirade Against the Symbol 'and/or'" 10 J.S.B. Calif. 187-190 (1935); Note, "In Defense of 'and/or,'" 45 Yale L.J. 918-919 (1936); Note, "Words and Phrases — Meaning of Words 'and/or,'" 20 Marq. L. Rev. 101-102 (1936); and see Note, "And/or," 154 A.L.R. 866, 867 (1945).

[94] See cases in Chapter XIII, notes 111-116.

[95] John W. Davis, in "An and/or Symposium," 18 A.B.A.J. 574, 575 (1932); Viscount Simon, L.C., in *Bonitto v. Fuerst Brothers & Co., Ltd.*, [1944] A.C. 75, 82.

[96] Cairns, L.C., in *Stanton v. Richardson*, 45 L.J.Q.B. (n.s.) 78, 82-83 (1875); see Scrutton, L.J., in *Gurney v. Grimmer*, 44 Lloyd's List L.R. 189, 194 (Eng. 1932).

(2) Others say it may include all of those possibilities, and is to be construed ". . . as will best accord with the equity of the situation . . ."[97]

(3) Some judges have said (not held) that *and/or* means that some, but not all, of the possibilities are included, and disagree on what to include.[98]

(4) Another group insists that *and/or* means either *and* or *or* but cannot mean both.[99]

(5) Other judges have turned away in disgust, and said that *and/or* is "meaningless."[100]

In the least complicated of situations there is little opportunity to misunderstand *and/or*.[101] A rule beginning

In all suits in rem against a ship, and/or her appurtenances . . .[102]

would be taken by most lawyers to be the equivalent of ordinary English

In all suits in rem against a ship, her appurtenances, or both . . .

But even here, the *and/or* way is not more precise than ordinary English. And it is only the simplicity of the facts — not the formula — that prevents confusion. Lawyers cannot depend on the generalization that ". . . the simple form 'A and/or B' . . . is unambiguous, . . ."[103]

With slight complication of legal setting, e.g., a bond account named A *and/or* B,[104] a gift by will to A *and/or* B,[105] *and/or* becomes ". . . an elliptical and embarrassing expression which endangers accuracy for the sake of brevity."[106] The depositor, the donor, may be indif-

---

[97] *State v. Dudley*, 159 La. 871, 877 (1925); *Black's Law Dictionary* (4th ed. 1951), under *and*.

[98] See Section 81; see also opinions in *Cuthbert v. Cumming*, 3 C.L.R. 401, 404 (1855), 3 W.R. 553, 554 (1855), 24 L.J. Ex. 310, 312 (1855); *Stanton v. Richardson*, 45 L.J.Q.B. 78, 82-83, 84-85, 85 (H.L. 1875).

[99] *Saylor v. Williams*, 93 Ga. App. 643, 645 (1955); see *Webster's New International Dictionary* (2d ed. 1934), under *and/or*.

[100] *State ex rel. Adler v. Douglas*, 339 Mo. 187, 190 (1936).

[101] See 7 Austl. L.J. 76, 77 (June 15, 1933).

[102] Adm. Rule 9, 28 U.S.C.A. (1950).

[103] Piesse and Smith, *The Elements of Drafting* 80 (2d ed. 1958).

[104] *Fadden v. Deputy Federal Commissioner of Taxation*, 68 Commw. L.R. 76 (Austl. 1943).

[105] *In re Lewis*, [1942] L.R. Ch. D. 424.

[106] *Fadden v. Deputy Federal Commissioner of Taxation*, 68 Commw. L.R. 76, 82 (Austl. 1943).

ferent to the outcome; the tax collector,[107] the beneficiaries,[108] are not. Ultimately the decision must be made, which is it — A or B or both? And this decision is not helped by *and/or*. That formula permits the one person who should know what he is talking about to dodge the decision, and fobs off the choice on a stranger — a lawyer, a judge — who may not have the slightest notion what the writer really meant. The formula also sometimes creates the suspicion that the draftsman himself didn't know what function he wanted *and/or* to serve — e.g., ". . . cancel any and/or all sales contracts in whole or in part,"[109] ". . . and shall in no manner or form be construed to be a partnership and/or limited partnership relationship."[110]

The law ordinarily requires of the practicing lawyer a more determined stretching after certainty than *and/or*. The indecisiveness of *and/or* will ruin:

an affidavit — "fraud and/or other wrongful act";[111]
a finding — "associate with and/or employ";[112]
a pleading — "officer and/or agent";[113]
a statute — driving while drunk "and, or" causing injury;[114]
an indictment — "cards, dice and/or dominoes";[115]
a judgment — in an action which described the plaintiff by the formula *A and/or B;*[116]

In a contract, *and/or* is the signal that the draftsman has abandoned his duty to speak for his client;[117] it gives the green light to a court bent on interpretation.[118]

The draftsman under pressure is tempted to avoid decision with

---

[107] *Fadden v. Deputy Federal Commissioner of Taxation*, 68 Commw. L.R. 76 (Austl. 1943).

[108] *In re Lewis*, [1942] L.R. Ch. D. 424.

[109] Nichols, *Cyclopedia of Legal Forms* §4.1047 (1955).

[110] Nichols, *Cyclopedia of Legal Forms* §7.371 (1936).

[111] *Rosenberg v. Bullard*, 127 Cal. App. 315, 321 (1932).

[112] *Strip City, Inc. v. Board of Police Commissioners*, Los Angeles Superior Ct., #718301, Los Angeles Daily J., April 13, 1959.

[113] *Vilardo v. County of Sacramento*, 54 Cal. App. 2d 413 (1942); and see *In re Bell*, 19 Cal. 2d 488 (1942); *Underhill v. Alameda Elementary School District*, 133 Cal. App. 733 (1933); *Shadden v. Cowan*, 213 Ga. 29 (1957); *Bonitto v. Fuerst Brothers & Co. Ltd.*, [1944] A.C. 75, 81-82; see also 3 *Words and Phrases*, 645-646 (perm. ed. 1962), "and/or," pleadings.

[114] *State v. Dudley*, 159 La. 871, 877 (1925).

[115] *Compton v. State*, 91 S.W.2d 732, 733 (Tex. Crim. App. 1936).

[116] *Sproule and/or Fidelity Life Ins. Co. v. Taffe*, 294 Ill. App. 374, 375 (1938).

[117] *Sproule and/or Fidelity Life Ins. Co. v. Taffe*, 294 Ill. App. 374, 375 (1938).

[118] 3 *Words and Phrases*, 642-643 (perm. ed. 1953), "and/or," contracts.

multiple *and/or's* and by pinning many items together with a single *and/or*.[119] There is an easy catchall ambiguity in:

> We will accept 100 tons of X, in fine and/or medium and/or coarse grades.

It is slightly longer but more precise to say:

> We will accept 100 tons of X all of one grade (fine, medium, coarse) or in any mixture of two or three of those grades.

And/or is sometimes shorter, but never more precise, than ordinary English. It is usually uncertain. It is completely unnecessary.

Forthwith

The fact that this is Middle English dating from an age when miracles were more common and kings were accustomed to being obeyed *right now* has given *forthwith* an air of imagined urgency. Like *presto!* and *off with his head!* But as with other time words, *forthwith* suffers from uncertainty if it is permitted to wander loose.

In the common speech where it originated, *forthwith* once had a hitching post. It was *forth with* = along with, at the same time with something else.[120] It is this sense of quick connection with another event that the dictionary gives us when it quotes the King James Bible:

> And immediately there fell from his eyes as it had been scales: and he received sight forthwith. . . .[121]

The law has rarely moved so fast, and when it did, *forthwith* was not the word. To avoid the rule that a dead man could not be a felon, a suicide used to be counted a felon *eo instante* (at the very instant) he killed himself.[122] In the swift metaphysics of real property, a particle of time was split to prefer a joint tenant's survivorship over his joint tenant's devise ". . . though they jump at one *instant* . . ."[123] Three centuries ago, a distinction was made between an order to plead *instanter* ("the same day") and an order to plead *forth-*

---

[119] *In re Bell,* 19 Cal. 2d 488, 499 (1942); Piesse and Smith, *The Elements of Drafting* 86-87 (2d ed. 1958); Am. Jur. *Legal Forms* 2:964 (1953), 12:650 (1955).

[120] *Oxford English Dictionary,* under *forth* and *forthwith*.

[121] Acts 9:18; *Webster's New International Dictionary* (2d ed. 1934).

[122] Jacob, *A New Law-Dictionary* (6th ed. 1750), under *instant*.

[123] Coke, *Commentary upon Littleton,* f. 185b, and see also ff. 297b, 298a (10th ed. 1703).

with ("such convenient time after as the court shall judge reasonable; . . . without delay").[124]

In the hundreds of years that *forthwith* has been known to lawyers,[125] it has remained flexible and ambiguous, the opposite of precise, and confusion has developed between meaning and application. Since *forthwith* is dependent on context,[126] the time it expresses is sometimes measured by the clock and sometimes by the calendar. Delays of three hours[127] and four and one-half hours[128] have been said to be *not forthwith*. Under different circumstances delays of thirty-three days[129] and fifty-three days[130] have been said to be *forthwith*. Because *forthwith* can be very quick, it is considered by some to be the same as *instanter*[131] and *immediately*.[132] Because *forthwith* can be quite slow, it has been said not to be the same as *instanter*,[133] and not the same as *immediately*.[134] *Forthwith* has been given every shade of meaning in the spectrum of time — from *instanter* and *immediately* through *without unnecessary procrastination or delay*[135] and *due diligence under all the circumstances*,[136] to *as soon as* necessary preliminaries are attended to,[137] and *within a reasonable time*.[138] The vast collections of litigated *forthwith's*[139] rather than pointing

---

[124] *Style's Practical Register* 452-453 (4th ed. 1707; 1st ed. 1657); see also 4 Blackstone, *Commentaries* °396 (Jones ed. 1916); compare 26 *C.J.* 997, 1000, and Jowitt, gen. ed., *The Dictionary of English Law* (1959), under *forthwith* and *instanter*.

[125] *Oxford English Dictionary*; *Style's Practical Register* 452-453 (4th ed. 1707); Carr, ed., *Pension Book of Clement's Inn*, 78 Selden Society 1, 4 (1960).

[126] 1 Bouvier, *A Law Dictionary* (1839); *Lewis v. Curry*, 156 Cal. 93, 101 (1909).

[127] *Ex parte Lamb,* 19 Ch. D. 169, 174 (1881).

[128] *Winston v. Commonwealth*, 188 Va. 386, 394-395 (1948).

[129] See *Woodlock v. Aetna Life Ins. Co.*, 225 S.W. 994, 998 (Mo. 1920).

[130] See *Solomon v. Continental Ins. Co.*, 11 Misc. 513, 514-517 (1895).

[131] *Hull v. Mallory,* 56 Wis. 355, 356 (1882); *Black's Law Dictionary* (4th ed. 1951), under *instanter*.

[132] *Trask v. State Fire & Marine Ins. Co.*, 29 Pa. 198, 200 (1858); *Black's Law Dictionary* (4th ed. 1951), under *forthwith*.

[133] *Queen v. Justices of the Isle of Ely*, 119 Eng. Rep. 563, 565 (Q.B. 1855).

[134] *Ballentine's Pronouncing Law Dictionary: Supplement* (2d ed. 1954), under *forthwith*.

[135] *Edwards v. Baltimore Fire Ins. Co.*, 3 Gill 176, 188 (Md. 1874).

[136] *Edwards v. Lycoming County Mutual Ins. Co.*, 75 Pa. 378, 380 (1874).

[137] See *Nicholls v. Chambers*, 149 Eng. Rep. 1129 (Ex. 1834).

[138] Under *forthwith* in *Black's Law Dictionary* (4th ed. 1951), Ballentine, *Law Dictionary with Pronunciations* (2d ed. 1948), and Jowitt, gen. ed., *The Dictionary of English Law* (1959).

[139] 26 *C.J. forthwith*, pp. 997-1000; 17 *Words and Phrases* 605-633 (perm. ed. 1958), 19 (Supp. 1962), "forthwith"; 2 *California Words, Phrases, and Maxims* (1960), "forthwith"; 3 *Words and Phrases: Judicially Defined* (1944), "immediately."

toward uniformity give color to any interpretation of the word which determined interest can imagine.

The varied meanings of *forthwith* leave a strong doubt with the profession. Does the user intend immediacy tied to some other event or merely what is reasonable? There is a tone of authority in "This order is final forthwith"[140] and ". . . you are therefore commanded forthwith to arrest . . . ,"[141] but what do they mean? If there is a time limit, why not say so? If there is a time limit by the clock, that should be stated; or if the reference is to the calendar, that should be stated; or if a more leisurely reasonableness is intended, that too should be stated. *Forthwith* is an archaic luxury that the law can do without.[142]

Hereafter

This Old English has been wandering in the wilderness of the common speech for more than a thousand years, now pointing to the-next-in-order, now to the-world-to-come.[143] For the law, *hereafter* is equally uncertain, usually looking to the future,[144] but never seeing it very clearly.

When legislators say *hereafter*, it sounds as if they mean as-soon-as-we-pass-this-law, and sometimes they do.[145] More often, the courts say they mean after-this-law-becomes-effective.[146] And so, when a statute is amended and republished, the *hereafter* may then refer to two effective dates, one for the old part of the law, one for the new.[147]

After you decide when *hereafter* starts, the battle is not over. Sometimes *hereafter* refers to activities commenced before,[148] sometimes

140 *In re Harmon*, Crim. No. 6719, Cal. Supreme Ct. minute order, Aug. 9, 1960, in 54 A.C., minutes p. 1, following p. 599 (1960).

141 Cal. Pen. Code §1197.

142 See and compare Piesse and Smith, *The Elements of Drafting* 114 (2d ed. 1958), and Dickerson, *Legislative Drafting* 78 (1954).

143 *Oxford English Dictionary*.

144 *Black's Law Dictionary* (4th ed. 1951); Ballentine, *Law Dictionary with Pronunciations* (2d ed. 1948); *contra: Hebblethwaite v. Cartwright*, 25 Eng. Rep. 643, 644 (Ch. 1734).

145 *Kendig v. Knight*, 60 Iowa 29, 31-32 (1882); see *Sawyer v. Gallagher*, 151 Iowa 64, 68-70 (1911).

146 *Allen v. California Mutual Bldg. & Loan Assn.*, 22 Cal. 2d 474, 488-490 (1943), disapproving dictum in *Allen v. California Mutual Bldg. & Loan Assn.*, 40 Cal. App. 2d 374, 379-380 (1940); *Bennett v. Bevard*, 6 Iowa 82, 89 (1858); and see *Charless & Blow v. Lamberson*, 1 Iowa 393, 401 (1855).

147 *Ely v. Holton*, 15 N.Y. 595, 599 (1857); *People v. McFall*, 158 N.Y. Supp. 974, 976 (Buffalo City Ct. 1916).

148 *Shreveport Long Leaf Lumber Co. v. Wilson*, 195 La. 814, 825-826 (1940);

only to activity commenced after the statute.[149] And how long does *hereafter* last? You can find any answer you look for:

permanently — in a statute ("Proceedings . . . shall hereafter be . . .");[150]

indefinitely — in an employment contract (". . . that hereafter the second party shall work as a salesman . . .");[151]

duration of contract — in a reference to designs made "preceding this contract, or hereafter";[152]

nine months after testator's death — in a bequest to grandchildren "now living or hereafter born";[153]

to the end of the period of postponement — in a conveyance (for life, remainder to children "born or hereafter to be born").[154]

Usually, *hereafter* must be interpreted. Sometimes it is best ignored. An English court did this two hundred years ago when *hereafter* unnecessarily intruded into the fee tail formula to make it read ". . . hereafter to be begotten." [155] An American court was of similar mind in the twentieth century when an enacting clause said that an old law was ". . . amended and re-enacted so as to read hereafter as follows . . ." *Hereafter,* said the judge, ". . . really means nothing . . ." for

The result of the amendment even without the word "hereafter," would be that the act would read thereafter as amended.[156]

In short, *hereafter* depends on which way the wind blows. If a definite time reference is intended, that should be stated.[157] If time is of no concern, that should be stated. In either case, *hereafter* adds nothing to ordinary English but confusion.[158]

Hereby

This is Middle English, not dignified by place in the standard law dictionaries in this country or England, but a great favorite with the

---

Nelson v. State, 17 Ind. App. 403, 407 (1897); see *Westwego Canal & Terminal Co. v. Louisiana Highway Commission,* 200 La. 990, 999 (1942).

[149] *Geddes & Moss Undertaking & Embalming Co. v. First National Life Ins. Co.,* 189 La. 891, 900 (1938).

[150] *Roccaforte v. Mulcahey,* 169 F. Supp. (D. Mass. 1958).

[151] *McManigal v. Hiatt,* 240 Iowa 541, 543, 546 (1949).

[152] *Strauss v. Borg,* 172 Ill. App. 466 (1912).

[153] *Merrill v. Winchester,* 120 Me. 203, 209, 213 (1921).

[154] 3 *Restatement of Property* §295u.

[155] *Hebblethwaite v. Cartwright,* 25 Eng. Rep. 643, 644 (Ch. 1734); see Coke, *Commentary upon Littleton,* f. 20b (10th ed. 1703).

[156] *Shreveport Long Leaf Lumber Co. v. Wilson,* 195 La. 814, 825 (1940).

[157] See, for example, Dickerson, *Legislative Drafting* 77, 83 (1954).

[158] Compare Piesse and Smith, *The Elements of Drafting* 48 (2d ed. 1958).

profession.[159]   *Hereby* is noteworthy for being vague in two dimensions — in space and time.   Its ordinary meaning is by-means-of-this,[160] and if no one is snapping at your heels, that's all there is to *hereby*.   But lawyers want to know first of all whether *hereby* means only by-means-of-this-writing,[161] or right-now-by-means-of-this-writing.[162]   And whichever choice is made, the answer still leaves in doubt whether this-writing refers to the entire document[163] or to only a part of it.[164]

Usually, no word need be substituted for *hereby*.   It is just unnecessary.   *I do hereby revoke*[165] is not more precise than *I revoke*.

If by-means-of-this must be tied to something, specific language is called for, something more substantial than *hereby*.   To minimize fumbling, the Book of Common Prayer says "With this ring I thee wed . . ."[166] rather than "Hereby, I thee wed."   A secular draftsman may speak of "the gifts listed in paragraph 3" rather than "their property hereby given."[167]

If right-now-by-means-of-this-writing is intended, the lawyer had best say so by reference to date or some notorious action.   *Hereby* cannot be depended upon.

Hereby gives only the flavor of law, which is probably what the linotyper had in mind when he produced this one:

> San Francisco — Repeal of California's guest statute law was recommended hereby the Conference of State Bar Delegates.[168]

[159] See, for example, Nichols, *Cyclopedia of Legal Forms* §2.520, pars. B, D, §§2.1184a, 2.1346 (1956); Neuhoff, *Standard Clauses for Wills*, Form Nos. 76.1, 76.3-76.7, etc.; *Am. Jur. Legal Forms* 3:1004 (1953), 9:88 (1954).

[160] *Webster's New International Dictionary* (2d ed. 1934); see *Oxford English Dictionary*.

[161] *Lane v. Kolb*, 92 Ala. 636, 648 (1890), and dissent at 665 (compare comment in 5 Ala. L. Rev. 61 (1952-1953)); see also *Home Ins. Co. v. Cobbs*, 20 Ala. App. 491, 493 (1925); *People v. Righthouse*, 10 Cal. 2d 86, 88 (1937); see also 19 *Words and Phrases* (perm. ed. 1940, Supp. 1962).

[162] *Hodges v. Dilatush*, 199 Ark. 967, 970 (1940); *Evans v. McCarthy*, 42 Kan. 426, 427, 429 (1889); *Custy v. Donlan*, 159 Mass. 245 (1893); *Chambers v. Sharp*, 61 N.J. Eq. 253, 257 (1901); see *Potter v. Eaton*, 26 Wis. 382, 383 (1870).

[163] *Essex Co. National Bank v. Harrison*, 57 N.J. Eq. 91, 93 (1898).

[164] *Renwick v. Smith*, 11 S.C. 294, 295, 307-308 (1877); and see *Bonner v. Bonner*, 33 Eng. Rep. 336 (Ch. 1807).

[165] Neuhoff, *Standard Clauses for Wills*, Form No. 76.6 (1958).

[166] *The Book of Common Prayer*, f. cxxiii b (Pickering, 1844).

[167] *Renwick v. Smith*, 11 S.C. 294, 295, 307-308 (1877).

[168] Los Angeles Daily J., Sept. 23, 1959, p. 1.

Herein

This is an Old English word of nonlegal origin. It combined older Old English *here* and the still older *in*, which has been a word of loose use for more than a millennium.[169] The big dictionaries do not brand *herein* as "archaic,"[170] but a courageous woman lists it in a sampling of "Legalistic Jargon,"[171] and an anonymous Englishman includes it in a *Chamber of Horrors*.[172] Litigated for years, *herein* has still not settled down to any fixed meaning. It means in-this[173] well enough, but in-this-what? This sentence, this paragraph, this contract, this statute? The exact point of reference remains obscure, and depends completely on "context,"[174] which is another way of saying that your writing is going to be "interpreted."

In a typical situation, interpreting *"Except as herein expressly provided,"* a trial court said *herein* meant the whole statute. An intermediate panel of three appellate judges thought it "manifest" that " 'herein' means 'in this section.' "[175] And four supreme court judges who held "Here it is clear that the word refers to the entire act" could not convince three colleagues that that was so.[176]

Sometimes *herein* is simply redundant — "enclosed herein," "the plaintiff herein,"[177] "as hereinafter stated herein."[178] But worse is the uncertainty it creates. It is a poor word of reference, which laymen scorn and no careful lawyer should use.[179] The antique flavor of *herein* gives the illusion of a precision whose substance is better obtained by ordinary English "in this paragraph," "in this statute," "in this contract."[180]

[169] *Oxford English Dictionary.*
[170] *Oxford English Dictionary; Webster's New International Dictionary* (2d ed. 1934).
[171] Hunter, *The Language of Audit Reports* 27 (1957).
[172] ["Vigilans"], *Chamber of Horrors* 69, 127 (1952).
[173] *Webster's New International Dictionary* (2d ed. 1934).
[174] *Miller v. Butterfield*, 125 U.S. 70 (1887); *Gatliff Coal Co. v. Cox*, 142 F.2d 876, 882 (6th Cir. 1944); *Saulsberry v. Maddix*, 125 F.2d 430, 434 (6th Cir. 1942); *In re Berkowitz*, 143 Fed. 598, 601 (E.D. Pa. 1906); *In re Pearsons*, 98 Cal. 603, 608 (1893); *San Gabriel County Water District v. Richardson*, 68 Cal. App. 297 (1924); *Curran v. Bradner*, 27 Ill. App. 582, 584 (1888); *Adams v. City of Hobart*, 166 Okla. 267, 272 (1933); *Gist v. Craig*, 142 S.C. 407 (1927); 19 *Words and Phrases* (perm. ed. 1940, Supp. 1962); 2 *California Words, Phrases, and Maxims* (1960); 2 *Words and Phrases: Judicially Defined* (1943).
[175] *Owen v. Off*, 218 P.2d 563, 566 (Cal. App. 1950).
[176] *Owen v. Off*, 36 Cal. 2d 751, 754 (1951).
[177] Hillyer, *Annotated Forms*, No. 2776, par. 2 (1938).
[178] Nichols, *Cyclopedia of Legal Forms* §4.1378 (1955).
[179] Dickerson, *Legislative Drafting* 75 (1954).
[180] See Piesse and Smith, *The Elements of Drafting* 48 (2d ed. 1958).

Hereinafter[181]

In the sixteenth century, someone (not at first lawyers) began adding to the uncertain reference of *herein* (in this list) the only slightly less uncertain Old English *after*. *After* means farther-from-the-front, but gives no clue to how far that might be, whether right next door or a long way off.[182] While ordinarily *hereinafter* should point to the right instead of the left, below rather than above,[183] it is a loose word, loosely used; and in at least two recorded instances judges have saved a cause if not the draftsman's reputation for alertness by interpreting *hereinafter* to mean *hereinbefore*.[184] Never definite, *hereinafter* was a makeshift road sign in the days when draftsmen did not number paragraphs (see Section 109) and were careless of punctuation. (Sections 82, 83, 84, 106.) It remains a trap for the dozing draftsman, permitting him to postpone the time for decision — sometimes indefinitely. Direct reference to "paragraph 12," to "Chapter X," to any landmark, requires the drafter to make up his mind and the reader to focus on what the draftsman intended.

There are instances where even though *hereinafter* is archaic, it can cause no direct harm.[185] But the habit of using *hereinafter* then calls for constant decision and extraordinary vigilance. In the same lease, for example, a harmless choice of *hereinafter* makes the introductory clause read, ". . . hereinafter called the lessors." But a confusing choice in paragraph "1" reads, ". . . *the agreements and stipulations hereinafter named*,"[186] leaving it open to speculation whether the reference is to the "agreements and stipulations" in paragraph "1" or in the whole lease. As with *herein*, if *hereinafter* means in-this-lease or in-this-paragraph, there is good reason for saying so.[187]

Heretofore

Just as *hereafter* (in this list) is a vague reference to the future, *heretofore* is a vague reference to the past. Since its birth in the com-

---

[181] See generally 19 *Words and Phrases* (perm. ed. 1940); ["Vigilans"], *Chamber of Horrors* 127 (1952).

[182] *Oxford English Dictionary.*

[183] *Webster's New International Dictionary* (2d ed. 1934).

[184] *Creighton v. Pringle*, 3 S.C. 77, 79, 94-95 (1870); *Waring v. Cheraw & Darlington R.R. Co.*, 16 S.C. 416, 425 (1881).

[185] See, for example, *A Uniform System of Citation* §24:4, pp. 79-80, 80 (10th ed. 1958).

[186] Nichols, *Cyclopedia of Legal Forms* §6.722 (1936).

[187] Dickerson, *Legislative Drafting* 75 and especially n.3 (1954); compare Piesse and Smith, *The Elements of Drafting* 32, 48 (2d ed. 1958).

mon speech of the fourteenth century, *heretofore* has not been firmly attached to any fixed point in time.[188] And it has been at the center of strife since the treaty ending the Revolutionary War (". . . debts, heretofore contracted").[189] *Heretofore* has been held to include the date of the document containing it,[190] and to exclude that date.[191] It has been said to refer to the time before the effective date of a statute,[192] and not to refer to that time — merely a " 'cautious redundancy.' "[193] It has also been held to mean *hereinbefore*.[194]

Heretofore is no help to a good verb in the past tense.[195] A "will made by me" is as well done as a ". . . will heretofore made by me . . ."[196] *Heretofore* succeeds only in stirring up ancient memories, filled with ambiguity and needless litigation.

Or/and

This is a little-used variant[197] of *and/or* (in this list) with as little to recommend it and as much to condemn it. This is a good time to abandon *or/and* before the virgule spreads its uncertainty — as it has already begun to do — with such flights from reality as *is/was*,[198] *was/were*,[199] *it/he*, *its/his*, *it/him*,[200] *for/to*.[201] There are more possibilities.[202]

---

[188] *Oxford English Dictionary.*
[189] *Ware v. Hylton*, 3 Dall. 199, 242, 249, 251, 280, 281, 282 (U.S. 1796).
[190] See *Miller v. State*, 55 Tex. Crim. App. 174, 175 (1909); *Wilson v. State*, 15 Tex. Crim. App. 150, 155 (1883).
[191] *Bixby v. Whitney*, 5 Me. 162, 165 (1827).
[192] *Charless & Blow v. Lamberson*, 1 Iowa 393, 401 (1855).
[193] *Commonwealth v. Rockwell Mfg. Co.*, 392 Pa. 339, 348 (1958).
[194] *Allison v. Chaney*, 63 Mo. 279 (1876).
[195] *Black's Law Dictionary* (4th ed. 1951); Ballentine, *Law Dictionary with Pronunciations* (2d ed. 1938); see *Skookum Oil Co. v. Thomas*, 162 Cal. 539, 547 (1912); *Andrews v. Thayer*, 40 Conn. 156, 157-158 (1873).
[196] Nichols, *Cyclopedia of Legal Forms* §9.1632, par. B (1936).
[197] 1 Holdsworth, *A History of English Law* 59 (3d ed. 1922); *Olsen Water & Towing Co. v. United States*, 21 F.2d 304, 305 (2d Cir. 1927); *Ralls v. E. R. Taylor Auto Co.*, 202 Ga. 107 (1947), 75 Ga. App. 136 (1947); compare Nichols, *Cyclopedia of Legal Forms* §8.1496 (1936), with §8.1496 (1960).
[198] Ross, *Etymology* 15 n.2 (1958).
[199] *Thibodeaux v. Uptown Motors Corp.*, 270 Ill. App. 191, 193 (1933); see *City National Bank & Trust Co. v. Davis Hotel Corp.*, 280 Ill. App. 247, 252-253 (1935).
[200] *City National Bank & Trust Co. v. Davis Hotel Corp.*, 280 Ill. App. 247, 253 (1935).
[201] *McEathron v. Township of Worth*, 315 Ill. App. 47, 53 (1942).
[202] See, for example, Sandwell, "The Which of and/or," 165 *Harper's* 244, 245 (1932); Evans and Evans, *A Dictionary of Contemporary American Usage* (1957), under *and/or*.

Said

This is an older Middle English relative of *aforesaid* (in this list), used in the language of the law with the same meaning — to talk about something that has already been talked about.[203] Where *aforesaid* blooms, *said* will also be found.[204] It is currently more popular than *aforesaid*, because lacking the Old English *afore*[205] *said* is not twice as archaic as it could be. But it shares with *aforesaid* the fault which is fatal to the claim of precision — uncertainty of reference.

For example. A will gives named grandchildren,

> . . . all of my right, title and interest in and to the lands of the T. M. Whetstone Estate of which I may die seized and possessed, except an undivided one-fifth (1/5) mineral rights and interest in and under said land, which I devise to my son William . . .[206]

Does *said land* refer to the whole of the Whetstone Estate lands, or only to the one-half interest which the testatrix owned? Does William take one fifth or one tenth of the whole? For the five-judge majority, the problem was simple. They said that "The intention of the testatrix is the guiding star," [207] and gazing upward, gave William one fifth of the whole. The spokesman for the four-judge minority was bitterly certain that it should be one tenth. "I know," he said,

> of no case in the books where similar words of reference have been held to mean anything other than the antecedent object to which they logically refer.[208]

To be sure — if you can find it.

As with *aforesaid*, if the antecedent is certain, *said* is unnecessary[209] — e.g., "said defendant" when there is only one defendant,[210] "said plaintiff" when there is only one plaintiff.[211] When there is any possibility of *said* referring to two things, whether both are in the same

---

[203] *Black's Law Dictionary* (4th ed. 1951); 38 *Words and Phrases* 25-32 (perm. ed. 1940), 7-9 (Supp. 1962); 4 *California Words, Phrases, and Maxims* 51 (1960).

[204] See Section 91; *Estate of Dubois,* 94 Cal. App. 2d 838 (1949).

[205] See Section 10; *Oxford English Dictionary.*

[206] *Ferguson v. Morgan,* 220 Miss. 266, 269 (1954).

[207] *Ferguson v. Morgan,* 220 Miss. 266, 270 (1954).

[208] *Ferguson v. Morgan,* 220 Miss. 266, 269-270, 272-276 (1954); see also *Baker v. Hugoton Production Co.,* 182 Kan. 210, 212 (1958), *rev'g* 181 Kan. 214, 221 (1957); compare *Reynaud v. Bullock,* 195 La. 86, 91, 94 (1940).

[209] Piesse and Smith, *The Elements of Drafting* 47-48 (2d ed. 1958).

[210] Hillyer, *Annotated Forms,* Nos. 3406, 3410 (1938).

[211] Hillyer, *Annotated Forms,* No. 3410 (1938).

writing[212] or one is in and another out,[213] reasonable men will differ; litigation is invited. Though some lay critics tell us that, worthless elsewhere, *said* is "traditional"[214] and "permissible"[215] in the law, it is either unnecessary or dangerous, and should be dropped.[216] (For better means of reference, see the discussion under *aforesaid*.)

ss

These "cabalistic characters"[217] are not precise in form or in meaning, and serve no good purpose at all.

They appear with the period,[218] and without it;[219] in small letters,[220] capitals,[221] and mixed (*Ss*).[222] And it is possible that the double *s* is a printer's error. (Section 54.)

The most widely held understanding is that *ss* abbreviates the Latin *scilicet* (towit),[223] but that understanding is not uniform. Current law dictionaries in England do not list *ss* as an abbreviation of *scilicet*, giving instead *scil.* and *sc.*[224] In this country also *sc.* has been used to abbreviate *scilicet*,[225] and so has *sst.*[226] Other variants are S.[227] and *s.*[228] While *ss* has been long used to abbreviate *scilicet*,[229] there is

---

[212] *Hershatter v. Colonial Trust Co.*, 136 Conn. 588, 592 (1950); *Chapman v. Groton*, 20 Conn. Supp. 333, 336-337 (1956).

[213] *Wennerholm v. Stanford*, 20 Cal. 2d 713 (1942), *rev'g* 113 P.2d 736, 740 (1941); see also *Trumbull Electric Mfg. Co. v. John Cooke Co.*, 130 Conn. 12 (1943); *Haughey v. Belmont Quadrangle Drilling Corp.*, 284 N.Y. 136 (1940); *Fort Quitman Land Co. v. Mier*, 211 S.W.2d 340 (Tex. Civ. App. 1948).

[214] Fowler, *A Dictionary of Modern English Usage* (3d ed. 1937).

[215] Partridge, *The Concise Usage and Abusage* (1955), under *said* and *the said*.

[216] Dickerson, *Legislative Drafting* 75 (1954); Cooper, *Effective Legal Writing* 16, 215 (1953).

[217] *Seay v. Shrader*, 69 Neb. 245, 247 (1903).

[218] Ballentine, *Law Dictionary with Pronunciations* (2d ed. 1948), under *ss.*; Brownlow, *Declarations, Counts, and Pleadings in English: The Second Part* 1, 3, 5 et seq. (1654); Nichols, *Cyclopedia of Legal Forms* §§1.864-1.873 (1936).

[219] *Legal Secretary's Handbook (California)* 486-488 (rev. ed. 1954); 39A *Words and Phrases* (perm. ed. 1953), "SS."

[220] Ballentine, *Law Dictionary with Pronunciations* (2d ed. 1948), under *ss.*; 39A *Words and Phrases* (perm. ed. 1953), "SS."

[221] *Black's Law Dictionary* (4th ed. 1951), under SS., and compare with S.S.

[222] 1 C.J.S. "*abbreviations*" 276 n.5 at p. 280.

[223] SS *What Does It Mean?* foreward (1939); Ballentine, *Law Dictionary with Pronunciations* (2d ed. 1948); *Black's Law Dictionary* (4th ed. 1951).

[224] Under *scilicet* in Jowitt, gen. ed., *The Dictionary of English Law* (1959), and *Wharton's Law Lexicon* (Oppé, 14th ed. 1938); see also Coke, *Commentary upon Littleton*, f. 282b (10th ed. 1703).

[225] 1 Harris, *Modern Entries* 698 (1801).

[226] 2 Bouvier, *A Law Dictionary* (1839), under *scilicet*.

[227] Martin, comp., *The Record Interpreter* 133 (2d ed. 1910).

[228] Kelham, *Domesday Book Illustrated* 317 (1788).

[229] Kelham, *Domesday Book Illustrated* 317 (1788); Martin, comp., *The Rec-*

no certainty that that is the way it started. The *ss* has also abbreviated *subscripsi* and *sans*,[230] *sacerdotes, sancti, sanctissimus, secundus, sensus, sestertii, Spiritus Sanctus, suis,* and *sunt*.[231] And it has been equated with the equally mystical S.S. collar of the Lord Chief Justice of England.[232]

If *ss* does abbreviate *scilicet,* then *towit* what? The standard answer is *towit,* the venue.[233] The explanation takes us back to the day of fictitious pleading to give foreign jurisdiction to the common law courts of England. As in Madrid, "towit in the parish of St. Mary le Bow in the Ward of Cheap," [234] which unusual geography no one was permitted to dispute. The explanation also tells us that *ss* was originally intended to spell out a particular locality from which the jurors must come, that the form of pleading continued even when the specification became unnecessary,[235] and that along the way *ss* got misplaced — outside the brace instead of in it.[236] Enough? While *ss* has been long used to particularize place of trial,[237] there is no certainty that that is the way it started, and a learned Lord Chancellor refused to accept the theory. Lord Hardwicke believed *ss* was nothing more than a division mark.[238]

Whether *ss* makes sense or not, it continues to decorate affidavits, as it has decorated the venue portion of a variety of forms for centuries.[239] Some lawyers believe it is necessary.[240] A formbook using *ss* for its affidavits cautiously advises that its omission is "not fatal," [241] a circumlocution not calculated to encourage innovators.

---

ord Interpreter 141 (2d ed. 1910); *contra:* Jordan, "The Cryptic 'SS,'" 8 B.U.L. Rev. 117, 124 (1928).

230 *Black's Law Dictionary* (4th ed. 1951), under SS.

231 Martin, comp., *The Record Interpreter* 141 (2d ed. 1910).

232 Jordan, "The Cryptic 'SS,'" 8 B.U.L. Rev. 117, 125 (1928).

233 *Black's Law Dictionary* (4th ed. 1951), under *SS.;* and see Ballentine, *Law Dictionary with Pronunciations* (2d ed. 1948), under *ss.*

234 5 Holdsworth, *A History of English Law* 140 (1924).

235 3 *Bouvier's Law Dictionary and Concise Encyclopedia* (3d rev. 8th ed. 1914), under *scilicet;* see 11 Holdsworth, *A History of English Law* 519-520, 521, 603 (1938).

236 Skinner, "Law and Philology: The Meaning of SS," 25 The Green Bag 59-64 (1913).

237 See, for example, Brownlow, *Declarations, Counts, and Pleadings in English: The Second Part* (1654).

238 *Jodderell v. Cowell,* 95 Eng. Rep. 222 (K.B. 1737).

239 Brownlow, *Declarations, Counts, and Pleadings in English: The Second Part* 105, 329 et seq. (1654); *Practical Forms,* Nos. 148, 162, 163, 242 et seq. (1823); Nichols, *Cyclopedia of Legal Forms* §§1.864-1.873 (1936).

240 *SS What Does It Mean?* foreward (1939).

241 1 Nichols, *Cyclopedia of Legal Forms* §1.856, p. 361 n.44 (1960).

Yet since 1829 a succession of American courts in dicta and decision have turned down arguments based on the omission of *ss*.[242] While one of the courts — in 1875 — thought it ". . . customary and more lawyer-like . . ." to use *ss*, it said an objection based on its omission was "untenable."[243] The learned Mr. Justice Story said the objection was ". . . clearly not maintainable . . .";[244] another called the omission "immaterial";[245] and another found *ss* to be without any ". . . peculiar virtue . . ."[246] One modern formbook uses *ss* when reproducing official affidavit forms that use *ss*,[247] but eliminates the *ss* in its own suggested form.[248] An *ss* adds nothing to precision; its omission is not missed.

Whereas

Condemned[249] and praised,[250] but most of all used,[251] *whereas* is one of the most persistently typical and most consistently vague words in the language of the law. It has as many meanings as you have patience, some of them poles apart. One moment *whereas* means the-fact-is,[252] and the next moment it reverses course to mean in-spite-of-

[242] See Story, J., in *United States v. Grush*, 26 Fed. Cas. 48, 52 (No. 15,268) (C.C.D. Mass. 1829); see *Smith v. Richardson*, 1 Utah 194, 195 (1875); see *McCord & Nave Mercantile Co. v. Glenn*, 6 Utah 139, 142 (1889); *Babcock v. Kuntzsch*, 92 N.Y. 33, 34 (1895); *Seay v. Shrader*, 69 Neb. 245, 247, 248 (1903); see *State v. Lucas*, 143 Kan. 245, 248 (1936); see also 1 *The American and English Encyclopaedia of Law* 311 n.1 (1887).

[243] See *Smith v. Richardson*, 1 Utah 194, 195 (1875).

[244] See *United States v. Grush*, 26 Fed. Cas. 48, 52 (No. 15, 268) (C.C.D. Mass. 1829).

[245] *Babcock v. Kuntzsch*, 92 N.Y. 33, 34 (1895).

[246] *Seay v. Shrader*, 69 Neb. 245, 247 (1903).

[247] *California Estate Administration* §§17.122, 17.123 (Continuing Education of the Bar, 1959).

[248] *California Estate Administration* §27.13 (Continuing Education of the Bar, 1959).

[249] For example, *Coffin v. Coffin*, 2 Mass. 358, 362 (1807); Beardsley, "Beware of, Eschew and Avoid Pompous Prolixity and Platitudinous Epistles!" 16 J.S.B. Calif. 65 (1941).

[250] Morton, "Challenge Made to Beardsley's Plan for Plain and Simple Legal Syntax," 16 J.S.B. Calif. 103, 104 (1941); see also Evans, *The Spoor of Spooks* 265 (1954).

[251] Lindey, *Motion Picture Agreements Annotated*, Forms I-A, III-C, VI-B (1947); *Am. Jur. Legal Forms* 3:580, 3:914, 3:915 (1953); *Am. Jur. Pleading and Practice Forms* 9:619 (1957); Nichols, *Cyclopedia of Legal Forms* §§6.594, 6.947, 6.1660 (1936); Rabkin and Johnson, *Current Legal Forms*, Form 1.53 (1961); Ind. Laws 1957, cc. 177, 179; Ky. Acts, Extra Sess. April, 1956, c. 1; see Ky. Acts 1940, c. 174, held unconstitutional in *Reeves v. Adams Hat Stores, Inc.*, 303 Ky. 633, 636 (1946) (rehearing denied, 1947); La. Acts 1957, Act No. 43; Miss. Laws 1956, c. 287; Nev. Stat. 1957, Resolutions and Memorials, File No. 1 et seq.; compare Lavery, "The Language of the Law," 8 A.B.A.J. 269, 274 (1922).

[252] *People v. Ennis*, 137 Cal. 263, 266 (1902).

the-fact (although);[253] now it is considering-that;[254] now it is on-the-contrary.[255] (The last is the popular meaning, and is also used in the law.) [256] Between these extremes are many soft gradations: the thing being so that,[257] that being the case,[258] being the case that,[259] since,[260] in view of the fact that,[261] considering that things are so,[262] while on the contrary,[263] when in fact,[264] while the contrary,[265] the fact or case really being that.[266]

Whereas has never been a lawyer's term of art. It was borrowed from the loose usage of the common speech of the Middle English period. (Section 53.) And equally loosely, it was used in law writings in England from the fifteenth to the eighteenth centuries, *whereas*[267] alternating with *where as*,[268] *where*,[269] *for as much*,[270] and,[271] *because*.[272] In the laws of seventeeth-century New England, it was indiscriminately *whereas*[273] and *forasmuch as*.[274]

---

253 *Hill v. Smith*, 95 Conn. 579, 584 (1920).

254 *Jones v. Paducah*, 283 Ky. 628, 632 (1940); *Katz v. New England Fuel Oil Co.*, 135 Me. 452, 455 (1938).

255 See *Worseley v. Demattos & Slader*, 97 Eng. Rep. 407, 415-416 (K.B. 1758).

256 See Fowler, *A Dictionary of Modern English Usage* (3d ed. 1937), under *where-*; Nicholson, *A Dictionary of American-English Usage* (1957), under *where-*; *Roper v. United States*, 54 F.2d 845, 846 (10th Cir. 1931); *People v. Fitzgerald*, 92 Mich. 328, 331 (1892).

257 *Dalton v. United States*, 127 Fed. 544, 547 (7th Cir. 1904); *Simpson v. Anderson*, 70 Atl. 696, 698 (N.J. Ch. 1908), *rev'd*, 75 N.J. Eq. 581, 584 (1909); *Dean v. Clark*, 80 Hun. 80 (N.Y. 1894).

258 *Jones v. Paducah*, 283 Ky. 628, 632 (1940).

259 *Katz v. New England Fuel Oil Co.*, 135 Me. 452, 455 (1938).

260 See *Hill v. Smith*, 95 Conn. 579, 584 (1920).

261 *Oxford English Dictionary*, under *whereas*, No. 2.

262 *Dalton v. United States*, 127 Fed. 544, 547 (7th Cir. 1904); *Simpson v. Anderson*, 70 Atl. 696, 698 (N.J. Ch. 1908), *rev'd*, 75 N.J. Eq. 581, 584 (1909); *Dean v. Clark*, 80 Hun. 80, 83 (N.Y. Sup. Ct. 1894).

263 *Dalton v. United States*, 127 Fed. 544, 547 (7th Cir. 1904); *Stoltz v. People*, 59 Colo. 342, 345, 346 (1915).

264 *Dalton v. United States*, 127 Fed. 544, 547 (7th Cir. 1904); *People v. Ennis*, 137 Cal. 263, 266 (1902); *Stoltz v. People*, 59 Colo. 342, 345, 346 (1915).

265 *People v. Ennis*, 137 Cal. 263, 266 (1902).

266 *Dalton v. United States*, 127 Fed. 544, 547 (7th Cir. 1904).

267 Decree, Star Chamber, 13 Car. (July 11, 1637).

268 *Oxford English Dictionary*, under *whereas*; 2 *The Paston Letters* 15-16 (Gairdner ed. 1904).

269 Stat. (1533) 24 Hen. VIII, cc. 7, 13; 2 *The Paston Letters* 15-16 (Gairdner ed. 1904).

270 Stat. (1533) 24 Hen. VIII, c. 1.

271 Decree, Star Chamber, 13 Car. (July 11, 1637).

272 Stat. (1533) 24 Hen. VIII, c. 8.

273 *The Laws and Liberties of Massachusetts*, p. 22, under "Ferries and Fines"; p. 23, under "Freeman"; p. 46, under "Rates and Records" (Farrand ed. 1929).

274 *The Laws and Liberties of Massachusetts*, p. 1, par. 1; p. 1, under "AnaBaptists"; p. 19, par. 13; p. 20, pars. 15, 16; p. 38, under "Marshal" (Farrand ed. 1929).

With the hardening of law forms in the eighteenth century (Section 95), *whereas* became the usual — though no more meaningful — translation for the Latin introducer *cum* of the thirteenth-century statutes,[275] as well as for Latin *quum, quandoquidem,* and *quoniam.*[276] *Whereas* also became the usual translation of the law French *la ou* (there where) of the Year Books,[277] a vague introduction — which in the days of oral pleading might be changed on the spot if it were troublesome. (Section 67.) *Whereas* appeared in English legal forms before the day of Blackstone's treatise,[278] and took its place in the earliest formbooks printed in America.[279]

From the moment *whereas* changed from a word nobody cared about to a fixed, written form, it caused litigation. More than two centuries ago, *whereas* (and *cum*) and *for that whereas* (and *quod cum*) were held bad in pleadings, no substitute for a positive declaration,[280] and not binding in a contract.[281] Ever since, courts have been telling lawyers the same thing,[282] sometimes sharply.[283] Even worse for the peace of mind of the bar, *whereas* is not even consistently held bad.[284]

---

[275] Stat. (1285) 13 Edw. I, Stat. 1; Statute of Marlborough, 1267, 52 Hen. III.

[276] *Dr. Adam Littleton's Latin Dictionary* (6th ed. 1735), under *cum* and *quoniam.*

[277] Kelham, *A Dictionary of the Norman or Old French Language* (1779), under *la ou;* 1 *Year Books of the Reign of King Edward I,* pp. 30-31 (Horwood ed. 1866); *Maneyswerthe v. Morton* (1302), in 3 *Year Books of the Reign of King Edward I,* pp. 190-191 (Horwood ed. 1863); *Charles v. Bishop of Norwich* (1306), in 5 *Year Books of the Reign of King Edward I,* pp. 246-247 (Horwood ed. 1879).

[278] Lilly, *Modern Entries* 405 (2d ed. 1741); see also Lilly, *The Practical Register* 602-603 (1735).

[279] For example: 1 Harris, *Modern Entries* 119, 553, 698 (1801); *American Precedents of Declarations* 191 (1802); Anthon, *American Precedents of Declarations* 317, 336 (new ed. 1810); *Practical Forms* 19, 20, 27, 167 et seq. (1823).

[280] *Amyon v. Shore,* 93 Eng. Rep. 739 (K.B. 1737); *Rex v. Crowhurst,* 92 Eng. Rep. 388 (K.B. 1736); see notes on English cases in *Lomax v. Hord,* 3 Hen. & M. (13 Va.) 271, 278-282 (1809), and discussion in *Hord's Executrix v. Dishman,* 2 Hen. & M. (12 Va.) 595, 601-602 (1808).

[281] *Walmesley and Booth,* 26 Eng. Rep. 412, 415 (Ch. 1739-1741).

[282] See *Wilder v. Handy,* 93 Eng. Rep. 1094 (K.B. 1740); *Coffin v. Coffin,* 2 Mass. 358, 364 (1807); *Taylor v. Rainbow,* 2 Hen. & M. (12 Va.) 423, 428 (1808); *Moore's Administrator v. Dawney,* 3 Hen. & M. (13 Va.) 127, 134 (1808); *Syme v. Griffin,* 4 Hen. & M. (14 Va.) 277, 280 (1809); *Spiker v. Bohrer,* 37 W. Va. 258, 260 (1892); *Dalton v. United States,* 127 Fed. 544, 547 (7th Cir. 1904).

[283] *Moore's Administrator v. Dawney,* 3 Hen. & M. (13 Va.) 127, 134-135 (1808).

[284] *Roper v. United States,* 54 F.2d 845, 846 (10th Cir. 1931); see: *People v. Ennis,* 137 Cal. 263, 266 (1902); *Stoltz v. People,* 59 Colo. 342, 345, 346 (1915); *People v. Fitzgerald,* 92 Mich. 328 (1892); *Simpson v. Anderson,* 70 Atl. 696, 698

The central issue in these cases is whether the utterer of a *whereas* means something by what he says or is only passing the time of day. Because *whereas* so frequently introduces recitals,[285] its effect is confused with the effect of the recital. That effect varies from state to state,[286] and does not depend on the word *whereas*. Sometimes recitals bind,[287] and sometimes they don't.[288] With its variety of meanings, *whereas* only clouds the decision.

When no rights or duties hang on a *whereas*, as in a presidential proclamation exhorting to civic virtue,[289] a half dozen *whereases* can do no harm, for no one will litigate civic virtue. But a large star or a small eagle would mean as much as the word *whereas*, and no sense would be lost by the substitution:

★

~~Whereas~~ it is our moral and civic obligation as free men . . .[290]

In other cases, in contracts and statutes, *whereas* — a muttering like "knock on wood" — gives a false sense of security. Once he has set down *whereas*, a lawyer feels relieved of the necessity of examining the effect intended by the words that follow. If a contract of sale reads:

Whereas there are 4000 square feet of floor space in Seller's house;

does it mean *Seller warrants* or *Seller represents*, or neither? Does it mean:

Buyer and Seller have examined the house and agree that whether the floor space is more or less than 4000 square feet will have no effect upon this contract. . . . ?

(N.J. Ch. 1908), *rev'd*, 75 N.J. Eq. 581, 584 (1909); *Benson v. Bennett*, 25 N.J.L. 166, 170 (1855); *Collier v. Moulton*, 7 Johns. 109 (N.Y. 1810).

[285] *Black's Law Dictionary* (4th ed. 1951), under *recital;* Cooper, *Effective Legal Writing* 170 (1953); Lindey, "On Legal Style," in *Motion Picture Agreements Annotated* xxi (1947); Lindey, "Let's Write Better Contracts," 3 Prac. Law. 32, 36 (1957); compare Lavery, "The Language of the Law," 8 A.B.A.J. 269, 274 (1922).

[286] 19 *Am. Jur.* "*estoppel*" §27.

[287] Cal. Civ. Proc. Code §1962(2); *Dean v. Clark*, 80 Hun. 80, 83-84 (N.Y. Sup. Ct. 1894).

[288] Cal. Civ. Proc. Code §1962(2); *Hill v. Smith*, 95 Conn. 579, 584 (1920); *Reeves v. Adam Hat Stores Inc.*, 303 Ky. 633, 635-636 (1946) (rehearing denied, 1947); *Jones v. Paducah*, 283 Ky. 628, 632 (1940); *Walmesley and Booth*, 26 Eng. Rep. 412, 415 (Ch. 1739-1741).

[289] Dwight D. Eisenhower, "The President's Proclamation," in 3 American Bar News 1 (Feb. 15, 1958).

[290] See and compare Dwight D. Eisenhower, "The President's Proclamation," in 3 American Bar News 1 (Feb. 15, 1958).

Does it mean:

> If the house has more or less than 4000 square feet of floor space, the purchase price will be adjusted by . . . ?

The easy mechanics of dropping history into a statute or of playing soft background music for a contract with a *whereas* dodges problems and stores them up for later. *Whereas* appears to include something in the writing, and yet it does not. *Whereas* has caused litigation for two centuries, and that is long enough.

121. *Does it have a definite meaning now?*

Many of the words that lawyers traditionally use have followed a language pattern of the common speech; they have changed meaning without changing their spelling.[291] Sometimes the change-of-meaning has been slight — an added use, a different sense or connotation; sometimes the change has been drastic.

As long as these changes in the language of the law are said to have taken place at a very early period, and especially when the direction of change is from the loose to the precise, the profession is prepared to accept the fact that such a process has been at work. Maitland has made lawyers proud to hear

> . . . that during the later middle age English lawyers enjoyed the inestimable advantage of being able to make a technical language. And a highly technical language they made. . . . English law was tough and impervious to foreign influence because it was highly technical, and it was highly technical because English lawyers had been able to make a vocabulary, to define their concepts, to think sharply as the man of science thinks.[292]

Lawyers are happy to recall the refinement of law French, creating the technicality of the *tort, devise, seisin, curtesy, words of purchase* (Section 63), *slander, partner, obligation, action, indictment, plaintiff,* etc. (Section 64.) So too with the Latin of *affidavit, alimony, corporation, deponent, minor, to subpoena,* etc. (Sections 49, 79.) Some lawyers have even found some cause to boast of precision in the hodgepodge of law French in its worst days. (Section 72.)

But indoctrination by massive repetition, at least since the age of printing (Section 78), has made the profession less ready to acknowl-

---

[291] Sections 111, 63, 64; see Collas, "Problems of Translation," in Introduction to *Year Books of Edward II,* 70 Selden Society xii-lxiv (1953); Trench, *A Select Glossary* (4th ed. 1873).

[292] Maitland, "Of the Anglo-French Language in the Early Year Books," in Introduction to *Year Books of Edward II,* 17 Selden Society xxxiii, xxxvi (1903).

edge that the whole process of change-of-meaning is continuous, and works in two directions.

Some law words have become more precise, and others less, much less precise than they once were. The words that helped to give the law a reputation for precision are not necessarily precise today. (This is not to speak of words which have died with changes in the law itself — neither the *bocland* and *wergild* of the Anglo-Saxons (Section 32), nor the later writs of *formedon* (Section 63), nor the special vocabulary of outmoded rules of pleading (Section 90).) Words which were once precise, or at least had some meaning in one environment — the Middle Ages, the Renaissance, the Age of Discovery, the Industrial Revolution — have been carried over into our completely different environment with the expectation that they would survive the journey. And so they have — but with a difference.

Words once sharp with precise meaning have been worn smooth. Words once tough enough to strangle an expressed intent (Section 89) have been emasculated. Words whose use was explicable in their day have been sucked dry of reason, with nothing poured back into the empty shell.

Some of these words travel their pedestrian courses in the law bothering no one, adding only an antique flavor and a false appearance of precision which delights lawyers and impresses the laity. Some are tested in court and the imposture is revealed. Yet so strong are the blandishments of tradition — and familiar spelling — that these words are used and reused in law writings as though their changed meanings continued to match their unchanged exteriors.

Here is a sampling of law words — old in the law, once serviceable, still used in the erroneous belief that they convey a definite meaning. Their age alone does not condemn them; neither does it validate them; age alone should dictate the desirability of re-examination. Lawyers will continue to find cause to use some of these words. But that cause should not be their supposed precision.

Civil death

Origin of the expression is discussed under *natural life* (in this list). At common law, *civil death* described mainly the loss of civil rights by the excessively spiritual and the excessively wicked — monks and nuns on the one side,[293] on the other those who today would be called

293 Coke, *Commentary upon Littleton*, ff. 132a-132b (10th ed. 1703).

felons.[294] The principal present instance of *civil death* is in a circumstance rare at common law[295] — the prisoner for life.[296] And this prisoner for life does not lose his property,[297] that an incident of common law felony unconnected with *civil death* except by lingering confusion.[298]

Each account of *civil death* (including this one) conjures up variant images,[299] and the statutes which now describe *civil death* gyrate through their own ritualistic word bending and mind twisting.[300] In Rhode Island, a life prisoner

> . . . shall thereupon, with respect . . . to the bond of matrimony . . . be deemed to be dead in all respects, . . . ; provided however, that the bond of matrimony shall not thereby be dissolved, . . .[301]

There is more to the statute than that, but nothing that makes it worthwhile to say, "I mean 'No' when I say 'Yes.'" In Utah, a life prisoner is "deemed civilly dead," but this zombi can make conveyances and be a witness.[302]

Take a will saying that *"If A dies, then to B."* A becomes *civilly dead.* Does B take? A split court said "No,"[303] but the articulate dis-

---

[294] Coke, *Commentary upon Littleton*, ff. 129b-130a, 132b-133a (10th ed. 1703).

[295] For example, see 5 Bacon, *Works* 91 and 100 (Montagu ed. 1826); Coke, *Commentary upon Littleton*, f. 130a (10th ed. 1703); see also 1 Pollock and Maitland, *The History of English Law* 49 (2d ed. 1898); 2 Pollock and Maitland, *The History of English Law* 516-517 (2d ed. 1898); 3 Holdsworth, *A History of English Law* 303, 306 (3d ed. 1923); Radin, *Handbook of Anglo-American Legal History* 239 (1936); 4 Blackstone, *Commentaries* °377 (Jones ed. 1916).

[296] For example: Cal. Pen. Code §§2600-2623; N.Y. Pen. Law §511 (Supp. 1960); Okla. Stat. Ann., tit. 21, §§66-68 (1958); R.I. Gen. Laws §13-6-1 et seq. (1956); Utah Code Ann. §§76-1-37 to 76-1-40 (1953); Vt. Stat. Ann., tit. 13, §7005 (1958); Note, 139 A.L.R. 1308-1325 (1942); Note, "Civil Death Statutes — Medieval Fiction in a Modern World," 50 Harv. L. Rev. 968-977 (1937).

[297] For example: Cal. Pen. Code §§2601, 2604; *Matter of Olson*, 202 Misc. 1113, 1114 (N.Y. 1953); *Avery v. Everett*, 110 N.Y. 317 (1888).

[298] *Beck v. Downey*, 191 F.2d 150 (9th Cir. 1951), *cert. granted, judgment vacated*, 343 U.S. 912 (1952), *prior opinion readopted*, 198 F.2d 626 (9th Cir. 1952), *cert. denied*, 344 U.S. 875 (1952); compare *Beck v. West Coast Life Ins. Co.*, 38 Cal. 2d 643 (1952); *Avery v. Everett*, 110 N.Y. 317, 334-336 (1888) (dissent).

[299] Compare 4 Bracton, *De Legibus* 310, 311 (°f. 421b) (Woodbine ed. 1942), with Littleton, *Tenures* §200, in Coke, *Commentary upon Littleton*, f. 131b-132a (10th ed. 1703); compare Coke, *Commentary upon Littleton*, ff. 130a, 132a-133b (10th ed. 1703), with 1 Blackstone, *Commentaries* °132 (Jones ed. 1916), and 2 Blackstone, *Commentaries* °121 (Jones ed. 1916).

[300] See statutes in note 296.

[301] R.I. Gen. Laws §13-6-1 (1956).

[302] Utah Code Ann. §§76-1-37 to 76-1-40 (1953); accord: Cal. Pen. Code §2603, §§2620-2623.

[303] See *Avery v. Everett*, 110 N.Y. 317 (1888).

senter warned of the danger in straying from fundamentalist interpretation while still clinging to fiction:

> What, then according to the conclusion reached by my brethern, is meant . . . by "civilly dead"? How much of the convict is civilly dead and how much is civilly alive? To solve these questions the legal wayfarer will find few blazed trees along his pathway, which must frequently be obscure, uncertain and easily missed.[304]

Again, a much litigated insurance policy unfolding the unhappy tale of Lila, her husband David, and her mother-in-law Jennie. Lila's life policies were made *to David . . . if living; otherwise to Jennie.* David murdered Lila and soon became civilly dead. Does Jennie take? "Yes," said the trial judge, because David is not "living" but dead, *civilly dead* that is. "No," said the Circuit, David may be dead, but he isn't "dead and buried." [305]

As with any other practical joke, there is always the risk that someone will take a legal fiction seriously. For the sake of preserving the fiction of *civil death,* which satisfied the logic and rules of an earlier day,[306] words are robbed of all ordinary meaning, yet nothing of technical sharpness results. As it is now, the rules that govern the civil rights of prisoners must still be spelled out in statute and case law.[307] In the confusion over the metaphysics of *civil death* even earnest men find themselves wandering. Much simpler to drop the whole *civil death* business.[308] Nothing would be lost.[309]

Heir

Once the mightiest in the common law,[310] *heir* has now become a second-class citizen. A distant relative from Roman law,[311] the word was known in the Latin of Glanvil (*heres*) long before it acquired its

---

[304] *Avery v. Everett,* 110 N.Y. 317, 335-336 (1888); see also note *u* to *The Archbishop of Canterbury's Case,* 76 Eng. Rep. 519, 525 (K.B. 1596), and discussion in 1 Pollock and Maitland, *The History of English Law* 433-438 and especially 435 (2d ed. 1898).

[305] *Beck v. Downey,* 191 F.2d 150, 152 (9th Cir. 1951), *cert. granted, judgment vacated,* 343 U.S. 912 (1952), *prior opinion readopted,* 198 F.2d 626 (9th Cir. 1952), *cert. denied,* 344 U.S. 875 (1952).

[306] Pages 336-338.

[307] See note 296.

[308] Note, "Civil Death Statutes — Medieval Fiction in a Modern World," 50 Harv. L. Rev. 968, 977 (1937).

[309] See, for example, Me. Rev. Stat., c. 154, §20 (1954), *repealed,* Me. Laws 1959, c. 276.

[310] Compare 39 *C.J.S. heir or heirs,* p. 881.

[311] Holmes, *The Common Law* 346-360 (1881); 1 Pollock and Maitland, *The History of English Law* 307-308 (2d ed. 1898).

present form from Old French.[312]   Through years of English history, *heir* struggled to attain eminence (see Sections 56, 89), and there is fit climax in the shuddering grandeur of Coke's definition, now almost unrecognizable:

> *Haeres* . . . is he to whom lands, tenements, or hereditaments by the Act of God, and right of blood do descend of some estate of inheritance, . . .[313]

This *heir* was savagely guarded by the common lawyers, with detailed protection down to the specification that a legitimate monster could not be an heir (though an idiot could), and a hermaphrodite,

> . . . shall be heir, either as male or female, according to that kind of the sex which doth prevail.[314]

The ultimate magic of the word *heir* was expressed with assured directness by Littleton, here as translated by Coke:

> For if a man would purchase lands or Tenements in Fee Simple, it behoveth him to have these words in his purchase, To have and to hold to him and to his Heirs; for these words (his Heirs) make the estate of the Inheritance.[315]

Without *his heirs*, the clearest intent foundered.   "To have and to hold to him and his Assigns for ever" — in a conveyance among the living — gave only a life estate.[316]   In a will those words would pass a fee,[317] but it was not recommended.   As Henry Swinburn wrote in 1590:

> . . . neverthelesse howe favorable soever the law be towards dead mens willes, the lawyers are not so favorable to their clients, and therefore if it were but to avoide long and costlie suites, it is meete that the testator utter his minde, as plainely and certainlie as he can.[318]

And today?   With the grantor dead or alive, a fee may pass without mention of *heirs*.[319]   The Rule in Shelley's Case (Section 89) falls by the wayside.[320]   The doctrine of worthier title has lost ground.[321]   And

---

[312] *Oxford English Dictionary.*
[313] Coke, *Commentary upon Littleton,* f. 7b (10th ed. 1703).
[314] Coke, *Commentary upon Littleton,* f. 8a (10th ed. 1703).
[315] Coke, *Commentary upon Littleton,* f. 1a (10th ed. 1703).
[316] Coke, *Commentary upon Littleton,* f. 1b (10th ed. 1703).
[317] Swinburn, *A Briefe Treatise of Testaments and Last Willes,* f. 190b (1590).
[318] Swinburn, *A Briefe Treatise of Testaments and Last Willes,* f. 193a (1590).
[319] For example: Cal. Civ. Code §1072; Cal. Prob. Code §107; Ill. Rev. Stat., c. 30, par. 12 (1957) (Conveyance Act §13); N.C. Gen. Stat. §39-1 (1950); Tenn. Code Ann. §64-101 (1955).
[320] For example: Cal. Civ. Code §779; Tenn. Code Ann. §64-103 (1955); 3 *Restatement of Property* §313.
[321] Cal. Civ. Code §1073; 3 *Restatement of Property* §314.

that stoutest of maxims, *Nemo est haeres viventis*[322] (No one is heir of the living), is legislated into oblivion. There are statutes — shocking to the common law conscience — which say that *heirs* may mean the *children* of the living.[323] This the result of legal technicality permitted to mingle with the people, and so become delinquent. (See Section 69.) This is the layman's notion of an *heir* — a child with a wealthy father; if the father is alive, so much the better.[324]

The older law dictionaries listed *heir* only in the singular,[325] as under the rules of primogeniture it usually was. Now *heirs* is added;[326] it is not *the heir* but more usually *heirs*, each entitled to something. Unlike the ancient if inaccurate maxim, freely rendered *Only God can make an heir,*[327] an *heir* today is as variously conceived and as unpredictable as the next session of the legislature.[328]

For lawyers, the passing of the technical rigidity of *heir* is not cause for rejoicing nor for wailing, but for awareness and caution. *Heir* is not the precise comfort it once was, yet the lawyer cannot assume that its technicality is dead.[329] If *heir* is to be used at all, it should not be glibly — only after close scrutiny and as a counsel of exhaustion.

What do you intend by *heirs?* Words of limitation or words of purchase? [330] A fee, or life estate with remainder? [331] To dispose of land alone, or land and chattels? [332]

Whom do you intend to benefit by *heirs?* Individuals or a class? [333]

---

[322] Broom, *A Selection of Legal Maxims* 349-351 (5th American from 3d London ed. 1864); see Coke, *Commentary upon Littleton,* f. 22b (10th ed. 1703); *Black's Law Dictionary* (4th ed. 1951); Jowitt, gen. ed., *The Dictionary of English Law* (1959).

[323] Ga. Code Ann. §85-504 (1955); N.C. Gen. Stat. §41-6 (1950).

[324] Compare Evans, *The Spoor of Spooks* 292 n.5 (1954), and Evans and Evans, *A Dictionary of Contemporary American Usage* (1957), under *heir.*

[325] Cowell, *The Interpreter* (ed. 1637); Blount, *Nomo-Lexikon* (1670); Blount, *A Law Dictionary and Glossary* (3d ed. 1717); *The Student's Law-Dictionary* (1740); Jacob, *A New Law-Dictionary* (6th ed. 1750).

[326] *Black's Law Dictionary* (4th ed. 1951), under *heir* and *heirs;* Ballentine, *Law Dictionary with Pronunciations* (2d ed. 1948), under *heirs.*

[327] See *Black's Law Dictionary* (4th ed. 1951), under "Deus solus haeredem facere potest, non homo"; Coke, *Commentary upon Littleton,* f. 7b (10th ed. 1703).

[328] See 3 *Restatement of Property* §305; and see Note, 139 A.L.R. 1107-1117 (1942).

[329] *In re Adkins' Estate,* 30 Del. Ch. 603, 607-610 (1947); see *Bost v. Johnson,* 175 Tenn. 232, 238 (1939); Note, 94 A.L.R. 112 (1935).

[330] Compare Tenn. Code Ann. §64-103 (1955) with *Hamby v. Northcut,* 25 Tenn. App. 11 (1940); see also Coke, *Commentary upon Littleton,* f. 26b (10th ed. 1703).

[331] *Hoge v. Hoge,* 17 Ill. 2d 209, 213-214 (1959).

[332] Note, 70 A.L.R. 581-591 (1931).

[333] *In re Adkins' Estate,* 30 Del. Ch. 603 (1947).

If *heir* is only a legal-sounding substitute for a flesh and blood Tom, Dick, or Mary, *heir* is a poor and expensive way to say it.[334]   If *heirs* is going to mean *children*,[335] why call them *heirs?*   If by *heirs* you mean that vast changing multitude who take property of various sorts in varying amounts, as determined by the statutes of distribution, then maybe *heirs* is the word.[336]

As he looks at the contrariety of possible meanings, wondering in what jurisdiction his client will die, or in what court his deed will be interpreted, a lawyer should scratch long and hard for something that better meets the facts than *heirs.*   When the well has run dry, that is time enough to use *heirs.*[337]

Last will and testament

This standard law phrase became English in the groping uncertainty of the probate law of the fifteenth and sixteenth centuries.   It has been perpetuated in the unfounded belief that perhaps a *will* or *last will* was appropriate to land and a *testament* only to chattels (Section 49), and that to be safe they had best be combined.   In former years the phrase also fitted the pattern of popular bilingual tautology (Sections 70, 71), *will* being Old English, *testament* its Latin synonym.   And it has been helped along by a distinctive rhythm. (Section 30.)   The words have been coupled as *testament and will, testament and last will* (Section 49), even *testament and latter will*,[338] but it is the lilting *last will and testament* that has survived.

For centuries *will* and *testament* have been used without other than nominal and occasional aberrant distinction.[339]   In mid-twentieth century the phrase *last will and testament* is not as precise as plain *will*,[340]

---

[334] See *Whitmore v. Starks,* 17 Ill. 2d 202 (1959).

[335] Ga. Code Ann. §85-504 (1955); N.C. Gen. Stat. §41-6 (1950).

[336] See 3 *Restatement of Property* §305.

[337] See 3 *Restatement of Property* §305, Comments *a, c;* Casner, "Construction of Gifts to 'Heirs' and the Like," 53 Harv. L. Rev. 207-250 (1939); see also Piesse and Smith, *The Elements of Drafting* 45-46 (2d ed. 1958).

[338] *Oxford English Dictionary*, under *will*, sb.[1], No. 23.

[339] Blount, *Nomo-Lexikon* (1670), under *will* and under *testament;* Blount, *A Law Dictionary and Glossary* (3d ed. 1717), under *will* and under *testament;* 2 Bouvier, *A Law Dictionary* (1839), under *will or testament; Black's Law Dictionary* (4th ed. 1951), under *last will,* under *testament,* and compare *will;* Jowitt, gen. ed., *The Dictionary of English Law* (1959), under *will*, and compare *testament;* compare Jacob, *A New Law-Dictionary* (6th ed. 1750), under *will, or last will and testament;* 45 *Words and Phrases* (perm. ed. 1940, Supp. 1962), "will-testament,"; 41 *Words and Phrases* (perm. ed. 1940, Supp. 1962), "testament"; 24 *Words and Phrases* (perm. ed. 1940, Supp. 1962), "last will and testament."

[340] Cal. Prob. Code §20; Del. Code Ann., tit. 12, §101 (1953); Ohio Rev. Code Ann. §2107.02 (Page, 1954).

which has the additional advantage of being understood by those who are asked to sign.

If *will* is used, *testament* is superfluous. And the subconscious knowledge that this is so leads draftsmen to forget that use of the same word to mean the same thing in the same context is an old virtue.[341] A statute that uses *last will and testament* in one section,[342] uses *will* in another section.[343] In the same state, one statute speaks of what is ". . . created by any will, testament, or codicil . . ."[344] and another gives the power only ". . . to devise and bequeath by will . . ."[345] A form that declares itself to be a "last will and testament" says that it revokes all "former wills and codicils,"[346] leaving former *testaments* roaming free, if the word had any independent meaning. The title of a case that fills the page "In the Matter of Last Will and Testament of Arthur Rutledge, Deceased" can be abbreviated as *In re Will of Rutledge,* and it is[347] — without loss of legal nuance.

The word *last* in the formula is even worse than the doubling of *will* and *testament.* At the least, *last* is ambiguous. In its earliest use in England, this *last* was associated with the imminence of death, the *last words* of the dying man (Section 49), and so antedates the clutter of our world of paper with whole processions of wills each proclaiming itself *last.* *Last words* in the nearness of death (allied to the *last illness, last breath,* and *last gasp*) are not necessarily the *last* in a succession of *wills,* and these expressions do not necessarily express that final or *last* intention of the testator which judges say they are looking for.[348]

And which *last will* is the *last will?* Calling it the *last will* does not make it so.[349] These words do not of themselves revoke an earlier will, but — like it or not — they do give room for an argument that

---

[341] 2 Locke, *An Essay Concerning Human Understanding* 164 (Fraser ed. 1894).

[342] Vt. Stat. Ann., tit. 14, §1 (1958).

[343] Vt. Stat. Ann., tit. 14, §3 (1958).

[344] Ill. Ann. Stat., c. 148, §31 (1936).

[345] Ill. Ann. Stat., c. 3, §42 (1961).

[346] *Murphy's Will Clauses,* Form No. 1:1 (1960); *accord:* Nichols, *Cyclopedia of Legal Forms* §§9.1110 (par. D), 9.1143 (1936).

[347] 5 Ill. App. 2d 355 (1955).

[348] *Webster's New International Dictionary* (2d ed. 1934), under *last;* and see *Estate of Salmonski,* 38 Cal. 2d 199, 212 (1951).

[349] 2 Bowe and Parker, *Revised Treatise on the Law of Wills* 408-409 (3d ed. 1960); 1 Jarman, *A Treatise on Wills* 189 (8th ed. 1951); notes, 59 A.L.R.2d 11, 69 (1958), 51 A.L.R. 652, 679 (1927), 123 A.L.R. 1395, 1402 (1939).

that was the intention.[350]   When a testator has been made will-conscious, and likes the habit, *last will* adds spice to a will contest.[351] For example: will No. 1 revoked by will No. 2; a later ". . . codicil to my last will" held to refer to No. 1, reviving it and revoking No. 2.[352] The testator was talking about his first, not his second, when he said his *last will*.

Trying to remember just what it was you called a *last will* is no easier for lawyers than for laymen.   Thus subdivision No. 1 of a statute speaks of a *last will in writing* to "dispose of his estate" and a later added subdivision No. 2 speaks of only a *will* to dispose of the testator's body.[353]   Does the *last* make a difference?

Last will and testament is redundant, confusing, and usually inaccurate.   The first American professor of law (Section 101) came closer to ordinary experience when he wrote of ". . . my testament, probablie the last." [354]

Mind and memory

In wills[355] and statutes[356] and instructions,[357] wherever lawyers gather to write or talk about testamentary capacity,[358] *mind and memory* pops up, as though these words of legal tradition were as fresh as the teachings of psychiatry.   And while it is possible that accents from the couch have made the package sound plausible to the twentieth century, *mind and memory* is a snatch of confusing nonsense, a further instance of several words being less precise than one.   (See *last will and testament* in this list.)

When Chaucer first joined these words,[359] he was coupling nonlegal

[350] See *Estate of Shute*, 55 Cal. App. 2d 573, 578 (1942); *Aldrich v. Aldrich*, 215 Mass. 164, 169 (1913).

[351] *In re Howard's Estate*, 3 Utah 76, 81 (1955); see *Gordon v. Whitlock*, 92 Va. 723, 728 (1896).

[352] *In the Goods of Van Cutsem*, 63 L.T.R. (n.s.) 252, 253 (Prob. Div. 1890).

[353] Minn. Stat. Ann. §525.18 (Supp. 1961); see also form in Cal. Prob. Code, p. 157 following §54 (Deering, 1959).

[354] 1 Wythe xxxvii (Va. Ch., ed. 1852).

[355] Nichols, *Cyclopedia of Legal Forms* §§9.1109, 9.1110 (par. D), 9.1143 (1936); compare 9 Nichols, *Cyclopedia of Legal Forms* 457 n.72, 458, 465 n.11 (1936); form in Cal. Prob. Code, p. 140 following §50 (Deering, 1959).

[356] Del. Code Ann., tit. 12, §101 (1953); Ohio Rev. Code Ann. §2107.02 (Page, 1954); Ill. Ann. Stat., c.3, §42 (1961).

[357] 4 Branson, *The Law of Instructions to Juries* §3192, pp. 1079-1106 and especially 1081, Forms (1), (2) (1936).

[358] *Black's Law Dictionary* (4th ed. 1951), under *testamentary capacity*; 41 *Words and Phrases* 424-426 (perm. ed. 1940), 153-155 (Supp. 1962), "testamentary capacity."

[359] *Oxford English Dictionary*, under *mind*, sb.[1], No. 5.

synonyms for poetic effect. His usage was related to the ancient sense of *mind* to mean *memory*, fastening Old English to Old French *memorie*, which in Chaucer's day was a newcomer to English.[360] Popular idiom still keeps the *memory* sense of *mind* alive, with *have, keep*, and *bear in mind*.[361]

With closer ties to both Latin and French (Chapters VII, IX), the law made the words completely convertible — not only *mind = memory* but *memory = mind*. The same word — Old French *memorie* (Latin *memoria*) — gives us both *the time of legal memory*[362] and *time out of mind*,[363] sometimes also *time out of memory*.[364] It appears also in *time whereof mind* (or *memory*) *runneth not to the contrary*.[365] Conversely, the Latin *non compos mentis* (not sound of mind) which speaks of the modern use of *mind = intellect* (as distinguished from *memory = recall*) was described by Littleton in his fifteenth-century Anglo-Norman as *de non sane memorie*.[366] And that was the phrase used in the statute explaining the Statute of Wills[367] — not *mind* but *memory, non sane memory*,[368] or as Coke also said it — *no sound memory*.[369]

It was in this era of movement of French words into English (Section 58), with bilingual synonyms the height of literary fashion (Sections 70, 71), that some English testators began certifying themselves mentally fit in two languages. They said they were ". . . in god mynde and saf memorye . . ." (1402),[370] and "Hole of mynde & in my gode memorie beyng" (1418), instead of sticking with English "good mynde," "full mende," and doubly English ". . . hole mynde & goode witte."[371] Repetition[372] and rhythm (Section 30) (it is *mind and memory* not *memory and mind*) made the phrase stick.

---

[360] *Oxford English Dictionary*, under *memory*.

[361] *Oxford English Dictionary*, under *mind*, No. 2b; L. P. Smith, *Words and Idioms* 184 (5th ed. 1943).

[362] See Coke, *Commentary upon Littleton*, f. 86a (10th ed. 1703), under *time of memory;* Jowitt, gen. ed., *The Dictionary of English Law* (1959), under *memory*.

[363] Coke, *Commentary upon Littleton*, ff. 113a, 113b (10th ed. 1703).

[364] *Black's Law Dictionary* (4th ed. 1951); *Oxford English Dictionary*, under *memory*, No. 6.

[365] Coke, *Commentary upon Littleton*, ff. 114a-114b (10th ed. 1703).

[366] Coke, *Commentary upon Littleton*, ff. 246b, 247a (10th ed. 1703).

[367] 1542-1543, 34 & 35 Hen. VIII, c. 5, s. xiv.

[368] Coke, *Commentary upon Littleton*, f. 246b (10th ed. 1703).

[369] Coke, *Commentary upon Littleton*, f. 246b (10th ed. 1703).

[370] Quoted in *Oxford English Dictionary*, under *memory*, No. 2b.

[371] Quoted in *Oxford English Dictionary*, under *mind*, No. 19b.

[372] See, for example, *Oxford English Dictionary*, under *memory*, No. 2b; Jacob, *A New Law-Dictionary* (6th ed. 1750), under *will; Every Man His Own Lawyer*

As in England,[373] American lawyers have long recognized that they were using *memory* here in a special way, in the sense of understanding[374] or mind,[375] and that *mind and memory* did no more for testamentary capacity than *mind* alone.[376] Confusion was inevitable, for ordinarily both people and lawyers speak of *memory* as a faculty of the *mind*, not the *mind* itself.[377] Coupling *mind and memory* today creates the unscientific impression that the *mind* can be split, that *memory* is not merely an aspect of *mind*, but that there are two independent tests for testamentary capacity, a *sound mind* and a *sound memory*,[378] with peculiar tests for each.

Many states have dropped the superfluous and confusing *memory*, and use only *mind* in the statutes dealing with testamentary capacity;[379] but that helpful step has not always stopped draftsmen from treading the worn path.[380] Nor does a statutory reference to *mind and memory*[381] produce a uniform use of the two words instead of the one.[382]

The joining of *mind and memory* creates no precise legal notion.

---

145 (Potter ed. 1834); 12A *Words and Phrases* (perm. ed. 1954), "disposing mind and memory," and in Supp. 1962 under "disposing memory," "disposing mind"; 39A *Words and Phrases* (perm. ed. 1953), "sound and disposing mind and memory," "sound mind and memory," and in Supp. 1962 under "sound and disposing mind"; 4 *California Words, Phrases, and Maxims* (1960), "sound and disposing mind and memory."

373 Jacob, *A New Law-Dictionary* (6th ed. 1750), under *non compos mentis;* see Coke, *Commentary upon Littleton,* f. 247a (10th ed. 1703); see Blount, *Nomo-Lexikon* (1670), under *non compos mentis.*

374 See 2 Bouvier, *A Law Dictionary* (1839), under *memory.*

375 See *United States v. Boylen,* 41 F. Supp. 724, 726 (D. Ore. 1941); *Black's Law Dictionary* (4th ed. 1951), under *memory;* see 57 *C.J.S. memory,* p. 1047.

376 *Yoe v. McCord,* 74 Ill. 33, 40-41 (1874); *Mairs v. Freeman,* 3 Redf. 181, 199 (N.Y. Surrog. Ct. 1877); *In the Matter of Forman's Will,* 54 Barb. 274, 286 (N.Y. 1869); Ballentine, *Law Dictionary with Pronunciations* (2d ed. 1948), under *sound mind and memory.*

377 *Oxford English Dictionary,* under *memory; Webster's New International Dictionary* (2d ed. 1934), under *memory;* Ballentine, *Law Dictionary with Pronunciations* (2d ed. 1948), under *memory, refresh the memory; Black's Law Dictionary* (4th ed. 1951), under *memory, refreshing the memory;* 27 *Words and Phrases* (perm. ed. 1961), "memory."

378 *Yoe v. McCord,* 74 Ill. 33, 39-41 (1874); see *In re Will of Rutledge,* 5 Ill. App. 2d 355, 359-361 (1955); *Couch v. Gentry,* 113 Mo. 248, 254-255 (1892).

379 For example: Cal. Prob. Code §20; Mass. Gen. Laws Ann., c. 191, §1 (1955); Minn. Stat. Ann. §525.18(1) (1947); Mo. Ann. Stat. §474.310 (1956); Vt. Stat. Ann., tit. 14, §1 (1958).

380 *Pulitzer v. Chapman,* 337 Mo. 298, 325-327 (1935); form in Cal. Prob. Code, p. 140 following §50 (Deering, 1959).

381 Ill. Ann. Stat., c. 3, §42 (1961).

382 See *Powell v. Weld,* 410 Ill. 198, 201-203 (1951); 4 Branson, *The Law of Instructions to Juries* §3192, p. 1081, Form No. (3) (3d ed. 1936).

On the contrary, there is no longer the one-time assurance that one word merely reinforces the other. When lawyers want to talk about *mind,* they should; and when they want to talk about *memory,* they should do that. The formula has outlived its origin, and makes no more sense today than the politician's cliché — "the hearts and minds of Americans."

Natural life

Occasionally a lawyer's phrase is so outrageously redundant no one can believe that any serious person would use it unless it had some special meaning. It is one thing for the untutored to gild the lily with *as nat'ral as life*[383] and a *natural lifer* (a life prisoner);[384] yet even in these ranks a feeling for economy of words has produced the abbreviated *not on your natural!* and *for all my natural.*[385] When a learned profession continues to use *natural life,*[386] it is assumed — out of decent respect — that there is a reason. And once — long ago — there was a reason, though ever so slim.

Natural life has historical association in the law with *civil death* (in this list), and their origins are discussed here together.

The loss of civil rights which we still fictionize as *civil death,* Justinian referred to under the heading *de capitis minutione*[387] (of loss of status).[388] The concept is mentioned by Glanvil,[389] and was verbalized in Bracton's thirteenth-century Latin *mors civilis* (civil death) in comparing the loss of an independent will by the monk and the villein.[390] Of more direct influence, Littleton said that the monk could not sue because he was *dead in the law* (*il est mort en ley*), and that

383 Wentworth, *American Dialect Dictionary* (1944), under *natural,* No. 1.

384 Partridge, *A Dictionary of the Underworld* (1950).

385 Partridge, *A Dictionary of Slang and Unconventional English* (4th ed. 1951), under *natural.*

386 N.Y. Pen. Law §511, No. 2, Supp. 1960; *Am. Jur. Legal Forms* 8:491, 8:492, 8:494, 8:495, 8:499, 8:500 (1954); Nichols, *Cyclopedia of Legal Forms* §§7.625 (1936), 9.1163 (1936).

387 Justinian, *Institutionum* 155-158 (lib. I, tit. 16), and see also 142-143 (lib. I, tit. 12) (Moyle, 5th ed. 1912); see Lewis and Short, eds., *A Latin Dictionary* (1879), under *caput,* IIIb; Smith and Hall, English-Latin Dictionary (1871), under *dead, death, civil.*

388 Justinian, *The Institutes* 23 (Moyle tr. 5th ed. 1913).

389 P. 159 (lib. XIII, cc. 5, 6) (Woodbine ed. 1932); 1 Pollock and Maitland, *The History of English Law* 434 and especially n.5 (2d ed. 1898).

390 4 Bracton, *De Legibus* 310, 311 (f. 421b) (Woodbine ed. 1942); 1 Pollock and Maitland, *The History of English Law* 433 and especially n.1 (2d ed. 1898); see also West, *Three Treatises, of the Second Part of Symbolaeographie* §17 (1594).

his son or his "next cousin incontinent" (a ruthlessly candid phrase) "shall inherit him, as well as though he were dead in deed." [391]

The *dead* here — as applied to the monk — was Christian metaphor. Coke drew it closer to its origin, glossing Littleton's French with Latin *civiliter mortuus* (civilly dead) and *mortuus seculo*.[392] As in the modern idiom describing the man asleep,[393] or drunk, the monk was *mortuus saeculo* (dead to the world, or worldliness).[394] That was the way the seventeenth century understood it: "He that is in a Monastery is dead to all worldly affairs." [395] That was the way the fourteenth-century monk had explained Christian theology: "He ssel by dyead to þe wordle, and libbe to god." [396] And that is what the Book said: "For I through the law am dead to the law, that I might live unto God." [397] All of this a part of the Christian emphasis on the contrast between the *spiritual* and the *natural*,[398] the *spiritual body* and the *natural body*.[399]

The monk's *civil death* was a practical accommodation of his own religious desires. He wanted out of this suing world and he wanted no property. He had his way. He could make his will upon *civil death* or have his property administered as intestate;[400] *civil death* took no property away from him. And unlike Blackstone's blurred account,[401] Coke made clear that this fictional death would not create new property rights or destroy old ones.[402] But in a hairsplitting and word multiplying age (see Sections 71, 85, 87, 88, 93), the logic of the unmixed metaphor suggested that if the Church could split *life* into

[391] Littleton, *Tenures* §200, in Coke, *Commentary upon Littleton*, ff. 131b-132b (10th ed. 1703).

[392] Coke, *Commentary upon Littleton*, f. 132a (10th ed. 1703); and see Smith and Hall, *English-Latin Dictionary* (1871), under *world* III, No. 2; Lewis and Short, eds., *A Latin Dictionary* (1879), under *saeculum; Medieval Latin Word-List* (1934), under *seculum.*

[393] See *Oxford English Dictionary*, compare *dead*, adv., C.1, with *dead*, a., Nos. 2b., 3, 4.

[394] See Lewis and Short, eds., *A Latin Dictionary* (1879), under *mortuus*, B; see Partridge, *A Dictionary of Slang and Unconventional English* (4th ed. 1951), under *dead to the world* and *world.*

[395] Quoted in *Oxford English Dictionary*, under *dead.*

[396] Quoted in *Oxford English Dictionary*, under *dead*, a., No. 3.

[397] Gal. 2:19; see also Rom. 7:4.

[398] For example, 1 Cor. 2:14, 15:46.

[399] 1 Cor. 15:44.

[400] Littleton, *Tenures* §200, in Coke, *Commentary upon Littleton*, ff. 132a, 133b (10th ed. 1703).

[401] 1 Blackstone, *Commentaries* °132 (Jones ed. 1916).

[402] Coke, *Commentary upon Littleton*, f. 132b (10th ed. 1703).

the *spiritual* and the *natural*, some lawyer might do it too. When you think of it, therefore, better make conveyances *during his natural life* (*durante vita sua naturali*)[403] instead of just *for life*, though neither Coke nor Blackstone cite any litigation where the distinction made a difference. Coke later explained that it was not as a fixed rule of law but only

> . . . to oust all scruples [that] Leases for life are ever made during the naturall life, etc.[404]

The figure of speech was used in and out of the law,[405] and it was not technical. Though *natural life* is preserved in Bridgman's *Conveyances*,[406] the master conveyancer did not follow the notion with any constancy. In the same settlement he speaks of *during the natural life* and *during the life*, without logical distinction.[407] For it was a distinction without substance at best, and lost even its rationalization when the Reformation ended monkdom.[408]

Civil death had even less effect on the property of the felon than of the monk. For without resort to fictitious death the law stripped the felon of his property as a part of his punishment, and another and separate fiction — *corruption of blood* — ended hope of inheritance from him. Even so, if the felon's life were spared as, for example, by banishment, his removal from civilized society did create problems for others. To these problems, the medieval mind found solution in the logic pattern of words suggestive of death. For example, the wife at common law could not litigate without her husband. Yet, if he were *civilly dead* then she

> . . . may bring an Action or may be impleaded during the naturall life of her husband.[409]

Thus *natural life* — which for the monk was the antithesis of *spiritual life* — became a wordy and untechnical contrast to *civil death*.

What place has *natural life* in the law today? None, but to clutter

---

[403] See *The Archbishop of Canterbury's Case,* 76 Eng. Rep. 519, 525 (K.B. 1596).

[404] Coke, *Commentary upon Littleton,* f. 132a (10th ed. 1703); compare *Strode v. Dennison,* 83 Eng. Rep. 594-595 (K.B. 1683); see and compare note *u* to *The Archbishop of Canterbury's Case,* 76 Eng. Rep. 519, 525 (K.B. 1596).

[405] *Oxford English Dictionary,* under *natural,* a., No. 9b.

[406] For example, pp. 15, 16, 291 (1682).

[407] *Sir Orlando Bridgman's Conveyances* 128, 131, 132 (1682).

[408] See 9 Holdsworth, *A History of English Law* 3 (1926); 4 Holdsworth, *A History of English Law* 489 (1924); 1 Blackstone, *Commentaries* °132 (Jones ed. 1916).

[409] Coke, *Commentary upon Littleton,* f. 133a (10th ed. 1703).

and confuse.[410] In life estates, there is only one kind of life to consider — this life — and *natural life* only creates suspicions that someone had something else in mind.[411] Where crime is involved, the ancient association of *natural life* and *civil death* still suggests that there is some secret sense to *during the term of his natural life,* and there is none.[412] Life means life. Naturally.

One

Here is pure pretentiousness, a parody of precision in the law, were it not accepted as genuine. The fogs of history obscure the origin of the law's current and peculiar use of *one:*

> One Eugene Rozanski was also a candidate . . .[413]

> . . . charging one Ernest O. Emery with the crime of murder . . .[414]

> Plaintiffs brought out that one C. W. Worthy previously owned both the Sawada property . . .[415]

Yet it is possible to find a past justification, which now has lost its force.

Lay use of *one* as an indefinite pronoun is traced to the thirteenth century, as in the later: "Then one brought hym a cup with wine." [416] This *one* is "a certain one," but unidentified, and translates the Latin *quidam,*[417] a shaded synonym of *aliquis.* Here the legal possibilities first appear, for *aliquis* rears up a distinction worthy of the profession; it means "some person obscurely definite." [418] And *quidam?* It was made for the circumspect:

> . . . *quidam* indicates not merely the existence and individuality of an object, but that it is known as such to the speaker, only that he is not acquainted with, or does not choose to give, its more definite relations.[419]

[410] Ballentine, *Law Dictionary with Pronunciations* (2d ed. 1948), under *natural life,* and compare with *during natural life.*
[411] *Doyle v. Andis,* 127 Iowa 36 (1905); *Collins v. Wickwire,* 162 Mass. 143 (1894); *Hill v. Guaranty Trust Co.,* 163 App. Div. 374, 376 (N.Y. 1914).
[412] *In re Stewart,* 24 Cal. 2d 344, 346-347 (1944), and see dissent at 348-353, especially 351-352; *People v. Wright,* 89 Mich. 70, 93 (1891); compare *Gray v. Stewart,* 70 Kan. 429 (1904).
[413] *State ex rel. Locke v. Peak,* 238 Ind. 468, 469 (1958).
[414] *State ex rel. Keast v. District Court,* 135 Mont. 545, 546 (1959).
[415] *Heil v. Sawada,* 187 Cal. App. 2d 633, 636 (1960).
[416] Quoted in *Oxford English Dictionary,* under *one,* No. 20a.
[417] Lewis and Short, eds., *A Latin Dictionary* (1879).
[418] Lewis and Short, eds., *A Latin Dictionary* (1879).
[419] Lewis and Short, eds., *A Latin Dictionary* (1879), under *aliquis.*

A word that could say all that was too good to lose in translation. Some of the Latin reserve was sloughed off when (also in the thirteenth century) personal names were tacked on after *one*, but this distinctive *quidam*-like *one* kept a full enough measure of implied disassociation to make it a favorite, as in "Oon Martyn luther . . ." from a sixteenth-century attack on Luther,[420]

> . . . and of *one* Jesus, which was dead, whom Paul affirmed to be alive.[421]

in the Biblical speech of the Roman Festus.

To lawyers beset by strong urges to hedge their every utterance (Sections 87, 88), anything "obscurely definite" had its appeal. Apart from that, the law had a special use for such a *one*, and the usage shows up in Latin records (*quidam, cuidam*)[422] and French Year Books (*un*)[423] of the fourteenth century. The practice is not uniform, and often names are introduced without the standoffish *one*,[424] yet as early as 1319 a Latin record of oral pleading exhibits a pattern of particularity[425] that becomes formula in later written pleadings. It goes like this:

(1) The first time a name is mentioned, prefix *quidam* (one), and follow the name with identification;

(2) After that, whenever the name appears, prefix *predictus* (aforesaid), or *dictus* (said), or *idem* (same).

Thus, Margery Russel's fourteenth-century lawyer says (in words here translated and much shortened) that:

> . . . one Henry, formerly abbot of Winchcomb, . . . bound himself . . . to one John Russel, her father, . . . to pay £100 to the same John . . . and though the aforesaid John often . . . requested the aforesaid Henry . . .[426]

---

[420] Quoted in *Oxford English Dictionary*, under *one*, No. 20b.

[421] Acts 25:19; quoted in *Oxford English Dictionary*, in earlier form, under *one*, 20b.

[422] *Utling v. Maudut*, 28 Edw. I (1300), in 66 Selden Society 227, 229 (1947); *Maulay v. Driby*, Mich., 1 Edw. II (1307), in 17 Selden Society 1, 2, No. 1, (1903).

[423] *Anon.* (1308-1309), in 17 Selden Society 162, No. 84 (1903); *Anon.* (1308-1309), in 17 Selden Society 150, No. 75 (1903).

[424] For example: *London v. Tynten* (1308-1309), in 17 Selden Society 145, No. 74a (1903); *De La More v. Thwing* (1308-1309), in 17 Selden Society 179, No. 98b (1903).

[425] *Russel v. Abbot of Winchcomb*, Easter, 12 Edw. II (1319), in 70 Selden Society 129, 131 (record), No. 12 (1953).

[426] *Russel v. Abbot of Winchcomb*, Easter, 12 Edw. II (1319), in 70 Selden Society 129, 131 (record), No. 12 (1953), with revised translation of record.

By such locution "Henry" and "John" are tied into neat packages, and in a meandering pleading the *one* stands out as a beacon warning that a new character is entering the drama. The device became more helpful, and more usual, as written pleadings became more usual,[427] more demanding of detail (such as *additions* — knight, esquire, Gentleman, etc.),[428] and beyond all, longer and longer and longer as in the one-sentence style of "Three Hogsheads of Cyder." (Section 91.)

But it was formula more than sense (Section 118), and where formula and sense collided, formula won. A seventeenth-century form of indictment ". . . translated into English out of the very Indictment it selfe" reads:

. . . to conferre and treat with one Edmond Coppinger Gentleman, and Henry Arthington Gentleman, . . .[429]

One *one* for two "gentlemen," because one *one* translated one *quidam*, though in Latin (unlike English) there was not the embarrassment of number, since *quidam* was the same in singular and plural.[430]

If reasons more than habit had dictated the choice of language, the *one Henry-said Henry* pattern might have continued to serve a purpose. As it turned out, the pattern became confused, for lawyers — like the laity — used *one Henry* where it served no purpose but snide derogation or pretended sophistication. The identifying *one* appears even where the name is mentioned only once.[431] And *one* is omitted or thrown in haphazardly, making it impossible to rely on any rule of usage.[432]

And so today. The pleader's standoffish *one* — faintly scornful, unmistakably unflattering — has continued on as meaningless rote.

[427] See, for example, *Panter v. Green*, St. Ch. 1, 2/89 (1489-1495), in 75 Selden Society 87, 88, 89, 90 (1958); *Abbot v. Moore*, 86 Eng. Rep. 692 (K.B. 1669); West, *Three Treatises, of the Second Part of Symbolaeographie* §319 at f. 152a, §365 at f. 161a (ed. 1632); Coke, *A Booke of Entries*, f. 356b (2d ed. 1671).

[428] Stat. (1413) 1 Hen. V, c. 5; see *Bromfield v. Lovejoy*, Quin. 237 (Mass. 1767); 2 Hawkins, *A Treatise of the Pleas of the Crown*, c. 23, §§103-125 (8th ed. 1824).

[429] West, *Three Treatises, of the Second Part of Symbolaeographie* §365 at ff. 160b, 161a (ed. 1632).

[430] See also Brownlow, *Declarations, Counts, and Pleadings in English: The Second Part* 383 (1654).

[431] *Mynn's Case*, 1 Mod. Rep. 1 (K.B. 1669), and compare report in 86 Eng. Rep. 681; *Redman's Case*, 86 Eng. Rep. 690 (K.B. 1669).

[432] *Dyer v. Clinton*, St. Ch. 1, 1.47 (1495-1505), in 75 Selden Society 111 (1958); *Chauncey v. Dacre*, St. Ch. 2, 8/247-250 (1500), in 75 Selden Society 123 (1958); *Daniel Appleford's Case*, 86 Eng. Rep. 750 (K.B. 1670); *Ambrose v. Ambrose*, 24 Eng. Rep. 407 (Ch. 1716); compare *King v. Inhabitants of Newington*, 99 Eng. Rep. 1136 (K.B. 1786), with *King v. Inhabitants of Old Alresford*, 99 Eng. Rep. 1138 (K.B. 1786).

Though statutes have attempted to simplify indictments,[433] the indictment remains a stronghold of *one*.[434] In opinions too the appendage hangs on,[435] giving a mock appearance of mathematical preciseness to old hokum.

Seisin

At the end of the last century legal historians whose work still has the mark of greatness wrote:

> In the history of our law there is no idea more cardinal than that of seisin.[436]

It should now be added that in the language of the law there is no word more disemboweled and yet alive.

For centuries the only short definition has been "seisin is possession." [437] It is beautifully short but it tells nothing about *seisin*, and is more translation than definition. (See Sections 55, 56, 63.)

Possession takes us to the literal past of *seisin* — to the ceremonial *delivery of possession* (law French, *livery de seisin*),[438] to the uncomplicated notion of a *seisin* "vacant" when the ". . . corpse was carried from the house . . ." [439] "Seisin is possession" before *seisin* became technical, before *possession* of the tenant was distinguished from the *seisin* of his lord.

When *seisin* became technical, it became technical in a dozen specific applications rather than in one neat definition. If as a working definition we call *seisin* the right to a freehold based on possession, we

[433] For example: Fed. R. Crim. P., Rule 58; Cal. Pen. Code §951; The Indictments Act, 1915, 5 & 6 Geo. V, c. 90, Rule 7 in 1st sched.; American Law Institute, *Code of Criminal Procedure* (official draft) §§152, 153, 157, 164, 167 (1930); Moreland, *Modern Criminal Procedure* 206-219 (1959).

[434] *People v. Silver*, 75 Cal. App. 2d 1, 2 (1946); see *Commonwealth v. Azer*, 308 Mass. 153, 154-155 (1941); *Archbold on Indictments*, app. I, forms, Nos. 2, 14, 21; app. II, p. 228 (Roome ed. 1916); 2 *Cowdery's Forms*, Nos. 2266, 2265, 2273 (1951).

[435] *People v. Mitman*, 184 Cal. App. 2d 685, 687-690 (1960); *Simmons v. Williams*, 251 N.C. 83 (1959); and cases in notes 413, 414, 415, page 339.

[436] 2 Pollock and Maitland, *The History of English Law* 29 (2d ed. 1898).

[437] 2 Pollock and Maitland, *The History of English Law* 29 (2d ed. 1898); Coke, *Commentary upon Littleton*, f. 153a (10th ed. 1703); 3 Holdsworth, *A History of English Law* 88 (3d ed. 1923); Cowell, *The Interpreter* (ed. 1637); Blount, *Nomo-Lexikon* (1670); *Les Termes de la Ley* (ed. 1708); Blount, *A Law-Dictionary and Glossary* (3d ed. 1717); *The Law-French Dictionary* (2d ed. 1718); *The Student's Law-Dictionary* (1740); Jacob, *A New Law-Dictionary* (6th ed. 1750); compare 2 Bouvier, *A Law Dictionary* (1839).

[438] Littleton, *Tenures* §59 and commentary, both in Coke, *Commentary upon Littleton*, f. 48a (10th ed. 1703).

[439] 2 Pollock and Maitland, *The History of English Law* 60, 61 and especially n.1 (2d ed. 1898).

still only hint at its complexity: *seisin in deed* and *seisin in law*;[440] *seisin* and *disseisin; seised* and *disseised;* a landowner who has never entered upon his land unable to will it, while a disseisor can;[441] "the hierarchy of seisins"[442] — with a quiver of special writs to guard them. In these and more involvements — above all, in these writs — *seisin* lived. It was an intellectual device in the working out of rules for the peaceful holding of property, a part ". . . of the process whereby Englishmen have thought themselves free of that materialism which is natural to us all."[443]

Lawyers and historians must talk among themselves of *seisin* to understand how their rules of law got that way — e.g., the destructibility of contingent remainders.[444] This history cannot be undone by repealing its vocabulary. But it is just as pertinent that the bygone precisions of history cannot be made to live again keeping only the form of words. A twentieth-century statute may use the words *livery of seizin*.[445] How strange it sounds among the skyscrapers. Words alone without the ancient symbolic demonstrations of public transfer. No twig; no clod of dirt. Words that once spoke of a ceremony have themselves become the only ceremony. And an uncertain ceremony it is.

What does *seisin* mean today? The law dictionaries give the seeker his own confused choice from a hodgepodge of historical scraps.[446] They accurately reflect the general uncertainty. There can be no definition of *seisin* which both preserves its historical flavor and gives guidance in an age that talks of *ownership* and stakes its existence on record *title* divorced from physical contact with the land. The tortured language that attempts still to make use of *seisin* meanders through redundancy and illogic, inaccuracy and chaos.

Are *seisin* and *possession* once more the same, as in Bracton's day? "Any person seized or possessed . . ." of a fee tail, says a statute, ". . . shall be held and deemed to be seized and possessed" of the

---

[440] Coke, *Commentary upon Littleton,* ff. 29a, 31a-31b (10th ed. 1703).

[441] Maitland, "The Mystery of Seisin," in 3 *Select Essays in Anglo-American Legal History* 591, 594-600 (1909).

[442] 2 Pollock and Maitland, *The History of English Law* 75 (2d ed. 1898).

[443] Maitland, "The Mystery of Seisin," in 3 *Select Essays in Anglo-American Legal History* 591, 602 (1909).

[444] Leach, *Cases and Materials on the Law of Future Interests* 55-56 (1935).

[445] N.J. Stat. Ann. §25:1-1 (1940); variant spellings in *Oxford English Dictionary,* under *seisin* and *seize.*

[446] Ballentine, *Law Dictionary with Pronunciations* (2d ed. 1948); *Ballentine's Pronouncing Law Dictionary: Supplement* (2d ed. 1954); *Black's Law Dictionary* (4th ed. 1951); Jowitt, gen. ed., *The Dictionary of English Law* 1959).

fee.[447] What does it mean when either word yields both? Is it *seisin*, *possession*, or gallantry that holds a Confederate general *seized and possessed* of a claim for longevity pay granted by the Federal government thirty years after his death? [448]

But no lawyer can rest his case or his conscience on any assumption that "seisin is possession." If you say, "I possess the title and am seized of the land," have you pleaded *possession?* "No," says Kentucky,[449] not when the statute requires a plaintiff to have ". . . both the legal title and possession . . ." [450] Well then, does *seisin* mean *title?* "No," says Minnesota,[451] not when the statute calls for an ancestor "seized or possessed." [452] Listen to the court:

> The title of the owner of a freehold estate is described by the terms "seizin" or "seizin in fee"; yet, in a proper legal sense, the holder of the legal title is not seized until he is fully invested with the possession, actual or constructive. When there is no adverse possession, the title draws to it the possession. . . .[453]

This sort of unnatural magnetism leads us back into blackness.

Wisps of *seisin* continue to float through the law — in dower[454] and curtesy,[455] in statutes of limitation,[456] in covenants of *seisin*,[457] in future interests,[458] etc. Its substance has been dissolved into notions of *title, ownership, possession*. And its incidents have either been per-

---

[447] Tenn. Code Ann. §64-102 (1955); see also *Bost v. Johnson,* 175 Tenn. 232, 234 (1939).

[448] *Wayne v. Hartridge,* 147 Ga. 127, 132-133 (1917).

[449] See *Smith v. Williamson,* 306 Ky. 467 (1948).

[450] Ky. Rev. Stat. §411.120 (1956).

[451] See *Seymour, Sabin & Co. v. Carli,* 31 Minn. 81, 83, 84 (1883), cited with approval in *Mellenthin v. Brantman,* 211 Minn. 336, 339 (1941); compare Lob, "Seisin in the Common Law," 15 Tul. L. Rev. 455, 465 (1941).

[452] Minn. Gen. Stat., c. 66, §4 (1878), now in Minn. Stat. Ann. §541.02 (1947, Supp. 1961).

[453] *Seymour, Sabin & Co. v. Carli,* 31 Minn. 81, 83, 84 (1883), quoted in *Mellenthin v. Brantman,* 211 Minn. 336, 339 (1941).

[454] Ark. Stat. §61-206 (1947); *Merrell v. Smith,* 228 Ark. 167, 171-172 (1957); *Maloney v. McCullough,* 215 Ark. 570 (1949); *Fletcher v. Felker,* 97 F. Supp. (W.D. Ark. 1951); Lob, "Seisin in the Common Law," 15 Tul. L. Rev. 455, 466 (1941).

[455] N.J. Stat. Ann. §§3A:36-1, 3A:36-2; *Hess v. Hess,* 162 Ore. 266 (1939), discussed in Buell, "The Law of Seisin in Oregon," 28 Ore. L. Rev. 12-25 (1948).

[456] Cal. C.C.P. §§318, 319, and compare §325; Minn. Stat. Ann. §541.02 (1947, Supp. 1961).

[457] Compare Cal. Civ. Code §3304 with N.J. Stat. Ann. §46:9-2 (1940); Nichols, *Cyclopedia of Legal Forms* §§3.1128, 3.1129 (1936); Lob, "Seisin in the Common Law," 15 Tul. L. Rev. 455, 466-467 (1941).

[458] Leach, *Cases and Materials on the Law of Future Interests* 55-56 (1935).

petuated as rules of law,[459] or abolished.[460] *Seisin* is history, not precision, and lives out a now useless life only by sufferance of the bar.[461]

122. *Does this way make meaning more exact than ordinary English?*

Most lawyers use traditional law language without doubting its precision. (Section 115.) And if in a moment of gloomy introspection (when the upper court has just refused to reverse) a lawyer is tempted to look around to see if there might have been some better way of saying what the court misunderstood, he is apt to look at anything but the toadstool under his doorstep. There are those who believe that ordinary English is beneath a professional's dignity;[462] as it should be — when ordinary English is bad English or when law language says it better.

But ordinary English is not always bad English, and law language does not always say it better, or more precisely. English has been refined by countless writers of good English and digested by millions of educated citizens, since those far-off days when English was a branch of chaos (Section 53) and the clergy and lawyers had a monopoly of literacy. (Sections 45, 51, 54, 59.) By contrast, lawyers have professed to be more interested in "the law" than in language (Section 114), and their language shows it. Nowhere is this long neglect more apparent than in the law's habit of doubling words.

Both law language and ordinary English have a history of using two words for one. From the earliest days of English, the oral tradition's preference for rhythm (Sections 30, 31) plus the mingling of English with other languages (Sections 27, 70, 97) have fostered the use of synonym. And there was a time when it was considered an accomplishment to double words, synonyms from two languages or one. (Sections 70, 71.) Outside of law language, most of these doublings are now considered clichés; for example, *rack and ruin*,[463] *safe and*

---

[459] See Leach, *Cases and Materials on the Law of Future Interests* 55-56 (1935); Bordwell, "Seisin and Disseisin," 34 Harv. L. Rev. 592-624, 717-740 (1921); Buell, "The Law of Seisin in Oregon," 28 Ore. L. Rev. 12-25 (1948).

[460] See Leach, *Cases and Materials on the Law of Future Interests* 105, 117, 118 (1935); Cal. Civ. Code §§741, 742; 2 *Restatement of Property* §164, Comment *c*.

[461] Compare 5 *Words and Phrases: Judicially Defined* (1945), under *seised*.

[462] Aiken, "Let's Not Oversimplify Legal Language," 32 Rocky Mt. L. Rev. 358, 364 (1960).

[463] Partridge, *A Dictionary of Clichés* (4th ed. 1950); Evans and Evans, *A Dictionary of Contemporary American Usage* (1957).

sound,[464] *might and main*,[465] *part and parcel*.[466] They are an aspect of the development of English but now to be avoided by those who have an interest in literary style.

Not so with the language of the law. A loathing for the redundant is not a generally respected lawyerly quality; here doubling is still fashionable. Like the buttons on his coat sleeve, the lawyer's doubled words are there without his awareness of any particular function. Generally, the lawyer is conscious only that he is being "traditional," probably therefore "precise." (Sections 115, 118.) And in a very few instances, doubled words have achieved a small but helpful technicality, so that what started as a pair of synonyms can properly be regarded as a single expression. Here are some of them.

Aid and comfort

"Treason against the United States," says the Constitution,

> shall consist only in levying War against them, or in adhering to their Enemies, giving them Aid and Comfort.[467]

Aid and *comfort* are Old French synonyms in the sense of support.[468] The law French of the fourteenth-century statute from which we inherit this language[469] rests in two handwritten versions, one joining the words with *or* (*ou*), the other making it *and* (*et*), both customarily translated to leave the phrase *aid and comfort*.[470] Since the conjunctions joined only redundancy, any significance that might have hinged on the conjunction was ignored, as it is today, even though — except for the law — *comfort* in this sense is obsolete.[471] *Aid* and *comfort* have become — in the law of the Constitution — one word [472] identifying a facet of treason. The nature of the *support* which is treasonable *aid and comfort* — the substance of the phrase — is still

---

[464] Partridge, *A Dictionary of Clichés* (4th ed. 1950); Evans and Evans, *A Dictionary of Contemporary American Usage* (1957).

[465] Partridge, *A Dictionary of Clichés* (4th ed. 1950); compare Evans and Evans, *A Dictionary of Contemporary American Usage* (1957).

[466] Partridge, *A Dictionary of Clichés* (4th ed. 1950); compare Evans and Evans, *A Dictionary of Contemporary American Usage* (1957).

[467] Art. III, §3.

[468] *Oxford English Dictionary*, under *aid, comfort*, v., No. 2, and sb., No. 1.

[469] Treason Act, 1351, 25 Edw. III, Stat. 5, c. 2.

[470] *Rex v. Casement*, [1917] 1 K.B. 98 (compare wording and translations at 134 with 98 n.1, and with 86 L.J.K.B. (n.s.) 467 n.1).

[471] *Webster's New International Dictionary* (2d ed. 1934).

[472] Ballentine, *Law Dictionary with Pronunciations* (2d ed. 1948); *Black's Law Dictionary* (4th ed. 1951); 1 Bouvier, *A Law Dictionary* (Rawle, 15th ed. 1892).

being defined by decision,[473] but the formula itself is warning to the profession that treason is up for discussion.

By and with

Another constitutional duplication is ". . . by and with the Advice and Consent of the Senate . . ." in the treaty-making and appointing powers of the President.[474] Both Old English words come to us through the English legislative formula:

> . . . by and with the advice and consent of the lords spiritual and temporal and commons of Great Britain in parliament assembled, . . .[475]

Were it not that the phrase is traditional, either of the words alone could do the job, as in the ancient *by your leave*[476] and *with your leave*.[477] As it is, *by and with* — in constitutional usage — are a unit, with a definite reference that would be obscured by simplification.[478]

Cease and desist

Both *cease* (French) and *desist* (from Old French) mean the same as English *stop*.[479] Any one of the three serves most purposes, and *stop* is most common in ordinary speech.[480] In the language of the law, there is a tendency (no more than that) to identify a *cease and desist order* as the order of an administrative agency, e.g., the Federal Communications Commission,[481] the Interstate Commerce Commission,[482] the National Labor Relations Board,[483] the Secretary of Agriculture.[484] Further, stockbrokers have a strong hold on the *stop order*

[473] 3 *Words and Phrases* (perm. ed. 1953); *Ballentine's Pronouncing Law Dictionary: Supplement* (2d ed. 1954).
[474] Art. II, §2, cl. 2.
[475] See Section 76, for this use in Records in English, 1731, 4 Geo. II, c. 26; compare 2 Holdworth, *A History of English Law* 440 n.3 (3d ed. 1923), and *Oxford English Dictionary*, under *with*, No. 33.
[476] *Oxford English Dictionary*, under *by*, No. 23c.
[477] *Oxford English Dictionary*, under *with*, No. 33.
[478] See Dickerson, *Legislative Drafting* 75 n.4 (1954).
[479] *Oxford English Dictionary*, under *stop*, *v.*, generally, and see especially No. 20 and No. 24.
[480] Evans and Evans, *A Dictionary of Contemporary American Usage*, under *stop*.
[481] 47 U.S.C.A. §312(b), (c), (e).
[482] 15 U.S.C.A. §21(b).
[483] *NLRB v. Colten*, 105 F.2d 179, 180, 183 (6th Cir. 1939).
[484] 7 U.S.C.A. §193(b); see also Cal. Lab. Code §1426; Cal. Pub. Util. Code §§1006, 1034, 1054, 1071, 4638; compare Cal. Bus. & Prof. Code §10084; N.Y. Ins. Law §§275, 276, 277; 4 *Ill. Law and Practice* 291 (1953); 73 *C.J.S. public administrative bodies and procedure* §151.

(or *stop-loss order*) as a term of art.[485]   Accordingly, *cease and desist*, when it connotes the order of an administrative agency, conveys a shade of meaning that one of the words alone would not, and avoids confusion with the broker's *stop order*.

Full faith and credit

Faith (from Old French from Latin)[486] and *credit* (French from Latin)[487] are ancient synonyms for belief, credence,[488] joined together in duplication at least as early as the fifteenth century in the phrase ". . . to gyve feith and credence . . ."[489] and in the sixteenth century ". . . to geve credite and perfait faith . . ."[490]   The present version, *full faith and credit*, appeared in the Articles of Confederation,[491] and though in two drafts of the United States Constitution the shortened *full faith* was suggested,[492] the older and longer phrase was written into the final report.[493]

Full faith and credit,[494] sometimes only *faith and credit*,[495] is also used without the sense of doubling.   In government bonds the two words are given distinctive meanings — *faith* in the sense of *faithfulness* plus *credit* in a money sense; so that a pledge of *full faith and credit* serves to distinguish general obligation from revenue bonds.[496] Despite this special use of the phrase in public finance, "the *full faith and credit* clause" has an explicit constitutional reference.   While there is great and continuing argument over application,[497] *full faith and credit* remains as a touchstone of federal union.   It is a convenient label for a concept sufficiently definite to work with.

---

[485] Engel, *How to Buy Stocks* 51-52 (Bantam ed. 1957); 40 *Words and Phrases* (perm. ed. 1940, Supp. 1962), "stop order."

[486] *Oxford English Dictionary.*

[487] *Oxford English Dictionary.*

[488] *Oxford English Dictionary,* under *credence.*

[489] Quoted in *Oxford English Dictionary,* under *faith,* No. 2.

[490] Quoted in *Oxford English Dictionary,* under *credence,* No. 4.

[491] U.S. Congress, *Documents Illustrative of the Formation of the Union* 28 (1927).

[492] U.S. Congress, *Documents Illustrative of the Formation of the Union* 480, 632-633 (1927).

[493] U.S. Congress, *Documents Illustrative of the Formation of the Union* 711 (1927); art. IV, §1.

[494] Ark. Acts 1959, Act 485, §3; Cal. State Construction Program Bond Act of 1958, §3; Cal. Educ. Code §7994.

[495] Del. Laws 1957, c. 283, §7; Ga. Laws 1960, No. 447, §18; N.J. Laws 1959, c. 10, §6.

[496] *Seward v. Bowers,* 37 N.M. 385, 391 (1933); Chermak, *The Law of Revenue Bonds* 144-145 (1954).

[497] 17A *Words and Phrases* 486-511 (perm. ed. 1958), 9 (Supp. 1962).

Had and received

Had (Old English)[498] and *received* (Anglo-Norman)[499] are ancient synonyms, but together are part of the name of one of the common counts.[500] When used in the phrase *money had and received*[501] the former synonyms are words of art,[502] peculiar perhaps, but part of a name, like "William Williams,"[503] or "John Johns."[504]

123. Worthless doubling

When doubled words have resulted in some utility (Section 122), there would be more loss than gain in dropping a synonym for the sake of brevity, or even to tailor law language to a more logical pattern of word usage. Language whose meaning is more precise than the ordinary is too rare and valuable a tool to be lightly discarded. Yet this point need not be labored, for lawyers need small encouragement to hold on to what they have.

It is habit rather than discrimination that perpetuates those doublings which have ultimately proved useful. And the same habit and lack of discrimination keep alive many more word doublings that do not make for precision, whose sense — where it is needed at all — can be rendered with more exactness in ordinary English. Some of these unnecessary doublings have already been discussed in detail — *last will and testament* (Sections 49, 121), *mind and memory* (Section 121), *seised and possessed* (Section 121), *to have and to hold* (Section 56). Here are some more that the law can get along without.

Fit and proper

It is now almost a hundred years since any form of *fit and proper* has been used to advantage. And when Lincoln made his "'. . . few

---

[498] *Oxford English Dictionary*, under *have*, No. 14.
[499] *Oxford English Dictionary*, under *receive*, No. 16.
[500] See 3 Blackstone, *Commentaries* °162 (Jones ed. 1916); 1 Chitty, *A Practical Treatise on Pleading* 339 (1809); 2 Chitty, *A Practical Treatise on Pleading* 41 (1809).
[501] 27A *Words and Phrases* (perm. ed. 1961); 2 *California Words, Phrases, and Maxims* (1960).
[502] Ballentine, *Law Dictionary with Pronunciations* (2d ed. 1948); *Ballentine's Pronouncing Law Dictionary: Supplement* (2d ed. 1954), under "assumpsit for money had and received"; *Black's Law Dictionary* (4th ed. 1951); 2 Bouvier, *A Law Dictionary* (Rawle, 15th ed. 1892); Jowitt, gen. ed., *The Dictionary of English Law* (1959).
[503] *Dictionary of American Biography* (subscription ed. 1958).
[504] *Dictionary of American Biography* (subscription ed. 1958).

appropriate remarks' " [505] at Gettysburg, it was not as lawyer but as orator that he included:

It is altogether fitting and proper that we should do this.[506]

In the sense of *suitable*[507] in which the law uses the combination, *fit*[508] and *proper*[509] are synonyms,[510] *fit* "perhaps" from Old English,[511] *proper* from Latin through French.[512] Each of the words has many shades of meaning, some completely individualistic;[513] but when the law says that a person is *fit and proper* (which is the usual reference),[514] it does not distinguish shades of meaning, nor draw lines between personal qualification and legal competency. It is simply saying the same thing twice.

Without perceptible change of sense, an opinion may switch from *fit and proper* to *proper*[515] or to *fitness*,[516] from *proper* alone to *fit* alone,[517] or wander over the field. An opinion — in the same context — speaks of parents *fit*,[518] *proper*,[519] *suitable*,[520] *fit and suitable*,[521]

[505] Peterson, ed., *A Treasury of the World's Great Speeches* 521-522 (1954).
[506] Peterson, ed., *A Treasury of the World's Great Speeches* 522 (1954).
[507] 2 *California Words, Phrases, and Maxims* (1960), "fit"; compare 17 *Words and Phrases* 140 (perm. ed. 1958), 6 (Supp. 1962), "fit."
[508] Ballentine, *Law Dictionary with Pronunciations* (2d ed. 1948); *Black's Law Dictionary* (4th ed. 1951); 26 *C.J.* 646; see 17 *Words and Phrases* (perm. ed. 1958, Supp. 1962), "fit."
[509] *Black's Law Dictionary* (4th ed. 1951); 2 Bouvier, *A Law Dictionary* (Rawle, 15th ed. 1892); 50 *C.J.* 721, 722; see 34A *Words and Phrases,* especially at 7 (perm. ed. 1957), "proper."
[510] Compare *Wojnarowicz v. Wojnarowicz,* 48 N.J. Super. 349, 353 (1958), with *Buehler v. Buehler,* 373 Ill. 626, 629 (1940).
[511] *Oxford English Dictionary;* see *Webster's New International Dictionary* (2d ed. 1934).
[512] *Oxford English Dictionary; Webster's New International Dictionary* (2d ed. 1934).
[513] For example, see Evans and Evans, *A Dictionary of Contemporary American Usage* (1957), under *proper;* Horwill, *A Dictionary of Modern American Usage* (2d ed. 1944), under *fit.*
[514] Cal. Ins. Code §1805; *Fantony v. Fantony,* 36 N.J. Super. 375, 380 (1955); *Moyer v. Moyer,* 75 N.J. Eq. 439, 443 (1909); *Legal Secretary's Handbook* (*California*) 193, 198 (1954); 2 *Words and Phrases: Judicially Defined* (1943), "fit and proper person"; compare 2 *Words and Phrases: Judicially Defined* (1943), "deem fit and proper."
[515] *Howard v. Howard,* 128 Cal. App. 2d 180, 187 (1954).
[516] *Guardianship of Walsh,* 100 Cal. App. 2d 194, 195, 199 (1950); see also Stat. (1845) 8 & 9 Vict., c. 70, §6, and compare §7; Stat. (1831) 1 & 2 Wm. IV, c. 38, §16.
[517] *Cohn v. Scott,* 231 Ill. 556, 557, 558 (1907).
[518] *Stafford v. Stafford,* 299 Ill. 438, 443 (1921).
[519] *Stafford v. Stafford,* 299 Ill. 438, 453 (1921).
[520] *Stafford v. Stafford,* 299 Ill. 438, 441 (1921).
[521] *Stafford v. Stafford,* 299 Ill. 438, 443, 446 (1921).

competent and fit,[522] and *fit and competent;*[523] and the case is digested in terms of *fit and proper.*[524] It is an area of law language where absence of technicality is the rule, as witness this flight of usage:

> Relatrix was pregnant at the time of the hearing in this case. We must take it that she now is a proper person to have custody and that the home . . . is a proper place to maintain the child. . . . the respondent father is also a proper person . . . and he presently is on the eve of marriage with a suitable person.[525]

Fit and proper serves no purpose, except occasionally to create doubt in the mind of a cautious lawyer. Thus, after hearings required by a statute which said a licensee must be a *fit and proper person,*[526] there were separate findings that the applicant was *not a fit person* and that he was *not a proper person.*[527] Together these were treated as though the finding had been *not a fit and proper person* — all supported by the same evidence.[528]

Fit and proper is so little regarded by the profession that its standard law dictionaries do not bother to define it. But its meaning is there, and as much of it as need be used is included under *fit*[529] and under *proper.*[530]

Force and effect

In the common parlance of laymen (and also of lawyers when they are not talking shop), a *force* customarily produces an *effect.*[531] So accustomed have we become to these words — their relationship as well as their individuality — that the mention of *force and effect* together leaves the vague impression that each must be at work serving some unspecified technical end. There is little occasion to reflect that when the law speaks of *force and effect* it is using the words as synonyms.

In the traditional phrasing *in full force and effect*[532] and negatively

---

[522] *Stafford v. Stafford,* 299 Ill. 438, 453 (1921).

[523] *Stafford v. Stafford,* 299 Ill. 438, 454 (1921).

[524] 12 *Ill. Digest* 219, §298 (5).

[525] *Commonwealth ex rel. Buell v. Buell,* 186 Pa. Super. 468, 471-472 (1958); see also *Edwards & Wise,* 27 Eng. Rep. 587-588 (Ch. 1740).

[526] Cal. Ins. Code §1805.

[527] *Newport v. Caminetti,* 56 Cal. App. 2d 557, 558 (1943).

[528] *Newport v. Caminetti,* 56 Cal. App. 2d 557, 560 (1943).

[529] See note 508.

[530] See note 509.

[531] *Webster's New International Dictionary* (2d ed. 1934), under *force,* No. 1; see Holmes, J., in *Schenck v. United States* 249 U.S. 47, 52 (1919), quoted in Section 134.

[532] Nichols, *Cyclopedia of Legal Forms* §5.745E (1956).

of no further force and effect,[533] the sense of *force* is effectiveness rather than causation.[534]   A law or contract that is *in force*[535] is one that is *in effect*,[536] and vice versa; stringing the words together does not change their meaning.[537]

Force and effect was never hammered out as a lawyer's term of art; it grew out of the general language usage of centuries ago. (Sections 70, 71.) Before *force and effect* became a stock phrase of lawyers, the same thought was expressed in other popular tautologies. In the fifteenth century, for example, Old English *strength* was doubled in French to say of a law that it ". . . be and stond in strenght and vertue . . . ,"[538] and in the same context there was an all-French double ". . . force and virtue."[539]   English was growing and versatile, with many interchangeable parts. (Section 79.) In the sixteenth century some said ". . . voyde and of noo fors,"[540] others ". . . woide and of non effect"[541] — both of these French doubles; a fancier version was an all-French triple: ". . . the vertue, force, and effecte of the sayd Sacrament";[542] but a lawyer's formbook outdid them all, with a grand bilingual extravaganza — doubled and redoubled — a bond form reading:

That then this present Obligation to be utterly voide and of none effect, or to stand, remaine and bee of full force, strength, power and vertue.[543]

From this point on the variations are endless.[544]   Though Blackstone was familiar with *force and effect* and used the words ". . . to

---

[533] Lindey, *Motion Picture Agreements Annotated,* Form IV-I (1947).

[534] *Oxford English Dictionary,* under *force,* Nos. 8, 9.

[535] Ballentine, *Law Dictionary with Pronunciations* (2d ed. 1948), under *in force;* Black's Law Dictionary (4th ed. 1951), under *force;* 5 *Words and Phrases* (perm. ed. 1940), "be in force."

[536] Ballentine, *Law Dictionary with Pronunciations* (2d ed. 1948), under *in effect;* see *Black's Law Dictionary* (1951), under *effect,* n.; see *Carlton v. Castranova,* 189 Cal. App. 2d 409, 414 (1961).

[537] See, e.g., 17 *Words and Phrases* (perm. ed. 1958), "force and effect."

[538] Quoted in *Oxford English Dictionary,* under *virtue,* No. 9e.

[539] *Oxford English Dictionary,* under *force,* No. 8c.

[540] *Oxford English Dictionary,* under *force,* No. 8b.

[541] *Oxford English Dictionary,* under *void,* No. 7.

[542] Quoted in *Oxford English Dictionary,* under *force,* No. 9.

[543] West, *The First Part of Symboleography* §111 (ed. 1598).

[544] For example: *Oxford English Dictionary* under *force,* Nos. 8, 9; under *virtue,* No. 9; under *strength,* No. 1h; Jacob, *A New Law-Dictionary* (6th ed. 1750), under *bond;* 2 Blackstone, *Commentaries* °353, app. III (Jones ed. 1916); 3 Blackstone, *Commentaries* °xx, °xxii (Jones ed. 1916); Lechford, *Notebook* 5, 8 (Wilson ed. 1885); 1 Burn, *The Justice of the Peace* 140 (16th ed. 1788); *Practical Forms,* Nos. 49, 50, 53, 60, 62, 64, 65 (1823).

consider the *force* and *effect* of a fine," [545] he preferred, for a bond, a shortened version of the sixteenth-century form: [546]

> . . . then this obligation to be void and of none effect, or else to be and remain in full force and virtue. [547]

Though this sense of *virtue* is obsolete in ordinary English, [548] it persists in the law's *by virtue of*, [549] and even *force and virtue* is not entirely cold. [550] Yet it is not now as common as it once was, and with the increased currency of *null and void* (in this list) for *void and of no effect*, the trend of fashion has been to pair *force and effect*. [551] But for all its years of use, the doubling of *force and effect* has added nothing to precision. The phrase still lacks the dignity of art, and wherever it is used, one of the words alone — most often *force* — can do the job every bit as well. [552]

Give, devise, and bequeath

Far from being precise, this collection of bilingual synonyms is evidence of the draftsman's lack of confidence in the tools he is using and in himself. It is an untechnical expression of a desperate hope that something (please God) will work.

Of the three words, the least technical is Old English *give*. [553] It is a making of *gifts* [554] in the broadest sense, including both Old English

---

[545] 2 Blackstone, *Commentaries* °353 (Jones ed. 1916).

[546] West, *The First Part of Symboleography* §111 (ed. 1598).

[547] 3 Blackstone, *Commentaries* °xxii (Jones ed. 1916); compare 3 Blackstone, *Commentaries* °xx (Jones ed. 1916), with 2 Blackstone, *Commentaries,* app. III (Jones ed. 1916).

[548] *Webster's New International Dictionary* (2d ed. 1934), under *virtue,* No. 10c.

[549] *Black's Law Dictionary* (4th ed. 1951); 5 *Words and Phrases* (perm. ed. 1940, Supp. 1962).

[550] For example, Nichols, *Cyclopedia of Legal Forms* §§2.892, 2.903B, 2.904A (1956).

[551] N.J. Stat. Ann. §46:9-2 (1940); *Stafford v. Stafford,* 299 Ill. 438, 442 (1921); *Fantony v. Fantony,* 21 N.J. 525, 536 (1956); 17 *Words and Phrases* (perm. ed. 1958), "force and effect"; Nichols, *Cyclopedia of Legal Forms* §§2.907-2.910, 5.745E (1956); Lindey, *Motion Picture Agreements, Annotated,* Forms I-M, II-G, IV-I, IV-J, and see IV-K (1947).

[552] Compare Nichols, *Cyclopedia of Legal Forms* §§5.745D with 5.745E, §§2.915 with 2.916 et seq. (1956); see also 17A *Words and Phrases* (perm. ed. 1958), "full force"; 21 *Words and Phrases* (perm. ed. 1960), "in full force"; Dickerson, *Legislative Drafting* 76 (1954).

[553] *Oxford English Dictionary.*

[554] See *gift* in *Oxford English Dictionary;* Jowitt, gen. ed., *The Dictionary of English Law* (1959); Jacob, *A New Law-Dictionary* (6th ed. 1750); Coke, *Commentary upon Littleton,* f. 301b (10th ed. 1703).

bequeath and Old French *devise*, and has been used in wills for more than five hundred years.[555]

Bequeath[556] (related to O.E. *cwyde* — saying, will (see Section 49)) and later *devise* (originally to divide, a division) [557] both took on the particular meaning of giving by will. As with *give*, these were still untechnical words, applied alike to real and personal property,[558] part of the mounting surplus of the growing English vocabulary. (Sections 70, 71.) A seventeenth-century law dictionary uses all of the words to tell us that

> *Devise* . . . Is properly that act, by which a Testator gives, or bequeaths his Lands or Goods by his last Will in Writing. . . .[559]

In the eighteenth century, some said that *devise* "properly" applied to wills of land,[560] but the same writers spoke of the *devise* of money.[561] Not until the nineteenth century did it become a lawyerly custom to *devise realty* and *bequeath personalty*, a subtlety contrary to the linguistic and legal history of the words and never uniform in practice. So persistent was the vacillation at the bar that the first American law dictionary recognized standards of regular and irregular usage. *Devise*, wrote John Bouvier in 1839,

> . . . properly and technically applies only to real estate, . . . Devise is also improperly applied to a bequest of personal estate, the proper terms being bequest or legacy . . .[562]

[555] *Oxford English Dictionary*, under *give*, No. 4.
[556] *Oxford English Dictionary*, under *bequeath*, No. 4; Bosworth and Toller, *An Anglo-Saxon Dictionary* (1898), *under becweðan*.
[557] Section 63; *Oxford English Dictionary*; compare Coke, *Commentary upon Littleton*, f. 111a (10th ed. 1703).
[558] *Webster's New International Dictionary* (2d ed. 1934), under *bequeath*, No. 2; see 2 Pollock and Maitland, *The History of English Law* (2d ed. 1898), 319, 326.
[559] Blount, *Nomo-Lexikon* (1670); see also *Les Termes de la Ley* (ed. 1671); and see Coke, *Commentary upon Littleton*, f. 111a (10th ed. 1703); Cowell, *The Interpreter* (ed. 1637), under *devise;* Statute of Wills, 1540, 52 Hen. VIII, c. 1; Statute of Frauds, 1677, 29 Car. II, c. 3, §5; *Hyde v. Parratt*, 24 Eng. Rep. 269 (Ch. 1695).
[560] *The Student's Law-Dictionary* (1740); Jacob, *A New Law-Dictionary* (6th ed. 1750), under *devise* and *will*.
[561] *The Student's Law-Dictionary* (1740), under *legacy;* Jacob, *A New Law-Dictionary* (6th ed. 1750), under *legacy;* and see 7 Bacon, *A New Abridgment of the Law* 303, 350, 367 (Gwillim, 5th ed. 1798); *Papillon v. Voice*, 24 Eng. Rep. 819 (Ch. 1728); Johnson, *A Dictionary of the English Language* (4th ed. 1775), under *bequeath*.
[562] 1 Bouvier, *A Law Dictionary* 322 (1839); see also 2 Bouvier, *A Law Dictionary* 15, 16 (1839); 1 Bouvier, *A Law Dictionary* (1839), under *bequest*.

Both usages are recognized today — the "proper"[563] and the "improper,"[564] which used to be the "proper." Only in the clearest case (when it makes no difference anyhow) can you be sure that the draftsman has been "proper" or "improper." More often he has been plain sloppy. Take for instance a misspelled, repetitious writing calling itself a *last will and testament,* others to be *null and void,* with six *jointly's* — one tacked onto a gift to a single person. In the portion of the will reproduced in the opinion, there are seven *give, devise and bequeath's.* Was this draftsman — a non-lawyer justice of the peace, once a probate judge — the sort who would use law words with their technical meanings?

Yes, said the trial judge,

> The context and language of said will as a whole exhibits a fair understanding of form, language and legal terms common to instruments of like character prepared by persons having legal training and experience.[565]

Preposterous, argued counsel,

> . . . a reading of the document involved discloses that the drawer thereof didn't have any legal knowledge because he used the word *"bequeath"* in devising real property and the word *"devise"* in bequeathing personal property.[566]

Unruffled, the appellate court replied:

[563] Under *devise:* Ballentine, *Law Dictionary with Pronunciations* (2d ed. 1948); *Black's Law Dictionary* (4th ed. 1951); Jowitt, gen. ed., *The Dictionary of English Law* (1959); 12 *Words and Phrases* (perm. ed. 1954, Supp. 1962); 1 *California Words, Phrases, and Maxims* (1960); 2 *Words and Phrases: Judicially Defined* (1943).
Under *bequeath: Black's Law Dictionary* (4th ed. 1951); Jowitt, gen. ed., *The Dictionary of English Law* (1959).
Under *bequest:* Ballentine, *Law Dictionary with Pronunciations* (2d ed. 1948); *Ballentine's Pronouncing Law Dictionary: Supplement* (2d ed. 1954); *Black's Law Dictionary* (4th ed. 1951); 5 *Words and Phrases* 369-370, 371 (perm. ed. 1940), 70-71 (Supp. 1962); 1 *California Words, Phrases, and Maxims* (1960).
[564] Under *devise: Ballentine's Pronouncing Law Dictionary: Supplement* (2d ed. 1954); Jowitt, gen. ed., *The Dictionary of English Law* (1959); 12 *Words and Phrases* 534-535, and see also 529-534 (perm. ed. 1954), 25 (Supp. 1962).
Under *bequeath:* Ballentine, *Law Dictionary with Pronunciations* (2d ed. 1948); *Black's Law Dictionary* (4th ed. 1951); Jowitt, gen. ed., *The Dictionary of English Law* (1959); 5 *Words and Phrases* 364-366 (perm. ed. 1940), 69 (Supp. 1962); 1 *Words and Phrases: Judicially Defined* 316-317 (1946).
Under *bequest:* Ballentine, *Law Dictionary with Pronunciations* (2d ed. 1948); *Black's Law Dictionary* (4th ed. 1951); 5 *Words and Phrases* 371, 372 (perm. ed. 1940), 70-71 (Supp. 1962).
[565] *Householter v. Householter,* 160 Kan. 614, 618 (1945).
[566] *Householter v. Householter,* 160 Kan. 614, 618 (1945).

Such indiscriminate usage is rather common.[567]

Not only are *bequeath* and *devise* being used as synonyms as a matter of careless practice; there are signs which point to a deliberate return to the old proprieties. Some statutes officially acknowledge the synonymous usage,[568] and the Restatement applies *devise* to both land and personalty.[569]

If the search for art or even pattern leads to the forms — those used or recommended — there lies frenzy compounded. Words without end and without consistent meaning. *Give, devise, and bequeath* is used for gifts of personalty alone,[570] realty alone,[571] and for both together.[572] But *give, devise, and bequeath* (even with the rhythm altered to *give, bequeath, and devise*[573]) has no monopoly of this triple role. *Give and bequeath* is used in the same way,[574] and so is *give* alone.[575] Realty is *devised* often enough,[576] yet sometimes in the same form realty is *given*.[577] Personalty is *bequeathed* often enough,[578] yet in the same form one paragraph will *give and bequeath* personalty and realty, and another will *give and bequeath* realty.[579] A lush if rare growth is *give, devise, and bequeath . . . the following devises*.[580] Often the clauses of gift dispense with *give* — e.g., *devise*

---

[567] *Householter v. Householter,* 160 Kan. 614, 618 (1945), citing *Breen v. Davies,* 94 Kan. 474, 475 (1915).

[568] For example, see Ind. Ann. Stat. §6-103 (1953); Iowa Code §633.15 (1946); Ky. Rev. Stat. §446.010(3) (1960); and see *Moore v. Dick,* 208 Iowa 693, 696-697 (1929); 29 *Indiana Law Encyclopedia* 515 (1960).

[569] 1 *Restatement of Property* §12; 3 *Restatement of Property* §314.

[570] *Am. Jur. Legal Forms* 13:1778.2 (Supp. 1962).

[571] *Modern Legal Forms* §9602 (rev. ed. 1957); Nichols, *Cyclopedia of Legal Forms* §9.1162 (1936).

[572] *Am. Jur. Legal Forms* 13:1771, 13:1773, 13.1780 (1955); *Cowdery's Forms,* Nos. 3751, 3752, 3753, 3756 (1951); *Modern Legal Forms* §§9561-9564, §9585 (rev. ed. 1957); Rabkin and Johnson, *Current Legal Forms,* Forms 7.03, 7.04, 7.04A (1961).

[573] Rabkin and Johnson, *Current Legal Forms,* Form 7.04B (1961).

[574] Nichols, *Cyclopedia of Legal Forms* §§9.1160C (realty and personalty; realty), 9.1176D (personalty) (1936).

[575] *Cowdery's Forms,* No. 3757 (1951), *Am. Jur. Legal Forms* 13:1771, 13:1778.2 (1955), Rabkin and Johnson, *Current Legal Forms,* Form 7.03 (1961) (personalty); *Cowdery's Forms,* No. 3755, (1951), *Am. Jur. Legal Forms* 13:1774 (1955) (realty); Rabkin and Johnson, *Current Legal Forms,* Forms 7.01, 7.02, (1961), Nichols, *Cyclopedia of Legal Forms* §9.1468a (Supp. 1958) (realty and personalty).

[576] *Modern Legal Forms* §9585 (rev. ed. 1957); *Cowdery's Forms,* No. 3764 (1951); Nichols, *Cyclopedia of Legal Forms* §§9.1143, 9.1144 (1936).

[577] *Cowdery's Forms,* No. 3764 (1951).

[578] *Modern Legal Forms* §§9564, 9565, 9584 (rev. ed. 1957).

[579] Nichols, *Cyclopedia of Legal Forms* §9.1160C (1936).

[580] *Am. Jur. Legal Forms* 13:1773 (1955).

and bequeath,[581] *bequeath and devise,*[582] *will and bequeath.*[583] On and on.[584]

Despite the vagaries of the forms and the tendency of courts to search out intent regardless of words,[585] there is a lingering sense within the profession that the weight of tradition — *devise* (realty), *bequeath* (personalty) — may tip the scales of interpretation. Yet if it sometimes does,[586] the use of *devise* and *bequeath* also raises questions that often are best unasked. When there is equitable conversion, should the words of gift be appropriate to the property in its original or changed form?[587] If you *give, devise, and bequeath* only one type of property, have you *bequeathed* realty, or *devised* personalty?[588] Do *bequeath* in one part of a will and *devise* in another part (or in a later will, or in a codicil)[589] mean different things? Or only that a lawyer was drowsing? Or that two lawyers had different habits, different formbooks, or secretaries who referred to different pages of the same formbooks?[590]

Combining all of these words joins their individual uncertainties without pointing conclusively to anything. Further, as with most formulas, *give, devise, and bequeath* lulls the draftsman into forgetfulness. The flourish of such a catchall can leave a power of appointment unexercised when it should have been, or exercised when it should not have been.[591]

At this point, *give* — uncontaminated by either *devise* or *bequeath* — has the advantage of all-encompassing neutrality and ease of uni-

[581] *Modern Legal Forms* §§9565, 9566, 9584 (rev. ed. 1957); *Am. Jur. Legal Forms* 13:1775 (1955).

[582] *Modern Legal Forms* §9589 (Supp. 1962); Nichols, *Cyclopedia of Legal Form* §9.1144 (1936).

[583] *Am. Jur. Legal Forms* 13:1777, 13:1778 (1955), 13:1891.1 (Supp. 1962).

[584] See, for example, *Cowdery's Forms*, Nos. 3754, 3757 (1951); *Modern Legal Forms* §9585, (rev. ed. 1957); Nichols, *Cyclopedia of Legal Forms* §§ 9.1316B, 9.1344C (1936).

[585] For example, *In re Pierce's Estate*, 111 N.Y.S.2d 525, 529 (N.Y. Surr. 1952).

[586] *In re Whamond's Will*, 124 N.Y.S.2d 45, 47, 48 (N.Y. Surr. 1953); *Phillips v. Beal*, 53 Eng. Rep. 545, 546 (Rolls Ct. 1858).

[587] See, for example, *In re Whamond's Will*, 124 N.Y.S.2d 45, 48 (N.Y. Surr. 1953); *Whicker v. Hume*, 51 Eng. Rep. 381, 385 (Rolls Ct. 1851).

[588] *Householter v. Householter*, 160 Kan. 614, 615, 616, 618 (1945).

[589] See, for example, *In re Whaley's Will*, 81 N.Y.S.2d 553, 554-555 (N.Y. Surr. 1948); *Whicker v. Hume*, 51 Eng. Rep. 381, 385 (Rolls Ct. 1851).

[590] Compare *Cowdery's Forms*, No. 3755 (1951), with *Am. Jur. Legal Forms* 13:1777, 13:1778 (1955); compare Nichols, *Cyclopedia of Legal Forms* §§ 9.1160A, 9.1160C, and 9.1160D (1936).

[591] See Leach, "Powers of Appointment," 24 A.B.A.J. 807 (1938).

form usage. It is not only the popular word, but one familiar to law-yers when striving for uncontroversial expression.[592] If *give* is used in a will,[593] it will carry any personal and real property to which it is directed.[594] *Appoint* when appointment is required,[595] but otherwise *give* alone can be as precise as the circumstances call for, and un-troubled by the conflicting proprieties of *devise* and *bequeath:*

> This is my will. I give Blackacre to Tom, my basset hound to Dick, and all other real and personal property to Mary.

Null and void

These French words are synonyms, but it was not always so, and even today — on occasion — each bears witness to independent origin. *Null,* from its ties to Latin *nullus* (not any, none, no) [596] can still mean amounting-to-nothing.[597] *Void* — distantly related to the Latin *vacuus* — is still used for *empty.*[598]

Void became an English word almost three hundred years before *null* was welcomed in from Old French, and during that time the gap between *empty* and *nothing* gradually narrowed. From its earliest thirteenth-century use to refer to a *vacant* church office, *void* called for explanation — ". . . voyde with-oute prelat . . ." Though not in-variably, such appendages continued later in other senses, as ". . . voyde wiþoute kynge . . . ," ". . . voyd and bare," ". . . voyde or emptie," ". . . holowe and voyde . . ." etc.[599] It was an imaginative use of language that converted this notion of emptiness (a ". . . voyd sadyl," for instance) [600] into ineffectiveness at law, and when this oc-curred in the fifteenth century, the draftsman with customary amplifi-cation wrote ". . . to be as voide and of noe valeure." [601] A century later, and it was ". . . woide and of non effect." [602]

[592] Statute of Wills, 1540, 32 Hen. VIII, c. 1; *Davis v. Gardiner,* 24 Eng. Rep. 693, 694 (Ch. 1723); Romilly, M.R., in *Whicker v. Hume,* 51 Eng. Rep. 381, 385 (Rolls Ct. 1851); *Black's Law Dictionary* (4th ed. 1951), under *bequeath.*
[593] *Estes v. Estes,* 200 Miss. 541, 546-547 (1946); compare *Poindexter v. Jones,* 200 Va. 372, 378 (1958).
[594] *Hoague v. Stanley,* 259 Mass. 200, 202-203 (1927); see *Polen v. Baird,* 125 W. Va. 682, 684, 687-688 (1943); 38 *C.J.S. give,* pp. 926, 927.
[595] Leach, "Powers of Appointment," 24 A.B.A.J. 807 (1938); Ritchie, "Draft-ing a Simple Will for a Moderate Sized Estate," 91 Trusts & Estates 724, 725 (1952); *Modern Legal Forms* §9581 and n.78 citing Ritchie (rev. ed. 1957).
[596] Lewis and Short, eds., *A Latin Dictionary* (1879).
[597] *Webster's New International Dictionary* (2d ed. 1934), under *null.*
[598] *Webster's New International Dictionary* (2d ed. 1934), under *void.*
[599] Quoted in *Oxford English Dictionary.*
[600] *Oxford English Dictionary,* under *void,* No. 2.
[601] Quoted in *Oxford English Dictionary,* under *void,* No. 7.
[602] Quoted in *Oxford English Dictionary,* under *void,* No. 7.

Early in the reign of Elizabeth I, *null* — with a long life as a negative in law French and in Latin[603] — became an English synonym for the law's use of *void*.[604] Another hundred years, and *null and void* were a team,[605] *null* taking the place of other explanatory nothingness (no value, no effect) that had often accompanied *void*. The combination stuck, despite frowns in[606] and out of the law.[607]

One of the historic explanations of repetition — the need for emphasis (Section 56) — supplies no present excuse for *null and void*. Worse than useless because of its beguiling sham, *null and void* does nothing to make voidness more emphatic.[608] While continuing to use it — especially in bonds,[609] options,[610] and on occasions of forfeiture[611] — the profession is in agreement with the lay authorities[612] that *null and void* together mean the same as either of the words separately.[613] And the phrase does nothing to avoid the confusion between *void* and *voidable*, Mr. Justice Holmes — among others — holding that in context *null and void*, like *void* alone, can mean *voidable*.[614]

Instead of strengthening the sense, *null and void* waters down whatever meaning there is in either of the words. *Null* has already been so weakened in the law by reliance on the association that its primary

[603] Magna Carta, pars. 8, 12, 16, 20, 22, 38, 39, 40, in Stubbs, ed., *Select Charters* 296, 298, 299, 301 (8th ed. 1905); *Vaus v. Babraham*, Y.B. Easter, 1 Edw. II (1308), 17 Selden Society 14 (1903); *Anon.*, Y.B., 2 Edw. II (1308-1309), 17 Selden Society 70 (1903); Extract from Record: De Banco Roll, Mich., 2 Edw. II (No. 173), r. 247d, Bed. (1308-1309), 17 Selden Society 84 (1903); Coke, *Commentary upon Littleton,* f. 3a (10th ed. 1703); see also *Black's Law Dictionary* 1215-1217 (4th ed. 1951).

[604] *Oxford English Dictionary,* under *null,* No. 1.

[605] *Oxford English Dictionary,* under *null,* No. 1b.

[606] Dickerson, *Legislative Drafting* 76 (1954).

[607] Partridge, *A Dictionary of Clichés* (4th ed. 1950).

[608] Compare Simon, "English Idioms from the Law," 76 L.Q. Rev. 283 (1960).

[609] Nichols, *Cyclopedia of Legal Forms* §§2.897, 2. 898a, and compare §§2.898, 2.890 (1956).

[610] Nichols, *Cyclopedia of Legal Forms* §7.496, and compare §7.495 (1936).

[611] Nichols, *Cyclopedia of Legal Forms* §§7.271, 7.272, 7.273A, 7.275A and C, and compare §§7.274, 7.275B, 7.273B (1936).

[612] *Webster's New International Dictionary,* under *null,* No. 1, *null and void,* and *void,* No. 7; *Oxford English Dictionary,* under *null,* No. 1b, *void,* No. 7.

[613] *Forrester & MacGinniss v. Boston & Montana Consolidated Copper & Silver Mining Co.*, 29 Mont. 397, 403 (1904); Ballentine, *Law Dictionary with Pronunciations* (2d ed. 1948), under *invalid, null, null and void, void; Black's Law Dictionary* (4th ed. 1951), under *null, void;* Jowitt, gen. ed., *The Dictionary of English Law* (1959), under *null and void, void;* and see 28A *Words and Phrases* (perm. ed. 1955), "null and void."

[614] *Stewart v. Griffith*, 217 U.S. 323, 329 (1910); see also *Soeker v. Kerr*, 202 Mo. App. 22, 27 (1919); 66 *C.J.S. null,* pp. 982-983; Ballentine, *Law Dictionary with Pronunciations* (2d ed. 1948), under *null and void, void; Black's Law Dictionary* (4th ed. 1951), under *null, void;* 28A *Words and Phrases* (perm. ed. 1955), "null and void."

meaning (*void*) [615] is not generally appreciated, and it is rarely used alone. To the inveterate word doubler, *void* alone seems a weak dose. After a time, *null and void* too fails to satisfy the word craving, so it becomes *totally null and void.*[616] And in extreme cases, doubles are heaped upon doubles, with *null and void and of no further force and effect.*[617] (See *force and effect* in this list.) What started out as a mild addiction to an old fashion — synonym for the sake of synonym — is caught up in a degenerative search for absolutes (Section 129) with no end in sight.

Because *void* itself is not a word of precision, meaning will often be made clearer if the effect of what is loosely called *void* is described in detail. When an accustomed contact with the law cannot be ignored, e.g., *void marriage,*[618] *void contract,*[619] saying *void, not voidable* will sometimes help. Whatever the weaknesses of *void, null and void* is no improvement.

Rest, residue, and remainder

Each of these words is a French way of referring to a leftover.

The fact that another kind of *remainder* is a particular sort of leftover[620] has recently inspired the specious explanation that *rest, residue, and remainder* somehow has some of the technicality of vested and contingent *remainders.*[621] And the fact that another kind of *rest* is Old English could at one time have furnished some reason for explaining that this was French residue *rest,* not English take-a-rest *rest.* (Section 37.)

It is far more likely that *rest, residue, and remainder* got that way from the ancient fashion of joining synonyms (Sections 70, 71), and stayed that way — and in that order — because of its appealing rhythm. (Section 30.) The first use of this tripled leftover has not been established, but the doubling is hundreds of years old and some of the earliest datings have nothing to do with the law. In the four-

---

[615] *Webster's New International Dictionary* (2d ed. 1934).

[616] Williams, "Language and the Law," 61 L.Q. Rev. 71, 76 (1945).

[617] Nichols, *Cyclopedia of Legal Forms* §7.496B (1936).

[618] 44 *Words and Phrases* (perm. ed. 1940, Supp. 1962); *Black's Law Dictionary* (4th ed. 1951).

[619] 44 *Words and Phrases* (perm. ed. 1940, Supp. 1962); 4 *California Words, Phrases, and Maxims* (1960); *Black's Law Dictionary* (4th ed. 1951).

[620] Coke, *Commentary upon Littleton,* f. 49a (10th ed. 1703); *Black's Law Dictionary* (4th ed. 1951); see Section 89.

[621] Mitgang, "It's Legal — But Is It English?" N.Y. Times Sunday Magazine 73, 76 (Nov. 13, 1960).

teenth century there is ". . . Residue and . . . remenaunt . . ." [622] (another synonym from French); in the sixteenth "Rest or resydue . . .";[623] and in seventeenth-century arithmetic ". . . the rest or remaine . . ." [624]

Rest, residue, and remainder has for years been a traditional law form, but even some of the formbooks which keep it active[625] say that it is not necessary,[626] and it has never been a standard of technical precision. Since the changeover from written Latin to written English (Sections 51, 80) made *residuum* less popular (though not dead),[627] writers have been using the widest range of words — in and out of wills — to refer to the leftovers of property. In the fifteenth century, some English testators used single words — *remainder,*[628] *remenent,*[629] *residue,*[630] *overplus.*[631] A sixteenth-century statute speaks of ". . . the Remain and Overplus . . . ," [632] just as the seventeenth century preached about ". . . the residuum or overplus . . ." of "corruption," [633] and in the next century Blackstone wrote that ". . . the surplus or *residuum* must be paid to the residuary legatee . . ." [634] The seventeenth century's master conveyancer used *all the rest and residue* in a living trust,[635] and the popular eighteenth-century *Bacon's Abridgment* alternates that phrase[636] with *rest, residue, and remainder.*[637]

Today's formbooks offer the flattery of a form to almost any whim

[622] *Oxford English Dictionary,* under *residue,* No. 1.
[623] *Oxford English Dictionary,* under *rest,* sb.[2], No. 4.
[624] *Oxford English Dictionary,* under *rest,* sb.[2], No. 1c.
[625] *Am. Jur. Legal Forms* 13:1771-13:1776, 13:2141, 13:2143 (1955), 13:2147.1, 13:2164.1 (Supp. 1962); Nichols, *Cyclopedia of Legal Forms* §§9.1433A, 9.1436B, 9.1437, 9.1439A and D (1936); *Murphy's Will Clauses,* Forms 5:52-5:54 (1961); Neuhoff, *Standard Clauses for Wills,* Class 20 (rev. ed. 1958).
[626] 13 *Am. Jur. Legal Forms* 838 (1955); 9 Nichols, *Cyclopedia of Legal Forms* 549 n.28 (1936); see also 69 *C.J. wills* §1473, p. 414; see also 4 *California Words, Phrases, and Maxims* (1960), "rest, residue, and remainder."
[627] See, for example, 37 *Words and Phrases* (perm. ed. 1950, Supp. 1962); 4 *California Words, Phrases, and Maxims* (1960); *Black's Law Dictionary* (4th ed. 1951).
[628] *Oxford English Dictionary,* under *remainder,* No. 1.
[629] *Oxford English Dictionary,* under *remenant,* No. 2.
[630] *Oxford English Dictionary,* under *residue,* No. 2.
[631] *Oxford English Dictionary,* under *overplus.*
[632] Quoted in *Oxford English Dictionary,* under *remain,* sb.[1], No. 2.
[633] Quoted in *Oxford English Dictionary,* under *residuum,* No. 1.
[634] 2 Blackstone, *Commentaries* *514 (Jones ed. 1916), quoted in *Oxford English Dictionary,* under *residuum,* No. 2; see also Jacob, *A New Law-Dictionary* (6th ed. 1750), under *residuary legatee.*
[635] *Sir Orlando Bridgman's Conveyances* 128, 131 (1682).
[636] 7 Bacon, *A New Abridgment of the Law* 324, 326, 342n (Gwillim, 5th ed. 1798).
[637] 7 Bacon, *A New Abridgment of the Law* 325, 355 (Gwillim, 5th ed. 1798).

of the most whimsical draftsman. Apart from *rest, residue, and remainder*, you can find *residue* alone;[638] *remainder* alone;[639] *rest* alone;[640] the combinations *residue and remainder*[641] and *remainder and residue*;[642] *rest and remainder*[643] and *rest and residue*;[644] variations within the same form, such as *rest* in one sentence, *residue* in another,[645] etc. In the cases, even the Americanism *balance*[646] — scorned by British grammarians[647] — has been recognized as an additional synonym on both sides of the Atlantic and Pacific.[648]

The sense of all of this language is not hard to find, and it need not be clothed in the bogus technicality of *rest, residue, and remainder*. Mechanical formula can only serve to distract the draftsman from attention to genuine technicality, such as — for example — the exercise of powers of appointment.[649] *Remainder* by itself has a better function to serve in the law of contingent and vested remainders. But *residue* is both adequate and clear to dispose of the leftovers of what the testator owned at his death,[650] and *rest* will also fill the bill.[651] None of the words of formula is essential. If *all other property* is what the testator is talking about, that is enough.[652]

[638] *Am. Jur. Legal Forms* 13:1778, 13:2144 (1955); Nichols, *Cyclopedia of Legal Forms* §§9.1432B, 9.1434A, 9.1435, 9.1438 (1936); see also 37 *Words and Phrases* (perm. ed. 1950, Supp. 1962).

[639] *Murphy's Will Clauses,* Form 5:54 (1961); Nichols, *Cyclopedia of Legal Forms* §9.1439C (1936); see also 36A *Words and Phrases* 496, 497, 499, 503-505 (perm. ed. 1962), "remainder."

[640] Rabkin and Johnson, *Current Legal Forms,* Form 8.30(b) (1961); *Am. Jur. Legal Forms* 13:2172 (1955); see also 37A *Words and Phrases* (perm. ed. 1950), "rest."

[641] Nichols, *Cyclopedia of Legal Forms* §§9.1439B, 9.1443 (1936).

[642] *Am. Jur. Legal Forms* 13:2168, 13:2170 (1955).

[643] *Am. Jur. Legal Forms* 13:2169 (1955).

[644] *Am. Jur. Legal Forms* 13:2171 (1955); *Murphy's Will Clauses,* Form 5:54 (1961); Nichols, *Cyclopedia of Legal Forms* §§9.1432A, 9.1440 (1936); see also 37A *Words and Phrases* (perm. ed. 1950, Supp. 1962), "rest and residue."

[645] Rabkin and Johnson, *Current Legal Forms,* Form 8.30(e) (1961).

[646] *A Dictionary of American English* (1938), under *balance,* No. 3.

[647] Fowler, *A Dictionary of Modern English Usage* (3d ed. 1937); compare Evans and Evans, *A Dictionary of Contemporary American Usage* (1957).

[648] 5 *Words and Phrases* (perm. ed. 1940, Supp. 1962); 1 *Words and Phrases: Judicially Defined* (1946); see also 5 *Words and Phrases* (perm. ed. 1940, Supp. 1962), "balance and residue . . ."

[649] See Leach, "Powers of Appointment," 24 A.B.A.J. 807 (1938).

[650] 37 *Words and Phrases* (perm. ed. 1950, Supp. 1962); 4 *California Words, Phrases, and Maxims* (1960); 4 *Words and Phrases: Judicially Defined* (perm. ed. 1944, Supp. 1958).

[651] *Casey v. Genter,* 276 Mass. 165, 171 (1931); see Leach, "Powers of Appointment," 24 A.B.A.J. 807, 811; see also note 640.

[652] *Sullivan v. Larkin,* 60 Kan. 545 (1899); Leach, *Cases and Text on the Law of Wills* 258 (par. VII) (2d ed. 1947); and see related expressions in *Equitable Trust Co. v. Delaware Trust Co.,* 30 Del. Ch. 348, 371 (1948); *Moffett v.*

124. *The pattern of two-words-for-one*

Legal tradition still makes it fashionable to use many phrases made up of synonyms (Sections 121-123, 27, 70, 71), and the repetition of these phrases accustoms the profession to the unprecise pattern of two-words-for-one. From the cases, from forms, from discussion in and out of court, doubled words insinuate themselves into the lawyer's subconscious. If a young lawyer is sufficiently steeped in *last will and testament, mind and memory, rest, residue, and remainder, force and effect, fit and proper, give, devise, and bequeath, null and void* (Section 123), etc., he soon comes to the conclusion that the proper lawyer which is the precise lawyer speaks mouthfuls. If the mature lawyer uses these phrases sufficiently long, pride rationalizes habit into conviction.

How is it possible to stop at *void* [653] when so many lawyers have for so long plunged on into *null and void?* What difference does it make that *null and void* is ridiculed as a cliché? [654] This is the way a lawyer says it; this is precise, no nonsense — *null and void.* And in this prideful vein, even more lawyerly, more precise, more emphatic is *null and void and of no further force and effect.*

True, there have been lawyers — even great ones — who have found means of emphasizing *void* in ways that no doubling of synonym or cliché could ever match. This, for example, from the lips of a seventeenth-century Lord Chancellor:

> It is a very hard Thing for a Son to tell his Father, that the Provision he has made for his younger Brothers is void in Law, but it is much harder for him to tell him so in Chancery. And if such a Provision be void, it had need be void with a Vengeance; it need be so clearly void, that it ought to be a Prodigy [a monstrous thing] if it be not submitted to.[655]

This is nice, but it is not stock, and some will dismiss it as "literary." Besides, there is not much of it around, and we write by what we read.

The drafting lawyer thinks big and fast. He wants to cover it all, and the quickest way to do it is in the manner it has most often been

---

Elmendorff, 152 N.Y. 475, 488 (1897); *Cogswell v. Armstrong,* 69 Eng. Rep. 764 (Ch. 1855).

[653] See, for example, Leach, "Perpetuities in Perspective: Ending the Rule's Reign of Terror," 65 Harv. L. Rev. 721, 731, 732 (1952).

[654] Partridge, *A Dictionary of Clichés* (4th ed. 1950).

[655] Lord Nottingham, in *The Duke of Norfolk's Case,* 22 Eng. Rep. 931, 953 (Ch. 1681).

done before, in the manner he is most familiar with. Include! Don't select. Adopt and multiply! Don't choose between *inhabitant* and *resident*. Make it *inhabitant actually resident*.[656]

A judge ponders a badly drawn paragraph of the Copyright Act — a single sentence:

> In case of failure of such manufacturer to pay to the copyright proprietor within thirty days after demand in writing the full sum of royalties due at said rate at the date of such demand, the court may award taxable costs to the plaintiff and a reasonable counsel fee, and the court may, in its discretion, enter judgment therein for any sum *in addition over* the amount found to be due as royalty in accordance with the terms of this title, not exceeding three times such amount. [Emphasis supplied.] [657]

How shall he phrase his determination to award the something additional? Shall he leave it at:

a royalty . . . plus treble damages?

Or shall it be enriched with English synonym of the cliché *over and above*[658] to make it:

treble damages over and above the . . . royalty?

Ah, but there is another — a French synonym. Interpretively plucked from the statute, *addition* might swell the chorus into a resounding:

treble damages . . . over, above, and in addition to the . . . royalty.

Which shall it be?

In the practice, no choice is made. The opinion quotes the statute, uses all three of the alternate phrasings, and repeats the flowing redundancy *over, above, and in addition to*.[659]

Here is a piece of paper with some writing on it. There is no tight definition that will tell us without fail when this paper becomes an *instrument*. Yet on one point there is agreement: without the writing the paper cannot be an *instrument*.[660] Sometimes lawyers will call

---

[656] See Section 104; U. S. Congress, *Documents Illustrative of the Formation of the Union* 492-494 (1927); and see 21 *Words and Phrases* 691-696 (perm. ed. 1960), "inhabit."

[657] 17 U.S.C. §1(e).

[658] Partridge, *A Dictionary of Clichés* (4th ed. 1950); compare *Oxford English Dictionary;* see 30 *Words and Phrases* (perm. ed. 1940), "over and above . . ."; 21A *Words and Phrases* 188 (perm. ed. 1960), "in lieu of."

[659] *ABC Music Corp. v. Janov*, 186 F. Supp. 443, 445, 446, 447, 448 (S.D. Cal. 1960).

[660] *Rich v. Ervin*, 86 Cal. App. 2d 386, 391-392 (1948); see *Rose v. Otis*, 5 Colo. App. 472, 473 (1895); Ballentine, *Law Dictionary with Pronunciations* (2d

this piece of paper an *instrument*,[661] but as often they will call it an *instrument in writing*[662] or a *written instrument*,[663] somewhat less frequently an *instrument of writing*.[664] And often they will call it by the one word and also by one of the longer phrases on the same piece of paper,[665] as though the sense had suddenly changed.

Why do they slip so easily from one to the other?

Because the words mean the same thing.[666]

Why then ever use phrases like *written instrument?* Is it to avoid confusion with *musical instrument*, so that no one will think you are talking about a French horn when you mean a lease? Is it to avoid arguments like that made in *State v. Nelson*,[667] that ". . . medicinal

---

ed. 1948); *Black's Law Dictionary* (4th ed. 1951); Jowitt, gen. ed., *The Dictionary of English Law* (1959).

[661] Cal. Civ. Code §§1169, 1170, 1172, 1180-1183.5, 1188, 1189, 1218, 1628, 3413, 3414; Iowa Code Ann. §556.17 (1950); Mass. Gen. Laws Ann., c. 36, §§12-15, §§20-23 (1961), and see c. 106, §3-102 (Supp. 1958); Minn. Stat. Ann. §555.02 (1947); N.J. Stat. Ann. §§46:14-3 (1940), 46:14-4 (1940, Supp. 1961), 46:16-1 (1940, Supp. 1961), 46-16-2 (1940), 46:16-5.1 (Supp. 1961); N.M. Stat. Ann. §§71-1-9, 71-1-10, 71-2-2, 71-2-4, 71-2-6 (1953); Wash. Rev. Code §9.44.060 (1956); Nichols, *Cyclopedia of Legal Forms* §§3.04 (Supp. 1956), 3.26 (1936), 8.285 (Supp. 1956), 8.320, 8.321 (1936).

[662] Cal. Civ. Code §§164, 1158(f), 1220, 3415; Cal. Civ. Proc. Code §337(1); N.J. Stat. Ann. §46:14-2 (1940, Supp. 1961); N.M. Stat. Ann. 71-2-3 (1953); *State v. Morse*, 38 Wash. 2d 927, 928 (1951); Nichols, *Cyclopedia of Legal Forms* §§1.1200 (1936), 2.780, 2.894 (1956).

[663] Cal. Civ. Code §§1614, 3412; Cal. Civ. Proc. Code §1962(2); Iowa Code Ann. §§556.1, 556.3 (1950); Mass. Gen. Laws Ann., c. 215, §6 (1955, Supp. 1961); Minn. Stat. Ann. §620.06 (1947); N.J. Stat. Ann. §46:15-3 (1940); 3 Nichols, *Cyclopedia of Legal Forms* §3.36 n.59, §3.38c, §3.55 n.93, §3.134 n.4, 3.137, 3.141 n.12 (Supp. 1956).

[664] N.M. Stat. Ann. §71-1-3 (1953); *Little v. Hilliard*, 117 Colo. 163, 165-166 (1947); *Hawley v. Barker*, 5 Colo. 118, 120 (1879); *Stephens Co. v. Lisk*, 240 N.C. 289, 293 (1954).

[665] Compare Cal. Civ. Code §1219 with §1220; compare Iowa Code Ann. §§556.1, 556.3 with §556.17 (1950); compare N.M. Stat. Ann. §§71-1-3, 71-1-5 with §71-1-10 (1953); Wash. Rev. Code §7.24.020 (1956); *Rose v. Otis*, 5 Colo. App. 472, 473 (1895); *Stephens Co. v. Lisk*, 240 N.C. 289, 293 (1954); 3 Nichols, *Cyclopedia of Legal Forms* §3.38c, and compare §3.36 n.59 with §3.38 n.68 (Supp. 1956).

[666] Under *instrument* in Ballentine, *Law Dictionary with Pronunciations* (2d ed. 1948); *Black's Law Dictionary* (4th ed. 1951); Jowitt, gen. ed., *The Dictionary of English Law* (1959); 21A *Words and Phrases* (perm. ed. 1960, Supp. 1962); 2 *California Words, Phrases, and Maxims* (1960); 3 *Words and Phrases: Judicially Defined* (1944).

Under *written instrument* in *Black's Law Dictionary* (4th ed. 1951); 45 *Words and Phrases* (perm. ed. 1940, Supp. 1962); 4 *California Words, Phrases, and Maxims* (1960); 5 *Words and Phrases: Judicially Defined* (1945); see also 21A *Words and Phrases* (perm. ed. 1960, Supp. 1962), "*instrument in writing*," "*instrument of writing*."

[667] 126 Conn. 412 (1940).

article or instrument for the purpose of preventing conception . . ." [668] might include a calendar used in the " 'rhythm system' "? [669]

Not at all. It is rather because we are dealing here not with the precise but the traditional. When lawyers give the wording some attention, they sometimes cut it short; for *instrument* is enough, easier to use consistently, and also has the sanction of history. [670]

But when their ears are not plugged against the ancient calls to verbosity — "ritual," "necessity," "fashion," "sanctioned," "precise," "safe" (see Part Two) — lawyers forget that one word will do, and fall under the spell of the centuries. Then come the words, the repetitions. Not *instrument* but *written instrument*, the law's mural on the wall.

125. The tradition of the long sentence: punctuation

Traditional imprecise words (Sections 119-123) and a traditional imprecise pattern of two-words-for-one (Section 124) have been carried into the twentieth century imbedded in the long sentence. [671] There are only two cures for the long sentence:

(1) Say less;

(2) Put a period in the middle.

Neither expedient has taken hold in the law.

The problem of lawyers saying too much is discussed in Chapter XIV. Right here let it be noted that the frequent complaint that lawyers and their long sentences are wordy (Section 114) focuses on only one part of the problem. It is at least as important that the long sentence is not precise, and can usually be made more precise by being chopped up and punctuated.

A characteristic lack of adequate punctuation is a major obstacle to precision in legal writing, and has been for centuries. Occasionally this lack may be traced to ignorance [672] or carelessness. [673] More often it is not accidental but deliberate, part of the tradition of legal

---

[668] *State v. Nelson,* 126 Conn. 412, 415 n.1 (1940).

[669] *State v. Nelson,* 126 Conn. 412, 427 (1940).

[670] *Oxford English Dictionary,* under *instrument,* sb., No. 5; West, *The First Part of Symboleography,* compare §1 with §§48, 49, 51, 52, 53 (ed. 1598).

[671] See examples in Sections 20, 91.

[672] For example: *Estate of Williams,* 113 Cal. App. 2d 895, 898 (1952); *Estate of Deering,* 29 Hawaii 854, 856 (1927).

[673] *Scott v. Powell,* 182 F.2d 75, 80 (D.C. Cir. 1950); *In re Schilling,* 53 Fed. 81, 83 (2d Cir. 1892); *Estate of Jones,* 55 Cal. 2d 531, 534 (1961), and see opinion in 9 Cal. Rptr. 126 (1960); see also *Baker v. Morrison,* 80 So.2d 805, 806-807 (Fla. 1956); *In re Potolsky's Estate,* 9 Misc. 2d 326, 327 (N.Y. Surr. 1957); and compare *In re Miller's Will,* 202 Misc. 763, 764-765 (N.Y. Surr. 1951).

composition. And both the ignorance and the carelessness have been fostered by the traditional injunctions to ignore punctuation. (Sections 82, 83, 84, 106.)

The evil stems from the false dictum that *Punctuation is no part of the statute*,[674] and has spread through all manner of law writings under the catchy but irrelevant slogan, *Punctuation is no part of the English language*.[675] The notion that words should stand by their own strength has been encouraged by professional grammarians of the "open" or "light" school of punctuation. Its most literate exponents have laid it down as ". . . sound principle that as few stops should be used as will do the work." [676] This has been restated for the lawyer-draftsman as: "In general punctuate no more than is necessary for understanding." [677] These "principles" have been reinforced by fear and flattery. It has been said that words are "masculine," punctuation marks are "feminine," [678] and "A good draftsman is able to express intention without their aid." [679]

All of these comments could be taken merely as warnings against sloppy writing and overpunctuation. But coupled with the law's traditional disdain for the art, they have been accepted as putting a curse on punctuation. It is something to be indulged in furtively, and only behind a very thick screen of words.

Lawyers are still reluctant to end a sentence, even though the old reasons for skimping on punctuation are gone. The ancient oral basis of punctuation as an aid to speakers and listeners — with ultimate appeal to the ear — has yielded to punctuation directed to the eye. Punctuation-for-pause — accepted by Noah Webster (Section 106) — is displaced by punctuation-for-meaning in the unabridged second edition of his famous dictionary.[680] In a world of general literacy where punctuation is the rule, the former unfamiliarity with the marks of punctuation has been supplanted by mass recognition. It is futile to insist that punctuation is an undesirable crutch when every schoolboy

---

[674] See Sections 83, 106; *contra: Commissioners v. Ellwood*, 193 Ill. 304, 308 (1901).

[675] *Holmes v. Phenix Ins. Co.*, 98 Fed. 240, 241 (8th Cir. 1899); *Clinton v. Miller*, 124 Mont. 463, 472 (1951); see 1 *Words and Phrases: Judicially Defined* 28 (par. 69) and compare 28-29 (pars. 70, 71) (1946).

[676] [Fowler and Fowler], *The King's English* 225 (1906).

[677] *A Uniform System of Citation* 102 (§37) (10th ed. 1958).

[678] Lavery, "Punctuation in the Law," 9 A.B.A.J. 225 and 228 (1923).

[679] 1 *Words and Phrases: Judicially Defined* 28 (par. 69) (1946).

[680] *Webster's New International Dictionary* (2d ed. 1934), under *punctuation;* compare *Webster's Third New International Dictionary* (1961), "Punctuation," pp. 48a-51a and especially 48a, pars. 0.1-0.4, and see also under *punctuation* at 1843.

has drilled into him the desirability of good punctuation. And it is dangerous for lawyers to believe that punctuation is ever really ignored. Can anyone — even a judge — accustomed to rely on punctuation in every other scrap of writing avoid being influenced by punctuation or the lack of it in the law?

A completely unpunctuated document is a rarity. When a court makes its preliminary determination that a writing is clear or ambiguous or worse, it has already consciously or not taken note of the marks that are there and the marks that are missing. As an experienced trial judge once remarked of his earlier encounters with the same litigants, a recollection that troubled him on motion for a mistrial, "I can strike it from the record, but I cannot strike it from my mind." [681]

Whether the punctuation is decisive or not, it is irrevocably in the record. Even when judges say that punctuation may be disregarded, they notice its presence and absence. Here one observes that a dispute ". . . is brought about largely by the punctuation . . ." [682] Another, years ago:

> The question would doubtless never have arisen had there been a comma inserted . . . thereby rendering the meaning too obvious for doubt or cavil. [683]

Even while paying lip service to the traditional abhorrence of punctuation, a court makes a sidling appeal to its authority.

> While it is true that punctuation is no part of a writing, it also may not be amiss to point out that there is no semi-colon separating the two portions of the sentence in question. [684]

The tug of the past is so strong that few courts will come right out and confess that the traditional snobbery toward punctuation has made a mess of legal writing. Instead we are treated to exercises in gamesmanship demonstrating how to ignore punctuation while really using it. The attempt to generalize rules out of the conflict between tradition and current mores [685] results in a higgledy-piggledy of double-talk, something like this:

Punctuation is ". . . always subordinate to the text, and is never

---

[681] Personal recall.
[682] *Snyder v. City of Alameda*, 58 Cal. App. 2d 517, 519 (1943).
[683] *Shriedley v. Ohio*, 23 Ohio St. 130, 140 (1872).
[684] *Randall v. Bailey*, 288 N.Y. 280, 287 (1942).
[685] For example: 12 *Am. Jur. contracts* §256, pp. 799-800; 17 *C.J.S. contracts* §306, p. 723; 10 Ann. Cas. 1080-1085.

allowed to control its meaning," [686] except when punctuation is dominant, and controls the meaning as it may ". . . in case of ambiguity . . ." [687] As a matter of fact, meaning should follow ". . . that indicated by the punctuation unless as punctuated the statute is inconsistent, absurd, or ambiguous." [688] Punctuation ". . . may always be disregarded . . ." [689] except when it must be regarded, as when disregarding it would ". . . create an ambiguity . . ." [690] or when supplying it helps in ". . . clearing up an ambiguity . . ." [691] At any rate, punctuation may be ". . . disregarded when necessary to ascertain the true intent and meaning," [692] but it may be ". . . resorted to when it tends to throw [or 'shed'] [693] light upon the meaning . . ." [694] In other words, ignore punctuation where without it the meaning is "obvious" [695] or "plain," [696] or the punctuation is ". . . not consistent with the general meaning and object . . ." [697] or "'. . . conflicts with the manifest intention . . .'" [698] At the same time, the ". . . manifest limitation . . ." of punctuation cannot be ignored even in the face of patent mistake, for that would change the ". . . manifest meaning of a statute . . ." [699]

This gibberish may not be dismissed as a compendium of conflict between jurisdictions or different ages. This is not a problem that can be resolved by counting cases and separating states into majority and minority rules. There are conflicting expositions in the same

[686] *Holmes v. Phenix Ins. Co.*, 98 Fed. 240, 242 (8th Cir. 1899); see *Stoddart v. Golden*, 179 Cal. 663, 664 (1919); *Snyder v. City of Alameda*, 58 Cal. App. 2d 517, 519 (1943); *Clinton v. Miller*, 124 Mont. 463, 472 (1951).

[687] *Travelers Indemnity Co. v. Pray*, 204 F.2d 821, 824 (6th Cir. 1953), and compare dissent at 825.

[688] *Baker v. Morrison*, 86 So.2d 805, 807 (Fla. 1956).

[689] *Shriedley v. Ohio*, 23 Ohio St. 130, 140 (1872).

[690] *Western Empire Petroleum Co. v. Davenport*, 318 S.W.2d 903, 905 (Tex. Civ. App. 1958) (writ of error refused).

[691] *Estate of Deering*, 29 Hawaii 854, 861 (1927).

[692] *Snyder v. City of Alameda*, 58 Cal. App. 2d 517, 519-520 (1943); see *Haskell v. United States*, 241 F.2d 790, 792 (10th Cir. 1957), *cert. denied*, 354 U.S. 921 (1957); *Slaten v. Travelers Ins. Co.*, 197 Ga. 1, 9 (1943); *In re Potolsky's Estate*, 9 Misc. 2d 326, 327 (N.Y. Surr. 1957).

[693] *Allen v. United States Fidelity & Guaranty Co.*, 269 Ill. 234, 239 (1915); *Osborn v. Farwell*, 87 Ill. 89, 91 (1877).

[694] *Georgiades v. Glickman*, 272 Wis. 257, 264 (1955); see *Lunt v. Aetna Life Ins. Co.*, 253 Mass. 610, 616 (1925).

[695] See *Holmes v. Phenix Ins. Co.*, 98 Fed. 240, 242 (8th Cir. 1899).

[696] *Osborn v. Farwell*, 87 Ill. 89, 91 (1877).

[697] *Jones v. Santa Cruz Co.*, 72 Ariz. 374, 377 (1951).

[698] Quoted in *Estate of Deering*, 29 Hawaii 854, 861 (1927).

[699] *In re Schilling*, 53 Fed. 81, 83-84 (2d Cir. 1892).

state,[700] the same court,[701] the same opinion,[702] even in the same sentence:

> In construing legal writings, generally the punctuation is subordinate to the text and the use of a period or other mark is not controlling upon the question of proper construction where such use would result in an unreasonable or absurd construction.[703]

Fortunately, an ancient spark of forthright professional interest in punctuation (Section 84) burns brighter every day. The old untruth that "punctuation is no part of the statute" has been directly and repeatedly challenged, here in the words of a Maine judge, early in this century:

> There is no reason why punctuation, which is intended to and does assist in making clear and plain the meaning of all things in the English language, should be rejected in the case of the interpretation of statutes.[704]

More and more, judges are giving open consideration to the marks of punctuation to see how they work with or against a proposed interpretation.[705] Professors of English have even been called to testify to the effect of punctuation.[706] The influence of punctuation is sometimes still rejected,[707] occasionally — in a hard case — violently,[708] just as words and spellings sometimes are.[709] But peculiar though some of the expressions of regard may be, there is growing inclination

[700] Compare *Estate of Jones*, 9 Cal. Rptr. 126, 128 (1960), with opinion in 55 Cal. 2d 531, 535-536 (1961), and both with *Snyder v. City of Alameda*, 58 Cal. App. 2d 517, 519-520 (1943), and see dissent at 527; compare *Baker v. Morrison*, 86 So.2d 805, 806-807 (Fla. 1956), with dictum in *Florida State Racing Commission v. Bourquardez*, 42 So.2d 87, 88 (Fla. 1949); compare *In re Miller's Will*, 202 Misc. 763, 764-765 (N.Y. Surr. 1951), with *In re Potolsky's Estate*, 9 Misc. 2d 326, 327 (N.Y. Surr. 1957).

[701] Compare *Baker v. Morrison*, 86 So.2d 805, 806-807 (Fla. 1956), with *Wagner v. Botts*, 88 So.2d 611, 613 (Fla. 1956).

[702] *Baker v. Morrison*, 86 So.2d 805, 807 (Fla. 1956).

[703] *Johnson v. Flex-O-Lite Mfg. Corp.*, 314 S.W.2d 75, 84 (Mo. 1958).

[704] *Taylor v. Caribou*, 102 Me. 401, 406 (1907); see also *Commissioners v. Ellwood*, 193 Ill. 304, 308 (1901).

[705] *Bill Curphy Co. v. Elliott*, 207 F.2d 103, 106 (5th Cir. 1953); *Ex parte Garrett*, 262 Ala. 25, 28 (1954); *Estate of Jones*, 55 Cal. 2d 531, 536 (1961), and see opinion in 9 Cal. Rptr. 126, 128 (1960); *West Hartford v. Thos. D. Faulkner Co.*, 126 Conn. 206, 210 (1940); *Wagner v. Botts*, 88 So.2d 611, 613 (Fla. 1956); *Lunt v. Aetna Life Ins. Co.*, 253 Mass. 610, 615-616 (1925); *Stephens Co. v. Lisk*, 240 N.C. 289, 293-295 (1954).

[706] *Leteff v. Maryland Casualty Co.*, 91 So.2d 123, 140-142 (La. 1956).

[707] For example: *Scott v. Powell*, 182 F.2d 75, 80 (D.C. Cir. 1950); *Jones v. Santa Cruz Co.*, 72 Ariz. 374, 376-377 (1951).

[708] *Clinton v. Miller*, 124 Mont. 463, 471-473 (1951).

[709] 1 *Words and Phrases: Judicially Defined* 32 (par. 79), 40-41 (par. 96) (1946); see Dickerson, *Legislative Drafting* 70 n.4 (1954).

.. to treat the rules of punctuation on a parity with other rules of interpretation." [710]

With courts accepting a view of punctuation more consonant with the common teachings of our day, there is less reason than ever for the long sentence. No twentieth-century lawyer need be reluctant to compose a paragraph with more than one period. The profession may now gracefully acknowledge what has always been true: that the tradition of the long sentence places too great a strain on hurried draftsmanship. A master craftsman may so weave a one-sentence paragraph that it becomes a thing of precision, clarity, and even beauty. No participles dangle, each remote reference is tied to its proper antecedent, each clause so sharply phrased that what is subordinate bows in humble submission to a harmonious and precise whole. What busy lawyer can work such a tapestry?

Consider the relative precision of the shorter sentence. Take note of the Wandering Afterthought, illustrated in shortened form by the clause:

. . . that shall have been stolen or taken by robbers.[711]

Does *by robbers* limit only *taken* or also *stolen?* This is a problem recognized by some lawyers in the sixteenth century (Section 84), and still troublesome four hundred years later.[712] For example, an employment contract contains this paragraph (here abbreviated):

The term "net income from operations" as used herein means (a) the gross income to employer, . . . less (b) all expenses . . . allowable under the Federal Income Tax Laws . . . less (c) an amount equal to the federal and Wiscon State income taxes . . . , computed as though the employer were a corporation and subject to income taxation as such; . . .[713]

In one sentence instead of two, what does this paragraph mean? What is to be *computed as though?* The case canvasses two of the possibilities.

A trial judge held there was no ambiguity. It meant the same as it would have meant if the sentence had ended before *computed,* and a second sentence had begun: *Item (c) shall be computed as though . . .*

A supreme court reversed, saying the comma before *computed*

710 *Wagner v. Botts,* 88 So.2d 611, 613 (Fla. 1956).
711 *Shriedley v. Ohio,* 23 Ohio St. 130 (1872).
712 *Estate of Jones,* 55 Cal. 2d 531 (1961), and see opinion in 9 Cal. Rptr. 126 (1960); see also *Casey v. Genter,* 276 Mass. 165 (1931).
713 *Georgiades v. Glickman,* 272 Wis. 257, 262 (1955).

made the paragraph ambiguous. It could mean what it would have meant if a second sentence had begun: *Items (b) and (c) shall be computed as though . . .*[714]

True, it is possible to tighten the sense in one good, long sentence, so that an afterthought does not wander, or may even appear to be forethought. But many have failed in the attempt. The Wandering Afterthought is often litigated, sometimes interpreted to apply to everything that precedes it,[715] sometimes to apply only to what immediately precedes it.[716] In *Estate of Jones*[717] the Wandering Afterthought was a roundabout way of saying *for life*, following four gifts to the wife in a one-sentence paragraph of a will. It was decided that the phrase limited only parcel number four; the rest were in fee. And all the while the unfortunate draftsman stood in the wings — waiting and willing — but not permitted to testify that his dead client had given instructions to draw the will so that the wife took only a life estate in all four parcels.

The Wandering Afterthought is related to another vice of long sentence composition — the Cascade of Words. For quick illustration, first observe the vice in its less deadly form — in the short sentence:

> The White Walnut Coal Co. is a corporation engaged in mining and selling coal, its mines and place of business being located at Pinckneyville, Perry County, Illinois. The Crescent Coal and Mining Co. is a corporation engaged in buying and selling coal, located in Chicago, Cook County, Illinois.[718]

Here the Cascade of Words is such that only at the end of the first sentence — like an O'Henry snapper — is the reader reassured that the White Walnut Coal Company is not selling "its mines and place of business." And — except to those who know Cook County best — it remains doubtful whether Crescent or its coal is located in Chicago. The Cascade of Words is so swift that the mind is carried from the beginning of the sentence to the end with confusing suddenness. It is worse in the long sentence.

Here is a litigated one-sentence paragraph:

[714] *Georgiades v. Glickman*, 272 Wis. 257, 263-264 (1955).

[715] *Gray v. General Construction Co.*, 250 S.W. 342, 343-344 (Ark. 1923) (noted without opinion in 158 Ark. 641); *Randall v. Bailey*, 288 N.Y. 280, 287 (1943).

[716] *Holmes v. Phenix Ins. Co.*, 98 Fed. 240 (8th Cir. 1899); *Cushing v. Worrick*, 75 Mass. 382 (1857); *Shriedley v. Ohio*, 23 Ohio St. 130 (1872).

[717] 55 Cal. 2d 531 (1961), and see opinion in 9 Cal. Rptr. 126 (1960).

[718] *White Walnut Coal Co. v. Crescent Coal & Mining Co.*, 254 Ill. 368, 369 (1912).

It is also mutually agreed that the balance of 6,500 acres shall be delivered upon the execution of this agreement with the express agreement that in the event a well is not completed or drilled to a depth of 3,500 feet on or before June 26, 1957, second party will pay rentals thereon; quitclaim to first party all of said acreage, or pay to first party the sum of $5.00 per acre for said leases.[719]

Apart from the choking redundancies — *mutually agreed . . . this agreement . . . express agreement* — the grammatical flow considered as one sentence makes possible the argument that there are three alternatives: rentals, quitclaim, or $5.00 per acre. The argument was twice made, and twice rejected; the sentence — says the appellate court — is unambiguous, its clarity reinforced by the semicolon before *quitclaim.* The paragraph is held to mean the same as if it had read:

> The balance of 6500 leased acres (the "Acreage") shall be delivered upon the execution of this agreement. If before June 27, 1957 a well is not either completed or drilled to a depth of 3500 feet, Western:
> (a) will pay the rental on the Acreage, and in addition
> (b) will either quitclaim the Acreage to Davenport, or pay him for the leases at $5.00 per acre.

An expensive victory for one-sentence draftsmanship and careless punctuation.

Whether it be Wandering Afterthought, Cascade of Words, or some other variety of long sentence involvement,[720] the traditional format of legal composition betrays even competent draftsmen. The pace of the long sentence reflects the pace of the draftsman's own thoughts. Taken at its charitable best, everything is clear to him. In the unrelieved onrush of the long sentence it is difficult to even consider that another may gather the pieces together differently — whether in good faith or bad. Nuance is blurred by merging phrases which give the temporary assurance that everything has been covered.

The breaking up of paragraphs is no automatic guarantee of precision.[721] But the habit of consciously shortening sentences — shorter than tradition dictates — encourages pause, however brief, to take stock of what has been thus far accomplished, to consider the connection between ideas, to fasten down what needs fastening. This process of fastening down is helped along by punctuation, and old prejudices should not be permitted to stand in the way. The emphasis of *as few*

[719] *Western Empire Petroleum Co. v. Davenport,* 318 S.W.2d 903 (Tex. Civ. App. 1958).

[720] See Section 20; see also *Minton v. Cavaney,* 56 Cal. 2d 576, 579 (1961); see also Nichols, *Cyclopedia of Legal Forms* §§1.1749D, 1.1759D (Supp. 1956).

[721] See, for example, *Johnson v. Flex-O-Lite Mfg. Corp.,* 314 S.W.2d 75 (Mo. 1958).

as and *no more than* needs changing. Legal writing cannot be hurt, and it may be improved if we punctuate *as much as* is helpful.[722]

126. The tradition of precision by precedent

Although neither traditional punctuation (Section 125) nor the traditional language of the law (Section 118) originated in collections of cases, another sort of tradition links the language of the law to the cases, and that is the tradition of precedent itself.

From faltering beginnings in the sixteenth and seventeenth centuries (Section 78), the rule of precedent has become the profession's consuming passion. Especially is this true in America, where a democratic itch to keep the people informed, diversity of jurisdiction, and a wildly expanding economy combined to flood the nation with law reports. (Section 110.)

In these ever more mountainous reports, lawyers continue to stalk the elusive law, with a now traditional faith that he who hunts long enough will find the law he wants. No matter that it lurks in some improbable cranny between law and equity, in some remote and dozing jurisdiction, covered with cosmic or atomic dust. Armed with *Shepard's* and a digest, the good lawyer will track down the law, drag it out, and parade it in triumph as a hand-bagged precedent. So strong is this faith that it fires counsel on opposite sides of most issues, and so rich is the accumulation of precedent that usually the faith of each is justified.

The sense in the search is that precedent deals not only with principle but with context. And whatever value there is in having more than a single precedent for any proposition in the law of property, contracts, or torts, arises from context, called in the law's bellowing redundancy — the *surrounding circumstances*.[723] Of these the variety is limitless. No lawyer, and only an unusual client, is shocked to hear it said that negligence is a lack of reasonable care, but there is inexhaustible surprise in the nuance of unreasonableness. It is this nuance, this nice distinction, that the lawyer is looking for, this that sometimes makes the precedent worth the search.

The qualification is important. Only "sometimes." For most of this accumulated circumstance is worthless, making no advance, no contribution to the law or to the lawyer's understanding of the law.

---

[722] Partridge, *You Have a Point There* 102 (1953).

[723] 40 *Words and Phrases* (perm. ed. 1940, Supp. 1962); *California Jury Instructions: Civil,* No. 101 (Revised) (Supp. 1962).

The heaped-up precedents of the substantive law swarm with trivia, with differences without instructive distinction, with repetitions that centuries ago attained the rank of platitude. (Section 131.) Even more so — the precedents for the language of the law.

As a thesaurus of circumstance, case law only rarely makes the pretension of being a dictionary of precise definition. Like soldiers who have been "in the army" but not "in combat," most of the words in the cases have been "in litigation" but not "litigated." (Section 112.) And even when the words themselves are litigated, they have seldom come to rest for more than a moment. With each change of circumstance, they are prodded, stretched, squeezed, and reshaped.

Yet the lawyer's traditional respect for the preserved word encourages him to believe that words uttered in court — as in some ancient temple — are sacrosanct. Blessed with the ritual phrase *stare decisis* (Section 78), they become "precise." It is on the strength of this belief that what is sanctioned by precedent is precise (Section 115), that indifferent scraps of language enjoy an undeserved reputation for precision. Their only claim to distinction — let alone precision — is that someone has tagged them with an official or an unofficial citation.[724]

Visit for a moment that ". . . comprehensive depositary . . . ," that ". . . vast storehouse of judicial definitions . . . ,"[725] known as *Words and Phrases*. (The ninety volumes — in Spring, 1973 — of this useful boneyard of words must be distinguished from the smaller and more selective English publication, *Words and Phrases: Judicially Defined*, and also from the more recent *California Words, Phrases, and Maxims*, which like its English cousin dates the selected cases.) To the extent that the publishers have done a good job, *Words and Phrases* is an impressive demonstration of lack of precision in the language of the law. And this lack of precision is demonstrated by the very device supposed to give law language its precision — precedent. Not everything in *Words and Phrases* is truly precedent. The volumes include expressions from cases long reversed,[726] dictum,[727] and sometimes

[724] See Llewellyn, *The Bramble Bush* 67-68 (ed. 1951); Hancock, "Fallacy of the Transplanted Category," 37 Can. B. Rev. 535-575 (1959).

[725] 1 *Words and Phrases* III (perm. ed. 1940).

[726] For example: 19 *Words and Phrases* 126 (perm. ed. Supp. 1962), "herein," citing "*Owen v. Off*, Cal. App., 218 P.2d 563, 566" (1950), *rev'd*, 36 Cal. 2d 751 (1951), *aff'g* trial court; 38 *Words and Phrases* 7 (perm. ed. Supp. 1962), "said," citing "*Wennerholm v. Stanford University*, Cal. App., 113 P.2d 736, 740" (1941), *rev'd*, 20 Cal. 2d 713, 720 (1942); 45 *Words and Phrases* 71 (perm. ed. 1940), "whereas," citing "*Simpson v. Anderson*, N.J., 70 A. 696, 698," (N.J. Ch. 1908), *rev'd*, 75 N.J. Eq. 581, 584 (1909).

[727] For example: 1 *Words and Phrases* 281 (perm. ed. 1940), "accident," citing

dictum and decision from the same case given equal billing.[728] But what gives *Words and Phrases* its bulk is language that the profession accepts as precedent. Scan these volumes, then, and observe the words with a strong affinity for the law — repeatedly involved in litigation, litigated and relitigated — and still wide open. Examine these words from only one point of view. Are they precise? Are they not merely repeated but exact in meaning? That the words may continue in use, that they may have utility though not precise, is now to one side. For the lawyer interested in knowing what he is doing, it is worth more than a random thought that despite years of precedent a large part of his vocabulary is untouched by precision. A number of these words have been discussed elsewhere, e.g., *and/or* (Section 120), *cancellation* (Section 116), *cause of action* (Sections 13, 116), *forthwith* (Section 120), *heir* (Section 121), *reasonable* (Section 119), *seisin* (Section 121). Here, from many more, are *accident* and *proximate cause*, old and unfaithful in the service of the law, each responsible for more than two thousand citations in *Words and Phrases*.

Accident

The current common understanding harks back to an origin in Classical Latin *accido* (to happen), where its special sense spoke ". . . of occurrences which take us by surprise . . . ," generally ". . . of an unfortunate occurrence." [729] An influential definition has been contributed by the *Oxford English Dictionary:*

> . . . an unusual event, which proceeds from some unknown cause, or is an unusual effect of a known cause; . . .[730]

The vagueness of these words of definition — *surprise, unfortunate, unusual, unknown* — has evoked a common sense skepticism about

---

"*Sloan v. Polar Wave Ice & Fuel Co.*, 19 S.W.2d 476, 481, 323 Mo. 363" (1929); 1 *Words and Phrases* 113 (perm. ed. Supp. 1962), "accident," citing "*Henderson v. Texas-New Mexico Pipe Line Co.*, 131 P.2d 269, 272, 46 N.M. 458" (1942); 2A *Words and Phrases* 386 (perm. ed. 1955), "aforesaid," citing "*In re Dubois' Estate*, 211 P.2d 895, 898, 94 Cal. App. 2d 838" (1949).

[728] For example: 3 *Words and Phrases* 643 (perm. ed. 1953), "and/or" (contracts), citing "*Ex parte Bell*, 122 P.2d 22, 29, 19 Cal. 2d 488"; 3 *Words and Phrases* 645 (perm. ed. 1953), "and/or" (ordinances), citing "*Ex parte Bell*, 122 P.2d 22, 29, 30, 32, 19 Cal. 2d 488" (1942).

[729] Lewis and Short, eds., *A Latin Dictionary* (1879); see also *Webster's New International Dictionary* (2d ed. 1934), under *accident*, n.; compare Evans and Evans, *A Dictionary of Contemporary American Usage* (1957), under *mishap; accident.*

[730] *Oxford English Dictionary*, under *accident* No. 1, b.

the element of chance in *accident*, expressed in the slang *accidentally-on-purpose*[731] and the more sophisticated *accident-prone*.[732] This basic uncertainty would be enough to disqualify *accident* in any contest of precision, but the clincher for laymen at least is that the word is applied indiscriminately to the widest scattering of ordinary events from an automobile collision[733] to an ". . . untimely call of nature."[734]

This is a word that fills the cases, and not only in the sense that there are many accidents and accordingly many cases which concern them. For years, opinions have been padded with definition of *accident* and its relatives *accidental* and *accidentally*. More than two hundred pages of *Words and Phrases* are devoted to epitome from the decisions, attempting to capture these words for lawyers.[735] Why? Is it because the lay speech is flabby, and that lawyers have been trying to firm it up — by deliberately using it and litigating it? If that were true, the attempt has failed, for despite manful and intricate distinction *accident* remains a blob of jelly. As the dissenting Cardozo warned with classical bitterness a quarter century ago:

> The attempted distinction between accidental results and accidental means will plunge this branch of the law into a Serbonian Bog.[736]

That's where we are now.[737]

Courts worry the word with the doubts of the laity, compounded with the metaphysics of causation. How much chance must there be to make it an *accident?* If someone acts intentionally, is there an *accident?* "Yes" [738] and "No." [739] If there is negligence, is it an *acci-*

731 Partridge, *A Dictionary of Slang and Unconventional English* (4th ed. 1951); *Dictionary of American Slang* (1960).

732 Masserman, *Principles of Dynamic Psychiatry* 49 and 264 (1946).

733 Evans and Evans, *A Dictionary of Contemporary American Usage* (1957), under *mishap; accident.*

734 *Oxford English Dictionary*, Supp., under *accident*, No. 1.b.

735 1 *Words and Phrases* 250-415 (perm. ed. 1940), 91-168 (Supp. 1962); see also 1 *California Words, Phrases, and Maxims* 16-19 (1960); 1 *Words and Phrases: Judicially Defined* 76-82 (1946), 5-7 (Supp. 1960).

736 *Landress v. Phoenix Mutual Life Ins. Co.*, 291 U.S. 491, 499 (1934); compare *Lewis v. Ocean Accident & Guarantee Corp. Ltd.*, 224 N.Y. 18, 20 (1918).

737 1 *Words and Phrases* 379-406 (perm. ed. 1940), 156-166 (Supp. 1962), "acidental means"; 1 *Words and Phrases* 407 (perm. ed. 1940), 166 (Supp. 1962), "accidental result."

738 *Jernigan v. Allstate Ins. Co.*, 269 F.2d 353, 355-357 (5th Cir. 1959); *Emergency Aid Ins. Co. v. Dobbs*, 263 Ala. 594, 599 (1955); and see Note, 33 A.L.R.2d 1027 (1954).

739 *M. R. Thomason, etc. v. United States Fidelity & Guaranty Co.*, 248 F.2d 417, 419 (5th Cir. 1957), and dissent at 419; *Scarborough v. World Ins. Co.*, 244 N.C. 502, 505 (1956).

dent? "Yes" [740] and "No." [741]   But these are abstract answers to abstract questions.   Look to context for an answer.

If you reach forward to stop a heavy crate from falling, and get a heart attack, that's an accident.[742]   But if you reach upward to stop heavy planks from falling, and get a heart attack, that's no accident.[743] A sunstroke is usually an *accident*,[744] but it is anyone's guess whether sunstroke is an injury by *accidental means*.[745]   If there is any doubt in your mind about what an *accident* is, just remember that if Mr. Schwartz picks his nose and it bleeds, that's an *accident*.[746]

An attempt to reduce all of this to precise generalization has produced the circular platitude:

> Where "design," "intent," and "volition" are considered as the opposites of "accident," definitions of the latter word exclude design, intent, or volition, confining an accident to something wholly involuntary.[747]

But that bold pronouncement has been watered down with:

> However, it has been held that the term does not absolutely exclude the idea of design on the part of any person, nor volition on the part of the person to whom it happens; . . .[748]

Without perceptible benefit, courts have for years repeated the lay definitions of *accident*, and are not even agreed that it has any technical meaning.[749]   This much is certain: *accident* is well documented.

---

[740] *Hardware Mutual Ins. Co. of Minn. v. C. A. Snyder, Inc.*, 242 F.2d 64, 67-68 (3d Cir. 1957); *Employers Ins. Co. of Ala., Inc. v. Rives*, 264 Ala. 310, 312-313 (1955).

[741] *Pinchback Planting Co. v. Cloud*, 305 S.W.2d 552, 555 (Ark. 1957); *Balfour v. Barty-King*, [1957] 1 All E.R. 156, 159.

[742] *Lareau v. Order of United Commercial Travelers of America*, 6 N.Y.2d 764, 765 (1959), and dissent.

[743] *Wilcox v. Mutual Life Ins. Co. of N.Y.*, 265 N.Y. 665, 666 (1934).

[744] 1 *Words and Phrases* 320-322 (perm. ed. 1940), 129-130 (Supp. 1962); see *Landress v. Phoenix Mutual Life Ins. Co.*, 291 U.S. 491, 497 (1934).

[745] 1 *Words and Phrases* 401-403 (perm. ed. 1940), 163 (Supp. 1962); *Landress v. Phoenix Mutual Life Ins. Co.*, 291 U.S. 491, 497 (1934), and dissent at 498-501.

[746] *Schwartz v. Commercial Travelers' Mutual Assn. of America*, 132 Misc. 200 (N.Y. 1928).

[747] 1 *C.J.S. accident*, p. 434.

[748] 1 *C.J.S. accident*, pp. 437-438.

[749] Compare *Landress v. Phoenix Mutual Life Ins. Co.*, 291 U.S. 491, 495-496 (1934), and dissent at 499, with *Lewis v. Ocean Accident & Guarantee Corp. Ltd.*, 224 N.Y. 18, 21 (1918); compare *Hardware Mutual Ins. Co. of Minn. v. C. A. Snyder Inc.*, 242 F.2d 64, 67 (3d Cir. 1957), with *Balfour v. Barty-King*, [1957] 1 All E.R. 156, 159; *Black's Law Dictionary* (4th ed. 1951); *Ballentine's Pronouncing Law Dictionary: Supplement* (2d ed. 1954); Jowitt, gen. ed., *The Dictionary of English Law* (1959).

Beyond that the certainty ends, for the precedent points overwhelmingly in every direction.

Proximate cause

This phrase took shape two thousand years ago in Classical Latin,[750] and as Latin *causa proxima* became an ornament of the common law late in the sixteenth century.[751]   *Proximate cause* — as an expression in the English language — had not yet been borrowed from the laity[752] when Sir Francis Bacon lent his weight to the maxim:

In jure non remota causa, sed proxima spectatur.[753]

This is now translated:

In law, the proximate, and not the remote, cause is regarded [754]

But an older style rendered *proxima* as *next*[755] or *immediate*,[756] which is closer to Bacon's comment that the law did not have time to discuss ". . . the causes of causes . . ." and would settle for ". . . the immediate cause . . ." of things.[757]   To this much-quoted statement Bacon noted a much-neglected exception and warning.[758] ". . . [T]he law," he wrote, "taketh heed to the corrupt beginning . . . ," [759] and in all things the law would look to ". . . the entire act . . ." [760]

These were generalized counsels of reason, not intended as a distillate of precision but of principle, instanced but not annotated, for Bacon thought it ". . . preposterous to prove rules and maxims . . ." [761]   This, like his other maxims, was to be of use ". . . in correcting unprofitable subtlety . . ." [762]

---

[750] Smith and Hall, *English-Latin Dictionary* (1871), under *proximate;* Lewis and Short, eds., *A Latin Dictionary* (1879), under *propior.*

[751] 13 Bacon, *Works* 145 (Montagu ed. 1831); 5 Holdsworth, *A History of English Law* 398-399 (1924).

[752] See, for example, Thomas Burnet, *Theory of the Earth* (1684-1690), quoted in Johnson, *A Dictionary of the English Language* (4th ed. 1755), under *proximate; Oxford English Dictionary*, under *proximate*, No. 2; *proxime, proxim*, No. 2.

[753] 13 Bacon, *Works* 145 (Montagu ed. 1831).

[754] *Black's Law Dictionary* 896 (4th ed. 1951); *accord:* Ballentine, *Law Dictionary with Pronunciations* 650 (2d ed. 1948); Jowitt, gen. ed., *The Dictionary of English Law* 948 (1959).

[755] See Jacob, *A New Law-Dictionary* (6th ed. 1750), under *causes and effects.*

[756] Broom, *A Selection of Legal Maxims* 152 (5th American from 3d London ed. 1864); 1 Bouvier, *A Law Dictionary* (1839), under *cause* and *damages.*

[757] 13 Bacon, *Works* 145 (Montagu ed. 1831).

[758] See, for example, Hart and Honoré, *Causation in the Law* 82 n.1 (1959).

[759] 13 Bacon, *Works* 146 (Montagu ed. 1831).

[760] 13 Bacon, *Works* 147 (Montagu ed. 1831).

[761] 13 Bacon, *Works* 141 (Montagu ed. 1831).

[762] 13 Bacon, *Works* 138 (Montagu ed. 1831).

Somewhere along the line this goal was lost,[763] and the Latin words which Bacon loved too well (see Section 79) became more sought after than their explanation. The deep boom of *causa proxima* extracted from the maxim could exalt into profundity[764] the thinnest finding of liability.[765] And it became the fashion to talk about this magic to juries, and to judges, and to lawyers.[766]

Though *proximate cause* has not become an indispensable part of the lawyer's vocabulary in England, it is used there.[767] And on occasion English bench and bar have indulged exquisitely in the sharp and learned word game. For example:

> *Mellor, J.* — Was not the spouting water the *causa causans* [causing cause] [768] of the accident?
>
> *Mellish, Q.C.* — But it was the unfenced excavation that was the *causa proxima.* . . . The *causa causans* is the aggregate of all things that have happened since the beginning of the world. . . .
>
> •   •   •   •   •   •   •
>
> *Mellor, J.* — . . . the spouting water was really the efficient cause, the *causa causans,* of the accident. But for the negligence of the defendants, the accident would not have happened, and that which did may fairly be termed the proximate cause of the injury to the plaintiff.[769]

Even so, *proximate cause* is not given independent definition in standard English law dictionaries.[770] Its body — though not its spirit — was similarly missing from the first American law dictionary.[771]

In modern America the story is quite different. You can get a definition of *proximate cause* at any supermarket,[772] and several definitions in any law dictionary. A favorite is:

---

[763] See *Bole v. Pittsburgh Athletic Co.,* 205 Fed. 468, 470-471 (3d Cir. 1913).

[764] See "Causation a Profound Subject," in 1 *California Jury Instructions: Civil* 30-31 (4th rev. ed. 1956).

[765] See Jeremiah Smith, "Legal Cause in Actions of Tort," 25 Harv. L. Rev. 102, 106 (1911).

[766] See *Bole v. Pittsburgh Athletic Co.,* 205 Fed. 468, 470-471 (3d Cir. 1913); and see also *Creech v. Blackwell,* 318 S.W.2d 342, 351 (Mo. 1958).

[767] 2 *Words and Phrases: Judicially Defined* (1943), under *direct or proximate cause.*

[768] *Oxford English Dictionary,* under *causa.*

[769] *Hill v. New River Co.,* 18 L.T.R. (n.s.) 355-356 (K.B. 1868); compare Jowitt, gen. ed., *The Dictionary of English Law* (1959), under *causa causans.*

[770] See entries under *proximate cause* and *causa causans* in Jowitt, gen. ed., *The Dictionary of English Law* (1959), and *Wharton's Law Lexicon* (Oppé, 14th ed. 1938).

[771] Bouvier, *A Law Dictionary* (1839), under *cause* and *damages,* and see *negligence.*

[772] *Webster's New International Dictionary* (2d ed. 1934).

That cause of an injury which, in natural and continuous sequence, unbroken by any efficient intervening cause, produces the injury, and without which the injury would not have occurred.[773]

It is also the *dominant*,[774] the *moving*,[775] the *producing*,[776] the *efficient*,[777] the *immediate*,[778] the *legal cause*.[779] It is also much more. *Words and Phrases* will give you more than two hundred pages of excerpted precedent.[780]

Whatever you have in mind about *proximate cause* you will find some wise man who has agreed with you, and some fool who has disagreed. You say that the *proximate cause* is the *direct cause?* [781] Judges have been reversed for saying so; it may also be *indirect.*[782] *Proxima* means *nearest.*[783] Is *proximate cause* the *next*, the *nearest?* Yes. Yes. But to the literal it means next in time and space,[784] and

[773] Ballentine, *Law Dictionary with Pronunciations* (2d ed. 1948); *accord: Black's Law Dictionary* (4th ed. 1951); see 1 *California Jury Instructions: Civil* 253, No. 104 (4th rev. ed. 1956).

[774] *Black's Law Dictionary* (4th ed. 1951), under *proximate cause;* 34A *Words and Phrases* (perm. ed. 1957), "proximate cause" (dominant cause), "proximate cause of injury" (dominant cause).

[775] *Black's Law Dictionary* (4th ed. 1951), under *proximate cause;* see *St. Louis Southwestern Ry. Co. of Texas v. Lowry*, 119 S.W.2d 130, 135 (Tex. Civ. App. 1938).

[776] *Black's Law Dictionary* (4th ed. 1951), under *proximate cause*, and compare *producing cause;* see 34 *Words and Phrases* (perm. ed. 1957, Supp. 1962), "producing cause."

[777] *Black's Law Dictionary* (4th ed. 1951), under *proximate cause*, and compare *efficient cause;* 34A *Words and Phrases* (perm. ed. 1957), "proximate cause" (efficient cause), "proximate cause of injury" (efficient cause); 14 *Words and Phrases* (perm. ed. 1952), "efficient cause" (proximate cause).

[778] *Black's Law Dictionary* (4th ed. 1951), under *proximate cause;* 34A *Words and Phrases* 636-637 and related entries at 665, 699-700, 748-753 (perm. ed. 1957), "proximate cause" (direct or immediate cause); 20 *Words and Phrases* (perm. ed. 1959), "immediate cause."

[779] *Black's Law Dictionary* (4th ed. 1951), under *legal cause;* 34A *Words and Phrases* (perm. ed. 1957), "proximate cause" (legal cause); see 24 *Words and Phrases* (perm. ed. 1940, Supp. 1962), "legal cause"; Jeremiah Smith, "Legal Cause in Actions of Tort," 25 Harv. L. Rev. 102, 106 (1911).

[780] 34A *Words and Phrases* 613-847 (perm. ed. 1957), "proximate" through "proximate result," 17-21 (Supp. 1962), "proximate cause" through "proximate or legal cause."

[781] 12A *Words and Phrases* (perm. ed. 1954, Supp. 1962), "direct cause"; 34A *Words and Phrases* 636-637 and related entires at 665, 699-700, 748-753 (perm. ed. 1957), "proximate cause" (direct or immediate cause); see Ballentine, *Law Dictionary with Pronunciations* (2d ed. 1948), under *direct; Ballentine's Pronouncing Law Dictionary: Supplement* (2d ed. 1954), under *direct* and *direct loss.*

[782] *Wills etc. v. Ashland Light, Power & Street Ry. Co.*, 108 Wis. 255, 261 (1900).

[783] Lewis and Short, eds., *A Latin Dictionary* (1879), under *proximus.*

[784] *Brogan v. Union Traction Co.*, 76 W. Va. 698, 705 (1915); see Hart and

to the sophisticated next in causal relation.[785]   And what is that
"causal relation"?   Well, as one reversed judge told a jury, *proximate
cause* is ". . . something without which the happening of the accident
would not have happened . . ."[786]   Judges not only disagree with
judges;[787] and professors with professors and judges;[788] it is a field
where a professor may disagree with himself.[789]

Yet of all, the most violent and long-standing disagreement is over
whether *proximate cause* has any meaning at all.   This argument has
not two but many sides.   One disunited faction agrees that *proximate
cause* has such a distinctively legal meaning that it must be defined
for laymen, i.e., jurors; disunited only for failure to agree on the distinctive legal meaning.[790]   Another large and split group says that
proximate cause needs no definition; split because one splinter slyly
insists that the terminology of definition is ". . . as accurately known
to jury as to court,"[791] and another that *proximate cause* cannot be
defined — only applied.[792]   Other schismatics complain that *proximate
cause* has so many meanings it should be dropped as one step away
from confusion[793] — a course followed by the Restatement of Torts,[794]

Honoré, *Causation in the Law* (1959); and see Jeremiah Smith, "Legal Cause in
Actions of Tort," 25 Harv. L. Rev. 102, 106 (1911).

[785] *Wills etc. v. Ashland Light, Power & Street Ry. Co.*, 108 Wis. 255, 261
(1900).

[786] *Detroit City Gas Co. v. Syme*, 109 F.2d 366, 369 (6th Cir. 1940).

[787] *Palsgraf v. Long Island R.R. Co.*, 248 N.Y. 339 (1928), per Cardozo, J., at
346, and Andrews, J., dissenting at 347-356.

[788] Jeremiah Smith, "Legal Cause in Actions of Tort," 25 Harv. L. Rev. 102-
128 (1911), 223-252, 301-327 (1912); compare Beale, "The Proximate Consequences of an Act," 33 Harv. L. Rev. 633-658 (1920), with McLaughlin, "Proximate Cause," 39 Harv. L. Rev. 149-199 (1925); compare Beale and McLaughlin
with Green, *Rationale of Proximate Cause* (1927), and Green, "Contributory
Negligence and Proximate Cause," 6 N.C.L. Rev. 3-33 (1927); compare Green
with Hart and Honoré, *Causation in the Law* (1959).

[789] Compare Prosser, *Handbook of the Law of Torts* 312-313 (1941), with
Prosser, *Selected Topics on the Law of Torts* 191-242 and especially 242 n.149, citing "*contra*, Prosser, Torts (1941), 313" (1953).

[790] Compare *Blanch v. Villiva*, 22 S.W.2d 490-491 (Tex. Civ. App. 1929), with
Southland Greyhound Lines, Inc. v. Cotten, 91 S.W.2d 326, 328-329 (Tex. Com.
App. 1936).

[791] *St. Louis Southwestern Ry. Co. of Texas v. Lowry*, 119 S.W.2d 130, 135
(Tex. Civ. App. 1938); *Brogan v. Union Traction Co.*, 76 W. Va. 698, 705 (1915).

[792] See *Bole v. Pittsburgh Athletic Co.*, 205 Fed. 468, 470-471 (3d Cir. 1913);
Meyette v. Canadian Pacific Ry. Co., 110 Vt. 345, 353 (1939); and see also *Merrill v. Los Angeles Gas & Electric Co.*, 158 Cal. 499, 503 (1910); *Creech v. Blackwell*, 318 S.W.2d 342, 351 (Mo. 1958); Pollock, *The Law of Torts* 28 (1887).

[793] Green, "Contributory Negligence and Proximate Cause," 6 N.C.L. Rev. 3, 33
(1927).

[794] 1 *Restatement of Torts* §9, 2 *Restatement of Torts* §431.

but not by the American bar.[795] Again, it is answered that *proximate cause* serves as ". . . a vague, rough, and general statement . . ."[796] of something the law has a use for.[797]

Does precedent make precision? Here, "No." Whatever else *proximate cause* may be, it is not precise, and two hundred more pages of precedent will not make it so.

127. *Precision and requirement*

The third category of repeated words which add bulk but seldom precision to the language of the law is language that is required. As with tradition (Sections 118-125) and precedent (Section 126), the lawyer is tempted here to call *exact* (precise) words that are only exactly-the-same-way. And as with the words bequeathed by tradition and precedent, any precision of required language is a matter of coincidence. (Section 116.)

The requirements of statutes and rules, orders and official "suggestions," are themselves the work of draftsmen accustomed to the ways of tradition and precedent,[798] too often accustomed to believing that those ways make for precision. Thus it is that the usual required form sharpens the authority but not the cutting edge of the imprecise language of tradition and precedent.

For example, the oath of the witness has been incorporated into statute,[799] and so is *required by law*.[800] It ends with the traditional flourish (Sections 15, 30, 86):

. . . *the truth, the whole truth, and nothing but the truth, so help you God*.[801]

[795] For example: *Am. Jur. Pleading and Practice Forms* 14:1044 (par. IV), 14:1059 (pars. VII, VIII) 1958, 14:1060 (pars. XV, XVII, XIX, XX) (Supp. 1963) 14:1151-14:1155, 14:1157 (1958); *West's Cal. Code Forms*. Cal. Civ. Code §1714, Form No. 11 (par. I, affirmative defense) (1960); Cal. Civ. Proc. Code §437a; Hillyer, *Annotated Forms*, No. 7869 (par. 6) (1939); *Nichols-Cahill Ann. N.Y. Civil Practice Acts*, Form 3:880, and compare Form 3:722 (1959); *contra:* 3 Marsh and Fishler, *N.J. Practice Forms* §§451, 464 (rev. ed. 1960).

[796] Prosser, *Selected Topics on the Law of Torts* 242 (1953).

[797] See and compare Hart and Honoré, *Causation in the Law* 81, 123, 273, 276 (1959).

[798] See, for example, Tex. Rev. Civ. Stat. Ann., tit. 24, art. 881a-8 (1953).

[799] Cal. Civ. Proc. Code §2094; Ga. Code Ann. §59-211 (1935); Ind. Ann. Stat. §2-1711 (1946).

[800] 37 *Words and Phrases* (perm. ed. 1950, 1962 Supp.), "required by law"; 3 *California Words, Phrases, and Maxims* (1960), "required by law."

[801] Cal. Civ. Proc. Code §2094; Ga. Code Ann. §59-211 (1935); Ind. Ann. Stat. §2-1711 (1946).

Has the redundant now become precise? If it is precise, what precisely does it mean?

In the intensely religious mood of the seventeenth century, such an oath might seem a logical reply to the medieval distinction between *truth* and *whole truth*. (Section 86.) Today, any metaphysical distinction between *truth* and *whole truth* has lost practical force.[802] The layman's expression — *half-truth*, which dates from the seventeenth century[803] — may logically suggest a *whole truth*, but it is enough that a *half-truth* departs from *truth*.[804] With three *truth's*, the oath is still an oath *to tell the truth*, if anything — as meaning goes — less precise than one *truth*, for its suggestion that perhaps truth is divisible. Let it be formal, rhythmical, traditional, even emphatically impressive (Section 135), but the oath is not precise, unless . . .

Unless like the ancient formulas, the ancient magic of the law, the oath has acquired a precise sense beyond the looseness of its individual parts. (Section 118.) No longer important that the witness assents to *truth* three times, but that when he has said it, it means that the witness *has been sworn*. If that is what the three *truths* now mean, then it may be said that a string of redundancy has become precise, not as words but as formula. And to that extent, requirement would tighten the sense of tradition, if the profession so understood the meaning of the formula. Does it?

There is some evidence that the profession takes the repetitious language, not as the law's way of saying *has been sworn*, but as a more precise way of spelling out a requirement of truth telling. Here are the traditional words dropped into another spread of required language. This is part of the oath of a grand juror:

> . . . but in all my presentments I will present the truth, the whole truth, and nothing but the truth, according to the best of my skill and understanding, so help me God.[805]

This is not an oath but a dicker; an effort to tie up the juror with three kinds of *truth*, and then to relieve him of his involvement. This is not the believer's *truth* or damnation, nor a definitive *has been sworn*. It is no longer an absolute, but a something of imprecise degree.[806]

---

[802] See, for example, 45 *Words and Phrases* (perm. ed. 1940), "whole truth."

[803] *Oxford English Dictionary*.

[804] See definition of *half-truth* in *Webster's New International Dictionary* (2d ed. 1934).

[805] Cal. Pen. Code §911.

[806] Compare Ga. Code Ann. §59-208, and compare that with §59-211 (1935).

The requirement is a requirement of repetition rather than precision. Imprecise language, similarly gleaned from tradition and precedent, is imbedded in jury instructions required by statute[807] and rule of court.[808] Sometimes the "requirement" is imposed by the realities of the practice — form instructions bearing the advance approval of the judges who will pass on the lawyer's proposed instructions.[809]

It is possible that required jury instructions — like the oath — may have a precision beyond the meaning of their words. Possible that even when the jurors are sent out, their ears ringing with imprecise gobbledygook, there is left for the record a precise essence of each instruction which means *has been instructed* (on causation, negligence, etc.). And this may perform some function in speeding the administration of justice. (Section 133.) But if instructions are so understood, it is a function and a sort of precision that needs separate definition, and should not be muddled with any feeling within the profession that a jury is being told something about the law in precise terms.[810] For in these required instructions may be found the cats and dogs of law language, defined and redefined, but not more precise for all of that. There is *proximate cause*, soft and well-litigated,[811] and continuously vague *and/or*,[812] and numbers of words that are deliberately flexible (Sections 16, 119) — *burden of proof*,[813] *preponderance of the evidence*,[814] *willfully*,[815] a profusion of *reasonably's*.[816]

807 For example: Cal. Civ. Proc. Code §2061; Cal. Pen. Code §§1127b, 1127c.

808 For example: Los Angeles County, Rules of the Superior Court, Rule 27-5; see Cal. Judicial Council, Rules for Superior Courts, Rules 16(a), 16(d); Ill. Supreme Court Rules, Rule 25-1.

809 For example: *Wisconsin Jury Instructions: Civil — Part 1*, note on endpaper, front cover (1960); see and compare *Jury Instruction Forms for Utah* VII, XIII (1957).

810 Yerkes, review of *Illinois Pattern Jury Instructions, Civil*, in 47 A.B.A.J. 505 (1961).

811 See Section 126; *California Jury Instructions: Civil*, Nos. 104, 116; *Illinois Pattern Jury Instructions, Civil*, Nos. 15.01, 21.02, and see No. 11.01; *Jury Instruction Forms for Utah*, No. 15.6.

812 See Section 120; *Jury Instruction Forms for Utah*, No. 34.1.

813 *California Jury Instructions: Civil*, Nos. 21, 22, 104-B.1; *Illinois Pattern Jury Instructions, Civil*, Nos. 21.01-21.04; *Jury Instruction Forms for Utah*, No. 2.1; *Wisconsin Jury Instructions: Civil — Part 1*, No. 210; see 5 *Words and Phrases* 923-938 (perm. ed. 1940), 190-193 (Supp. 1962), "burden of proof," and related words at 921-923 (perm. ed. 1940), 189-190 (Supp. 1962).

814 See Section 109; Cal. Civ. Proc. Code §2061(5); *California Jury Instructions: Civil*, Nos. 21, 103.3, 104-F; *Jury Instruction Forms for Utah*, Nos. 3.1, 34.1; *Wisconsin Jury Instructions: Civil — Part 1*, No. 210; see 33 *Words and Phrases* 389-402 (perm. ed. 1940), 90-92 (Supp. 1962), "preponderance of evidence," and related words at 388, 402-405 (perm. ed. 1940), 90, 92 (Supp. 1962); see also 3 *California Words, Phrases, and Maxims* 388-390 (1960).

815 *California Jury Instructions: Civil*, No. 30-B; *Illinois Pattern Jury Instructions,*

There is even included the reasonably uncertain *reasonable certainty.*[817] A related monstrosity of imprecision — *reasonably possible* — occurs in the required language of a standard insurance policy.[818]

Little of the law's past has been overlooked in the required language of some mid-twentieth-century form, often interesting enough but not related to precision. A fine collection is on exhibition in Minnesota — the Uniform Conveyancing Blanks (1947) intended to standardize forms, with lower recording fees offered as inducement to the profession to use them.[819]   Here lurk the mysterious *ss.,*[820] the redundant *duly sworn on oath,*[821] the flavorous *Know all men by these presents,*[822] etc.   Not only are ancient words preserved — *grant, bargain, sell, and convey; to have and to hold* — but a form bears witness to the grammatical inversion left over from the translation of Latin (Section 80):

> And the above bargained and granted lands and premises, in the quiet and peaceable possession of the said part .... of the second part, ... heirs and assigns, against all persons lawfully claiming or to claim the whole or any part thereof, subject to incumbrances, if any, hereinbefore mentioned, the said part .... of the first part will Warrant and Defend.[823]

Wherever the lawyer turns, he may find the accumulated imprecision of the ages required for some legal purpose.   A standard form policy with the traditional long sentence,[824] an affidavit with the unnecessary *said's,*[825] a candidly indefinite notice intended only to alarm — "This contract limits our liability — read it." [826]

Civil, Nos. 14.01, 14.02; *Jury Instruction Forms for Utah,* Nos. 3.12, 34.10, 34.12; see 45 *Words and Phrases* 186-344 (perm. ed. 1940), 48-121 (Supp. 1962), "willful, willfully," and related words; 4 *California, Words, Phrases, and Maxims* 564-582 (1960), 11-12 (Supp. 1961), "wilful, wilfully," and related words.

[816] See Section 119; Cal. Civ. Proc. Code §2061(5); *California Jury Instructions: Civil,* Nos. 101, 104-C; *Illinois Pattern Jury Instructions, Civil,* Nos. 10.01, 10.02, 160.05, 160.07, 160.08, and compare p. 115; *Jury Instruction Forms for Utah,* No. 15.1; *Wisconsin Jury Instructions: Civil — Part 1,* No. 1005.

[817] *California Jury Instructions: Civil,* No. 176; *Wisconsin Jury Instructions: Civil — Part 1,* No. 210; see 36 *Words and Phrases* (perm. ed. 1962), "reasonable certainty"; 3 *California Words, Phrases, and Maxims* (1960), "proof to reasonable certainty."

[818] Ill. Ann. Stat., c. 73, §969a (Smith-Hurd, 1937, effective 1952).

[819] 29 Minn. Stat. Ann., pp. 301-434 (1947); Minn. Stat. Ann. §§507.08-507.14, and especially §§507.13, 507.12 (1947).

[820] See Section 120; 29 Minn. Stat. Ann., pp. 387-389, Form No. 67 (1947).

[821] 29 Minn. Stat. Ann., p. 387, Form No. 67 (1947).

[822] See Section 56; 29 Minn. Stat. Ann., pp. 400-402, Form Nos. 76-78 (1947).

[823] 29 Minn. Stat. Ann., p. 304, Form No. 1 (1947).

[824] Mass. Gen. Laws Ann., c. 175, §99(12th) (1959).

[825] Cal. Judicial Council, Rules for Superior Courts, Rule 20.

[826] Cal. Civ. Code §1630; see also Cal. Civ. Code §1803.2(c)(3).

This is not the whole story of required language. Some of it — like *order of,*[827] *nonnegotiable, not negotiable*[828] required by the Uniform Bills of Lading Act — is precise. More of it is not precise but passes for precision because it is "official," mistaken for *exact* because it is exactly-the-same-way. It is repeated by the year and by the yard, without consideration of the possibility of its improvement.

Most important of all is that the profession recognize this language for what it is. Is it used because it is precise? Or only because it is required? Or is there a reason other than precision that makes it both required and useful? If it is precise language, perhaps it is worth using again, and elsewhere. If it is imprecise, perhaps a client needs further protection. If it is required because it serves a purpose unrelated to precision, that too is worth knowing, so that it may be used again where the reason is, and dropped where the reason ends.[829]

128. *The limits of precision: The small area*

On any detailed inspection, the dogma that the language of the law is precise (Section 115) turns out to be something less than a compliment to the profession. One look at any digest of cases, a study of the litigation that has turned repeatedly (and in many directions) on the interpretation not of layman's words but of law words (Sections 120-123, 126), brings a conviction of imprecision or incompetency, or of both. Can it be that the language is precise, and the trouble is simply that lawyers don't know how to use it? Or won't use it properly even if they know how to? Some, but not the thousands of lawyers who have urged a losing interpretation of law words, have been inept lawyers or venal ones. Some, but not the hundreds of judges whose interpretations have been rejected, have been unfit judges. If Augustus Hand can disagree with Learned Hand over the meaning of the words in a bill of lading,[830] and the Justices of the Supreme Court of the United States side some with Augustus and more with Learned,[831] doubt of the precision of law language cannot be heresy.

While not as immediately comforting as the dogma of precision, it is more accurate — and also more helpful to the practitioner — to

---

[827] Uniform Bills of Lading Act §2(g); Cal. Civ. Code §2126a.

[828] Uniform Bills of Lading Act §8; Cal. Civ. Code §2126g.

[829] For example, compare *Rolando v. Everett,* 72 Cal. App. 2d 629 (1946), with *In the Matter of Hurt,* 129 F. Supp. 94, 101-102 (S.D. Cal. 1955).

[830] *Alcoa S.S. Co. v. United States,* 175 F.2d 661 (2d Cir. 1949), and dissent at 663-665, *rev'g* 80 F. Supp. 158 (S.D.N.Y. 1948).

[831] *Alcoa S.S. Co. v. United States,* 338 U.S. 421 (1949), and dissent at 429, *aff'g* 175 F.2d 661 (2d Cir. 1949).

appreciate that the chief peculiarity of law language is its peculiarity and not its precision. *The language of the law has never been generally precise, and it is neither possible nor desirable that it become completely so.* If the language of the law is to be used most effectively, and then improved some, those limits of its precision must be recognized and understood. We examine them in turn, first *the small area of precision.*

The defect in the dogma of precision is that it claims too much. Law language is but rarely precise. In a few particulars, "Yes"; as a whole pattern of communication, "No." And it is as important to the lawyer to make himself aware that his language is not generally precise as it is for him to know the precision that is there.

If the language of the law is stripped first of its overwhelming mass of ordinary English (Section 7), and next of the repeated words and phrasings of tradition (Sections 118-125), precedent (Section 126), and requirement (Section 127) which are occasionally precise but only by coincidence (Section 116), there still remains a distinctive nubbin of precision. It is achieved by the discriminating use of *terms of art* (Section 13) and some of the law's *argot* (Section 14), and by a striving for precision — for limitation of meaning (Section 17), a striving that can be detected in the works of draftsmen of every degree of competency.

This small part — this precise part — of the language of the law is almost lost in any given square foot of law language. Put to better use, with some of the dross skimmed off, the precise part could make a better showing. As it is, the sprinkling of precision is no more representative of the whole than the nuggets in a salted gold field.

This has been true in the law's past (see Sections 90-95, 104), and it is true today. (See Section 112.) Take an "adjudicated" form for "Requirement of Acceptance of Surrender by Lessor," and follow its possible metamorphosis:

Before	*After*
"This lease can be modified and changed only by an instrument in writing signed by the landlord and by the tenant and no surrender of this lease before the expiration of the demised term or any renewal thereof shall be valid unless accepted by the landlord in writing." [832]	This lease can be changed only by an instrument signed by landlord and tenant. No surrender shall be valid unless accepted by the landlord in writing.

[832] *Am. Jur. Legal Forms* 8:315 (1954), with note "Adapted from *Jackson*

Of the original forty-eight words, four terms of art are useful — *lease, landlord, tenant, surrender.* The word *valid,* which started with the law, is today simply a legal application of common usage.[833] One other word not of the law — *only* — becomes a vital part of the scheme of tightening the sense. Half of the rest — despite its legal flavor — is worthless, inconsistent with an intention to speak precisely. It may be deleted without loss of meaning and with a gain in preciseness. See what the draftsman has done:

He has fallen into the traditional pattern of two-words-for-one. (Section 124.) Why *modified and changed?* The greater evil of redundancy is not its length — which is bad enough (Chapter XIV) — but the increased possibility it provides for error. A standard rule of construction requires that whenever possible meaning be given to each word used.[834] Since *modified* is included in *changed,*[835] how are we to understand *modified and changed?* Is this intended to emphasize *modification,* meaning *changed by being modified,* and so exclude more drastic *change?* Or are there merely extra words?

Similarly with *instrument in writing.* With normal clients, the only kind of *instrument* designed to be *signed* (as this one is) is one *in writing.* (Section 124.) If the passage were to be redrafted, *a writing* could as well supplant *instrument. Instrument* is lawyer's argot, used here not for rapid communication (Section 132) and not for any extra sense of preciseness, but only through habit. If the word added anything to either speed or precision, it would not be encumbered as *an instrument in writing signed.*

And what of that term of art *surrender?* Here is technicality used without respect for its technical sense. The precise part of *surrender,* the only reason for using the word, is that it makes unnecessary the next fourteen words; after expiration there will be nothing left to *surrender.*[836] If *surrender* is to be gilded as in *Before,* why not embrace the vernacular, forget law words, and say:

Heights, Inc. v. 171-24th Street, 274 App. Div. 1070, 85 N.Y.S.2d 618," and compare *Jackson Heights, Inc. v. 171-24th Street,* 274 App. Div. 1070, 85 N.Y.S.2d 618 (1949).

[833] *Oxford English Dictionary; Black's Law Dictionary* (4th ed. 1951).

[834] See, for example, 1 *Words and Phrases: Judicially Defined* 26-27 (par. 64) (1946); and see Cal. Civ. Code §§1641, 3541.

[835] *Webster's New International Dictionary* (2d ed. 1934), under *modify;* 27 *Words and Phrases* (perm. ed. 1961), "modify" (change).

[836] See *Black's Law Dictionary* (4th ed. 1951), under *surrender;* Coke, *Commentary upon Littleton,* ff. 337b-338a (10th ed. 1703).

*and nothing you do or I do will let you squirm out of this deal unless
I give the word — in writing that is?*

Why not? Because years of the law of landlord and tenant are
compressed into *surrender*. Older in the law than in the common
speech,[837] *surrender* speaks here of special situations that have arisen
recurrently in the leasing of land through the centuries — a *surrender
in law*[838] (or *by operation of law*),[839] for example. As a term of art,
properly used, *surrender* is more precise than any equivalent of the
common speech.

The specimen *Before* also uses technicality where it serves no purpose whatever, merely filling space with the empty tinkle of precision.
Why the *demised term?* Apart from the fact that *surrender* makes
the whole expression unnecessary, the only *term* we are talking about
here is the *term* of the *lease*. *Term* needs no description. And if one
were in order, the surest departure from the path of precision is the
switch from *lease* to *demise*. To each word a meaning? Perhaps.
For the layman, *demise* has only the sound of *death*.[840] For the lawyer it brings an uncertain echo of the *covenant for quiet enjoyment*,[841]
when probably all that was intended was traditional extra wordage.[842]

What was intended here? The ultimate vice of this combination of
traditional redundancy and long sentence construction (Section 125)
is that intention is so shrouded in words that both writer and reader
have difficulty in focusing on what is essential to the deal the parties
are making. What are the limits of the deal? Has something been
left out that was intended to be there? Has something been put in
that was not intended? When *Before* (forty-eight words) has been
worked down to *After* (twenty-six words), it will be easier to examine
the lines of intention. Perhaps neither *Before* nor *After* quite expressed

[837] *Oxford English Dictionary;* Cowell, *The Interpreter* (ed. 1637).

[838] Cowell, *The Interpreter* (ed. 1637), under *surrender;* Coke, *Commentary
upon Littleton*, f. 338a (10th ed. 1703).

[839] 40 *Words and Phrases* (perm. ed. 1940, Supp. 1962), "surrender by operation of law"; and see 4 *California Words, Phrases, and Maxims* (1960), "surrender"; and compare 5 *Words and Phrases: Judicially Defined* (Supp. 1960),
"surrender."

[840] See Nicholson, *A Dictionary of American-English Usage* (1957); Evans and
Evans, *A Dictionary of Contemporary American Usage* (1957); Partridge, *Usage
and Abusage* (new ed. 1957); see also ["Vigilans"], *Chamber of Horrors* (1952).

[841] *Trimble v. City of Seattle*, 231 U.S. 683, 688-689 (1913); *Spencer's Case*,
77 Eng. Rep. 72, 75 (K.B. 1583); Note, 62 A.L.R. 1257, 1262 (1929); 12 *Words
and Phrases* (perm. ed. 1954), "demise"; Jowitt, gen. ed., *The Dictionary of
English Law* (1959), under *demise*.

[842] Nichols, *Cyclopedia of Legal Forms* §5.1866a (par. C.1) (1956).

that intention. Perhaps what the parties really intended may be expressed in only fifteen words:

> *This lease cannot be either changed or surrendered without written approval of landlord and tenant.*

Terms of art make such compression and such relative precision possible. And whenever such precision is both possible and desirable, the competent lawyer uses the terms of art at his command. When precision is the dominant consideration, it is no objection to the immediate use of terms of art that they are not completely precise. It is sufficient for the lawyer's purpose of the moment that with the terms of art the effect of context on meaning has become more limited than for most words. That is the essence of the *term of art*. (Section 13.) Through long use in a recurrent context, *plaintiff* conveys a workably clear notion to the lawyer. It was not always so (Section 64), but it is now. Law students study about *plaintiffs*. Lawyers represent them, and oppose them. Judges decide their cases. *Plaintiff* makes quick and general sense; that's *the man who sued me*. Having learned it so well, lawyers will not (nor should they) drop their accustomed use of *plaintiff* simply because they discover that in a particular context — e.g., a cross-complaint — *plaintiff* may mean *defendant*.[843] The sense of the term of art is so generally accepted that it is no longer dependent upon supporting precedent, and not overturned at once by adverse precedent, until — like *seisin* (Section 121) — it arrives at a time of life when the world has passed it by so completely — with new customs and new reasons — that it must be dropped.

Correct use of his terms of art marks the lawyer. If it is to be *for life*, that says it precisely, and that it should be — not *during her natural life*,[844] nor (even worse) *in fee simple . . . as long as he lives*.[845] Correctly used, the terms of art make for precision; used haphazardly, or for their sound alone (e.g., *sworn on oath*),[846] they become confusing and worthless.

So it is — to a lesser degree — with some of the lawyer's *argot*. (Section 14.) Restricted to its proper sphere, for rapid, immediate communication between members of the profession, *argot* can be the most precise possible, and also as precise as necessary. For if a law-

---

[843] 32A *Words and Phrases* (perm. ed. 1956), "plaintiff" (defendant).
[844] See Section 121; Nichols, *Cyclopedia of Legal Forms* §1.04 (1936).
[845] *Shoemaker v. Coats*, 218 N.C. 251, 252 (1940).
[846] 29 Minn. Stat. Ann., p. 387, Form No. 67 (1947).

yer argues to a judge that "This case is *on all fours* with *the case at bar*," both judge and opposing counsel know what he is talking about even if they don't agree with him. And they will set him straight if need be. But where *argot* does not serve this swift, correctable purpose — as in leases, and wills, and contracts — the *aforesaid's* and the *hereafter's*, the *hereby's* and the *whereases* (Section 120), are both unnecessary and imprecise.

These possibilities of a more precise language through terms of art and argot have overexcited the profession. And in the feverish search for precision, the sense of fitness has suffered. It has been assumed that the only avenue of precision lay in specialized usage, and that one equaled the other. Yet the striving for precision — and its limited successes — may be there without any law words at all. And the most confused imprecision may be swathed in sheets of law words. (Section 20.) *Mutually agree*[847] says nothing that is not better said by *agree*. *If it is proven*[848] is archaic, but not on that account more legal than *proved*.[849] A pleading in ordinary English that John *married* Mary is more precise than John and Mary *were intermarried*,[850] and *intermarry with each other*[851] is only puzzling.

Use and non-use of language are equally important. Over the years, the profession has built up such a vast supply of words — some precise, more not — that it suffers not from an embarrassment of riches but from a continuous strain of choice between good and bad. And it has been easier to use than to choose. Easier to use than not to use. The lack of discrimination causes trouble.

How is a lawyer to know then whether a particular word is more precise than the common speech, whether a particular word is term of art, a more precise bit of argot, or just traditional claptrap?

Answer: This is what the lawyer learns in law school and in the practice of his profession. The term of art is that — not merely because it has been used, but because it contains within it the substance

[847] Section 125; see *Alcoa S.S. Co. v. United States*, 80 F. Supp. 158, 165 (S.D.N.Y. 1948) (see later history in notes 830, 831); Mass. Gen. Laws Ann. c. 175, §99 (12th) (1959).

[848] Cal. Prob. Code §930.

[849] *Webster's New International Dictionary* (2d ed. 1934), under *proven;* compare *Oxford English Dictionary*, under *proven*, with entry under *prove*, No. 5; Ballentine, *Law Dictionary with Pronunciations* (2d ed. 1948), under *prove* and *proved*.

[850] See Hillyer, *Annotated Forms*, No. 3606 (1938).

[851] Cal. Pen. Code §285.

of the learned law. Mention the magic word *lease*, and unbeknownst to the layman who signs it, the word without more incorporates the centuries of the law of *landlord and tenant;* the incidents follow the relationship whether they are expressed or unexpressed. This is what the student learned in law school, and of this his practice gives him constant reminder. Mention the once-magic *seisin*, and it speaks of a relation that no longer has its ancient significance; this too the student learned in law school — the ancient meaning and the ceasing of the reasons that called it into life. (Section 121.) This too he can see in his daily world of law. And if the lawyer continues then to use *seisin,* it is through habit and not through a striving for precision.

It is for the lawyer to know what is more precise — within the possibilities of knowing. (Section 129.) This is his job; this that he studies, in law school and in practice; this that makes it a learned profession. This is what he *is* paid for.

The lawyer cannot assume that what is in the formbook is precise, for it is the unsegregated repository of the repeated (tradition, precedent, requirement) as well as the precise. And unless the lawyer knows a reason for a usage, knows what a word means, knows why he uses it, then the course of honesty and safety for a member of a learned profession is not to use it.

129. *The limits of precision: The impossible and the undesirable*

Along with his continued striving for precision in the small area where law language can be more precise than the ordinary speech (Section 128), the lawyer can take a surer hold on the instruments of his craft, can flog himself less with vague and debilitating misgivings, if he recognizes once and for all that it is impossible that the language of the law become completely precise. Not that this should signal an end of the striving, nor license sloppy pleading and general literary mush. Only that the striving must not be confused with arriving, and the attainability of near goals not discouraged by the unattainability of absolutes.

It would be a most strange and wonderful thing if lawyers had indeed been able to succeed where the rest of talking and writing humanity had failed. The quest for a precise language is as ancient as the search for the fountain of youth, and less capable of fulfillment than the alchemist's dream of turning lead into gold. Marvelous it would be if lawyers had fashioned an exact instrument out of language — a substance that Plato found "more pliable than wax." [852] But they have not done so.

Maitland spoke of his prize specimen of law French precision (Section 63) in glowing, prideful words:

> Precise ideas are here expressed in precise terms, everyone of which is French: the geometer or the chemist could hardly wish for terms that are more exact or less liable to have their edges worn away by the vulgar.[853]

These words, applied to the merest speck of the language of the law, suggest a comparison between the languages of law, mathematics, and the natural sciences (Section 115), a comparison that can only be embarrassing to the lawyer and disappointing to his clients.

The geometer may speak with assurance of a *line*, for it lives only in a succession of moving dots. The law's most bloodless abstractions — a *corporation, property, justice* — concern living people, their hopes, their whims, their aching backs. Tomorrow the back no longer aches, and the concept of *justice* and *property* has changed a little with the relief.

Nor does the lawyer — unlike his fellow professional, the chemist — deal with universal phenomena, with fixed points of boiling and freezing. The common law speaks of "Willy the milman: Robin the pannierman, &c." (Section 87), each with his own unpredictable thoughts and acts. If the law is a science, it is not an exact science, and its language must share some of the ambiguity of life.[854]

The common law is built for such ambiguity, hand-tailored for people. Its basic notion is that things cannot be too precise, that no matter how thin a principle is sliced, particularization is always possible. There was a reason for the original proposition, and when that reason falters ever so little, a man may still overcome the precedents.[855] This flexibility of the common law is reflected in its language. The continuing vogue of *reasonable* (Sections 119, 127), a nation built on *due process*, are symbols of the imprecision of law language, and their

---

[852] *The Republic,* Book IX, in 1 Jowett, transl., *The Dialogues of Plato* 848 (Random House, 1937).

[853] Maitland, "Of the Anglo-French Language in the Early Year Books," in Introduction to *Year Books of Edward II,* 17 Selden Society xxxiii, xxxvi (1903).

[854] Levin, "Language, Symbol Cycles, and the Constitution," 71 U.S.L. Rev. 258, 265 (1937).

[855] See Broom, *A Selection of Legal Maxims* 113 (5th American from 3d London ed. 1864).

firm roots in our jurisprudence is some measure of the impossibility of pounding law language into a precise mold.

Made for people, the common law has long suffered a further tribulation largely unknown to the exact sciences. The law must not only speak about people but to them. Not that the law has always done this. Quite the contrary. But when the law speaks in a "hidden tongue," it is occasionally berated — if not reformed. The scientist has been able to talk to himself unmolested. The day may now be here, but it is still not officially recognized of science, as it long has been of law, that *ignorance is no excuse.*[856]

As a corollary to that maxim, there is an underlying feeling in the nations of the common law that law must in some degree be comprehensible not merely to those who work at it but to those who are expected to be governed by it. Accordingly, the law must communicate within professional ranks and beyond — into an ever-widening area of literacy. And the wider that area of communication becomes the more impossible the attainment of precision. The finest minds may sharpen the finest tools — e.g., symbolic logic (Section 17) — and use them to analyze the problems of the law, but ultimately the law must talk with people — many people — about their problems. And in that communication it is impossible to speak in the precise measures of the mathematician. The law ministers to living needs, and in speaking to the living its language shares some of the imperfections of the common tongue.

Ordinary English, for example, reflects a skepticism about the whole vocabulary of absolutes — those one-word generalizations like *void* (Section 123), *all,*[857] and *never*[858] — which run counter to human experience. As lawyer Gilbert has explained, if questioned, the layman's *never* quickly reduces to *hardly ever.*[859] The ex-layman who becomes lawyer or judge remembers that *never* is not necessarily the last word. We are told that as long ago as ancient Athens the chief judges took an oath,

856 See Broom, *A Selection of Legal Maxims* 174 (5th American from 3d London ed. 1864).

857 *In re Hittson,* 39 Cal. App. 91 (1918); see *People v. McDonald,* 2 Idaho 10, 12 (1881); *West Branch State Bank v. Farmers Union Exchange,* 221 Iowa 1382, 1384 (1936); *Guiterrez v. Gober,* 43 N.M. 146, 155, 158 (1939); *Jackson v. Harris,* 8 Johns. 141, 145, 146 (N.Y. 1811); *In re Estate of Sowards,* 105 Ohio App. 239, 242 (1957).

858 *Pfleiderer v. Brooks,* 122 Kan. 647 (1927), and compare *Dimock v. Corwin,* 19 F. Supp. 56, 61, 62 (E.D.N.Y. 1937), aff'd, 306 U.S. 363 (1939), with dissent at 373-374.

859 In "I Am Captain of the Pinafore," from *H.M.S. Pinafore.*

"That they would observe the laws and administer justice without partiality; would never be corrupted by bribes, or if they were, . . . they would dedicate a statue of gold to the Delphinian Apollo." [860]

Unfortunately, the lawyer cannot rest assured that someone won't take an absolute seriously — an insurance company for instance. Here is part of an application for insurance:

"What is your practice as regards the use of spirits, wines, malt liquors, or other alcoholic beverages?"

The insured replied,

"Kind, nothing. Amount, none. How often, never."

This sounded like a member of the Anti-Saloon League, but when the widow tried to collect the $1000 the company turned up evidence of strong drink. What to do about the absolutes?

The Supreme Court of Kentucky found that the insured's answers were "not responsive" to the question about the insured's "practice as regards the use of spirits." It observed:

The effect of all this is that the applicant occasionally took a toddy or a drink of whiskey, and, on one occasion, according to the testimony of two witnesses, he was in an intoxicated condition, though neither of them saw him drink anything.

.   .   .   .

When this evidence is critically analyzed, it is apparent that, if the applicant had stated in the application that he took as many as four or five drinks in the course of a year, no insurance company would have rejected the risk on this ground.

And what of evidence of the "Keeley treatment"? Well, that could have been for something else. Judgment for the widow affirmed. [861]

Never, for all its absoluteness, means one thing to an insurance company, something else to a live insured, and something yet different to a Kentucky gentleman and judge trying to help a poor widow. This is a part of what the semanticists have been telling us, [862] that words have not one but many meanings, that a word is not the same thing as reality.

The language of the law shares the imperfections of the common language and of language itself. And while it can be better understood, better used, refined, it will not become completely precise

---

[860] Quoted in Tyler, *Oaths* 298 (1834).

[861] *Columbia Life Ins. Co. v. Tousey*, 152 Ky. 447, 451, 453 (1913); see also *Higbee v. Guardian Mutual Life Ins. of N.Y.*, 66 Barb. 462, 472-474 (N.Y. 1873).

[862] See Section 115; and see Holmes, "The Theory of Legal Interpretation," 12 Harv. L. Rev. 417 (1899).

as long as it *is* to be an instrument of communication — person-to-person.[863]

Added to the difficulties of making any language precise, law language has its unique obstacle. Nowhere else can so much hinge on a word — not merely billions of dollars, but weightier intangibles —

> *Loss of reputation . . . unending humiliation . . . legal and moral chaos . . .*[864]

And since that is so, in no other discipline are words subjected to such extraordinary tugging and hauling, such pounding and chipping, such filing and chiseling. These language arts, which are part of the lawyer's routine and among the indexes of his professional skill, sometimes produce refinements of word usage more precise than the common speech. But more often the whole process results not in refined words, precise words, but mangled words — distorted out of recognizable shape to achieve the object of the moment.

A statute says the trial judge shall hear a motion for new trial,

> . . . provided, however, that in case of the inability of such judge or if . . . he is absent from the county . . .

another judge shall hear the motion.[865] The exceptions seem clear enough, two of them — *inability* and *absence*. There is a third, *death*,[866] despite a learned opinion in an intermediate court of appeal, demonstrating beyond the cavil of linguists that both *inability* and *absence* from Los Angeles County are misfortunes of the living.[867] Perhaps the draftsman was forgetful, but whatever other defect may be charged to him, his word usage was without fault. Against the hazard of such interpretation, the draftsman is helpless. (See Section 16.)

If the lawyer had only to write language that fools could not misunderstand and knaves could not twist,[868] the problem of precision would be vastly simpler than it is. A greater difficulty, an insuperable one, is to write language that time will not change. It is more often

[863] See Thring, *Practical Legislation* 81-82 (Little, Brown, 1902); Cairns, "Language of Jurisprudence," in Anshen, ed., *Language* 232, 256-257 (1957).

[864] McReynolds, J., dissenting, in *Perry v. United States*, 294 U.S. 330, 381 (1935).

[865] Cal. Civ. Proc. Code §661.

[866] *Telefilm, Inc. v. Superior Court*, 33 Cal. 2d 289, and dissent at 296-297 (1949).

[867] 194 P.2d 542 (1948).

[868] Lavery, "Language of the Law," 7 A.B.A.J. 277, 281 (1921); and see also Thring, *Practical Legislation* 9 (Little, Brown, 1902).

changed circumstance and changed minds rather than foolishness or knavery that strains the language of the law. The hard cases which make bad law also strain language beyond the breaking point of the precise. This is no philosopher's search for abstract truth, but for lawyers something more precious because more attainable — right as individual men know it. And if judges have to choose between a word and a widow, the word may bend a little, ". . . to the end that justice may not be the slave of grammar." [869]

In a more immediate, controllable sense, complete precision is sometimes also incompatible with some of the other desirables of law language — durability, intelligibility, brevity, for instance. And it cannot be accepted as axiom that all else must always be sacrificed for the sake of precision. (Section 115.) There are times when precision may kill a deal that should not be killed, or confuse an issue that should be immediately clear, times when precision is *undesirable* even if possible. There are other considerations of policy and expediency which can influence a lawyer's choice of language. The rest of this book discusses those considerations.

[869] *Black's Law Dictionary* (4th ed. 1951), under *may.*

CHAPTER XIV

Shorter

130. *An independent factor*

As precision is the loudest virtue of the language of the law (Section 114), so wordiness is its noisiest vice. Even the untutored can see that law language is too long, and some of them have not hesitated to say so. (Sections 78, 93, 114, 115.) For lawyers glorying in the illusion of precision (Section 115), the virtue outshouts the vice, and most often they let it go at that.

Yet from the long past, distinguished lawyers — More, Hale, Coke, Bacon (Sections 93, 94), Bentham (Sections 109, 115), Jefferson (Section 107) — have added their indorsement to the layman's complaint of verbosity in the law. As a result, even the most verbose lawyer occasionally recognizes brevity as a disembodied virtue — like charity, materializing in moments of convenience and as conveniently evaporating. Brevity is given perfunctory recognition — a salute to the most junior second lieutenant — and as quickly ignored. It is more difficult to convince lawyers that anything should be done about their verbosity than to account for its intrusion and presence in the language of the law.

The influences most responsible for wordiness in the law (as distinct from wordiness in writing generally) have lost their original force. The redundancies of primitive word magic and metaphysical ritual; the solemn repetitions coaxing barbarians to accept an unestablished law; the need and fashion of bilingual duplication; the involvements brought on by the translation of Latin, by Elizabethan literary styles, and by a pay-by-the-word legal economy; the overcautious repeating of the repeated to circumvent the harshness of the law and to mask an ignorance of its content (Part Two) — all of these have burdened the law with language unnecessary, confusing, and wasteful.

What remains of these influences is the comfort of familiar spirits. This is no inexorable progression from ". . . terseness to prolixity"[1]

[1] Compare Cairns, "Language of Jurisprudence," in Anshen, ed., *Language* 232, 237 (1957).

but habit. There is wordiness in the most ancient texts (Sections 29, 30) yet the staccato brevity of terms of art peppers the tedious repetitions of seventeenth- and eighteenth-century legal prose. (Sections 39, 91.) The terse stays and the prolix stays, sometimes side by side, leaving an impression of random selection. Look, for example, at this squidgy *and/or* (makes for brevity, say its friends),[2] here jammed in tight by the verbosity of a vague indictment:

> . . . keeping a certain building, room and place to bet and wager, and to gamble cards, dice *and/or* dominoes then and there played; and as a place where people did then and there resort to gamble, bet and wager on games played with cards, dice *and/or* dominoes against the peace and dignity of the State.[3]

This is brevity without conviction. The lawyer is not beguiled by the quick lay sentiment that any shortening of law language — no matter what — is pure gain.[4] But neither is he sufficiently alarmed that anyone can hold such belief. If legal prose ends up long or short, it is more accident or habit than consistent design. The well-intentioned preface:

> . . . the singular number includes the plural, and the plural the singular . . .[5]

grows muzzy with the passage of words, and no one bothers to shorten the *person or persons,*[6] *horse or horses,*[7] *tire or tires,*[8] *instalment or instalments*[9] that follow in the body of the statute. So with *will includes codicil,*[10] followed by the recitation of both.[11]

The long and the short mingle haphazardly, wordy habitual usage defended as "precise," shorter habitual usage recommended for its "brevity," with no attempt to further reconcile the choices.

---

[2] See Section 120; Mumper, "The Unfair Tirade Against the Symbol 'and/or,' " 10 J.S.B. Calif. 187, 188 (1935); Morton, letter, in "For and/or on Behalf of; or Against and/or," 10 J.S.B. Calif. 89-91 (1935); note, "In Defense of 'and/or,' " 45 Yale L.J. 918-919 (1936).

[3] *Compton v. State,* 91 S.W.2d 732, 733 (Tex. Crim. App. 1936).

[4] See, for example, Flesch, *The Art of Plain Talk* 170-171 (1946), and compare Aiken, "Let's Not Oversimplify Legal Language," 32 Rocky Mt. L. Rev. 358, 361-362 (1960).

[5] Cal. Pen. Code §7; see also Cal. Civ. Code §14; N.Y. Retail Instalment Sales Act §401(18) (1957); Dickerson, *Legislative Drafting* 95 (1954); compare 3 Bentham, *Works* 265 (Bowring ed. 1843); and see Section 109.

[6] Cal. Pen. Code §597a (docking horse tails).

[7] Cal. Pen. Code §597a (docking horse tails).

[8] Cal. Pen. Code §499c.

[9] Cal. Civ. Code §1807.1; N.Y. Retail Instalment Sales Act §409(1) (1957).

[10] Cal. Pen. Code §7(14).

[11] Cal. Pen. Code §470, and compare §§2603, 5061.

Who would force such reconciliation? The laity without the knowledge, and the profession without a sense of urgency. For this "brevity" that lawyers sometimes speak of is a vague kind of goodness, subordinate to every other consideration of necessity or convenience, especially subordinate to "precision." Flexible as the concept of brevity is, it will never become part of the lawyer's credo until the reasons for brevity in the law become as compelling as the ancient reasons for verbosity.

A necessary step toward brevity in the language of the law is the recognition that brevity is an independent factor, to be weighed apart from precision, intelligibility, or anything else.

What is precise may incidentally be brief — *surrender* (Section 128), *or order* (Sections 13, 127), *voir dire* (Sections 12, 60) — shorter than equivalent expressions in ordinary English. But it does not follow that precision and brevity are inseparable companions, nor that the shorter way of saying things in the law is always the precise or the best way. As law words go, *and/or* is short, but precision is not in it. (Section 120.) *Will* is shorter and more precise than *last will and testament*. (Section 121.) As used in a will, *give, devise, and bequeath* is longer and less precise than *give* (Section 123); *give and appoint* increases the wordage, but also affords coverage that *give* alone does not.[12] Precision is not to be determined by counting words; the only similarity between wordiness and imprecision is that both are undesirable.[13]

So too, brevity and intelligibility may be poles apart. A few words may produce instant understanding — *not guilty, overruled, stop* — or concise gibberish — *proximate cause*. (Section 126.) And a multitude of words may befog, as with the ordinary jury instruction (Sections 20, 126, 133), or impress with its clarity, as with almost anything touched by the lively wordiness of Frederic William Maitland.[14]

If brevity can be made to coincide with goals of precision and intelligibility, so much the better. But brevity, like precision or intelligibility, stands on its own, desirable for its own sake, for what only brevity can accomplish. It is to be used thoughtfully, in proportion to the purpose to be served by being briefer, more precise, clearer, etc.

[12] Section 123; see Leach, "Powers of Appointment," 24 A.B.A.J. 807, 808, 811 (1938).

[13] Leach, "Powers of Appointment," 24 A.B.A.J. 807, 808 (1938); Casner, "Construction of Gifts to 'Heirs' and the Like," 53 Harv. L. Rev. 207, 250 (1939).

[14] For example: "English Law and the Renaissance," 1 *Select Essays in Anglo-American Legal History* 168, 200-202 (1907); "The Mystery of Seisin," 3 *Select Essays in Anglo-American Legal History* 591, 602, 609-610 (1909).

First then, brevity minimizes the possibility of error. (Section 128.)
The more he writes the greater opportunity the draftsman gives himself to bungle. The pleader of an older day who could have passed muster pleading *one hundred sheep* made his declaration uncertain and bad by saying *one hundred sheep, ewes and wethers*.[15] And today too, saying too much can ruin a good general pleading.[16] This is not the worst. By the end of the traditional long, long sentence, the most astute draftsman has forgotten just a little of what he said at the beginning. (Section 125.) In the toils of excess words, the sharpest minds lose their bearings, unable to concentrate on what is essential, and so to be insisted upon, and what trifling or worthless, to be bargained away graciously. (Section 128.) The more he writes the greater opportunity also the draftsman gives to those who are able to misunderstand — or at least to interpret.

Secondly, and related to the error that creeps into many words, bulk leads to ignorance.

By the time he has found his way to the end of an insurance policy, the alert and unusual householder (layman or attorney) cannot know what he is covered for — because there is more in an insurance policy than he can read and retain, even if he understood each word as he read it. (Section 112.) The reading has left him — nay, made him — ignorant. More fundamental to the profession, with every word that is written the practitioner finds himself more ignorant of more of the law itself. In part this arises incurably — from the expansion of the law. And for that reason, the part that is curable takes on a greater urgency. Every unnecessary word placed into an opinion, a statute, a regulation, puts that much extra strain on the strained minds of busy men, and the worth of their professional opinions suffers accordingly. This is an old complaint (Sections 78, 94), sharpened today with the greater ease of getting things into writing, printed, and circulated.

Every mechanical aid the law has seized upon to make itself more available has increased its bulk. Thus with the switch from oral to written pleadings, from written to printed precedents (Section 78), from oral to written and printed opinions (Section 110), from private formbooks to commercial ones (Sections 110, 112), from human beings to office machinery (Section 108).

The latest in this dismal procession has the mouth-filling title (an

---

[15] See Section 90; *More v. Clipsam*, 82 Eng. Rep. 538 (K.B. 1648).
[16] See *Green v. Palmer*, 15 Cal. 411, 414 (1860); and see *Powell v. Powell*, 112 Utah 418 (1948); 49 *C.J. pleading* §111, p. 119.

evil omen) — *Electronic Data Retrieval* (E.D.R.), in one plant appropriately under the jurisdiction of a *Synthetic Intelligence Department.*[17] Like its predecessors in the arts of availability, E.D.R. is ruled by a corollary of Parkinson's Law:[18] *The data to retrieve increases as it becomes more retrievable.* The ease of feeding the machine will encourage wholesale dumping rather than selection, the perpetuation even of those unreported reports still safely unreported. (Section 110.) The ease of retrieval will extend the magic of precedent (Section 126) into dustbins unprobed and unmissed. The whirling lawyer will spin in yet more directions in a desperate effort to preserve his repute as a member of an unignorant profession.

Though there are increasing signs that the machine has bitten the lawyer,[19] there is as yet no evidence that what electronics makes more available will be useful law rather than extra words. The machine stores what it receives. Will it retrieve the lean or the fat or lick the platter clean? The machine cannot be stopped, but the fat can be trimmed before it gets to the hopper.

Third, and working against the ignorance that bulk produces, brevity can save the time of the bar and the public.

Here, a distinction between composing time and reading time. It takes more time to write briefly than verbosely. One page of brief literary composition represents ten in the wastebasket. The time-saving of brevity comes in the reading, not the writing,[20] but this saving more than overbalances the time spent (not lost) in writing briefly. For one thing, the extra time in the composition is spent by the one person who should know what he wants to say. And it will

[17] Los Angeles Daily J., vol. 74, No. 103, May 24, 1961, p. 1.

[18] See Parkinson, *Parkinson's Law* 2 (1957).

[19] For example: P. James, *Mechanized Legal Research,* draft proposal for evaluation by the Electronic Data Retrieval Committee of the American Bar Association, pp. 1-23, and bibliography, pp. 16-18 (1959); Modern Uses of Logic in Law (MULL) (quarterly newsletter of the Electronic Data Retrieval Committee of the A.B.A., first published Sept. 1959); item in "Report of the Board of Governors," 85 Reports of the A.B.A. 354 (1960); *Applications of Electronic Data Processing Systems to Legal Research* (1960); Melton and Bensing, "Searching Legal Literature Electronically: Results of a Test Program," 45 Minn. L. Rev. 229-248 (1960); Freed, "Prepare Now for Machine-Assisted Legal Research," 47 A.B.A.J. 764-767 (1961); Dickerson, "The Electronic Searching of Law," 47 A.B.A.J. 902-908 (1961).

[20] *King v. Gildersleeve,* 79 Cal. 504, 507-508 (1889); McComb, "A Mandate from the Bar: Shorter and More Lucid Opinions," 35 A.B.A.J. 382, 383 n.4 (1949); Martin, "The Problem of Reducing the Volume of Published Opinions," 26 J. Am. Jud. Soc. 138, 141 (1943); compare Beardsley, "Judicial Draftsmanship," 24 Wash. L. Rev. 146, 149 (1949); compare also Gibson, "Literary Minds and Judicial Style," 36 N.Y.U.L. Rev. 915, 923 n.19 (1961).

take him less time to figure out a way of saying what he means than
for a stranger to sift his meaning out of too many words. Again, some
writing is intended for wide readership, and it is a balancing of one
man's time against the time of many. Even though the one counts
himself a dollar and the others as dimes, there is enough of small
change to overbalance the account. Furthermore, since the writer —
in less violent mood — is also a reader, the writer's contribution of
time to the cause of brevity works ultimately to his own advantage.

As long as the discussion of brevity is kept in terms of "literary composition," "writing," "writers," most lawyers (and judges) will nod
agreement. This is talk about someone else — mostly literary chaps
(Section 114), or perhaps even clients who write long letters. A lawyer may also appreciate its application to a judge's adverse opinion[21]
and a judge to a lawyer's brief.[22] Yet nothing is more fundamental
to the survival of the profession in a world of expanding law. Brevity is the last best hope for an informed and effective bar, while verbosity wastes its time (and money) multiplying the bar's capacity for
ignorance and error.

Though the case for brevity deserves emphatic statement, brevity
is still but one of a number of qualities that shape the language of the
law. In short, the language of the law is not uniformly long or short,
nor should it be. But the decision of longer or shorter need not be
left to chance. (See Section 131.)

131. Contagious verbosity

The most effective way of shortening law language is for judges and
lawyers to stop writing, a cruel and unusual expedient yet not without its advocates. Some of them have said that the need is for fewer
laws, no commentaries,[23] fewer opinions,[24] an end to law reviews.[25]

---

[21] See and compare Llewellyn, *The Common Law Tradition: Deciding Appeals*
464 (1960); compare "Report of the Special Committee on Legal Publications and
Law Reporting," in 65 Reports of the A.B.A. 263, 270 (1940).

[22] *King v. Gildersleeve,* 79 Cal. 504, 507-508 (1889); and compare McComb,
"A Mandate from the Bar: Shorter and More Lucid Opinions," 35 A.B.A.J. 382
(1949).

[23] More, *Utopia,* in *Ideal Empires and Republics* 127, 203 (1901); Swift,
Gulliver's Travels 152 (Crown ed. 1947); "The Fundamental Constitutions of
Carolina," arts. 79, 80, in 5 F. Thorpe, *The Federal and State Constitutions,
Colonial Charters, and Other Organic Laws* 2782 (1909); and see also Moyle,
General Introduction in Justinian, *Institutionum* 75-76 (Moyle, 5th ed. 1912).

[24] Martin, "The Problem of Reducing the Volume of Published Opinions," 26
J. Am. Jud. Soc. 138-141 (1943); see also Prince, "Law Books Unlimited," 48
A.B.A.J. 134-137 (1962).

[25] Rodell, "Goodbye to Law Reviews," 23 Va. L. Rev. 38 (1936).

In a free society this is a call for a refined and unappealing asceticism. So easy for the writing lawyer to convince himself that the wrong people might heed the call. Is my opinion, my dissent, is my book necessary? Who will be his own executioner? Whatever the abstract advantages of total abstinence, moderation is attainable. At least it is possible to demonstrate that if it must be written, it can be shorter.

As a preliminary: the fewest words that accomplish the purpose is brevity enough, whether the word count is high or low. Beyond that the words are worthless, to be systematically rooted out whether they be many or few. The antidote for verbosity is not haphazard brevity (Section 130), which sometimes succeeds in achieving the paradoxically bad: language too short and too long at the same time. For if law language does not accomplish its purpose, even one word is too many. So it is with some of the archaisms which the laity has discarded, leaving lawyers holding the bag — *aforesaid, forthwith, hereafter, hereby, herein, hereinafter, heretofore, said, whereas* (discussed in detail in Section 120). So it is too when words of changing technicality such as *seisin* (Section 121) and *heirs*[26] are used without notice of the change, and words of variable construction such as *children*[27] and *issue*[28] are used without more to chart the course of construction.[29]

It is possible to shorten by ceasing to act as lawyer — by leaving out protection that a client wants even when he doesn't know enough to ask for it. A lease can be made shorter by omitting a covenant against assignment.[30] A consent to assignment is shorter when it ignores the rule in *Dumpor's Case*,[31] a will shorter which fails to exercise a power

---

[26] Section 121; Casner, "Construction of Gifts to 'Heirs' and the Like," 53 Harv. L. Rev. 207-250, 250 (1939).

[27] See 7 *Words and Phrases* 3-150 (perm. ed. 1952), 3-8 (Supp. 1962), "child; children" and related entries; 1 *California Words, Phrases, and Maxims* (1960), "children"; 1 *Words and Phrases: Judicially Defined* 429-434 (1946), 87-89 (Supp. 1960), "child; children" and related entries.

[28] 22A *Words and Phrases* 553-629 (perm. ed. 1958), 18-20 (Supp. 1962), "issue-descendants"; 2 *California Words, Phrases, and Maxims* (1960), "issue-descendants"; 3 *Words and Phrases: Judicially Defined* 155-162 (1944), 32-33 (1960 Supp.), "issue," "offspring"; 3 *Words and Phrases: Judicially Defined* 168 (1944), "issue living," "issue of cousins"; 22A *Words and Phrases* (perm. ed. 1958), "issue of marriage"; 3 *Words and Phrases: Judicially Defined* (Supp. 1960), "issue of our marriage"; 22A *Words and Phrases* (perm. ed. 1958), "issue of the body."

[29] Leach, "Powers of Appointment," 24 A.B.A.J. 807, 808, 811 (1938).

[30] Nichols, *Cyclopedia of Legal Forms* §5.1865 (1956).

[31] 76 Eng. Rep. 1110 (K.B. 1603); for example, Nichols, *Cyclopedia of Legal Forms* §§5.2377B, 5.2378A, and compare §§5.2381A, 5.2381B (1956).

of appointment,[32] or ignores the tax collector. Saying not enough can be as disastrous to the professional as saying too much but at least it does not take so much of his colleagues' time. Let us assume competence and pass on to unadulterated wordiness.

In other parts of this book are illustrations of worthless doubling (Section 123), of the unprecise pattern of two-words-for-one (Section 124), of the traditional and evil long sentence (Section 125), of forms that give ways of saying things worse with more words. (Sections 112, 120, 121.) These are curable ills, uncured, with the cumulative effect contagious verbosity. The profession has come to expect that a good contract or opinion will be a long one. Purposeless repetition conforms to the accustomed literary rhythms of the law, so that it passes without sustained protest,[33] almost without notice.

Only rarely is there a sign of the self-consciousness which can be the prelude to self-correction. A fleeting awareness of verbosity comes to the surface in phrases like *As above stated,*[34] *As before stated,*[35] *As heretofore noted,*[36] *as we said above,*[37] *at the risk of redundance.*[38]

More often the heart is pure, the mind untroubled by doubt. This, for example, from an opinion decrying the vagueness of a *common drunkard* statute. The meaning of *habitual,* says the court, is undefined,

> ". . . left as a matter of fact to be determined by those who might differ widely in regard to it." [39]
>
> . . . Consequently, each judge and jury is free to define the crime in any manner that it sees fit, . . .[40]
>
> . . . Thus, it was left to the jury to determine according to their individual views and concepts when in their respective opinions a person . . .[41]
>
> . . . By its terms the statute leaves to the individual judge or jury

[32] See Leach, "Powers of Appointment," 24 A.B.A.J. 807, 811 (1938).

[33] Compare Beardsley, "Judicial Draftsmanship," 24 Wash. L. Rev. 146-153 (1949); McComb, "A Mandate from the Bar: Shorter and More Lucid Opinions," 35 A.B.A.J. 382-384 (1949); "Report of the Special Committee on Legal Publications and Law Reporting," 65 Reports of the A.B.A. 263-300 (1940).

[34] *Thilman v. Thilman,* 30 Wash. 2d 743, 774 (1948).

[35] *Ex parte Cook,* 270 Ala. 31, 32 (1959).

[36] *Estate of Karkeet,* 56 Cal. 2d 277, 283 (1961).

[37] *Scandinavian Airlines System, Inc. v. County of Los Angeles,* 56 Cal. 2d 11, 42 (1961).

[38] *People v. Daniel,* 168 Cal. App. 2d Supp. 788, 799 (1959), and see also 791, 802.

[39] *In re Newbern,* 53 Cal. 2d 786, 796 (1960), quoting from *State v. Ryan,* 70 Wis. 676, 685 (1888).

[40] *In re Newbern,* 53 Cal. 2d 786, 796 (1960).

[41] *In re Newbern,* 53 Cal. 2d 786, 796 (1960).

the determination of the meaning of the law as well as what proven
facts render the accused guilty or innocent.[42]

. . . It is not difficult to visualize the divergence of decisions or
verdicts that must ensue when the law leaves its definition and meaning to be determined by judges and juries who might differ widely in
regard to it.[43]

. . . That provision will not tolerate a criminal law so lacking in
definition that each defendant is left to the vagaries of individual
judges and juries.[44]

Precious reading time wasted in giving busy lawyers the same
thought six times in the space of little more than a page. This is
talking, not writing. And were it not recorded, it would seem less
inappropriate. Oral delivery calls for some repetition, for the ear
cannot wander back over lost sounds as the eye does over passed
print. And this difference between eye and ear partly explains how
— willy-nilly — the repetitions get into legal writings, especially opinions. They are dictated repetitions, not written ones. The oral opinion of the past (Section 110) remains oral even though it is now called
a "written" opinion. It is oral but it has been mechanically captured,
and all of it has been preserved, not just its substance or its beauty.
The opinion talker suffers the same physical limitations of the opinion
listener; he has got to repeat so that he can keep in ear (and so in
mind) what it is he is talking about. That is why an opinion gives a
contract verbatim,[45] and later repeats verbatim passages;[46] gives the
contentions of a party,[47] and repeats them;[48] says what "The first point
of inquiry concerns . . ."[49] and wanders away from it, to return pages
later with repetitive vigor: "Therefore, it is of primary importance to
determine . . ."[50] — the substitution of *primary* for *first* the only faint
evidence of literary embarrassment.

The orally prepared "written" opinion also falls easily into excited
wordiness — an attention-getting device more characteristic of speaking (or shouting) than of writing. The sound of spoken words — his
own — arouses the latent orator. It is no longer written legal prose,
but the booming artillery of the rostrum. Hear this (read it aloud),

[42] *In re Newbern,* 53 Cal. 2d 786, 796 (1960).
[43] *In re Newbern,* 53 Cal. 2d 786, 796 (1960).
[44] *In re Newbern,* 53 Cal. 2d 786, 797 (1960).
[45] *Williams v. Chastain,* 221 Ore. 69, 72-73 (1960).
[46] *Williams v. Chastain,* 221 Ore. 69, 77-78 (1960).
[47] *Williams v. Chastain,* 221 Ore. 69, 74 (1960).
[48] *Williams v. Chastain,* 221 Ore. 69, 76 (1960).
[49] *Williams v. Chastain,* 221 Ore. 69, 74 (1960).
[50] *Williams v. Chastain,* 221 Ore. 69, 76 (1960).

if you doubt that women must have a cause of action for loss of *consortium*:

> In such circumstances, when her husband's love is denied her, his strength sapped, and his protection destroyed, in short, when she has been forced by the defendant to exchange a heart for a husk, we are urged to rule that she has suffered no loss compensable at the law. But let some scoundrel dent a dishpan in the family kitchen and the law, in all its majesty, will convene the court, will march with measured tread to the halls of justice, and will there suffer a jury of her peers to assess the damages. Why are we asked then, in the case before us, to look the other way? Is this what is meant when it is said that justice is blind? [51]

Impressed with that "brilliant opinion," [52] another judge not only reproduces it, but improves upon it — like this:

> The flesh and blood of our American civilization is the family. Without children, not only our civilization but the race itself would perish. Does it not mean something to the law to protect this right; and punish for its destruction? Are we to understand from the decision rendered by this Court today that a wife may bring an action against any person who steals her pocket book, steps on her foot, or injures her dog, but she may not bring an action for the loss of her most valued privilege? [53]

> . . . The Majority has written a long opinion, but I do not find in its entire length any justification or even attempted rationalization for its conclusion that a wife may not recover for the loss of her possibility to procreate children. The opinion does not even mention the word Motherhood.
>
> To enter into any eulogy on Motherhood would be "to gild the vernal morn," but it may be relevant to say that Motherhood is a privilege and responsibility so sacred and divine that women have been known to accept poverty, contumely, and untold sacrifice to achieve it within the sanctified sphere of matrimony. The pages of the human race are golden with instances of women who have married worthless men, even scamps, so as to produce children who would engladden their lives and enrich the world, hoping that with the advent of the children, the husbands might become better men and be worthy of the accolade of father.[54]

Dictation by lawyers and judges increases a traditional insensitivity to wordiness. It sounds all right — even the repetitions and the bombast, even the long sentences (which originated in an oral tradition). (Sections 82-84.) Mediated by the voice, wordage that would cause the eye to wander loses some of its deadliness. Especially is this true when it is the voice of the author talking to himself — dictating. Thus

[51] *Montgomery v. Stephan*, 359 Mich. 33, 48-49 (1960).
[52] Musmanno, J., dissenting, in *Neuberg v. Bobowicz*, 401 Pa. 146, 161 (1960).
[53] *Neuberg v. Bobowicz*, 401 Pa. 146, 161 (1960).
[54] *Neuberg v. Bobowicz*, 401 Pa. 146, 162 (1960).

charmed, the author easily forgets that he is talking to those who may read, but will not listen.

Beyond the physical and psychological differences between listening and reading is a related distinction between prose suitable only for ephemeral speech and prose fit to be preserved. If only those within hearing distance in court or lecture room suffer a platitude, the damage is minimal. But let a legal platitude be dropped into print, and the suffering is widespread and daily.

The least harmful platitude takes a form familiar to laymen:

> Without fear of contradiction, it can be stated that the counselling of clients is probably one of the most important phases of a lawyer's professional work.[55]

Here the circulation is restricted.

The more vicious platitude is the hornbook legal principle[56] clogging the reports and bulging the digests so that working lawyers cannot avoid them. A high court tells us (1951):

> Before there can be a legally enforceable obligation there must be an offer and an acceptance.[57]

This startling intelligence[58] is dutifully headnoted:

> An offer and an acceptance thereof, are necessary to create a legally enforceable obligation.[59]

It is carefully indexed, and pads a digest already amply endowed.[60]

A lower court (1960) says it differently:

> To constitute a "contract" there must be an offer made by one person or body to another, and an acceptance of that offer by the person to whom it was made.[61]

The system — like a tired echo — preserves this too:

> To constitute a contract, there must be an offer made by one person to another, and acceptance of offer by other person.[62]

---

[55] Mehler, "Language Mastery and Legal Training," 6 Vill. L. Rev. 201, 207 (Winter, 1960-1961), and see also 201.

[56] Beardsley, "Judicial Draftsmanship," 24 Wash. L. Rev. 146, 150 (1949).

[57] *Mathieu v. Wubbs,* 330 Mich. 408, 412, 47 N.W.2d 670, 673 (1951).

[58] Compare Holmes, *The Common Law* 303 (1881).

[59] *Mathieu v. Wubbs,* 47 N.W.2d 670, 671 (1951), and see headnote in 330 Mich. 408.

[60] *Mathieu v. Wubbs,* 330 Mich. 408, 47 N.W.2d 670, noted in 6 *Sixth Decennial Digest* 1096 (1957), and 4 *Mich. Digest,* pt. 1, p. 104.

[61] *Riegel v. Holmes,* 171 N.E.2d 553, 562 (Ohio Ct. Com. Pl. 1960).

[62] *Riegel v. Holmes,* 171 N.E.2d 553, 554 (Ohio Ct. Com. Pl. 1960), noted in 15 *West's General Digest* 3d 361 (1961).

Yearly the tonnage of banality mounts, through *contracts*, definitions of *negligence*,[63] *summary judgment*,[64] on and on. Yearly the profession pays its money, wastes its time, and strains its eyes rereading what it already knows too well trying to discover answers to what it does not know. The barrier is artificial and unnecessary.

How to end it? How end the platitudes, the old quotes, the repetitions, the bombast, the endless gossipy statements of irrelevent evidence? Better organization of opinions?[65] A concentration on the important?[66] A sharper focus on the audience?[67] All to the good. A cynic has been even blunter:

> "The judge might accomplish this desired end by writing a long opinion, if he wished the mental exercise. He could then give it adequate headnotes and throw the opinion in the wastebasket. This would tend to clarity of expression and crystallize the thoughts of the judge."[68]

These appeals to reason and to pride break up on the sharp limits of time. Granting an awareness of verbosity and of its harm to the profession, judge and lawyer need time to reorganize and cut. The crowded docket places a premium on the rambling opinion quickly produced. For want of calm minutes, a will follows the long sentence tradition into ambiguity — and a client dies, his wishes unfulfilled.[69] The time-worried lawyer reaches for the word-encrusted form, gives the printer his swollen brief,[70] and sends to the law magazines his speeches designed for listening rather than reading.[71] Rewrite takes time. Get it off. File it on time.

---

[63] For example: *Turnell v. Mahlin*, 171 Neb. 513, 518, and headnote at 514, 106 N.W.2d 693, 697, and headnote at 694 (1960); *Jackson v. Stancil*, 253 N.C. 291, 297-298, and headnote at 292, 116 S.E.2d 817, 822, and headnote at 818 (1960).

[64] *Mastercraft Lamp Co. v. Mortek*, 28 Ill. App. 2d 273, 274-275, 171 N.E.2d 427, 428 (1960), *rehearing denied* (1961); *Teague v. Reid*, 340 S.W.2d 235, 240, and headnote at 235 (Ky. Ct. App. 1960).

[65] McComb, "A Mandate from the Bar: Shorter and More Lucid Opinions," 35 A.B.A.J. 382-384 (1949).

[66] Martin, "The Problem of Reducing the Volume of Published Opinions," 26 J. Am. Jud. Soc. 138-141 (1943).

[67] Gibson, "Literary Minds and Judicial Style," 36 N.Y.U.L. Rev. 915-930 (1961).

[68] Excerpt from testimony, "Report of the Special Committee on Legal Publications and Law Reporting," in 65 Reports of the A.B.A. 263, 270 (1940).

[69] *Estate of Jones*, 55 Cal. 2d 531, 539 (1961), and see opinion in 9 Cal. Rptr. 126, 130 (1960).

[70] See *King v. Gildersleeve*, 79 Cal. 504, 507 (1889).

[71] Anderson, "Medical Testimony in the Courts," 43 J. Am. Jud. Soc. 79-86 (1959); Doub, "Recent Trends in the Criminal Law," 46 A.B.A.J. 139-142 (1960); Levin, "Traffic Courts: The Judge's Responsibility," 46 A.B.A.J. 143-146, 223-224 (1960); Friendly, "A Look at the Federal Administrative Agencies," 60 Colum.

Somewhere there must be a beginning of a change. For these extra words take more time to read, which gives less time to write, which makes more extra words to read, which . . .

Wordy complaints invite wordy answers.[72] Extra words by lawyers stimulate extra words from the bench.[73] A long-talking majority produces a longer dissent.[74] One mixed-up metaphor begets another. Here is one from the majority:

> The roots which at one time, if ever, gave nurture and a legitimate birth to the husband's right to assert a claim for loss of consortium have long since `wizened and died. They owe their origin to a seed of thought which, when viewed by the eyeglass of the present day, none should accept, much less implant anew.[75]

And a capper from the dissenter:

> The defendants in this case, . . . have reduced the [husband] plaintiff to a physical wreck. The wife plaintiff is a victim of that wreck . . .[76]

Look at the opinion in *Thilman v. Thilman* (1948), sprawling over thirty-three pages of official reports[77] and seventeen pages of unofficial,[78] reduced by a careful lawyer to a law review page.[79] See contagious verbosity at work from trial through appeal. Here are parts of the opinion on appeal, a picture of judges wrestling with too many words:

> Many witnesses were sworn, the testimony comprising over one thousand pages of the statement of facts. . . .
>
> . . . .
>
> After a lengthy oral decision, the trial court filed a written memorandum opinion, and . . . entered the decree, which refers to the court's oral decision.[80] . . .
>
> . . . .
>
> At the close of the case, the trial court delivered a lengthy and comprehensive oral summation of the testimony and, later, when ruling

---

L. Rev. 429-446 and especially 429n (1960); Rives, "The Scope of Review of Facts by United States Courts of Appeals," 11 Ala. L. Rev. 70-78 (Fall, 1958).

[72] *Jones v. City of Petaluma*, 36 Cal. 230, 232-233, 234, 236, 237 (1868); *Racouillat v. Rene*, 32 Cal. 450, 454, 455, 456 (1867); see *Meyers v. Huschle Bros. Inc.*, 75 N.Y.S.2d 350, 352, 353-354 (1947), aff'd, 273 App. Div. 107 (1947).

[73] *Green v. Palmer*, 15 Cal. 411 (1860); *Van Grutten v. Foxwell*, 84 L.T.R. (n.s.) 545, 546, 547, 549 (H.L. 1901); *Bonitto v. Fuerst Brothers & Co. Ltd.*, [1944] A.C. 75.

[74] *Neuberg v. Bobowicz*, 401 Pa. 146 (1960).

[75] *Neuberg v. Bobowicz*, 401 Pa. 146, 150 (1960).

[76] *Neuberg v. Bobowicz*, 401 Pa. 146, 164 (1960).

[77] 30 Wash. 2d 743-777 (1948).

[78] 193 P.2d 674-692 (1948).

[79] Beardsley, "Judicial Draftsmanship," 24 Wash. L. Rev. 146, 152-153 (1949).

[80] *Thilman v. Thilman*, 30 Wash. 2d 743, 759 (1948).

upon appellant's motion for judgment notwithstanding the decision of the court or, in the alternative, for a new trial, filed a written memorandum opinion. Both opinions are contained in the statement of facts.

Respondent Margaret Thilman testified on the trial as a witness on her own behalf, her testimony comprising over two hundred pages of the statement of facts . . .[81]

Too much to hear, too much to read, too little time to write. But the time taken to cut at any stage of the proceedings would have made the effort at brevity easier for those who followed.

Here is the contagion again, in *People v. Daniel* (1959),[82] testing a *common drunkard* statute. The opinion (of the appellate department of a trial court) covers thirteen pages of official reports, eight pages of unofficial. Aware of verbosity at the bar, the judge yet succumbs to it:

> The matter has been exhaustively briefed by both parties, and so many authorities have been cited that the task of even coordinating them has been Herculean. They range in time from the delivery of the commandments and laws to his people by Moses as related in Deuteronomy, wherein he advises his people to take the stubborn and rebellious son without the walls of the city and stone him to death as a glutton and a *drunkard* (emphasis added) so that they shall purge the evil from their midst, and all Israel should hear and fear. They cover the entire English speaking world from the ancient common law to the present date. It would be tedious, and in our opinion, unnecessary to here attempt any detailed discussion of these authorities, but . . .[83]

> .   .   .   .

> The words, both singly and conjunctively, have been in common use and generally understood since Moses delivered the commandments and the law to his people, and up to the present time . . .[84]

> .   .   .   .

> We regret the length of this opinion. In spite of diligent effort, we have been unable to shorten it, and still give the difficult problem proper consideration.[85]

.   .   .   .

And the result of this verbosity and torment? One year later a disapproval, in thirteen pages.[86]

It is possible to make the same point verbosely or briefly. For instance, the point that sex can make a constitutional difference:

[81] *Thilman v. Thilman*, 30 Wash. 2d 743, 761 (1948).
[82] 168 Cal. App. 2d Supp. 788-802 (1959).
[83] *People v. Daniel*, 168 Cal. App. 2d Supp. 788, 790-791 (1959).
[84] *People v. Daniel*, 168 Cal. App. 2d Supp. 788, 798 (1959).
[85] *People v. Daniel*, 168 Cal. App. 2d Supp. 788, 802 (1959).
[86] *In re Newbern*, 53 Cal. 2d 786, 797 (1960), and see also 793-794.

Brewer, J.

The limitations which this statute places upon her contractual powers, upon her right to agree with her employer as to the time she shall labor, are not imposed solely for her benefit, but also largely for the benefit of all. Many words cannot make this plainer. The two sexes differ in structure of body, in the functions to be performed by each, in the amount of physical strength, in the capacity for long-continued labor, particularly when done standing, the influence of vigorous health upon the future well-being of the race, the self-reliance which enables one to assert full rights, and in the capacity to maintain the struggle for subsistence. This difference justifies a difference in legislation, and upholds that which is designed to compensate for some of the burdens which rest upon her.[87]

Holmes, J.

If Montana deems it advisable to put a lighter burden upon women than upon men with regard to an employment that our people commonly regard as more appropriate for the former, the Fourteenth Amendment does not interfere by creating a fictitious equality where there is a real difference.[88]

It is possible for brevity to become fashionable, even habitual. The pressure against too many words can become stronger than the pressure of too little time — and so make the time last longer.

In a World War II prison camp, with a six-line limit imposed by the enemy, a British lawyer composed this workable power of attorney:

"I, John Blank, a prisoner of war, hereby irrevocably appoint for one year my wife, Mary Blank, of 4 High Street, Nosuchtown, to be my attorney for all purposes with power to do anything I might myself do including the execution and delivery of any document. And I indemnify any person acting hereunder." [89]

The pressure for brevity comes in better grace from the bar itself — self-criticism,[90] the conscientious efforts of some of the judiciary,[91]

---

[87] *Muller v. Oregon*, 208 U.S. 412, 422-423 (1908).

[88] *Quong Wing v. Kirkendall,* 223 U.S. 59, 63 (1912).

[89] Quoted in Greene, "Shorter Deeds, or Multum in Parvo," 110 L.J. 84 (Feb. 10, 1961).

[90] For example, "Report of the Special Committee on Legal Publications and Law Reporting," 65 Reports of the A.B.A. 263-300 (1940).

[91] For example, McComb, "A Mandate from the Bar: Shorter and More Lucid Opinions," 35 A.B.A.J. 382-384 (1949), and see opinions of McComb, J., in *Gonzalez v. Derrington*, 56 Cal. 2d 130 (1961), and *Spector v. Superior Court,* 55 Cal. 2d 839 (1961); Martin, "The Problem of Reducing the Volume of Published Opinions," 26 J. Am. Jud. Soc. 138 (1943).

a looking to the best rather than the worst of the law's literary tradition. A part of that best is another six lines, an opinion:

> The Court below erred in giving the third, fourth, and fifth instructions. If the defendants were at fault in leaving an uncovered hole in the sidewalk of a public street, the intoxication of the plaintiff cannot excuse such gross negligence. A drunken man is as much entitled to a safe street, as a sober one, and much more in need of it.
> The judgment is reversed and the cause remanded.[92]

[92] *Robinson v. Pioche,* 5 Cal. 460, 461 (1855).

CHAPTER XV

More Intelligible

132. *The areas of misunderstanding*

Intelligible and *unintelligible* have an overpowering sound of absoluteness that limits their usefulness in discussion of the language of the law. It is a very empty phrase that someone, somewhere, cannot squeeze a drop of sense from, yet some glittering nonsense discourages the effort. Take this specimen, spawned by a current vogue for legislation about emergency calls on party lines: [1]

> In every telephone directory . . . there shall be printed in type not smaller than any other type appearing on the same page, a notice preceded by the word "warning" printed in type at least as large as the largest type on the same page, . . .[2]

This is no misprint. It had models in the laws of sister states,[3] and in turn has become a model for others.[4] Take comfort that some draftsmen have refused to buy this pre-wrapped shoddy, stopping the word flow when they had had enough for law, for good English, and for people — after the word *warning*.[5] Take comfort too that complete gibberish is not the typical instance of language mangling by lawyers. It is still aiming too low to be satisfied with language that is only "capable of being understood," the standard definition of *intelligible*.[6] The general antipathy to absolutes (Section 129) has for centuries split *intelligible* into degrees,[7] and as used in this book it means "easily

---

[1] Bruno, Note, "Legislation — Surrender of Party Line Telephones in Emergency . . . ," 36 Notre Dame Law. 392-396 (1961).

[2] N.J. Stat. Ann. §48:17-15.1 (1955).

[3] For example: Mich. Stat. Ann. §28.808(2) (1952); N.Y. Pen. Law §1424-a(3) (1954).

[4] For example: Cal. Pen. Code §384(c); Conn. Gen. Stat. §16-256 (1957); compare Md. Ann. Code, art. 27, §629A(c) (1957).

[5] For example: Ill. Ann. Stat., c. 134, §16.9 (1959); Wash. Rev. Code §70.85.040 (1953); see also Wis. Stat. §941.35(4) (1959).

[6] *Webster's New International Dictionary* (2d ed. 1934).

[7] *Oxford English Dictionary,* under *intelligible,* No. 2.

understood,"[8] what some mean by clear[9] or plain.[10]   Its opposite —
unintelligible — covers the full muddy spectrum available to lawyers.
From the shortest nonsense — *ss.* (Section 120.)   Through long rows
of unnecessarily unclear words (Sections 20, 129) and constructions
(Sections 125, 127), variously distinguished as obscure,[11] vague,[12]
ambiguous,[13] and in other circles called doubletalk,[14] officialese,[15]
gobbledygook,[16] federal prose,[17] etc.[18]   Down into the scraps of language which at best are not easily understood, such as *and/or* and
or/and. (Section 120.)

This breadth of range is a further reminder that intelligibility is not
synonymous with brevity, though verbosity does make it easier for the
writer to lose himself while losing his reader. (Section 130.)

Likewise, intelligibility is not dependent upon precision, which
sometimes must be sacrificed for quick understanding (Section 129),
as in the traffic signs which tell pedestrians to WAIT (without saying
for how long), and to WALK (without adding, "if you want to").
The sacrifice of precision for intelligibility needs mention, not to encourage sloppiness but appropriateness, and to offset the single-minded
teaching which reverses the rites — making intelligibility always the
goat. (Section 115.)   There are still times when magic words make
a legal difference[19] — e.g., *consideration for the lease* (instead of *prepaid rent*),[20] or the weaker magic of *liquidated damages*[21] (instead of

---

[8] Partridge, *Usage and Abusage* (new ed. 1957), under *intelligent.*

[9] Evans and Evans, *A Dictionary of Contemporary American Usage* (1957),
under *intelligent.*

[10] Gowers, *Plain Words* (London, 1948).

[11] 8 Bentham, *Works* 304-305 (Bowring ed. 1843).

[12] 43 *Words and Phrases* (perm. ed. 1940), "vague" and related headings; and
see 5 *Words and Phrases: Judicially Defined* (1945), "vagueness."

[13] 8 Bentham, *Works* 304-305 (Bowring ed. 1843).

[14] *Webster's Third New International Dictionary* (1961); Evans and Evans, *A
Dictionary of Contemporary American Usage* (1957), under *persiflage.*

[15] Partridge, Introduction to ["Vigilans"], *Chamber of Horrors* 13, 15 (1952).

[16] *Webster's Third New International Dictionary* (1961).

[17] Masterson and Phillips, *Federal Prose* (1948).

[18] See generally Hunter, *The Language of Audit Reports* 27-32 (1957); Partridge, *Usage and Abusage* (new ed. 1957), under *jargon;* Orwell, "Politics and
the English Language," in *Shooting an Elephant* 84-101 (London ed. 1950);
Quiller-Couch, *On the Art of Writing* 83-103 (1916).

[19] See Leach and Tudor, *The Rule Against Perpetuities* 16 (1957); Williams,
"Language and the Law," 61 L.Q. Rev. 71, 78-80 (1945).

[20] See 36 *C.J. landlord and tenant* §1064.

[21] See 25 *Words and Phrases* 555-586 (perm. ed. 1961), 5 (Supp. 1962); 2
California Words, Phrases, and Maxims 567-568 (1960); 3 *Words and Phrases:
Judicially Defined* 263-264 (1943).

forfeiture or *penalty*). Even so, there is little legal prose of any sort which cannot be made more intelligible than it usually is.

Once the draftsman starts with a clear understanding of what it is he wants to say, making himself understood is more a matter of how than of what. If the simplest truth goes in fuzzy, it will come out that way. And if complexity goes in clear, it can come out that way — gospel or not. Even ". . . Holmes was sometimes clearly wrong; but . . . when this was so he was always wrong clearly." [22]

Any legal prose can be made more intelligible if the draftsman is striving for intelligibility, but even the careful draftsman sometimes finds more pressing concerns — some legitimate. There is, for example, the deliberate use of language which everyone recognizes as being easily misunderstood, accepted for the sake of quick agreement. This sort of *calculated ambiguity* [23] is left for later. (Section 135.) Also left for later is the deliberate use of language which though not always easily understood is quickly felt, the language of ceremony and persuasion. (Section 135.)

On the blacker side is the art of planned confusion, which has its advocates,[24] its gray and off-white shadings, and above all its patterns for identification. The patterns are so strong that at times the "planned" aspect has dropped deep into the inner lawyer, to become merely habitual without taint of sinister purpose.

Planned confusion takes two major forms: (1) saying-nothing and making it look like something, and (2) saying-something and making it look like nothing, or like something else. The law has no monopoly on either form, but as wholesale dealers in words lawyers have found the patterns too useful.

At its mildest, nonprofessional saying-nothing takes the form of small talk, the polite lying that is the mark of civilized society. Thus,

we say	*instead of*
I find it stimulating	Absolute nonsense
Most interesting	What a bore
Very stately	Real ugly
We must get together soon	Thank God, you're leaving town

Related to this is the lawyer's

[22] Hart, "Positivism and the Separation of Law and Morals," 71 Harv. L. Rev. 593 (1958).

[23] Cox, "Internal Affairs of Labor Unions Under the Labor Reform Act of 1959," 58 Mich. L. Rev. 819, 852 (1960); see also Arnold, "Professor Hart's Theology," 73 Harv. L. Rev. 1298, 1312 (1960); and see Section 104.

[24] See Coulson, book review, in 44 A.B.A.J. 55 (1958).

"progress" letter	*instead of*
Your matter is being given due consideration in the light of the pertinent statutes and case law, and you will be further advised in due course.	Right now it looks like you're stuck. But don't go shopping for another lawyer.

A more widespread malady of nothingness at the bar is the *one-legged subjunctive*. Its most prevalent forms are *it would seem*[25] and *it may well be*,[26] which make no more sense when joined together like this:

> It would seem also that a further and more far reaching effect of the instant judgment may well be to encourage other persons to breach their obligations . . .[27]

Variants are *one might wish*[28] and the emphatically spurious *it may very well be*.[29]

Unlike the bald fraud of *yes and no,* these phrases equivocate even on being equivocal. *It would seem* (that is the appearance of things, says the writer) — and you wait in vain for the other shoe to drop. Not *it would seem to be, but the fact is,* just way up in the air, *it would seem.* So that the writer can never be called to account. Not what I thought or believed or what the fact was, just what it seemed to be. And then again, *it may well be* something completely different, or *it may well not be.* I'm not sure or won't say; at least I haven't said.

The lawyer's addiction to *it would seem* is related to the old and continuing law use of French *semble* (it seems).[30] But that is a technical expression of uncertainty [31] and lack of authority [32] which still

[25] For example: *In re Higdon,* 30 Wash. 2d 546, 555 (1948); Cox, "Internal Affairs of Labor Unions Under the Labor Reform Act of 1959," 58 Mich. L. Rev. 819, 852 (1960); "Note from the Temple," 94 Ir. L.T. 127, 128 (May 28, 1960); and see discussion in Rodell, "Goodbye to Law Reviews," 23 Va. L. Rev. 38, 39 (1936); Levitan, "Dissertation on Writing Legal Opinions," Wis. L. Rev. 22, 37 (Jan. 1960); see also Evans and Evans, *A Dictionary of Contemporary American Usage* (1957), under *will, would.*

[26] See Cox, "Internal Affairs of Labor Unions Under the Labor Reform Act of 1959," 58 Mich. L. Rev. 819, 852 (1960); McGowan, "Lawyers and the Uses of Language," 47 A.B.A.J. 897 (1961).

[27] *Caplan v. Schroeder,* 56 Cal. 2d 515, 523 (dissenting opinion, 1961); see also *Wentham v. State,* 65 Neb. 394, 401 (1902).

[28] Pierce, "Form Versus Substance," 46 Va. L. Rev. 1150, 1155 (1960).

[29] Lecture, Oct. 11, 1959.

[30] *Oxford English Dictionary; Webster's New International Dictionary* (2d ed. 1934).

[31] *A Uniform System of Citation* 91 (10th ed. 1958).

[32] *Black's Law Dictionary* (4th ed. 1951); Jowitt, gen. ed., *The Dictionary of English Law* (1959).

has a place (in footnotes), and should be kept there. A more intelligible statement of guess is *one of the possibilities is,* and a candid *I don't know* would win the law some friends.

A more vicious way of saying-nothing is the lawyer's *agreement to agree,*[33] or — as it frequently appears by design or accident — *subject to change by mutual consent.*[34] Of course. It always is. Like the *whereas* recital (Section 120), this phrase gives the hurried bargainer the false impression that something has been taken care of. It is eyewash or worse.

One step deeper into bad morals is saying-something calculated to mislead. This is a species of unintelligibility related to the practice of using fine print to make contracts illegible.[35] The object of each is the same — to force law on the victim without arousing suspicion that it is there. Various paths lead to the same sinkhole.

One of them is using words so ordinary in appearance that the reader thinks he understands. Here is a sample. Without counsel, the citizen in the hurried sanctuary of the voting booth ponders "Yes" or "No" on a —

Ballot	*Meaning*
ASSESSMENT OF GOLF COURSES. Assembly Constitutional Amendment No. 29. Establishes manner in which non-profit golf-courses should be assessed for purposes of taxation.[36]	Private golf courses shall be taxed less than other private property.[37]

These ballot words are carefully designed to produce a "yes" vote (which they did).[38] First, they speak of the "manner" of *doing something* — "assessment," "establishes," "assessed," "taxation." So that atttention is diverted from the fact that the words are consistent with a way of *not doing something* — not assessing, not taxing. Second, they speak of *non-profit,* which (if it means anything to the voter) has a vaguely charitable sound,[39] unconnected with expensive mem-

---

[33] See 1 Williston, *Contracts* §45 (3d ed. 1957).

[34] *Beech Aircraft Corp. v. Ross,* 155 F.2d 615, 616 n.3 (10th Cir. 1946), *rehearing denied;* and see *Modern Legal Forms* §8171 (1957).

[35] Mellinkoff, "How to Make Contracts Illegible," 5 Stan. L. Rev. 418-432 (1953).

[36] Proposition 6, on general election ballot, California (Nov. 8, 1960).

[37] See O'Connell, "Argument Against Assembly Constitutional Amendment No. 29," in *Proposed Amendments to Constitution . . . General Election Tuesday, Nov. 8, 1960,* p. 10 (California official election pamphlet, 1960).

[38] Cal. Const., art. XIII, §2.6.

[39] See *Webster's Third New International Dictionary* (1961), under *non-profit.*

berships. Yet on the statute books, the words will mean what they mean to lawyers — ". . . not designed primarily to pay dividends . . ." [40] If the ballot measure had said what it meant, the issue would have been clear and the vote in doubt.

Another form of saying-something is the disarmingly disingenuous letter agreement. Here boring repetition and amiable fairness combine to mask the one sharp tooth:

> We agree to pay all bills in full promptly as they come in, including without limitation of the generality of the foregoing all bills for labor, services, and materials, supplies, utilities, taxes, permits, fees, royalties, and everything else directly or indirectly for or used in connection with the construction of your building, you of course to reimburse us for everything spent for labor, services, and materials, supplies, utilities, taxes, permits, fees, royalties, overhead, and everything else directly or indirectly for or used in connection with the construction of your building.

Even without the overreaching minority of the profession, there is trouble enough. For the word *intelligible,* to be intelligible, raises a question more pointed with law language than with the language generally: Intelligible to whom?

The brief but classic dialogue about intelligibility runs something like this:

LAYMAN: Say it in English! (Sections 51, 59, 65, 73, 76.)
LAWYER: You'll be just as ignorant in English. [41]
LAYMAN: Not just English, plain English! (Sections 95, 96, 103, 108.)
LAWYER: The old way is better. [42]   Besides, "habeas corpus" would sound silly in English. [43]

This script has varied little in six hundred years, [44] though it took shape in England at a time when few lawyers made any pretense of trying to be understood by laymen. They preferred law French (Sections 59, 65) and law Latin (Sections 47, 51, 76), smug in the knowledge that they would not be overheard — or at least not understood — outside the dress circle. (Sections 59, 65.)

[40] *Black's Law Dictionary* (4th ed. 1951), under *non-profit.*
[41] See Sections 72, 74, 76; see 3 Blackstone, *Commentaries* *322 (Jones ed. 1916).
[42] See Sections 25, 72, 74, 76; see North, *A Discourse on the Study of the Laws* 11-14 (1824).
[43] See 3 Blackstone, *Commentaries* *323 (Jones ed. 1916).
[44] See, for example, Mitgang, "It's Legal — But Is It English?" N.Y. Times Sunday Magazine 73, 76 (Nov. 13, 1960), and compare Morton, "Challenge Made to Beardsley's Plan for Plain and Simple Legal Syntax," 16 J.S.B. Calif. 103-106 (1941).

If that script told all the story, the language of the law would be in a worse mess than it is. Fortunately, the problem of intelligibility does not resolve itself into a head-on clash between those who know and those who don't know, nor between those who should know and those who should be content with paying the bills. The language of the law has at least three separate areas of varying intelligibility and unintelligibility, and the dunce cap shifts from head to head.

First is the area of strictly professional concern, in communication lawyer-to-lawyer.

There is no reason other than sociability that a plumber should interrupt his conversation with an assistant to translate for a meddlesome householder: "Hey Charley, get me a one-inch *union.*"

Similarly, if in their day-to-day contacts, lawyers can get their work done faster, understanding each other better in terms of art and argot which to the outsider are gobbledygook, there is advantage, and no harm — unless. Unless esoteric speech becomes so habitual (Sections 124, 130) that it gushes uncontrolled, slopping over into fields that have no need of it.

Unlike the plumber, who is a *doing* man, the lawyer is primarily a *communicating* man. His words are more and more overheard by non-lawyers — in trial, in legislatures, in public meetings of all sorts. His words are more and more intended for the understanding of non-lawyers — in contracts, and statutes, and myriad regulations. He runs the constant risk of misjudging or forgetting his audience.[45]

Even when his audience is within the profession, the lawyer who wallows in law language cannot be sure that his own friends will recognize him. Daily the old legal forms become more strange to lawyers themselves, the incidental language more out of tune with the language that commands their attention everywhere else but in the law. The traditional circumlocutions of the law (Sections 119-124), the long sentences (Section 125), are not the most readily understood. Why should brother lawyers, let alone judges, take the time to crack hard nuts, unless it is necessary?

Orally, lawyer to lawyer, involvement is subject to quick correction. What do you mean by that, counsel? In writing, the lawyer's problem of communication with his own kind is but a little different from his problem of communication to the layman. More technical knowledge can be taken for granted. A small group of words can accomplish

[45] Gibson, "Literary Minds and Judicial Style," 36 N.Y.U.L. Rev. 915-930 (1961).

shorthand precision. (Section 128.) But if he wants to be under-stood — within the time that busy lawyers will allot to other lawyers — the lawyer had best say as little as necessary in terms of art and argot, and as much as possible in accents that are most familiar to all men, including lawyers.

In short, the lawyer's language problem is that he has too much to choose from — too many decisions.

Second is the area where the layman wrestles with law language that is intelligible to lawyers.

Unlike the lawyer, the layman has not too much but too little to choose from. When he comes to the law he is plain ignorant.

From its earliest days the bar has recognized that at least some laymen — nobles and gentlemen, for instance — should have some knowledge of the law.[46] (Blackstone thought that in a pinch a little law might come in handy even to a doctor — say, something about wills.)[47] Whatever the ancient need, it is greater today, as law multi-plies and spreads even faster than literacy. (Section 110.) Yet even without a training in the substance and technicality of the law which lawyers learn, the layman's path can be smoothed a little. He may still stumble, but it need not be so often.

In Coke's day, making the law intelligible to non-lawyers meant pulling it out of Littleton's French into English; and that even Coke was willing to do. (Section 72.) He would reach the limits of a circle of literacy that had grown but was still small. Today, a larger part of law language is directly addressed to laymen. That part still in-cludes strange and misleading words and phrases (Section 9) unnes-sary to the layman no matter what their utility to the lawyer. As well put it back into Latin or French, which had at least the virtue of being patently unintelligible. For his daily needs — with no lawyer to hold his hand — the layman is less concerned with more precision than with getting a modicum of intelligibility. That can be supplied him without hurting the law or lawyers. (Section 133.)

Third is the area of misunderstanding — the largest one — that has nothing to do with the requirements of legal learning, where lawyers and laymen suffer a common frustration from unintelligible wordage.

---

[46] See Section 72; Plucknett, *A Concise History of the Common Law* 225 (5th ed. 1956); 2 Holdsworth, *A History of English Law* 416 and especially n.6, 494 (3d ed. 1923); Harno, *Legal Education in the United States* 44 (1953); Warren, *A History of the American Bar* 563-566 (1911).

[47] 1 Blackstone, *Commentaries,* introduction °14 and see generally °5-°17 (Jones ed. 1916).

Make allowance first for the extraordinary strains to which law language is subjected — the Donnybrook Fair of legal interpretation which can shred the most precise, intelligible, sedate words. (Section 129.) Make further allowance for the involved facts which the law must reduce to writing. Then look at the horrors that remain, unforgiven. The unnecessarily long and involved sentences. (Section 125.) Unnecessary and mystifying word duplication. (Section 123.) Unnecessary old words that have lost their grip on the twentieth century. (Section 121.) Confusing dictated verbosity. (Section 131.) And also some plain bad writing, verging on the illiterate.[48]

Lawyers are no better equipped than others to cope with such obscurity. They have no special key to unlock its secrets, unless it be the patience born of resignation. Making law language more intelligible will help the profession even more than it will delight the laity, for the lawyers suffer more of it. And it can be made more intelligible, if there is more patience but less resignation. Turn to the next section.

133. *To make the language fit*

After hours, lawyers talk just like people. The off-duty lawyer will tell you, as any other citizen might, that he *needs help fast when his life or property* (in that order) *is in danger.* But let him sit down at the office desk to put the same thing into law. He switches on the dictating machine. The bell rings. He commences to salivate and to gibber. Somehow it gets all mushed up, like this:

> "Emergency" as used in this section means a situation in which property or human life is in jeopardy and the prompt summoning of aid is essential.[49]

What happened?

It is a lawyer's rather than a Marxian explanation for the precedence of *property* over *human life*. If you said *human life or property*, this might also be understood to say *human property* (Section 84, 125), which even to a lawyer is nonsense. But why *human life* at all? Well, to the precisionist (Section 17) there was a fleeting glimpse of a *dog's life*, and the glimpse was too fleeting to let the possibility rest in the concept of *property*. And — come to think of it — there are other

48 See Cooley, "A Law School Fights Graduate Illiteracy," 44 *Saturday Review* 39-41 (1961); "Current Issues in Legal Education (A Survey)," 9 Clev.-Mar. L. Rev. 582, 590-591 (1960).
49 Cal. Pen. Code §384(a); see also N.Y. Pen. Law §1424-a (par. 2).

possibilities.   No one is going to drive a wild jackass through my statute!

And *jeopardy?* It has a lawyerly sound, though here it serves no lawyer's purpose.   It diverts the lawyer's attention to more accustomed thoughts of *double jeopardy* [50] and danger-of-being-convicted,[51] which are his proper uses of the word.   It also slows down the layman.   His *property* would be in *danger,* and he would think it an *emergency* if an outhouse were on fire, but he would let it burn to the ground before saying "My privy is in jeopardy."

The phrase *the prompt summoning of aid is essential* has its syntactic roots in Bentham's "substantive-preferring principle," [52] no contribution to intelligibility.   The individual words as used here have no precise legal meaning: *prompt* (fast or quickly),[53] *aid* (help),[54] *essential* (need fast, i.e., "demanding maximum attention"),[55] and *summoning* (calling) [56] — which is incidental to the help that is needed.

The draftsman — as he approached a legal subject — had vague stirrings of conscience that somehow he must "talk like a lawyer," his ferment fed by the myth that he is dealing with a language that is precise.   (Chapter XIII.)   If he does not write in this obscure way, perhaps he will be suspected of not holding a union card.   So he prefers the roundabout and the uncommon, which the law does not require nor bless as "precise."   He uses words and phrases that have a legal flavor, language that stops the ordered progress of eye and mind to make lawyers and laymen ponder whether some special meaning is hinted at.   The draftsman ends up by being less intelligible even to lawyers.

There is no inherent vice in the law which requires it be written unintelligibly.   (That sentence should be a platitude but it isn't.   See Section 115.)   And it can be demonstrated that the evil is in the mind of the beholder.

Observe two lawyers putting the same bit of law into words, and

50 *Black's Law Dictionary* (4th ed. 1951).

51 Jowitt, gen. ed., *The Dictionary of English Law* (1959), under *jeopardy.*

52 See Section 109; and see Cavers, "The Simplification of Government Regulations," 8 Fed. B.J. 339, 355 (1947).

53 34 *Words and Phrases* (perm. ed. 1957, Supp. 1962); see *Webster's New International Dictionary* (2d ed. 1934).

54 *Black's Law Dictionary* (4th ed. 1951), under *aid;* compare Section 122.

55 *Webster's Third New International Dictionary* (1961); see *Black's Law Dictionary* (4th ed. 1951).

56 *Webster's Third New International Dictionary* (1961), and compare *Black's Law Dictionary* (4th ed. 1951).

see if you misundersand both of them. You will be at once suspicious when you find that though they cover the same ground, they do not say the same things. One starts your mind running in several directions at once, and (if you have the time) you will reread more than once to make sure that there is indeed a central theme. Everything is hedged but the obvious, and that well documented. Oftener than not the grammar is dubious, the sentences long ones — with words to spare. There are so many obstacles to quick comprehension that it will be startling to discover that another has said it so easily.

Take for example the hoary dogma that *an appellate court will affirm when a judgment rests on the credibility of witnesses.* If it needs saying, it can be said like that — hornbook style — and like this:

> Inasmuch as the issues arising out of this contention are mainly factual, almost every material part of the testimony is in dispute, and plaintiff relies only on the evidence favorable to her, we point up the fundamental rule that this court has "no power to judge of the effect or value of the evidence, to weigh the evidence, to consider the credibility of the witnesses, or to resolve conflicts in the evidence or in the reasonable inferences that may be drawn therefrom" (*Overton v. Vita-Food Corp.*, 94 Cal. App. 2d 367, 370 [210 P.2d 757]), nor may it substitute its deductions for those of the trial court (*Grainger v. Antoyan*, 48 Cal. 2d 805 [313 P.2d 848]). Thus, the presumption being in favor of the judgment we view the evidence in the light most favorable to the defendant giving him the benefit of every reasonable inference and resolving all conflicts in favor of the judgment. (*Crawford v. Southern Pacific Co.*, 3 Cal. 2d 427 [45 P.2d 183]); *Estate of Bristol*, 23 Cal. 2d 221 [143 P.2d 689]). Over 1100 pages of testimony produced 11 witnesses and numerous exhibits, all of which resulted in considerable conflict. The trial judge heard and observed the witnesses; and that the circumstances occurred over 20 years ago in a foreign country, interpreters were needed by some witnesses and others were unavailable or testified by way of deposition, the claim involved extensive property and was vigorously tried, and some of the witnesses showed more than the ordinary bias, were all factors for the judge's consideration in determining that which was worthy of belief. Further, when a finding is attacked for insufficiency of the evidence, "the power of an appellate court *begins* and *ends* with the determination as to whether there is any substantial evidence *contradicted* or *uncontradicted* which will support the finding of fact. [Citations.]" (*Primm v. Primm*, 46 Cal. 2d 690, 693 [299 P.2d 231].) (Emphasis added.) [57]

And it can also be said most intelligibly like this:

> I do not profess to understand the reasoning of the magistrate; but, as he saw the defendant and heard him cross-examined, it would be

---

[57] *Fernandez v. Fernandez*, 194 Cal. App. 2d 782, 787-788 (1961).

impossible for us to say that there was no evidence on which he could come to his conclusion of fact. . . .[58]

No lawyer likes to be reminded that it was his witness who was not believed, but every lawyer has long learned the rule of law that these opinions deal with. The second opinion applies the rule, making its factual basis comprehensible to anyone. The first opinion repeats the rule with ruffles and flourishes, so unnecessary and so involved that the reader loses himself trying to figure out which comes first, the witness or his testimony. Nothing is gained in restating the rule for lawyers, nor in hiding it from laymen. For the proposition that the law discusses here is old and simple in the common experience of all men — a distrust of liars.

But suppose the law itself is uncertain. What is *commerce?* (Section 104) a *reasonable doubt?* (Section 119) *proximate cause?* an *accident?* (Section 126.) It is less a rebuke to either language or law than to the writer that the uncertainty of a legal concept results in language that is unintelligible. The gobbledygook comes when the writer does not know that the concept is uncertain or pretends that it is certain.

Extreme cruelty is about as uncertain as you could wish for. The words are flabby individually[59] and get no support by leaning upon each other.[60] A statute which says that

> Extreme cruelty is the wrongful infliction of grievous bodily injury, or grievous mental suffering, . . .[61]

does tell us that cruelty can be physical or mental, but beyond that it talks uncertainly about uncertainty. *Wrongful* begs the question, and *grievous*[62] is as indefinite as *extreme*. This is no definition at all,[63] and other attempts to firm it up make no improvement. For example:

---

[58] Lord Goddard, C.J. in *Wilson v. Inyang*, [1951] 2 K.B. 799, 802.

[59] *Extreme* in 15A *Words and Phrases* (perm. ed. 1950), 1 *California Words, Phrases, and Maxims* (1960), and *Webster's New International Dictionary* (2d ed. 1934); *cruelty* in 10 *Words and Phrases* 614-628 (perm. ed. 1940), 188-193 (Supp. 1962), 1 *California Words, Phrases, and Maxims* 410, 1 *Words and Phrases: Judicially Defined* 597-598 (1946), 119-121 (Supp. 1960), and *Webster's New International Dictionary* (2d ed. 1934).

[60] *Extreme cruelty* in *Black's Law Dictionary* (4th ed. 1951), 15A *Words and Phrases* 707-729 (perm. ed. 1950), 56-58 (Supp. 1962), and 1 *California Words, Phrases, and Maxims* 712-713 (1960).

[61] Cal. Civ. Code §94.

[62] *Black's Law Dictionary* (4th ed. 1951); 18A *Words and Phrases* (perm. ed. 1956).

[63] See *McFall v. McFall*, 58 Cal. App. 2d 208, 211 (1943).

> . . . any unjustifiable and long practiced course of conduct . . .
> which utterly destroys the legitimate ends and objects of matri-
> mony . . .[64]

Worse yet:

> . . . that degree of cruelty, either actually inflicted or reasonably in-
> ferred, which endangers the life or health of the aggrieved party, or
> renders his or her life one of such extreme discomfort and wretched-
> ness as to incapacitate him or her, physically or mentally, from dis-
> charging the marital duties.[65]

If there could be agreement on what *destroys* a marriage, or *utterly
destroys* what is left of its redundant *ends and objects*, then *destroy*
could be the ground of divorce rather than the catchphrase *extreme
cruelty*. So too with a life of *extreme discomfort and wretchedness*,
which ventures further into the nuance of sensibility that defies definition. Better to recognize that *extreme cruelty* is a ground for divorce,
see what he did, and see if it bothers you.

For example. A Gay Nineties court takes a decree away from a
wife — a bitter woman whose drunken husband called her "whore,"
"damned bitch," and "damned bitch from hell." [66] Does that bother
you? Either the conduct of husband or of court? This language of the
dissenter would apply to both:

> And while extreme cruelty of either kind [i.e., physical or mental]
> cannot, in the very nature of things, be accurately defined, there is
> often misconduct so far outside of and beyond that produced by the
> ordinary weaknesses and passions of men that the common judgment
> of mankind pronounces it extremely cruel.[67]

That is no definition either, and it doesn't make *extreme cruelty* a solid
legal concept. But it is the sort of uncertainty that all men live with
every day. "How was it?" you ask. The old man shakes his head
and says, "It was real bad." *Extremely cruel.*

Jurors don't often have to be bothered with divorce, but if they did,
even a juror could understand language like that, or like this charge:

> There is but little difficulty in deciding whether certain facts do or
> do not amount to extreme cruelty, but there is great difficulty in giving
> a general definition of extreme cruelty; perhaps, however, it may be said
> to be such conduct on the part of one of the parties, whether manifested
> by words alone, or by personal violence, or by both, as by the common
> understanding and judgment of mankind, living in civilized societies,

---

[64] *Paul v. Paul,* 183 Kan. 201, 206 (1958).
[65] *Friedman v. Friedman,* 37 N.J. Super. 52, 58 (1955).
[66] *Waldron v. Waldron,* 85 Cal. 251, 253 (1890).
[67] *Waldron v. Waldron,* 85 Cal. 251, 268 (1890).

ought not to be borne or tolerated by the other, which is probbably [*sic*] as near a definition as the court can give, to aid you in coming to a conclusion upon the point.[68]

The law was uncertain; it remains uncertain; and the language says so. The language is more certain than the law. That is intelligible enough.

In these samplings — an appellate court affirming and *extreme cruelty* — nothing is discussed that requires language peculiar to the law. The language is customarily addressed more to lawyers than to laymen, but there is no reason why the intelligent of each species should not understand all of it. No reason to accentuate the trend of our age to shut off intelligent beings from intelligible communication. No reason for lawyers to strive after differences that don't help anyone.

Even if it were certain that no layman would ever lay eyes on it, why make things difficult for other lawyers?

A rule of court says that if a notice of appeal is received after the deadline for filing, a petition may request relief. The petition is to give the date of the order or judgment, the steps toward timely filing,

. . . and any other information which has, or which the party believes has, a bearing upon the circumstances which caused the notice of appeal to arrive late.[69]

So many barriers stand between him and the late arrival that a lawyer feels he must examine each, closely — *information, believes, bearing, circumstances, caused.* Comb the words as he will, the lawyer cannot get over the impression that it all still seems to say: "*any explanation of the delay.*" But he will go away muttering. And in his near-sleeping hours fret over the difference between what *has a bearing* (and is rejected) and what his client *believes has a bearing* (and is also rejected). And would it make any difference if he put in something that *had a bearing* even if his client *didn't believe it had a bearing?* etc. It takes some time to decide that it all comes to the same thing. And the draftsman could have taken that time once — for all the lawyers.

Where unintelligible language only gives the lawyer insomnia, it crushes the layman.

Take him at his pitiful best, neither eavesdropping nor reading over a lawyer's shoulder. Imagine him invited in. Worse; ordered to read

[68] *Gaskins v. Gaskins,* 1 Lab. 381, 383 (Cal. Dist. Ct. 1857).
[69] Cal. Judicial Council, Rules on Appeal, Rule 31 (1961).

or to listen or both. One sentence is enough to finish him. (Section 112.)

This is how the government talks to a produce man. This is *Lime Order 4:*

> . . . no handler shall handle:
> (i) Any limes, including the group known as true limes (also known as Mexican, West Indian, and Key limes and by other synonyms) and the group known as large fruited or Persian limes (including Tahiti, Bearss, and similar varieties) . . . unless such limes grade at least U.S. No. 2 Mixed Color: Provided, That no requirement as to color shall be applicable to any limes except those known as large fruited or Persian limes (including Tahiti, Bearss, and similar varieties).[70]

For no good reason, the lawyer has recast non-lawyer's language into the one-paragraph, one-sentence mold of law language. It doesn't work for law language (Sections 82-84, 106, 125), and it doesn't work here. Draftsman confuses draftsman and reader. The sentence chases itself through the paragraph with its tail in its mouth.

If the traditional formula of the law is abandoned, the thoughts sorted out, the paragraph split, it makes sense like this:

> . . . no handler shall handle:
> (i) Any limes of the group known as true limes (also known as Mexican, West Indian, and Key limes and by other synonyms) . . . which do not meet the requirements of at least U.S. No. 2 grade for Persian (Tahiti) limes, except as to color; or
> (ii) Any limes of the group known as large fruited or Persian limes (including Tahiti, Bearss, and similar varieties) . . . which do not grade at least U.S. No. 2, Mixed Color.[71]

With these limes — whether Mexican or Persian — the draftsmanship problem is not translating law language for laymen. The law argot is minimal even though unnecessary: the formula of alias (*also known as*) applied strangely to fruit, and — in the first version — an unfortunate *Provided* that introduced too much. The problem is weaning lawyers away from accustomed pattern. And in one way or another that is the problem with most of the writings which lawyers prepare for the eyes of laymen. Here — and often — it is the pattern of the one-sentence paragraph which makes it too easy to be unintelligible. In other places it is a pattern of strange words which have the crowning vice of being unnecessary.

The party line emergency statutes (Section 132) — bad enough in a lawyer's library — also invade the sanctity of the home. They re-

[70] 22 Fed. Reg. 2873 (1957).
[71] 7 C.F.R. §1001.309 (1960); 25 Fed. Reg. 13684 (1960).

quire a notice in telephone books explaining the law to laymen. This
is a part of one notice:

> California Penal Code section 384 makes it a misdemeanor for any
> person who shall wilfully refuse to immediately relinquish a telephone
> party-line when informed that such line is needed for an emergency
> call to a fire department or police department or for medical aid or am-
> bulance service. Also, any person who shall secure the use of a tele-
> phone party-line by falsely stating that such line is needed for an emer-
> gency call, shall be guilty of a misdemeanor.[72]

With almost the same statute to work from,[73] another draftsman has
tailored the same part of the notice to his audience, striving to eliminate the frightening lawyer smell:[74]

> New York State law requires you to hang up the receiver of a party
> line telephone immediately when told the line is needed for an emer-
> gency call to a fire department or police department or for medical
> aid or ambulance service. It is unlawful to take over a party line by
> stating falsely that the line is needed for an emergency.[75]

The California draftsman has taken the easy way — following the
language of the statute,[76] thus passing on to laymen technicality they
don't need and words they don't understand. The New Yorker gives
as much as the layman needs. He has avoided repetitions and chosen
the ordinary, the direct, rather than the strange and roundabout. This
is how he did it:

California	*New York*
Penal Code section 384 makes it a misdemeanor	State law requires
for any person who	you
shall willfully refuse to immediately relinquish a telephone party line	to hang up the receiver of a party line telephone immediately
when informed	when told
that such line	the line
is needed for an emergency call . . .	is needed for an emergency call . . .

---

[72] Marin County, California, Telephone Directory, p. 1 (April, 1961).
[73] N.Y. Pen. Law §1424-a(3) (1954).
[74] See Cavers, "The Simplification of Government Regulations," 8 Fed. B.J. 339,
354 (1947).
[75] Manhattan, New York, Telephone Directory, p. 1 (1961-1962).
[76] Cal. Pen. Code §384.

Also, any person who	It is unlawful
shall secure the use of a telephone party line	to take over a party line
by falsely stating	by stating falsely
that such line	that the line
is needed for an emergency call	is needed for an emergency.
shall be guilty of a misdemeanor.	....

There is a small terroristic value in California's brandishing of the words *Penal Code, section 384, guilty, misdemeanor.* But for most citizens it is enough to learn from a telephone directory that conduct is against the law. Beyond the level of the parking ticket, when a layman needs to weigh the specific consequences of law-breaking, he is on his way to a lawyer or to prison. The New York draft is both shorter and more intelligible, with nothing essential lost.

For ordinary doses of law, the layman should not be expected to bother himself with the technicality useful to a lawyer. Accordingly, in addressing laymen, the lawyer can eliminate many of the terms of art and argot he may find convenient in talking to other lawyers. The lawyer has a two-level vocabulary, and he ought to use it if he wants to be quickly understood. For example:

For the lawyer	*For the layman*
talk easily about *consideration*	Call it whatever it is — *$10,000,-000.00* or a *pig.* The law word starts the layman's mind running on the familiar, which is the wrong, track. (Section 9.)
stipulate that *Jones v. Jones* be heard at 10:00 A.M., October 9, 1961, in *Department* 25	"I have agreed with your husband's lawyer that the case goes to court on Monday morning, October 9th. It will be in Judge Smith's courtroom. That's Room 201, on the 2d floor of the City Hall. Be sure to be there at 9:45 A.M."
plaintiff alleges	Make it *Jones says.* Courts have approved the various forms of *allege,*[77] but don't use it if you are

[77] See *Heidemann v. Kelsey,* 7 Ill. 2d 601, 605 (1956); *Smith v. Henline,* 174

looking for neutral expression. Current lay usage — probably influenced by the press — shows an increasing feeling that it refers to something that *can't be proved*.[78] The point here is not what will pass, but what will be more easily understood.

demur

"We filed a legal objection." (Section 9.)

motion for a continuance

"We asked the court to postpone the case."

constructive possession

"It will be just as bad [good] as if you were really there."

constructive notice

"If you didn't see it, it's just too bad."

nunc pro tunc

"The judge can back date it."

"This is *on all fours*."

"I've found a case just like ours."

waive notice

"I told his attorney not to bother sending me a paper telling me something I already knew."

intestate

"If you die without a will, or if for some legal reason your will is no good . . ."

"The tax is *due* November 1, and becomes *delinquent* November 30."

"You can pay this tax bill at any time before December 1."

"*Title* to the car does not *pass* until the purchase price is paid in full."

"Until you have paid in full for the car you are buying, we still own it, and we can take it back if you don't keep up the payments."

In most of these instances the layman is getting a partial explanation rather than an exact equivalent. While there is always the risk that the explanation will not be full enough, against that you must balance

Ill. 184, 200 (1898); *State v. Hostetter*, 222 S.W. 750, 754 (Mo. 1920); see *Webb Estate*, 391 Pa. 584, 588 (1958).

[78] See and compare *Webster's New International Dictionary* (2d ed. 1934), under *allegation* and *allege*, with *Webster's Third New International Dictionary* (1961), under *allegation, allege, alleged;* see also Evans and Evans, A *Dictionary of Contemporary American Usage* (1957), under *allege*.

the greater risk of talking to a blank wall. It is the job of the lawyer to say what has to be said, and to say it so that it can be understood by those who must understand it.

There are times when technicality cannot be avoided. And when that time comes, a further question taxes the lawyer's power of discrimination: Is an explanation worth the time and effort?

If a will must *exercise a power of appointment,* no word but *appoint* will fill the bill.[79] This is strange talk to a layman, and the testator who needs a will of this sort can do with an oral briefing by his lawyer. The writing itself expresses the testator's will, yet mostly so that other lawyers will understand it, and see to it that that will is carried out. So with *quiet enjoyment, community property, marital deduction,* and others that lie within the specialist's realm. On occasion they must be used. As time permits they may be explained. But their use can be cut to the minimum. Further, sometimes no explanation at all is in order; and if an explanation is given, it need not be one that would satisfy a bar examiner.

The *jury instruction* is a case in point. Imagine the climax of a five-day trial. The perplexed but earnest jurors take their places brightly, to hear the judge clear away the confusions of strange talk, conflicting witnesses, and two sets of lawyers — equally confident. All eyes are on the bench. From that height will come the wisdom to guide these troubled laymen. The judge speaks, and this is what he says:

> During the course of these instructions the term *burden of proof* will be used. By *burden of proof* is meant the duty resting upon the party having the affirmative of an issue to satisfy or convince the jury to a reasonable certainty of the truth of the contentions of that party.
>
> .   .   .   .
>
> By *preponderance of the evidence* is meant the evidence which possesses the greater weight or convincing power. It is not enough that the evidence of the party upon whom the burden of proof rests is of slightly greater weight or convincing power; it must go further and satisfy or convince the minds of the jury before the burden of proof is discharged.[80]

What a letdown!

The judge would have done his job much better telling the jury:

> Jones brought this case to court and it is his job to satisfy you that Smith hit him.

[79] See Leach, "Powers of Appointment," 24 A.B.A.J. 807, 811 (1938).
[80] *Wisconsin Jury Instructions: Civil — Part 1,* No. 210 (1960).

True, unlike the room-shaking form instruction, the shorter one would have to be recast and repeated as the charge progressed:

> Smith says that if he hit Jones, he struck in self-defense.   It is Smith's job to satisfy you on that point.

But that is an aid to intelligibility, not a hindrance.   The form instruction is gobbledygook partly because it tries to cover too much, once and for all, and for that very reason it is too cumbersome to be repeated at the places where it would do the most good.

Burden of proof and *preponderance of the evidence* are not the only soporifics administered to the jury.   There is more and more of the same.   (Section 127.)   By the time the voice has droned on through fleeting moments of *proximate cause* (Section 126), *contributory negligence* (Section 20), and the rest, even the few things which seemed at first intelligible have slipped away.   *Reasonable doubt* seemed plain enough until it had been defined.   (Section 119.)

One explanation of the needless explanations and the needless confusion is that many of these instructions are not designed for the quick understanding of listening laymen, but rather for more or less intelligible reading by appellate judges.[81]   "More or less," because when the instructions have become standardized and commonplace, with pet names like BAJI,[82] JIFU,[83] IPI,[84] etc., almost all the reviewing judge need do is hold them up to the light, to see if the paragraph indentations and periods are in the right places.[85]   So that he may say: *This jury has been instructed.*   (Section 127.)   That speeds the administration of justice,[86] even if the juror understands nothing of what is said to him.   In his confusion — and fidgeting over the prospect of being late to dinner — he reverts to his somewhat muddled common sense, and brings in a verdict that does not shock the sense of justice.

Another explanation of the typical jury instruction is that the instruction makers confuse precision and intelligibility.   (Section 132.)   It is said that the jury must be given ". . . accurate statements of the law . . . ,"[87] and that it must be said ". . . dogmatically in certain

---

[81] See Hager, "Let's Simplify Legal Language," 32 Rocky Mt. L. Rev. 74, 80 (1959).

[82] *California Jury Instructions: Civil,* title page (4th rev. ed. 1956).

[83] *Jury Instruction Forms for Utah,* cover (1957).

[84] *Illinois Pattern Jury Instructions, Civil* (1961).

[85] Compare Shinn, J., concurring, in *Werkman v. Howard Zink Corp.,* 97 Cal. App. 2d 418, 428-431 (1950).

[86] See Cunningham, "Instructing Juries," 32 J.S.B. Calif. 127, 129 (1957).

[87] *Illinois Pattern Jury Instructions, Civil* xviii (1961).

terms," [88] even when the law itself is uncertain. It is assumed that out of this chaos will come understanding.

Yet for the purpose of deciding legal right in *Smith v. Jones,* a jury can do better given an intelligible essence than it can with painfully accurate statements of the law.

What is that "intelligible essence" to tell the jury about damages in defamation? Here is what it is not:

> If you find from the evidence that the plaintiff is entitled to recover in this action, it will then be your duty to assess the amount of damages which, in your judgment, she should recover. In assessing such damages you may take into consideration any mental suffering produced by the publishing of the words to others, if you find from the evidence that any such suffering has been endured by her, and the injury, if any, to the plaintiff's character and reputation, which the evidence shows she has sustained as a proximate result of the publishing of the alleged words. And you should assess her damages at such a sum as in your judgment will compensate her for an injury sustained as the proximate result of defendant's wrongful conduct as alleged in the complaint and as shown by the evidence in the cause. [89]

Here is that "intelligible essence," coming in strong and clear, even through the barrier of a third person report:

> But if the jury took the view that this was not fair comment, but that it was so strong that no fair-minded man could honestly have held it, then the defendants failed and the jury would have to consider the question of damages.
>
> Lord Silkin had said that he was not seeking enormous damages. This was not a case where punitive damages were asked for or where the defendants had persisted in bringing charges which they did not seek to justify. If the question of damages arose, the jury should bring in such a figure, not unreasonable, as in their good judgment they thought fit. [90]

But let us not overemphasize the importance of making law language intelligible to laymen. [91] The massive litigation of the centuries (Sections 115, 126) tells us better than any text that the lawyer's most recurrent difficulty is in writing intelligibly for other lawyers. His woes are not to be blamed on the government. [92] For behind every

---

[88] Yerkes, review of *Illinois Pattern Jury Instructions, Civil,* in 47 A.B.A.J. 505 (1961).

[89] 4 Branson, *The Law of Instructions to Juries* 216, §2133(1) (Reid, 3d ed. 1936).

[90] Diplock, J., in *Silkin v. Beaverbrook Newspapers Ltd.,* The Times, June 11, 1958, p. 5 (Q.B.).

[91] Cavers, "The Simplification of Government Regulations," 8 Fed. B.J. 339, 343, 352 (1947).

[92] Compare McGowan, "Lawyers and the Uses of Language," 47 A.B.A.J. 897, 900 (1961).

snatch of federal gobbledygook sits a lawyer, justifying habit by throwing stones (*baby-talk, henny-penny, pidgin English*)[93] at other lawyers who strive for intelligibility. Lawyers have themselves and their history (Part Two) and their myth of precision (Chapter XIII) to thank for what is now a habit of unintelligible writing. If lawyers but concentrate on writing more intelligibly for each other, with the same strokes they will write more intelligibly for laymen.

[93] Cavers, "The Simplification of Government Regulations," 8 Fed. B.J. 339, 340 (1947).

CHAPTER XVI

More Durable

134. *Rememberable*

It is a most refined notion that the law might be something different from *the letter of the law*.[1] The idiom itself is an expression of the more primitive (and recurrent) identification of words with what they refer to.[2] In the beginning, the letter, the word was the law,[3] for it was the magic that worked. The oath-swearing man who stumbled over the words of an oath was a gone soul. (Section 29.) The lawyer who lost a syllable had lost his cause. (Section 87.) The judge who departed from the letter of the law had ceased to be a judge, and had become a legislator.[4] So the word *law*, which meant something fixed (Section 24), and the law words which made up the law must themselves be enduring if the law were to endure. If the law were to remain unchanged, then — in Coke's words — "neither ought legal terms to be changed." (Section 72.) Change the words; you lose the law. This was the fear, and this the urge to make the language of the law durable.

Is there a workable scheme for a durable language, a language of the law? Something has apparently worked, for at the very least this language has preserved a body of law, given it continuity from backwater beginnings to world eminence. This is an achievement worth talking about.

The essence of durability is that the language of the law be rememberable. It must be right there when you wake up in the morning, or the law is gone. The sentry recites the parole to his relief, and if he has heard the word enough times or if there is something perhaps poetic about this shibboleth, the relief remembers, and passes it on

---

[1] *Oxford English Dictionary*, under *letter*, No. 5; see also Rom. 7:6, 2 Cor. 3:6; *The Scofield Reference Bible* 1199 n.1 (new ed. 1945).

[2] Ogden and Richards, *The Meaning of Meaning* (6th ed. 1944).

[3] See John 1:1.

[4] 2 Bacon, *Works* 214 (Montagu ed. 1825); 8 Bacon, *Works* 378 (Montagu ed. 1827); see Simon, "English Idioms from the Law," 76 L.Q. Rev. 283, 302 and n.25 (1960).

in a never-ending changing of the guard. Something else too discourages forgetting — "drunk or sober, asleep or awake": my life depends upon this word; only this word will save me and the lives of those who have their sleeping trust in me.

This was the early history of the language of the law — made rememberable by repetition, rhythm, rhyme, alliteration, and an awestruck respect for the magic potency of certain words. (Sections 29, 30, 34.) Planned for that effect or willy-nilly, these features fastened upon the language of the law in a time of illiteracy when the very survival of law depended on mnemonic device (Sections 28, 29), and where the memory of man did not run — there was no law. (Sections 83, 121.)

The necessity for repetition and the tricks of verse to insure the law's survival passed long ago. The written word spared men's memories, and the printing press could remember — even if it were the word of man rather than the word of God. (Sections 78, 79.) But there is a limit to the number of times a lawyer can say "I'll look it up" and still keep his clients or face the same judge. The books take care of long-run remembering — the memory of the race. In addition to that, the lawyer — like the sentry — has got to remember some things on his feet. The very writings which have made the law more secure for posterity have made the personal task of remembering the more difficult. There is so much more to remember (Sections 110, 130, 131), and no nudging supernatural to stimulate the lawyer's recollection.

No wonder then that the lawyer wants the same words repeated in the same way, is more interested in conforming than reforming. While rationalizing his language conservatism with talk of "precision," he is really hanging on to repetition as the oldest and dearest of his remaining mnemonic devices. No longer, though, for fear the law itself will be forgotten if the language changes, but that the lawyer might forget it.

Thus their descendants carried the word magic of the ancients one small but important misstep further. With a little positive thinking, the lawyers converted the old fear that different words would make different law into the new salvation that the same words would mean the same law. Little dreaming that old words, like old wineskins, could be refilled.[5]

---

[5] Compare Matt. 9:17, Mark 2:22, and Luke 5:37-39, with Holmes, J., in *Towne v. Eisner*, 245 U.S. 418, 425 (1918); see also Howe, *Justice Oliver Wendell Holmes: The Shaping Years* 23 and n.67 (1957); and see Section 121.

How something was to be remembered became confused with what was to be remembered. The mnemonic device became the sense, the repetitions the essence. Lawyers slaughtered each other over misspelled words and a thousand meaningless inadvertencies. (Sections 87, 88, 90.) They fought to keep their Latin (Sections 51, 74, 76), their bastard French (Sections 72, 74), their court hand (Section 76), and cried out in anguish when even a part of these were snatched away — though the law managed to survive the changes. Still today, the profession clings to the imprecise words and the changed words of the past, still repeats the *said's*, the *whereases*, and the *herein's*. But it is the device (repeat, repeat, repeat) that is being remembered, while the sense — confused by the very device for remembering — is itself forgotten. (Sections 120, 121.) Like the fascinating singing commercial whose sponsor and product no one can recall.

When it comes to mnemonic devices (and the legal mind needs them as does any overworked brain), lawyers have too often backed the wrong horse. They have bet on the constancy, the precision of the repeated word, and it has let them down in centuries of litigation. (Section 126.) They have continued swinging with rhythms (Section 30) which make words easy to remember and ideas easy to forget — *mind and memory, force and effect, give, devise, and bequeath, fit and proper,* etc. (Sections 121, 123.) They have plumped for the forms — the same ones, easy to remember; only the blanks are different. And the device, the repeated form, is remembered and reused, though error creeps in (Section 112) and though time eats out the heart of the words that are in the form. (Sections 121, 127.)

To the mnemonic device with the greatest possibilities — writing (in prose or in rhyme) so unhackneyed that it pricks the dozing reader and disturbs the peace of the quiet memory — lawyers give their least efforts. They have accustomed themselves to the dullest prose in the world (Section 22) as though it were inevitable. (Sections 114, 115.) Yet when something shows up with some sparkle to catch up the loose ends of a legal problem, lawyers hug it — sometimes almost to death:

For an action of *deceit,*

There must be a misstatement of an existing fact; but the state of a man's mind is as much a fact as the state of his digestion.[6]

[6] Bowen, L.J., in *Edington v. Fitzmaurice,* 29 Ch. D. 459, 483 (1885).

Income — any word for that matter — does not always mean the same thing, for

A word is not a crystal, transparent and unchanged, it is the skin of a living thought and may vary greatly in color and content according to the circumstances and the time in which it is used.[7]

The *exclusionary rule*[8] amounts to this:

The criminal is to go free because the constable has blundered.[9]

And *wiretapping?* It is a *dirty business.*[10] Etc.

For each generation of lawyers, these words glitter anew, and call up for action the reasoning which gave them birth. These words do not go by any rule, unless it be the rule that pattern can be deadly. A metaphor — for all its dangers when misused (Section 131) — may fix a reason shortly and sharply, making it not only remember-able but memorable.

While warning against overadornment (Section 114), Coke knew how to turn a phrase, and turn it to the cause of remembering legal principle. Nice to come upon this simile in the middle of the *Littleton* desert:

Note that the Lord shall not have an Action of Debt for relief or for escuage due unto him, because he hath other remedy, but his Executors or Administrators shall have an action therefore, because it is now become as a Flower faln from the stock, and they have no other remedy.[11]

How remember that mere number of *lives in being* does not create a perpetuity? In the vivid logic of a Restoration judge:

If all the Candles be light at once, good.[12]

Thirty years later, his inspiration picked up, Twisden, J., became immortal:

For let the lives be never so many, there must be a survivor, and so it is but the length of that life; for Twisden used to say, the candles were all lighted at once.[13]

---

[7] Holmes, J., in *Towne v. Eisner*, 245 U.S. 418, 425 (1918).
[8] *Elkins v. United States*, 364 U.S. 206, 216 (1960).
[9] Cardozo, J., in *People v. Defore*, 242 N.Y. 13, 21 (1926).
[10] Holmes, J., dissenting, in *Olmstead v. United States*, 277 U.S. 438, 470 (1928).
[11] Coke, *Commentary upon Littleton*, f. 47b (10th ed. 1703).
[12] Twisden, J., in *Love v. Wyndham & Wyndham*, 86 Eng. Rep. 724, 726 (K.B. 1669).
[13] *Scattergood v. Edge*, 1 Salk. 220 (K.B. 1699); see also Leach, ed., *Langdell Lyrics of 1938*, p. 12 (1938).

In our own day, Mr. Justice Frankfurter — with an interest in words, words long ("a *temerarious man*")[14] and short — drafts a metaphor of the common speech into the service of the constitutional lawyer:

> The crux of that doctrine is that a search is a search by a federal official if he had a hand in it; it is not a search by a federal official if evidence secured by state authorities is turned over to the federal authorities *on a silver platter.* [Emphasis supplied.] [15]

The law of the sanctimonious federal — his hands unsoiled by the illegal search, yet claiming the damning proceeds — could be remembered more easily as *the silver platter doctrine,*[16] and in vicissitude as "*The Tarnished Silver Platter.*" [17]

Sometimes legal writing is beautiful; that will help it (and its burden) to be remembered.

Of many possible samplings from Mr. Justice Holmes, here is one, discussing — of all things — *police power,* in words that are literature as well as law:

> We have not that respect for art that is one of the glories of France. But to many the superfluous is the necessary, and it seems to me that Government does not go beyond its sphere in attempting to make life livable for them.[18]

And the language of law reviews, usually "dignified and ignored"? [19] That too can be beautiful. This, from Maitland, on the law's preference for possession, a preference based on

> . . . a mental incapacity, an inability to conceive that mere rights can be transferrred or can pass from person to person. Things can be transferred; that is obvious; the transfer is visible to the eye; but how rights? You have not your rights in your hand or your pocket, nor can you put them into the hand of another nor lead him into them and bid him walk about within their metes and bounds. . . . A very large part of the history of Real Property Law seems to me the history of the process whereby Englishmen have thought themselves free of that materialism which is natural to us all.[20]

If the writing is beautiful, so much the better, but beauty depends on taste, and some like it sour. Besides, the end is not beauty. The

---

14 *Clay v. Sun Ins. Office Ltd.,* 363 U.S. 207, 210 (1960), and see also Black, J., dissenting at 227.

15 *Lustig v. United States,* 338 U.S. 74, 78-79 (1949).

16 *Elkins v. United States,* 364 U.S. 206, 208 and especially n.2 (1960), and see also Harlan, J., at 252.

17 J. A. C. Grant, in 8 U.C.L.A.L. Rev. 1-43 (1961).

18 Dissenting, in *Tyson & Brothers v. Banton,* 273 U.S. 418, 447 (1927).

19 Rodell, "Goodbye to Law Reviews," 23 Va. L. Rev. 38 (1936).

20 Maitland, "The Mystery of Seisin," in 3 *Select Essays in Anglo-American Legal History* 591, 602 (1909).

words are there to help the lawyer (and sometimes a layman) remember an idea by remembering the language that refers to it. So
that he does not find himself clutching beautiful or ugly, or merely
old words that sift through his fingers leaving nary an idea behind.

There need be no straining after literary masterpiece, nor waiting
for that right moment of portentousness, to depart from the commonplace. For the bar, rememberable writing is an everyday affair.

Let it be as prosaic as personal injury — here summarized by a reporter:

> Plaintiff's claimed injuries were a black eye and bloody nose which
> discomforted him for two weeks and worried him for several months.[21]

Or a condemnation case, with an appellate opinion leading off like
this:

> An almost unbelievable accumulation of procedural snarls in this emi-
> nent domain proceedings has led to the present appeal . . .[22]

Or a dissent on Sunday closing:

> I find this ordinance bad for so many reasons that I scarcely know where
> to begin.[23]

Humor may also be an aid to remembrance, and need not be an
outcast of legal writing. All that a lawyer has to fear from humor is
failure, and with the stakes so high (an end to unmitigated dullness)
(Section 22), the risk is sometimes worth taking.

Judge Woolsey took it, when — seeking definition of "obscenity"[24]
— he contrasted "dirt for dirt's sake"[25] with the appropriateness he
found in the language of *Ulysses*:

> The words which are criticized as dirty are old Saxon words known
> to almost all men and, I venture, to many women, and are such words
> as would be naturally and habitually used, I believe, by the types of
> folk whose life, physical and mental, Joyce is seeking to describe. In
> respect of the recurrent emergence of the theme of sex in the minds of

[21] *Darden v. Louisville & Nashville Rd. Co.*, 171 Ohio St. 63 (1960).

[22] *Mountain View Union High School District v. Ormonde*, 195 Cal. App. 2d
89, 91 (1961).

[23] *People's Appliance, Inc. v. City of Flint*, 358 Mich. 34, 48 (1959).

[24] *Commonwealth v. Gordon*, 66 Pa. D. & C. 101, 104 (1948); 29 *Words and
Phrases* 68-73 (perm. ed. 1940), 23-28 (Supp. 1962), "obscene; obscenity," and
related words; 3 *California Words, Phrases, and Maxims* 133-134 (1960); 4 *Words
and Phrases: Judicially Defined* 4-5 (1944).

[25] *United States v. One Book Called "Ulysses,"* 5 F. Supp. 182, 184 (S.D.N.Y.
1933), *aff'd sub nom. United States v. One Book Entitled Ulysses*, 72 F.2d 705
(2d Cir. 1934).

his characters, it must always be remembered that his locale was Celtic and his season Spring.[26]

An ancient tradition[27] — still lovingly nurtured by some lawyers — calls upon humor to help make the law of real property more rememberable.

In the writings of Professor W. Barton Leach, the irresistible Rule Against Perpetuities meets the immovable presumption of lifelong fecundity in the *Fertile Octogenarian Cases*, and from there the path is downward:

> With the Fertile Octogenarian doctrine on the books and with the cases breeding much more successfully than the octogenarians it was inevitable that sooner or later a will drawn by some hapless lawyer would produce the *Case of the Precocious Toddler* and stumble into raising the question whether babies, too, can have babies in this Never Never Land of the Rule. My attempts to concoct such a gift for classroom purposes seemed labored and farfetched to me and to my students. But the mother country came to my rescue in Re *Gaite's Will Trusts* . . .[28]

A life tenant given property to use ". . . for her own individual benefit . . ." as well as support, has a vast power to amuse herself at the expense of remaindermen. A California judge once explained it like this:

> Having ample means — the value of the estate amounting to some ninety thousand dollars — the not unnatural desire arises in her to remove to California, or at least to live there during a part of the year. Should she leave her husband toiling and moiling in Chicago?[29]

Few who read the casebook version of this opinion will ever forget what it stands for, nor forget that Judge Kerrigan's whimsical question got its matching answer in a resounding footnote: "No! No! A thousand times, No!"[30]

A less boisterous departure from the dreariness of legal footnotes is this one:

> * There is no merit in plaintiff's contention made at the oral argument that the ruling of the Supreme Court was not binding since it appeared in the footnote in the opinion. A footnote is as important a part of an

[26] *United States v. One Book Called "Ulysses,"* 5 F. Supp. 182, 183-184 (S.D.N.Y. 1933).

[27] See Sections 22, 30; see also Blount, *Fragmenta Antiquitatis* (Beckwith, new ed. 1784); 6 Holdsworth, *A History of English Law* 611 and especially nn.13, 14 (1924).

[28] Leach, "Perpetuities in Perspective: Ending the Rule's Reign of Terror," 65 Harv. L. Rev. 721, 732 (1952).

[29] *Colburn v. Burlingame*, 190 Cal. 697, 704 (1923).

[30] Leach, *Cases and Materials on the Law of Future Interests* 241 n.19 (1935).

opinion as a matter contained in the body of the opinion and has like binding force and effect. See cases cited 21 *C.J.S.* (1940) p. 407, Courts, footnote 3.[31]

Whether it be humor, or metaphor, or beauty, or some other artistic device which also happens to be mnemonic, the choice of how to say things is but rarely made for the lawyer. (Section 133.) The great variety of the English language usually makes it possible for him to choose dullness or to reject it. Here, for example, are two ways of saying that the constitutional guaranty of free speech has limits. One — rambling, pontifical, sweeping — digs its own unmarked grave in the field of forgettable generalities. The other — tight, and tied to human beings — is adapted to easy remembering. (In each quote, only the interrupting citation of cases has been omitted.)

It is a fundamental principle, long established, that the freedom of speech and of the press which is secured by the Constitution, does not confer an absolute right to speak or publish, without responsibility, whatever one may choose, or an unrestricted and unbridled license that gives immunity for every possible use of language and prevents the punishment of those who abuse this freedom. . . . Reasonably limited, it was said by Story in the passage cited, this freedom is an inestimable privilege in a free government; without such limitation, it might become the scourge of the republic.[32]

But the character of every act depends upon the circumstances in which it is done. . . . The most stringent protection of free speech would not protect a man in falsely shouting fire in a theatre and causing a panic. It does not even protect a man from an injunction against uttering words that may have all the effect of force. . . . The question in every case is whether the words used are used in such circumstances and are of such a nature as to create a clear and present danger that they will bring about the substantive evils that Congress has a right to prevent. It is a question of proximity and degree.[33]

As with contagious verbosity (Section 131), the practice of improving the rememberable qualities of legal composition spreads itself. Association is still the best bet in the unsolved riddle of creativeness, as in and out of the law — one good word begets another.

In his dissent to wiretapping, Mr. Justice Brandeis wrote these words:

And it is also immaterial that the intrusion was in aid of law enforcement. Experience should teach us to be most on our guard to protect liberty when the government's purposes are beneficient. Men born to freedom are naturally alert to repel invasion of their liberty by evil-

[31] McComb, J., in *Melancon v. Walt Disney Productions,* 127 Cal. App. 2d 213, 214n (1954).
[32] Sanford, J., in *Gitlow v. New York,* 268 U.S. 652, 666-667 (1925).
[33] Holmes, J., in *Schenck v. United States,* 249 U.S. 47, 52 (1919).

minded rulers. The greatest dangers to liberty lurk in insidious encroachment by men of zeal, well-meaning but without understanding.[34]

The ringing *men born to freedom* has roots in Scripture:

And the chief captain answered, With a great sum obtained I this freedom. And Paul said, But I was free born.[35]

Beyond that, the Justice footnoted his inspiration with reference to an amicus brief. A part of the brief reads:

. . . but, in any event, it is better that a few criminals escape than that the privacies of life of all the people be exposed to the agents of government, who will act on their own discretion, the honest and the dishonest, unauthorized and unrestrained by the courts.[36]

Those words penned by telephone company lawyers were not lost upon Mr. Justice Holmes, who reshaped them for posterity as:

We have to choose, and for my part I think it a less evil that some criminals should escape than that the government should play an ignoble part.[37]

When do words make a promise without saying so? The lawbooks are full of answers.[38] A half century ago, Mr. Justice Scott gave this one:

It is true that plaintiff does not by precise words engage to employ defendant for the term specified, but the whole contract is instinct with such an obligation on its part and there can be no doubt that upon a fair construction it imports a hiring by the plaintiff as well as an obligation to serve by defendant.[39]

Five years later, Mr. Justice Cardozo took the phrase in hand:

There are times when reciprocal engagements do not fit each other like the parts of an indented deed, and yet the whole contract, as was said in *McCall Co. v. Wright* . . . , may be "instinct with . . . an obligation," imperfectly expressed.[40]

By 1917, that master craftsman — taking care to preserve the provenance — had added a high polish:

[34] *Olmstead v. United States*, 277 U.S. 438, 479 (1928).

[35] Acts 22:28; see also Justinian, *The Institutes*, 6-7 (Moyle, transl. 5th ed., 1913).

[36] *Olmstead v. United States*, 277 U.S. 438, 479 n.12 (1928); see also Fortescue, *De Laudibus*, c. XXVII, p. 65 (Chrimes ed. 1942).

[37] Dissenting, in *Olmstead v. United States*, 277 U.S. 438, 470 (1928).

[38] For example, 20 *Words and Phrases* 343-366 (perm. ed. 1959), "implied contract."

[39] *McCall Co. v. Wright*, 133 App. Div. 62, 68 (N.Y. 1909).

[40] *Moran v. Standard Oil Co.*, 211 N.Y. 187, 198 (1914).

The law has outgrown its primitive stage of formalism when the precise word was the sovereign talisman, and every slip was fatal. It takes a broader view today. A promise may be lacking, and yet the whole writing may be "instinct with an obligation," imperfectly expressed.[41]

Sacrilege perhaps when that delicacy is mauled in the bustle of court life:

Wood v. Duff-Gordon . . . is cited in arguing that although a promise to remain in Yonkers may be lacking, yet the writing is instinct with an obligation to do so.[42]

Yet even the fragments of Cardozo's masterpiece are helping lawyers to remember.

135. *Impressive*

Rememberability is only one of the elements that makes for the durability of the language of the law. (Section 134.) Another is the power of that language to instill in its hearers and readers a respect for the law which it represents. The language of the law was originally designed to impress laymen (Section 29), and that has never ceased to be one of its functions; although the way in which it has accomplished this purpose has varied from age to age.

The awe which the ancient oaths inspired (Sections 29, 30) was grounded in the supernatural, in the identity of letter and law — together magical and unchanging. And even when the role of the supernatural weakens, an unchanging language of the law has been the reverent tie with antiquity, with the power — spiritual or temporal — that comes from beyond the mists.

This is what the magnificent William had in mind when, unaccustomed as he was to the English language, he nonetheless saw to it that his charter to the City of London was cast in Old English. (Section 42.) This not a matter of intelligibility or precision, but of what was best at the moment for impression's sake: a continuity of the old and the good and the powerful.

So it once was with Latin in the law (Chapter VII), described by Bacon as ". . . the aptest for memory, and of the greatest authority and majesty . . ."[43]

Even when he finds it unintelligible (Chapter XV), perhaps because of its muddiness, the layman today is still awed by the "authority and majesty" of some of the language of the law — Latin or not.

[41] *Wood v. Duff-Gordon*, 222 N.Y. 88, 91 (1917).
[42] *Matter of Otis Elevator* (*Carney*), 6 N.Y.2d 358, 361 (1959),
[43] See Section 79; 13 Bacon, *Works* 140 (Montagu ed. 1831).

The unaccustomed sounds of the courtroom for instance. (Section 15.)

A sharp rap for order; then:

All rise!

Hear ye! hear ye! hear ye! This honorable court is now in session . . .

May it please the court . . .

Your Honor . . .

Counsel, approach the bench . . .

Swear the witness! (You hear it? He says *swear him*, not *at him*.)

And then it is the oath, the rolling:

. . . truth, the whole truth, and nothing but the truth. So help you God! (Sections 30, 86, 127.)

Impressive still.[44] Even when it leaps out suddenly, barely audibly — in the clerk's blasé mumble —

YOUSWEAR . . . tatellthetruththewholetruthnothingbutthetruthsahelp-yaGODBESEATED& STATE YOUR NAME!

This is far away from the world beyond the courtroom door. Sounds that evoke a dim but not forgotten past. A strangeness. A minuet amidst rock-and-roll. A sense of things well ordered. A detachment — here no ordinary backfence brawling. This is a court of law. Here — at last — is justice.

Here, in this ritual of working justice, the old law words still have a place. The words but one part of a legal setting, as much a part as raised bench, robed judge, armed bailiff, the railing, the box, the flag. Precise or not. Brief or not. Intelligible or not. Here the words continue their ancient function — instilling respect for the process of law, and misleading no one.

For some traditionalists, all of the wasteful nonsense of law language (Section 115) has the same impressive quality of the courtroom ritual. This is what Dickens spoke of as he described the layman listening to the droning of the solicitor:

[44] 6 Wigmore, *Evidence* §1815, p. 285 (3d ed. 1940); compare Silving, "The Oath," 68 Yale L.J. 1329, 1389, and 1527, 1552-1553 (1959).

Sir Leicester in a great chair looks at the fire, and appears to have a stately liking for the legal repetitions and prolixities, as ranging among the national bulwarks.[45]

A lawyer may find it difficult to hand an old and profitable will-changer a *Will* instead of a *Last Will and Testament.* (Section 121.) Or to sell a confirmed landlord on a lease without a *Witnesseth.* Or to convince a businessman — a seasoned plainclothes lawyer — that his contract doesn't need a *said* or a *herein* (Section 120), a *null and void* (Section 123), or even a *Whereas.* (Section 120.) The client may feel cheated. Or let down. Adrift. Lawyerless. In such cases, diplomacy is called for, and small continued doses of word opiate may still be the better part of valor. But most clients get the word habit from their lawyers. And where the words serve no good purpose, most lawyers (if they will) can convince most clients that the time for a change has arrived.

There are other words that lawyers use in court which are designed to impress laymen, words of persuasion. These, though, are not a part of the continuity with the past, and only occasionally and by coincidence do they instill respect for the process of law. Once the lawyer has uttered his *Ladies and gentlemen of the jury,* he is strictly on his own. Apart from some incidental law words anticipating the judge's charge (Section 133), the jury speech is a personal creation. Cheap, or great,[46] it is more related to the good and bad speeches in other forums than to the jury speeches of other lawyers. Books have been written on the subject,[47] and the jury speech is not discussed in this book as a separate aspect of the language of the law.

In and out of the courtroom, lawyers use other law words — a whole category of words — also impressive, but in a distinctive way. These are the flexible words, the words that can be squeezed into any shape, or stuffed into any hole that needs plugging — with a soft plug. The *reasonable's* and the *substantial's,* the *satisfactory's* and the *extraordinary's,* etc. (Sections 16, 119, 129.)

These words lack the antique formality of the words of courtroom

---

[45] *Bleak House,* c. 2 (Gadshill ed. 1897).

[46] Weinberg, ed., *Attorney for the Damned* 491-531 (1957).

[47] For example: Philbrick, *Language and the Law: The Semantics of Forensic English* (1951); Stryker, *The Art of Advocacy* (1954); Weinberg, ed., *Attorney for the Damned* (1957); and see also I *The Papers of Benjamin Franklin* 328, 330 (Labaree ed. 1959).

ritual. Here no comforting, booming "Mesopotamia,"[48] no swing, no word sparkle. But like the words of ritual they have the deep appeal of the primitive identification of law and language (Section 134), giving the appearance — even when spurious — of a continuity of the law itself. Impressive? Respect instilling? Indeed yes! This is the word that was touched by the hand. These the very words of ". . . the enlightened patriots who framed our Constitution . . ."[49]

How can a short written Constitution last one hundred and seventy-five years and still come up strong? Don't break with the past. Interpret it.

> Such is the character of human language, that no word conveys to the mind, in all situations, one single definite idea; and nothing is more common than to use words in a figurative sense.

(That not the expression of a twentieth-century semanticist, but of the great Chief Justice almost one hundred and fifty years ago.)[50]

All language can be interpreted. All the language of the law is. (Sections 16, 129.) But the flexible words make that task the easier, the connection with the past the more discernible.[51]

There it is in the Constitution — just as it was written:

> To make all Laws which shall be necessary and proper. . . .[52]

You say that *necessary* is an absolute, that it means only those laws ". . . most direct and simple"?[53]

Well, no. You see,

> Almost all compositions contain words, which, taken in their rigorous sense, would convey a meaning different from that which is obviously intended. It is essential to just construction, that many words which import something excessive, should be understood in a more mitigated sense — in that sense which common usage justifies. The word "necessary" is of this description. It has not a fixed character peculiar to itself. . . . A thing may be necessary, very necessary, absolutely or indispensably necessary.[54]

[48] *Webster's New International Dictionary* (2d ed. 1934), under *blessed word;* Warren, *Spartan Education* 30 (1942).

[49] Marshall, C.J., in *Gibbons v. Ogden,* 9 Wheat. 1, 188 (U.S. 1824).

[50] Marshall, C.J., in *McCulloch v. Maryland,* 4 Wheat. 316, 414 (U.S. 1819).

[51] See Levin, "Language, Symbol Cycles, and the Constitution," 71 U.S.L. Rev. 258, 266 (1937).

[52] Art. I, §8, cl. 18.

[53] Marshall, C.J., *arguendo,* in *McCulloch v. Maryland,* 4 Wheat. 316, 413 (U.S. 1819).

[54] *McCulloch v. Maryland,* 4 Wheat. 316, 414 (U.S. 1819); compare *Commonwealth v. Morrison,* 9 Ky. 75, 80-84 (1819); see 28 *Words and Phrases* 209-244

Thus is the link with the past preserved — an impressively aged Constitution, still flexible in its joints with *freedom* of speech,[55] *unreasonable* searches and seizures,[56] *due* process,[57] *equal protection* of the laws,[58] and a *commerce* clause[59] deliberately left so vague (Section 104) that it has survived to regulate televised Bingo.[60] We see the process continuing in our own day. A marvelously flexible phrase is added to the constitutional vocabulary, fetched up from another century to douse a sizzling bomb — *with all deliberate speed.*[61]

The flexibles are the words which make the small, slow changes possible, the gradual adjustment of principle to fact which is the heart of the common law. (Section 129.) These are the words which absorb the shock of social change, leaving the law with a semblance of stability impressive to the beholder. And that is a valuable function, as long as the appearance is not mistaken for substance.[62] As long as the distinctive services of the flexible words in the language of the law are not confused with the goals of precision, or intelligibility.

The impressive appearance of continuity that the flexible words give to the law is a lasting result of the more workaday function of these words in making agreement possible in the first place. This, a sort of magic more impressive to lawyers than to laymen.

Enter the arena. Duck the brickbats. Strive to reconcile reasonable and unreasonable men, strive for an armistice — let alone for that will-o'-the-wisp, that beautiful metaphor of the law — *a meeting of the minds.*[63] Sometimes it is only the flexible, the *calculated ambiguity,*[64]

(perm. ed. 1955), 10-12 (Supp. 1962), "necessary"; 3 *California Words, Phrases, and Maxims* 72-73 (1960); 3 *Words and Phrases: Judicially Defined* 459-461 (1944), 84-85 (Supp. 1960).

[55] Amend. I.

[56] Amend. IV.

[57] Amends. V, XIV.

[58] Amend. XIV.

[59] Art. I, §8, cl. 3.

[60] *Caples Co. v. United States,* 243 F.2d 232 (D.C. Cir. 1957).

[61] *Brown v. Board of Education,* 349 U.S. 294, 301 (1955); Thaler, "With All Deliberate Speed," 27 Tenn. L. Rev. 510-517 (1960); compare *with all convenient speed* in Court Rules, 2 Tyr. 341-352, 349, Rule No. 87 (Ex. 1832), and *Oxford English Dictionary,* under *speed,* No. 5.

[62] See Section 119; see also Levin, "Language, Symbol Cycles, and the Constitution," 71 U.S.L. Rev. 258, 266 (1937).

[63] See *Oxford English Dictionary,* under *meet,* No. 8d; Ballentine, *Law Dictionary with Pronunciations* (2d ed. 1948); 27 *Words and Phrases* (perm. ed. 1961), "meeting of minds"; 2 *California Words, Phrases, and Maxims* (1960), "meeting of the minds."

[64] See Section 132; Cox, "Internal Affairs of Labor Unions Under the Labor Reform Act of 1959," 58 Mich. L. Rev. 819, 852 (1960); see also Arnold, "Professor Hart's Theology," 73 Harv. L. Rev. 1298, 1312 (1960).

that will bring men to any agreement at all, whether in constitutions (Section 104), statutes,[65] or contracts.

If each time someone has a stubborn idea it must be reduced to the most definite of propositions, there is no end to the drafting of a contract or a law. For instance.

When culture came to the West, a gallant legislature added to the exemption statute not only "sucking calves" but

one piano, in actual use in a family, or belonging to a woman; . . .[66]

Four years later, "sucking pigs" were freed from threat of execution, but that "piano" (which could be used in a house as well as a home) was once more subject to levy.[67] Twenty-one years later, culture squeezed in again, this time in strange, compromising company. Exempt, as a package deal —

also, one piano, one shotgun, and one rifle.[68]

The "piano" has stuck; a radio (1935)[69] and then "one television receiver" (1955)[70] were added. On other fronts, every imaginable sort of widget has been made part of the exemption statutes, from a "whim"[71] to a wooden leg.[72]

If that same tugging and hauling had characterized the legislature's consideration of items of *wearing apparel* to be exempt from execution, the original session would still be going. Instead, the flexible *necessary* came to the rescue. It became the rule that whatever is *necessary wearing apparel* is exempt.[73] True it is that this is vague talk, whether in exemption statutes or elsewhere. My clothing *luxuries*[74] are your *necessaries*.[75] Yet it is a manageable, durable vague-

---

[65] See Cox, "Internal Affairs of Labor Unions Under the Labor Reform Act of 1959," 58 Mich. L. Rev. 819, 852 (1960).

[66] Cal. Civ. Proc. Code §690 (1872).

[67] Cal. Civ. Proc. Code §690 (1875-1876).

[68] Cal. Civ. Proc. Code §690 (1897).

[69] Cal. Civ. Proc. Code §690.2; compare *Lader v. Gordon,* 88 N.Y.S.2d 758, 759 (Supp. App. T. 1949).

[70] Cal. Civ. Proc. Code §690.2; compare *Michealson v. Elliott,* 209 F.2d 625 (8th Cir. 1954).

[71] Cal. Civ. Proc. Code §690.6.

[72] Cal. Civ. Proc. Code §690.5.

[73] *Estate of Millington,* 63 Cal. App. 498 (1923), and compare *Los Angeles Finance Co. v. Flores,* 110 Cal. App. 2d Supp. 850, 852, 853, 855-856 (1952); *Arch Lumber Co., Inc. v. Dohm,* 98 A.2d 840, 842 (R.I. 1953); 28 *Words and Phrases* 431-432 (perm. ed. 1955), "necessary wearing apparel"; 3 *California Words, Phrases, and Maxims* 76-77 (1960).

[74] See 25A *Words and Phrases* (perm. ed. 1961).

[75] See *Arch Lumber Co., Inc. v. Dohm,* 98 A.2d 840, 842 (R.I. 1953); 28 *Words and Phrases* 170-201 (perm. ed. 1955), 8-9 (Supp. 1962); 3 *California Words,*

ness, with chaos the alternative. A debate on whether or not "mink" is a *necessary* would send brave men running for cover, and leave any legislative session in tatters. But a judge with a sharp pencil and an appraising eye can tell rather quickly that this particular lady has mink coming to her.[76]

Note here that a flexible word — even more than other words — varies in content according to who uses it and who listens to it. Laymen as well as lawyers live by such usage. If a seller starts a dicker by remarking ever so casually that he will sell for "*about* $100,000," he is understood to mean that he will take "*less than* $100,000." But if the buyer starts the dicker over the same property by saying that he will buy for "*about* $100,000," that means that he will pay "*more than* $100,000." [77]

Extraordinary[78] is another such word, at its spongy best in the law's *extraordinary services.*[79] In that form it relieves the legislator of a problem insoluble in bulk, by shifting the problem to judge and lawyer, who are able to cope with it in the common law way — piecemeal.

To judges in probate and to lawyers, *extraordinary services* is a workable convenience. Both are accustomed to its vagaries. But in every probate there is a layman — viewing with alarm each nibbling inroad upon his dwindling patrimony. To him there is nothing *extraordinary* about an executor's lawyer defending a lawsuit.[80] What is a lawyer for anyhow? [81] Unless the layman in probate is given patient and clear explanation, he will look upon *extraordinary services* as a devious lawyer's gimmick to get more money. Exit respect.

For all the usefulness of both flexible words and ritual words in promoting a respect for the law, there is a limit beyond which neither

---

Phrases, and Maxims 69-70 (1960); 3 *Words and Phrases: Judicially Defined* 454-459 (1944).

[76] See *Gimbel Brothers, Inc. v. Pinto,* 188 Pa. Super. 72, 74 (1958).

[77] See 1 *Words and Phrases* 107-108 (perm. ed. 1940), 51 (Supp. 1962), "about" (estimate of value).

[78] *Fry v. National Rejectors, Inc.,* 306 S.W.2d 465, 468 (Mo. 1957); 15A *Words and Phrases* 677-700 (perm. ed. 1950), 54-55 (Supp. 1962), "extraordinary," and related phrases; 1 *California Words, Phrases, and Maxims* 711-712 (1960); 2 *Words and Phrases: Judicially Defined* 265-268 (1943), 58 (Supp. 1960).

[79] 15A *Words and Phrases* 697-699 (perm. ed. 1950); 1 *California Words, Phrases, and Maxims* 712 (1960); Cal. Prob. Code §§469, 902, 910.

[80] See *In re Will of Jewe,* 201 Iowa 1154, 1156 (1926).

[81] *Webster's New International Dictionary* (2d ed. 1934), under *lawyer;* see also *Roberts v. Veterans Cooperative Housing Assn.,* 88 A.2d 324, 327 (D.C. Mun. Ct. App. 1952).

can be pushed, lest that respect turn to disgust. That point is reached where the law requires the layman personally to understand the law, and the language of the law prevents understanding. (Sections 132, 133.) In most ancient times when the layman's role in the law was simply that of oath-swearer, awe was sufficient. (Section 29.) It is not today. The diminished hold of religion diminishes the impressive capacity of even the oaths. And as the ordinary layman's role in legal affairs increases — as witness, juror, businessman, and citizen — more and more his respect for the law itself depends upon his understanding in the idiom of today what is going on, rather than being overawed and confused with unnecessary nonsense syllables.

When the juror is told that he must follow the law as laid down by the judge,[82] and he cannot follow the words — let alone the law — this frustration does not promote respect. When the harried businessman is overwhelmed with the language confusions of the government he is taxed to support and of the professionals he pays to help him, his feelings for the law and for lawyers are not properly described as respectful. (Section 133.)

Respect for law is no mere matter of words; neither intelligibility nor precision nor ritual will sell bad law indefinitely. But bad language usage can hurt good law; good language usage can promote respect for good law. And for the rest of this language-conscious century, an important part of the layman's attitude toward the law will be determined by what the profession does with its language. (Section 136.)

136. The priesthood

Beyond its rememberable and impressive qualities, the language of the law depends for survival upon those it unites in priesthood — the lawyers.

Law language is no longer — as lawyers once wanted it — bottled in bond, "that their discipline might not be made common among the vulgar." (Section 25.) Like it or not, the law has become common (Section 135), the possession of all men far more immediately than when the *common law* got its name.[83] Yet in becoming common, it did not become simple. The law in its most ordinary operations has

---

[82] *California Jury Instructions: Civil*, No. 1 (4th rev. ed. 1956).
[83] 1 Pollock and Maitland, *The History of English Law* 176-178 (2d ed. 1898); *Oxford English Dictionary.*

sufficient technicality to baffle the untrained. Only the lawyer can exploit the capabilities of the language of the law, he alone even recognize some of its limitations.

Here as elsewhere, the layman looks to the lawyer for guidance. For all his complaining, he even looks up to the lawyer. Almost any live lawyer is introduced as a *distinguished member of the bar;* almost any dead one eulogized as a *successful attorney.* The lawyer's daily mail showers him with the polite flattery of the archaic addition *Esquire* or *Esq.*[84] Small signs to be sure, but indicative of a basic respect for an ancient profession, still honorable.

Responsibility for law language is fixed upon the profession. And the urgent cries for improvement can be heard above the croaking of "precision" and the moaning over the impossibility of perfection.

In making the language of the law work in the twentieth century, it is neither necessary nor desirable that the profession break with its past — only that it be more selective of what it takes from that varied past. More of principle than words. More of fact than sentiment.

What has made the common law great is less *reason*[85] than an endless succession of *reasons.*[86] What has made the language of the law less than great is a tendency of its users to accept a single reason ("precision"), rather than to search for reasons, their beginnings and their ceasing to exist. When that search is made, the reasons are many, not the least of them "habit," and the most spurious "precision."

It is a lawyer's — not a robot's — job to know when a reason and a word are done for. It is a steady job, not ended with yesterday's pleading, today's opinion, nor with this book. Cleansed of words without reason, much of the language of the law need not be peculiar at all. And better for it.

---

[84] See Section 121; *Oxford English Dictionary,* under *esquire,* sb.1, Nos. 2, 3; compare Mencken, *The American Language Supplement I* 550 (1945), and Mencken, *The American Language* 278 (4th ed. 1936); see also Post, *Etiquette* 507 (9th ed. 1955); 2 *A Dictionary of American English* (1940), under *Esq., Esqr.,* and *Esquire;* Evans and Evans, *A Dictionary of Contemporary American Usage* (1957), under *Esquire; Black's Law Dictionary* (4th ed. 1951), under *Esquire;* Ballentine, *Law Dictionary with Pronunciations* (2d ed. 1948), under *esquire;* 15 *Words and Phrases* (perm. ed. 1950, Supp. 1962), "Esquire."

[85] See Coke, *Commentary upon Littleton,* f. 97b (10th ed. 1703).

[86] See Coke, *Commentary upon Littleton,* f. 183b (10th ed. 1703); Littleton, *Tenures,* Epilogus, and comment, in Coke, *Commentary upon Littleton* (10th ed. 1703); see also Fraunce, *The Lawiers Logike* 62a (1588).

Selected Bibliography

(Separate alphabetical lists for Dictionaries, p. 455; Language, p. 458; History, p. 466; Law Treatises, p. 472; Formbooks, p. 475; Miscellany, p. 477.)

DICTIONARIES

American Dialect Dictionary. [See Wentworth, Harold.]
An Anglo-Saxon Dictionary. [See Bosworth, Joseph, and T. Northcote Toller.]
An Anglo-Saxon Dictionary: Supplement. [See Toller, T. Northcote.]
Bailey, Nathan. *An Universal Etymological English Dictionary.* London: 1721.
———— ———— 2d ed. London: 1724.
———— ———— Two parts (in one). London: 1727.
———— ———— Joseph Nicol Scott, ed. London: 1755.
Ballentine, James A. *Law Dictionary with Pronunciations.* 2d ed. Rochester, N.Y.: Lawyers Co-operative Publishing Company, 1948.
Ballentine's Pronouncing Law Dictionary: Supplement. 2d ed. Rochester, N.Y.: Lawyers Co-operative Publishing Company, 1954.
Bartlett, John Russell. *Dictionary of Americanisms.* 4th ed. Boston: Little, Brown and Company, 1896.
Black's Law Dictionary. 4th ed. St. Paul: West Publishing Co., 1951.
Blount, Thomas. *Glossographia.* London: 1656.
———— *Nomo-Lexikon: A Law Dictionary.* In the Savoy: John Martin and Henry Herringman, 1670.
———— *A Law-Dictionary and Glossary.* W. Nelson, ed. 3d ed. In the Savoy: Printed by Eliz. Nutt and R. Gosling, 1717.
[————, ed.] *Les Termes de la Ley* (1671). [See.]
Bosworth, Joseph, and T. Northcote Toller. *An Anglo-Saxon Dictionary.* London: Oxford University Press, 1898. [See also Toller, T. Northcote.]
Bouvier, John. *A Law Dictionary.* Philadelphia: T. & J. W. Johnson, 1839. 2 vols.
———— ———— 3d ed. Philadelphia: 1848. 2 vols.
———— ———— Preface by Francis Rawle. 15th ed. Philadelphia: J. B. Lippincott Company, 1892. 2 vols.
Bouvier's Law Dictionary and Concise Encyclopedia. 3d rev. 8th ed. St. Paul: West Publishing Co., 1914. 3 vols.
California Words, Phrases, and Maxims. San Francisco: Bancroft-Whitney Company, 1960. 4 vols.
Cowell, John. *The Interpreter.* London: William Sheares, 1637. [1st ed. 1607.]
A Dictionary of American English: On Historical Principles. Sir William A. Craigie and James R. Hulbert, eds. Chicago: University Press, 1938-1944. 4 vols.

Dictionary of American Slang. Harold Wentworth and Stuart Berg Flexner, eds. New York: Thomas Y. Crowell Company, 1960.

Evans, Bergen, and Cornelia Evans. *A Dictionary of Contemporary American Usage.* New York: Random House, 1957.

Farmer, John S. *Americanisms — Old & New.* London: Printed by Thomas Poulter & Sons, 1889.

Fowler, H. W. *A Dictionary of Modern English Usage.* Oxford: University Press, 1926.

Godefroy, Frédéric. *Lexique de L'Ancien Français.* J. Bonnard and Am. Salmon, eds. New York: G. E. Stechert & Co., 1928.

Grandsaignes d'Hauterive, R. *Dictionnaire D'Ancien Français: Moyen Age et Renaissance.* Paris: Librairie Larousse, 1947.

Halliwell, James Orchard. *A Dictionary of Archaic and Provincial Words.* 10th ed. London: John Russell Smith, 1881. 2 vols.

Harrap's Standard French and English Dictionary. J. E. Mansion, ed. With supplement, new ed., R. P. L. Ledésert, comp. London: George G. Harrap & Company Ltd., 1955.

Horwill, H. W. *A Dictionary of Modern American Usage.* 2d ed. Oxford: University Press, 1944.

Jacob, Giles. *A New Law-Dictionary.* 6th ed. In the Savoy: R. Ware and others, 1750.

Johnson, Samuel. *A Dictionary of the English Language.* 4th ed. Dublin: Thomas Ewing, 1775. 2 vols. [1st ed. 1755.]

Jowitt [Earl], gen. ed. *The Dictionary of English Law.* Clifford Walsh, ed. London: Sweet & Maxwell Limited, 1959. 2 vols.

Kelham, Robert. *A Dictionary of the Norman or Old French Language.* London: Edward Brooke, 1779.

The Law-French Dictionary. To which is added, The Law-Latin Dictionary. 2d ed. In the Savoy: D. Brown and others, 1718.

Lewis, Charlton T., and Charles Short, eds. *A Latin Dictionary.* Oxford: University Press, 1879.

Littleton, Adam. *Dr. Adam Littleton's Latin Dictionary: In Four Parts.* 6th ed. London: J. Walthoe and others, 1735.

Mathews, Mitford, ed. *A Dictionary of Americanisms: On Historical Principles.* Chicago: University Press, 1951. 2 vols.

Medieval Latin Word-List. Prepared by J. H. Baxter and Charles Johnson, with assistance of Phyllis Abrahams. London: Oxford University Press, 1934.

Middle English Dictionary. Hans Kurath, ed., Sherman M. Kuhn, assoc. ed. Photolithoprinted. Ann Arbor: University of Michigan Press, 1954- Fascicles.

A Middle-English Dictionary. By Francis Henry Stratmann. New edition, re-arranged, revised, and enlarged by Henry Bradley. London: Oxford University Press, 1891.

Mozley and Whiteley's Law Dictionary. 5th ed. London: Butterworth & Co. (Publishers), Ltd., 1930.

Nicholson, Margaret. *A Dictionary of American-English Usage.* New York: Oxford University Press, 1957.

The Oxford English Dictionary. Oxford: University Press, 1933. 13 vols.

Partridge, Eric. *The Concise Usage and Abusage.* New York: Philosophical Library, 1955.

—— *A Dictionary of Clichés.* 4th ed. London: Routledge & Kegan Paul Ltd., 1950.

—— *A Dictionary of Slang and Unconventional English.* 4th ed. New York: The Macmillan Company, 1951.

—— *A Dictionary of the Underworld: British & American.* New York: The Macmillan Company, 1950.

—— *Usage and Abusage.* New edition. London: Hamish Hamilton, 1957.

Pickering, John. *A Vocabulary.* Boston: Cummings and Hilliard, 1816.

Rastell, William. [See *Les Termes de la Ley.*]

Skeat, Walter W. *A Concise Etymological Dictionary of the English Language.* New York: Harper & Brothers, 1882.

—— *An Etymological Dictionary of the English Language.* New edition revised and enlarged. Oxford: University Press, 1909.

Skene, M. John. *De Verborum Significatione: The Exposition of the Termes and Difficill Wordes Conteined in the Foure Buikes of Regiam Majestatem.* 1681. [1st ed. 1597.]

The Slang Dictionary. London: John Camden Hotten, 1872.

Smith, William, and Theophilus D. Hall. *A Copious and Critical English-Latin Dictionary.* New York: American Book Co., 1871.

Spelman, Sir Henry. *Glossarium Archaiologicum.* 3d ed. London: Thomas Braddyll, 1687.

Stratmann, Francis Henry. [See *A Middle-English Dictionary.*]

The Student's Law-Dictionary. In the Savoy: James Hodges, 1740.

Sweet, Henry. *The Student's Dictionary of Anglo-Saxon.* Oxford: University Press, 1896.

Taylor, Archer, and Bartlett Jere Whiting. *A Dictionary of American Proverbs and Proverbial Phrases: 1820-1880.* Cambridge, Mass.: Harvard University Press, 1958.

Les Termes de la Ley. Newly corrected and enlarged edition [of William Rastell's dictionary]. Thomas Blount, ed. London: Printed by John Streater and others, 1671.

—— Now corrected and enlarged edition [of William Rastell's dictionary]. London: Printed by Samuel Roycroft and James Rawlins, 1708.

Thornton, Richard. *An American Glossary.* Philadelphia: J. B. Lippincott Company, 1912. 2 vols.

Toller, T. Northcote. *An Anglo-Saxon Dictionary: Supplement.* Oxford: University Press, 1921. [See also Bosworth, Joseph, and T. Northcote Toller.]

Trench, Richard Chenevix. *A Select Glossary.* 4th ed. London: Macmillan and Co., 1873.

["Vigilans."] *Chamber of Horrors: A Glossary of Official Jargon Both English and American.* London: Andre Deutsch, 1952.

Webster, Noah. *A Compendious Dictionary of the English Language.* New Haven: Hudson & Goodwin and others, 1806.

—— *An American Dictionary of the English Language.* New York: S. Converse, 1828. 2 vols.

Webster's New International Dictionary of the English Language. 2d ed. Unabridged. Springfield: G. & C. Merriam Company, 1934.

Webster's Third New International Dictionary of the English Language: Unabridged. Springfield: G. & C. Merriam Company, 1961.

Wentworth, Harold. *American Dialect Dictionary.* New York: Thomas Y. Crowell Company, 1944.
Wharton's Law Lexicon. 14th ed., by A. S. Oppé. London: Stevens and Sons Limited, 1938.
Words and Phrases: Judicially Defined. Roland Burrows, general ed. London: Butterworth & Co. (Publishers), Ltd., 1943-1946. 5 vols.
Words and Phrases: Permanent Edition. St. Paul: West Publishing Co., 1940-1973. 90 vols.

LANGUAGE

Aiken, Ray J. "Let's Not Oversimplify Legal Language," 32 *Rocky Mountain Law Review* 358-364 (1960).
Alderman, Sidney S. "The French Language in English and American Law," 28 *Canadian Bar Review* 1104-1123 (1950), reprinted in 12 *Alabama Lawyer* 356-374 (1951).
Alford, Henry. *A Plea for the Queen's English.* With preface to 2d ed. (1864). London: Strahan & Co., 1869.
Allen, Layman E. "Symbolic Logic: A Razor-edged Tool for Drafting and Interpreting Legal Documents," 66 *Yale Law Journal* 833-879 (1957).
"And/or," editorial in 18 *American Bar Association Journal* 456 (1932).
"And/or," note in 118 *American Law Reports* 1367-1377 (1939).
"And/or," note in 154 *American Law Reports* 866-874 (1945).
"And/or -iana," editorial in 18 *American Bar Association Journal* 524 (1932).
"An and/or Symposium," letters in 18 *American Bar Association Journal* 574-577 (1932).
Anglo-Norman Political Songs. Isabel S. T. Aspin, ed. Anglo-Norman Texts, XI. Oxford: Anglo-Norman Text Society by Basil Blackwell, 1953.
Applications of Electronic Data Processing Systems to Legal Research. Washington, D.C.: Bureau of National Affairs, Inc., 1960.
Arnold, Thurman W. *The Folklore of Capitalism.* New Haven: Yale University Press, 1937.
Baugh, Albert C. *A History of the English Language.* New York: Appleton-Century-Crofts, Inc., 1935.
Beardsley, Charles A. "Beware of, Eschew and Avoid Pompous Prolixity and Platitudinous Epistles!" 16 *Journal of the State Bar of California* 65-69 (1941).
——— "Judicial Draftsmanship," 24 *Washington Law Review* 146-153 (1949).
——— "Wherein and Whereby Beardsley Makes Reply to Challenge," 16 *Journal of the State Bar of California* 106-107 (1941).
Bentham, Jeremy. *The Works of Jeremy Bentham.* John Bowring, ed. Edinburgh: William Tait, 1843. 10 vols.
Benthamiana. John Hill Burton, ed. Edinburgh: William Tait, 1843.
Beutel, F. K. "Elementary Semantics: Criticisms of Realism and Experimental Jurisprudence," 13 *Journal of Legal Education* 67-75 (1960).
Bodmer, Frederick. *The Loom of Language.* Lancelot Hogben, ed. New York: W. W. Norton & Company, Inc., 1944.
Bryant, Margaret M. *English in the Law Courts.* New York: Columbia University Press, 1930.

———— Review of *Language and the Law* by Frederick A. Philbrick [see], in 24 *American Speech* 201-293 (1949).

Burrow, Sir James. "A Few Thoughts upon Pointing and Some Other Helps Towards Perspicuity of Expression," in *A Series of the Decisions of the Court of King's Bench upon Settlement Cases.* London: 1768.

Cairns, Huntington. "Language of Jurisprudence," in Ruth Nanda Anshen, ed., *Language: An Enquiry into Its Meaning and Function.* New York: Harper & Brothers, 1957. Chap. XIV, pp. 232-269.

Cambridge Anglo-Norman Texts. O. H. Prior, gen. ed. Cambridge: University Press, 1924. Vol. I.

Campbell, George. *The Philosophy of Rhetoric.* 2d ed. London: A. Strahan and others, 1801. [1st ed. 1776.] 2 vols.

Cardozo, Benjamin N. *Law and Literature, and Other Essays.* New York: Harcourt, Brace and Company, 1931.

Casner, A. James. "Construction of Gifts to 'Heirs' and the Like," 53 *Harvard Law Review* 207-250 (1939).

Cavers, David F. "The Simplification of Government Regulations," 8 *Federal Bar Journal* 339-356 (1947).

Chafee, Zechariah, Jr. "The Disorderly Conduct of Words," 41 *Columbia Law Review* 381-404 (1941).

Chase, Stuart. *The Tyranny of Words.* New York: Harcourt, Brace and Company, 1938.

Cohen, Felix S. "Transcendental Nonsense and the Functional Approach," 35 *Columbia Law Review* 809-849 (1935).

Collas, John P. "Problems of Translation," in Introduction to *Year Books of Edward II: Vol. XXIV. 12 Edward II. Hilary and Part of Easter, 1319.* John P. Collas and Theodore F. T. Plucknett, eds. Selden Society, Vol. 70. London: Bernard Quaritch, 1953. Pp. xii-lxiv.

Cook, Robert N. *Legal Drafting.* Revised ed. Brooklyn: The Foundation Press, Inc., 1951.

Cooley, Thomas M., II. "A Law School Fights Graduate Illiteracy," 44 *Saturday Review* 39-41 (1961).

Cooper, Frank E. *Effective Legal Writing.* Indianapolis: The Bobbs-Merrill Company, Inc., 1953.

"Current Issues in Legal Education (A Survey)," 9 *Cleveland-Marshall Law Review* 582-591 (1960).

Dickerson, Reed. "The Electronic Searching of Law," 47 *American Bar Association Journal* 902-908 (1961).

———— *Legislative Drafting.* Boston: Little, Brown and Company, 1954.

Doherty, Ella Tormey, and Elsie E. Cooper. *Word Heritage.* Chicago: J.B. Lippincott Company, 1929.

Earle, John. *The Philology of the English Tongue.* 4th ed. Oxford: University Press, 1887.

[Field, David Dudley.] Untitled manual, reprinted in *Cal. Civ. Proc. Code* following §426 (Deering, 1959). Pp. 162-181.

Flesch, Rudolf. *The Art of Plain Talk.* New York: Harper & Brothers, 1946.

———— *The Art of Readable Writing.* New York: Harper & Brothers, 1949.

"For and/or on Behalf of; or Against and/or," letters in 10 *Journal of the State Bar of California* 89-93, 95 (1935).

[Fowler, H. W., and Francis George Fowler.] *The King's English.* Oxford: University Press, 1906.

Freed, Roy N. "Prepare Now for Machine-Assisted Legal Research," 47 *American Bar Association Journal* 764-767 (1961).

Funk, Charles Earle. *Heavens to Betsy! And Other Curious Sayings.* New York: Harper & Brothers, 1955.

Gerhart, Eugene C. "Improving Our Legal Writing," 40 *American Bar Association Journal* 1057-1060 (1954).

———— "Improving Our Legal Writing: Maxims from the Masters," 20 *Lawyers Journal* (Manila) 159 (1955).

Gibson, Walker. "Literary Minds and Judicial Style," 36 *New York University Law Review* 915-930 (1961).

Gowers, Sir Ernest. *Plain Words: A Guide to the Use of English.* London: His Majesty's Stationery Office, 1948.

———— *Plain Words: Their ABC.* New York: Alfred A. Knopf, 1954.

———— *The Complete Plain Words.* 4th impression, with amendments. London: Her Majesty's Stationery Office, 1957.

Greene, W. A. "Shorter Deeds, or Multum in Parvo," 110 *Law Journal* 84-86 (1961).

Greenough, James Bradstreet, and George Lyman Kittredge. *Words and Their Ways in English Speech.* London: Macmillan & Co. Limited, 1902.

Hager, John W. "Let's Simplify Legal Language," 32 *Rocky Mountain Law Review* 74-86 (1959).

Hancock, Moffatt. "Fallacy of the Transplanted Category," 37 *Canadian Bar Review* 535-575 (1959).

Harris, James. *Hermes: Or a Philosophical Inquiry Concerning Universal Grammar.* 5th ed. London: F. Wingrave, 1794.

Hayakawa, S. I. *Language in Action.* New York: Harcourt, Brace, and Company, 1941.

Hexner, Erwin. *Studies in Legal Terminology.* Chapel Hill: University of North Carolina Press, 1941.

Hogan, John C. "Legal Terminology for the Upper Regions of the Atmosphere and for the Space Beyond the Atmosphere," 51 *American Journal of International Law* 362-375 (1957).

Hogben, Lancelot. *From Cave Painting to Comic Strip.* London: Max Parrish & Co. Ltd., 1949.

Hohfeld, Wesley Newcomb. "Some Fundamental Legal Conceptions as Applied in Judicial Reasoning," 23 *Yale Law Journal* 16-59 (1913).

———— "Fundamental Legal Conceptions as Applied in Judicial Reasoning," 26 *Yale Law Journal* 710-770 (1917).

Holmes, Oliver Wendell, Jr. "The Theory of Legal Interpretation," 12 *Harvard Law Review* 417-420 (1899).

Hulbert, James Root. *Dictionaries British and American.* London: Andre Deutsch, 1955.

Hunter, Laura Grace. *The Language of Audit Reports.* U.S. General Accounting Office. Washington, D.C.: Government Printing Office, 1957.

"In Defense of 'and/or,'" note in 45 *Yale Law Journal* 918-919 (1936).

Jackson, E. Hilton. *Law-Latin.* Washington, D.C.: John Byrne, 1897.

Jackson, Kenneth. *Language and History in Early Britain.* Edinburgh: University Press, 1953.

Jacobs, Noah Jonathan. *Naming-Day in Eden; The Creation and Recreation of Language.* New York: The Macmillan Company, 1958.

James, Peter. *Mechanized Legal Research.* Pamphlet; proposal drafted for evaluation by Electronic Data Retrieval Committee of the American Bar Association (Feb. 1, 1959).

"Jargon," editorial in *The Listener* 584 (April 2, 1959).

Jenkinson, Hilary. *The Later Court Hands in England from the Fifteenth to the Seventeenth Century.* Cambridge: University Press, 1927.

Jespersen, Otto. *Growth and Structure of the English Language.* Doubleday Anchor reprint. 9th ed. (1938). Garden City: Doubleday & Company, Inc., 1955. [1st published, 1905.]

Johnson, Alexander Bryan. *A Treatise on Language.* David Rynin, ed. Berkeley: University of California Press, 1959. [1st published, 1828, as *The Philosophy of Human Knowledge, or A Treatise on Language.*]

Johnson, Charles, and Hilary Jenkinson. *English Court Hand AD 1066 to 1500.* Oxford: University Press, 1915.

Johnson, Edwin Lee. *Latin Words of Common English.* Boston: D.C. Heath and Company, 1931.

Jones, Hugh. *A Short English Grammar.* London: 1724.

Jones, Richard Foster. *The Triumph of the English Language.* Stanford: University Press, 1953.

Jordan, Michael J. "The Cryptic 'SS,' " 8 *Boston University Law Review* 117-125 (1928).

Korzybski, Alfred. *Science and Sanity.* 2d ed. Lancaster, Penn.: Science Press, 1941.

Laird, Charlton. *The Miracle of Language.* Premier reprint. New York: Fawcett Publications, Inc., 1957. [1st published, 1953.]

"The Language of Law, a Symposium," Walter Probert, ed., in 9 *Western Reserve Law Review* 115-198 (1958).

"Language of the Law," 22 *Law Times* 200-201 (1955).

Latin for Lawyers. 2d ed. London: Sweet & Maxwell Limited, 1937.

Lavery, Urban A. "The Language of the Law," 7 *American Bar Association Journal* 277-283 (1921), 8 *American Bar Association Journal* 269-274 (1922).

———— "Punctuation in the Law," 9 *American Bar Association Journal* 225-228 (1923).

Leach, W. Barton, ed. *Langdell Lyrics of 1938.* Chicago: The Foundation Press, Inc., 1938.

———— "Powers of Appointment," 24 *American Bar Association Journal* 807-811, 855 (1938).

Legge, M. Dominica. "French and the Law," in Introduction to *Year Books of Edward II: 10 Edward II, A.D. 1316-1317.* M. Dominica Legge and Sir William Holdsworth, eds. The Year Book Series, vol. XXI. Selden Society, vol. 54. London: Bernard Quaritch, 1935. Pp. xxxviii-xliv.

———— "The Salient Features of the Language of the Earlier Year Books," in Introduction to *Year Books of Edward II: 10 Edward II, A.D. 1316-1317.* M. Dominica Legge and Sir William Holdsworth, eds. The Year Book Series, vol. XX. Selden Society, vol. 52. London: Quaritch, 1934. Pp. xxx-xlii.

Levin, A. J. "Language, Symbol Cycles, and the Constitution," 71 *United States Law Review* 258-267 (1937).

Levitan, Mortimer. "Dissertation on Writing Legal Opinions," *Wisconsin Law Review* 22-38 (Jan. 1960).

Lindey, Alexander. "Let's Write Better Contracts," 3 *Practical Lawyer* 32-38 (1957).
————"On Legal Style," in Lindey, *Motion Picture Agreements Annotated*. Pp. xvii-xxx. [See under Formbooks.]
Linton, Calvin D. *Effective Revenue Writing*. Vol. 2. U.S. Treasury Department, Internal Revenue Service. Training No. 83-0 (Rev. 5-61). Washington, D.C.: Government Printing Office, 1961.
Littler, Robert. "Legal Writing in Law Practice," 31 *Journal of the State Bar of California* 28-36 (1956).
———— "Reader Rights in Legal Writing," 25 *Journal of the State Bar of California* 51 (1950).
Locke, John. *An Essay Concerning Human Understanding*. Alexander Campbell Fraser, ed. Oxford: University Press, 1894. 2 vols.
[Lowth, Robert.] *A Short Introduction to English Grammar*. 2d ed. London: 1763.
Luders, Alexander. "On the Use of the French Language in Our Ancient Laws and Acts of State," Tract VI, in Luders, *Tracts on Various Subjects in the Law and History of England*. Printed by Richard Cruttwell. Bath: 1810. [Tract VI first published, 1807.] Pp. 341-430.
Lyly, John. *Euphues: The Anatomy of Wit*. English Reprints. London: Constable, 1928. [1st published, 1579.]
McComb, Marshall F. "A Mandate from the Bar: Shorter and More Lucid Opinions," 35 *American Bar Association Journal* 382-384 (1949).
McGowan, Carl. "Lawyers and the Uses of Language," 47 *American Bar Association Journal* 897-901 (1961).
McKnight, George H. *English Words and Their Background*. New York: D. Appleton-Century Company, 1923.
Maitland, Frederic William. "Of the Anglo-French Language in the Early Year Books," in Introduction to *Year Books of Edward II: 1 & 2 Edward II. A.D. 1307-1309*. Frederic William Maitland, ed. The Year Book Series, vol. I. Selden Society, vol. 17. London: Bernard Quaritch, 1903. Pp. xxxiii-lxxxi.
Marckwardt, Albert H. *American English*. New York: Oxford University Press, 1958.
Marsh, George P. *The Origin and History of the English Language, and of the Early Literature It Embodies*. 3d ed. New York: Charles Scribner & Co., 1869.
Martin, Charles Trice, comp. *The Record Interpreter: A Collection of Abbreviations, Latin Words and Names Used in English Historical Manuscripts and Records*. 2d ed. London: Stevens and Sons, Limited, 1910.
Martin, John D. "The Problem of Reducing the Volume of Published Opinions," 26 *Journal of the American Judicature Society* 138-141 (1943).
Masterson, James R., and Wendell Brooks Phillips. *Federal Prose: How to Write in and/or for Washington*. Chapel Hill: University of North Carolina Press, 1948.
Mathew, Theobald. "Law-French," 54 *Law Quarterly Review* 358-369 (1938).
Matthews, Thomas A. *Drafting Municipal Ordinances*. Chicago: Callaghan & Company, 1956.

Mehler, I. M. "Language Mastery and Legal Training," 6 *Villanova Law Review* 201-217 (Winter, 1960-1961).

Melton, J.S., and R. C. Bensing. "Searching Legal Literature Electronically: Results of a Test Program," 45 *Minnesota Law Review* 229-248 (1960).

Mencken, Henry L. *The American Language.* 4th ed. New York: Alfred A. Knopf, 1936.

————— ————— *Supplement I.* New York: Alfred A. Knopf, 1945.

————— ————— *Supplement II.* New York: Alfred A. Knopf, 1948.

Millar, Robert Wyness. "The Lineage of Some Procedural Words," 25 *American Bar Association Journal* 1023-1029 (1939).

Mitgang, Herbert. "It's Legal — But Is It English?" *New York Times Sunday Magazine* 73, 76 (Nov. 13, 1960).

Modern Uses of Logic in Law (MULL). Quarterly Newsletter of the Electronic Data Retrieval Committee of the American Bar Association. [1st published, Sept. 1959.]

Morton, Robert A. "Challenge Made to Beardsley's Plan for Plain and Simple Legal Syntax," 16 *Journal of the State Bar of California* 103-106 (1941).

Mulcaster, Richard. *The First Part of the Elementarie.* London: 1582.

Mumper, Hewlings. "The Unfair Tirade Against the Symbol 'and/or,'" 10 *Journal of the State Bar of California* 187-190 (1935).

Ogden, C. K. *Bentham's Theory of Fictions.* 2d ed. London: Routledge & Kegan Paul Ltd., 1951.

Ogden, C. K., and I. A. Richards. *The Meaning of Meaning.* 6th ed. New York: Harcourt, Brace and Company, 1944. [1st published, 1923.]

Oliphant, T. L. Kington. *The New English.* London: Macmillan and Co., 1886. 2 vols.

Oppenheimer, Reuben. "Legal Lingo," 2 *American Speech* 142-144 (1926).

Orwell, George. "Politics and the English Language," in Orwell, *Shooting an Elephant and Other Essays.* London: Secker and Warburg, 1950. Pp. 84-101. [Written 1945-1949.]

Parsons, Harry H. "And/or," 10 *Journal of the State Bar of California* 77-80 (1935).

Partridge, Eric. *Slang: Today and Yesterday.* 3d ed. London: Routledge & Kegan Paul Ltd., 1950.

————— *You Have a Point There: A Guide to Punctuation and Its Allies.* With a chapter on American practice by John W. Clark. London: Hamish Hamilton, 1953.

Pei, Mario. *The Story of English.* Philadelphia: J. B. Lippincott Company, 1952.

Philbrick, Frederick A. *Language and the Law: The Semantics of Forensic English.* New York: The Macmillan Company, 1949.

Piesse, E. L., and J. Gilchrist Smith. *The Elements of Drafting.* 2d ed. London: Stevens & Sons Limited, 1958. [1st published, 1946.]

Pope, Mildred K. *The Anglo-Norman Element in Our Vocabulary.* Manchester University Lecture Series No. XXXVII. Manchester: University Press, 1944.

Prince, Eugene M. "Law Books, Unlimited," 48 *American Bar Association Journal* 134-137 (1962).

Probert, Walter. "Law and Persuasion: The Language-Behavior of Lawyers," 108 *University of Pennsylvania Law Review* 35-58 (1959).

"Punctuation in the Eye of the Law," 51 *Albany Law Journal* 76 (Feb. 2, 1895).

Quiller-Couch, Sir Arthur. *On the Art of Writing*. Cambridge: University Press, 1916.

Reed, Joseph W., Jr. "Noah Webster's Debt to Samuel Johnson," 37 *American Speech* 95-105 (1962).

Reliquiae Antiquae: Scraps from Ancient Manuscripts Illustrating Chiefly Early English Literature and the English Language. Thomas Wright and James Orchard Halliwell, eds. London: William Pickering, 1841-1843. 2 vols.

"Report of the Special Committee on Legal Publications and Law Reporting," in 65 *Reports of the American Bar Association* 263-300 (1940).

The Reports of Sir Edward Coke, Kt. in Verse. In the Savoy: Worrall, 1742.

Ritchie, John, III . "Drafting a Simple Will for a Moderate Sized Estate," 91 *Trusts and Estates* 724-728 (1952).

Rodell, Fred. "Goodbye to Law Reviews," 23 *Virginia Law Review* 38-45 (1936).

────── *Woe unto You, Lawyers!* New York: Reynal & Hitchcock, 1939.

Ross, Alan S. C. *Etymology: With Especial Reference to English*. London: Andre Deutsch, 1958.

Rossman, George. "The Lawyer's English," 48 *American Bar Association Journal* 50-51 (1962).

Runes, Dagobert D. "Our Obsolete Legal English," 99 *New York Law Journal* 1964 (April 23, 1938).

Sandwell, B. K. "The Which of And/or," 165 *Harper's* 244-247 (1932), reprinted in 18 *American Bar Association Journal* 576-577 (1932).

Schele De Vere, Maximilian. *Americanisms: The English of the New World*. New York: Charles Scribner and Company, 1872.

Schuyler, Daniel M. "Conservative Draftsmanship Is Constructive," in "Drafting Legal Documents," 39 *Illinois Bar Journal* 49-119 (Sept. 1950, Supplement). Pp. 57-65.

Serjeantson, Mary S. *A History of Foreign Words in English*. London: Routledge and Kegan Paul Ltd., 1935.

Setzler, Edwin Boinest, Edwin Lake Setzler, and Hubert Holland Setzler. *The Jefferson Anglo-Saxon Grammar and Reader*. New York: The Macmillan Company, 1938.

Sheard, J. A. *The Words We Use*. London: Andre Deutsch, 1954.

Shelly, Percy Van Dyke. *English and French in England: 1066-1100*. Philadelphia: University of Pennsylvania, 1921.

Simon, Sir Jocelyn. "English Idioms from the Law," 76 *Law Quarterly Review* 283-305, 429-446 (1960).

Simpson, Percy. *Shakespearian Punctuation*. Oxford: University Press, 1911.

Skeat, Walter W. *The Science of Etymology*. Oxford: University Press, 1912.

Skelton, Reginald. *Modern English Punctuation*. 2d ed. London: Sir Isaac Pitman, 1949.

Skinner, Joseph Osmun. "Law and Philology: The Meaning of SS," 25 *The Green Bag* 59-64 (1913).

Smith, Jeremiah. "The Use of Maxims in Jurisprudence," 9 *Harvard Law Review* 13-26 (1895).

Smith, Logan Pearsall. *Words and Idioms.* 5th ed. London: Constable & Company, Ltd., 1943.

SS *What Does It Mean?* Foreword by Charles V. Imlay. Washington, D.C.: Judd & Detweiler, 1939.

Starnes, De Witt T., and Gertrude E. Noyes. *The English Dictionary from Cawdrey to Johnson: 1604-1755.* Chapel Hill: University of North Carolina Press, 1946.

Strunk, William, Jr. *The Elements of Style.* Revised by E. B. White. New York: The Macmillan Company, 1959.

Summers, Robert S. "A Note on Symbolic Logic and the Law," 13 *Journal of Legal Education* 486-492 (1961).

Thaler, Alwin. "With All Deliberate Speed," 27 *Tennessee Law Review* 510-517 (1960).

Thring [Lord]. *Practical Legislation.* Boston: Little, Brown and Company, 1902. [1st ed., 1877.]

Thurber, James. *The Wonderful O.* New York: Simon and Schuster, 1957.

Tollett, Kenneth S. "Verbalism, Law, and Reality," 37 *University of Detroit Law Journal* 226-244 (1959).

Trench, Richard Chenevix. *English, Past and Present.* 10th ed. London: Macmillan and Co., 1877.

―――― *On the Study of Words.* 21st ed. rev. by A. L. Mayhew. London: Kegan Paul, Trench, Trubner, & Co., Ltd., 1890.

―――― *A Select Glossary.* [See under Dictionaries.]

Tur-Sinai, N. H. "The Origin of Language," in Ruth Nanda Anshen, ed., *Language: An Enquiry into Its Meaning and Function.* New York: Harper & Brothers, 1957. C. III, pp. 41-79.

A Uniform System of Citation: Forms of Citation and Abbreviations. 10th ed. Cambridge, Mass.: Harvard Law Review Association, 1958.

Vising, Johan. *Anglo-Norman Language and Literature.* London: Oxford University Press, 1923.

Vizetelly, Frank H. *Punctuation and Capitalization.* New York: Funk & Wagnalls, 1921.

[Ward, Nathaniel.] *The Simple Cobler of Aggawamm in America.* By Theodore de la Guard. 3d ed. London: 1647.

Warren, Edward H. *Spartan Education.* Boston: Houghton Mifflin, 1942.

Webster, Noah. *Letters of Noah Webster.* Harry R. Warfel, ed. New York: Library Publishers, 1953.

Weekley, Ernest. *The English Language.* With a chapter on the history of American English by John W. Clark. London: Andre Deutsch, 1952.

Weissman, David L. "The 'No-Nonsense, Straight-from-the-Shoulder' School: Another Note on Legal Style," 20 *Lawyers Guild Review* 24-26 (1960).

―――― " 'Supremecourtese': A Note on Legal Style," 14 *Lawyers Guild Review* 138-139 (1954).

Welch, George N. "And/or," 44 *Massachusetts Law Quarterly* 98 (1959).

Wells, John Edwin. *A Manual of the Writings in Middle English 1050-1400.* New Haven: Yale University Press, 1916.

Whitney, William Dwight. *The Life and Growth of Language: An Outline of Linguistic Science.* New York: D. Appleton and Company, 1875.

Williams, Glanville. "Language and the Law," 61 *Law Quarterly Review* 71-86, 179-195, 293-303, 384-406 (1945); 62 *Law Quarterly Review* 387-406 (1946).

——— *Learning the Law.* 6th ed. London: Stevens and Sons Limited, 1957.

Wilson, John. *A Treatise on English Punctuation.* 13th ed. Boston: Crosby, Nichols and Company, 1856.

Witherspoon, Gibson B. "Why Write," 64 *Commercial Law Journal* 152-155 (1959).

Woodbine, George E. "The Language of English Law," 18 *Speculum* 395-436 (1943).

"Words and Phrases — Meaning of Words 'And/or,' " note by Roger Sherman Hoar, in 20 *Marquette Law Review* 101-102 (1936).

Wright, Andrew. *Court-Hand Restored.* 3d ed. London: Andrew Wright, 1786.

HISTORY

Adams, John. *Diary and Autobiography of John Adams.* Vol. I, L. H. Butterfield, ed. Cambridge, Mass.: Harvard University Press, 1961.

Adams, John [and Daniel Leonard]. *Novanglus and Massachusettensis.* Boston: Hews & Goss, 1819.

Appendix to Reports from the Commissioners Appointed by His Majesty . . . Respecting the Public Records of the Kingdom. London: 1819 [1820].

Bacon, Francis. *The Works of Francis Bacon, Lord Chancellor of England.* Basil Montagu, ed. London: William Pickering, 1825-1834. 17 vols.

Baildon, William Paley, ed. *Select Cases in Chancery A.D. 1364-1471.* Selden Society, vol. 10. London: Quaritch, 1896.

Bayne, C. G., and William Huse Dunham, Jr., eds. *Select Cases in the Council of Henry VII.* Selden Society, vol. 75. London: Quaritch, 1958.

Bigelow, Melville Madison. *History of Procedure in England from the Norman Conquest.* Boston: Little, Brown and Company, 1880.

——— *Placita Anglo-Normannica.* Boston: Soule & Bugbee, 1881.

Blount, Thomas. *Fragmenta Antiquitatis.* New ed. by Josiah Beckwith. York: 1784. [1st ed., 1679.]

Bolland, William Craddock. *A Manual of Year Book Studies.* Cambridge: University Press, 1925.

———, ed. *Select Bills in Eyre A.D. 1292-1333.* Selden Society, vol. 30. London: Quaritch, 1914.

The Book of Oaths. [Attributed to Richard Garnet.] London: 1649.

Bowen, Catherine Drinker. *John Adams and the American Revolution.* Boston: Little, Brown and Company, 1950.

——— *The Lion and the Throne: The Life and Times of Sir Edward Coke (1552-1634).* Boston: Little, Brown and Company, 1957.

[Bowen.] Charles Synge Christopher, Baron Bowen. "Progress in the Administration of Justice During the Victorian Period," in *Select Essays in Anglo-American Legal History* [see]. Vol. I (1907), pp. 516-557.

Burke, Edmund. "Conciliation with America," speech, in *Modern Eloquence.* Thomas B. Reed, ed. Philadelphia: John D. Morris and Company, 1903. Vol. XI, pp. 368-428. [Speech delivered March 22, 1775.]

Carey, Walter. "The Present State of England," in *The Harleian Miscellany* [see]. Vol. III (1809), pp. 552-561.

Chroust, Anton-Hermann. "The Dilemma of the American Lawyer in the Post-Revolutionary Era," 35 *Notre Dame Lawyer* 48-76 (1959).

"Civil Death Statutes — Medieval Fiction in a Modern World," note in 50 *Harvard Law Review* 968-977 (1937).

Cohen, Herman. *A History of the English Bar and Attornatus to 1450.* London: Sweet & Maxwell Limited, 1929.

Collas, John P., and Theodore F. T. Plucknett, eds. *Year Books of Edward II: Vol. XXIV. 12 Edward II. Hilary and Part of Easter, 1319.* Selden Society, vol. 70. London: Bernard Quaritch, 1953.

Collections of the New York Historical Society for the Year 1912. New York: New York Historical Society, 1913.

Crèvecoeur, Michel-Guillaume Jean de. *Letters from an American Farmer.* Philadelphia: 1793. [First published, 1782.]

Davis, John F. *Historical Sketch of Mining Law in California.* Los Angeles: Commercial Printing House, 1902. [First published, 1901.]

Dickinson, John. *Letters from a Farmer in Pennsylvania to the Inhabitants of the British Colonies.* Boston: Edes & Gill, 1768.

Dictionary of American Biography. Subscription edition. New York: Charles Scribner's Sons, 1958. 11 vols. and index.

Elyot, Sir Thomas. *The Boke Named the Governour.* Everyman's Library. London: J. M. Dent & Co., 1937. [1st published, 1531.]

Encyclopedia of American History. Richard B. Morris, ed. New York: Harper & Brothers, 1953.

Everett, C. W. "Bentham in the United States of America," in George W. Keeton and Georg Schwarzenberger, eds., *Jeremy Bentham and the Law: A Symposium.* London: Stevens & Sons Limited, 1948. C. 9, pp. 185-201.

Feiling, Keith. *A History of England.* London: Macmillan & Co. Ltd., 1950.

Fortescue, Sir John. *De Laudibus Legum Angliae.* With notes by John Selden. London: 1672.

——— ——— [2d ed.] In the Savoy: 1741.

——— ——— S. B. Chrimes, ed. and tr. Cambridge Studies in English Legal History. Cambridge: University Press, 1942.

Foss, Edward. *A Biographical Dictionary of the Judges of England.* London: John Murray, 1870.

——— *The Judges of England.* London: John Murray, 1848-1864. 9 vols.

Franklin, Benjamin. *The Autobiography of Benjamin Franklin.* Frank Woodworth Pine, ed. Garden City: Garden City Publishing Co., 1916.

——— *The Papers of Benjamin Franklin.* Leonard W. Labaree, ed. New Haven: Yale University Press, 1959-   Vols. 1 and 2 (1960).

Freeman, Edward A. *The History of the Norman Conquest of England.* Vols I and II, 3d ed. (1877); vol. III, 2d ed. (1875); vol. IV, 2d ed. (1876); vol. V, 1st ed. (1876). Oxford: University Press, 1875-1877. 5 vols.

Goebel, Julius, Jr., and T. Raymond Naughton. *Law Enforcement in Colonial New York: A Study in Criminal Procedure.* New York: Commonwealth Fund, 1944.

Hale, Sir Matthew. "Considerations Touching the Amendment or Alteration of Lawes," in Francis Hargrave, ed., *A Collection of Tracts Relative to the Law of England.* Dublin: 1787. Vol. I, pp. 249-289.

Hargrave, Francis, ed. *A Collection of Tracts Relative to the Law of England.* Dublin: 1787. Vol. I.

The Harleian Miscellany. New edition. London: Robert Dutton, 1808-1811. 12 vols.

Harno, Albert J. *Legal Education in the United States.* San Francisco: Bancroft-Whitney Company, 1953.

Haskins, George Lee. *Law and Authority in Early Massachusetts.* New York: The Macmillan Company, 1960.

Helper, Hinton Rowan. *The Land of Gold.* Republished as *Dreadful California,* Lucius Beebe and Charles M. Clegg, eds. Indianapolis: The Bobbs-Merrill Company, 1948. [1st published, 1855.]

Holdsworth, Sir William. *Charles Dickens as a Legal Historian.* New Haven: Yale University Press, 1928.

———— *A History of English Law.* Boston: Little, Brown and Company, 1922-1932. 9 vols. and index.

———— ———— London: Methuen & Co., 1938-1952. Vols. 10-13.

———— ———— Introductory essay by S. B. Chrimes. 7th ed. London: Methuen & Co., 1956. Vol. 1.

Howe, Mark De Wolfe. *Justice Oliver Wendell Holmes: The Shaping Years 1841-1870.* Cambridge, Mass.: Harvard University Press, 1957- Vol. I.

Howell, T. B., comp. *A Complete Collection of State Trials.* London: 1816. 21 vols.

James, Sir Henry, ed. *Facsimiles of National Manuscripts from William the Conqueror to Queen Anne.* London: 1865-1868 [1869]. 4 parts.

Jefferson, Thomas. *The Complete Jefferson.* Saul K. Padover, ed. New York: Duell, Sloan & Pearce, Inc., 1943.

———— *The Papers of Thomas Jefferson.* Julian P. Boyd, ed. Princeton: University Press, 1950- . Vols. 1-16 (1961).

———— *The Writings of Thomas Jefferson.* Andrew A. Lipscomb, ed. Washington, D.C.: Thomas Jefferson Memorial Association, 1905. 20 vols.

Jones, John. *The New Returna Brevium.* London: 1650.

Kelham, Robert. *Domesday Book Illustrated.* London: Edward Brooke, 1788.

Kent, James. "An American Law Student of a Hundred Years Ago," in *Select Essays in Anglo-American Legal History* [see]. Vol. I (1907), pp. 837-847.

Kiralfy, A. K. R. *A Source Book of English Law.* London: Sweet & Maxwell Limited, 1957.

The Laws and Liberties of Massachusetts. Reprinted from the copy of the 1648 ed. in the Henry E. Huntington Library. Introduction by Max Farrand. Cambridge: Harvard University Press, 1929.

Lechford, Thomas. *Notebook Kept by Thomas Lechford, Esq., Lawyer (June 27, 1638-July 29, 1641).* Cambridge, Mass.: John Wilson, 1885.

Lévy-Ullmann, Henri. *The English Legal Tradition: Its Sources and History.* Tr. by M. Mitchell, rev. and ed. by Frederic M. Goadby, foreword by Sir William Holdsworth. London: Macmillan & Co. Ltd., 1935.

Lewis, Walker. "The Right to Complain: The Trial of John Peter Zenger," 46 *American Bar Association Journal* 27-30, 108-111 (1960).

McGroarty, John Steven. *Los Angeles from the Mountains to the Sea.* Chicago: American Historical Society, 1921. 3 vols.

Madox, Thomas. *Formulare Anglicanum: Or a Collection of Ancient Charters and Instruments of Divers Kinds Taken from the Originals.* London: 1702.

Maine, Sir Henry Sumner. *Ancient Law.* Introduction and notes by Sir Frederick Pollock. New ed. London: John Murray, 1930.

Maitland, Frederic William. *Domesday Book and Beyond.* Cambridge: University Press, 1921. [1st published, 1897.]

——— "English Law and the Renaissance," in *Select Essays in Anglo-American Legal History* [see]. Vol. I (1907), p. 168. Also in *Selected Historical Essays of F. W. Maitland* [see]. Pp. 135-151.

——— Introduction to *Political Theories of the Middle Age* by Otto Gierke. Frederic William Maitland, tr. Beacon Paperback. Boston: Beacon Press, 1958. [1st published in English, 1900.] Pp. vii-xlv.

——— "The Mystery of Seisin," 2 *Law Quarterly Review* 481-496 (1886). Also in *Select Essays in Anglo-American Legal History* [see]. Vol. III (1909), pp. 591-610.

——— *Selected Historical Essays of F. W. Maitland.* Helen M. Cam, ed. Cambridge: University Press, in association with the Selden Society, 1957.

———, ed. *Year Books of Edward II: 1 & 2 Edward II.* A.D. 1307-1309. The Year Book Series, vol. I. Selden Society, vol 17. London: Bernard Quaritch, 1903.

Maitland, Frederic William, and William Paley Baildon, eds. *The Court Baron.* Selden Society, vol. 4. London: Quaritch, 1891.

Maxwell, W. Harold, and Leslie F. Maxwell, comps. *A Legal Bibliography of the British Commonwealth of Nations: Vol. 1: English Law to 1800.* 2d ed. London: Sweet & Maxwell Limited, 1955.

Milton, John. *Areopagitica.* English Reprints. Edward Arber, ed. London: 1868. [1st published, 1644.]

Monumenta Historica Britannica: Or Materials for the History of Britain. Vol. I (extending to the Norman Conquest). Henry Petrie, John Sharp, and Thomas Duffus Hardy, eds. London: Commissioners of the Public Records, 1848.

Osgood, Herbert L. *The American Colonies in the Eighteenth Century.* New York: Columbia University Press, 1924. 4 vols.

Palgrave, Sir Francis. *The History of Normandy and of England.* London: Macmillan & Co., Ltd., 1864. Vol. 3.

[———] Review of *The History of England* by David Hume (new ed. London: 1825), in 34 *Quarterly Review* 248-298 (1826).

The Paston Letters. New Complete Library ed. James Gairdner, ed. London: Chatto & Windus, 1904. 6 vols.

Phillips, William. *Studii Legalis Ratio, or Directions for the Study of Law.* 3d ed. London: 1675.

Plucknett, Theodore F. T. *A Concise History of the Common Law.* 5th ed. Boston: Little, Brown and Company, 1956.

——— *Early English Legal Literature.* Cambridge: University Press, 1958.

——— *Statutes and Their Interpretation in the First Half of the Fourteenth Century.* Cambridge: University Press, 1922.

Pollock, Sir Frederick, and Frederick William Maitland. *The History of English Law: Before the Time of Edward I.* 2d ed. Cambridge: University Press, 1898. 2 vols.

Pound, Roscoe. "Legal Education in the United States," in 13 *Encyclopaedia Britannica* 874 (1948).

Powell, T. G. E. *The Celts.* London: Thames and Hudson, 1958.

Quincy, Josiah, Jr. *Quincy's Massachusetts Reports.* Boston: Little, Brown and Company, 1865.

Radin, Max. *Handbook of Anglo-American Legal History.* Hornbook Series. St. Paul: West Publishing Co., 1936.

The Record Commissioners. "An Historical Survey of Ancient English Statutes," in *Select Essays in Anglo-American Legal History* [see]. Vol. II (1908), pp. 169-205.

The Records of the Society of Gentlemen Practisers. London: The Incorporated Law Society, 1897.

Records of the Suffolk County Court 1671-1680. Preface by Samuel Eliot Morison, ix-xiii; introduction by Zechariah Chafee, Jr., xvii-xciv. Publications of the Colonial Society of Massachusetts, vol. 29. Boston: 1933. Parts I and II.

Reeves' History of the English Law. With notes and introduction by W. F. Finlason. New American ed. Philadelphia: M. Murphy, 1880. 5 vols.

Reinsch, Paul Samuel. "The English Common Law in the Early American Colonies," in *Select Essays in Anglo-American Legal History* [see]. Vol. I (1907), pp. 367-415.

Rice, William B. *The Los Angeles Star: 1851-1864.* John Walton Caughey, ed. Berkeley: University of California Press, 1947.

Richardson, H. G., and George Sayles. "The Early Statutes," 50 *Law Quarterly Review* 201-223, 540-571 (1934).

Robertson, A. J., ed. *Anglo-Saxon Charters.* 2d ed. Cambridge: University Press, 1956. [1st ed. 1939.]

————, ed. and tr. *The Laws of the Kings of England from Edmund to Henry I.* Cambridge: University Press, 1925.

Robinson, W. W. *Lawyers of Los Angeles.* Los Angeles: Los Angeles Bar Association, 1959.

Robson, Robert. *The Attorney in Eighteenth-Century England.* Cambridge: University Press, 1959.

Sayles, G. O., ed. *Select Cases in the Court of King's Bench Under Edward III.* Vol. V. Selden Society, vol. 76. London: Bernard Quaritch, 1958.

Schlesinger, Arthur M., Jr. *The Age of Jackson.* Boston: Little, Brown and Company, 1945.

Selden, John. "The Reverse or Back-face of the English Janus," tr. by Redman Westcot, in *Tracts Written by John Selden.* London: Thomas Basset and Richard Chiswell, 1683.

Select Cases of the Mayor's Court of New York City 1674-1784. Richard B. Morris, ed. American Legal Records, vol. 2. Washington, D.C.: American Historical Association, 1935.

Select Essays in Anglo-American Legal History. Compiled and edited by a Committee of the Association of American Law Schools. Boston: Little, Brown and Company, 1907-1909. 3 vols. [Vol. I, 1907; vol. II, 1908; vol. III, 1909.]

Shinn, Charles Howard. *Land Laws of Mining Districts.* Johns Hopkins

University Studies in Historical and Political Science. Herbert B. Adams, ed. Second Series, XII. Baltimore: Johns Hopkins University, 1884.

—————— Mining Camps: A Study in American Frontier Government. Introduction by Joseph Henry Jackson. New York: Alfred A. Knopf, 1948. [1st published, 1885.]

Steinberg, Sigfrid Henry. Five Hundred Years of Printing. Pelican Book. Harmondsworth: Penguin, 1955.

Stokes, Anthony. "Directions for Holding Court in Colonial Georgia," edited by Edwin C. Surrency and reprinted in 2 American Journal of Legal History 321 (1958). [1st published, 1771.]

Stubbs, William, ed. Select Charters. 8th ed. Oxford: University Press, 1905.

Thorne, Samuel E., ed. Readings and Moots at the Inns of Court in the Fifteenth Century. Vol. I. Selden Society, vol. 71. London: Quaritch, 1954.

Thorpe, Benjamin, ed. Ancient Laws and Institutes of England. London: Record Commission, 1840. 2 vols.

—————— Diplomatarium Anglicum aevi Saxonici: A Collection of English Charters, from the Reign of King Aethelbirht . . . to That of William the Conqueror. London: Macmillan & Co. Ltd., 1865.

Thorpe, Francis Newton, ed. The Federal and State Constitutions, Colonial Charters, and Other Organic Laws of the States, Territories, and Colonies Now or Heretofore Forming the United States of America. Washington, D.C.: Government Printing Office, 1909. 7 vols.

Tocqueville, Alexis de. Democracy in America. Henry Reeve text, rev. by Francis Bowen, ed. by Phillips Bradley. New York: Vintage Books, 1958. 2 vols.

Turner, G. J., ed. Brevia Placitata. Selden Society, vol. 66. London: Quaritch, 1951.

Tyler, James Endell. Oaths: Their Origin, Nature, and History. London: John W. Parker, 1834.

U.S. Bureau of the Census. Historical Statistics of the United States. 1789-1945. Washington, D.C.: 1949.

—————— Congress. House. Documents Illustrative of the Formation of the Union of the American States. Selected, arranged, and indexed by Charles C. Tansill. 69th Congress, 1st Session, House Doc. No. 398. Washington, D.C.: 1927.

—————— Department of Interior, Census Office. The United States Mining Laws. 10th census, vol. 14. Washington, D.C.: 1885.

—————— Library of Congress. Copyright in Congress: 1789-1904. Prepared by Thorvald Solberg. Copyright Office Bulletin No. 8. Washington, D.C.: 1905.

Van Caenegem, R. C. Royal Writs in England from the Conquest to Glanvill. Selden Society, vol. 77. London: Quaritch, 1959.

Vinogradoff, Sir Paul. The Growth of the Manor. 2d ed. London: George Allen & Unwin, 1932.

—————— "Ralph of Hengham as C. J. of the Common Pleas," in A. G. Little and F.M. Powicke, eds., Essays in Medieval History Presented to Thomas Frederick Tout. Printed for the subscribers. Manchester: 1925.

Warren, Charles. *A History of the American Bar.* Boston: Little, Brown and Company, 1911.
Watt, Ian. *The Rise of the Novel.* Berkeley: University of California Press, 1957.
Whitmore, William Henry. *A Bibliographical Sketch of the Laws of the Massachusetts Colony from 1630 to 1686.* Boston: City Council of Boston, 1890.
Winfield, Percy H. *The Chief Sources of English Legal History.* Cambridge, Mass.: Harvard University Press, 1925.
Woodbine, George E. Review of *Records of the Suffolk County Court 1671-1680,* vols. 29, 30 [see], in 43 *Yale Law Journal* 1036-1043 (1934).
Yunck, John A. "The Venal Tongue: Lawyers and the Medieval Satirists," 46 *American Bar Association Journal* 267-270 (1960).

LAW TREATISES

The American and English Encyclopaedia of Law. Northport: 1887-1896. 31 vols.
American Jurisprudence. San Francisco: Bancroft-Whitney Company, 1936-1952. 58 vols. and 4 index vols.
Archbold on Indictments. By Henry Delacombe Roome. London: Sweet & Maxwell Limited, 1916.
Bacon, Matthew. *A New Abridgment of the Law.* 5th ed. with additions by Henry Gwillim. London: T. Cadell and others, 1798. 7 vols.
Barrington, Daines. *Observations upon the Statutes.* 2d ed. London: 1766.
————— ————— 5th ed. London: 1796.
Bishop, Joel Prentiss. *Commentaries on the Written Laws and Their Interpretation.* Boston: Little, Brown and Company, 1882. [1873 ed., Cambridge, Mass.]
————— *New Criminal Procedure.* 4th ed. Chicago: T. H. Flood, 1895. 2 vols.
Blackstone, Sir William. *Commentaries on the Laws of England.* William Carey Jones, ed. San Francisco: Bancroft-Whitney Company, 1916. 2 vols. [1st published, 1765-1769.]
Bowe, William J., and Douglas H. Parker. *Revised Treatise on the Law of Wills.* 3d ed. Cincinnati: W. H. Anderson, 1960. 8 vols.
Bracton. *De Legibus et Consuetudinibus Angliae.* George E. Woodbine, ed. New Haven: Yale University Press, 1915-1942. 4 vols.
Branson, Edward R. *The Law of Instructions to Juries.* 3d ed. By A. H. Reid. Indianapolis: The Bobbs-Merrill Company, 1936. 5 vols.
Brooke, Richard. *A Treatise on the Office and Practice of a Notary of England.* Leone Levi, ed. 4th ed. London: Stevens, 1876.
Broom, Herbert. *A Selection of Legal Maxims, Classified and Illustrated.* 5th American from 3d London ed. Philadelphia: T. & W. Johnson & Co., 1864.
Burn, Richard. *The Justice of the Peace, and Parish Officer.* Continued by John Burn. 16th ed. London: T. Cadell, 1788. 4 vols.
Chitty, Joseph. *A Practical Treatise on Pleading, and on the Parties to Actions.* New York: Robert M'Dermut, 1809. 2 vols.
————— *A Treatise on Pleading, and Parties to Actions.* 9th American from

6th London ed. with additions by H. Greening, John A. Dunlap, E. D. Ingraham, and J. C. Perkins. Springfield: G. & C. Merriam, 1844. 3 vols. [1st ed. 1808.]

Clark, Charles Edward. *Handbook of the Law of Code Pleading.* Hornbook Series. St. Paul: West Publishing Co., 1928.

Coke, Sir Edward. *The First Part of the Institutes of the Laws of England, or a Commentary upon Littleton.* 10th ed. London: William Rawlins and Samuel Roycroft, 1703. [1st published, 1628.]

—————— —————— Charles Butler, ed. 19th ed. London: J. & W. T. Clarke and others, 1832. 2 vols.

The Complete English Lawyer: Or Every Man His Own Lawyer. 3d ed. London: c. 1810.

Corpus Juris. New York: American Law Book Co., 1914-1937. 72 vols.

Corpus Juris Secundum. Brooklyn: American Law Book Co., 1936-1960. 120 vols.

Dalton, Michael. *The Countrey Justice.* London: 1618.

Dane, Nathan. *A General Abridgment and Digest of American Law.* Boston: Cummings, Hilliard, 1824. 8 vols.

A Discourse upon the Exposicion & Understandinge of Statutes. With Sir Thomas Egerton's Additions. Samuel E. Thorne, ed. San Marino: Huntington Library, 1942.

Doderidge, Sir John. *The English Lawyer.* London: 1631.

Dwarris, Sir Fortunatus. *A General Treatise on Statutes.* 2d ed. London: William Benning, 1848.

Every Man's Own Lawyer: Every Man His Own Lawyer. 68th ed. London: Technical Press, 1955. [1st ed. 1863.]

Fearne, Charles. *An Essay on the Learning of Contingent Remainders and Executory Devises.* London: 1772.

Fraunce, Abraham. *The Lawiers Logike.* London: 1588.

Green, Leon. *Rationale of Proximate Cause.* Kansas City, Mo.: Vernon Law Book Co., 1927.

Hart, H. L. A., and A. M. Honoré. *Causation in the Law.* Oxford: University Press, 1959.

[Hatton, Sir Christopher.] *A Treatise Concerning Statutes.* London: 1677.

Hawkins, William. *A Treatise of the Pleas of the Crown.* 8th ed., John Curwood. London: 1824. [1st ed. 1716-1721.] 2 vols.

Holmes, Oliver Wendell, Jr. *The Common Law.* Boston: Little, Brown and Company, 1881.

Jacob, Giles. *Every Man His Own Lawyer.* 6th ed. London: 1765. [1st ed. 1736.]

Jarman, Thomas. *A Treatise on Wills.* 8th ed. By Raymond Jennings, assisted by John C. Harper. London: Sweet & Maxwell Limited, 1951. 3 vols.

Justinian. *Imperatoris Iustiniani Institutionum: Libri Quattuor.* With introduction, commentary, and excursus by J. B. Moyle. 5th ed. Oxford: University Press, 1912.

—————— *The Institutes of Justinian.* J. B. Moyle, tr. 5th ed. Oxford: University Press, 1913.

Leach, W. Barton, and Owen Tudor. *The Rule Against Perpetuities.* Boston: Little, Brown and Company, 1957.

Lieber, Francis. *Legal and Political Hermeneutics.* 3d ed. with notes by William G. Hammond. St. Louis: F. H. Thomas and Company, 1880.

Llewellyn, Karl N. *The Common Law Tradition: Deciding Appeals.* Boston: Little, Brown and Company, 1960.

Malynes, Gerard. *Consuetudo vel Lex Mercatoria, or, the Antient Law-Merchant.* London: 1636. [1st ed. 1622.]

Maxwell, Sir Peter Benson. *On the Interpretation of Statutes.* London: William Maxwell, 1875.

May, Thomas Erskine. *A Treatise upon the Law, Privileges, Proceedings and Usage of Parliament.* London: Charles Knight, 1844.

———— ———— 10th ed. London: 1893.

Park, James Allan. *A System of the Law of Marine Insurances.* London: T. Whieldon, 1787.

Plowden, Edmund. *The Commentaries or Reports of Edmund Plowden.* Now first rendered in English. London: 1779. [1st French ed. 1571-1578, 1st English ed. 1761.]

Poldervaart, Arie. *Manual for Effective New Mexico Legal Research.* Albuquerque: University of New Mexico Press, 1955.

Pollock, Sir Frederick. *Essays in Jurisprudence and Ethics.* London: Macmillan & Co., Limited, 1882.

———— *A First Book of Jurisprudence.* 4th ed. London: Macmillan & Co., Limited, 1918.

———— *The Law of Torts.* London: Stevens, 1887.

Pomeroy, John Norton. *Code Remedies.* Walter Carrington, ed. 5th ed. Boston: Little, Brown and Company, 1929.

Powell, J. J. *A Treatise on the Law of Mortgages.* Reprinted from 6th English ed. with notes by Thomas Coventry. Notes and references to American cases by Benjamin Rand. Boston: Wells & Lilly, 1828. 2 vols.

Prosser, William L. *Handbook of the Law of Torts.* St. Paul: West Publishing Co., 1941.

———— *Selected Topics on the Law of Torts.* Ann Arbor: University of Michigan Law School, 1953.

Restatement of the Law of Property. St. Paul: American Law Institute Publishers, 1936-1944. 5 vols. [Vols. 1 and 2, 1936; vol. 3, 1940; vols. 4 and 5, 1944.]

Restatement of the Law of Torts. St. Paul: American Law Institute Publishers, 1934-1939. 4 vols. [Vols. 1 and 2, 1934; vol. 3, 1938; vol. 4, 1939.]

St. Germain, Christopher. *Doctor and Student.* 1598. [1st dialogue published in Latin, 1523; next in English, 1530; both in English, 1532.]

Scrutton, Sir Thomas Edward. *Charterparties and Bills of Lading.* 16th ed. By Sir William Lennox McNair and Alan A. Mocatta. London: Sweet & Maxwell Limited, 1955.

Spence, George. *The Equitable Jurisdiction of the Court of Chancery.* Philadelphia: Lea & Blanchard, 1846. 2 vols.

Stephen, Henry John. *New Commentaries on the Laws of England.* London: Henry Butterworth, 1841-1845. 4 vols.

———— *A Treatise on the Principles of Pleading in Civil Actions.* London: Joseph Butterworth, 1824.

Stephen, Sir James Fitzjames. *A Digest of the Law of Evidence.* 2d ed. St. Louis: Soule, Thomas & Wentworth, 1876.

Style, William. *Style's Practical Register.* 4th ed. London: C. Harper and others, 1707. [1st ed. 1657.]

Swinburn, Henrie. *A Briefe Treatise of Testaments and Last Willes.* London: John Windet, 1590.

Wharton, Francis. *Wharton's Criminal Evidence.* 12th ed. By Ronald A. Anderson. Rochester, N.Y.: Lawyers Co-operative Pub. Co., 1955. 8 vols.

Wigmore, John Henry. *A Treatise on the Anglo-American System of Evidence in Trials at Common Law.* 3d ed. Boston: Little, Brown and Company, 1940. 10 vols.

Williston, Samuel. *A Treatise on the Law of Contracts.* 3d ed. By Walter H. E. Jaeger. Mount Kisco, N.Y.: Baker, Voorhis, 1957. Vol. 1.

FORMBOOKS

Abbott, Benjamin V., and Austin Abbott. *The Clerks' and Conveyancers' Assistant.* Clarence F. Birdseye, ed. 3d ed. New York: Baker, Voorhis, 1911. [1st ed. 1866, 2d ed. 1881.]

———— *A Collection of Forms of Pleadings in Actions Under the Code of Procedure of the State of New York.* New York: John S. Voorhies, 1858.

American Jurisprudence Legal Forms Annotated. San Francisco: Bancroft-Whitney Company, 1953-1955. 14 vols.

American Jurisprudence Pleading and Practice Forms Annotated. San Francisco: Bancroft-Whitney Company, 1956-1959. 21 vols. and 2 index vols.

American Precedents of Declarations. Boston: Barnard B. Macanulty, 1802.

Anthon, John. *American Precedents of Declarations.* New York: 1810. [1st ed. 1802.]

The Attorney's Companion. Poughkeepsie: P. Potter and another, 1818.

BAJI. [See *California Jury Instructions: Civil.*]

Bridgman, Sir Orlando. *Sir Orlando Bridgman's Conveyances.* Compiled by Thomas Page Johnson. London: 1682.

Brownlow, Richard. *Declarations and Pleadings in English.* London: Henry Twyford, 1652.

———— *Declarations, Counts, and Pleadings in English: The Second Part.* London: Matthew Walbancke and another, 1654.

———— *Brownlow Latine Redivivus: A Book of Entries.* London: 1693.

California Jury Instructions: Civil. 4th rev. ed. William J. Palmer, ed.-in-chief. St. Paul: West Publishing Co., 1956. 2 vols.

California Jury Instructions: Criminal. Rev. ed. St. Paul: West Publishing Co., 1958.

CALJIC. [See *California Jury Instructions: Criminal.*]

Coke, Sir Edward. *A Book of Entries.* 2d ed. London: 1671.

Covert, Nicholas. *The Scrivener's Guide.* 5th ed. London: T. Woodward and others, 1740. 2 vols.

Cowdery's Forms. San Francisco: Bancroft-Whitney Company, 1951. 3 vols.

Crosby, Franklin. *Everybody's Lawyer and Book of Forms.* Rev. by S. J. Vandersloot. Philadelphia: John E. Potter, 1869.

Every Man His Own Lawyer. Poughkeepsie: P. Potter, 1834.

Griffith, William. *The Scriveners Guide.* Newark: 1797.

Harris, Thomas. *Modern Entries.* Anapolis: 1801. 2 vols.

Hillyer, Curtis. *Annotated Forms of Pleading and Practice in Civil Cases.* San Francisco: Bender-Moss Company, 1938-1939. 11 vols.

Hutchinson, A. *Manual of Juridical, Ministerial and Civil Forms, Revised, Americanized, and Divested of Useless Verbiage.* Jackson, Miss.: 1852.

Illinois Pattern Jury Instructions, Civil. Chicago: Burdette Smith Co., 1961.

IPI. [See *Illinois Pattern Jury Instructions, Civil.*]

JIFU. [See *Jury Instruction Forms for Utah.*]

Jury Instruction Forms for Utah. J. Allan Crockett, ed. Salt Lake City: Utah Bar Association, 1957.

Legal Secretary's Handbook (California). Inez Ingram and B. Rey Shauer, eds. Rev. ed. Los Angeles: Legal Secretaries, Inc., 1954.

Lilly, John. *Modern Entries.* 2d ed. Translated into English. In the Savoy: 1741. [1st ed., Latin, 1723.]

Lindey, Alexander. *Motion Picture Agreements Annotated.* New York: Matthew Bender & Company, Incorporated, 1947.

Marsh, Theodore McCurdy, and George S. Fischler. *New Jersey Practice: Forms.* Rev. ed. Vols. 3, 4, and 4A in *New Jersey Practice.* Newark: Soney & Sage, 1960-1962. 23 vols. Vol. 3 (1960).

Modern Legal Forms. Revised. Edmund O. Belsheim and others, eds. Kansas City, Mo.: Vernon Law Book Co., 1957. 10 vols.

Murphy, Joseph Hawley. *Murphy's Will Clauses.* New York: Matthew Bender & Company, Incorporated, 1960.

Neuhoff, Ralph R. *Standard Clauses for Wills.* Rev. ed. New York: Fiduciary Publishers, Inc., 1958.

The New American Clerk's Magazine, and Complete Practical Conveyancer. 2d ed. Hagers-town: Jacob D. Dietrick, 1807.

Nichols, Clark A. *Cyclopedia of Legal Forms Annotated.* Chicago: Callaghan & Company, 1936-1960. 10 vols.

The Pocket Companion: Or Every Man His Own Lawyer. 5th ed. Philadelphia: S. Parmele, 1818.

Pocket Conveyancer: Or Attorney's Useful Companion. 2d ed. London: 1773. 2 vols.

The Pocket Lawyer, or Self-Conveyancer. 5th ed. Harrisburg: G. S. Peters, 1833.

Practical Forms. Windsor, Vt.: Simeon Ide, 1823.

Precedents. Reading: George Getz, 1822.

Rabkin, Jacob, and Mark H. Johnson. *Current Legal Forms with Tax Analysis.* New York: Matthew Bender & Company, Incorporated, 1959. 6 vols.

Revised Law and Form Book for Business Men. San Francisco: Bancroft, 1892. [1st ed. 1888.]

Richardson, James R. *Florida Jury Instructions.* St. Paul: West Publishing Co., 1954.

Rodman, Robert M. *Massachusetts Procedural Forms Annotated.* Boston: Boston Law Book Co., 1949. [1st ed. 1941.]

Van Heythuysen, F. M. *The Equity Draftsman.* Rev. by Edward Hughes. New York: 1832.

West, William. *The First Part of Symboleography.* London: 1598. [1st ed. 1590.]

—— *Three Treatises, of the Second Part of Symbolaeographie.* London: 1594.

West's California Code Forms with Practice Commentaries: Civil. David H. Adams, ed. St. Paul: West Publishing Co., 1960. 3 vols.

Wisconsin Jury Instructions: Civil — Part 1. John E. Conway, ed. Madison: University of Wisconsin Extension Law Dept., 1960.

MISCELLANY

[Anstey, John.] *The Pleader's Guide, a Didactic Poem.* London: 1796.

[Arbuthnot, John.] *Law Is a Bottomless Pit.* 6th ed. London: John Morphew, 1712.

————— ————— London: Benjamin Motte, 1732.

Arnold, Thurman. "Professor Hart's Theology," 73 *Harvard Law Review* 1298-1317 (1960).

Beale, Joseph H. "The Proximate Consequences of an Act," 33 *Harvard Law Review* 633-658 (1920).

The Book of Common Prayer. Printed by Whitechurch March 1549. Commonly called The First Book of Edward VI. London: William Pickering, 1844.

Bordwell, Percy. "Seisin and Disseisin," 34 *Harvard Law Review* 592-624, 717-740 (1921).

Boswell, James. *Boswell's Life of Johnson.* Oxford: University Press, 1922. 2 vols.

Buell, James K. "The Law of Seisin in Oregon," 28 *Oregon Law Review* 12-25 (1948).

Chaucer, Geoffrey. *The Canterbury Tales.* Walter W. Skeat, ed., with introduction by Louis Untermeyer. Modern Library. New York: Random House, 1929.

Cunningham, Thomas J. "Instructing Juries," 32 *Journal of the State Bar of California* 127-136 (1957).

Evans, Bergen. *The Spoor of Spooks: And Other Nonsense.* New York: Alfred A. Knopf, 1954.

Frank, Jerome. *Law and the Modern Mind.* With preface to the 6th printing, by the author. New York: Coward-McCann, Inc., 1949. [1st published, 1930.]

Frazer, Sir James George. *The Golden Bough: A Study in Magic and Religion.* 1 vol. abridged ed. New York: The Macmillan Company, 1951.

Freud, Sigmund. *The Basic Writings of Sigmund Freud.* A. A. Brill, ed. Modern Library. New York: Random House, 1938.

Green, Leon. "Contributory Negligence and Proximate Cause," 6 *North Carolina Law Review* 3-33 (1927).

Haley, Andrew G. "Space Law and Metalaw — A Synoptic View," 23 *Harvard Law Record* 3-5 (Nov. 1, 1956).

Holmes-Laski Letters. Mark DeWolfe Howe, ed. Cambridge, Mass.: Harvard University Press, 1953. 2 vols.

Holmes-Pollock Letters. Mark DeWolfe Howe, ed. Cambridge, Mass.: Harvard University Press, 1946. 2 vols. in 1. [1st published, 1941.]

Jeremy Bentham and the Law: A Symposium. George W. Keeton and Georg Schwarzenberger, eds. London: Stevens & Sons Limited, 1948.

Leach, W. Barton. *Cases and Materials on the Law of Future Interests.* Chicago: The Foundation Press, Inc., 1935.

————— *Cases and Text on the Law of Wills.* 2d ed. Cambridge, Mass.: published jointly by the editor and the Law School Press, Los Angeles, 1947.

——— "Perpetuities in Perspective: Ending the Rule's Reign of Terror,"
65 *Harvard Law Review* 721-749 (1952).

Llewellyn, Karl N. *The Bramble Bush: On Our Law and Its Study.* New
York: Oceana, 1951. [1st published, 1930.]

Lob, Ferdinand Michel. "Seisin in the Common Law," 15 *Tulane Law Review* 455-468 (1941).

[Lowell, James Russell.] *The Biglow Papers.* Cambridge, Mass.: George
Nichols, 1848.

McLaughlin, James Angell. "Proximate Cause," 39 *Harvard Law Review*
149-199 (1925).

Marquand, John P. *Lord Timothy Dexter.* New York: Minton, Balch,
1925.

——— *Timothy Dexter Revisited.* Boston: Little, Brown and Company,
1960.

Mathes, William C. "Some Suggested Forms for Use in Criminal Cases,"
20 *Federal Rules Decisions* 231-295 (1958).

Mellinkoff, David. "How to Make Contracts Illegible," 5 *Stanford Law
Review* 418-432 (1953).

More, Sir Thomas. *Utopia.* Reprinted in *Ideal Empires and Republics.*
Cambridge Library of Law Classics. New York and London: M. Walter Dunne, 1901. Pp. 127-232.

North, Roger. *A Discourse on the Study of the Laws.* London: Charles
Baldwyn, 1824.

"Objects and Work of the Selden Society," in *Select Civil Pleas: Vol. I.   AD
1200-1203.* William Paley Baildon, ed. Selden Society, vol. 3. London: Quaritch, 1890. Pp. 1-28 following p. 128.

The Oxford Dictionary of Nursery Rhymes. Iona and Peter Opie, eds. Oxford: University Press, 1951.

Parkinson, C. Northcote. *Parkinson's Law: And Other Studies in Administration.* Boston: Houghton Mifflin Company, 1957.

Pension Book of Clement's Inn. Sir Cecil Carr, ed. Selden Society, vol. 78.
London: Quaritch, 1960.

The Scofield Reference Bible. C. I. Scofield, ed. New ed. New York: Oxford University Press, 1945.

Silving, Helen. "The Oath," 68 *Yale Law Journal* 1329-1390, 1527-1577
(1959).

Smith, Jeremiah. "Legal Cause in Actions of Tort," 25 *Harvard Law Review* 102-128 (1911), 223-252 (1912), 301-327 (1912).

Swift, Jonathan. *Gulliver's Travels.* New York: Crown Publishers, 1947.
[1st published, 1726.]

Thayer, James B. "Bedingfield's Case: Declarations as a Part of the Res
Gesta," 15 *American Law Review* 1-20, 71-107 (1881).

——— *Legal Essays.* Cambridge, Mass.: Harvard University Press, 1927.

"Toward a Cosmic Law: Hope and Reality in the United Nations," 5 *New
York Law Forum* 333-347 (1959).

U.S. Congress. House. *Survey of Space Law.* Staff Report of the Select
Committee on Astronautics and Space Exploration. Prepared by Spen-
cer M. Beresford and Philip B. Yeager. 86th Congress, 1st Session.
House Doc. No. 89. Washington, D.C.: 1959.

Wigmore, John Henry. *A Panorama of the World's Legal Systems.* Library
ed. Washington, D.C.: Washington Law Book Company, 1936.

Word and Phrase Index

chattels, 58
cheap, 40
cheat, 120, 241
cheater, 120
child, 48, 58, 121
children, 331, 405
choate, 76
choate lien, 76, 272
choateness, 76
chose in action, 16
Christ, 50
citation, 76
civil death, 326, 336
civilly dead, 327
claim, 15
claimed, 185
Classical Latin, 72
clean and neat condition, 21
clear, 28
clear and convincing, 21
clear and present danger, 444
clearly erroneous, 21
clearly expressed, 28
clearly justified, 27
clearly pointed out, 28
clearly results, 28
clemency, 143
clerk, 15
codicil, 400
codification, 262
codifier, 262
codify, 262
co-heir, 110
colloquium, 14
colon, 153
come here, 19
comes now the plaintiff, 19
comfort, 346
comitatus, 72
comma, 153
commerce, 21, 234, 426, 450
common barrator, 215
common counts, 17
common drunkard, 406, 412
common law, 453
community property, 433
comparable, 21
comparative negligence, 17
competent and fit, 351
complains, 110
complaint, 18, 110
complete, 76

completion, 21
conclusion, 18
conclusive force of the view we have
    stated, 28
condition, 15
conditional fee, 273
conditional sales contract, 270
conditional use, 273
conqueror, 61
consider, 47
consideration, 12, 180, 431
consideration for the lease, 416
consortium, 408
constable, 58
constables, 15
constitute, 254
constituted, 214
constitution, 244
Constitution-shrieker, 244
constitutional, 244
constitutional amendment, 244
constitutional construction, 244
constitutional law, 244
constitutional lawyer, 244
constitutional right, 244
constitutionality, 244
constructive notice, 432
constructive possession, 432
continuance, 432
continuance for settlement, 107
contract, 15, 101, 270, 297, 409
contracts, 410
contributory negligence, 17, 26, 434
convenient, 21
convey, 7
conviction, 15, 108
co-parcener, 110
co-partners, 215
coram nobis, 14
corporation, 143, 325, 394
corpus delicti, 14
corruption of blood, 177, 338
cosmic law, 273
counsel, 15, 80, 119, 447
counselor, 80
count, 15, 72
counterpart, 12
county, 72
court, 15, 58, 62, 68, 109
court below, 19
court hand, 86, 127
courtesy, 107

General Index

References are to pages

rise and fall: twelfth to fifteenth centuries, 95

Bill of lading
judges disagree over, 387
Uniform Bills of Lading Act, precision, 387

Birkenhead, Sir John, critic of law in English statute, 128

Bishop, Joel, on punctuation, 251

Blackstone. *See also* William the Conqueror, tale that he made French law language
bond form, 352
Commentaries have good sale in colonial America, 221
contracts, small part of *Commentaries,* 270
Jefferson's opinions of, 222, 227
residue words, 361
said to be precise, 290
writing on
brevity of Latin, 146, 189
civil death, 336
Georgian regulation of law language, 134
illiteracy, 41
Latin, 73, 74, 146, 189
law for doctors, 422
purchase, 108
witchcraft, 137

Blount, Thomas, lawyer-lexicographer, 143

Boilerplate, 93, 234, 278

Bonds
Blackstone form, 352
general obligation and revenue, 348
language transplanted in America, 213

Book of Common Prayer. See Husband and wife, marriage ritual words

Boswell's *Johnson,* on attorneys, 198

Bouvier, John
deletes useless words, 254
first American law dictionary, 247
on punctuation, 251
on usage of *devise,* 354

Bracton
as seen by young Thomas Jefferson, 222
Latin, 82, 113

on civil death, 336
punctuation, 154
said to be precise, 290

Brandeis, on wiretapping, 444

Brevity. *See also* Verbosity
distinguished from intelligibility and precision, 401
early Massachusetts forms, 236
haphazard, 400, 405
hole in the sidewalk opinion, 414
minimizes chance of error, 402
sex discrimination: two versions, 413
sometimes vicious, 405
takes time, 403, 410
tendency toward in early New England documents, 216
test of, 405
Thomas Jefferson on, 222
time saver, 403

Bridgman, Sir Orlando
Conveyances, 338
master conveyancer, 181
residue clause, 361
trustees to preserve contingent remainders, 181

Briefs
amicus brief, wiretapping, 445
massive briefs produce massive opinion, 412

Britton, 99, 113

Brownlow, Richard
formbook in English, 129
formbook in Latin, 129

Bulstrode, Edward, critic of law in English statute, 128

Burrow, Sir James
criticizes Georgian regulation of law language, 135
punctuation for meaning, 165

Butler, Samuel, contributes a law word, 172

CALIFORNIA
Field code, rejected and adopted, 263
statute: emergency calls on party lines, 430

California Words, Phrases and Maxims, 375

Campbell's *Rhetoric,* on Latin brevity, 146

clear understanding by draftsman, 417

draftsman can't testify to his instructions, 372

helpless against some interpretation, 397

Jefferson, on legislative draftsmanship, 252

not all draftsmen seek intelligibility, 417

of marine insurance policy criticized, 150

punctuation. *See also* Punctuation
    need for, 371
    warnings against, 367

recitals, 190, 324

seventeenth century: some expert, more incompetent, 194

sex discrimination: two versions, 413

telephone book notice: confusion and cure, 429

verbosity's burden, 389, 390, 402

Drunkenness
    bilingual drunks, 143
    common drunkard statute cases, 406, 412
    drinking habits of insured, 396
    hole in the sidewalk opinion, 414
    whisky, 37

Dull writing, 28

Durability. *See also* Latin
    "impressive" language
        limits, 452
        link with the past, 449
        to lawyers, 450
        to laymen, 446
    lawyers' role, 453
    letter and the law, 437, 440, 108
    mnemonic devices
        beauty in writing, 441
        humor in writing, 442
        metaphor and simile, 440
        of traditional law language, 438
        unhackneyed writing, 439
    of Constitution, how, 449
    "rememberable" language
        the key, 437
        with and without books, 438

Dutch contributions to English, 144, 205, 206

EDWARD THE CONFESSOR
    custom of sealing, 60
    Norman-French influences, 60
    reared in Normandy, 60

Electronic data retrieval, 402

England: population figures, 63, 137

English
    acquires French law words, 109, 118
    after the Conquest. *See also* William the Conqueror, tale that he made French law language
    one of languages of written law, 65
    one of spoken law languages, 67
    scarcity of borrowing from French in first century, 97
    American and British, 7, 80, 81, 198. *See also* American English
    ancient mixture with Latin, 39
    chancery petitions switch from French to English, 116
    chancery's equity records in, 116
    competes with French, 95. *See also* Bilingualism
    competes with Latin law words, 77
    conjunctions, 148
    dialect expressions, 148
    Elizabethan, 12
    gradual change: oral French to oral English pleading, 114
    grammar
        adaptation of Latin genitive, 146
        Latin inverted word order, 146, 233, 386
        long neglect, 145, 147
        sixteenth-century distinctive English, 145
    increasing necessity for law use, 130, 131
    Indo-European language, 39
    judicial notice of meanings, 10
    lawbooks written in, 131
    law dictionaries, 84, 131
    lawyers and judges reared in English use law French, 100
    London English, 137
    mass borrowing from French in Middle English period, 97
    Middle. *See* Middle English

Frankfurter, Felix, interest in words, 441

Franklin, Benjamin
critical of lawyers and their language, 230
his punctuation, 248
sells legal forms, 232

Free bench, in rhyme, 44

French
abbreviations, 88
after the Conquest. *See also* William the Conqueror, tale that he made French law language
not a language of written law, 65
one of languages of learning, 70
one of spoken law languages, 67
scarcity of loans to English in first century, 97
Anglo-French, 103
Anglo-Norman. *See also* Literature
defined, 104
follows independent course, 96
other names, 104
central French, 103
chancery petitions switch from French to English, fifteenth century, 116
development in England, 95
development on the Continent, 96
Francien, 102
in Louisiana, 8
law French. *See* Law French
mass borrowing by English in Middle English period, 97
Middle, 101
Modern, 101
Normand, 102
Norman-French
defined, 103
in England under Edward the Confessor, 60
Treason Act (1351), 169
Old French
defined, 101
dialects, 102
peculiar law use, 16
Pollock and Maitland list of law words, 15
varieties of, 101

GENERAL SEMANTICS, 294

Glanvil
first important book on English law, 73, 82
said to be precise, 290
translated into French, 113
vulgar Latin, 73

Gold complicates life and law in Old West, 260

Gowers, Sir Ernest
apologist for law language, 291
Plain Words
cited on legal style, 292
quoted, 291, 292

Grammar. *See* English, and Latin

Greek. *See also* Punctuation
law language of ancient Brittains, says Coke, 37
Puritans dislike, 203
Renaissance interest in, 142
words into English, 143

HALE, SIR MATTHEW
History of the Common Law, 221
Pleas of the Crown, 132
writing on
bulk of the law, 141, 269
competition for court business, 188
costly verbosity, 190
disreputable attorneys, 196
tenacity of forms, 194

Hamilton, Alexander
first use of *constitutionality*, 244
writes *Federalist* papers, 239

Hamilton, Andrew
his reputation, 227
Zenger trial, 222

Hatton, Sir Christopher, on punctuation, 165

Hawaii
English official, 6
Hawaiian language, 6, 8

Headnotes repeat platitudes, 409

Hohfeld, Wesley Newcomb, viii, 294

Holdsworth, Sir William, writing on
language of the law, 3
law French, 106
Magna Carta's use of *vel*, 149

Holmes, Oliver Wendell
clear and present danger, 444
dissent, *Haddock v. Haddock*, 28

Made in the USA
Las Vegas, NV
19 January 2021